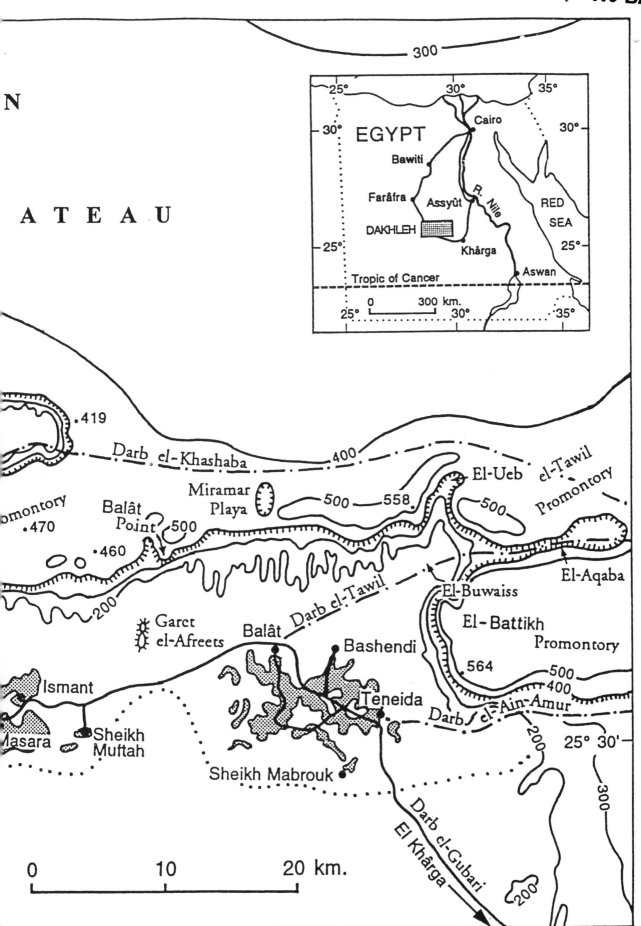

N

A T E A U

300

EGYPT

25°   30°   35°

30°   Cairo   30°

Bawiti

Farâfra   •   RED
Assyût   R. Nile   SEA

DAKHLEH

25°   25°
Khârga

Tropic of Cancer   Aswan

0   300 km.
25°   30°   35°

.419

Darb el-Khashaba   400

El-Ueb   el-Tawil
Miramar   500   558   Promontory
Playa   500

romontory   Balât
.470   Point   500

.460   El-Aqaba
200   El-Buwaiss
Garet   El-Battikh
el-Afreets   Balât   Darb el-Tawil   Promontory
Bashendi   564   500
400
Teneida   Darb el-Ain-Amur
Ismant   200   25° 30'
Sheikh
Masara   Muftah   300
Sheikh Mabrouk
Darb el-Gubari
El Khârga   200

0   10   20 km.

REPORTS FROM THE SURVEY OF THE DAKHLEH OASIS WESTERN DESERT OF EGYPT, 1977–1987

Dakhleh Oasis Project: Monograph 2

REPORTS FROM THE SURVEY OF THE DAKHLEH OASIS WESTERN DESERT OF EGYPT 1977–1987

Edited by

C. S. Churcher and A. J. Mills

Contributing Authors

C.S. Churcher, R.A. Frey, A.F. Hollett, C.A. Hope, M.R. Kleindienst, K.S. Khan, J.E. Knudstad, J.C. Krug, M.M.A. McDonald, A.J. Mills, J.C. Ritchie, H.P. Schwarcz, P.G. Sheldrick, D.M. Tangri, M.F. Wiseman, and A.K. Zielinski

Oxbow Monograph 99
1999

The Monographs of the Dakhleh Oasis Project
are published by Oxbow Books
Park End Place, Oxford OX1 1HN

Dakhleh Oasis Project Monographs

Editorial Committee

Iain Gardner
Colin A. Hope
Olaf E. Kaper
Anthony J. Mills
Klaas A. Worp

ISBN 1 900188 49 X

*This book is available direct from
Oxbow Books, Park End Place, Oxford OX1 1HN
(Phone: 01865–241249; Fax: 01865–794449)*

and

*The David Brown Book Company
P.O. Box 511, Oakville, CT 06779
(Phone: 860–945–9329; Fax: 860–945–9468)*

Printed in Great Britain
at the Short Run Press, Exeter

EDITORS' PREFACE

This volume reports on major aspects of the survey of Dakhleh Oasis for sites of archaeological, anthropological, biological and geological significance. The papers are, in general, reviews or surveys in which detailed investigations or considerations are not presented. The purpose of the volume is to present general aspects of the Oasis on which a reader interested in a particular aspect of Egypt, whether archaeological or from another disciplinary view, may gain an introduction to the Oasis as a basis for the pursuit of a more focused topic.

The major topics presented are geomorphology, stratigraphy and palaeontology, recent biology, Pleistocene and Holocene lithic cultures, pottery from Neolithic to Islamic times, and Roman Period Settlement. Chapter 1 reports on the surficial Quaternary deposits within a historical geomorphological framework and presents for the first time a developmental paradigm by which landsurfaces and conditions of erosion or deposition are explained. The chapter goes into more details and presents new observations not available in earlier works mainly because Kleindienst and her co-workers were able to walk over more of the Oasis surface than had previous geologists. Chapter 2 has a review of the vertebrate fossils found in the late Cretaceous formations exposed mainly in the Libyan Escarpment. This represents a further step in the description of the Tethyean marine reptiles and fishes recorded by Karl von Zittel or mentioned by subsequent authors and the first records of terrestrial dinosaurs from this Oasis. Chapter 3 is a brief report on soil fungi, about which nothing previously has been recorded for the Western Desert. Chapter 4 records the macroflora of the Oasis, with consideration for some archaeological materials and the pollen record. Chapter 5 is the first attempt at a description of the Pleistocene lithic sequence in the Oasis and how its distribution relates to the sequence of geomorphological developmental features. Some relations to those of nearby Kharga Oasis are apparent. Chapter 6 considers a problematic lithic culture that does not easily conform to the general palaeolithic framework for the Eastern Sahara. Chapter 7 describes the cultural sequence of lithic artifacts produced by the Neolithic oasis dwellers and constitutes a first description of these peoples for the Oasis. Chapter 8 discusses the faunal remains from mainly Neolithic Cultural sites and their bearing on the Neolithic peoples' diets and on wild and domestic animals. Chapter 9 presents annotated lists of the animals (exclusive of insects and lower invertebrates) seen or obtained as specimens in the Oasis. Avian records constitute the major portion of the taxa recorded. Chapter 10 discusses the influence of Pharaonic Egyptians in the Oasis and the general paucity of surviving evidences of occupation. Chapter 11 records the presence of an unusual skeletal aberration in the human population of the Oasis. Chapter 12 discusses some of the problems and their solutions in preserving major sandstone buildings in the Oasis. Chapter 13 gives a plan for the well-preserved Roman Period settlement at Ismant el-Kharab (Kellis) and details of some of its buildings. Although the Roman Period is represented by a large number of sites in the index (Appendix 2), it was felt that a site-specific chapter such as this would present greater detail about the period and the condition of its sites than would a more general survey of all the sites of the period. Chapter 14 reports on the progression of pottery fabrics and styles from Neolithic to Islamic times. Correlations with the pottery of the Nile Valley are discussed and aspects of trade and communication deduced. Appendix I constitutes a bibliography of all publications by members of the Dakhleh Oasis Project up to December, 1997, as an easy reference list for persons interested in the overall project. Appendix II is a complete list of all the sites recorded in the Oasis and the surrounding desert. This list includes all archaeological sites but excludes geological and palaeontological locations. Appendix III lists all palaeolithic and neolithic archaeological sites both within the present oasis and within the greater area of the palaeoasis and atop the Libyan Escarpment by a series of Locus Numbers as the grid reference system used for Appendix II is anapplicable for unmapped areas.

The indices of archaeological sites are up to date to March, 1997. New sites are constantly being discovered and reviews of previously indexed sites result in new components or even reidentification; so, the list is in continual flux. However, all cross-references, the identification code, and the brief sketches of a site's major features have been carefully checked. There are bound to be errors, but there is no redendancy in the index by which an error might be detected. We accept responsibility for these hidden flaws.

We thank all those who assisted us in our endeavours to bring this series of discoveries into print for all interested researchers to read. They are far too many to name, but particular recognition must be made of Ms. Marijka Mychajlowycz, who first patiently retyped the manuscripts into a single format. The reviewers of individual chapters and of the volume as a whole also performed a most valuable service. The particular assistence of Professor Maxine Kleindienst (Pleistocene), Dr. Mary McDonald (early Holocene), and Dr. Colin Hope (historical periods) in checking the site Index (Appendix II) has been invaluable.

In addition, we also thank Dr. Nicholas B. Millet, of the Royal Ontario Museum, who generously allowed the facilities of his (then, Egyptian) department to be used by Churcher, and supplied the means by which the halftones in chapter 14 were reproduced in the museum's Photography Department by Mr. Brian Boyle. Ms. Roberta Shaw assisted in verifying the Egyptological references. Other photographs and diagrams were reproduced by Mr. John Glover of the Photographic Facility, Faculty of Arts and Science, University of Toronto. We thank the National Science and Engineering Research Council of Canada for Grant A1760 to Churcher which paid the salary of Ms. Mychajlowycz while she was Churcher's scientific assistant. This grant also paid for the photography performed by Mr. Glover and for laboratory supplies and sundries used in the preparation of the final copy. We are also grateful to Mr. David Brown and Ms Val Tomlin of Oxbow Books, our publishers, for their patience and the efforts needed to produce this book, and to our various contributors for their great patience in waiting for this work to close. Not least, the long suffering wives of the editors must also be congratulated for their persistent patience while the editors worked at getting this volume to go forward to its conclusion.

Finally, such a volume of reports about an ever expanding body of material is difficult to conclude. Authors wish to update manuscripts in the light of new data, opinions and interpretations change, even new disciplines are brought into the project and ought to be included in such a preliminary grouping. The end of 1997, however, has been elected as the final closing date of the work (the latest of several) but must not be taken as the final word on any of the subjects covered in the volume. No synthesis of our data and results has been formed as yet as much of the work is in its infancy when the richness of evidence about the Dakhleh Oasis is considered.

The Editors

CONTENTS

INTRODUCTION

A. J. Mills

In 1972, a few months prior to his death, Dr. Ahmed Fakhry gave a lecture in Toronto to the Society for the Study of Egyptian Antiquities (S.S.E.A.). In it he discussed his recent work in the western oases of Egypt. His discovery of large, Old Kingdom mastaba tombs together with an adjacent town site at Balat particularly piqued Geoffrey Freeman's and my interest, but it was Fakhry's positive enthusiasm for the whole Dakhleh Oasis and its historical importance that impelled us to consider it as an area for field research.

In November, 1977, Mr. Freeman, then Chairman of the S.S.E.A., and I visited the oasis to see it first-hand, with the idea of developing a specific research project, should the region prove suitable. Our reaction from this visit was one of enthusiasm for the modern oasis and fascination with the archaeological potential which could be seen in the standing monuments and the general spread of artifacts across the oasis. Our journey of a fortnight was greatly eased by the welcoming reception everywhere to be encountered in the oasis, and by the eager assistance of various Egyptian Antiquities Organisation officials. The interest of a number of colleagues in Toronto and elsewhere was soon engaged and the project formulated.

The initial proposal of the project averred that the project was

"Designed to study the whole area of the Dakhleh Oasis, approximately 3125 km², throughout the period from about 5000 BC until 500 AD ... three major aspects of this oasis will be elucidated: its environmental composition and evolution, its internal cultural development and its relationships with a number of external forces and areas."

The multi-disciplinary approach required by this direction has been maintained throughout the research. However, it was quickly realised that the original restricted time frame was impractical for a number of reasons in such a regional study. Human activity had been demonstrated, by the work of Schild and Wendorf (1977), to have extended well back into the Old Stone Age; and it has continued unbroken since 500 AD into the 20th Century. Environmental change occurs whether humans are present or not, and it was soon evident that all the Pleistocene and Holocene features and events would have to be understood in detail for a full appreciation of the information to be obtained. The Dakhleh Oasis is being studied as a single entity, not as a series of sites and isolated data. The various archaeological sites and occurrences within Dakhleh, from flint-knapping workshop floors to large Romano-Byzantine towns, are each considered as component parts of the whole regional study. Indeed, it is the study of the region that is the goal of the Dakhleh Oasis Project and, while human activity within the region is a major concern, the physical environment in which the activity occurred is equally important in our considerations. The environmental background to all human activity is seen as a major influence on development and change, just as human activity can have a profound effect on environmental conditions and the landscape. It is only by understanding development on a regional scale that it is possible to begin to assess this symbiotic relationship. Human activities are all too frequently modified by the land forms and bedrock composition, especially when they influence settlement or site distribution, land uses, and building or technology. Human cultural development is much more easily described and assessed from the loci that archaeologists generally regard as 'sites'. But when regional or inter-regional forces are involved, natural or anthropocentric, initially the effects can appear to be localised, only subsequently permeating the whole population. Conversely, the effects may only be retained at a local level, due to specialised activity or specific conditions. Without understanding the forces and their effects on a broad scale, it is inadequate to attempt a specific localised interpretation.

The program established by the project began with a series of five seasons, during which a walking survey of the entire oasis floor was designed to search everywhere for evidence of human occupation and of natural events and features. As a regional study was, for Egypt, an

'Reports from the Survey of Dakhleh Oasis, Western Desert of Egypt, 1977–1987', edited by C.S. Churcher and A.J. Mills. Dakhleh Oasis Project: Monograph 2. Oxbow Monograph 99.

unusual concept, it was decided that a study of the whole space, rather than employment of a random sampling technique, would be more convincing. However, the survey did not investigate land which was under crops and, thereby, has left unexplored about one-sixth of the modern oasis. The rest of the region, together with some of the area outside the present periphery, was walked over in five winter seasons between 1978 and 1982. A total of 410 archaeological loci, ranging from Old Stone Age to Islamic in cultural affinity, were indexed (List of Archaeological Sites, Appendix II, this volume). The greatest number of these belong to the historical periods of the last five millennia. The field technique was to walk both controlled transects and notable topographic features, noting and testing occurrences. The archaeological survey data include information on the location of a site, apparent horizontal extent, state of preservation and buried depth, its dating or cultural affinities and associations with both natural features and other sites, and any special features that are apparent from a surface inspection.

Generally speaking, present environmental conditions have prevailed during the last 5000 years and human activity, apart from trans-desert travel, has been more or less confined to today's oasis zone. However, much of the earlier Holocene enjoyed different conditions and human occupation, as a result, was not necessarily confined to the same area. The work of the prehistorians of the project, as a result, continues to lead them to seek material increasingly distant from the 'historical' heart of the oasis, into what is termed the 'palaeoasis'. So, in part, surveying continues to be an important field technique as we expand and develop our information. Indeed, some 200 additional loci have been added to our index since 1982, principally from the areas beyond the edges of the present oasis.

Environmental information can be collected in different ways. Floral and faunal collections of present-day oasis populations have been made to provide a datum and for comparative material. Excavated material from dated contexts provides much of the necessary palaeoenvironmental data. Geologic and topographic changes to the oasis are recorded in the remnants of former structures and stratified surfaces. This information can be sought on the ground and from air photographs and, because of the wider ramifications of geomorphologic changes, in neighbouring regions as well. All interrelate to provide a complete picture of Dakhleh and it behooves our various colleagues to work closely together in the field whenever disciplines overlap or intermingle.

Surveying began at Maohoub, at the extreme north-western end of the oasis, and gradually worked eastwards to and beyond Teneida. Because of the length of the oasis, about 80 km, it was decided that a permanent single expedition headquarters would be less useful than a moveable one. So, we live in rented accomodation in the village most convenient to the current work. In 1978, we were established at Maohoub in the house of Sheikh Sabr Ahmed, the son of the sheikh who entertained Winlock in 1908 (Winlock 1936). In 1979, our camp was first at Maohoub again, and subsequently at the village of Gedida. The following two seasons we worked in the central zone of the oasis from the village of Sheikh el-Aweina. Finally, in 1982, accomodation was taken in Esbet Bashendi for our survey of the eastern end of Dakhleh. At that point, it was decided to finish the investigation of the eastern end of Dakhleh before returning to a more western camp.

Following the survey, our intention became to supplement the information gained by the surveying techniques through more intensive examination of specifically selected locations, chosen for their potential to provide the maximum amount of information relative to specific problems and questions. This involves, to some extent, a major alteration in the integration of our multi-disciplinary approach, although it does not change our overall goals of understanding the relationships of man and environment and human cultural evolution in Dakhleh. It does mean a more concentrated focus on relatively specific matters by various individual investigators. This is a natural progression from the generalities of the survey and will, eventually, be superceded by a phase of synthesis, when data from all the project's facets will be integrated.

The present volume is a collection of papers which arise from our surveying activities. There is no attempt to present all our data, nor to synthesise material across disciplines. The former will appear as a series of topically organised reports, which will be produced as one or another topic is completed. The latter will, of course, be the subject of later writings. The papers here are a presentation of current thinking on some of our material. Papers by C.A. Hope, R.A. Frey and J.E. Knudstad, and A.J. Mills are based on information gathered during the initial five seasons from historical arenas. Those of M.M.A. McDonald, M.R. Kleindienst, C.S Churcher and J.E. Ritchie include, in part, material mainly gathered up to the closing of this manuscript in 1997 and represent not more up-to-date material so much as that based in wider-ranging and different techniques. The essay by A.K. Zielinski has been included in this collection because the often experimental nature of field conservation techniques depends on areal information about conditions and raw materials.

There are other parts of the project which are not fully reported or represented here, notably the petroglyphs recorded by L. Krzyzaniak and K. Kroeper, Islamic archaeology and ethnography, and physical anthropology by J. E. Molto and others. The latter is really the adjunct of an excavation, while the others are insufficiently advanced for inclusion.

This group of papers will seem diversified in style and approach. This is inevitable in such a project, where each investigator is responsible for the conduct and publication of his own special avenue of research and the opinions that he derives from it. Apart from imposing some uniformity in format, and collating the cross-referencing and data as far as possible, the main editorial work has been to ensure standardised spellings of Arabic names and words, consistency both within and between reports, and a general format. Renderings of Arabic words or terms into European languages is always a thorny subject and no particular rationale is offered here. Some words have been taken from one or another published source; others have been 'invented' by the project as need has arisen. The map (Fig. 1.1), that serves as the Frontispiece, is part of this introduction, and has been compiled from many sources, and some of the less prominent features bear local names of restricted currency. This map relates to most of the contributions and should be used freely by readers: it is the basic map to most chapters.

Another standardised system adopted by the project has been an index numbering of individual archaeological locations. The maps supplied to the expedition in 1978 were the best currently available in Egypt. The Project's 1 × 1 km grid is therefore based upon the 13 sheets of the 1932 Egyptian Government Survey 1:25,000 maps. Surveying for these maps took place in 1929-30 with the major emphasis on agricultural land use. As a result, the parts of the oasis where habitation or farming was either absent or impossible were left unmapped. The alphanumeric index system adopted was based on the 1-kilometre grid of the maps and is fully explained in Mills (1979). Our exploration of the unmapped areas, as well as those adjacent to the 'historical' oasis zone, have had no published grid system to which to relate. Our numbering system will eventually have to be altered, to accomodate this deficiency, to one using specific co-ordinates. In recent years, air photo coverage of the oasis, by KLM Aerocarto NV, 1:20,000, 1958, has been obtained from the Egyptian military authorities and will make the location of information on new maps a simpler process. A new basemap was prepared by Ian A. Brookes from 1:100,000 photogrammetric maps by "Geofizika", Zaghreb, Yugoslavia, which became available in 1986. Some sites are also being located by geopositional coordinates (latitude and longitude) obtained by Global Positioning Systems navigational aids.

The project will continue for a number of years. The gathering of environmental information must go on as long as the archaeologists are at work. Until the details of the cultural evolution of Dakhleh, and the dynamics that affect it and are created by it, can be documented and understood, the archaeologists will not be satisfied. Already, intensive mapping and excavation are taking place at a great variety of loci, including a number of later Pleistocene and early Holocene locations, the town of Ismant el-Kharab (Roman 'Kellis'), a Roman temple, and a cemetery at 'Ein Tirghi which has been in use for almost the last 4000 years. We have published annual news reports on our field activities in the Journal of the Society for the Study of Egyptian Antiquities, as well as various other venues, and a long series of specialist and general publications can be expected before the work is ended.

Acknowledgements
Such a major undertaking as the Dakhleh Oasis Project could never succeed without support from many individuals and institutions. First, I would like to record our appreciation for the interest, kindness and great assistance from our many Egyptian colleagues. Ali el-Bazidi, Ahmed el-Haggar, Adel Hussein, the late Safi el-Din Khalil and Ibrahim el-Sayidi were Antiquities Organization officers present with us in the field during the various seasons of the survey. Their problems in administring and controlling such a diverse group were always overcome cheerfully and efficiently and with as little trouble to ourselves as possible. In fact, the attitude of everyone in the Egyptian Antiquities Organization was always welcoming, interested and helpful and we are very grateful to the chairmen of the Organization – Dr. Gamal Mokhtar, then the late Dr. Ahmed Kadry – and all their innumerable officers in Cairo and in the New Valley for all their kindnesses.

Miss Nadia Ayad undertook to be our representative in Cairo during the first couple of seasons of the survey and toiled endlessly at administrative chores as well as locating food supplies, spare parts for vehicles and all the small items that are so important to have once one is in the field, several hundred kilometres away from the Cairo shops. It is also a great pleasure to record the assistance, first of Dr. Ronald J. Leprohon and later, Mr. Edwin C. Brock, directors of the Canadian Institute in Egypt, who afforded administrative and logistical help for the expedition throughout the time of the survey and subsequently.

It is impossible to quantify the amount of support given to myself and all the Dakhleh Oasis Project team by Mr. Geoffrey Freeman of the Society for the Study of Egyptian Antiquities and by Dr. Nicholas B. Millet of the Royal Ontario Museum. These two have ensured the survival of the Dakhleh Oasis Project through the energy and expertise that each brought year after year to both practical and intellectual matters of the field work and our results. We are deeply in their debt.

Of course, all the various project members are the crux of the matter. I thank you all for bringing your great intellects and expertises, for your good humour under very trying conditions, and for your continuing loyalty to our common interests and to each other, and for all the hard work work that goes into the research of the Dakhleh Oasis Project. I would also like to record here that virtually all the editorial work on this volume has been done by C.S. 'Rufus' Churcher in a most selfless and meticulous manner.

Funding for the work of the survey of the Dakhleh Oasis came principally from the Canada Council, the Social Sciences and Humanities Research Council of Canada and the National Science and Engineering Research Council of Canada.

REFERENCES

Mills, A.J. 1979. Dakhleh Oasis Project: Report on the first season of survey, October-December 1978. *Journal of the Society for the Study of Egyptian Antiquities* **9**: 163–185.

Schild, R.F. and F. Wendorf. 1977. *The prehistory of the Dakhla Oasis and adjacent desert.* Warsaw, Polish Academy of Sciences, Warsaw, 259p.

List of Archaeological Sites indexed by the Dakhleh Oasis Project. This volume, Appendix II, 251–266.

Winlock, H.E. 1936. *Ed Dakhleh Oasis. Journal of a camel trip made in 1908.* Metropolitan Museum of Art, New York, 77p.

LIST OF CONTRIBUTORS

CHARLES S. CHURCHER
Department of Zoology, University of Toronto, Ontario,
CANADA M5S 3G5; Department of Palaeobiology,
Royal Ontario Museum, Queen's Park, Toronto,
Ontario, CANADA M5S 2C6 and R.R.1, Site 42,
Gabriola Island, British Columbia, CANADA V0R
1XO (mailing address)

ROSA A. FREY
Cassacawn Cottage, Blisland, Bodmin, Cornwall,
ENGLAND PL30 4JU

ALAN F. HOLLETT
Department of Near Eastern and Asian Civilisations,
Royal Ontario Museum, Queen's Park, Toronto,
Ontario, CANADA M5S 2C6 and Box 512, 51 Fox
Street, Lunenburg, Nova Scotia, CANADA B0J 2C0
(mailing address)

COLIN A. HOPE
Department of Greek, Roman and Egyptian Studies,
Monash University, Clayton, Melbourne, Victoria,
AUSTRALIA 3168

SHAH K. KHAN
Department of Botany, University of Toronto, Toronto,
Ontario, CANADA M5S 3B2 and Department of
Zoology, University of Toronto, Ontario, CANADA
M5S 3G5

MAXINE R. KLEINDIENST
Department of Anthropology, University of Toronto at
Mississauga, Ontario, CANADA L5L 1C6; Department
of West Asian Studies, Royal Ontario Museum,
Queen's Park, Toronto, Ontario, CANADA M5S 2C6
and 1762 Angela Crescent, Mississauga, CANADA L5J
1B9 (mailing address)

JAMES, E. KNUDSTAD
Cassacawn Cottage, Blisland, Bodmin, Cornwall,
ENGLAND PL30 4JU

JOHN C. KRUG
Department of Botany, University of Toronto, Ontario,
CANADA M5S 3B2 and Centre for Biodiversity and
Conservation Biology, Royal Ontario Museum, Queen's
Park, Toronto, Ontario, CANADA M5S 2C6

MARY M.A. McDONALD
Department of Archaeology, University of Calgary,
Calgary, Alberta, CANADA T2N 1N4

ANTHONY J. MILLS
Department of Near Eastern and Asian Civilisations,
Royal Ontario Museum, Queen's Park, Toronto,
Ontario, CANADA M5S 2C6 and The Barn, Above
Town, Egloshayle, Wadebridge, Cornwall, ENGLAND
PL27 6HW (mailing address)

JAMES C. RITCHIE
Department of Botony, University of Toronto,
Scarborough College, West Hill, Ontario, CANADA
M1C 1A4 and Pebbledash Cottage, Corfe, Taunton,
Somerset, ENGLAND TA3 7AJ (mailing address)

HENRY P. SCHWARCZ
School of Geography and Geology, McMaster
University, Hamilton, Ontario, CANADA L8S 4M1

PETER G. SHELDRICK
209 Victoria Avenue, Chatham, Ontario, CANADA
N7L 3A7

MARCIA F. WISEMAN
Department of Social Sciences, Scarborough College,
University of Toronto, West Hill, Ontario, CANADA
M1C 1A4

ADAM K. ZIELINSKI
P.O. Box 356, Wellington, Ontario, CANADA K0K
3L0

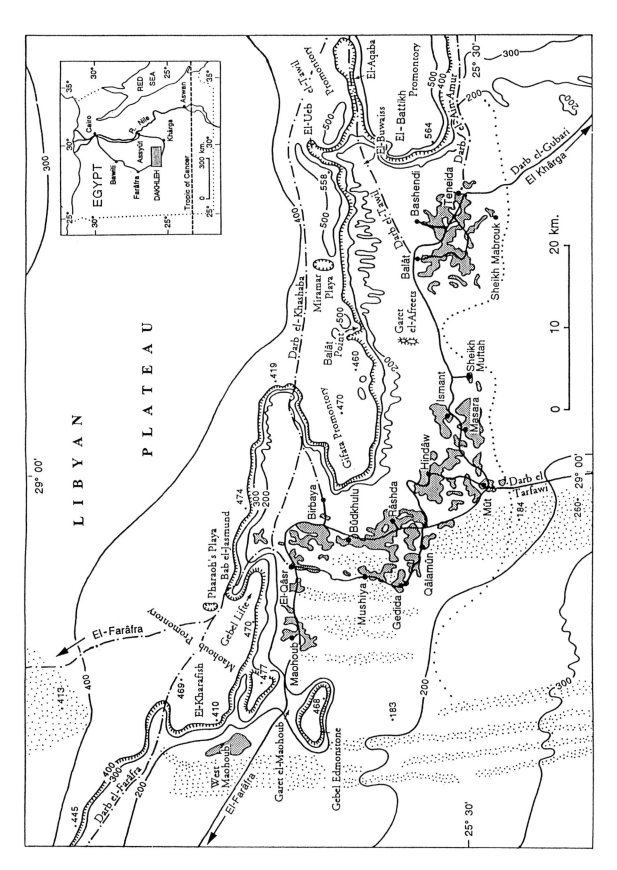

Fig. 1.1. Map of the Dakhleh Oasis, with location of the oasis within Egypt (inset map). Areas of cultivation (ca. 1970) shown cross hatched, towns and villages (solid dots), main roads (heavy lines), caravan roads (dot-dash lines), Libyan Escarpment (parallel contours topped by scarp symbol), and sand dunes (stippled). Names are derived from 'Egypt1:25,000' series of maps, from local residents, explorers' notes and from usage by members of the Dakhleh Oasis Project. Contours and spot heights in metres.

1

GEOGRAPHY, GEOLOGY, GEOCHRONOLOGY AND GEOARCHAEOLOGY OF THE DAKHLEH OASIS REGION: AN INTERIM REPORT

M.R. Kleindienst, C.S. Churcher, M.M.A. McDonald
and H.P. Schwarcz

"The challenge to all geoarchaeologists is to ... incorporate the geological and cultural worlds. The geologic realm is more than a context within which human societies act and their remains are entombed.... The geologic realm is a source and a recipient of cultural meaning" (Leach 1992: 415).

I. INTRODUCTION

Background

In 1978, W.K. Hodges (1980) made preliminary observations on geomorphology and hydrology for the Dakhleh Oasis Project (DOP). Detailed geological and geoarchaeological reconnaissance for the DOP was initiated by C.S. Churcher during the 1979, 1980 and 1981 seasons (1980, 1981, 1982), followed by I.A. Brookes who completed seven weeks of fieldwork in 1982 and 1986 (1983, 1986), and another seven weeks from January to March, 1987 (1989a, 1989b). Brookes subsequently conducted selective pitting into Holocene sediments with Campbell in January-February, 1990 (Brookes 1993). Regional subdivisions of landforms have been mapped from 1:100,000–scale aerial photographic index sheets and from interpretation of selected 1:20,000–scale airphotos (Brookes 1986, pl. I); and Kleindienst and McDonald have identified geological resources (Kleindienst, this volume, Chapter 5,). A tentative sequence for environmental changes over the estimated 350,000–400,000 year span of human occupation has been constructed. Brookes' preliminary stratigraphic scheme (Brookes 1986, pl. II; 1993, fig. 4, tab. 2) has been substantially modified (see Table 1.1) to allow greater flexibility in referring to geological units.

Location and Environment

Dakhleh Oasis lies ca. 280 km southwest of Assiyut in the Arab Republic of Egypt, and its administrative centre, Mut is located at 25° 30′N; 29° 07′E (Fig. 1.1). It occupies one of a semi-circle of structurally-controlled depressions – Kharga, Dakhleh, Farafra and Bahariya – around and within the southern and western borders of the Libyan Plateau, the 'oasis crescent'.

Dakhleh Oasis is composed of several discrete oases, and occupies a lowland at 92–140 m above sea level (a.s.l.), in which local relief largely reflects differential fluvial and aeolian erosion, with some bedrock control. It is oriented west-northwest – east-southeast, and extends ca. 60 km from Ezbet Sheikh Maohoub, near Gebel Edmonstone (Qaret el-Maohoub) in the west, to a few kilometres southeast of Teneida, at Ain el-Sheikh Mabrouk Badr, southwest of the 'el-Battikh Promontory' (previously called 'Tawil Plateau' [Hermina *et al.* 1961, pl. II], 'Gebel Abu Tartur' [Brookes 1983, 1986, 1993, fig. 3], or 'Wadi el Battikh Plateau' [Hermina 1990, fig. 14.5]). An extension of the cultivated lands has been recently established northwest of Gebel Edmonstone at Gharb Maohoub, in an area which Hermina called 'West Dakhla'. North-south width varies from about 15 km through Mut to a few kilometres at each extremity, with a maximum width of 25 km from Qasr to Mut. To the

'Reports from the Survey of Dakhleh Oasis, Western Desert of Egypt, 1977–1987', edited by C.S. Churcher and A.J. Mills. Dakhleh Oasis Project: Monograph 2. Oxbow Monograph 99.

Table 1.1. General stratigraphic framework for Dakhleh Oasis. The bedrock geology follows Hermina (1990). Recent subdivision of capping Plateau limestones not shown (Tarawan Group comprised of Tarawan Formation in west equivalent to Kurkur formation in east, overlain by Garra Formation. See pp. 5–6 for details.)

AGE (Ma)	PERIOD/EPOCH	STAGE		FORMATION	THICKNESS (m)	LITHOLOGY	LANDFORM
37	EOCENE	(undivided)		THEBES	300	Fossiliferous limestone, with chert and marl bands	Plateau, scarp
				ESNA	50–100	Green-grey shales	Cuestas, vales Plateau
52				TARAWAN	20–60	Whitish limestone, marls and chalk beds cherts	Plateau, scarp
64	PALEOCENE	DANIAN					
		MAASTRICHTIAN		DAKHLA	> 250	Grey shale, fossiliferous limestone interbeds	Scarp-face badland
72				DUWI	10–20	Siliceous limestone phosphatic beds	Cuesta
80	LATE CRETACEOUS	CAMPANIAN	SERIES	QUSSEIR (Mut)	20–85	Red shales 'chert balls'	Lowland
		SANTONIAN		TAREF	>100	Buff sandstones, quartzites	Cuesta
91		CONIACAN TURONIAN					
		CENOMANIAN	NUBIA				
100	EARLY CRETACEOUS	ALBIAN		MAGHRABI	600–1300	Sandstones, minor conglomerate, shale, quartzites	Cuesta, residual hills, plain

north, the lowland is overlooked by a 300 m high scarp, which marks the southern edge of the Libyan Plateau at between 420 and 560 m a.s.l. To the south, it is bounded by a rocky ridge and a rough, sand- and gravel-covered desert plain with isolated hills, from the oasis rim at ca. 140–150 m rising to >200 m a.s.l.

Located in the eastern Sahara, and now far removed from oceanic influences, the one recording station at Mut receives rainfall so infrequently that annual totals and the annual average for the oasis are effectively nil (Sutton 1947, tab. 10, 15; World Meteorological Organization 1971, 62300 [2]). Rain falls somewhere in Dakhleh in most years, either as extended and extensive drizzle, or as brief, highly localized storms, as shown by even the earliest records (1905–1911) (Bates 1970 [1914]). The hydrologic, geomorphic, and biological significances of these rains have not been studied.

Weather in the Western Desert is related to the passage of large depressions along the Mediterranean in winter months. Depressions from the Sahara influence weather during the summer (Bagnold 1933; Shaw 1936; Sutton 1950; Soliman 1953). "These 'Saharan depressions' were well-known to French and British meteorologists in the 1930's; they are by no means rare" (Flohn and Nicholson 1980, 7). Rain usually occurs in January-February, the pattern for Lower Egypt (Sutton 1947; Soliman 1953). Sutton (1947, tab. 6) records 0 to 1 mm annual precipitation

from 1932 to 1947, with records of 4 mm in 1944/45, and 10 mm in 1941/42. He gave 8 mm as the maximum for a 1 day rainfall (Sutton 1947, tab. 12, February 15, 1942; Ezzat 1974a). The record from 1948 to 1967 shows zero annual precipitation except for 1 mm recorded in 1956 (Shahin 1985, App. A1). The coefficient of variation for annual rainfall at Dakhleh is 450%, the extreme for the Western Desert (Shahin 1985, fig. 4.7).

Sustained local precipitation is rare. Jordan reports (1875a, 24) that, at the time of the famous rainfall experienced by the Rohlfs expedition at 'Regenfeld' in the Great Sand Sea: "In Dachel fiel an diesem Tage auch Regen, aber viel weniger." Beadnell (1901a, 84) reports that: "Quite recently (February, 1901) Dakhla was visited by a violent downpour, which is said to have lasted 40 hours and done incalculable damage." While camped at Deir el Hagar in western Dakhleh, Winlock (1936, 28) experienced a storm lasting over 45 minutes on May 18, 1908: "The sudden drop in temperature at 3 P.M. was due to an extraordinary little storm which Jones described as follows: 'It grew warmer in the afternoon; clouds gathered; at 2:20 P.M. rain began to patter, and 10 minutes later we were in the midst of a cyclonic disturbance that kept things lively around the tent for half an hour. The wind came from the W., blowing the sand ahead of it and moving the dunes to the SW. of us right along. It was very heavy and the rain quite heavy for some 15 minutes.

The wind then whipped around to the N., and both it and the rain were still heavy for another 15 minutes. Then the wind came in from the E., still heavy with rain for about 5 minutes, and finally the storm ended with a hot heavy S. wind, without rain, which dried out everything in short order and which had dropped to a dead calm by 3:15 P.M.'" The temperature change during the storm was marked: at 2:00 pm., 111°F (= 44°C), and at 3 pm., 92°F (= 33°C). Conditions related to summer storms are described by Sutton (1950).

Hume (1925, 83) noted: "A heavy rain storm is stated to have destroyed many of its [Dakhleh's] houses some years ago, but no official records are available." Evidence of local storms is observed from year to year by DOP fieldworkers, mainly as mud-cracked thin silt layers deposited in depressions in veneered surfaces or in wadi bottoms, or as rain drop impressions and rilling on sand ripples, although no rain may be registered at Mut. Over December 31, 1993 and January 1, 1994, a heavy rain lasting ca. 20 hours was experienced at Ezbet Beshendi by the DOP. Although no official figures are available, standing water in depressions lasted for some days depositing silts, and rainfall caused minor damage to mud walling. The wadis did not run, so that there was apparently little precipitation on the Plateau, and the storm was localized in the Beshendi-Tenida-Balat area so that it did not register on the official rain guage at Mut. Hollows in the roadside verges near cultivation and formed by bulldozer scrapes filled with water, and contained fine silt veneers over mudcracks. Moisture penetrated into the soil sufficient for vegetation to germinate in the depressions and to be still living some weeks later in February. Bashendi experienced a similar storm on February 7, 1999, lasting several hours with heavy rain at times (A.J. Mills, pers. comm., Feb. 10, 1999).

In October, 1994, when heavy rains fell in the central Nile Valley, heavy rain also damaged the main Kharga road and filled pans and wadis in the Zayat area between Dakhleh and Kharga, while no rain fell in either oasis (S. Zemzemi, pers. comm., December, 1994). Some standing water was still observed there in mid-December; pans near Zayat showed deep sink holes and heavy mud cracking, and soils were darkened by the wetting. However, there was no widespread generation of vegetation, suggesting that no viable seeds persisted in the soil away from the main road or cultivation. Green vegetation, mainly in drainages near the road, persisted in late February, 1995, and grew again in 1996, suggesting considerable moisture remaining in the soil.

It is not known when last any of the major Dakhleh wadis may have carried significant runoff, although Beadnell's (1901) storm is a likely episode. Limestone boulders in the wadi beds often show marked aeolian erosion, some remaining only as windwardly hollowed-out 'case hardened' leeward shells and proving that major runoffs are very infrequent. Northwesterly winds prevail, but local orientations of small aeolian landforms (dunes, yardangs) reflect the influences of the Libyan Escarpment, whose promontories and embayments deflect and channel winds in directions from northwest to northeast. High winds and sand or duststorms are most frequent from March through June, while January and February have the highest percentage of calm days (Shahin 1985, tab. 3.10a). Mean monthly relative humidities at Mut vary from 38% (May to August) to 60% (December) (Shahin 1985, tab. 3.8); and mean daily relative humidities from 30% in June and July, to 53% in December (Shahin 1985, tab. 3.4). Sling psychrometer readings at Ezbet Bashendi in January-February, 1984 and 1985, show near-surface relative humidities ranging from 22% in mid-afternoon to 78% in early morning (A.F. Hollett, pers. comm., 1988). Dew formation, therefore, may contribute to some plants' and animals' water budgets, as well as to rock weathering. Morning fog banks are frequently observed on top of the Plateau in January-February, and sometimes descend into adjoining lowland areas.

Mean monthly temperatures in Dakhleh range from 12.3°C in January to 30.8°C in July, with an annual mean of 22.8°C (Shahin 1985, tab. 3.2). With low cloudiness, wide daily ranges of temperature are common (20°–30°C, measured at Ezbet Bashendi), but monthly averages are not as disparate (15.5°C in September, 19.1°C in April) (Shahin 1985, tab. 3.3). Mean daily temperatures range from 22° to 5°C in January, and from 39° to 23°C in July. Daily extremes reach 49°C (121°F) in summer ; and winter night temperatures drop below freezing (minimum recorded 25°F or -4°C) (Sutton 1950), especially on the Plateau; wind chill is high during the winter, and can be a hypothermic hazard in fieldwork. Mean monthly cloudiness ranges from 0.0 oktas (eighths of the celestial dome covered by cloud) for August and September, to 1.4 in January, with a yearly mean of 0.6 (Shahin 1985, tab. 3.8). Based on data from Kharga, mean evaporation rates are between 6.0 and 6.5 mm/day (Shahin 1985, figs 5.8, 5.10); the annual potential evapotranspiration as extrapolated is ca. 2,250 mm (Shahin 1985, fig. 6.2); but this is only possible locally through ground water discharge or irrigation. The evapotranspiration requirement for crop cultivation in Dakhleh is estimated at 1,900–2,000 mm/yr (Shahin 1985, fig. 6.16). Today, oasis cultivation is dependent upon artesian water obtained from the Nubian aquifer (Beadnell 1901a; Thorweihe 1990, fig. 28.5) and mostly depends upon the deep boreholes.

Consequently, evidence for past regional, as opposed to local, vegetation cover is surrogate evidence for an ameliorated water budget. There are botanical as well as geological indications that Dakhleh was more humid in past times (Ritchie, this volume, Chapter 4): for example, coppice dunes built around living *Tamarix* in the southern desert fringe and around living or dead trees on the Plateau. Evidence for past vegetation exists as molds and casts in playa and other sediments, and as seeds or fragments in Holocene sediments. Phytoliths also occur (U. Thanheiser, pers. comm., 1995).

II. PRE-QUATERNARY GEOLOGY

Early geological and meteorological observations in the Dakhleh region date from 1818 by Edmonstone (1822) and 1820 by Cailliaud (1826). Geological studies begin with the work of Karl von Zittel in 1874 (1883), a member of Rohlfs' expedition (Rohlfs 1875), who recognised a sedimentary sequence of Upper Cretaceous to Eocene age. Lyons made observations on structure and physiography (1894a, 1894b). Mapping and hydrogeological studies were carried out by Beadnell in 1898 (1901a); and remains of a survey camp which he established (Camp 40) may be seen northeast of Tenida. We suspect that some particularly well-built survey beacons also can be attributed to Beadnell. Hume's 1925 overview of Egyptian geology summarizes the literature to 1923, although his 1:2,000,000 'Revised Geological Map of Egypt (Provisional Issue)' shows only 'Cretaceous limestone' overlying 'Nubian Sandstone'. Recent literature is summarized in Said (Hermina 1990; Said 1990a). A report on hydrogeology in Kharga and Dakhleh appeared in 1954 (Paver and Pretorius 1954). Work intensified with the building of the Sidd el 'Ali (High Dam) at Aswan, and with plans for development in the Wadi el-Gedid (New Valley Project) in the 1960's (Ezzat 1974a, 1974b, 1975); the Geological Survey and Mineral Research Department carried out field mapping from December, 1959 to May, 1960. Hermina *et al.* (1961) gave a number of measured geological sections, and suggest trends of inferred faults, synclines and anticlines. Said (1962a, 68) gave a simple bedrock sequence at Dakhleh as (top to base): "Chalk; Dakhla shale; Phosphatic beds; Variegated shales; Nubia sandstone". Later Abbas and Habib (1971) and Mansour *et al.* (1982) published on the area west of Gebel Edmonstone, and clarified the stratigraphic terms.

The Project's work in Dakhleh is based on the 1982 1:1,000,000 Dakhla Sheet (Egyptian Geological Survey and Mining Authority 1982). More recently, remapping of the Western Desert at 1:500,000 has been undertaken by German geologists (Fay and Hermann-Degen 1984; Klitzsch *et al.* 1979, 1987a, 1987b; Klitzsch and Schrank 1987), based mainly on satellite imagery with some ground control (List *et al.* 1990). They suggest raising the Nubia Formation to the status of a group and its subdivison into a number of formations. The most recent stratigraphic synthesis for the Kharga-Dakhleh area is by Hermina (1990). The revisions of geological nomenclature in the Western Desert have recently been criticized by Issawi (1993). Here, we will continue to follow some older nomenclature and stratigraphic subdivisions because boundaries between the various proposed formations are not easily detected on the ground. However, we will use the term 'Mut Formation' (Fay and Hermann-Degen 1984; Klitzsch *et al.* 1987a), which includes both shale/claystone and sandstone facies, to refer to the local facies of the Qusseir or Variegated Shales Formation.

Dakhleh Oasis and surroundings are underlain by sedimentary rocks of Late Cretaceous to Eocene age (Table 1.1), which dip east of north at less than 5 degrees (Fig. 1.2). These rocks were deposited in deltaic and marine environments on the southern margin of Tethys Ocean (Hermina *et al.* 1961; Hendriks *et al.* 1984; Hermina 1990). The sinuous trend of the northern Escarpment has been interpreted (Hermina *et al.* 1961, pls VIII, IX) as reflecting northeast-trending anticlines (marked by embayments) and synclines (marked by intervening promontories) with amplitudes up to 100m. While apparently topographically influential, these are not immediately noticeable on the ground. Several normal faults with throws up to ca. 100 m are inferred (Hermina *et al.* 1961, pls V, X, IX). The most prominent trend is northeast-southwest, following the Wadi el-Battikh and the western face of the 'Gifata Promontory' (Hermina 1990, fig. 14.5). [This promontory has been termed the 'Budkhulu promontory' (Hermina *et al.* 1961) or 'Gebel Gifata' (Brookes 1983, 1993, figs. 1, 3; Fay and Hermann-Degen 1984); Gebel Gifata is actually a small hill on top of the promontory.]

The oldest bedrock exposed in Dakhleh is an upper part of the Nubia Formation (or Group) of Cenomanian-Turonian age (Egyptian Geological Survey and Mining Authority 1982; Fay and Hermann-Degen 1984; Hermina 1990, tab. 14.1) (Fig. 1.2). This contains the shallow aquifers tapped by historic wells. The older, deeper Nubia members (or formations) have been tapped by deeper wells since the 1950's (Paver and Pretorius 1954; Ezzat 1974a, 1975; Thorweihe 1990). Dakhleh Oasis sits over the northern portion of the Dakhla basin, which is the most extensive and important in the Nubian aquifer system of Egypt. Contrary to earlier assumptions (e.g., Hammad 1970; Shahin 1985), the Nubian aquifer is "... a fossil ground water reservoir which gets recharged from other fossil reservoirs (Kufra basin, northern Sudan) but, compared to discharge, the recharge is small, ..." (Thorweihe 1990, 601). The Mut and Dakhla formations are the confining beds for the aquifer. The modern piezometric head for ground water at Dakhleh Oasis is calculated at 150 m a.s.l. (Thorweihe 1990). Brookes (1993, 530) notes that recent work has shown that " ... both Holocene and Late Pleistocene rains from Atlantic sources were responsible for local recharge across the presently arid Sahara." This presumably reflects a southerly extension of the northern storm belts.

On reconnaissance with Mills and Wiseman in 1991, Kleindienst noted an unusal outcrop on the east rim of 'Big Pan', south of Ismant, which stands above the Nubia sandstones at ca. 155 m a.s.l. In 1992 Schwarcz identified the rock as an igneous plug; it apparently intrudes into the Taref sandstone, possibly adjacent to a fault line. 'Basaltic' dykes and plugs are mapped in Nubia terrain ca. 130 km south-southeast (Klitzsch *et al.* 1987a); 'basalt' outcrops ca. 260 km to the southwest (Egyptian Geological Survey and Mining Authority 1982) and also southeast of Baharīya and northward (Meneisy 1990, fig. 9.3), but this is the first igneous outcrop recognized near Dakhleh. On analysis

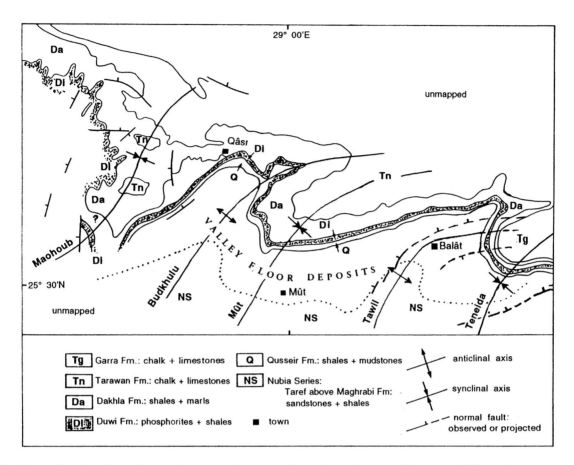

Fig. 1.2. Generalised geological map showing bedrock and formations, based on Hermina (1990), with terminology used here. The Qusseir Formation is locally termed the Mut Formation.

it proves to be a heavily weathered calcareous volcanic, probably a carbonatite (V. Vertolli, pers. comm., Aug. 18, 1994), and is unexpected. The closest known outcrops of carbonatites occur in the southern Eastern Desert, or Sinai (Meneisy 1990).

Above the Nubia Taref Fm. sandstones, red claystones with grey, black and light green beds and sub-vertical clastic dikes underlie the Dakhleh Lowland. These are the 'Variegated Shales' (Klitzsch *et al.* 1979) which are correlated with the Qusseir Formation of the Red Sea coast (Hermina 1990), and which Fay and Hermann-Degen (1984) term the Mut Formation. While red and green muds predominate and are interposed between the eroded Nubia sandstone dip slope and the succeeding Duwi Formation near the foot of the Escarpment, locally sandstone tongues penetrate the Lowland, forming small topographic highs, particularly in eastern Dakhleh. A low sandstone scarp and bench is a prominent feature northeast of Balat to northeast of Ezbet Bashendi (see 'Sandstone Ridges', below).

The succeeding Duwi Formation of Late Campanian-Maastrichtian age (Hermina 1990) comprises >20 m of shales, limestones and several interbedded phosphorites, each 1–2 m thick, and contains an extensive vertebrate and invertebrate fauna (Churcher 1988, this volume, Chapter 2). Where capped by siliceous limestone (Said

1962a), a series of Duwi Fm. cuestas termed the 'Sio'h Ridge' run from south of Gebel Edmonstone northeast past Ezbet Maohoub. The Duwi Fm. is overlain by the latest Cretaceous Dakhla Formation of Maastrichtian age. This is a thick (~250 m) sequence of finely stratified, dark, gypsiferous shales and limey marls, with a 1–5 m shelly limestone(s) in its upper mid-section, the 'Overwegi Bed', which may form a resistant bench in some sections, e.g., Upper Wadi el-Tawil. The type section is established in the Escarpment north of Mut (Said 1962b). The dark shales form a distinctive scarp where dissected by the heads of recent wadis. Across most of the Escarpment face they are protected from erosion by a colluvial mantle and an overlying 20–30+ m thick cap of limestones.

The capping Paleocene to early Eocene limestones and chalks, originally termed 'Chalk' (Said 1962a) or the Tarawan Formation (Issawi 1977), are now divided into three formations, the Tarawan, Garra, and Kurkur (Egyptian Geological Survey and Mining Authority 1982; Klitzsch *et al.* 1987a; Hermina 1990, fig. 14.5), but variable facies confuse the stratigraphy. According to the geological maps, the youngest Garra Formation outcrops on the el-Battikh Promontory and to the northeast. The Kurkur Formation underlies the Garra, partly replacing the upper Dakhla Formation. It consists of marl and marly limestone with dolomite beds and is exposed on the main Abu Tartur Plateau and in the cliff west of Wadi el-Battikh. The Tarawan is also older than the Garra, and seems to be correlative to the west with the upper part of the Kurkur. It consists of white, occasionally cherty, limestone and dolomite, and crops out over the Plateau and scarp face from Wadi el-Tawil westward (Egyptian Geological Survey and Mining Authority 1982), or, alternatively, from Gifata Promontory westward (Klitzsch *et al.* 1987a). However, Hermina (1990, fig. 14.5) considers that the Kurkur Formation caps only the Abu Tartur Plateau, while the Garra Formation outcrops on the Escarpment at Dakhleh from Wadi el-Battikh westward to Gifata Promontory, which is capped by the Tarawan Formation. The Tarawan caps the Escarpment westward from north of Qasr along the edge of the El-Karafish Plateau north of the Qur el-Malik and West Dakhleh/Gharb Maohoub.

Whatever the formational boundaries, the east-to-west change in chalk facies or formations, from Kurkur to Garra to Tarawan, correlates with chert abundances in the Piedmont gravels. Below the cliffs formed in the Kurkur and possible Garra formations, chert fragments are rare to absent in the gravels below the el-Battikh Promontory, and are lacking in the surface veneer on the Plateau north to Wadi el-Tawil; chert fragments are abundant in the gravels from west of Wadi el-Tawil westward to Bab el-Jasmund north of Qasr, and on areas of the Plateau to the north, leading to the contrasts in the oasis between cherty desert pavements across the central piedmont and limestone-rich pavements to east and west (Kleindienst, this volume, Chapter 5). This is not an exact correlation, however.

At varying distances north of the Plateau rim, the greyish green Esna Formation shales form isolated hills and a low escarpment, and are exposed for 5–10 km until overlain by the Thebes Formation's massive limestone with marl and chert bands (Egyptian Geological Survey and Mining Authority 1982). Formations mapped in this northern area by Hermina (1990, fig. 14.5) are more complex, with formations of the Thebes Group overlying the Esna Shale. The Plateau surface has as yet been little explored by the Project's geoscientists.

The biogeology and palaeontology of these formations and units is poorly known. Churcher (this volume, Chapter 2) reports on the vertebrate faunas as so far known, but there has been little recent work on the invertebrate or botanical fossils. All formations but the sandstone facies of the Nubia Group are fossiliferous, even though some are sparingly or unevenly so, with both terrestrial, fluviatile and near shore and deep water marine bioassocies. Von Zittel (1883) made the first report on the fossils from the more obvious Duwi Formation's Phosphorites and possibly some specimens from the overlying Dakhla Formation or underlying Mut Formation's Variegated Shales, but, as he reported no large bones of the obvious larger vertebrates, e.g., chelonians, elasmosaurs or mosasaurs, the specimens apparently were not obtained by his personal examinations of the better fossiliferous outcrops.

The palaeontological resources of Dakhleh Oasis are extensive but will be only briefly reviewed here as Churcher (this volume, Chapter 2,) considers the Cretaceous vertebrate faunas at greater length. The fossil record in the oasis is divisible into two or three periods: 1 – the late Cretaceous terrestrial to deltaic and near shore, to deeper fully marine deposits of the Santonian to Danian or early Palaeocene stages; 2 – the Quaternary record associated with deposits of lacustrine origin; and 3 – deposits with a cultural context in middens, mainly Roman, Byzantine, Islamic or modern, or less concentrated within scatters of Masara, Bashendi or Sheikh Muftah Cultural Units (see McDonald, this volume, Chapter 7, and Churcher, this volume, Chapter 8). Deposits containing mid-Pleistocene fossils were found only in 1996 on the southern and southeastern margins of the present oasis (see below).

The terrestrial Taref Formation sandstones so far have proven barren of any fossil evidence despite the presence of fine clay stringers and coarse channel deposits representing fluviatile conditions conducive to the preservation of small or large animals. The superior or interfingering muds of the Mut Formation are generally barren and no invertebrate remains have been recovered. Three lenses, possibly representing swale or back bar conditions, have yielded mixed assemblages of weathered or water rolled bones and teeth of reptiles and fishes; one has specimens generally less than 5 mm and the others specimens up to 50 mm in diameters. One badly eroded site yielded remnants of the large crocdilian *Dyrosaurus* and a sauropod, possibly *?Aegyptosaurus*, both of which have been recovered from equivalent beds at Kharga Oasis (Pause 1979). Some fossil wood, seeds, cones and fruits, and a few isolated vertebrae, lungfish tooth plates, and teeth have also been found.

The Duwi Formation produces vertebrate bones and teeth of sharks, rays, teleosts, and large reptiles, usually as isolated or partial fragments such as vertebral centra or chelonian carapaxial units which are usually water worn and lack processes. These are usually found within the upper two phosphatic strata, from which they are hard to remove, and are associated with many small peloids, up to 40 mm long, probably of teleost origin. The under surfaces of the phosphatic strata bear internal casts of interlacing burrows in the underlying mud, presumably made by crabs (Fig. 1.3, Top). Isolated vertebral and other bony elements are sparsely present in the intervening shales.

The Dakhla Formation is composed of mainly black shales with greenish and reddish strata, interspersed with marl beds of limited extent, and interrupted by a thick (1–2 m) oyster shell bed (the Overwegi Bed, mainly composed of *Exogyra overwegi*). Scattered and usually disarticulated isolated teeth or skeletal elements of sharks, teleosts (Fig. 1.3, Bottom), mosasaurs, plesiosaurs and turtles are found and occasional decapod crustacean fragments, and ammonite or cephalopod shells also occur, especially above the Overwegi Bed.

The capping Tarawan, Kurkur and Garra formations

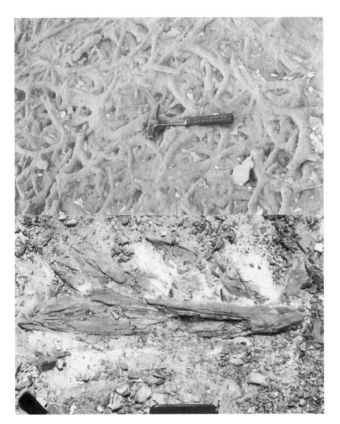

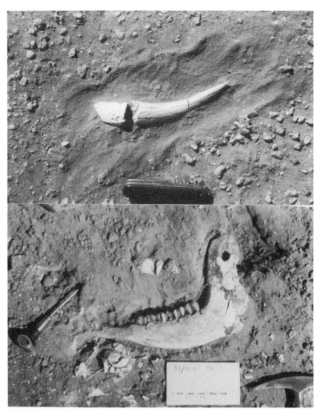

Fig. 1.3. TOP, Underside of phosphorite block from Duwi Formation, north of Bashendi. A web of branching passages, presumably constructed by crabs, was excavated in soft black mud (now shale), and later cast in phosphate rich detritus. C.S.C., Feb., 1987. BOTTOM, Bonyfish (Enchodus sp.) lower jaw in middle Dakhla Formation shale, upper valley of Wadi el-Tawil. Symphysis is to the right, angle to left and three teeth are visible. Knife is 100 mm long. C.S.C. Feb., 1991.

Fig. 1.4. TOP, Horn core of gazelle (Gazella cf. leptoceros) from Neolithic deposits near Sheikh Muftah (Loc. 092, 31/420–F9–3). Breaks are natural taphonomic damage. Area around horn core has been brushed clear of debris. Knife is 100 mm long. C.S.C., Feb., 1987. BOTTOM, Immature bovid dentary (cf. Bos sp.) from Neolithic deposits east of Teneida (Loc. 100, 31/420–P6–1). Jaw has been exposed for preserving and jacketting. Note other bone fragments near jaw. C.S.C., Dec., 1982.

chalks and limestones contain many bivalve molluscs, at least two ammonites, bryozoa, corals, snails, and crabs, which weather out onto the slopes below as haematite stained fossils. No vertebrate remains have been found in these capping deposits.

No attempt has been made to investigate the invertebrate faunas of these formations and that for the vertebrates has depended on chance discoveries.

The Holocene faunas are represented by scattered and broken bones and teeth of wild and possibly domestic animals in lacustrine littoral muds (e.g., Loc. 006, 32/390–D2–2; Bashendi Cultural Unit) or in playa deposits of silty aeolian sand as in the eastern basins (Sheikh Muftah Cultural Unit) shown by the gazelle horncore and bovid dentary (Fig. 1.4). These archaeozoological specimens derive from contexts in which direct linkages to humans are usually unavailable but artifacts and green breaks exposing marrow cavities are present, as in the Bashendi Cultural Unit, even if sparse and, in the Sheikh Muftah Cultural Unit, reflects human modification of ostrich shell into beads, and bones with punctured holes or made into needles.

III. REGIONAL GEOMORPHOLOGY AND QUATERNARY GEOLOGY

The Western Desert has attracted many scientific explorers: early travellers returned with information on meteorology, topography, geology, hydrography, biology, ecology, archaeology and ethnology, e.g., (Ball 1900, 1927; Beadnell 1901a, 1909; Forbes 1921; Hassanein Bey 1925; Rohlfs 1875; Shaw 1929; Wingate 1934; Winlock 1936). Improved equipment (e.g., Bagnold 1931, 1933, 1939) facilitated more detailed work in the 1930's (e.g., Bagnold 1941; Clayton and Spencer 1934; Sandford 1933a, 1933b, 1933c; Shaw 1936; Peel 1941). Wendorf and Schild (1980) have reviewed the history of work in the Western Desert/Eastern Sahara (see Mills, this volume, Chapter 10).

An archaeological record of protracted human occupation in northern Kharga Oasis was discovered by G. Caton-Thompson and E.W. Gardner during three seasons' work in 1930 to 1933 (Caton-Thompson 1931a, 1931b, 1932, 1952, 1983; Caton-Thompson and Gardner 1932; Gardner

1932, 1935; Sandford 1933a). They produced a regional archaeological and geological sequence which now needs to be reassessed, but which has been used as a widely-applied reference sequence in the later work at Western Desert oases and elsewhere (cf. Brookes 1993). In this work, Caton-Thompson pioneered the application of quantitive methods in Pleistocene archaeology, and the use of air survey and multidisciplinary regional studies in African archaeology.

Following 1960's surveys in the Nile Valley in Nubia and Upper Egypt, archaeological work by the Combined Prehistoric Expedition (CPE) extended into the Egyptian oases and intervening desert in the 1970's (Close 1987a, 1987b; Kobusiewicz 1987; Schild 1987; Schild and Wendorf 1975, 1977, 1981; Wendorf and Schild 1976, 1980; Wendorf *et al.* 1976, 1977; 1987; 1993). Brief observations on Quaternary geology in Dakhleh were made by Haynes (1983), Hermina *et al.* (1961), and Issawi (1977; Wendorf and Schild 1980).

IV. QUATERNARY GEOMORPHOLOGY AND GEOLOGY

Chronometric Dating

The sedimentary deposits of the Dakhleh region are potentially dateable by some methods of Quaternary geochronology. Detrital, siliceous windblown sediments

can be dated by optically stimulated luminescence (OSL: Godfrey-Smith *et al.* 1988), over a possible time range from 1 to 150 kiloyears (ka). This method has not yet been applied in the oasis area, although Stokes (1993) used it to date sediments in the Bir Tarfawi area of southern Egypt. Similarly, thermoluminescence dating (Aitken 1985, 1990) may be applicable to some primary quartz deposits formed in siliceous sinters in spring mounds.

Uranium-series dating (U/Th) is applicable to chemically or biologically precipitated carbonate deposits such as those found scattered through the Dakhleh lowland (Schwarcz 1989; Latham and Schwarcz 1991). The method is based on the assumption that freshly deposited fresh-water carbonates contain trace amounts of uranium (U) but contain negligible amounts of thorium (Th). The age of the deposit is determined from measurement of the amount of the daughter isotope ^{230}Th that has formed from its parent ^{234}U. The half life of this formation is about 75,000 years, and dates can be determined to a limit of about 350,000 yrs. The precision of the method is about ± 5–10% when isotopic measurements are made by alpha spectrometry. A much higher precision is now available (>± 1%) using thermal ionization mass spectrometry (TIMS). In principle, U-series dating is applicable to any fresh-water carbonate deposit such as travertine, caliche, or playa-lake marl. In practice, however many such surficial and near-surface deposits are contaminated with windblown dust containing an 'old' thorium component that leads to erratic dating behaviours. These problems can generally be recognized

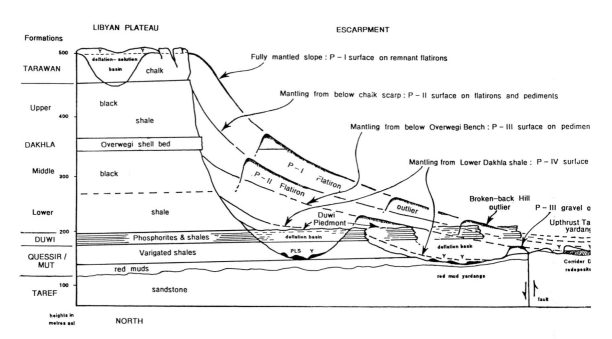

Fig. 1.5. *N-S sectional view through the Libyan Escarpment and the eastern Dakhleh Oasis west of Balat. This idealised section shows a generalised stratigraphic section, faults, and erosional surfaces and features. Yardangs (Y) are common and may occur in Tarawan Formation Chalk, Pleistocene Laminated Sediments (PLS), Mut Formation Red Muds or Taref Formation Sandstones. Deflation basins occur on the Libyan Plateau, at the escarpment foot within or outside the Duwi Formation Piedmont, in the oasis basin proper, and in the sand covered pans south of the southern Taref Formation sandstone boundary ridge of the oasis. The Libyan Plateau basins may penetrate into the upper Dakhla Shale (Upper Wadi*

through the presence of contaminant [232]Th, an isotope which is not formed by radioactive decay, but accompanies contaminant (non-radiogenic) [230]Th.

Schwarcz has applied U-series dating to some samples from the Dakhleh region, in order to determine the times in the past when carbonate-charged, fresh-water deposits (spring, or runoff/seepage) were forming. We believe that these would also have been times of greater rainfall recharge of shallow aquifers, and probably would have been coincident with times of human occupation of the area. Artesian springs, anciently or recently active in the lowland, have not deposited calcium carbonate ($CaCO_3$), and were presumably undersaturated with it. Calcite depositing springs would presumably have been fed by shallower aquifers which were recharged locally through the capping limestones and dolomites on the Libyan Plateau, and which would have then emerged from the Escarpment to deposit $CaCO_3$ precipitates. Conditions favouring spring deposition of travertines would therefore be restricted to times of at least intermittant pluvial activity. Overland runoff, or near-surface seepage might also have supplied $CaCO_3$–charged water into the Dakhleh Lowland during such periods.

The samples studied from the Dakhleh region are of two types: a) Isolated fragments of spring-deposited tufa found by Churcher, Kleindienst or Schwarcz on colluvial slopes or in Piedmont gravels near the base of the Escarpment, and in isolated remnants further south; presumably these eroded from larger, undiscovered fossil spring deposits similar to those described at Kharga ('wadi tufa' of Caton-Thompson 1952) or b) Dense, silty carbonate sheets (CSS) that form caps on eroded remnants of pediment-related surfaces in the Dakhleh Lowland. Unfortunately, there has been little success so far in attempts to date the second type of deposit, largely because some feature of their chemical composition makes it difficult to obtain adequate chemical yields during extraction of U and Th. Results of the U-series dating are reported here in the context of the discussion of the sites where each sample was obtained (see below). U-series determinations are cited plus/minus 2 sigma yr BP.

Cited radiocarbon determinations are uncalibrated, and cited plus/minus 1 sigma yr BP. Where noted, determinations on ostrich egg shell are adjusted only for fractionation.

Archaeological sites are designated by DOP Grid References (Appendix II), based on 1:25,000 map sheets which mainly cover the inhabited oasis. Prehistorians working outside that area, and for other reasons, designate archaeological find areas by Locality Numbers (Appendix III), and by Grid when possible (see Kleindienst, this volume, Chapter 5). Both 'Loc.' and Grid references may apply to locations noted below.

Quaternary Geomorphology and Geology

Brookes (1983, 1986) mapped the geomorphology of Dakhleh Oasis in six units – 1) northern plateau, 2) northern

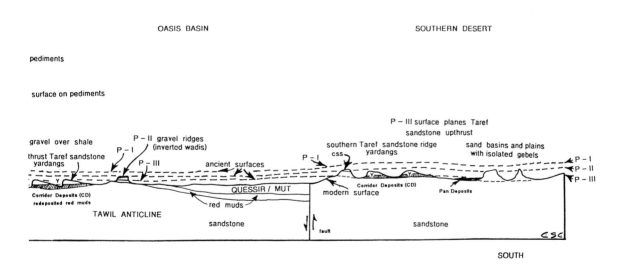

el-Tawil, Pharaoh's Playa) or not (Miramar Basin). PLS yardangs are formed in aqueously deposited sediments, red mud yardangs in in situ Mut Formation red muds or claystones, and sandstone yardangs in Taref Formation Sandstones which may contain infilling Corridor Deposits to 6 m depth, chiefly formed of aeolian sand and red mud particles. Past pediments are capped by boulder layers (fringed surfaces). Calcareous Silty Sediments (CSS, see Fig. 1.6) cap some Taref Formation sandstone yardangs along the southern oasis boundary ridge. The surface of the oasis basin is being continually lowered by aeolian erosion. Horizontal distance approximately 30 km, not to scale.

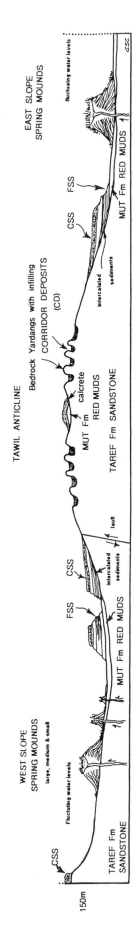

Fig. 1.6. Schematic W-E cross-sectional view through Tawil anticline at lattitude of Sheikh Muftah, showing sequences and distribution of Quaternary deposits on the Nubia Group bedrocks. The Cretaceous Nubia Group comprises the Taref Formation sandstone with Mut Formation red muds or claystones and Mut Formation red muds or claystones. The Quaternary deposits are both Pleistocene and Holocene and comprise Ferruginous Sandy Sediments (FSS), Calcareous Silty Sediments (CSS), Corridor Deposits (CD), and Spring Mound deposits. The history and genesis of FSS, CSS and their interbedded sediments are at present unclear: CSS may have been deposited in more than one episode or in a prograding manner ascending the anticline's flanks. Water levels appear to have varied and may have reached heights > 150 m a.s.l. when CSS to the west was deposited. Aeolian sculpted N-S oriented bedrock yardangs and corridors on the anticline crest represent a desiccation episode in contrast to the humid episode(s) represented by the CSS, FSS, CD and spring mound deposits.

escarpment, 3) northern piedmont, 4) central lowland, 5) fossil spring-related sediments, and 6) southern sandstone ridge and plain. These can be condensed into four main areas (Mabbutt 1977, fig. 9A; Brookes 1989b) as 1), 2), 3+4+5), and 6). Brookes (1993, 531) has recently simplified his classification into "(1) Libyan Plateau, (2) Dakhla Scarp and Piedmont, (3) Dakhla Lowland, (4) Southern Cuesta and Plain". A slightly different organization will be followed here. The surficial units recognized are shown in Figure 1.2. Figure 1.5 is a schematic north-south geologic section across eastern Dakhleh, illustrating the geomorphic regions, and the settings for Quaternary sedimentary units discussed below. The numerical designations for the sedimentary units previously used by Brookes (1986) are replaced here by descriptive labels and initials in the legend to Fig. 1.5 (cf. Brookes 1993, fig. 4). Figure 1.6 is a schematic west-east geologic section across the Tawil Anticline (Fig. 1.2) at about the latitude of Sheikh Muftah.

1) Northern Plateau

Satellite images and aerial photographs show that the Libyan Plateau to the north of Dakhleh Oasis comprises several geomorphological zones reflecting rock outcrop patterns and geomorphic processes (Brookes 1989b, fig. 2; 1993, fig. 3). The broadest division is into a southern zone ending at the edge of the Libyan Escarpment, where limestones are eroded into extensive fields of closely-spaced yardang hills, and a northern zone, from 4 to 14 km north of the scarp, marked by west-east, shallow crests, with smooth dip slopes and straight scarps, marking the outcrop of weaker beds (Brookes 1986, 1993). Over the northern zone, dip slopes are crossed by north-directed, joint-controlled, dendritic, dry-valley systems. The apparent lack of aeolian erosion here suggests a recent origin, probably during Holocene wet episodes recorded in sediments in some Plateau basins (Miramar Basin', see below) (Brookes 1986, figs 1–5).

As reported by Brookes (1986), in the southern zone, the gently north-dipping limestone formations are cut by an erosional surface which slopes gently upwards to the north, from about 500 m a.s.l. at the plateau edge (maximum 564 m on the western el-Battikh Promontory, minimum 419 m in the central re-entrant). Prominent regional joint systems trend between 135° and 150°, and weaker ones between 010° and 050°. Locally, these influence yardang distribution and morphology, as well as the orientation of parts of the Escarpment.

It appears that an older rolling topography once existed on the Plateau, which may have been strongly influenced by karstic processes. Evidence of such processes is preserved on the west flank of the local Miramar Basin, where Kleindienst discovered a solutional conduit opening onto a joint-controlled gully. The conduit and adjacent fissures are lined with large, euhedral, varicoloured calcite crystals. An attempt was made to date a sample of these by U-series analysis but the sample was too contaminated to provide a meaningful date (cf. Brookes 1993). The actual age may be late Tertiary. Extensive karst topography, less obscured by subsequent aeolian erosion, has been recognized in the Eocene limestone plateau around Bahariya Oasis north of Dakhleh (El Aref *et al.* 1987), and solution caves are known on the Plateau (C. Bergmann, pers. comm., Feb. 8, 1992). Said (1990b) notes that boreholes on the Abu Tartur Plateau penetrated virtual solution cavities.

The mechanically strong limestone formations of the Plateau have been sculptured by wind into extensive fields of parallel yardangs (Brookes 1986), a topography termed 'kharafish' by Beadnell (1909, 35; Hobbs 1917). "The Arabic term 'Karafish (p. Khurfush)' (Charaschaf of Rohlfs Expedition) is used to denote a particular type of desert, that produced by sand erosion of hard limestone, which leaves a rocky surface closely resembling a rough sea" (Beadnell 1901b, 13). He noted this topography as charcteristic of the Plateau surface along the southern part of the camel track leading from Bab el-Jasmund to Farafra, later called the El Karafish Pleateau (Hermina 1990). The term *yardang* ('*jardang*') appears to have been first applied to the Western Desert by Hobbs (1917, 39). Yardang morphology varies with bedrock lithology and three forms are recognized in the Dakhleh area: 1) Linear, tabular forms up to 2 km long, 300 m wide, and 30 m high are separated by narrow (<100 m wide), straight, V-shaped corridors or *couloirs* (Grolier *et al.* 1980): this form occurs only locally adjacent to the plateau edge north of Balat (Fig. 1.7). 2) Short (<1 km long), blunter, streamlined forms, usually with narrow crests, and up to 60 m high, often with rock-controlled, stepped profiles, are separated by corridors which range from narrow V's to broad and level-floored U's. This form crosses bedrock lithologies, and may ring deflated basins as at Miramar (Brookes 1989b, fig. 4a). 3) Linear (<1 km long), narrow (<100 m wide) and generally low yardangs (<20 m high) are generally restricted to the northern fringe of the Garra limestone outcrop. Solution and mechanical erosion along intersecting joints have imparted an *en echelon* pattern to yardang fields, but yardang orientation is parallel to wind directions, which vary with the promontories and embayments in the plateau edge. Where least affected yardangs trend at 005°–185°; the range is from ca. 160° in the west to ca. 200° in the east (Brookes 1993).

Yardang-free areas occur on the Plateau. Within yardang fields, basins with areas up to 4 km² are deeply deflated. The Miramar Basin (Fig. 1.8; and see below) in limestone contains lake and fluvial sediments and archaeological sites. A more extensive basin ('Pharaoh's Playa') with archaeological remains north of Maohoub is floored by Dakhla Formation shales (basins 'B' and 'A', respectively, in Brookes 1993, fig. 3). The upper reaches of both wadis el-Tawil and el-Battikh appear to be basins that penetrated the Dakhla Fm. shale boundary and, probably by hydrological sapping through these shales, breached

Fig. 1.7. Close-set bedrock yardangs in Tarawan Formation limestones northeast of Miramar Basin forming a peneplain surface to the Libyan Plateau, looking north-northeast. Note weathered greyed crests, windscoured flanks and fluvial deposits on floors. M.R.K., Jan., 1986.

Fig. 1.8. TOP, Miramar Basin on the Libyan Plateau. View from first limestone yardang on the northwest rim, looking SSE to areas of low yardangs in Holocene/latest Pleistocene sediments in the central and eastern parts of the basin. Silt haze, due to strong northerly wind. M.R.K., Jan., 1986.
BOTTOM, Miramar Basin. View northeast to yardangs formed in Holocene/latest Pleistocene sediments from south-central edge of 'lacustrine' sediments. Greyed limestone caps bedrock yardang gebels which rim the basin. Note lighter colour marking probable former elevation of basin filling, and current level of aeolian erosion. M.R.K., Jan., 1986.

Fig. 1.9. Linear yardang hills formed in Garra Formation limestone on surface of Libyan Plateau, looking south from the south crest of upper valley of Wadi el-Tawil across el-Battikh Promontory. C.S.C., Feb., 1994.

the chalk or limestone rim to join shorter wadi reentrants, forming the modern longer valleys. Other basins have yet to be explored. Such depressions on the Plateau appear to be analogous to the *dayas* of northwestern Africa (Clark *et al.* 1974; Mitchell and Willimott 1974).

Some yardang-free areas are more extensive (Brookes 1993), such as the smooth surface on top of Gebel Edmonstone, where a 6 km long, flat-topped oval remnant, with a surface area of approximately 16 km², stands about 6 km from the crest of the western 'Maohoub Promontory' of the Plateau. To the north, a small outlier which has recently been partially severed from the plateau edge of the Maohoub Promontory bears traces of yardangs on only its upwind northern edge. The central Gifata Promontory (Fig. 1.1) is also free of yardangs, as is the area immediately north of Wadi el-Tawil ('Tawil Promontory', termed 'Wadi el Tawil Plateau' by Hermina 1990, fig. 14.5). The surface of the el-Battikh Promontory has long, low limestone yardangs separated by wide valleys (Fig. 1.9)

In the yardang free areas the Plateau surface is covered by a chert-rich lag, which includes Pleistocene, and in some places Holocene, artifacts. Although no systematic archaeological survey has been done, it is reported that artifacts can be found across the entire length of the Libyan Plateau north of Dakhleh (C. Bergmann, pers. comm., Feb., 1992, observed from camel traverses).

Miramar Basin
In 1986, Brookes (1986, fig. 2) identified on aerial photographs a closed basin, 2.1 × 1.2 km and area of ca. 2.5 km², at 25° 41'12" N & 29° 14'48" E, within an extensive bedrock yardang field on the Plateau (Fig. 1.1). The basin contains a small field of yardangs at the north end sculptured in obviously unconsolidated sediments. It lies 7 km north of the plateau edge, on the longitude of Balat (Brookes 1989b, fig. 4, 'Area B') (Fig. 1.10). A three-day reconnaissance in January, 1986, by Brookes, Churcher, Hollett, Kleindienst and McDonald established that the

Fig. 1.10. TOP, Miramar Basin on the Libyan Plateau. Dead recent Holocene vegetation, probably Cornulaca monacantha, *grown on eroded laminated Holocene/latest Pleistocene silts, looking northeast to greyed limestone yardangs which rim basin. Lighter coloured sediments in background mark elevation of recent aeolian erosion, and possible original level of basin infilling. Holocene limestone artifacts on small bench in foreground; geological hammer at base of bush for scale. M.R.K., Jan., 1986. BOTTOM, Miramar Basin, looking north from northeast corner along corridors between limestone yardangs capped by greyed limestone rubble. High section of laminated Holocene/latest Pleistocene sediments on left; geological hammer for scale. M.R.K., Jan., 1986.*

fine-grained sediments in the north end of the basin are stratified and lacustrine (or similar) in type. Brookes and C. Campbell returned for a second visit in 1990, and Campbell grid-collected surface material from a Masara archaeological occurrence found weathering out of the sediments in the northwestern part of the basin by McDonald in 1986 (Loc. 166, 33/435–C7–2, Campbell 1990).

The stratified sediments overlie an undulating, deflated, fluted limestone floor exposed only in the northwest corner. Four metres of sediments are exposed in yardangs near the western margin but a greater depth of sediments probably exists lower in the basin (Brookes extrapolated a minimum depth of 8 m), but aeolian erosion limits the height of exposures to ca. 4 m. The sediments are horizontally stratified, alternating beds of silty clay and clayey silt with minor sand and gravel beds (Fig. 1.10). Cyclothem beds are 1–5 cm thick and usually yellowish brown. Samples from several levels yielded no contemporary organic remains, although vegetation, mostly dead, once grew in coppice dunes in wadis cut through the sediments or on the sediments. The sediments are mixed with angular bedrock fragments near the eastern margin of the basin, which derive from tributary wadis and basin walls, but stratified muds suggest calm-water sedimentation well in-shore. No shoreline features could be identified. In the many sections examined, Brookes noted a single mud-cracked bed near the base of the exposed sequence, and evaporite horizons are absent. Therefore, he interpreted the lake as perennial, except for the one episode of desiccation. An indurated, halite-rich crust caps the sediments, where preserved, around the margins of the basin. The crust is overlain by up to 25 cm of crudely-bedded fluvial gravels, consisting of unsorted, platy fragments of friable limestone which extend upslope into the main tributary wadis at the south edge of the basin. In the north-central area the gravels and the crust have been dissected to expose the lake muds to wind erosion, forming the small yardangs. More recent wadis from the southwest, southeast, and northeast corners of the basin have incised the fluvial gravels, with those from the southwest and southeast extending into the yardang area and deflated basin floor (Brookes 1989b). Brookes (1993, 535) subsequently revised his interpretation, and now describes the sediments as 'playa sediments', laid-down in an '... intermittent lake by episodic rain-fed runoff ...'

Archaeological reconnaissance by McDonald and Kleindienst of the former lake-floor area and surrounding gebels established that all artifacts are typical of Holocene occupations: indeed, no Pleistocene artifacts were found either in the basin or on the surrounding yardangs except for obvious 'holoports' (see Kleindienst, this volume, Chapter 5). Local raw materials are poor quality grey cherts to the south and north of the basin, and an outcrop of excellent quality translucent brown chert nodules in the limestone of the eastern side of the basin, used by the Holocene peoples.

The earliest industry is represented by small knapping areas on the surface of the lacustrine sediments, and is similar to Epipalaeolithic Masara Unit sites in the Dakhleh lowland (McDonald 1986, 1987, 1991a, 1991b, this volume, Chapter 7). A ^{14}C date of 8,270 ± 160 yr BP (Beta-17022) from Loc. 166 (33/435–C7–2) (Brookes 1989b, tab. 2; McDonald 1990a, fig. 4; 1990b) was obtained on ostrich eggshell from the surface scatter. It suggests deposition of the sediments during Later Pleistocene or earliest Holocene times. The archaeological aggregate, collected by Campbell from Loc. 166 in 1990, comprises artifacts with charcoal, ostrich egg shell and bone fragments (gazelle) weathering out of a yardang, from a calcareous horizon, about 4.5 m below an eroded surface overlain by wadi gravel (Campbell 1990). Brookes (1993: 535) has obtained two radiocarbon dates for this material: 8,650 ± 170 yr BP (Gd-4563) on ostrich eggshell

(adjusted for fractionation = 9,050 ± 170); and 8,170 ± 110 yr BP (TO-2360) on charcoal; while a small charcoal sample from about 1.5 m higher in the sediments gave a date of 7,380 ± 80 yr BP (TO-2362).

A second locality (Loc. 165, 33/435–C7–1) on wadi gravels, just below the eroded edge of the salt-crusted lake sediments, contains Bashendi Unit, phase B artifacts (McDonald 1990c). Ostrich eggshell from that surface was dated at 6,210 ± 130 yrs BP (Beta-17023, adjusted for fractionation = 6,480 ± 130), which gives a minimum age for the gravel surface.

A third locality lies on the upper surface of the wadi gravels on the east side of the basin. It contains an amorphous flake industry, without ground stone. A date of 4,720 ± 330 yr BP (Beta-17021) is suspect as it is based on a single piece of eggshell which yielded only 0.15 g of carbon. The tentative sequence of basin sedimentation is (cf. Brookes 1989b):

1) Deposition of at least 8 m of stratified sediments over an undulating limestone basin floor in a shallow, perennial lake. Stratified sediments were supplied by periodic (?seasonal) fluvial input from a catchment basin where environmental conditions reduced the influx of aeolian sand.
2) Desiccation of the lake and evaporative concentration of salts in the surface sediments to form an indurated crust.
3) Deposition of fluvial gravels over the basin floor from one or more intense storms. The lack of horizontal partings in the gravels makes it possible that they were emplaced in one intense event. (The basin to the north is completely mantled by gravel cover.)
5) Aeolian deflation of the north-central part of the basin to form yardangs and a level floor in the lake beds, accompanied or followed by down-cutting in the wadis crossing the basin floor. Aeolian action continues today.

The existence of an open water body on the Plateau raises an important question. Maintenance of a lake over any extended period in a basin underlain and surrounded by porous, well-jointed limestone, at latitude about 26°N, where potential evapotranspiration today is extremely high, calls for a special combination of climatic, hydrogeologic, and vegetative conditions.

To provide sufficient runoff, an elevated water table and vegetative cover, rainfall would have had to increase greatly. Brookes (1993) notes that runoff was energetic enough to transport gravel into the basin at least eight times. The Plateau sediments record only one episode of marked desiccation, which suggests that the ground water table may have been raised sufficiently to maintain the lake through the dry season, or that strong seasonality did not exist. (In the western Sahara, a marked seasonal regime was only established ca. 7500 BP [Casey 1993, 29–30].) Rarity of aeolian sands in the lake sediments indicates minimal erosion of the Plateau upwind of the lake, which

Fig. 1.11. Libyan Escarpment on the north face of el-Battikh Promontory, showing mature greyed-limestone colluvium on rolling slumped topography now undergoing modification by recent gully incision. The terrace in foreground is capped by light coloured P-III limestone/chert gravels and cut into the Duwi Formation. This terrace traces up the Wadi el-Tawil to below the head of the lower valley section. Although historic reports site the Darb el-Tawil camel road along the wadi floor, air photographs show that an ancient donkey and foot track ascends the Escarpment here. C.S.C., Feb., 1994.

Fig. 1.12. TOP, Columnar limestone blocks of the Garra Formation falling away from the west face of el-Battikh Promontory. Note shear fissure of crest of central hill. Northeastern Dakhleh Piedmont and Libyan Escarpment in background. M.R.K., Jan., 1986. BOTTOM, Shear fissures parallel to and at right angles to Escarpment lip at south margin of el-Battikh Promontory. The fissures are partly filled with sand and limestone fragments, but still >2 m deep. Duwi Formation Piedmont gebels and cultivation near Teneida visible in left distance. Wadi el-Tawil P-III and P-IV outwash plain visible beyond the scarp edge. C.S.C., Feb., 1996.

probably reflects a dense ground cover (Brookes 1989b, 1993) and/or reduced windiness. However, a ground cover of grasses, trees and shrubs would increase water loss through transpiration (Todd 1980, fig. 6.14). Reduced evapotranspiration could have been achieved through decreased temperatures and/or by increased cloudiness. Unfortunately, the drainage basin area for the lake cannot be determined in the surrounding yardang-and-corridor terrain. Other basins have yet to be explored.

2) Northern or Libyan Escarpment

The Northern or Libyan Escarpment is a 300 m high feature, visible from almost everywhere in Dakhleh Oasis. A general west-northwest to east-southeast orientation is broken by four main promontories and their flanking embayments (from east to west, termed here the el-Battikh Promontory east of Tenida, the el-Tawil Promontory north of Wadi el-Tawil, the Gifata Promontory north of Ismant, and the Maohoub Promontory northwest of Ezbet Sheikh Maohoub) which may reflect northeast-trending synclines and anticlines (Hermina *et al.* 1961) (Fig. 1.1). Dips on the fold limbs are visually imperceptible, but structural contours of the top of the Nubia Formation (Ezzat 1975, pl. III.7) show dips of 0.5°–5°.

The Escarpment crest, usually sharp but occasionally smoothed by colluvial cover or weathered to a convex profile (Fig. 1.11), truncates Plateau yardangs, so its present position post-dates the aeolian landforms on the Plateau (Brookes 1993, fig. 5a). While the bedrock yardangs post-date a (possibly Tertiary?) period of

karstification, climates humid enough to promote cliff-sapping have returned more than once since yardang formation, and yardangs have probably been rejuvenated in the drier intervals. The Dakhleh Escarpment is a typical caprock scarp in which more competent chalk formations overlie the less resistant Dakhla Shales (Oberlander 1989, figs 4.1, 4.9A). Although none of the other resistant beds are as thick as the caprock, it can be classed as a complex scarp (Shumm and Chorley 1966). The scarp crest displays a series of steep arcuate or amphitheatral embayments (Mabbutt 1977, 143) resulting from cliff-sapping at the heads of ravines (Brookes 1993, fig. 5c). The geology of the Escarpment facilitates this process, which has also affected the scarp around Kharga Oasis (Caton-Thompson and Gardner 1932). In places, collapse-movement has been arrested by colluvium so that the Plateau edge displays a tessellated pattern of joint-bounded limestone blocks in precarious array (Fig. 1.12), for instance, on the western

Fig. 1.13. TOP, Colluvium mantling Libyan Escarpement, north of Bashendi, with large limestone collapse block incorporating chert nodules, resting in wadi draining beheaded flatiron, and acting to channel wind downslope. White limestone and dark chert cobbles in wadi heavily abraded and ventifacted. M.R.K., Feb., 1992. BOTTOM, Escarpment north of Sheikh Maohoub. Collapsed blocks of Tarawan Formation limestone, rubble and shale overlying the Overwegi Shell Bed, within the Dakhla Formation black shale, exposed on side of new wadi. Note ancient weathered surface at top left and sand lining wadi floor. C.S.C., Feb., 1995.

contact with the Overwegi bed where modern seepage springs emerge (Kleindienst, this volume, Chapter 5). Saturated shales would have disaggregated and deformed plastically under the weight of the overlying caprock (Brookes 1983, pl. XVIb, 1986; cf. Grunert *et al.* 1979 for evidence of Pleistocene landslides on the Nubia sandstone escarpments in southern Libya, at about the same latitude as Dakhleh). Grunert and Busche (1980, 859) note among the places where landslides are known in the Sahara are "... the margins of the oases of Al Kharga, Dakhla and Bahariyah in the Egyptian Western Desert." Evidence of plastic deformation and flow in Dakhla Shale can be seen on the north side of the lower Wadi el-Tawil (Fig. 1.14), and in typical slump topography and rotated slump blocks along the faces of the el-Battikh and el-Tawil promontories, and elsewhere (Fig. 1.12, Top). W.J. Vreeken also noted evidence of debris flow on the west face of el-Battikh Promontory (Brookes 1993, 535, footnote, fig. 5d).

A large rotated slump block is prominent near the head of upper Wadi el-Tawil, and another, representing a much more ancient event in Escarpment retreat, is a rotated block of Duwi Formation sediments, 'Broken-back Hill',

face of the el-Battikh Promontory, or north of Ezbet Sheikh Maohoub (Brookes 1983, pl. XVIa). Northwest-southeast joints often control the orientation of the eastern rim of an embayment, while sympathetic perpendicular tensional fractures control the west rim (Brookes 1986). Occasional huge limestone blocks are found resting on the colluvium (Brookes 1993, fig. 5b), in some cases showing collapse from the caprock which predates deep incision separating the beheaded colluvial slope from the Escarpment face, as seen north of Bashendi (Fig. 1.13).

Precipitation would reach the Dakhla Shales directly where basins on the Plateau surface penetrate the limestone caprock, as at Pharaoh's Basin, or where broad upper valleys develop at the head of major reentrants, as in Wadi el-Tawil or Wadi el-Battikh. Water would also have percolated through the porous and fractured limestone cap, to emerge in springs at the contact with the more impervious Dakhleh Shales or within the shales at the

Fig. 1.14. TOP, North side of Wadi el-Tawil, near head of older, lower valley section, showing debris flow into pre-existing valley. The underlying Dakhla Formation shales are contorted and squeezed into the overlying colluvium, indicating wet plastic flow. C.S.C., March, 1992. BOTTOM, Wadi el-Tawil, lower part. Debris slumped over Dakhla Formation shales. C.S.C., March, 1992.

Fig. 1.15. TOP, Rotated slump block at head of upper valley of Wadi el-Tawil, looking south, showing old greyed limestone rubble surface on east slope. Level of valley bottom is bench supported by Overwegi Bed, overlain by thin capping of Upper Dakhla Formation shales. M.R.K., March, 1992. BOTTOM, Broken-back Hill, an ancient rotated slump block of Mut and Duwi Formations on the northern margin of the Dakhleh Lowland, northwest of Balat. It is capped by P-I gravels, has a P-III grave-capped terrace at its foot, and is seen from the southwest across a modern wadi. The Libyan Escarpment is visible between the gebels and on the right. Hermina et al. (1961) probably interpreted the slump fault as a linear bedrock fault. M.R.K., Feb., 1996.

However, the debris-flow topography flanking the northeastern reentrants (Wadi el-Tawil and 'North Wadi' or el-Ueb: Jordan 1875b, taf. 11) may belong to a later colluvial episode (C-III). Scarp retreat by cliff sapping and collapse must have taken place over an extended period, but preliminary U/Th dating on tufa blocks by Schwarcz shows that some are beyond dating range, indicating that the Dakhleh escarpment may have reached approximately its present position over 350,000 years ago (MRK1988/DAK 1). Butzer and Hansen (1968) argued that scarp retreat of 10–15 km after the late Pliocene is implied by outliers of plateau tufa interpreted to be of that age in Kurkur, Dungul, and Kharga oases. There is no evidence to suggest such a magnitude of scarp retreat at Dakhleh, and Oberlander uses it as an example of a 'stagnant' erosional form (Oberlander 1989, fig. 4.9A; misidentified as Kharga in Oberlander, 1994, fig. 2.5,b; Brookes 1983). If such did occur, we must account for the removal of much larger masses of debris from the area by aeolian and/or fluvial transport (cf. Said 1983, 1990b)!

On the Libyan Escarpment today, earlier erosional ravines that are filled with thicker colluvial rubbles than

Fig. 1.16. TOP, Erosion of limestone rubble mantling Dakhla Formation shales on northwest face of el-Battikh Promontory. A P-III terrace is visible in the foreground. C.S.C., Feb., 1994. BOTTOM, Cliff foot recesses at base of Garra Formation limestone on west face of el-Battikh Promontory, at Military Road. Note weathered honeycombed limestone of cliff face and unweathered white recesses. Stone walled structures are disused weapons pits. Johannes Walter for scale. M.R.K., Feb., 1996.

in the piedmont on the northern rim of the central Lowland (Fig. 1.15). Thus, there is evidence both of caprock collapse and debris flow in the formation of the Escarpment. Masses of shale and limestone rubble have progressively mantled the Escarpment-face (Fig. 1.16, Top), and are now being stripped away. 'Cliff foot recesses' (Smith 1978) have only been noted on el-Battikh Promontory, where the limestone meets the debris slope, at the summit of the road up the Escarpment from Teneida (Fig. 1.16, Bottom). The lighter colour of the limestone in the basal zone suggests recent exposure and weathering. Apparently, some of these small shelters were prepared as light gun emplacements during the First World War.

Brookes (1986) recognized only two major phases of colluvial deposition, correlated with erosion surfaces and gravel deposition below the scarp: colluvial unit I (C-I), and colluvial unit II (C-II) (see 'Piedmont', below).

Fig. 1.17. TOP, Libyan Escarpment from an outlier remnant hill north of Sheikh Maohoub, showing irrigated cultivation with grain, thorn trees (Acacia nilotica), cattle and donkey. The Escarpment crest is formed in Tarawan Formation limestones. The ancient rolling surface with slight relief reaches to the crest without a scarp being formed (right centre); elsewhere, the limestones form a scarp. Deeply eroding wadi channels have cut off earlier flanking buttresses to form flatirons on the left. Sand glacis/falls mantle many of the slopes at the heads of the wadis. The Overwegi Bed is visible midway in the Dakhla Formation as the upper resistent stratum, mainly left and centre. C.S.C., Feb., 1994.

BOTTOM, 'Scalloped' rim of Libyan Escarpment north of Sheikh Maohoub, formed in sectioned leeward ends of large Tarawan Formation limestone yardangs. C.S.C., Feb., 1994.

are deposited on the adjacent ridges have more strongly resisted re-excavation, so that modern ravine formation is concentrated on the earlier ridge areas. This results in an inverted topography, with reverse scarps and flatirons (Brookes 1993) (Fig. 1.17, Top). Aeolian erosion has straightened the ravine walls, forming a parallel pattern of wind-scoured corridors extending across the Piedmont surface (Brookes 1983, 1986). The scarp truncates the Plateau yardangs as a series of scalloped headlands with sandslopes debouching from the interyardang ravines (Fig. 1.17, Bottom).

A major contrast between the geologic sequences in Dakhleh and Kharga oases is the absence in Dakhleh of the Plateau or Wadi Tufas described in Kharga by Caton-Thompson (1952) and Gardner (1932; also Ball 1900;

von Zittel 1883), which were interpreted as indicating wetter periods. This contrast is unlikely to reflect differences in palaeoclimates. Indeed, it has long been recognised that Dakhleh-Kharga form one physiographic unit (Rohlfs 1874). Tufas at Kharga are preserved on the west-facing Escarpment above the Tarawan limestones, but are not mapped on the south-facing scarp that continues to Dakhleh around the Abu Tartur Plateau (Klitzsch *et al.* 1987b), although Gardner reported tufa on the south side of the reentrant below the spring of Ain Amur (Caton-Thompson 1952) (confirmed by R.F. Giegengack, Jr., pers. comm., 1994).

At Kharga, primary exposures of 'wadi tufa' were mapped as interstratified with detrital sediments containing lithic artefacts in the Refuf Pass (Caton-Thompson and Gardner 1932; Caton-Thompson 1952; Gardner 1932). Schwarcz has begun U-series analyses of tufa samples obtained there in 1992. A high-precision, mass-spectrometric date on a sample (HPS1992 REF 2) from the highest level ('Tufa 4, Upper Tufa Terrace' (Caton-Thompson 1952, pl. 127), east of 'Km 147' on the abandoned Western Desert Railway from Oasis Junction, northwest of Farshut, to Kharga, gives an age of 166,000 ± 2,000 yr BP. Tufa further down the wadi from this sampled point, near 'Km 148', and correlated with 'Tufa 4', overlay a Middle Stone Age workshop (Caton-Thompson 1952, Locus VII, fig. 20, 96–97). (A sample obtained from this locus [MRK 1996/REF 3, McM #96004] gives an age of 125,000 ± 1,600 [2] yr BP.

No tufas have yet been found in place along the Dakhleh Escarpment, although spring tufa has been found as float blocks on colluvial slopes or in Piedmont terraced gravels (see 'Chronometric dating', above; also Kleindienst, this volume, Chapter 5). These tufa deposits must have formed at an earlier stage in the retreat of the Escarpment to have almost entirely vanished from the present geological suites.

A sample (MRK1988/DAK 1) from a large tufa float-block, incorporated in P-II gravels at Loc. 187E below Balat Point, was analyzed by U-series methods. Its isotope ratios (^{230}Th/^{234}U = 1.03 ± .02; ^{234}U/^{238}U = 1.135 ± .014) indicate that it was deposited more than 350,000 years ago. The ^{234}U/^{238}U ratio is close to that observed in younger materials from this region; this ratio decays to 1.00 with a half life of 250,000 yr, and these data therefore suggest that the age is not much more than 500,000 yr BP (or earlier Middle Pleistocene).

A float-tufa block similar in appearance to that found in P-II further east was recovered from the surface of P-III gravels in the 'North Wadi' (MRK1988, DAK 2). Schwarcz obtained finite U-series ages of 122 ± 9 and 145 ± 6 × 10³ yr for two aliquots of this sample. The ^{234}U/^{238}U ratios for these samples are essentially identical (1.341 and 1.337) and we conclude that the travertine deposition occurred somewhere on the Escarpment, above this site, at 134 ± 12 × 10³ yr ago, that is, near to the Isotope Stage 5/6 boundary. (Lacustrine deposition occurred at Bir Tarfawi at about this date also [Schwarcz and Morawska 1993].)

Fig. 1.18. Tufa block from surficial limestone debris north of Sheikh Maohoub. This is probably that referred to by Brookes (1993, 537) and dated at 176,000 ± 14,000/170,000 ± 12,000 yr BP. C.S.C., March, 1985.

The U/Th determinations on a tufa boulder cited by Brookes and ascribed to P-II gravels (Brookes 1993, 537) appear to be on a specimen collected by Churcher from the colluvial surface of the Escarpment face north of Maohoub (Fig. 1.18). Thus the 'ages' on the boulder have no clear relationship to any of the terraced gravels, although they do indicate that water was issuing from the Escarpment face in western Dakhleh at 176,000 ± 14,000/ 170,000 ± 12,000 yr BP.

Thus, *contra* Brookes (1993, 530), it appears that spring-deposited tufas did form in major wadi reentrants, but have been removed by subsequent erosional episodes. Mansour *et al.* (1982, 261) report Quaternary 'tufa silts and sands' associated with 'interbedded sands and limestones' from the El-Karafish Plateau somewhere north of West Dakhleh. The older Kharga date falls between the two dated Dakhleh samples, and is consistent with deposition in Isotope Stage 6. This is also consistent with observations at Bir Tarfawi, namely that spring activity in southern Egypt was most intense toward the end of the penultimate glacial stage (Isotope Stage 6), rather than in the last interglacial (Schwarcz and Morawska 1993).

3) Piedmont

Two sub-zones comprise the Dakhleh Piedmont: a cuesta developed on the Duwi Formation, the Sio'h ridge, the top of which varies from 1 to 8 km in width depending on the local dip (Fig. 1.2); and a zone of dissected, gravel-covered pediments/erosion surfaces which extends from the scarp foot at about 200 m a.s.l. for between 1 and 8 km into the Lowland, with outliers as much as 12 km from the Escarpment. Also in the Peidmont zone, fluvial and aeolian erosion have exposed several palaeobasins containing horizontally stratified shaly sands and silts, a process which continues today (Brookes 1983, 1986, 1993; Hermina 1990, fig. 14.5).

Fig. 1.19. TOP, Duwi Piedmont, south of Sheikh Maohoub. Duwi Formation exposed in the Sio'h Ridge, looking west with southern half of Gebel Edmonstone in distance. Formation topped by three main phosphorite beds dipping to north or slightly west of north and interrupted by drainage channels from basin between Sio'h Ridge and the foot of Gebel Edmonstone or the Libyan Escarpment; channels developed in lower Duwi Formation shales and underlying Mut Formation red muds. C.S.C., Feb., 1994.
BOTTOM, Duwi Formation Piedmont east of Tenida, eastern Dakhleh oasis, with el-Battikh Promontory in distance. Note limestone filled wadi floor with remnant yardangs of Nubia Group, Mut Formation red muds in fore distance. The Duwi Formation stands out in the middle distance as two closely spaced layers, above a thinner layer visible beyond the flat, limestone rubble-covered terrace (P-III gravels). The gravels overlie hidden Quseir/Mut Formation shales. Remnant hills of Dakhla Formation shale formed in earlier erosional cycles and capped by scarps formed of consolidated limestone debris rise above the Duwi Formation (?P-I gravels). El-Battikh Promontory is capped by Garra Formation limestones, which form scarps where more recent erosion has reached the Escarpment crest, and flatirons may be formed, as on the western skyline. The Overwegi Bed is visible in two places (right of photo), middle of Dakhla Formation. C.S.C., Feb., 1994.

Duwi Cuesta

The Duwi Formation is a >20 m thick sequence containing several resistant limy phosphorite beds alternating with thicker zones of shales and mudstones (Hermina 1990). Where the resistant horizons are thicker or more siliceous limestones, these cap the benches, or larger cuestas. West of Gebel Edmonstone, a resistant calcareous caprock floors the eroded surface south of the paved road.

The Piedmont zone (varying from 1 to 8 km wide and with a variable dip) is formed or underlain by these rocks. It is widest across synclinal axes southwest of Gebel Edmonstone (Fig. 1.19, Top) and south and southwest of the Gifata Promontory. It is least prominent around the entrance to Wadi el-Tawil and the footslopes of el-Battikh Promontory where, as part of the Libyan Escarpment, it is exposed on steep slopes or heavily mantled by colluvium. The gently sloping cuesta form is best developed south of Gebel Edmonstone where it lies farthest from the Libyan Escarpment, but is heavily dissected. The dip slope is more broken but still largely intact south of Gifata Promontory at up to 5 km from the Escarpment, where the caprock is siliceous limestone with a residual lag cover. Elsewhere, except below the el-Battikh Promontory (Fig. 1.19, Bottom), the cuesta is broken into a line of stepped residuals with the elongate or circular plan indicative of aeolian erosion (Fig. 1.19, Top). In detail, dip slopes on resistant limestones show a range of abrasion and deflation features, such as polishing, fluting, and basin development, which indicate strong aeolization. The P-I and P-II Piedmont gravel sheets (see below) overlie the Duwi Formation; P-III is the only Piedmont gravel sheet which consistently breaches the Duwi Cuesta (Sio'h Ridge) southwards through valleys dissecting the dip slope, and extends far across the Lowland in front of the scarp slope (see below). The cuts through the Duwi Cuesta provide the nickpoints determining the level of downstream terraces in P-III gravel deposits.

Pediments and Gravels – Alluvial Fans

A pediment is taken as '... a gently-inclined slope of transportation and/or erosion that truncates rock and connects eroding slopes or scarps to areas of sediment deposition at lower levels' (Oberlander 1989, 56, fig. 4.1A). Those at Dakhleh are similar to those originally described by Gilbert (1877), later differentiated as '*glacis d'erosion*' (Coque 1966; Mabbutt 1977), or '*glacis*' (Brookes 1993) Such pediments/erosion surfaces are often mantled by alluvial gravels derived from more resistant highland formations. In Dakhleh, these gravel covers are up to 10 m or more thick (Brookes 1993, fig. 5f). Transverse slopes on remnant terraces, and sometimes clear association of fan-morphology with recent scarp-face ravines, suggest that the gravel sheets formed as coalescent alluvial fans, or *bajada* (Harvey 1989, 136; Mabbutt 1977; Brookes 1993).

Probably Wadi el-Battikh provides the best modern analogue at Dakhleh for the process of gravel deposition by a wadi which finally debouches into an 'end pan' depression containing playa lake sediments, where the fines are laid down and then subsequently removed by aeolian erosion. Fan deposition is confined to the northern-most steep wadi-head zone, while the main wadi gravel deposition is in a confined, broad, braided bed rather than an alluvial fan. This form of coarse to fine gravel to fine

Fig. 1.20. TOP, View of Piedmont and Libyan Escarpment from high point on Duwi Formation north of Sheikh Wali, looking north and northeast. Balat Point is the highest point on the horizon. Modern wadi dissecting P-III gravel terraces in foreground; P-III gravel-capped terraces in middle ground at foot of escarpment to north. P-II gravel-capped terraces and fan heads standing above P-III to northeast. M.R.K., Feb. 25, 1988.
RIGHT, P-II gravel-capped terrace (Loc. 187) at foot of Libyan Escarpment, below Balat Point, with fan heading in colluvial flatiron. Looking north-northwest from head of P-III gravel-fan at Loc. 189A. M.R.K., Jan., 1995.

Fig. 1.21. View westward across Dakhleh Piedmont and Lowland from el-Battikh Promontory. Sinuous drainage on mature rolling slumped topography of the west face of the promontory, with the Military Road built by the British Army in World War I ascending the slope. Note shallow drainage channels on surface of slope that drain into rejuvenated channels either side of road. Oasis cultivation near Teneida in distance. C.S.C., Feb., 1994.

sediment deposition may also have occurred in the past. It is interpreted by Gerson (1982) as pertaining to different erosional conditions than those which produce collasced alluvial fans.

Three generations of mantled pediment/erosion surface formation have been recognized in the Dakhleh Piedmont, and a fourth is weakly developed in places (Brookes 1983, 1986). (Brookes [1993] refers to these as 'piedmont bajada, P/B'.) The youngest (fifth) fluvial erosion episodes are those of recent wadi incision. The oldest surface, here

termed 'Pediment-I' (P-I), which replaces 'Unit IIa' of Brookes (1986), is preserved as isolated fragments, usually as gravel-capped, narrow-crested or knife-edge ridges, found up to ca. 5 km from the scarp crest. These appear to be the remains of headward fan deposits near the original scarp which have been detached and dissected. Close to the scarp, some P-I remnants pass steeply upslope into fragments of coarse colluvium (C-I), a few of which mantle the cliff face. The surface slopes of outlying P-I remnants also project to near the cliff-top, so that at its fullest development this colluvial-fluvial sediment sheet may have completely mantled part or all of the Libyan Escarpment. Subsequent dissection of the colluvium has left reverse scarps at the heads of steep flatirons (Figs 1.17; 1.20). A mantled Escarpment is seen today in places between Kharga and Dakhleh on the Abu Tartur Plateau.

The second generation of pediment formation, 'Pediment-II' (P-II), correlated with colluvium C-II (also previously included in 'Unit IIa'), is better preserved as elongated gravel-capped and veneered terraces with crests ca. 50 m below those of the P-I remnants close to the Escarpment, and extends south from there for <5 km. Isolated remnants occur up to 15 km from the scarp crest. Headward, P-II terraces pass abruptly upslope into a colluvial sheet, C-II, similar in appearance to C-I but less dissected and weathered, which continues upslope as far as the Overwegi Bed bench to the foot of the limestone cliff, rather than to the top of the scarp. It is not always easy to distinguish P-II from P-I remnants in areas where one is lacking; if sufficient surface area is preserved, P-I limestone fragments show greater weathering, with a greater depth of fine sediment below the desert pavement, producing a 'softer' surface. Broader P-II terrace remnants often slope towards a median shallow, sinuous wadi from

Fig. 1.22. View from Libyan Escarpment north of Sheikh Maohoub, south over the Piedmont to the Dakhleh Lowland. Mature topography on colluvium mantling the Escarpment. Note: new gulley heads almost meeting in mid-foreground forming an incipient flatiron; limestone boulders fallen into gullies; yardangs of PLS in basin in left middle distance; limestone mantled remnant hills on either side of nearer cultivation; and buildings and cultivation of Sheikh Maohoub in distance. C.S.C., Feb., 1994.

Fig. 1.23. TOP, Recent gully erosion cutting into older coalescing fan heads, looking east at base of el-Battikh Promontory and south of mouth of Wadi el-Tawil. Terraced clastic gravels overlie lower Dakhla Formation shales. C.S.C., Feb., 1994. BOTTOM, Terraced gravels and fan heads in the Piedmont zone, Bab el-Jasmund, northeast of El-Qasr, looking northwest. An outlier of Maohoub Promontory is on the left, yardangs in PLS lie in the middle ground and several terrace levels (?P-II and P-III) in the re-entrant. The eroded sanded surface in the foreground is on the Duwi Formation, and is overlain by a thin layer of irrigation sediments formed into low yardangs on right. Phreatophyte dunes and tamarisk suggest a higher water table here than in most of the oasis. M.R.K., Jan., 1987.

steeper flanks (Brookes 1983, pl. XVIIa; 1993, fig. 5g) (Figs 1.21; 1.22). Heavy cementation of P-I and P-II gravels by silica, gypsum and calcite also contribute to their preservation (Brookes 1983, pl. XVIIb).

The third generation of pediment formation, 'Pediment-III' (P-III), 'Unit IIIa' of Brookes (1986), is poorly developed near the Escarpment, beginning as fan-heads in valleys incised below the P-II terraces (Fig. 1.23, Top). These widen downslope, are often constricted in passing through canyons in the Duwi Fm. cuesta, and then form the main Piedmont surface between the cuesta and the Lowland. Locally, the distal parts are divisible into two terrace surfaces, seen flanking Wadi el-Battikh, or northwest of Balat, where P-III is much dissected, or northwest of Qasr (Fig. 1.23). P-III gravels appear to have been deposited in quantity from the North Wadi-Wadi el-Tawil drainage on the northeast, and to correlate with a surface planed across the sandstones north and east of

Bashendi, leaving inverted wadi deposits of P-II gravels standing above that surface. No colluvial correlate is yet mapped ('C-III'), but the slumped deposits flanking the Tawil Promontory may represent the coeval episode of colluvial mass movements, *contra* Brookes (1993, 534), who interprets these gravels as P-II. In a few localities, such as north of Bashendi, a weakly developed erosion surface incised into P-III and capped by small-sized gravels can be recognized; this is tentatively termed 'Pediment IV' (P-IV). Experience shows that while the generalized sequence may be recognized across the Dakhleh Piedmont, each drainage bears a singular imprint, and much more extensive mapping and survey is required to correlate human usages of the changing palaeogeography. For instance, it is not yet clear that all P-II gravels belong within the same depositional episode, and some recent wadis are discharging onto fan heads of the 'P-III' surface west of North Wadi (el-Ueb).

Fig. 1.24. TOP, Libyan Escarpment from the main road between Ismant and Balat, showing the highest point, Balat Point (519 m a.s.l., centre), the Piedmont formed in Duwi Formation phosphorites and, at edge of plain, P-II terrace remnants above P-III terraces. In the foreground, the gravel plain (dissected P-III or 'P-IV' surface) bears unevenly distributed limestone and chert fragments resulting from historic gravel stripping for industrial and local uses. C.S.C., Feb., 1994. BOTTOM, Mechanical extraction of gravel from P-III and P-IV terraces between Ismant and Balat, north of the main road. View northeast across modern wadi with lorry tracks to Escarpment and southern P-II remnant (Loc. 216). P-III gravels south of remnant entirely stripped by mechanical means since 1987: gravels extracted are exported to the Nile Valley for industrial uses. Duwi Piedmont in right background below Balat Point. M.R.K., Feb., 1996.

Limestones in P-III gravels are always visibly a lighter grey and less eroded by weathering than are P-I or P-II limestone clasts. The buildup of soil beneath the P-III veneer is thinner than on the older surfaces, and the gravels are less cemented. The P-III terraces are highly dissected in the central area and extend into the Lowland between Balat and the ridge of Duwi Fm. gebels just east of Ismant. Further south a lag spread of P-III/P-II-derived gravels overlies the Mut Fm. P-III gravels and lags are much modified by cultural practices, especially by collection of gravel as industrial aggregates, which has occurred at least since Roman times (Fig. 1.24, Top). Pleistocene artifacts as well as potsherds were used in chinking vaults at Ismant el-Gharab (Romano-Byzantine Kellis, 31/420 D6–1), and

are incorporated into modern paved roads. When DOP began surveys, gravel collection was still mainly by individual hand screening and donkey cart: today it is a mechanized operation which rapidly strips the lower-lying P-III/P-IV gravels from the oasis surfaces, and stripping has already begun on P-II surfaces well away from the main road (Fig. 1.24, Bottom). Although the exact time of extraction is not known, areas selectively stripped for larger cobbles and boulders have not regenerated into a surface desert pavement since, and are easily recognized as having been selectively stripped.

Deposits of each generation of alluvial gravels consist mainly of limestone with chert and other minor bedrock constituents in the zone between Maohoub and el-Battikh promontories (Figs 1.25; 1.26). Cherts are sparse or absent to the west of Maohoub or east of Teneida. Detailed fabric comparisons among the three gravel sheets have not yet been undertaken, but components other than limestone and chert are included, *contra* Brookes' statement (1993, 537) that "... only limestone and chert survived deconstitution". In general, the Pleistocene gravels become

Fig. 1.25. TOP, Coarse clastic gravels capping P-II terrace at north end of Loc. 187E, looking north to dissected head of P-III fan (Loc. 189A) and Escarpment. Balat Point on right skyline; P-II gravel-capped terrace (Loc. 187A) on left below Escarpment. M.R.K., March, 1987. BOTTOM,. Fluted limestone boulder pavement in coarse P-II gravels exposed where soil cover has been removed, in small drainage at Loc. 187A. Strong aeolian erosion postdates the water action. M.R.K., Feb., 1987.

somewhat finer grained and better stratified downslope, but thicknesses do not change systematically and large boulders continue to occur, suggesting that powerful floods maintained competence in distal fan zones dispite the low gradient into the central Lowland. Whether or not the fine sediments still in place in the Lowland to the south relate to the gravel depositions is unclear (see 'Calcareous Silty Sediments', below).

Where chert fragments are abundant on Piedmont terraces their distribution is not uniform. Several factors can account for this, some undoubtedly post-depositional, and some humanly created. Some relief on the terrace remnants may still reflect the original bars and channels of the stream systems which deposited the gravels, and cherts would be more abundant as denser lags on the bars (Brookes, pers. comm. 1987) (Fig. 1.26, Bottom). Later fluvial erosion has caused variations in exposure to wind abrasion which has influenced chert density, increasing the amounts in exposed areas where limestone clasts have suffered greater abrasion. Humans have fragmented large volumes of this chert (Kleindienst, this volume, Chapter 5).

Fig. 1.27. Pit section at Set VI, Loc. 187A, dug by I.A. Brookes. Red silty soil underlying limestone/chert veneer, showing vertical sand-filled cracks, and accumulation of calcite and gypsum in lower portion. Base of consolidated gravels of P-II terrace. M.R.K., Feb., 1987.

To initiate a study of chert fragment and artifact density by Kleindienst and Brookes in 1987, surface densities were compared with those in pits, to permit approximations of the volumes (thickness/m²) of limestone or other rock potentially removed from a sample surface to produce the chert densities observed (Kleindienst, this volume, Chapter 5). The distal edge of the P-II remnant chosen lies 11.5 km northwest of Balat and 13.5 km northeast of Ismant (Loc. 187) (Brookes 1993, fig. 5e). All chert fragments were collected from the surface of six 1 m² plots showing different chert densities, at roughly 500 m intervals near the median line of the terrace. Pits were dug at the lower, middle, and upper locations below collected plots. Obtaining adequate samples from the heavily cemented underlying gravels proved extraordinarily difficult. Surface cherts were all heavily varnished, whereas anciently-broken fragments from pits show only hydration rinds. A specific gravity of 2.64 for chert was confirmed from one near-spherical nodule collected in the wadi to the east. Weights of cherts collected from the six 1 m² 'density squares' ranged from 0.93 to 7.75 kg. Converted to volumes and using the mean chert volume of two pits, the results indicate that 1.0 m is a maximum depth for surface lowering since gravel deposition. The pits were dug in

Fig. 1.26. TOP, View from main road north across terraced P-III gravels, with modern wadi cutting in foreground, northwest of Balat. The southernmost P-II remnant, in central middle ground, bears Aterian Dakhleh Unit workshops (Loc. 216). Libyan Escarpment forms the distant horizon. C.S.C., Feb., 1994. BOTTOM, Chert-rich gravels in foreground cap a P-III terrace on Darb el-Tawil, north of Bashendi. View northeast to west face of el-Battikh Promontory. C.S.C., Feb., 1994.

areas free of obvious severe wind abrasion. (As noted above, aeolian abrasion is evident on parts of the terrace, where sectioned micro-fluted limestone boulders form much of the surface.) Below the surface pavement of heavily varnished chert and aeolized limestone fragments is a gravel-free layer 15–30 cm thick of pale brown (7.5 YR 6/4) calcareous sandy silt with columnar structure, and sand within desiccation cracks regularly spaced at 7–8 cm intervals (Fig. 1.27). The sandy silt soil profile overlying cemented or partially cemented gravels is aeolian dust or loess; a similar sediment is found in some basins within the entirely different sandstone terrain downwind of the Piedmont zone (Brookes 1989b, 1993, fig. 5h).

The mechanism by which the heavily desert-varnished cherts arrive and remain at the surface is considered similar to that proposed for the formation of desert pavements in the Mojave Desert by McFadden *et al.* (1987), described as an accretionary mechanism of soil formation by Breed *et al.* (1989; Cooke *et al.* 1993, 74–75). In opposition to older hypotheses on the formation of desert pavements by deflation and/or upward migration of gravel through fines (e.g., Cooke 1970, Mabbutt 1977), it is argued that the desert pavement clasts were present on an original sediment surface, and are then continuously maintained at an aggrading surface through infiltration of the aeolian sediment as it gradually accumulates below the surface veneer. The 'accretion hypothesis' has profound implications for desert geoarchaeology: any clasts or features left below the soil horizon, which did not migrate upward with the veneer, are sealed archaeological deposits which may have suffered little horizontal displacement (Kleindienst, this volume, Chapter 5)! In fact, in some surface samples at Dakhleh conjoining artifacts indicate minimal horizontal displacement.

Little is yet known about the age of the several generations of Dakhleh pediments and their mantles. Survey by Kleindienst (this volume, Chapter 5) on P-II remnants located clusters of Balat Unit bifaces, and Levallois workshop debitage belonging to an older, larger-sized Middle Stone Age (MSA) unit, and to younger units including the (Aterian) Dakhleh Unit. A few isolated Upper Acheulian bifaces have also been found. Thus, the oldest artifacts suggest human occupation during the later Middle Pleistocene, and Balat Unit bifaces are probably later Middle Pleistocene in age. These provide only minimum ages for P-II gravel deposition. The gravels themselves lack artifact content: only one biface and a few flakes have been found *in situ* (Loc. 84, 31/420–E5–1) in a small remnant that may be less cemented, distal P-II fan gravels, or a later deposit; the biface could Acheulian but is probably Balat Unit. (Unfortunately, the duricrust matrix of the gravels at Loc. 084 is unsuitable for U-series dating.) Formation of and deposition on P-I and P-II surfaces are inferred to be Pleistocene in age, but P-I at least could be older. Middle Stone Age (MSA) workshop material observed near the edges of P-I terraces overlooking

broader P-II or P-III surfaces, interpreted by Kleindienst as 'out-look' sites, have no relation to the age of the P-I gravel deposition.

The oldest clusters of artifacts on the P-III surfaces all appear to belong to the MSA (Aterian) Dakhleh Unit, although P-III gravels are incompletely surveyed. This suggests a broad minimum age range during the later Pleistocene of <90,000 to ca. 20,000 yr BP for human use of that surface, based on comparisons with southern Egypt and the central or western Sahara (Tillet 1989; Wendorf *et al.* 1993).

The oldest pediment P-I predates P-II by a long interval, long enough for its almost complete removal from the Piedmont. Because more extensive areas of P-II remain after ca. >200,000 years, it might be argued that P-I predates it by much more than that. The P-II surfaces have passed through fewer arid-humid-arid cycles than P-

Fig. 1.28. TOP, Side view from the west of yardang field carved in cyclical Pleistocene Laminated Sediments, in basin between Sio'h Ridge (Duwi Formation) and foot of Libyan Escarpment, north of Sheikh Maohoub (cf. Fig. 1.17 TOP). Foreground is lower Dakhla Formation with residual limestone fragments. In right middle distance a more recent limestone lag is still intact. C.S.C., Feb., 1994.
BOTTOM, Windward (north) end-view of same yardang field showing aeolian carved corridor between rows of yardangs. Residual limestone fragments present in right foreground, and limestone lagged conical hill in right far distance cover lower Dakhla Formation shales. White streak in front of hill is isolated sand sheet. C.S.C., Feb., 1994.

I (Gerson 1982, 127, fig. 4). P-II gravels cap the crest of the Duwi cuesta where it approaches within 2 km of the Escarpment, but deflated chert lags derived from P-I/P-II gravels litter the Duwi Piedmont surface farther south. The Duwi cuesta has been eroded since the P-II gravels were deposited; in places aeolian erosion has reduced it to elongated yardangs and conical residuals nearer the Escarpment. P-II predates the 'Pleistocene Laminated Sediments' (see below), because these were laid down in basins eroded below the P-II surfaces.

Pleistocene Laminated Sediments (PLS)

Brookes' (1986) sedimentary 'Unit Ia/Unit Ib' is here renamed 'Pleistocene Laminated Sediments' (PLS) to reflect their less certain stratigraphic position. They are no longer considered the oldest sediments in the Dakhleh sequence. They are extensively exposed in partially exhumed Piedmont deflation basins (Brookes 1983, pl. XVIII) (Fig. 1.28), as well as south of the Piedmont. Similar extensive outcrops occur in larger basins west and east of Dakhleh Oasis. These were noted by Hermina *et al.* (1961, Hermina 1990) and Mansour *et al.* (1982) who considered them lacustrine deposits despite some evidence of torrent bedding nearer the Escarpment. Churcher (1980), who first investigated PLS outcrops for DOP, also considered them lacustrine (cf. Wendorf and Schild 1980).

Exposed in a discontinuous belt over 150 km long, from Gharb Maohoub, west of Dakhleh, to east of Zayat between Dakhleh and Kharga oases, these sediments are similar in structure, texture, and lithology, and in basin geometry (Winlock 1936; Brookes 1986). Usually grey shale particles derived from the Dakhla Fm. predominate in the lithology. Red and brown particles reflect sources in the Mut and Duwi formations, while minor quartzose additions in the eastern exposures derive from the Nubia sandstones. Sandy shale beds predominate, but silt and clay stringers are generally intercalated. The PLS sediments are structurally variable. While the dominant characters of bedding horizontality and lateral continuity suggest lacustrine origin, other structures indicate current bedding (Fig. 1.29). Brookes (1986) emphasised the high-energy sedimentary structures and a fluvial/terminal floodplain origin was postulated, by analogy to 'fan-tail' sediments in northern Sinai (Sneth 1983). He now terms them 'Pleistocene lacustrine sediments' (Brookes 1993). Similar deposits have long been noted in Kharga Oasis (Beadnell 1909 as 'lake'), and their genesis similarly disputed (e.g. Beadnell 1933; Caton-Thompson 1932; Caton-Thompson and Gardner 1932, 380, 'loess-like deposits'; Caton-Thompson 1952, 10, 'aeolian silt'; Grolier *et al.* 1980, 86, 'lacustrine'; Busche 1988, 1054, 'lake and playa-type deposits').

Lacustrine features include graded vertical bedding and mud drapes over rippled sands. Fine- and medium-grained sand layers are occasionally very finely interbedded over tens of meters, which is more easily explained under calm

Fig. 1.29. TOP, Pleistocene Laminated Sediments, in flank of yardang in same field north of Sheikh Maohoub (Fig. 1.28). Note slumping, mud curls, and fossil dehydration cracks. C.S.C., Feb., 1994. BOTTOM, Features preserved in Pleistocene Laminated Sediments in side of yardang in same field. Note cut-and-fill, coarse sandy and fine muddy layers, limestone fragments in coarse pocket, desiccation cracks, and mud curls. M.R.K., Jan., 1987.

lacustrine processes. The PLS occupy elongated north-south and steep-walled basins at the foot of the Escarpment, and 'rock tank' basins northeast of Bashendi (where they are unlaminated red muds or clays), and rectangular or irregular and shallow basins in the Nubia sandstone plain to the southeast of Teneida (e.g., 'Southeast Basin') and eastward (Egyptian Geological Survey and Mining Authority 1982; Klitzsch *et al.* 1987a). In both situations, beds abut the basin walls without changes in texture, structure, or lithology, as at a lake margin, and support blocks fallen from the yardangs showing a sequence of deposition. Brookes (1993, figs. 6, 9) now identifies four facies of PLS, 'Facies A', 'B', 'C' and 'D', occupying basins in different areas, although he considers them all to occupy an equivalent stratigraphic position.

Bedding structures and such features as mudballs or transported blocks of sediment clearly indicate high rates of sediment influx onto and across basin floors, although coarse clasts are usually lacking, and basal gravels are rarely observed. Proximity to the Escarpment would provide hydraulic energy and, where visible, grain-sizes increase towards the Escarpment, although structural

Fig. 1.30. Conical gebel with white Pleistocene Laminated Sediments at Zayat, between Dakhleh and Kharga, at Km 94. The sediments extend south from the lee of the gebel to the foreground with, in the left middle distance, a white calcareous band within the sequence. C.S.C., March, 1994.

complexity does not. On almost horizontal depositional slopes the structures observed imply large volumes of turbid, fine sediment-charged water. High rates of northward input could have been maintained across the basin floor by wind-generated currents (flow indicators are south-directed), yet graded beds and mud drapes suggest still water at other times. Transportation of fine sediments from the Dakhla Fm. shale of the Escarpment imply rainfall and runoff rates which did not move coarser material. Northeast of Qasr, in western Dakhleh, shale beds are densely intercalated, even replaced, by beds of quartzose aeolian sand probably flushed from scarp ravines, where analogous sand drifts and falling dunes accumulate today (Brookes 1986, figs 8, 9). Occasional desiccation is marked by mud curls and cracks, some curls ripped up and some intact beneath overlying beds. Other features have been noted that may represent animal burrows or root channels. The evidence suggests deposition under conditions of increased but intermittent precipitation (Brookes 1993, figs 6a, b, c – 'Facies A').

More convincing evidence for a lacustrine/playa origin for PLS is at an extensive exposure about 2 km east of the Zayat checkpoint on the Kharga road, at Km 94 from Mut, north of the paved road and opposite a fenced microwave installation (Brookes' 'Facies B') (Fig. 1.30). There a 20 m high conical sandstone gebel to the north protects an elongated, tear-drop-shaped PLS 'slab' from aeolian erosion (Brookes 1993, fig. 6d, e). In this section, horizontal gypsum evaporite beds are interbedded with massive pale brown sand-silt beds. Ripple marks in the thin gypsum laminae, with crests trending east to west, indicate shallow water with currents generated by longitudinal winds. The deposit, about 9 m thick, stands centrally in a broad plain floored with clastic beds bearing Holocene ('Neolithic') artifacts in the surface lag, which continue onto the base of the sandstone hill. Between Km 56 and Km 120 from Mut the road to Kharga crosses similar plains

floored with these sediments (Egyptian Geological Survey and Mining Authority 1982; Klitzsch *et al.* 1987a). 'Facies C' and 'D' are found flanking or flooring the basins southeast of Teneida (Brookes 1993, figs 6 f, g, h) (see below).

There is no chronological evidence derived from the PLS at Dakhleh (the Combined Prehistoric Expedition also found none: Wendorf and Schild 1980). PLS postdate a major interval or intervals of aeolian erosion, because they occupy basins possibly initiated by fluvial erosion but showing such aeolian features as closed floors and definite orientations. South of the Mut to Balat road, in the Taref sandstone ridge east of Sheikh Muftah, and northeast of Ezbet Bashendi PLS are found in preexisting closed sandstone basins. Southeast of Teneida PLS can be found preserved up to 6 m above the base of the present surface in the eroded sediment on the flanks of bedrock yardangs (Brookes 1993, fig. 8g). Clearly these resistent yardangs existed before PLS deposition in the basins. No artifacts have been found in association, nor is it known whether there is more than one generation of PLS sediments. PLS lie in basins eroded below Pleistocene P-II gravel-capped surfaces, and are capped in places by gravels on the third (P-III) and the fourth (P-IV) generation surfaces. At Kharga, Caton-Thompson (1952) found 'aeolian silts' overlain by gravels including MSA artifacts east of Gebel el-Shams, and 'Epi-Levalloisian' *in situ* at another locality (KO15) in northern Kharga, which suggests more than one phase of Pleistocene deposition. Brookes (1993, 539) has obtained a ^{14}C determination of 39,620 ± 1,100 yr BP (BETA-54659, corrected to 39,920 ± 1,150), and a U/Th determination of 61,980 ± 7,600 yr BP (UQT 0618 and 0619) on marl from 'Facies B' at Zayat, both of which appear to be far too young if 'Facies B' is equivalent in age to 'Facies A' in Dakhleh. The U/Th determination, however, is in the range of those obtained for CSS caprock at Dakhleh (see below). As Beadnell noted (1933, 529), "But the last word has by no means been said on the correct subdivision, age, and methods of accumulation of these beds ..."

4) Central Lowland

The Dakhleh Lowland, mainly lying below the 130 m contour, is underlain by the red and green claystones of the Mut Fm. (Fig. 1.2); this zone contains most of the agricultural land and settlements of the oasis, because here ground water can be tapped at the shallowest depths. The Lowland varies in width from about 15 km northsouth at Mut in the centre and at Gedida, to 2 km near Sheikh Maohoub in the west, to about 6 km in the east through Balat, and is 30 km across from Mut to Qasr, variations which reflect geological structure. The modern cultivated lands are interrupted by uninhabited desert and bedrock ridges between Balat and Ismant (Fig. 1.1), although there is evidence of earlier agricultural uses and habitation in the lowlands, including the major settlement of Ismant el-Kharab (Romano-Byzantine Period Kellis,

Fig. 1.31. Recent barchan dunes southeast of Muzzawaka, mantling Pleistocene spring mounds (foreground), and lower eroded surficial and Mut Formation surfaces. Archaeological evidence in this area ranges from Middle Pleistocene to Romano-Byzantine in age. View is northeast towards Qasr and shows groundwater irrigated cultivation near Sheikh Maohoub in background and el-Gifata Promontory on horizon. M.R.K., Jan., 1986.

31/420 D6–1). This uninhabited area provides a convenient division between 'eastern' and 'western' Dakhleh (Beadnell 1901a; Brookes 1986, 1993).

The central Lowland of Dakhleh is difficult to assess. The lower altitude and relief limit geological exposures; large areas are intensively cultivated, and surfaces have been much modified by cultural processes. Apart from farmsteads, settlements and cemeteries, both ancient and modern, field patterns, irrigation canals or 'aqueducts', and dredgeate from well digging and clearing are prominent features. Particularly in the west, recent mobile dune fields overlie earlier sediments and landforms (Fig. 1.31).

Holocene morphological and sedimentary units recognized include: a) salt-crusted or rhizolith-strewn level traces similar to, and possibly genetically related to and synchronous with, true lacustrine/playa sediments within the sandstone terrain south of the Lowland; b) closely associated traces of deflated tabular sand sheet deposits; c) tabular bodies of fluvio-aeolian sandy sediment accumulated in association with irrigation agriculture; and d) linear chains or 'belts' of active sand dunes (King 1918; Brookes 1983, 1986, 1989b). Radiocarbon dates for these Holocene sediments come mainly from samples collected by McDonald at archaeological occurrences. Older, Pleistocene sediments occur as terraces and terrace remnants in the southern Lowland and western Dakhleh, with outliers southeast of Teneida, and as deposits marking the vents of fossil artesian springs (Brookes 1983, 1986, 1993; Issawi 1977; Wendorf and Schild 1980).

Sandstone Ridges
In the eastern oasis Lowland, two areas of higher elevation are formed by Taref Fm. sandstone. The ridge of sandstone forming the eastern rim of the Sheikh Muftah Embayment

Fig. 1.32. TOP, Yardangs cut into Nubia Group, Taref Formation sandstone, which underlies the eastern flank of Sheikh Muftah valley and forms the prominent ridge separating the Balat cultivation from the central Lowland. View southward from just south of the main tarmac road between Ismant and Balat. Pleistocene Laminated Silts red mudstones underlie talus slopes on sides of yardangs (Fig. 1.33) and are exposed at yardang heads to about 3.5–4.0 m above floor to rear of Landrover. C.S.C., Feb., 1994.
BOTTOM, Sandstone yardangs and conical remnants in a rock tank basin, northwestern portion of 'Bashendi Rock Art Basin', northeast of Bashendi, looking north to Wadi el-Ueb. Basin is floored in sandstone veneered by a thin sandsheet. Older fill of Pleistocene Laminated Silts red mudstones represented by remnants on gebel flanks, and less eroded in north end of basin. Gebel crests contain Holocene occupations and the basin floor contains much displaced Dakhleh Unit (Aterian Technocomplex) occupational debris (Loc. 283) east of central pillar. M.R.K., Feb., 1991.

trends north-northeast to ca. 2 km north of the main road. The ridge follows the crest of the Tawil Anticline (Fig. 1.2) showing minor faulting (downthrows to the northwest) and strong jointing. The higher ground, >150 m a.s.l. in the south, and dipping to ~145 m a.s.l. in the north, divides the eastern oasis into two depressions at <130 m a.s.l.). The western area, once cultivated around the Roman Period town of Kellis, but now only worked in the south around Sheikh Muftah, and 2). The larger area now cultivated from southwest and west of Balat to Teneida, and south to Sheikh Mabrouk.

The crest of the Tawil Anticline (Fig. 1.6) is incised into yardangs north of Bashendi and just south of the main road between Ismant and Balat for ca. 2 km southward (Fig. 1.32). Here, the corridors between the

Mut claystone occur and higher remnants of green Mut shales, including the landmark 'Bashendi Hills', but most of the Mut Fm. has been stripped away. Shallow well heads are dug into the southern margin of this Taref (Tawil Anticline) sandstone ridge, at ca. 132 m a.s.l., where waters can reach the surface along the bounding fault. Some of these are still running.

The northern side of the upthrust is cut into sandstone yardangs of various heights, many plastered with red mud derived from then nearby Mut Fm. claystones, to >25 m above their bases. These redeposited muds exhibit poorly defined stratification and are more massive and blocky than are those to the west lying south of the main road.

A row of rock tank basins of various depths has been deflated into the sandstone from 0.5 to 1 km south of the northern rim. These appear to vary in age of formation:

Fig. 1.33. TOP, Side view of Taref Formation sandstone yardang with red-brown sandy sediments, on crest of Tawil Anticline, south of main tarmac road. Remnant sediments are being removed by aeolian action and exhuming an older aeolian modelled surface. These ancient yardangs represent a former period of strong aeolian action, subsequently inundated by water-laid sediments. Figure at foot of yardang gives scale. M.R.K., Feb., 1996. BOTTOM, Close-up of flank of Taref Formation sandstone yardang being exumed from beneath red-brown sandy sediments. Note that the red-brown sediments enter into crevices in the sandstone and also support 'float' rockfalls. C.S.C., Feb., 1996.

Fig. 1.34. TOP, View looking south up the Taref Formation dipslope. Sand sheet and Taref Formation sandstone gebel-yardangs on the southeast flank of Tawil Anticline southeast of Sheikh Muftah Embayment. Eroded surface on yardang crests is at >160 m a.s.l. Masara Loc. 085 lies between large yardangs on horizon. M.R.K., Feb., 1996.
BOTTOM, Yardangs in Holocene sediments in Eastern Halfa Grass Basin. Three main depositional units in these waterlaid sediments are visible: two units of brown sediment overlie and are separated by a gypsum-rich layer from a basal reddish unit. The upper units yield sherds and stone artifacts (Loc. 222, 30/435–J6–2). Taref sandstone yardangs form the distant basin rim with sediments at base of yardangs. Geological hammer for scale. M.R.K., Feb., 1996.

yardangs were once filled to a maximum depth of >10 m with a red brown sediment, which was deposited in layers 1–2 cm thick, and composed of a mixture of sand grains from the Taref sandstone and fragments of the Mut red muds (Fig. 1.33, Top). This is now being removed by aeolian erosion and exists as extensive fillets against the walls of the corridors (Fig. 1.33, Bottom). Further south, isolated sandstone gebels, which reach 180 m a.s.l., stand above a sandsheet veneering the Taref sandstone dip slope (Fig. 1.34, Top).

A second area of elevated Taref sandstone lies north and northeast of Bashendi (Fig. 1.32, Bottom), where the sandstone marks the upthrust side of a normal fault that trends northeasterly towards Wadi el-Tawil (Fig. 1.2). On the north, the planed-off sandstone surface lies at 150 – 165 m a.s.l., rising eastward where it is deeply cut by the lower Wadi el-Tawil. Isolated gebels on the east reach 185 m a.s.l. On the south, some residual patches of red some are being stripped of deep red mud infilling, to >5 m thickness (e.g., Loc. 283, 32/435–M9–1, Fig. 1.32, Bottom); others with thinner, brown waterlaid, Holocene/ latest Pleistocene infilling, are also now being deflated (e.g., Loc. 297, 32/435–M10–2). Some basins carry only a thin sand and gravel lag over a sandstone bedrock floor, and may never have contained infilling sediments (e.g., Loc. 161, 32/435–K10–1 & L10–1, Bashendi Rock Art Basin).

The general surface level of the east-west trending sandstone ridge is equivalent to that of the broad P-III terraced gravels overlying the Mut Fm. to the north, flanking the Darb el-Tawil. Isolated P-II gravel-capped gebels stand above that elevation, and inverted P-II wadi gravel ridges rise above the sandstone, as does one calcrete capped knoll (Fig. 1.6). P-III lag limestone gravels here, therefore, are derived from P-II deposits. These include numerous 'chert balls', as do the P-II wadi gravels, probably derived from now vanished stratigraphically higher Mut Fm. shales (Kleindienst, this volume, Chapter 5).

The southern rim of the oasis is also formed in Taref Fm. sandstone, and is similarly incised into north-south oriented yardangs and corridors. These change in the south to scattered gebels and sand plains (Fig. 1.34, Top). The crests of the yardangs on the northern rim and the higher swells to the south carry remnants of a CSS sheet that once mantled most of the southern sandstone rim.

The corridors are floored with sand and infilling sediments can rarely be observed. Where the corridors widen out to the south, they may form 'Halfa' grass basins or plains, with coppice dunes formed around tamarisk (see Ritchie, this volume, Chapter 4). These plants root in a sand-covered PLS sheet composed of a basal reddish brown horizontally stratified mud topped by a layered gypsum crust, in turn overlain by two or three sandy silt units that are less distinctly stratified (Fig. 1.34, Bottom). Sheikh Muftah Unit artifacts occcur above the basal layer.

Western Dakhleh Oasis is less complex. Tongues of Taref Fm. sandstone project into the southern Lowland south of Qâlamûn and Gedida (Fig. 1.1), and mark the crest(s) of the Budkhulu Anticline (Fig. 1.2). The bedrock is masked by sandsheets and dunes. Scattered high sandstone gebels (trig points) reach 184 m a.s.l. southwest of Mut, and 166 m to the west-northwest at Loc. 123 (31/ 405–B6–1). The southern boundary of the western oasis is also formed by the eroded Taref sandstone dip slope which reaches elevations >230 m a.s.l. ca. 16 km west of Mut.

Terraced Pleistocene Sediments in the Lowland
Terraces formed by Pleistocene sediments are observed along the central portion of the boundary between the Dakhleh Lowland and the sandstone terrain to the south. Two units have been recognized in the area south and east of Sheikh Muftah, westward to south and west of Mut: the stratigraphically lower unit is ferruginous, here termed 'Ferruginous Sandy Sediments' (FSS), and the higher calcareous or calichefied unit is termed 'Calcareous Silty

Sediments' (CSS). The designations 'Unit IIb' and 'Unit IIIb' of Brookes (1986) are replaced, although it is clear that the calcareous unit is superimposed on the ferruginous in the central and southern 'Sheikh Muftah Embayment' or valley. (These units are Brookes' (1993) 'Ferruginous Spring Sediments' and 'Calcareous Spring Sediments'.) Existence of remnants of the calcareous unit southwest of Balat was first noted by Issawi (1977, fig. 7), which he termed 'tufa'. Terrace remnants are usually small (100– 300 m long by ~100 m wide), but their distribution and nearly horizontal bedding suggest former extensive sediment sheets. Two larger terrace exposures have been noted: the ferruginous unit flanking the Sheikh Muftah Embayment on the east, which can be traced for 3 km and is up to 750 m wide with outliers in the embayment; and a 1.5 × 0.75 km remnant of the calcareous unit located about 7 km southeast of Teneida, north of the paved road. Terraced sediments are clearly water deposited, and may reflect deposition by artesian spring-waters (Brookes 1983, 1986, 1993) or overland flow.

Ferruginous Sandy Sediments (FSS) are exposed at the eroding edges of a series of erosional terraces on the east flank of the Sheikh Muftah Embayment, flanking a sandstone ridge, and within the embayment (Brookes 1986, fig. 23; 1993, fig. 8a) (Figs 1.35; 1.36). Terrace remnants parallel the western sandstone rim, the largest being 'Dune Hill', at 150 m a.s.l. Small exposures indicate that FSS overlapped the sandstone both east and west of the embayment, to elevations of at least 150 m a.s.l. At several localities FSS is seen underlying the calcareous unit (Brookes 1986, fig. 27; 1993, fig. 8b) (Fig. 1.36, Top). FSS extend north along the eastern sandstone ridge and remnants are found to ca. 0.5 km west of it; some small remnants also occur east of the ridge.

Residuals of the Calcareous Silty Sediments (CSS) are found within the embayment north to the road, to the east of the ridge, and on the sandstone ridges south of this and other embayments to the west and east. The former are also at elevations >150 m a.s.l. The distribution implies that the zone of deposition of calcareous sediments had a greater southerly extent than did FSS (Brookes 1993), or that FSS was removed prior to CSS deposition. The CSS terrace remnants south and southeast of Teneida or a small remnant of CSS duricrust northeast of Bashendi at an elevation >150 m a.s.l. may be unrelated to those in the central Lowlands. Probable FSS remnants in western Dakhleh (Brookes 1983) have not been examined.

Ferruginous Terraced Sediments (FSS)
The east flank and southern end of the Sheikh Muftah Embayment consists of a dissected terrace of Ferruginous Sandy Sediments (FSS) against a sandstone cliff. Viewed northwards across the valleys which dissect it, it appears as an intact surface dipping northwards 1.0–1.5° over nearly 3 km, but also dipping more gently westward to the valley axis (Fig. 1.36, Bottom). The terrace is underlain by reddish brown, ferruginous sands, largely derived from

Fig. 1.35. TOP, View eastward across Sheikh Muftah Valley from large mound, 'Dune Hill', on western flank, showing westerly-dipping Ferruginous Sandy Sediments (FSS) draped along the Taref Formation sandstone eastern margin of the valley or embayment. The valley is floored with aeolian sand, overlying either thin Mut Formation claystones or Taref Formation sandstones. C.S.C., Feb., 1994.
BOTTOM, Consolidated Ferruginous Sandy Sediments (FSS, ferricrete) overlying lighter coloured sandy ?spring deposits on the east side of Sheikh Muftah Valley. A high spring mound or large residual FSS terrace, 'Dune Hill' (trig point, 150 m a.s.l.), is visible at left across the valley. C.S.C., Feb., 1994.

Fig. 1.36. TOP, View southward along the east flank of Sheikh Muftah Valley, showing westerly-dipping Ferruginous Sandy Sediments. The Taref Formation sandstone ridge forms the southern skyline. C.S.C., Feb., 1994. BOTTOM, Basal, current-bedded Ferruginised Sandy Sediments (FSS), at westernmost of eastern exposures ('FSS Ridge', Loc. 328) in Sheikh Muftah Valley. Sediments rest on eroded surface of Mut Formation, with fine gravel at base; root casts are throughout the section. No indurated ferricrete occurs here. A remnant of the overlying Calcareous Silty Sediments caps the highest knoll at left. J. O'Carroll for scale. M.R.K., Feb., 1995.

the Nubia bedrock, with local sandstone and quartzite gravel fragments which in places reach boulder size (Fig. 1.35, Bottom). The sands may be massive, or bedded and/or crossbedded. One biface of Acheulian/Balat Unit type, similar to that found in ?P-II gravels (Loc. 084), was found *in situ* in a gravel by Kleindienst in 1992 (Loc. 323, 31/420–F10–3); other rare finds of artifacts have been less diagnostic (Loc. 155, Occ. 2), but none indicates a date later than the Acheulian/Balat Unit. Sections through FSS commonly show several units; claystone-derived muds with included rafts and balls of claystone are indicative of vigorous erosion of the claystone lenses within the sandstone on which these sediments lie. Hollow ferruginous root casts indicating vegetation often penetrate several horizons. A section measured by Brookes at the southeastern end of the Sheikh Muftah embayment shows:

Depth of Unit (cm)	Description	Cumulative Depth (m)
20	Indurated ironstone with vesicular structure.	3.70–3.95
150	Ferruginous brown silt.	3.50–3.75
100	Ferruginous, highly coloured silt, consolidated, laminar, with thick ferruginised rhizoliths.	2.00–2.25
20	Very pale green silt with vertical grey-green mottles; top 2 cm laminar.	1.00–1.25
20–30	Ferruginous clay-silt with rhizoliths.	0.80–1.05
5–20	Gravely sand in red clay matrix, with ferruginous rhizoliths filled with grey-green silt.	0.60–0.75

| 55 | Contorted grey-green claystone with red claystone clasts. | 0.55 |

[Eroded Surface/ Disconformity]

Cretaceous:
| Taref Formation, sandstone. | 0 |

Other terrace bluffs show poorly developed bedding, picked out by sandier and siltier layers, and dipping gently with the terrace slope away from the sandstone ridge. Occasionally there is a coarse gravel component. Sediment exposures are frequently capped by indurated horizons, sometimes tufaceous in structure, showing wavy laminae of indurated 'ironstone' and including casts and molds of plant fragments. Some casts of tree fragments show fine woody structure preserved in the ironstone. In places cracks in the iron crust are filled by calcareous sediments. They may be rhizoliths or precipitates within the cracks that remain after removal of superimposed calcareous sediments. The indurated horizons also occur as massive, coarsely crystalline hematitic or ferruginous pisolites which developed *in situ* (Brookes 1993).

Such ferricrete horizons may relate to groundwater (Dewolf 1976) or soil forming conditions (Nahon 1980a, 1980b) which concentrated iron during erosion of FSS sediments, and thus be post-depositional phenenomena. An indurated ferricrete (<1 m thick) caps the east-central FSS ridge in the Sheikh Muftah Embayment, and protects it from rapid erosion. To the west this is seen to wedge-out into ferruginized sediments, where a thicker section of FSS conformably overlain by CSS is preserved. Both Dakhleh Unit and 'small-sized MSA' ('Sheikh Mabruk Unit') artefacts lie on the ferricrete surface (Loc. 328, 30/420–E1–3 & F1–3).

Calcareous Terraced Sediments (CSS)

Calcareous Silty Sediments (CSS) are more widespread than FSS. In places there is a basal gravel rich in red or green claystone clasts, some sandstone fragments, small chert nodules, occasional fragments of indurated ironstone, and rare but undiagnostic chert artifacts (Loc. 151; Loc. 362, 31/420–F9–4: Churcher 1982, 1983; McDonald, pers. comm., 1988) (Fig. 1.37, Top). This basal gravel is discontinuous, and most commonly present where CSS overlies claystone bedrock rather than FSS. In several similar sections those gravels contain small, irregular, deeply hydrated chert nodules. Although Brookes (1993) suggests derivation from long eroded P-I gravels, they differ from cherts seen in the limestones capping the Libyan Escarpment or their derivatives in the Piedmont gravels and lags. Kleindienst (this volume, Chapter 5) has noted small grey chert nodules deriving from the Mut Fm. Similar nodules have been noted in red Nubia Group claystones near Kharga (S. Eichelkamp, pers. comm., 1987). Churcher found *in situ* large and small varicoloured chert balls up to 60 cm diameter in the upper strata of the Mut. Fm. shales northeast of Teneida in 1994 (Fig. 1.37, Bottom).

These suggest the CSS derived its cherts at least in part from the Mut Fm. The gravels pass upwards abruptly into greyish-green calcareous muds, containing variable but small amounts of rounded, frosted quartz. These muds are highly consolidated with columnar structure, abundant slickensides and moderately dense iron oxide mottling. The muds pale upwards as the carbonate content increases until they pass more or less abruptly into a light grey to white, indurated, massive or laminar, calcareous cap or caliche/calcrete duricrust. At a few localities, large irregular masses of dark organic(?) matter occur near the base of the calcareous cap and may represent a disrupted organic mat (Brookes 1993, fig. 8d).

Brookes (1983, pls XXII, XXIIIa; 1986, figs 24–26) described a section in a CSS sequence from 'Bone Butte' (Loc. 31/420–F9–4) (Fig. 1.38, Top) southeast of Sheikh Muftah:

Depth of Unit (cm)	Mineralogy and Remarks	Cumulative Depth (m)
50	Strongly indurated, white, massive caliche with faint laminae, vertical joints, and hollow root molds.	3.20
20	Powdery to semi-indurated, greyish-white, calcareous mud; base of overlying unit.	2.70
100	Grey-green mud with semi-indurated fragic columnar/ prismatic structure; abundant slickensides, oxidised mottles: upper 20 cm black mottled (?Mn); strong HCl reaction.	2.50
100	Grey-green mud with columnar structure, scattered granules and pebbles up to 40 mm diameter, usually 5 mm, including 10 mm diameter ferruginous pisolites.	1.50
50	Finely stratified, gravely and sandy, reddish silt; discontinuous. Moderate reaction with HCl from disseminated carbonates in non-reactive matrix.	0.50

[Eroded Surface/Disconformity]

Cretaceous:
| Mut Formation, red claystone. No HCl reaction. | 0 |

A bone of a large mammal (Churcher 1983) lying on the disconformity between the basal silt and the underlying Mut Formation was ^{14}C-dated at 15,755 ± 380 yrs (S-2499) on the CO_2 fraction; this is likely to be unreliable. Collagen and apatite were insufficient for dating (Brookes 1986).

Sequences similar to that described are common, but vary in detail and in the texture and structure of the caliche/calcrete cap. At the top of Bone Butte, near Sheikh Muftah, and in the Lowland southwest of Balat, east of the sandstone ridge, some CSS terrace remnants are capped by caliche-

Fig. 1.37. TOP, West end of 'Bone Butte', a residual 'mesa' southeast of Sheikh Muftah. The hillock is capped by a calcareous limey marl or calcrete (CSS) grading downwards into subaqueous clays, which overlie the Mut Formation red claystones. The top of the lower bench at left is where a large mammalian bone was found, which was ¹⁴C dated at 15,755 ± 380 yr BP. C.S.C., Feb., 1994. BOTTOM, Chert balls weathering out of upper Mut Formation shales, northeast of Teneida. An extensive field of these spheroidal cherts exist at Loc. 347, 31/435–P6–1), with balls from 3 to 80 cm in diameter weathered from (two large, foreground) or in the process of emerging from the shales (top halves only visible). They appear to be biogenic in origin and vary internally in hardness and colour. M.R.K., Feb., 1996.

Fig. 1.38. TOP, Horizontal root casts (rhizoliths) in limey marl (CSS) capping 'Bone Butte', southeast of Sheikh Muftah. Detached blocks show biogenic casts of plant remains and possible animal burrows (bioturbations). C.S.C., Feb., 1994. BOTTOM, Horizontal and vertical rhizoliths developed in calcareous sediments (CSS) on east side of Sheikh Muftah Valley. Hammer for scale. C.S.C., Feb., 1994.

fied sediment showing cross-bedding and delicate, straw-like, rhizoliths (Fig. 1.38). Some show more than one heavily indurated layer, and the underlying members are sandier than in the section described above (Brookes 1993).

In CSS exposed southeast of Tenida, silty and sandy sediments capped by ~1 m of caliche/calcrete overlie sandstone bedrock. The main terrace slopes upward at a low angle to the north. On the terrace surface, Kleindienst noted scattered patches of a vitreous material in 1987, which may be a form of 'Libyan Desert Silica Glass' (Giegengack and Issawi 1975; Said 1990b; Schwarcz 1962) because no cultural material is associated that would suggest an industrial slag. A sample collected in 1992 included plant impressions of grass/reed/sedge and others (U. Thanheiser, pers. comm., 1992), and other samples were submitted to Schwarcz for identification.

Genesis of Ferruginous and Calcareous Terraced Sediments

The association of ferruginous and calcareous units with the contact between the claystone Lowland and the sandstone ridges south of and within the central oasis suggests ground water discharge as the medium for transporting local clastic components downslope northward and into the valley axes. Discharge from the sandstone rim surrounding the Sheikh Muftah Embayment would account for the predominantly sandy composition of FSS. Greenish clays within the Nubia sandstones or Mut Fm. claystones could provide the muddier component of the CSS (Brookes 1986).

However, the source of the carbonate in CSS is a problem. The hydrochemistry of deep ground waters from Dakhleh boreholes (Ezzat 1974b) indicates insufficient carbonate to deposit that of the caliche. In the modern environment calcite is a major constituent of the dust blown from the limestone Plateau and gravel Piedmont to the north, which is a possible source (Brookes 1986, 1993). The lack of carbonate in FSS would then indicate accumulation under a different climatic regime. Another interpretation suggested by Schwarcz is that, while FSS probably relate to iron-rich ground water derived from the Nubian aquifer, the carbonate in CSS comes from carbonate-rich water draining from the north, either as direct overland flow or as near-surface groundwater seepage. Carbonate in a caliche/calcrete may also derive from gypsum rather than calcite, by reduction of sulfate (Lattman and Lauffenburger 1974); gypsum occurs commonly in the stratigraphically higher bedrock formations to the north, but can also be found in the underlying Nubia sandstones. (The waters issuing from fossil spring vents deposited jarosite in the eye sediments, producing yellow sulfate colorings [Gardner 1932; Schild and Wendorf 1977; Wendorf and Schild 1980].)

Stratigraphic Position of the Ferruginous and Calcareous Terraced Sediments

At the two localities where he reports CSS superimposed on FSS in the southern end of the Sheikh Muftah Embayment, Brookes (1993) considers the FSS to be capped by an indurated ferricrete horizon indicative of surface exposure. At several other localities in that vicinity CSS directly overlies shale bedrock, indicating erosion of any previously existing FSS before its deposition. Therefore, deposition of CSS may have been temporally separated from that of FSS by weathering and erosion over sufficient time for removal of FSS from the Embayment. However, in a clean section along the west face of the central FSS ridge (Loc. 328), thin CSS sediments are apparently conformable on FSS, and no indurated horizon is present. Elsewhere in eastern Dakhleh it is impossible to say whether FSS was ever deposited.

No satisfactory chronometric dates have been obtained for either FSS or CSS. The FSS is intrinsically unsuitable for U-series dating; it is lacking in calcite or any other minerals that would have acted as closed systems after deposition. The CSS is, in principle, more promising for U-series dating. Samples of CSS provided by Brookes either gave very poor yields of U and Th, or exhibited anomalous isotope ratios which could not be interpreted as U-series ages. Inspection of outcrops in the southern Sheikh Muftah Embayment by Schwarcz in 1992 indicated that most deposits were unsuitable for dating.

A single sample (MRK1991/Dak 3, McM #91080) from the southernmost outcrop south of the Sheikh Muftah valley gave a poorly-defined date. Its isotopic data are: $^{230}Th/^{234}U = 0.550 \pm .042$; $^{234}U/^{238}U = 1.183 \pm .080$; $^{230}Th/^{232}Th = 3.00, \pm 0.24$. The last ratio shows that the sample is highly contaminated with detritus; isotopic ratios for any sample with $^{230}Th/^{232}Th <20$ must be corrected for the effect of detrital contamination. If we assume that the contaminant had a $^{230}Th/^{232}Th$ ratio of 1.25, then the corrected age is 57 ± 13 kya. A sample from 'Bone Butte' (Loc. 362, 31/420–F9–4) (MRK1991/Dak 2, McM #91079), ca. 30 cm below the surface of the indurated caprock, gave adequate Th and U yields, but had a $^{230}Th/$

$^{234}U = 1.336 \pm 0.120$, and $^{230}Th/^{232}Th = 2.26 \pm .084$, clearly outside the range of datable samples, and indicating severe detrital contamination.

The series of samples collected by Brookes in 1990 from the gebel to the southwest of Bone Butte but stratigraphically equivalent, and analysed earlier, had given very low $^{230}Th/^{238}U$ ratios that could not be interpreted as ages; one sample also gave an anomalously low $^{234}U/^{238}U = 0.9$. However, one sample from this locality, at a depth of 25–30 cm below surface of the caprock, gave acceptable Th and U yields (IAB1990 DAK 2, McM #90056): $^{230}Th/^{234}U = 0.804 \pm 0.179$ and $^{230}Th/^{232}Th = 1.25 \pm 0.231$. If the three cited analyses are combined to define a leachate-only isochron as described by Schwarcz and Latham (1989), the resultant $^{230}Th/^{234}U$ ratio of 0.33 gives an approximate age of 40 ± 10^3 yr BP. This age, although rough, suggests that water-deposited carbonates were reaching the lowland during Isotope Stages 4 to 2. What this age applies to, however, is unclear, and the analytic problems underscore the need for further investigation into the genesis of CSS. It is unclear whether the indurated calcareous sediments are mainly duricrusts or marls, or some combination of these types of deposits.

On the basis of a single diagnostic biface, and included cores and flakes, FSS deposition is not older than later Middle Pleistocene. Surface occurrences on FSS or deflated FSS are Middle Stone Age, including Dakhleh Unit occurrences on deflated FSS (Loc. 325, 31/420–E1–2 & F1–2) in the Sheikh Muftah Embayment. The few surface artifacts from CSS are MSA, or undiagnostic flakes on the terrace southeast of Tenida (Loc. 211). Both terraced sediment units are older than some spring mounds (see next section) which erupted through the floors of valleys eroded into them, but FSS (and ?CSS) may well be coeval with others that include Acheulian/Balat Unit bifaces in the eye sediments (DOP finds and Schild and Wendorf 1977). Viewed from a distance, FSS appears to wrap around or incorporate the oldest, highest spring mounds (Fig. 1.39). Both FSS and CSS are older than (some) Pleistocene Laminated Sediments (PLS) because the basins containing PLS in southeastern Dakhleh are eroded through CSS into Taref sandstone (Brookes' 'Facies C' and 'D', 1993, fig. 8f–h). At the north end of the Sheikh Muftah Embayment the northernmost butte of the CSS (Loc. 322, 31/420 H5–2) occupies a position altitudinally below the projected distal profile of P-I, which would therefore have to be eroded before CSS could be deposited and, since CSS overlie FSS, FSS must also postdate P-I, *contra* Brookes (1993, 545, tab. 2). Based *only* on the rare archeological finds *in situ*, ?distal P-II gravels at Loc. 084 and FSS may be approximately coeval in age. The erosion which affected FSS flanking the Sheikh Muftah Embayment before CSS were deposited, and the deposition of CSS, would then post-date P-II, and pre-date P-III gravels which flank CSS remnants, suggesting that CSS were deposited during the downcutting from P-II surfaces. Alternatively, both FSS and CSS correlate with the P-II gravels' deposition; or, less likely CSS correlates with P-III gravels' deposition.

A final alternative is that CSS and capping duricrusts in fact relate to more than one episode of accumulation. A small calcrete-capped remnant stands at elevation of >150 m a.s.l., on the sandstone ridge northeast of Bashendi (= P-II level), and small duricrust outliers (calcrete and/or silcrete) occur on the Taref sandstone rim ca. 12 km south of the Masara cultivation (elevations 155–160 m a.s.l.). These indicate a complex history of deposition, that probably relates to more than one cycle of deposition and duricrust formation. This interpretation differs considerably from that of Brookes (1993, tab. 2) who considers FSS to predate P-I gravels, and CSS to fall between P-I and P-II in age.

Spring Mounds

'Spring mounds' are a second landform associated with former artesian ground water discharge in Dakhleh Oasis. These mounds were built by now defunct artesian springs, and/or are remnant erosional landforms surrounding fossil spring vents or eyes. Where spring mounds occur in close association with the terraced sediments, in some cases they erupted through the floors of wide valleys cut through the terraces (*contra* Brookes 1986, figs 20, 28), in others they were probably exhumed from terraced FSS deposits (Fig. 1.34). More than one phase of mound building is now recognised (Brookes 1986, 1993), but the chronology of these mounds or vents is uncertain.

No active mound-building springs are present in Dakhleh today. The only descriptions of such a spring in the Western Desert appear to be those for Ain el-Dalla which, however, has been subjected to anthropogenic alterations (Haynes 1983): "The second [spring], Ain Iddaila, is in the western branch of the depression, 63 kilometres W.N.W. of Qasr Farafra as the crow flies. This is a beautiful running spring of very sweet water, warm to the hand, and which runs to waste into a small pool. The spring is hidden by a dense mass of green reeds lining the sides and bottom of a large hole, from the base of which the water rises" (Beadnell 1901b, 13). "There are two motor passes into the [Ain el-Dalla] depression from the northern cliffs, one north-west and the other north-east of the spring. Both are full of drift sand, which forms a ramp down the otherwise steep cliffs. The sand is hard if not too much disturbed by previous cars. The spring has been cleared by Prince Omar Toussoon. The water, rather warm and sulphurous but quite good to drink, flows out in a decent stream from the top of a sandy mound 30 feet [≈ 9.1 m] high in the centre of the depression" (Bagnold 1931, 18). "At Dalla the vegetation is concentrated on the low sandy hill at the top of which the spring emerges. Here were a few date palms, *Tamarix mannifera* Ehrenb.; a willow, *Salix Safsaf* Forsk.; a reed, *Phragmites communis* Trin., which is one of the main constitutents of the marsh types of vegetation in the northern part of the continent; and *Alhagi Maurorum* Medic., a desert plant of wide

distribution" (Shaw 1931, 535). Haynes (1983) reports that back-dirt from clearing the spring vent includes MSA artifacts.

Hundreds of ancient spring mounds are present in Dakhleh Oasis, generally restricted to the southern Lowland near the sandstone-claystone boundaries, but also in the sandstones between Gedida and Maohoub. Few spring mounds have been found east of Balat, where the regional northerly dip steepens, narrowing the claystone outcrop and shifting its contact with the Nubia sandstones towards the northern Escarpment. No spring mounds are known farther east until fossil artesian spring vents reappear in Kharga Oasis, where geological structures are, as in Dakhleh, more complex (Hermina 1990). There are many fewer fossil spring vents in Kharga than in Dakhleh, although no systematic mapping has been done since the 1930's; and these often seem to show evidence of repeated rejuvenation (Gardner 1932; Haynes 1983). In 1992, Churcher, Kleindienst and Wiseman located vents on the southern margin of Kharga Oasis with surface artifacts ranging from Upper Acheulian through later MSA in type, on the eastern flanks of Gebel Qarn, far south of those previously reported (Caton-Thompson 1952; Simmons and Mandel 1985, 1986).

No systematic measurements have yet been made of mound geometry, but reconnaissance of several groups of mounds by Brookes and Kleindienst, and air photographs, suggest that diameters and heights have modal values of ca. 15–25 m and 6–12 m, although some are much smaller with the smallest ca. 6 by 2 m or even less, and the largest ca. 200 by 25 m (Brookes 1993: fig. 7a, b). The heights and mounded nature of these features are probably accentuated by erosion of surrounding sediments and bedrock in many cases. The largest and most complex structures appear to be concentrated north of Gedida, where two that are not covered by migrating dunes (Fig. 1.31) consist of rings of contiguous vents around a large central depression ca. 200 m across. One of these has a small central cone which probably indicates rejuvenation. The central vent sediments are more easily eroded, and the surrounding matrix is left in various stages of 'ring' formation around the central areas as mounds are planed-down by erosion (Figs 1.39; 1.40).

Spring mounds are superficially similar in lithology and structure (Brookes 1993). When seen in section, greyish white, fine quartz sand and silt conveyed by the Nubian aquifers feeding the vent forms a central mass within a surrounding matrix of altered mudstones and muds. Spring vent sediments were deposited rapidly through high-volume discharge, and occasionally contain blocks of sandstone, or wall gravels. Sediments are more highly mineralised near the top and in the eye, with thinly stratified, varicoloured ochreous silt, commonly penetrated by ferruginised root casts up to 30 mm in diameter. Many mounds with eroded or humanly-breached perimeters show sub-horizontally bedded ochreous yellow sediments near the summit, reflecting a larger original diameter (Brookes

Fig. 1.39. TOP, Large spring mounds to west of Sheikh Muftah Valley, looking southeast, with western margin of valley to left. Note many mounds at different heights and stages of decay. Mounds are originally capped by 'ironstone' or 'sandrock', which erodes to expose coloured sediments of the central spring eye (right). Taref Formation sandstone yardang-gebels visible on the horizon. C.S.C., Feb., 1994. BOTTOM, View southeast from 'Dune Hill', northwest Sheikh Muftah Valley. A remnant mound lies this side of and the ring signature of a planed-off mound beyond and to the left of a less eroded mound containing MSA artifacts (Loc. 146, 31/420–E10–3). M.R.K., Jan., 1986.

Fig. 1.40. TOP, Small spring mounds on west side of Sheikh Muftah Embayment near 'Dune Hill'. Each small yardang comprises half the eye deposits which have protected a slice of the softer mound deposits to the south. The nearest mound shows the unstratified eye conduit in front, and the stratified mound deposits on the sides. Holocene artifacts and bone fragments are found scattered in the surrounding area. The large FSS mound to right, 'Dune Hill', is still capped by 'ironstone' or 'sandrock', and is older than others shown in Figure 1.39, Top. C.S.C., Feb., 1994. BOTTOM, View from southwest of Balat, looking north from edge of terrace remnant (foreground) of Calcareous Silty Sediments across plain with decayed and sectioned spring mounds, to the central re-entrant and Balat Point in the Libyan Escarpment (cf. Figs 1.20, 1.24). M.R.K., Jan., 1986.

1993, fig. 8c). Uneroded summits may therefore have originally contained a shallow pool confined within a low rim, as at Ain el-Dalla. In detail, stratigraphy is highly variable (cf. Gardner 1932; Caton-Thompson 1952; Schild and Wendorf 1977).

Many of the mounds still recognisable after prolonged erosion (many have been planed-off) are protected by a crust of indurated ferricrete or 'ironstone'. This commonly includes casts and molds of plant remains and is therefore original (Brookes 1993). Vegetation probably facilitated the accumulation of sediments around the vent. Ironstone crusts are lacking in the main masses of mound vent-sediments, which may indicate that deposition was too rapid to permit iron concentration until the mounds had reached a height at which the artesian head was insufficient to maintain strong spring activity. The complex geo-chemistry implied has not been studied (cf. Schild and Wendorf 1977).

Most Dakhleh spring mounds are geographically clustered: a likely result of continual efflux through localised bedrock fractures, as seen flanking the sandstone Tawil Anticline southwest of Balat, or south of Ezbet Sheikh Muftah (Brookes 1986, fig. 20) or Muzzawaka (Brookes 1986, fig. 28). No regular pattern has been noticed, however, such as the rectilinear, joint-controlled pattern of mounds reported in Kharga Oasis by Gardner (1932). Within a mound group, many springs could have been active simultaneously; with time, after reaching artesian head height, vents would become clogged with sediment, and the eyes may have shifted. If shifts were rapid, dating techniques would be unlikely to distinguish serial eruptions unless changes in secular geomagnetism can be detected in the ferruginous cappings.

Fig. 1.41. TOP, View southwest of Balat across salt-encrusted sediments, looking northeast to el-Battikh Promontory. The salted sediments overlie Mut Formation red muds and surround low spring mounds in middle distance. M.R.K., Jan., 1986. BOTTOM, Diaporic sediments showing plastic deformation due to dewatering and a capping halite crust at Ain Duma (Loc. 105, 30/420–P1–1). Trowel on crust for scale. C.S.C., Feb., 1983.

Brookes (1986) concluded that the Dakhleh spring mounds formed during a single period because of included fresh Earlier Stone Age (ESA) chert artifacts (Schild and Wendorf 1977; McDonald 1982). He continues to recognize only one set of Pleistocene mounds, stratigraphically placed between P-II and the PLS (Brookes 1993, tab. 2). Kleindienst (this volume, Chapter 5) identified mounds in the Sheikh Muftah Embayment including fresh MSA artifacts in 1986 and, subsequently, south of Balat, a younger generation of mounds of probable Holocene age was discovered by McDonald, Kleindienst and Brookes, formed in what is now an area of salt-crusted sediments, and standing up to 6 m high (Fig. 1.41, Top, also see next section). Scatters of mid-Holocene Sheikh Muftah Unit material are found on the flanks of spring mounds just north and northwest of Mut, where the surface elevation is 100–110 m a.s.l., suggesting Holocene spring activity. Scatters are also found just south of the modern cultivation belt between Mut and Sheikh Muftah around the 130 m contour, often close to mounds for which Holocene activity can be inferred.

Finds of *in situ* artifacts in spring mounds suggest that there are several generations of fossil artesian springs (Kleindienst, this volume, Chapter 5), and McDonald's survey indicates artesian spring activity at least into mid-Holocene times. Further detailed mapping and excavation is required to place these within the general Quaternary chronology. The oldest spring deposits apparently contain Upper Acheulian in western Dakhleh, but their relationship to other sediments or features is unknown. Excavated eyes with Balat Unit content (Brookes 1993, fig. 7d) in eastern Dakhleh are coeval with or post-date P-II gravels, as shown west of Balat at archaeological occurrences excavated by the Combined Prehistoric Expedition (Schild and Wendorf 1977), and by DOP finds.

Holocene Sediments in the Lowland
Salt-Crusted Areas
Salt-crusted areas in the Lowland are restricted to eastern Dakhleh, in a zone south of the cultivated land, extending from southwest of Balat to south of Teneida (Beadnell 1901a, pl. VI; Brookes 1983; 1989b, fig. 1, 'Area C'). Its northern boundary is defined by cultivation, which in places has slightly encroached on the salt crust. The southern boundary is the junction with the Nubia Group (Taref Fm.) sandstones where they dip beneath the crust. The apparent absence of enclosing higher terrain to the north prevents this zone from being conclusively identified as a Holocene playa, although Issawi (1977, fig. 7) designated deposits to the west of Balat cultivation as 'playa' (Fig. 1.2). There is no evidence that sediments underlying this tract once continued as far north as the distal margins of the Piedmont gravel fans which at present are the only features which could have contained a large water body; and there is no evidence that Holocene erosion along the northern boundary of this zone could have removed a hypothetical bedrock dam. It is possible, therefore, that sediments similar to those deposited in true playas could have been deposited in this area in an extensive unconfined wetland (Brookes 1989b, 1993), although the exposed deposits all lie below ca. 130 m a.s.l.

Sediments are rarely exposed to a depth of more than 0.5 m, but sections show two sub-units: a lower one of reddish-brown, stratified, muddy, quartz sands, densely riddled with mud-filled root and stem casts of aquatic plants, probably reeds (Churcher 1983). One exposure shows deflated sections across the tops of diapiric dewatering structures. Above an abrupt, wavy contact, an upper sub-unit consists of 30–50 cm of loosely consolidated, massive, pale brown, silty, quartz sand, often with thin gypsum partings and crystalline calcareous rhizoliths, and with few plant remains (Brookes 1986) (Fig. 1.41, Bottom). This sub-unit contains Sheikh Muftah Unit chert tools and sometimes pottery; broken ostrich eggshell and occasionally bone fragments. Churcher (1983) identified hartebeest, gazelle, and a large bovid amongst bones from Loc. 105, (30/420–P1–1, Ain Duma,

Fig. 1.43. Salt-encusted abandoned irrigation area north of Sheikh Mabrouk. Note salt-encusted soil slabs being mined in left foreground and naturally tented in the area. Distant vegetation is date palms, Nile acacia and tamarisk. Man on cycle in centre distance for scale. C.S.C., Feb., 1994.

Fig. 1.42. TOP, Neolithic artifact cluster at Ain Duma (Loc. 105, 30/420–P1–1). Note inverted pot lacking base and containing ashes, and surrounding pottery and bone fragments and charcoal. Trowel for scale. C.S.C., Feb., 1983. BOTTOM, View from the oasis' southern sandstone rim, south of the Balat cultivation, looking northeast across well-preserved field of spring mounds. M.R.K., Jan., 1986.

Fig. 1.42, Top) in this terrain. This unit passes abruptly upwards into a disrupted silt-rich halite crust, with 'teepee' or 'tented' structures up to 50 cm high (Brookes 1983, pl, XXIIIb; 1989b, 1993).

Artifacts within sub-aqueous sediments imply human occupation of a periodically inundated land surface. In the southwest sector this terrain is dotted with low spring mounds (<6 m high, usually ca. 3 m) (Fig. 1.42, Bottom). The flanks of these mounds up to ~2 m above the present surface are composed of the same halite-crusted silts which cover the surrounding flats. Above that level, mounds are littered with disrupted fragments of a thin ironstone crust densely riddled with thin ferruginised root casts. These mounds may therefore have been the source of water in which the surrounding sediments were deposited. Elsewhere in the encrusted zone, where Holocene spring mounds are lacking, water could have been supplied directly by rainfall and/or by seepages from a recharged shallow aquifer (Brookes 1989b, fig. 5a).

Only one radiocarbon date is available on ostrich eggshell fragments probably deflated from the upper sub-

unit of these playa-like sediments, at Loc. 108 (30/435–B3–2, Ain Tauwabit): 7,860 ± 80 yr BP (Beta-23685) (Brookes 1989b, tab. 2; 1993). Some of the shell fragments were large, sharp-edged, almost unvarnished and showed pores on the outer surface, indicating recent emergence from the host sediment. Eroding patches of sediment lie only a few metres from the scatter of chert artifacts, artiodactyl bones and shell fragments sampled. This and other scatters lie on the surface of the lower sub-unit of the playa-like sediments, and the two can be seen superposed near the site. Although this determination may 'date' the shell fragments, and possibly some level in the sediments, McDonald doubts its validity as a date for the Sheikh Muftah aggregate, based upon comparisons with 'Late Neolithic' mid-Holocene dates at Kharga (Wendorf and Schild 1980, 265) and other dates on Dakhleh localities with identical ceramics and distinctive chipped lithic assemblage (see 'Halfa Grass Basins', below). Loc. 108 contained a fragment of copper (McDonald 1983, fig. 1,k), and a similar Sheikh Muftah surface scatter about 500 m away contained a Dynasty I storage jar (4440–4220 BP) (Loc. 111, 30/435 C5–1). (Several Sheikh Muftah localities include both Sheikh Muftah and Old Kingdom cultural materials.)

Brookes (1983) suggested that the salt-encrustation resulted from salinization related to Roman irrigation practices (1986: fig. 29). However, the mounds and surrounding sediments are clearly much older. There is evidence of more recent salinization: southwest of Ein Shams, on the eastern border of the encrusted zone, a village ruin on coppice dunes (31/435 D10–1) is built of blocks of salt-crust; the area has been affected by later salt encrustation after abandonment. Sherdage was identified as 'Ottoman' (D. Whitcomb, pers. comm., 1987). Some salt-crust blocks were also used as building material at the larger settlement of El-Qasaba (31/435 D9–1) to

Fig. 1.44. TOP, Remnant yardangs in irrigation sediments at Loc. 006, Site 32/390–D2–2, near Bir Talata el-Maohoub (vegetation in middle distance), 2 km southwest of Deir el-Hagar and 4 km south of Sheikh Maohoub, looking west from crest of barchan dune similar to that in left middle distance. Sio'h Ridge, Duwi Formation, forms far wall of valley. Landrover for scale. C.S.C., Feb., 1994.
BOTTOM, Remnant yardang in left foreground (TOP) at Loc. 006, Site 32/390–D2–2, showing tilted bedding in irrigation sediments. Note fox den at base. C.S.C., Feb., 1994.

the north, where the surrounding area also shows effects of salinization. Salinization related to modern irrigation practices can be seen towards Sheikh Wali, between Masara and Mut, where salt blocks are also used in construction, and north of Sheikh Mabrouk (Fig. 1.43) (see 'Irrigation Deposits', below), and unrelated on coppice dunes in the 'Halfa Grass Basins' southwest of Sheikh Mabrouk (see 'Southern Sandstone Ridge', below).

Tabular Sand Sheets
Tabular sand sheet deposits are not easily mapped because they do not present a distinctive surface in the field or on airphotos, exposures are discontinuous and often shallow 'windows' eroded through younger sediments, and they may be or have been cultivated and consequently have had their distinctive internal structure obscured or obliterated. They have been identified in western Dakhleh, at Loc. 006, 32/390 D2–2 (Fig. 1.44), and in the east at

Loc. 101, 31/420 P5–1, Loc. 100, 31/420 P6–1, and Loc. 116, 31/435 A6–3, closely grouped on the west edge of the Balat cultivation and north of the salinized ground (Brookes 1986, 'Unit V').

Brookes (1986, 1989a) reported that sands and derivatives of the bedrock predominate in both areas, and comprise variable mixtures of grey and red shales, sandstone, spring-derived quartz, and minor limestone. Exotic grains of rounded, frosted quartz sand in the coarse fraction and angular, clear quartz sand and silt in the fine fraction have been introduced by wind.

Structurally, these sediments are tabular with generally southerly dips, sub-horizontally bedded, and with occasional poorly-developed low-angle cross-beds (Fig. 1.44, Bottom). Horizontally ramified root-cast networks cover deflation surfaces, with individual casts often 5 cm diameter, but occasionally larger (Fig. 1.45). They represent an anchoring mat of sparse woody shrubs such as *Tamarix* or *Acacia*. No vertical tubules are seen as in the lower sub-unit below the salt crust, where they indicate reed growth in still or slowly moving water. Texture, structures, and lithology of these tabular sediments all indicate aeolian deposition. In the eastern exposures their marginal location with respect to salt-crusted, possible

Fig. 1.45. Cast of large tree (?Acacia nilotica)in remnant yardang (Fig. 1.44, Bottom) at Loc. 006, Site 32/390–D2–2. Note rhizoliths and stratification of sandy matrix, and termite galleries in righthand trunk cast. C.S.C., Feb., 1994.

playa/marsh sediments suggests sand sheet deposition anchored by shrub vegetation around water bodies (Brookes 1986). Both archaeological evidence and radiocarbon dates suggest that these sediments are penecontemporaneous with the now salt-encrusted, mid-Holocene water-deposited sediments.

An age for these sediments in eastern Dakhleh at Loc. 116, 31/435–A6–3, 6.8 km southwest of Balat, is given by a radiocarbon date of 5,170 ± 90 yr BP [(Beta-17020) for ostrich eggshell fragments *in situ* with other artifacts, and at Loc. 101, 31/420–P5–1, 6.5 km southwest of Balat, for eggshell fragments deflated with other artifacts from the sediments, of 5,310 ± 160 yr BP (Beta-17019). A third date on surface material is from Loc 104, 31/420–M9–2, 4 km futher south: 5,745 ± 80 yr BP (S-2149). All of these localities lie near the 130 m contour. The associated cultural material is assigned to Bashendi B. Some Sheikh Muftah Unit localities (Loc. 100 and scatters to the south) are also associated with tabular sand sheet deposits; a few artifacts were found *in situ* at Loc. 100, but no dateable material was obtained. In western Dakhleh, at Loc. 006, 32/390–D2–2, 5 km south of Maohoub, eggshell fragments from a tight surface cluster collected by Brookes resting *on* similar sediments yielded an age of 5,800 ± 60 yr BP (Beta-6873) (Brookes 1989b). (The archaeological unit represented is unknown.)

Irrigation Deposits
Sediments, here termed 'irrigation deposits', were previously identified as 'coppice dune' (*nebkha*) of Old Kingdom age (approx. 2,200 BC) (Brookes 1986, figs 17, 18) and 'tabular dune' of Graeco-Roman age (approx. 300 BC to 400 AD) (Brookes 1986, fig. 16a,b), and as 'Units VI' and 'VII' in Brookes (1986). The term 'tabular dune' is not entirely inappropriate because the texture, structure, lithology and morphology of these sediments all indicate some aeolian activity in their genesis. However, in 1987 Brookes recognized that these sediments are associated with irrigated field systems (1989a, 1993). Their anthropomorphic genesis was confirmed by DOP observations in 1987 at Gebel Gala in Kharga Oasis south-southeast of Algiers village, where Caton-Thompson and Gardner (1932, Caton-Thompson 1952) recognised the anthropogenic origin of comparable sediments which they termed 'historic well deposits'. Haynes referred to 'Shurafa Hill' (Haynes 1983, 1985), conducted more detailed studies in 1978, 1979 and 1983, and terms such deposits 'semiplaya', following Embabi (1972).

Irrigation deposits occur in two forms in the central lowland. One is an irregularly shaped, tabular sheet with low relief (<2 m) and steeper, eroded margins (up to 5 m high over 50 m). These may cover several square kilometres and are either still being cultivated or are more-or-less severely deflated (Fig 1.46, Top). The other form is as groups of yardangs up to 5 m high, carved from similar sheets, mainly found in areas more prone to severe wind erosion such as near the escarpment foot or in alignment

Fig. 1.46. TOP, *Irrigation deposits mantling 'Ein Birbeyeh temple (31/435–K5–1) rise and structure, northwest of Teneida, looking northwest. The well is located near the tall date palm on the mound's crest. Old water channels for the field system show as horizontal lines in middle distance, and as a discontinuous ridge in the foreground. C.S.C., Feb., 1994. BOTTOM, Irrigation sediments burying 'Ein Birbeyeh temple. Note the dip of the sediments compared to the horizontal roof courses at the back of the temple, and the contained stones, potsherds, and charcoal. M.R.K., Feb., 1996.*

with a piedmont valley (Brookes 1989a) (Fig. 1.44, Top). Examples of the former can be seen near the temple of 'Ein Birbiyeh (31/435–K5–1) or to the east of the main road near Budkhulu and, of the latter, north of Bashendi, northeast of Teneida or south of Muzzawakka.

Evidence of associated irrigation agriculture comes from deflated field patterns, aqueducts, and rare enclosed potsherds. Sherds are more abundant on deflation surfaces where up to 5 m of sediment have been removed. Reconnaissance of irrigation deposits in an area south of Ein Shams by Brookes, Kleindienst, and Whitcomb showed that they once contained sherds of wares made between the 10th and 17th Centuries AD (D. Whitcomb, pers. comm., 1987; Brookes 1989a, fig. 4a) which are now scattered over deflation surfaces.

Brookes' earlier conclusion (Brookes 1983, pl. XIXb; 1986) that a 'coppice dune' at Bir Talata el-Maohoub, western Dakhleh (Loc. 006, 32/390–D2–2), containing an Old Kingdom sherd (approx. 2,200 BC), had accumulated at that time may be erroneous (cf. Haynes 1983, fig. 19). Similar deposits south of Muzzawaka (32/390–H8–1) are related to Islamic Period irrigated agriculture, based upon archaeological contents (Brookes 1989a, fig. 2b). In fact, all securely-dated bodies of irrigation sediment so far encountered appear to be Roman or younger, i.e., 1st Century AD or later).

For example, the 1st Century AD Roman temple at 'Ein Birbiyeh (31/435–K5–1) (Brookes 1989a, fig. 2a; Mills, this volume, Chapter 10), about 25 × 21 m, is buried to the roof slabs in eight metres of dune sand and irrigation deposits (Fig. 1.46, Bottom). Contrary to Brookes (1983, 1986), it is now established that abandonment of the temple, probably no later than 400 AD, was followed by a Christian occupation which built on the temple roof after its entombment in sand. Although the irrigation deposits here may all post-date the Christian occupation, the earlier deposits could be contemporary (Mills, pers. comm., 1994).

Irrigation deposits are usually dominated by medium to coarse-grained sands, with significant proportions of silt and even clay (Figs 1.44, Bottom; 1.46, Bottom). They vary lithologically and contain components from most of the local bedrock types and Quaternary sediments. They are distinctive, however, in the high proportion of irregularly shaped, therefore locally derived, pale brown sand-sized grains derived from deflated older counterparts or other upwind deposits (e.g., playa sediments and/or tabular sand sheets) (Brookes 1989a).

The structure of the bedding gives the main clues to the origin of the sediments; these are:

1) 15–50 cm thick sub-horizontal beds with occasional low-angle cross-bedding, alternating with or frequently parted by

2) 10–20 cm thick horizontal wavy and rippled beds, and

3) less frequent 50–150 cm thick, steeply dipping beds, bounded by types 1 or 2.

Each bedding type is penetrated by mainly vertical rhizomorphs, typically small and <20 mm diameter but some up to 50 mm (Fig. 1.44, Bottom). The rhizomorphs contrast with the horizontal, robust ones in earlier tabular sand sheets, discussed above, and point to an anchoring mat of grassy and herbaceous vegetation. An intact mold of a bifurcating *Acacia* trunk penetrates bedding type 3 at Bir Talata el-Maohoub (Loc. 006, 32/390–D2–2) (Brookes 1983, pl. XXa; 1986, fig. 19c; 1989a, fig. 2c) (Fig. 1.45).

Brookes notes (1989a) that frequent southerly orientation of low-angle cross-bedding in type 1 beds, over areas crossed in all directions by ancient aqueducts, strongly suggests aeolian deposition. Conditions for deposition could have been provided by a crop which reduced surface wind velocity, and a moist surface, probably periodically flooded, which held the sand. The deposits can thus be interpreted as largely aeolian, but the type 2 plane-to-

wavy-bedded layers may reflect periodic water flowing over the surface.

Irrigation deposits are being formed today in Dakhleh in two topographic situations, either in low, level tracts bordering an aqueduct fed from a *saqia* (water wheel) or a natural spring, or bordering raised fields flooded by a *saqia* or pump from a perimeter aqueduct onto lower ground, as at Bashendi or Sheikh Mansour. In both situations, palm fronds are placed across the wind to trap fresh sediment. Low ridges are then raised around small rectangular plots which are inundated and planted. The plants then trap more sand. Cultivation of a surface which is gradually rising above its surroundings should limit the surface accumulation of salts, because these sandy sediments are freely draining. Surrounding lower areas would be susceptible to salination as water drains into them. Cultivation of lower areas without intentional creation of irrigation deposits will lead to salination, as shown by recently salinised ground east of Mut (Brookes 1989a, figs. 5–7).

Accumulation of irrigation deposits appears to have begun in Dakhleh with Roman rule, roughly 1,900 years ago, when hydraulic techniques were introduced that greatly expanded the agricultural areas of the oasis. [There are relatively few Pharaonic or Ptolemaic sites within the oasis, implying a smaller agrarian community (Mills, pers. comm., 1994), and no associated sediments have been identified.] No evidence yet recovered from Dakhleh bears on whether Roman agricultural expansion was aided by an ameliorating environment, but Mawson and Williams (1984, 50) report: "... the limnological, archaeological and archival evidence from Sudan, Egypt, Ethiopia, Chad, Libya, and Ghana is entirely consistent with a regional climate somewhat wetter than today... some 2,000 years ago". However, the particular conditions under which agriculture is practiced in Dakhleh Oasis do not need climatic change to effect a production increase. Increased production could derive from more efficient well sinking and the introduction of *saqias* to allow for expansion of field systems.

Well or Irrigation Canal Dredgeate

Another series of anthropogenic sediments are the piles of dredgeate which mark the digging and maintenance of dug wells during Historic times, and those which relate to the construction and maintenance of the large irrigation canals ('aqueducts'). These have not been systematically mapped or sampled.

Ancient clearance of blocked wells or springs was by hand carried baskets of wet mud, which was moved a minimal distance away from the eye or channel to form 'key-hole' shaped mounds around the eyes and parallel 'track' mounds leading away from them. In Figure 1.44 (Top), showing the multiple component site of Loc. 006, 32/390–D2–2, three large but low mounds between the irrigation sediment yardangs and the distant vegetation are key-holes. Their channels and tracks run away to the right behind the righthand two further yardangs. From the contained pottery and association with remains of Roman-style water jars, the dredging here was done in late Roman or Byzantine times.

The ancient mounds of dredged wet muds ('dredgeate') have a distinctive structure, being composed of many lenticular units of muds, often with differing colours or minerals, depending on the source within the eye or channel and the track the worker took away from the source. As the eyes had to be cleared more frequently or to greater depths (Beadnell 1901a), the key-hole mounds are usually higher than the track mounds, as at Loc. 006, 32/390–D2–2 (Fig. 1.44, Top).

It is impossible to date these dredging operations except by their contained pottery fragments. However these only provide a *datum ante quem* as Roman sherds may be found in modern dredgeate. It is also unfortunate that, as wells and springs have been cleared since earliest times, modern or more recent operations have obscured or removed any signs of earlier works.

The dredgeate also yields remains of aquatic molluscs, particularly the large wet-land apple snail *Pila ovata*, and the small conical water snail *Melanoides tuberculata*. These are found both within the dredgeate and gathered into windrows after exposure by erosion. Only the water snail is still extant in the oasis (see Hollett and Churcher, this volume, Chapter 9).

Mobile Dunes and Sands

Pervasive in western Dakhleh and beyond its western border in West Dakhleh, mobile dunes are among the youngest deposits assignable to a specific geomorphic context (excluding the deposits related to agricultural practices) (Brookes 1993). 'Dune belts' comprise three groups organised into dune forms varying from transverse to barchan to longitudinal whose distribution and size depend on sand supply and wind directions (Embabi 1990, fig. 4). These were noted by the earliest visitors to the oasis (e.g., Cailliaud 1826; Rohlfs 1875) and, together with those at Kharga, have provided a laboratory for studies of dune sands (e.g., Ball 1900; Beadnell 1910; King 1916, 1918; Bagnold 1935, 1941; Busche 1988; Embabi 1982, 1990). To the north, dune rows are oriented nearly north-south, but veer towards 165° (south-southeast) at their southern extremities as air flows around the western Maohoub Promontory and converge downwind.

Coarse sand granules are derived locally from mixed lithologies, but the bulk is finer, far-traveled sand, probably from the southeast edge of the Great Sand Sea to the northwest or more directly from a smaller sand sea southeast of the Farafra Depression (Brookes 1986, 1993; Embabi 1990, fig. 3; Hermina 1990, fig. 14.6). Beadnell (1901b) in 1898 reported that the downwind end of the NNW-SSE-trending parallel dunes flanking the camel track from Dakhleh to Farafra over the el-Karafish Plateau ended 20 km north of the Dakhleh escarpment edge; the latest geological map based on satellite imagery (Klitzsch *et al.* 1987a) shows the dunes ending only ca. 9 km to the

north along the track, suggesting substantial downwind sand movement or accretion over some 85 years, or ca. 130 m/yr!

Barchans and other dunes are today migrating over uninhabited areas and cultivated fields in western Dakhleh (Brookes 1986, fig. 21) (Fig. 1.31). At Dakhleh single barchans have slip faces up to ca. 10 m high. Bagnold (1941) estimated ca. 7,000 years for advance of the dunes to Dakhleh and Kharga from source. Following Embabi (1982), Brookes (1993, 542) estimates ca. 5,300 years for "...a barchan travelling ... from the proximal edge of the Farafra sand sea ..." which, however, ignores the fact that the dunes on the Libyan Plateau are not of barchan type. However, the dunes that invaded Islamic villages in Dakhleh during the last 1,000 years can be viewed as relatively late arrivals that do not necessarily indicate a recent intensification of aridity. (Brookes [1993, 530] refers to ^{14}C determinations on dead vegetation from 20 km outside Dakhleh of ca. 650 and 350 BP.) Pre-Islamic sand drifting is manifest in the burial of a 4th Century house complex at the Roman Period town of Kellis (Ismant el-Kharab) (Hope 1985, 1986, 1988; Hope *et al.* 1989). More-or-less stabilized dunes ring Bashendi and sand blankets the area of the Old Kingdom town of Ain Aseel (31/435–I1–1).

The northern Escarpment north of Qasr is almost completely mantled by sand fall, the falling dunes showing megarippling in places. The central portion of the Escarpment is today less affected, and sand has accumulated only in ravine heads. Large dunes block the North Wadi or el-Ueb, and sand blankets its amphitheatral head ramping up to the limestone caprock, while several dunes have formed across lower Wadi el-Tawil, blocking the drainage. These have existed long enough for polygonally cracked sediments bearing vegetation to accumulate behind the dunes; surface sherdage here is Islamic to modern in age. These dunes in their present form are at least post-World War I in age, because they cover lorry ruts cut into wet sediments along the earlier army road up the wadi. Further deposit of sand in these dunes and against the south walls of minor wadis continues and was noted by Churcher (pers. comm., 1994). Thus, it appears that the location of mobile dune formations may shift across the oasis through time.

A thin sand veneer blankets, and often blows across, portions of the central and western parts of the eastern oasis and up the Mut and Taref dip slopes; but the only extensive sand sheet is that southwest of the 'Southeast Basin' (see below). This overlies a surface which carries abraded Dakhleh Unit (Aterian) artifacts.

5) The "Palaeoasis": Regions East, South and West of the Lowland

The regions outside the oasis proper are here termed the 'palaeoasis' (Kleindienst, this volume, Chapter 5), extending the interests of DOP investigations some 50 km beyond modern oasis margins. On the south and east the Dakhleh central lowland is confined by dissected Taref Formation (Nubia Group) sandstone ridges, while on the southwest and west the Mut Fm. claystone/sandstone boundary lies considerably further south (Hermina 1990, fig. 14.5); the Duwi Fm. cuesta or Sio'h ridge partially confines the Lowland south of Gebel Edmonstone, and upper strata of the Duwi Fm. also outcrops on the southwest (Fig. 1.19, Top).

East of Dakhleh, and east of the 'Southeast Basin' and the mouth of Wadi el-Battikh, a range of high gebels stretches south from the Escarpment; these retain an ancient, heavily ironstone encrusted surface. West of the wadi mouth, north-south oriented sandstone yardangs bearing abundant rock art stand above P-III gravels which mantle PLS in places (Krzyzaniak and Kroeper 1990, Krzyzaniak 1987). Holocene settlements are located on ridges above the eastern rim of the Basin (McDonald 1990b). The higher sandstone area to the west (>150 m a.s.l.) has not yet been fully explored. Southeast Basin sediments extend ca. 10 km north-northeast to south-southwest, with numerous associated Holocene archaeological localities (mainly Bashendi Unit, but also a few of Old Kingdom age). The 'Western Lobe' or 'Embayment' of the basin is particularly rich in Holocene archeological occurrences (Loc. 228, 30/450 A9–1). Masara Unit occurrences with stone slab structures are found on the higher ground to the southeast of the 'Southeastern Lobe' of the depression (McDonald 1991b). Limited surveys suggest that Pleistocene remains are scattered and sparse; many are obviously recycled holoports associated with Holocene localities, although a few isolated Dakhleh Unit tanged points probably indicate use of the area during the Pleistocene.

A sandsheet-mantled sandstone surface extends southward from the confining margin of the Western Lobe (McDonald 1990a) of the Southeast Basin. The surface rises gently southward to >220 m a.s.l., until it falls off into a broad depression between a ridge of low gebels and three prominent high residual cuestas/buttes, outliers of the Taref sandstones (Klitzsch, et al. 1987a), and termed 'Taohin Berge' by Rohlfs' expedition (Jordan 1875b, Taf. 11). These stand as landmarks on the southeastern horizon when viewed from Dakhleh. The true desert margin is marked by a south-facing escarpment, south of the high gebels (McDonald 1990a), which approximates the boundary between the Maghrabi and Sabaya formations' sandstones (Klitzsch, et al. 1987a).

A few traverses by DOP members have located archaeological occurrences ranging from MSA, including Dakhleh Unit, to Historic across this terrain (McDonald 1990a; Kleindienst, this volume, Chapter 5). Sheikh Muftah Unit artifacts from a small rockshelter in a low gebel (Loc. 244) have been radiocarbon dated to 4,310 ± 80 yr BP (Gd-4492) (McDonald 1990d). Little reconnaissance has yet been done to the west or southwest of the oasis, although one traverse in 1992 by Churcher,

Kleindienst and Wiseman located both Pleistocene and Holocene archaeological occurrences. Archaeological and geological survey, mainly by McDonald and Brookes, has concentrated on the southern Sandstone Ridge and Plain, from Sheikh Mabruk westward to Mut (Brookes 1989b, 'Area A', 'Area D'; McDonald 1986, 1987, 1990a, 1990b, 1990c, 1990d). This is an aeolian erosional landscape, on which features and topography are largely controlled by bedrock structure and lithology.

Southern Sandstone Ridge and Cuesta/Plain, and Deflation Basins

Brookes (1989b, figs 1, 2) terms the zone south of oasis cultivation the 'Nubia Sandstone Cuesta/Plain', or 'southern Cuesta and Plain' (cf. Brookes 1993). Southwest of Balat the sand-mantled Mut Fm. claystones slope gradually upward and southward to meet the underlying Taref sandstones along a relatively smoothly-planed dip slope between scattered, linear, north-south-oriented sandstone yardangs, but the contact is more abrupt to the east and west. To the east, south of the salt-encrusted zone, the oasis Lowland margin is marked by a low escarpment and ridge of resistant quartzitic sandstone and quartzite, through which aeolian erosion has incised corridors between broader benches that open into basin and ridge terrain to the south. To the west, south of the cultivated areas between Ismant and Mut, the claystones stand as small buttes or conical hills fronting a low sandstone escarpment. In the Sheikh Muftah Embayment, and for a distance westward, the sandstone outcrops are fronted by a series of spring mounds or exposures of FSS and/or CSS (Figs 1.39, 1.40, Top).

In the central area, south of the cultivation between the Sheikh Muftah and Mut, the sandstone terrain can be subdivided into northern and southern zones. The northern surface "... rises gently [southward] for up to a kilometer to the crest of a 10–15 m scarp ... fronted by a 1–4 km wide zone of small residual hills, often linear in plan and usually aligned parallel to the dominant north-south wind direction. ... The Taref sandstone dip slope is marked on airphotos by an unusual pattern of intersecting, nested sets of concentric, imperceptibly low swells and intervening swales. These structures are planed sets of large-scale fluvial point bars" (Brookes 1986, 44, fig. 31). The low escarpment of the 'Taref rim', which lies as much as 12 km south of the oasis rim, marks the contact between the Taref and the Maghrabi sandstones; it has been affected by intense aeolian erosion that cut corridors and yardangs in it.

On the present terrain, aside from a few heavily aeolized ESA/Balat Unit bifaces, the oldest archeological occurrences appear to belong with the Dakhleh Unit or with earlier Holocene Masara Units (McDonald 1986, 1991a, 1991b), suggesting that this is essentially a later Pleistocene landscape. Evidence for mid-Holocene or Historic period remains is scanty, suggesting that this was used only as a 'transit zone', although Churcher and Kleindienst dis-

Fig. 1.47. Art Mobilier from Old Kingdom lookout, Site 30/ 420–F3–1. Left stone shows Libyan facing right above hind parts of a tsem *hound; right stone shows gazelle (right) pursued by a* tsem *hound (forequarters only); Old Kingdom potsherd on central stone; base slab shows patterns and cryptic sequences, e.g., 3 × 3 lozenge grid and OII≡IIO. C.S.C., Feb., 1996.*

Fig. 1.48. View of terrain ca. 7 km south of Sheikh Muftah Valley, 4 km south of oasis rim, looking southeastward from an isolated ironstone-capped gebel. Aeolian erosion picks out features of point bars in Cretaceous Taref Formation sandstones. Resistant beds form higher ridges, and less resistent beds are eroded to form depressions containing early Holocene sediments and Masara Unit occupations. The residual surface lags include MSA and ESA artifacts. M.R.K., Jan., 1995.

covered and Old Kingdom 'outpost' with structures, artifacts and petroglyphs atop an isolated hill on February 5, 1996 (30/420 F3–1) (Fig. 1.47). McDonald noted another on the highest gebel southwest of Balat (30/420–H3–1), south of the oasis' southern rim. Several have been located on high sandstone prominences on the margins of Camel Thorn and El Akoulah Basins in the southeast (30/450–C4–1, 30/450–D4–2, 30/450–D4–6, 30/450–F9–1).

The desert pavement is mainly comprised of ferricrete

and quartzite fragments, but in places includes heavily weathered white chalcedony chunks and nodules not found elsewhere in Dakhleh Oasis, but seen in southern Kharga Oasis in surface lag from north of Baris southward to Dush and Maks Qibli, and also reported by Haynes (1983, 284) from southwest of Qasr el-Gyb in northern Kharga weathering from 'salty maroon mudstones'. Said (1990b, 496) notes that similar lag chalcedonies found in southern Egypt may be residuals from eroded bedrock, or ancient playa deposits, and that they "... could well be older than the Quaternary." At Dakhleh and Kharga they could also relate to ancient, completely destroyed artesian spring conduits. A localized occurrence of heavily-battered 'chert ball' nodules probably indicates the former presence of ancient gravels in which they were transported ca. 5 km south of the present oasis rim (Kleindienst, this volume, Chapter 5). The nodules were flaked by Upper Acheulian/ Balat artisans, and continued to be used until Holocene times (Pleistocene Loc. 340 and Holocene Loc 207, 30/ 420–C4–1), so that they must predate later Middle Pleistocene times in this location.

The southern rim of the Taref sandstones is at ca. 150 m a.s.l. Small patches of calcrete and/or silcrete duricrusts overlie sandstone above the rim, implying an old soil cover now nearly eroded away. The southern zone, south of the low rim, is a more level but broken plain cut across the north-dipping sandstones, rising gently southward to >200 m a.s.l., and stretching south 35–40 km to a low south-facing escarpment that marks the margin of the desert and overlooks a broad sandsheet (Darb el-Arba'in Desert [Haynes 1982]) (Fig. 1.48). Here, wide sand-covered basins are rimmed by low residual swells, sometimes crowned by craggy or flat-topped gebels. Ferricrete capped and encrusted sandstone residuals suggest a prior planation surface of considerable antiquity. This area has not yet been surveyed.

Rock-walled Basins

Sandstone-rimmed basins deflated into the northern sandstone terrain contain two types of sedimentary record (Brookes 1989b). The first type floors basins lying south and southwest of the Sheikh Muftah Embayment. These are contained within steep 5–10 m high sandstone walls, which are often breached to link neighbouring basins at different levels. Selective pitting (Brookes 1989b, 'Area A', figs. 3a, 3b) showed that the sediments are uniformly reddish brown (5YR 5/4) silty sands, less than 1 m thick. Stratification is faintly apparent in sandier sediments, but those with more fine sand and silt appear massive. The top 10 cm is polygonally cracked, with polygon diameters of 20–30 cm, and cracks filled with aeolian quartz sand (Fig. 1.49). This upper horizon is penetrated by gypsum filaments and dispersed calcite, probably originally aeolian and concentrated pedogenically. Profile characteristics, particularly the cracking pattern and dispersed carbonate, are similar to 'stage III' soil profiles on earlier Holocene sand sheets in southern Egypt (Haynes 1985). Brookes

Fig. 1.49. TOP, View southward across I.A. Brookes' rock tank basin 'A-5', showing sandstone yardang and conical gebels capped by resistent quartzite or ironstone beds, and sand veneer on basin floor. Pit dug by Brookes is in centre of photograph. M.R.K., March, 1991. BOTTOM, Wall of I.A. Brookes' pit in rock tank basin 'A-5', showing sectioned deposits of recent sand overlying reddened laminated silty sediments over unconsolidated aeolian sand. Geological hammer for scale. M.R.K., March, 1991.

now considers (1993, 546) that these "... massive compact, reddish-brown muddy sands that overlie sandstone bedrock at ≤1 m depth ..." are representative of PLS 'Facies C' rather than belonging to the earlier Holocene playa sediments in the basins.

Representative of the earlier Holocene deposits, in one of these basins (Brookes 1989b, 'A4', 1993) a low central floor is veneered with the usual sand layer, with an admixture of calcareous rhizolith fragments winnowed from eroded younger water-laid sediments. They give the area formerly covered by the sediments a distinctively paler colour than the surrounding yellow-brown surface. The veneer is only 2 cm thick and is underlain by about 30 cm of wavy-bedded reddish-brown (5YR 5/4) mud, in 1–2 cm thick beds, containing granule-size fragments of rhizolith and sun-dried mud curls (cf. Fig. 1.49, Bottom). These are interbedded with 5 mm wavy beds of iron-stained aeolian quartz sand (Brookes 1989b, fig. 3c). The depositional environment is inferred to have alternated between wet and dry intervals: 1) erosion of desiccated muds and rhizoliths, and their inclusion in the reddish-brown muds occurred

during maximum shallow basin inundation, and 2) deflation and accumulation of thin sand sheets was by aeolian action. Beneath the banded muds and sands lie loose sands and gravels from prior slopewash deposition or disintegrated bedrock. This section "... suggests the brief existence of a playa" (Brookes 1989b, 142). Masara Unit Phase B chert artifacts, with ostrich eggshell fragments, are concentrated on a low terrace 2 m above this water-laid sediment, below a low marginal sandstone cliff at Loc. 200, 30/420 C5-1. Eggshell from a cluster associated with artifacts yielded a radiocarbon date of 8,110 ± 110 yr BP (Beta-23687).

In another basin (Brookes 1989b, 'A1') (Loc. 075, 30/420 C1-1,), floored by faintly stratified silty sands, at ca. 10 cm below surface, McDonald recovered a large sample of broken eggshell associated with worked chert flakes and debitage. The eggshell fragments have fresh edges and surfaces and are considered coeval with the deposit. Three fragments with internal percussion flake scars were conjoined showing a deliberate perforation, suggesting that the fragments belonged to an *in situ* eggshell water container. A ^{14}C age of 8,650 ± 150 yr BP (Beta-23694) on the shell dates the occupation and the enclosing sediment (McDonald 1982, 1986).

Dates on two other eggshell surface scatters from similar nearby basins are 8,830 ± 110 yr BP (Beta-23693) for 'A5' (Loc. 194, 30/420 D1-1) and 8,630 ± 130 yr BP (Beta-23696) for 'A2' (Loc. 197, 30/420 E3-1) (Brookes 1989b, tab. 2). (The date of 8,720 ± 100 yr BP [Beta-23684] from Brookes' 'A3' is from Masara Loc. 085 [31/420 H10-1], a shallow depression between scattered sandstone gebels on the sandstone dip slope east-southeast of the sandstone ridge flanking the Sheikh Muftah Embayment [Brookes 1989b, tab. 2].) The three dates (uncalibrated, not adjusted for fractionation) from rock-walled basins indicate that sediments were accumulating well before 8,700 radiocarbon years ago, because 45 to >60 cm of sediment underlay the eggshell clusters. The sediments in those basins that indicate intermittent standing water record different responses of individual basins to the same climatic regime (increased rainfall is implied), which may reflect the ratio of each basin to its catchment area. A small catchment area would have yielded insufficient runoff to generate standing water in a large basin, whereas the converse would produce standing water (Brookes 1989b). Archaeological occurrences associated with these basin sediments found by McDonald's surveys are predominantly of earlier Holocene age, belonging to Masara Unit Phase B (McDonald 1991a, 1991b); but during brief visits, MSA concentrations (Locs 291, 292, 293) have been found by Kleindienst and Wiseman on the sandstone rims of the largest basin ('Big Pan') to the west of Brookes' 'Area A', and along the Taref sandstone rim. These indicate earlier, Upper Pleistocene occupation(s), probably during earlier humid periods affecting the deflation basins. Scattered, extremely aeolized ESA/earlier MSA bifaces are also found. Further survey for Pleistocene material and sediments is required.

Fig. 1.50. TOP, 'Halfa' Grass Plain south of Sheikh Mabrouk and within southern Taref Formation sandstone ridge. Note living grass clumps in foreground and left and dead grass sheared by sand blasts to right, and coppice dune in central far distance. View is to northeast with sandstone ridge to left and remnant yardangs to right. C.S.C., Feb., 1996.
*BOTTOM, Vegetation and phreatophyte dunes on floor of westernmost low rock basin ('Camel Thorn Basin'), southeast of Teneida, cut into Taref Formation sandstone of the oasis' southern rim. View to the east. Vegetation is mainly tamarisk (*Tamarix nilotica*) on dunes with dead twigs forming surface blankets. Small isolated plants between dunes are the spiny Alhagi maurorum. Sandstone gebels in background bear remants of possible Pleistocene Laminated Silts on their flanks to ca. 2–3 m above the present basin floor. Marginal areas of the basin bear Sheikh Muftah Unit occupations. C.S.C., Feb., 1994.*

Halfa Grass Basins

The second type of sedimentary record noted by Brookes occurs in the Halfa Grass Basins, deflation basins found from south of Sheikh Mabrouk westward, which occupy shallow depressions below the 135 m contour, between gentle dip slopes to the south and a low escarpment on the north (Brookes 1989b, fig. 1, western portion of 'Area D', 1993). Drainage into these depressions is from the sandstone highs to the north, and the sandstone terrain to the south. They are floored with lacustrine/marsh and/or playa sediments, with included mid-Holocene artifacts belonging to the Sheikh Muftah Unit. The present vegetation in these areas is either a pure stand of the false 'halfa'

grass (*Desmostachya bipinnata*) (Fig. 1.50, Top) or phreatic dunes built around tamarisk (*Tamarix nilotica*) bushes with smaller xerophytes in between (Fig. 1.50, Bottom), both growing through a layer of aeolian sand. Brookes described the sediments as similar to those beneath salt-crusted areas in the central Lowland, identified above as possible wetland sediments (see 'Salt-Crusted Areas', above), and these can be included within the same archaeological zone (see below). They comprise a lower member of stratified, silty sands, rich in local sandstone and shale, with subsidiary aeolian quartz. These sediments are darkly coloured due to a high iron content, commonly penetrated by sub-horizontal root casts up to 30 mm diameter, and contain dense ramifying root networks related to reeds or sedges which are replaced by black iron oxide. The root casts are the only direct subaquatic indicators within these sediments. A lower member in these basins is overlain by an upper member comprising up to 1 m of pale brown (7.5YR 6/4) quartzose, loosely consolidated sandy silt with minor gypsum and calcite. The silt is mainly massive with faint horizontal partings and profuse crystalline calcareous rhizoliths about 10 mm in diameter. In its upper part this member contains thin wavy laminae of gypsum, indicative of periodic desiccation. Brookes (1989b) considers this to be playa sediment. Sheikh Muftah artifacts including ceramics are occasionally found *in situ* in the gypsiferous member, but more commonly are seen littering the surface of the lower member, where the upper has been deflated (e.g., Locs 135, 143, 222). Loc. 222 yielded complete pots in situ in the upper unit, but the base of one penetrated into the lower unit: it could have been set into the lower sediments, however, suggesting that the lower unit formed the surface at that time (Fig. 1.34, Bottom).

Above the gypsiferous silt, these basinal sediments are usually capped by a 10–20 cm crust of halite-rich, pale-brown silt and sand. Salt precipitation may indicate the final desiccation of the playas, or it may be later. Dark grey, shale-rich sand has accumulated as *Tamarix*-anchored coppice dunes or 'phreatophyte mounds' (Mabbutt 1977) on the playa sediments and is salt-crusted (Fig. 1.50, Bottom). Similar dunes dot the halite crust of other playas, built around other *Tamarix* which survive to the present day, so that salt crust formation is a continuing process. However, it is difficult to understand how the unconsolidated sediment below the crust could have survived deflation if salt precipitation had not begun earlier in the Holocene.

Although the areas with depressions lying north and south, or east and west, of the dissected sandstone ridge which marks the physiographic edge of the oasis (ca 135–140 m a.s.l.) are considered as separate geomorphic areas, with different drainage catchments, they can be considered as a single archaelogical area. Elevations in depressions are between 131 and 135 m a.s.l.; they contain analogous sediments; and both areas are sprinkled with similar Sheikh Muftah Unit cultural scatters. It is possible that any marsh

Fig. 1.51. TOP, 'Halfa' grass plain southwest of Balat area of cultivation. False 'Halfa' grass(Desmostachya bipinnata) is seen growing through a sandsheet into Pleistocene Laminated Silts below. Visible are young growing and mature flowering plants, and dead plants whose leaves have been sheared by sand blasting (left foreground). Taref Formation sandstone gebels form the oasis rim on the horizon. C.S.C., Feb., 1994. BOTTOM, 'Halfa' grass root systems in Pleistocene Laminated Silts in the West Lobe, Southweast Basin. Horizontal rhizomes with aerial shoots at joints run linearly across the surface. M.R.K., Jan., 1987.

or lake conditions would have been coterminous in both areas, or that the areas in some cases may have been linked through corridors eroded across the sandstone oasis boundary ridge Fig. 1.51). The boundary for the mid-Holocene palaeoasis and for Sheikh Muftah habitation was further south and east than it is today, extending to the closure of the 140 m contour with the Escarpment.

One radiocarbon date has been obtained on ostrich eggshell from a Sheikh Muftah occurrence at Loc. 143 (30/435 B6–1) in the Halfa Grass basins. McDonald again considers the date of 7,100 ± 290 yr BP (Beta-17018) to be too old for the archaeological unit based upon comparisons with other dates on Sheikh Muftah occurrences. (It might date the eggshell, however; among other possibilities, Holocene peoples may have used old eggshell.) This date, and that on Sheikh Muftah occurrence (Loc. 108) north of the sandstone ridge bordering the 'salt-crusted land' in the oasis Lowland (above), are suspect when compared with that of 4,720 ± 80 yr BP

(Beta-23690) obtained at Loc. 135 (30/450 B4–1) on the margin of the westernmost basin southeast of Tenida (below), or that of ca. 4,300 BP on charcoal from the rockshelter (Loc. 244) in the desert south of the Southeast Basin (above). The alternative, which seems less likely, is that the Sheikh Muftah Unit has an extended time span, overlapping that of the Bashendi Unit.

Basins Southeast of Teneida
Deflation basins cut into sandstones southeast of Teneida are floored by PLS (Brookes' [1993, 545–546] 'Facies C' and 'D'), with younger Holocene sediments usually found closer to or on the basin margins. The westernmost ('Camel Thorn Basin') lies within the 140 m contour, marginal to the oasis and separated from it by a dissected sandstone ridge. Sheikh Muftah Unit localities occur on the northern and southeastern (Loc. 135) rims, and this basin can be considered as within the same archaeological zone as that of the Halfa Grass Basins (above, & Fig. 1.50).

Two large, interconnected basins to the east, 'El Akoulah' on the north, and 'Al Belizeiah' to the south, are closed by the 150 m contour; the basin floors lie at or just below the 145 m contour. Together, these areas have been termed the 'Southeast Basin' by McDonald (1982, 1990a, 1990b, 1990c). Al Belizeiah and a small basin higher in elevation to the east of a sandstone high, are end-pan catchments for drainage from the Wadi el-Battikh. All these basins are fed by drainage from the Plateau. The northern margins of basins closest to the Piedmont were overlapped by P-III gravels, which have subsequently been deflated into a residual thin scatter of limestone pebbles on sedimented surfaces. On the sandstone margins, low fans of granules and sand obscure otherwise abrupt basin boundaries. In areas of greater wind exposure basin sediments are carved into fields of low yardangs; lag Holocene artifacts commonly lie on the corridor surfaces between the yardangs (Fig. 1.52, Top). (Note: Brookes' [1989b, fig. 1] descriptions of 'Area D' sediments are not typical for this set of depressions, although he shows them as an eastward extension of that zone.)

Reconnaissance by Brookes in the northern part in 1986, and by Kleindienst, Hollet and O'Carroll to the southwest in 1987, established that artifact scatters of mid-Holocene age are found in many parts of the Southeast Basin, on its margins or on the PLS flooring the basin. McDonald has conducted intensive survey and excavations on this area since 1988 (McDonald 1990a, 1990b, 1990c). In Al Belizeiah Basin's 'Western Lobe', McDonald has defined two mid-Holocene cultural units, Bashendi A and B, each from different geomorphological contexts (McDonald 1990c) (Fig. 1.52, Top). On the Western Lobe's floor, Bashendi Phase A cultural scatters are associated with a layer, now up to 40 cm thick, of nearly pure silts. The archaeological evidence – hearths and associated artifacts and animal bone – are found lying over and under the silts, or in thin sandy layers within the silts (McDonald 1990a, fig. 6; 1990d). Casts of large tree roots (one 180

Fig. 1.52. TOP, View of yardangs developed in Pleistocene Laminated Sediments flooring the northern Southeast Basin (El Akoulah), looking northward to el-Battikh Promontory. Holocene artifacts occur in the corridors between the low yardangs. M.R.K., Jan., 1986. BOTTOM, View south-southeast across the Western Lobe of the Southeast Basin(Al Belizeiah) (Loc. 228, 30/450–A9–1). Bashendi Unit occupations occur on the basin's margins and on eroded Pleistocene Laminated Sediments in the central areas. M.R.K., Feb., 1988.

mm in diameter, and another 110 mm in diameter and >7 m long) and trunks (one with an oval cross-section measured 240 × 410 mm) are observed in places in the Holocene basin floor silts, together with smaller root or stem casts from grasses or shrubs (Fig. 1.51, Bottom). Lag rhizoliths are found on the surface.

Bashendi Phase B scatters, the campsites of pastoralists, are confined to the sandy-floored strip above the current level of the floor silts (PLS and Holocene) in the Lobe, and to the band of gravels lying at higher elevation than the sands along the rim (McDonald 1990c, fig. 1). In one test trench with 1 m of sediments above sandstone bedrock (Loc. 228, Cluster C, Test Trench 3) some cultural remains were found within the upper 40 cm of layered reddish sands overlying a thin coarse sand bed; the lower 60 cm of bedded greyish sands were sterile. The sands possibly were deposited as slopewash from the Nubia sandstone margin. Most of the Bashendi B material – hearth mounds and associated debris – lies on the deflated modern surface.

Eleven of 14 radiocarbon dates for Bashendi A localities in the Western Lobe fall between 7,600 and 6,940 BP (McDonald 1990b, tab. 1). Occupation of the area seems to have been more dense toward the end of this time span. Along the eastern margin of the Southeast Basin, Loc. 174 is a cluster of hearth mounds covering ca. 4000 m², while Loc. 270, on the sandstone ridge just east of the Southeast Basin, consists of some 200 probable stone slab structures. Both of these localities date ca. 6,900 BP. Dates for Bashendi B from the Western Lobe (McDonald 1990c, tab. 2) fall between 6,370 and 5,180 BP. (Elsewhere, as noted above, sites falling toward the end of the Bashendi B time range are associated with tabular sand sheets; and sites are known on the Plateau, e.g., Miramar Basin.) Other dates for Bashendi B come from artifact scatters on the deflating surface of PLS and could relate to now completely-eroded Holocene sediments which once overlay them: 5,130 ± 120 yr BP (Beta-23697) from Loc. 212 (30/450 C6–1) on the southern margin of El Akoulah pan; and 5,530 ± 120 yr BP (Beta-23688) from Loc. 210 (30/450 F8–6) further south. Dense scatters of resistant calcareous rhizolith lag on the surface at these sites suggest that they do relate to completely eroded, once-vegetated sediments on playa margins. An additional date is from Loc. 181 (30/450 F7–3)on the sandstone ridge to the east of the Southeast Basin: 5,610 ± 180 yr BP (Beta-23958). Early Holocene occurrences representing the Masara Unit, both scatters of Masara Phase A artifacts (Locs 242, 243, 261, 263), and some with stone slab structures termed 'Masara Phase C' (Locs 260, 264, 265, 267, 268), are located to the south and southeast of the southeastern embayment of Al Belizeiah Basin, in the sandstone terrain within ca. 1.5 km of the basin margin (McDonald 1990b, 1991b). McDonald, Mumford and Tangri have noted that these occupy small depressions or corridors within the sandstone ridges. Each of the small hollows containing an archaeological site seems to support one or two living shrubs, which were green in the 1990 season; foliage probably related to a rainstorm in the preceding two years indicating that these small hollows still act to concentrate drainage. Only one Masara C locality which lacks structural evidence has been found elsewhere, to the north of the Western Lobe (Loc. 274, 30/435 P8–2).

Masara C localites have yielded a similar range of radiocarbon dates when eggshell dates are adjusted for isotopic fractionation (McDonald 1990b, tab. 2): Loc. 262 (29/450 H3–1) at 8,280 ± 80 yr BP (Gd-5718) on ostrich eggshell (adjusted, 8,650 ± 80 yr BP); Loc. 264 (29/450 G3–1) at 8,340 ± 70 yr BP (Gd-5720) on eggshell (adjusted, 8,730 ± 70 yr BP), and 8,660 ± 90 yr BP (Gd-6318) and 8,950 ± 120 yr BP (Gd-6320), both on charcoal. These fall within the same time range as Masara Unit dates associated with sediments in the rock-walled basins in the sandstone terrain south of Ezbet Sheikh Muftah, or from Miramar Basin on the Plateau.

V. SUMMARY

Geological and geomorphological observations provide a provisional regional chronology for Quaternary events which have shaped the Dakhleh region. This is based on relative stratigraphic position, except for Holocene basin and later sediments where chronometric or ceramic dating is available. Relative chronology based only upon included archaeological remains is unsatisfactory, at least for the archaeologists.

Pleistocene

The earliest sediments so far recognised from the Dakhleh region are the P-I gravels overlying the remnants of a once more extensive erosion surface or pediment, and the correlated C-I colluvia. There are no cultural associations. In the central area of the oasis, P-II gravels, which overlie a younger erosion surface at lower elevations (and C-II colluvia), on the tenuous grounds of correlation by *rare* archaeological finds, may correlate with the Ferruginous Sandy Sediments (FSS) exposed as terraces bordering the embayment in the sandstone terrain south of Ezbet Sheikh Muftah, those to the east of the central Taref sandstone ridge, and in western Dakhleh. Probably deposited as sheets of ferruginous sand and gravel by ground water issuing from springs in the Nubia Group (Taref Fm.) sandstone, FSS were deposited under climatic conditions allowing aeolian transport of sand grains into the sediments, but also allowing at least a localized vegetation cover and human occupation. Calcareous Silty Sediments (CSS) in places overlie eroded FSS, but whether this erosion relates to the downcutting from the P-II surface is unclear. Local erosion on the southern margins of the Lowland may not be correlated with any major cutting closer to the northern Escarpment. If included CSS carbonates originate from the north, it is not clear whether they arrived by wind transport, or whether the contemporary climate was humid enough to generate powerful braided streams, fed both from rains and scarp-face springs, to deposit fine sediments far south in the Lowland. In the latter case, CSS may be the distal deposits of either P-II or P-III sedimentation, or of a downcutting episode, and caliche formation would parallel cementation of the Piedmont gravels; some may even be older. Some spring mounds including Acheulian and Balat Unit artifacts may be older than or coeval with FSS and P-II gravels; others are clearly younger. The CSS are older than a generation of spring mounds formed in valleys eroded into them, which include MSA artifacts. Middle Stone Age artifacts also remain in the lag/pavements on FSS and CSS, indicating human use of those surfaces, as well as of the P-I and P-II gravel surfaces.

Pleistocene Lacustrine Sediments (PLS) are younger than P-II gravel surfaces, and at least some are younger than some CSS, because PLS occupy basins eroded through CSS and P-II levels. There are no archeological associations, which in itself may indicate an environment unattractive for human habitation, although PLS were probably deposited from rain-fed runoff into fluctuating Piedmont lakes/playas. (Possible equivalents are found in isolated basins in the southern sandstone terrain.) P-III gravels cover some PLS, and dissected P-III gravels wrap around eroded remnants of CSS and spring mound stumps incorporating Balat Unit artifacts. The gravels are therefore younger than these PLS, and are possibly younger than CSS, but can only be broadly dated by surface archaeological remains, the oldest with cultural associations belonging to the Dakhleh Unit.

After P-III deposition, wadis have become incised only ca. 10 m in outer and inner Piedmont zones, leaving a floodplain terrace up to 1 km wide in the lower reaches of the main wadis (Wadi el-Tawil, Wadi el-Battikh). The terrace and modern wadi floors show heavy aeolian abrasion, with the severest effects in areas unprotected by major bends or higher terraces. Wadi incision and severe deflation have stripped P-III gravels from the PLS in middle and outer reaches of PLS basins along the Piedmont. Large and small fields of yardangs carved in Piedmont PLS are among the most dramatic landforms observed. The strongest effects of post-P-III erosion occur where winds have been channeled down larger scarp ravines. Rock tank basins in sandstone terrain northeast of Bashendi in eastern Dakhleh Oasis, floored with PLS and once overlapped by P-III gravels, were similarly deflated by ≥6 m in this interval, leaving patches of PLS on flanks of sandstone yardangs, as were those southeast of Teneida. This erosion phase may indicate hyperaridity correlated with the Late Pleistocene glacial maximum (Oxygen Isotope Stage 3), postulated by Close and Wendorf (1990, 1992), because aeolized Dakhleh Unit artifacts lie on deflated P-III surfaces. However, there is some indication in the U-series dates obtained from CSS calcrete that water was available during Stage 3.

Certain chronological relationships are not yet established between or within all the Pleistocene sedimentary units. The processes of landscape evolution are likely to have been complex in their relationships to erosional and depositional episodes in the different geomorphic regions. The applicability of various chronometric dating techniques to Dakhleh sediments is only now being tested. Uranium/thorium dating holds promise, at least for defining the time periods when springs issued from the northern Escarpment, and comparisons can be made with Kharga tufas; possibly thermoluminescence can be used for dating spring eye sediments, or soils overlying terraced gravels.

Holocene

Radiocarbon dating is available for the earlier Holocene sedimentary units, and later units can often be dated by included Historic period artifacts. The oldest Holocene sediments are variably textured and structured, reddish-brown, basin sediments within the sandstone terrain south of central Dakhleh, and in Miramar basin on the Plateau.

Artifactual ostrich eggshell and charcoal from the upper part of these sediments is dated ca. 8,050 to >8,800 BP (eggshell adjusted only for fractionation, >9,000 ya), so that the more humid climate which allowed fluvial and lake/marsh/playa deposition probably began somewhat earlier. Torrential wadi gravels over the sediments in Miramar Basin, and coarse aprons of sediment around southern sandstone basins may mark more rigorous conditions for human occupation towards the end of that phase. The youngest date yet for Masara Unit occupation in the southern sandstone terrain is >8,100 BP, suggesting that the humid phase may have been ending by then, but dates on sediments in Maramar Basin, and on surface eggshell both in the Dakhleh Lowland and in the Halfa Grass basins suggest that deposition continued after ca. 7,000 BP. Localities adjacent to the Southeast Basin also fall within the >8,000 BP time range, although no playa sediment has been dated to that period.

Geographically separated from these early Holocene basin sediments, and therefore never seen superimposed on them, are pan/lacustrine sediments confined in shallow sandstone basins in the Halfa Grass basins and southeast of Dakhleh, as well as similar sediments overlying the claystone surface north of the sandstone ridge and southwest of Balat. Radiocarbon dates allow tentative placement of these sediments, and some of the associated Holocene occupations, ranging between ca. 7,800 and 5,100 BP. It is likely that more than one humid-arid-humid cycle is involved, and archaeological evidence of playa use suggests at least three such cycles on the basis of human occupations: 1) Bashendi A as in the Western Lobe of the Southeast Basin, followed by a break; 2) then Bashendi B on the Southeast Basin margins; and 3) Sheikh Muftah Unit occupations on the edges of salt-crusted sedimented areas which may indicate a third cycle continuing into Old Kingdom times.

Tabular bodies of aeolian, muddy sands in western Dakhleh, phytogenetically accumulated, are dated to about 5,800 BP, while in eastern Dakhleh similar sediments marginal to playas/marshes contain Bashendi B occupation debris dated at >5,000 BP. It thus appears that moisture sufficient to generate at least seasonal standing water in one place generated only shrub-anchored tabular sand sheets in another, although western Dakhleh is as yet poorly surveyed. There are some indications in included Sheikh Muftah Unit artifacts that tabular dune sand accumulation continued after 5,000 BP in eastern Dakhleh.

Clearly, much more detailed work remains to be done on mapping and dating the Holocene sedimentary units. However, it does appear that distributions of Holocene archaeological units associated with basins or water-deposited sediments show a change through time. Sites of the early Holocene Masara Unit extend further south than do those of the Bashendi Unit, although both are found flanking the southern Southeast Basin. Sites indicating Bashendi occupation are far more numerous. The distributions of Bashendi and Sheikh Muftah Units' artifacts

overlap in the central Lowland south and southwest of Balat, but some Sheikh Muftah localities are found as far east as the Camel Thorn Basin area. Sheikh Muftah and later occupations in Dakhleh seem mainly to be confined to the central Lowland.

Two hypotheses can be advanced on the basis of the available evidence: 1) that there is a temporal pattern of human occupation observed, from the earlier through mid-Holocene times, of a decreasing perimeter of occupation, with the boundary of oasis habitation moving inward toward the central Lowlands; and 2) that the pattern of oasis occupation sufficiently intensive to leave a marked archaeological signature took place mainly at the beginning of or during *drier climatic episodes* when more scattered desert dwellers moved into the better-watered oasis areas. These will be tested by further work in eastern Dakhleh, and detailed surveys in western Dakhleh.

Aside from anthropogenic sediments at archaeological sites, no sedimentary units have yet been recorded in Dakhleh which can be assigned to the interval between ca. 4,500 BP and the Roman period (1st Century BC). Extensive bodies of muddy sand accumulated over the central Lowland during and since Roman occupation of the oasis could mask sediments of this missing interval. This is considered unlikely, however. Thus, it appears that the later Holocene was dominated by non-depostion or deflation, at least until Roman hydraulic engineering opened larger areas for cultivation and concomitant sediment build-up through agricultural practices. Evidence of erosion can be seen near the Roman town of Amheida (33/390–L9–1), where Old Kingdom brick architecture (33/390–K9–1) and graves (33/390–L9–2) have been planed down to bedrock and then buried, at least partly if not completely, by Roman agricultural sediments (Mills 1980). Evaporation of Roman irrigation water may have caused induration of the planed-off Old Kingdom brick-work. If such hardening occurred before deflation, higher remnants should have survived unless deflation was not solely responsible for levelling the Old Kingdom structures.

Irrigation deposits built up during and since Roman times are firmly dated by archaeological associations at several localities to Roman, Romano-Byzantine, early Islamic and later periods. Variations in their sedimentary structures, facies and stratigraphy result from spatial and temporal variations in cultivation, and it is not expected that these sediments will be divisible into well defined stratigraphic units. Comparable irrigation deposits continue to be created, abandoned, and deflated to-day.

More recently, mobile trains of dunes have invaded Islamic and modern settlements, but the sand mobilised may derive from an upwind source and may take 5,000 to 8,000 years to reach Dakhleh. Evidence for earlier episodes of sand accumulation affecting human habitation occurs at archeological sites, as at Ismant el-Kharab (Roman Periods Kellis).

VI. ACKNOWLEDGEMENTS

We are extremely thankful for all the help that other members of the Dakhleh Oasis Project have given us during the many field seasons when we have been in the Dakhleh Oasis. Foremost in our thanks is A.J. Mills who, as Field Director, made our sojourns in the oasis' villages most memorable and enabled us to reach far distant sites on the Libyan Escarpment, in the nearby desert, or even in Kharga Oasis. Others who have assisted in the field or have aided us by driving vehicles to almost inacessible places are Hussein Ali Abdel Halim, Alan Hollett, Jim Knudstad, John O'Carroll, Peter Sheldrick and Zemzemi Shahab Zemzemi. We acknowledge the extensive field work carried out by Ian Brookes during the period he was with the Project, despite our scientific disagreements.

We also thank Tony Mills for his efficient operation of the field house, for overseeing the complex feeding, staffing, and maintainance of facilities and vehicles. Special thanks are due to Rosa Frey who did much to train the domestic staff in catering, to Alan Hollett who performed some excellent photography when in the field and noted interesting outcrops or features, to Peter Sheldrick who acted as Mary McDonald's field partner during many seasons, to Marcia Wiseman who assisted Maxine Kleindienst as a field investigator, to Bee Churcher who acted as photographer and field assistant to Rufus Churcher, and to Airlie Armstrong Browne and Marijka H. Mychajlowycz who were Churcher's field assistants and assisted in editing the chapters. We also thank the other scientists in other disciplines of the Project, our graduate students, visitors, and many others who took an interest in the geomorphological features of Dakhleh Oasis and reported observations of interest to us. Without the asssitance of all these persons, this synthesis could not have been compiled. The authors gratefully acknowledge research support from: the Social Sciences and Humanities Research Council of Canada; the Natural Sciences and Engineering Research Council of Canada; the National Geographic Society, Washington D.C.; the Royal Ontario Museum, Toronto; the University of Toronto and the Department of Anthropology; the University of Calgary and the Department of Archaeology; and all private donors.

Addressess for Authors
C.S. Churcher, Department of Zoology, University of Toronto, Ontario M5S 3G5, and R.R.1, Site 42, Box 12, Gabriola Island, British Columbia V0R 1X0 CANADA for correspondence.
M.R. Kleindienst, Department of Anthropology, University of Toronto at Mississauga, Mississauga, Ontario L5L 1C6, and 1762 Angela Crescent, Mississauga, Ontario L5J 1B9, CANADA for correspondence
M.M.A. McDonald, Department of Archaeology, University of Calgary, Calgary, Alberta T2N 1N4, CANADA
H.P. Schwarcz, School of Geography and Geology, McMaster University, Hamilton, Ontario L8S 4M1, CANADA

REFERENCES

Abbas, H.L. and M. Habib. 1971. Stratigraphy of west Mawhoob area, south Western Desert: Egypt. *Desert Institute Bulletin* **19**: 48–108.

Aitkin, M.J. 1985. *Thermoluminescence Dating*. London: Academic Press, 359p.

Aitkin, M.J. 1990. *Science-based Dating in Archaeology*. London: Longman, 274.

Bagnold, R.A. 1931. Journeys in the Libyan Desert, 1929 and 1930: A paper read at the evening meeting of the society on 20 April 1931. *Geographical Journal* **78**: 13–39.

Bagnold, R.A. 1933. A further journey through the Libyan Desert. *Geographical Journal* **82**: 103–129, 211–235.

Bagnold, R.A. 1935. The movement of desert sand. *Geographic Journal* **85**: 342–369.

Bagnold, R.A. 1939. An expedition to the Gilf Kebir and Uweinat, 1939. *Geographical Journal* **93**: 281–313.

Bagnold, R.A. 1965 (1941). *The Physics of Blown Sand and Desert Dunes*. London: Methuen, 265p.

Ball, J. 1900. *Kharga Oasis: Its Topography and Geology*. Cairo: Public Works Ministry, 116p.

Ball, J. 1927. Problems of the Libyan Desert. *Geographical Journal* **70**: 21–28, 105–108, 209–224.

Bates, O. 1970 (1914). *The Eastern Libyans: An Essay*. London: Frank Cass, 298p.

Beadnell, H.J.L. 1901a. *Dakhla Oasis: Its Topography and Geology*. Cairo: Survey Department, Public Works Ministry, 107p.

Beadnell, H.J.L. 1901b. *Farafra Oasis: Its Topography and Geology*. Cairo: Survey Department, Public Works Ministry, 39p.

Beadnell, H.J.L. 1909. *An Egyptian Oasis: An Account of the Oasis of Kharga in the Libyan Desert with Special Reference to its History, Physical Geography and Water Supply*. London: John Murray, 248p.

Beadnell, H.J.L. 1910. The sand dunes of the Libyan Desert. *Geographical Journal* **25**: 379–395.

Beadnell, H.J.L. 1933. Remarks on the prehistoric geography and underground waters of Kharga Oasis. *Geographical Journal* **81**: 128–134.

Breed, C.S., J. F. McCauley and M. I. Whitney. 1989. Wind erosion forms, 284–307. *In* Thomas, D.S.G., ed., *Arid Zone Geomorphology*. New York/Toronto: Halsted Press, 372p.

Brookes, I.A. 1983. Dakhleh Oasis – a geoarchaeological reconnaissance. *Journal of the Society for the Study of Egyptian Antiquities* **13**: 167–177.

Brookes, I.A. 1986. *Quaternary Geology and Geomorphology of Dakhleh Oasis Region and Environs, South-central Egypt: Reconnaissance Findings*. York University, Toronto: Department of Geography, Discussion Paper no. 32, 90p.

Brookes, I.A. 1989a. Above the salt: sediment accretion and irrigation agriculture in an Egyptian oasis. *Journal of Arid Environments* **17**: 335–348.

Brookes, I.A. 1989b. Early Holocene basinal sediments of the Dakhleh Oasis region, south-central Egypt. *Quaternary Research* **32**: 139–152.

Brookes, I.A. 1993. Geomorphology and Quaternary geology of the Dakhla Oasis region, Egypt. *Quaternary Science Reviews* **12**: 529–552.

Busche, D. 1988. Post-Neolithic changes of aeolian morphodynamics in the Kharga and Toshka depressions, southern Egypt. *Bulletin de la Société Géologique de France, 8e série*, **4**: 1053–1061.

Butzer, K.W. and C.L. Hansen. 1968. *Desert and River in Nubia: Geomorphology and Prehistoric Environments at the Aswan Reservoir*. Madison, Wisconsin: University of Wisconsin Press, 562p.

Cailliaud, F. 1826. *Voyage a Méroé, au fleuve Blanc, au-delà de Fazoql dans le midi du Royaume de Sennâr, a Seyouah et dans cinq autres oasis, fait dans les années 1819, 1820, 1821, et 1822.* Paris: L'Imprimerie Royale [1972, facsimile edition, Farnborough, Hampshire: Gregg International Publishers, vol. I], 429p.

Campbell, C. 1990. Fieldnotes. Unpublished, on file, Egyptian Department, Royal Ontario Museum.

Casey, J.L. 1993. *The Kintampo Complex in Northern Ghana: Late Holocene Human Ecology on the Gambaga Escarpment.* Ph.D. thesis, Department of Anthropology, University of Toronto, 291p.

Caton-Thompson, G. 1931a. Kharga Oasis. *Antiquity* **5**: 221–226.

Caton-Thompson, G. 1931b. Royal Anthropological Institute's Prehistoric Research Expedition to Kharga Oasis, Egypt. Preliminary outline of the season's work. *Man* **31**: 77–84.

Caton-Thompson, G. 1932. Recent discoveries in Kharga Oasis. *British Association for the Advancement of Science 102nd Meeting, London,* 74.

Caton-Thompson, G. 1952. *Kharga Oasis in Prehistory.* London: Athlone Press, 213p.

Caton-Thompson, G. 1983. *Mixed Memoires.* Gateshead, Tyne and Wear: Paradigm Press, 346p.

Caton-Thompson, G. and E.W. Gardner. 1932. The prehistoric geography of Kharga Oasis. *Geographical Journal* **80**: 369–406.

Churcher, C.S. 1980. Dakhleh Oasis Project: Preliminary observations on the geology and vertebrate palaeontology of northwestern Dakhleh Oasis: A report on the 1979 fieldwork. *Journal of the Society for the Study of Egyptian Antiquities* **10**: 379–395.

Churcher, C.S. 1981. Dakhleh Oasis Project: Geology and palaeontology: Interim report on the 1980 field season. *Journal of the Society for the Study of Egyptian Antiquities* **11**: 193–212.

Churcher, C.S. 1982. Dakhleh Oasis Project: Geology and palaeontology: Interim report on the 1981 field season. *Journal of the Society for the Study of Egyptian Antiquities* **12**: 103–114.

Churcher, C.S. 1983. Dakhleh Oasis Project: Palaeontology: Interim report on the 1982 field season. *Journal of the Society for the Study of Egyptian Antiquities* **13**: 178–187.

Churcher, C.S. 1988. Marine vertebrates from the Duwi Phosphorites, Dakhleh Oasis, Western Desert of Egypt. *Abstracts of Papers, Forty-Eighth Annual Meeting, Society of Vertebrate Paleontology, Drumheller, Alberta, Journal of Vertebrate Paleontology,* **8** (Supplement to no. 3): 11A.

Churcher, C.S. This volume. Chapter 2. The Late Cretaceous formations and faunas of Dakhleh Oasis, 55–67.

Clark, D.M., C.W. Mitchell and J.A. Varley. 1974. Geomorphic evolution of sediment filled solution hollows in some arid regions (Northwestern Sahara). *Zeitschrift für Geomorphologie Supplementband* **20**: 130–139.

Clayton, P.A. and L.J. Spencer. 1934. Silica-glass from the Libyan Desert. *The Mineralogical Magazine* **23**: 501–508.

Close, A.E. 1987a. Preface. *In* Close, A.E., ed., *Prehistory of Arid North Africa. Essays in Honor of Fred Wendorf.* Dallas: Southern Methodist University Press, 357p.

Close, A.E. 1987b. Overview, 317–324. *In* Close, A.E., ed., *Prehistory of Arid North Africa, Essays in Honor of Fred Wendorf.* Dallas: Southern Methodist University Press, 357p.

Close, A.E. and F. Wendorf. 1990. North Africa at 18 000 BP, 41–57. *In* Gamble, C. and O. Soffer, eds, *The World at 18 000 BP. 2. Low Latitudes.* London: Unwin Hyman, 394p.

Close, A.E. and F. Wendorf. 1992. The beginnings of food production in the eastern Sahara, 63–72. *In* Gebauer, A.B. and T.D. Price, eds, *Transitions to Agriculture in Prehistory.* Monographs in World Archaeology 4. Madison, Wisconsin: Prehistory Press, 180p.

Cooke, R., A. Warren and A. Goudie. 1993. *Desert Geomorphology.* London: UCL Press Limited, 526p.

Cooke, R.U. 1970. Stone pavements in deserts. *Annals of the Association of American Geographers* **60**: 560–577.

Coque, R. 1966. Le Quaternaire en Tunesie. *Quaternaria* **8**: 139–154.

Dewolf, Y., J. Dresch, F. Joly and R. Raynal. 1976. Cuirasses et ocres du Mouydir (Sahara central). Genése et signification. *Zeitschrift für Geomorphologie* N.F. **20**: 468–475.

Edmonstone, A. 1822. *A Journey to Two of the Oases of Upper Egypt.* London: John Murray, 153p.

Egyptian Geological Survey and Mining Authority. 1982. *Geological Map Sheet NG-35 Dakhla, 1:1,000,000.* Cairo: Geological Survey of Egypt.

El Aref, M.M., A.M. Abou Khadrah and Z.H. Lotfy. 1987. Karst topography and karstification processes in the Eocene limestone plateau of El Bahariya Oasis, Western Desert, Egypt. *Zeitschrift für Geomorphologie* **31**: 45–64.

Embabi, N.S. 1972. The semi-playa deposits of Kharga depression, the Western Desert, Egypt. *Bulletin de la Société Géographie d'Égypte* **41–42**: 73–87.

Embabi, N.S. 1982. Barchans of the Kharga depression, 141–155. *In* El-Baz, F. and T.A. Maxwell, eds, *Desert Landforms of Southwest Egypt: A basis for comparison with Mars.* Washington, D.C.: NASA Scientific and Technical Information Branch, National Aeronautics and Space Administration, Report CR-3611, 372p.

Embabi, N.S. 1990. Dune movement in the Kharga and Dakhla Oases depression, the Western Desert, Egypt, 79–105. *In* El-Baz, F., I.A. El-Tayeb and M.H.A. Hassan, eds, *Proceedings of the International Workshop on Sand Transport and Desertification in Arid Lands 17–26 November 1985, Khartoum, Sudan.* Singapore: World Scientific, 469p.

Ezzat, M.A. 1974a. *Hydrogeologic Conditions in the Dakhleh-Kharga Area.* Cairo: Ministry of Agriculture and Land Reclamation, 106p.

Ezzat, M.A. 1974b. *Regional Hydrogeologic Conditions.* Cairo: Ministry of Agriculture and Land Reclamation, 121p.

Ezzat, M.A. 1975. *Exploitation of Ground Water, Dakhleh Oasis.* Cairo: Ministry of Agriculture and Land Reclamation [maps].

Fay, M. and W. Hermann-Degen. 1984. Mineralogy of Campanian/ Maastrichtian sand deposits and a model of basin development for the Nubian Group of the Dakhla Basin (southwest Egypt). *In* Klitzsch, E., R. Said and E. Schrank eds, *Research in Egypt and Sudan, Sonderforschungsbereich 69: Results of the Special Research Project Arid Areas, Period 1981–1984. Berliner Geowissenschaftliche Abhandlungen* **50**: 99–115.

Flohn, H. and S. Nicholson. 1980. Climatic fluctuations in the arid belt of the 'Old World' since the Last Glacial maximum; possible causes and future implications. *In* Sarnthein, M., E. Seibold and P. Rognon, eds, *Sahara and Surrounding Seas. Sediments and Climatic Changes. Proceedings of an international symposium, Akademie der Wissenschaften und der Literatur, Mainz, 1–4 April 1979. Palaeoecology of Africa and the Surrounding Islands* **12**: 3–21.

Forbes, R. 1921. *The Secret of the Sahara: Kufara.* New York: George H. Doran, 356p.

Gardner, E.W. 1932. Some problems of the Pleistocene hydrography of Kharga Oasis. *Geological Magazine* **69**: 386–421.

Gardner, E.W. 1935. The Pleistocene fauna and flora of Kharga Oasis, Egypt. *Quarterly Journal of the Geological Society of London* **91**: 479–518.

Gerson, R. 1982. Talus relicts in deserts: a key to major climatic fluctuations. *Israel Journal of Earth-Sciences* **31**: 123–132.

Giegengack, R.F. and B. Issawi. 1975. Libyan Desert silical glass, a summary of the problem of its origins. *Annals of the Geological Survey of Egypt* **5**: 108–118.

Gilbert, G.K. 1877. *Report on the Geology of the Henry Mountains.* United States Geological Survey of the Rocky Mountain Region. Washington, D.C.: Department of the Interior, 170p.

Godfrey-Smith, D.I., D.J. Huntley and W.-H. Chen. 1988. Optical dating studies of quartz and feldspar sediment extracts. *Quaternary Science Reviews* **7**: 373–380.

Grolier, M.J., J.F. McCauley, C.S. Breed and N.S. Embabi. 1980. Yardangs of the Western Desert. *Geographical Journal* **146**: 86–87.

Grunert, J., and D. Busche. 1980. Large-scale fossil landslides at the Msak Mallat and Hamadat Manghini Escarpment, 849–860. *In* Salem, M.J. and M.T. Busrewil, eds, *The Geology of Libya, III*. New York: Academic Press, [781–1158].

Grunert, J., D. Busche, H. Hagedorn, A. Skowronek and E. Schulz. 1979. Contributions to the geo-ecology and landscape history of the Messak/Mangueni Escarpment (Central Sahara). *Palaeoecology of Africa and the Surrounding Islands* **11**: 45–63.

Hammad, H.Y. 1970. *Ground Water Potentialities in the African Sahara and the Nile Valley*. Beirut: Beirut Arab University, 112p.

Harvey, A.M. 1989. The occurrence and role of arid zone alluvial fans, 136–158. *In* Thomas, D.S.G., ed., *Arid Zone Geomorphology*. London: Belhaven, 372p.

Hassanein Bey, A.M. 1925. *The Lost Oasis*. New York: The Century Company, 363p.

Haynes, C.V. 1982. The Darb El-Arba'in Desert: A product of Quaternary climatic change, 91–117. *In* El-Baz, F. and T.A. Maxwell, eds, *Desert Landforms of Southwest Egypt: A Basis for Comparison with Mars*. Washington, D.C.: NASA Scientific and Technical Information Branch, National Aeronautics and Space Administration, Report CR-3611, 372p.

Haynes, C.V. 1983. Quaternary studies, Western Desert, Egypt and Sudan, 1975–1978. *National Geographic Society Research Reports* **15**: 257–293.

Haynes, C.V. 1985. Quaternary studies, Western Desert, Egypt and Sudan, 1979–1983 field seasons. *National Geographic Research Reports* **19**: 269–341.

Hendriks, F., P. Luger, H. Kallenbach and J.H. Schroeder. 1984. Stratigraphical and sedimentological framework of the Kharga – Sinn El-Kaddab stretch (western and southern part of the upper Nile Basin), Western Desert, Egypt. *In* Klitzsch, E., R. Said and E. Schrank, eds, *Research in Egypt and Sudan, Sonderforschungsbereich 69: Results of the Special Research Project Arid Areas, Period 1981–1984. Berliner Geowissenschaftliche Abhandlungen* **50**: 117–151.

Hermina, M. 1990. The surroundings of Kharga, Dakhla and Farafra oases, 259–292. *In* Said, R., ed., *The Geology of Egypt*. Rotterdam/Brookfield: A.A. Balkema, 734p.

Hermina, M.H., M.G. Ghobrial and B. Issawi. 1961. *The Geology of the Dakhla Area*. Cairo: Egyptian Geological Survey and Mineral Research Department, 33p.

Hobbs, W.H. 1917. The erosional and degradational processes of deserts, with especial reference to the origin of desert depressions. *Annales of the Association of American Geographers* **7**: 25–60.

Hodges, W.K. 1980. Patterns of Environmental Change and Land-Use Hydrology in a Hyperarid Desert: A Preliminary Survey of Ed Dakhleh Oasis, Western Desert, Egypt. Manuscript, on file, Egyptian Department, Royal Ontario Museum, 102p.

Hollett, A.F. and C.S. Churcher. This volume. Chapter 9. Notes on the Recent fauna of Dakhleh Oasis, 153–170.

Hope, C. 1988. Three seasons of excavations at Ismant el-Gharab in Dakhleh Oasis, Egypt. *Mediterranean Archaeology* **1**: 160–178.

Hope, C.A. 1985. Dakhleh Oasis Project: Report on the 1986 excavations at Ismant El-Gharab. *Journal of the Society for the Study of Egyptian Antiquities* **15**: 114–125.

Hope, C.A. 1986. Dakhleh Oasis Project: Report on the 1987 excavations at Ismant El-Gharab. *Journal of the Society for the Study of Egyptian Antiquities* **16**: 74–91.

Hope, C.A. This volume. Chapter 14. Pottery manufacture in the Dakhleh Oasis, 215–243.

Hope, C.A., O.E. Kaper, G.E. Bowen and S.F. Patten. 1989. Dakhleh Oasis Project: Ismant el-Kharab 1991–92. *Journal of the Society for the Study of Egyptian Antiquities* **19**: 1–26.

Hume, W.F. 1925. *The Surface Features of Egypt, their Determining Causes and Relation to Geological Structure*. Cairo: Government Press, 408p.

Issawi, B. 1977. 2. The Geology, 11–17. *In* Schild, R. and F. Wendorf, eds., *The Prehistory of Dakhla Oasis and Adjacent Desert*. Warsaw: Institute for the History of Material Culture, Polska Akademia Nauk, 259p.

Issawi, B. 1993. 2. Contribution to the stratigraphy of the area of Bir Tarfawi and Bir Sahara East, 11–14. *In* Wendorf, F., R. Schild, A.E. Close and Associates, *Egypt during the Last Interglacial. The Middle Paleolithic of Bir Tarfawi and Bir Sahara East*. New York/London: Plenum Press, 596p.

Jordan, W. 1875a. *Die Geographischen Resultate der von G. Rohlfs geführten Expedition in die Libysche Wüste. Oeffentlicher Vortrag, gehalten in Museum zu Carlsruhe am 16. Dezember 1874*. Berlin: C.B. Lüderitz'sche Verlagsbuchhandlung, 32p.

Jordan, W. 1875b. Dr. G. Rohlfs' Expedition in die Libysche Wüste, 1873/4. Erläuterungen zu der Originalkarte (Tafel 11). *Petermann's Geographische Mittheilungen* **21**: 201–214.

King, W.J.H. 1916. The nature and formation of sand ripples and dunes. *Geographical Journal* **47**: 187–209.

King, W.J.H. 1918. Study of a dune belt. *Geographical Journal* **51**: 16–33.

Kleindienst, M.R. This volume. Chapter 5. Pleistocene archaeology and geoarchaeology: a status report, 83–108.

Klitzsch, E., J.C. Harms, A. Lejal-Nicol and F.K. List. 1979. Major subdivisions and depositional environments of Nubia strata, southwestern Egypt. *Bulletin of the American Association of Petroleum Geologists* **63**: 967–974.

Klitzsch, E., F.K. List and G. Pöhlmann. 1987a. *Geological Map of Egypt NG 35 SE Dakhla, 1:500,000*. Cairo: The Egyptian General Petroleum Corporation.

Klitzsch, E., F.K. List and G. Pöhlmann. 1987b. *Geological Map of Egypt NG 36 SW Luxor, 1:500,000*. Cairo: The Egyptian General Petroleum Corporation.

Klitzsch, E. and E. Schrank. 1987. Research in Egypt and Sudan. *Sonderforschungs bereich 69: Results of the Special Research Project in Arid Areas, Period 1984–1987. Berliner Geowissenschaftliche Abhandlungen* **75**: 1–967.

Kobusiewicz, M. 1987. The Combined Prehistoric Expedition: the first twenty-five years, 325–344. *In* Close, A.E., ed., *Prehistory of Arid North Africa: Essays in Honor of Fred Wendorf*. Dallas: Southern Methodist University Press, 357p.

Krzyzaniak, L. 1987. Dakhleh Oasis Project: Report on the first season of recording of petroglyphs, January/February 1988. *Journal of the Society for the Study of Egyptian Antiquities* **17**: 182–191.

Krzyzaniak, L. and K. Kroeper. 1990. The Dakhleh Oasis Project: Interim report on the second (1990) and third (1992) seasons of the recording of petroglyphs. *Journal of the Society for the Study of Egyptian Antiquities* **20**: 77–88.

Latham, A.G. and H.P. Schwarcz. 1991. Carbonate and sulphate precipitates, 423–459. *In* Ivanovich, M. and R.S. Harmon, eds, *Uranium Series Disequilibrium: Application to Environment Problems in the Earth Sciences* (Chapter 12). Oxford: Oxford University Press, 910p.

Lattman, L.H. and S.K. Lauffenburger. 1974. Proposed role of gypsum in the formation of caliche. *Zeitschrift für Geomorphologie Supplementband* **N.F. 20**: 140–149.

Leach, E.K. 1992. On the definition of geoarchaeology. *Geoarchaeology: An International Journal* **7**: 405–417.

List, F.K., B. Meissner and G. Pöhlmann. 1990. Application of remote sensing and satellite cartography in preparing new geologic map 1:500,000, 27–44. *In* Said, R., ed., *The Geology of Egypt*. Rotterdam/Brookfield: A.A. Balkema, 734p.

Lyons, H.G. 1894a. Notes sur la géographie physique des oasis de Khargueh et de Dakhel. *Bullein de la Société Khédiviale de Géographie, Caire* **4**: 241–265.

Lyons, H.G. 1894b. On the stratigraphy and physiography of the Libyan Desert of Egypt. *Quarterly Journal of the Geological Society* **50**: 531–547.

Mabbutt, J.A. 1977. *Desert Landforms*. Cambridge, MA: The MIT Press, 340p.

Mansour, H.H., B. Issawi and M.M. Askalany. 1982. Contribution to the geology of west Dakhla Oasis area, Western Desert, Egupt. *Annals of the Geological Survey of Egypt* **12**: 255–281.

Mawson, R. and M.A.J. Williams. 1984. A wetter climate in eastern Sudan 2,000 years ago? *Nature* **309**: 49–51.

McDonald, M.M.A. 1982. Dakhleh Oasis Project: Third preliminary report on the lithic industries in the Dakhleh Oasis. *Journal of the Society for the Study of Egyptian Antiquities* **12**: 115–138.

McDonald, M.M.A. 1983. Dakhleh Oasis Project: Fourth preliminary report on the lithic industries in the Dakhleh Oasis. *Journal of the Society for the Study of Egyptian Antiquities* **13**: 158–166.

McDonald, M.M.A. 1986. Dakhleh Oasis Project: Holocene prehistory: Interim report on the 1987 season. *Journal of the Society for the Study of Egyptian Antiquities* **16**: 103–113.

McDonald, M.M.A. 1987. Adaptations in Dakhleh Oasis in the early- to mid-Holocene. *Society for American Archaeology, 52nd Annual Meeting, Toronto, Program and Abstracts*, 98.

McDonald, M.M.A. 1990a. The Dakhleh Oasis Project: Holocene prehistory: Interim report on the 1988 and 1989 seasons. *Journal of the Society for the Study of Egyptian Antiquities* **20**: 24–53.

McDonald, M.M.A. 1990b. The Dakhleh Oasis Project: Holocene prehistory: Interim report on the 1990 season. *Journal of the Society for the Study of Egyptian Antiquities* **20**: 54–64.

McDonald, M.M.A. 1990c. The Dakhleh Oasis Project: Holocene prehistory: Interim report on the 1991 season. *Journal of the Society for the Study of Egyptian Antiquities* **20**: 65–76.

McDonald, M.M.A. 1990d. New evidence from the early to mid-Holocene in Dakhleh Oasis, South-Central Egypt, bearing on the evolution of cattle pastoralism. *Nyame Akuma* **33**: 3–8.

McDonald, M.M.A. 1991a. Systematic reworking of lithics from earlier cultures in the early Holocene of Dakhleh Oasis, Egypt. *Journal of Field Archaeology* **18**: 269–273.

McDonald, M.M.A. 1991b. Technological organization and sedentism in the Epipalaeolithic of Dakhleh Oasis, Egypt. *The African Archaeological Review* **9**: 81–109.

McDonald, M.M.A. This volume. Chapter 7. Neolithic cultural units and adaptations in Dakhleh Oasis, Egypt, 117–132.

McFadden, L.D., S.G. Wells and M.J. Jercinovich. 1987. Influence of eolian and pedogenic processes on the origin and evolution of desert pavements. *Geology* **15**: 504–508.

Meneisy, M.Y. 1990. Vulcanicity, 154–172. *In* Said, R., ed., *The Geology of Egypt*. Rotterdam/Brookfield, A.A. Balkema, 734p.

Mills, A.J. 1980. The Dakhleh Oasis Project: Report on the second season of survey, September – December, 1979. *Journal of the Society for the Study of Egyptian Antiquities* **10**: 251–282.

Mills, A.J. This volume. Chapter 10. Pharaonic Egyptians in the Dakhleh Oasis, 171–178.

Mitchell, C.W. and S.G. Willimott. 1974. Dayas of the Moroccan Sahara and other arid regions. *Geographical Journal* **140**: 441–453.

Nahon, D. 1980. Soil accumulations and climatic variations in western Sahara. *In* Sarnthein, M., E. Seibold and P. Rognon, eds, *Sahara and Surrounding Seas. Sediments and Climatic Changes. Proceedings of an international symposium, Akademie der Wissenschaften und der Literatur, Mainz, 1–4 April 1979.*

Palaeoecology of Africa and the Surrounding Islands **12**: 63–68.

Nahon, D., A.V. Carozzi and C. Parron. 1980. Lateritic weathering as a mechanism for the generation of ferruginous ooids. *Journal of Sedimentary Petrology* **50**: 1287–1298.

Oberlander, T.M. 1989. Slope and pediment systems, 56–84. *In* Thomas, D.S.G. ed., *Arid Zone Geomorphology*. New York/Toronto: Halsted Press, 372p.

Oberlander, T.M. 1994. Global deserts: a geomorphic comparison, 13–35. *In* Abrahams, A.D. and A.J. Parsons, eds, *Geomorphology of Desert Environments*. London: Chapman and Hall, 674p.

Pause, M. 1979. Über eine fossile Schildkröte (*Podocnemis*) aus der mittleren Kreide der südlichen Kharga-Oasen (SW-Ägypten). *Diplom-Arbeit, Institut für Geologie und Paläontologie* der Technischen Universität Berlin, 42p.

Paver, G.L. and D.A. Pretorius. 1954. *Report on Hydrogeological Investigations in Kharga and Dakhla Oases*. Heliopolis: l'Institut du Desert d'Egypte, 108p.

Peel, R.F. 1941. Denudational landforms of the central Libyan Desert. *Journal of Geomorphology* **4**: 3–23.

Ritchie, J. This volume. Chapter 4. Flora, vegetation and palaeobotany of the Dakhleh Oasis.

Rohlfs, G. 1874. Chargeh-Dachel die Oasis Herodot's. *Petermanns Geographische Mittheilungen* **19**: 360.

Rohlfs, G. 1875. *Drei Monate in der libyschen Wüste*. Cassel: Theodor Fischer, 340p.

Said, R. 1962a. Chapter VI. Geology of Western Desert oases Dakhla, Kharga, Farafra and Baharia, 67–86. *In* Said, R., ed., *The Geology of Egypt*. New York: Elsevier, 377p.

Said, R. 1962b. *The Geology of Egypt*. New York: Elsevier, 377p.

Said, R. 1983. Remarks on the origin of the landscape of the eastern Sahara. *Journal of African Earth Sciences* **1**: 153–158.

Said, R. 1990a. *The Geology of Egypt*. Rotterdam/Brookfield: A.A. Balkema, 734p.

Said, R. 1990b. Quaternary, 487–507. *In* Said, R., ed., *The Geology of Egypt*. Rotterdam/Brookfield: A.A. Balkema, 734p.

Sandford. K.S. 1933a. Further remarks on the Kharga Oasis, III. *Geographical Journal* **81**: 530–531.

Sandford, K.S. 1933b. The geology and geomorphology of the southern Libyan Desert. *Geographical Journal* **82**: 219–222.

Sandford, K.S. 1933c. Past climate and early man in the southern Libyan Desert. *Geographical Journal* **82**: 219–222.

Schild, R. 1987. Unchanging contrast? The Late Pleistocene Nile and Eastern Sahara, 13–27. *In* Close, A.E., ed., *Prehistory of Arid North Africa. Essays in Honor of Fred Wendorf*. Dallas: Southern Methodist University Press, 357p.

Schild, R. and F. Wendorf. 1975. New Explorations in the Egyptian Sahara, 65–112. *In* Wendorf, F. and A.E. Marks, eds, *Problems in Prehistory: North Africa and the Levant*. Dallas: Southern Methodist University Press, 462p.

Schild, R. and F. Wendorf. 1977. *The Prehistory of the Dakhla Oasis and Adjacent Desert*. Warsaw: Polish Academy of Sciences, Institute for the History of Material Culture, 259p.

Schild, R. and F. Wendorf. 1981. *The Prehistory of an Egyptian Oasis*. Warsaw: Polish Academy of Sciences, Institute for the History of Material Culture, 155p.

Schwarcz, H.P. 1962. A possible origin of tektites by soil fusion at impact sites. *Nature* **194**: 8–10.

Schwarcz, H.P. 1989. Uranium series dating of Quaternary deposits. *Quaternary International* **1**: 7–17.

Schwarcz, H.P. and A.G. Latham. 1989. Dirty calcites. 1. Uranium series dating of contaminated calcites using leachates alone. *Isotope Geoscience* **80**: 35–43.

Schwarcz, H. and L. Morawska. 1993. Uranium-series dating of carbonates from Bir Tarfawi and Bir Sahara East, 205–217. *In* Wendorf, F., R. Schild, A.E. Close and Associates, *Egypt during* the Last Interglacial. The Middle Paleolithic of Bir Tarfawi and Bir Sahara East. New York/London: Plenum Press, 596p.

Shahin, M. 1985. Hydrology of the Nile Basin. Amsterdam: Elsevier, 575p.

Shaw, W.B.K. 1929. Darb el Arba'in. The Forty Days' Road. Sudan Notes and Records 12: 63–71.

Shaw, W.B.K. 1931. Journeys in the Libyan Desert, 1929 and 1930: note on the map by Major R.A. Bagnold, remarks by Mr. W.J. Harding King, Appendicies on survey methods and results, barometric heights and meteorology, the Kufara-Egypt caravan route, 'Ain el Kiyeh, and botanical notes. Appendix IV: Botanical notes. Geographical Journal 78: 534–535.

Shaw, W.B.K. 1936. An expedition in the southern Libyan Desert. Geographical Journal 87: 193–221.

Shumm, S.A. and R.J. Chorley. 1966. Talus weathering and scarp recession in the Colorado plateaus. Zeitschrift für Geomorphologie N.F. 10: 11–36.

Simmons, A.H. and R.D. Mandel. 1985. Human Occupation of a Marginal Environment: An Archaeological Survey near Kharga Oasis, Egypt. Lawrence, Kansas: University of Kansas Museum of Anthropology, Project Report Series 57, 243p.

Simmons, A.H. and R.D. Mandel. 1986. Prehistoric Occupation of a Marginal Environment: An Archaeological Survey near Kharga Oasis in the Western Desert of Egypt. Oxford: British Archaeological Reports, International Series 303, 242p.

Smith, B.J. 1978. The origin and geomorphic implications of cliff foot recesses and tafoni on limestone hamadas in the northwest Sahara. Zeitschrift für Geomorphologies N.F. 22: 21–43.

Sneth, A. 1983. Desert stream sequences in the Sinai Peninsula. Journal of Sedimentary Petrology 53: 1271–1279.

Soliman, K.H. 1953. Rainfall over Egypt. Quarterly Journal of the Royal Meteorological Society 79: 389–397.

Stokes, S. 1993. 15. Optical dating of sediment samples from Bir Tarfawi and Bir Sahara East: an initial report, 228–233. In Wendorf, F., R. Schild, A.E. Close and Associates, Egypt during the Last Interglacial. The Middle Paleolithic of Bir Tarfawi and Bir Sahara East. New York/London: Plenum Press, 596p.

Sutton, L.J. 1947. Rainfall in Egypt: Statistics, Storms, Run-off. Cairo: Government Press, 129p.

Sutton, L.J. 1950. The climate of Egypt. Weather 5: 59–62.

Thorweihe, U. 1990. Nubian aquafer system, 601–614. In Said, R., ed., The Geology of Egypt. Rotterdam/Brookfield: A.A. Balkema, 734p.

Tillet, T. 1989. L'Atérian saharien: essai sur le comportement d'une civilisation paléolithique face à l'acroissement de l'aridité. Bulletin de la Société Géologique de France, 8e série, 5 (1 – Sahara, 2e partie): 91–97.

Todd, D.K. 1980. Groundwater Hydrology. New York: John Wiley and Sons, 539p.

von Zittel, K. 1883. Beiträge zur Geologie und Pälaeontologie der Libyschen Wüste und der abgrenzenden Gebiete von Aegypten. Cassel: Gustav Fischer, 147p.

Wendorf, F., A.E. Close and R. Schild. 1987. Recent work on the Middle Palaeolithic of the Eastern Sahara. The African Archaeological Review 5: 49–63.

Wendorf, F. and R. Schild. 1976. Prehistory of the Nile Valley. New York: Academic Press, 404p.

Wendorf, F. and R. Schild. 1980. Prehistory of the Eastern Sahara. New York: Academic Press, 414p.

Wendorf, F., R. Schild, A.E. Close and Associates. 1993. Egypt during the Last Interglacial. The Middle Paleolithic of Bir Tarfawi and Bir Sahara East. New York/ London: Plenum Press, 596p.

Wendorf, F., R. Schild, C.V. Haynes, M. Kobusiewicz, A. Gautier, N. El Hadidi, H. Wieckowska and A.E. Close. 1977. Late Pleistocene and Recent climatic changes in the Egyptian Sahara. Geographical Journal 143: 211–234.

Wendorf, F., R. Schild, R. Said, C.V. Haynes, A. Gautier and M. Kobusiewicz. 1976. The prehistory of the Egyptian Sahara. Science 193: 103–114.

Wingate, O. 1934. In search of Zerzura. Geographical Journal 83: 281–308.

Winlock, H.E. 1936. Ed-Dakhleh Oasis: Journal of a Camel Trip Made in 1908. New York: The Metropolitan Museum of Art, 61p.

World Meteorological Organization. 1971. Climatolological Normals (CLINO) for CLIMAT and CLIMAT Ship Stations for the period 1931–1960. Geneva: World Meteorological Organization. unpaginated.

2

A NOTE ON THE LATE CRETACEOUS VERTEBRATE FAUNA OF THE DAKHLEH OASIS

Charles S. Churcher

INTRODUCTION

Investigations into the bedrock and subsoil deposits of Dakhleh Oasis have made me aware of the local distinctions of the various strata, rock units and formations, and distributions of the vertebrate and invertebrate fossils in Dakhleh Oasis compared to coeval deposits elsewhere in Egypt. The base level of the oasis lies in the terrestrial sandstones and shales of the Middle Cretaceous Nubia Series Taref Formation and rises through the deltaic or riverine Early Campanian Qusseir Clastic Member or Variegated Shales, also known as the Mut Formation, into the littoral or nearshore marine Late Campanian Duwi Formation Phosphorites or Bone Beds at the base of the deeper marine Dakhla Formation Black Shales, with its *Exogyra overwegi* bed, which span from Late Cretaceous Campanian, through Maastrichtian to the Early Tertiary Late Palaeocene times, and topped by the deepwater marine Eocene Tarawan Group Chalks. The Cretaceous-Tertiary Boundary is unrecognised at present. The Nubia deposits form much of the surface of Dakhleh Oasis, with the Qusseir (=Mut), Duwi, Dakhla and Tarawan formations exposed in the piedmont and face of the Libyan Escarpment. The surface of the Libyan Plateau at the edge of the scarp is formed in the Eocene Tarawan Fm. Chalks, with Late Cretacaeous Esna Formation shales and Thebes Formation Chalks to the north. Vertebrate fossils are relatively numerous throughout the section, and are often well preserved although usually represented by disarticulated isolated elements.

BEDROCK GEOLOGY OF DAKHLEH OASIS

Dakhleh Oasis lies in an uneven sequence of depressions that skirt the foot of the Libyan Escarpment between 25° 25′ and 25° 45′ N latitude and 28° 45′ and 29° 25′ E longitude, at altitudes between 92 and 140 m above sea level (asl) (Fig. 2.1). It extends over 75 km west-northwest to east-southeast as a discontinuous sequence of cultivated areas interspersed with Cretaceous sandstone ridges, Pleistocene terraces and spring deposits and piedmonts, Holocene fluvial gravel plains, and modern dune fields situated to the south of the Libyan Escarpment (see Kleindienst *et al.*, this volume, Chapter 1).

The western limit is near Gebel Edmonstone, where there is an isolated basin northwest of the Gebel at Gharb or West Maohoub. The eastern limit is about 2 km east of Teneida, north of the road to Kharga Oasis (Darb el-Ghobari). The southern limit is south of the main town, Mut, on the road south to el-Sherg el-Uweinat and Bir el-Tarfawi. The oasis lies near the geographical midpoint of Egypt and about 300 km west of the Nile Valley at about the latitude of Luxor.

The northern margin of the oasis is a small section of the Libyan Escarpment which rises about 300 m above the oasis, to between 420 and 560 m asl, and extends northwards as the Libyan Plateau at about 400 m asl. The eastern margin is also formed by the southerly projecting spur of the el-Battikh Promontory northeast of Teneida. The southern margin is formed by an unnamed lengthy sandstone ridge of the Taref Fm. which underlies the Nubia deposits at about 150 m elevation. The western margin is formed by lines of migrating barkhan dunes to the west of Mut, Gedida and Qâlamûn, and by an extension of the Duwi Formation piedmont (Sio'h Ridge) southeast of Gebel Edmonstone. Gharb Maohoub lies in an isolated depression north of the western end of G. Edmonstone

'Reports from the Survey of Dakhleh Oasis, Western Desert of Egypt, 1977–1987', edited by C.S. Churcher and A.J. Mills. Dakhleh Oasis Project: Monograph 2. Oxbow Monograph 99.

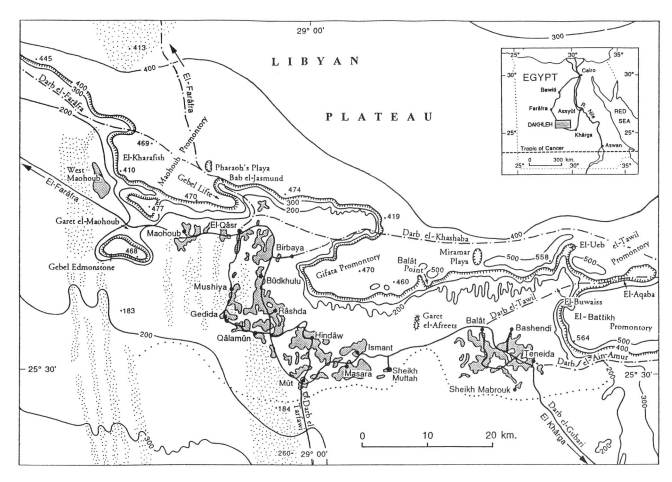

Fig. 2.1. Map of Dakhleh Oasis showing settlements, main roads, the Libyan Escarpment and dune areas.

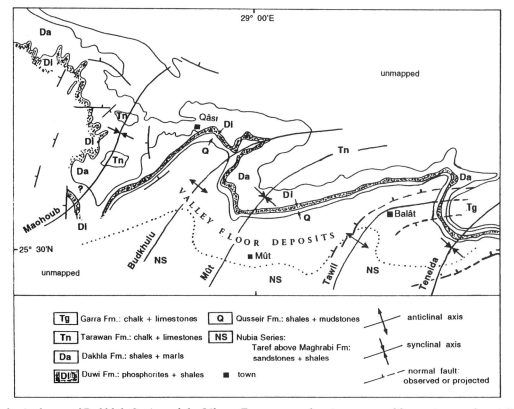

Fig. 2.2. Geological map of Dakhleh Oasis and the Libyan Escarpment showing extent of formations and anticlina-synclinal folding and faults (modified from Hermina et al., 1961).

Table 2.1. Stratigraphy of the Dakhleh Oasis region. The vertebrate fossil bearing units are the Qusseir (=Mut), Duwi and Dakhla Formations, from about 80 to 64 mya.

AGE (Ma)	PERIOD/EPOCH	STAGE		FORMATION	THICKNESS (m)	LITHOLOGY	LANDFORM
— 37 —				THEBES	300	Fossiliferous limestone, with chert and marl bands	Plateau, scarp
	EOCENE	(undivided)		ESNA	50–100	Green-grey shales	Cuestas, vales Plateau
— 52 —				TARAWAN	20–60	Whitish limestone, marls and chalk beds cherts	Plateau, scarp
— 64 —	PALEOCENE	DANIAN		DAKHLA	> 250	Grey shale, fossiliferous limestone interbeds	Scarp-face badland
— 72 —		MAASTRICHTIAN		DUWI	10–20	Siliceous limestone phosphatic beds	Cuesta
— 80 —	LATE CRETACEOUS	CAMPANIAN	NUBIA SERIES	QUSSEIR (Mut)	20–85	Red shales 'chert balls'	Lowland
		SANTONIAN		TAREF	>100	Buff sandstones, quartzites	Cuesta
— 91 —		CONIACAN					
		TURONIAN					
		CENOMANIAN					
—100—	EARLY CRETACEOUS	ALBIAN		MAGHRABI	600–1300	Sandstones, minor conglomerate, shale, quartzites	Cuesta, residual hills, plain

and west of an embayment in the escarpment. The eastern cultivated portion centred on Balat is separated by a rise of Taref sandstone from the main body of the oasis at Sheikh Muftah. Gharb Maohoub is separated from the area around Maohoub by the neck between G. Edmonstone and the main escarpment.

The inhabited parts of the oasis are discontinuous and separated by dune areas, gravel plains extending from the foot of the escarpment, old piedmont ridges, sandstone areas and salinated deposits. Bedrock is revealed in deflated areas where the lag gravels, and fluviatile or lacustrine deposits have been removed by aeolian action (Fig. 2.2). The gravel plains are old valley fans of Pleistocene or Holocene age (Kleindienst *et al.*, Chapter 1, this volume). There are numerous remnant deposits of laminated lake sediments or laminated irrigation silts and sands that, when in modern use, support cultivation or, when highly deflated, may form isolated or complex yardang fields. These Quaternary deposits rest on Nubia Group sandstones, silts, clays or mudstones, or on the variegated shales of the Qusseir Fm., over most of the oasis, with some above the Duwi piedmont and formed in the Dakhla Fm. lower shale at Maohoub.

The bedrock formations in Dakhleh Oasis and surround-

ing it are sedimentary and date from the Middle Cretaceous (Mesozoic, Turonian or Cenomanian) to Early Tertiary (Cenozoic, Eocene) (Table 2.1). The floor of the oasis is formed mainly in the sandstones and red muds or claystones of the Nubia Series' Taref Fm (terminology will generally follow classical use and not that of Fay and Hermann-Degen, 1984). Above the Taref Fm lies the Qusseir Fm or Variegated Shales (= Mut Fm of Fay and Hermann-Degen, 1984), the Duwi Fm phosphorites, the Dakhla Fm black shales, and topped by the Tarawan Fm (= Tarawan Group with Tarawan, Tartur and Garra Fms of Fay and Hermann-Degen, 1984) chalks. The Tarawan chalks are overlain by Esna Formation shales and Thebes Formation chalks which form isolated linear hills or yardangs on the Tarawan surface until they form a second but lower scarp about 25 km back from the main escarpment rim on the Libyan Plateau.

These Cretacous bedrock formations mainly lie conformably over one another with a general dip of some 5° at about 010° T with strikes at 280–100° T ± 5°. The scarp face is about 300 m high and is formed by the resistant caprock of Tarawan chalks above the easily eroded Dakhla shales (Fig. 2.3). A piedmont of variable width is formed by the harder but thin phosphoritic limestone bands of the

Fig. 2.3. The Libyan Escarpment from the oasis floor near Maohoub, looking northwest. The Tarawan Formation chalks form the Plateau top and the Dakhla Formation black shales the main slope. The Exogyra Overwegi Bench is visible in the slope of Gebel Maohoub to the left. The surface is Cenozoic colluvium and fan deposits over the Duwi Formation piedmont. Date palms and acacia trees with camels in middle distance.

Duwi Fm, with a surface eroded in the lower Dakhla shale and usually mantled with chalk and limestone debris from the Tarawan deposits.

Table 2.1 gives a précis of the stratigraphic sequence and lithologies for the formations exposed in Dakhleh Oasis. Previous workers' systems are summarised in comparison with the schema proposed by Fay and Hermann-Degen (1984). All accounts here follow terminologies based on earlier works and not that of Fay and Hermann-Degen (1984).

The first geological descriptions of the oasis were provided by Karl A. von Zittel (1883) who, as member of Röhlfs' Expedition, visited Dakhleh Oasis twice, commented on its geological structure and palaeofaunas, and left his name as 'Carl Zittel' carved on the First Century AD Roman temple at Deir el-Haggar, near Maohoub. Zittel noted the relatively simple stratigraphic sequence and assigned ages to the strata on their invertebrate fossils. Beadnell (1901) assigned an Upper Senonian (=Campanian) age to the Nubia Fm sandstone and claystone sequence, and a Danian age to the Tarawan chalks and chalky limestones on the top of the escarpment. He (1901, 92–93) noted "Clays with interbedded bone-beds" and that there was "good reason for believing the [Duwi Fm] bone-beds to be of Upper Senonian (Campanian) age from the [taxonomic] determinations which have already been made" by Zittel. It is worth remarking that Zittel apparently did not climb the escarpment, even in part, as he omits any record of turtles, elasmosaurs or mosasaurs, reptiles that are commonly represented by obvious bone fragments, and thus his mainly dental samples probably represent surface materials collected by untrained Egyptian field assistants.

Beadnell (1901) was the first to refer to 'bone-beds',

Ball and Beadnell (1903) noted the phosphate beds of the Hefhuf Formation in Baharia Oasis, and Zittel (1883) noted the phosphorites in Dakhleh and Kharga Oases. Domnik and Schaal (1984) review the phosphate beds from Baharia Oasis, through Farafra, Dakhleh and Kharga Oases, to Qusseir on the Red Sea, and assign them a Late Campanian age because of the presence of the ammonite *Bostrychoceras polyplocum*, which is characteristic of Late Campanian faunas. Previous workers have dated the Duwi Fm, whether referred to as bone-beds, phosphorites, or phosphate beds, as Santonian (Blanckenhorn 1921), Campanian (Stromer and Weiler, 1930), or Campanian-Early Maastrichtian (Hendriks *et al.* 1987), and correlated it with exposures at Mahamid or the Rakhiyat Formation in the Nile Valley, and with the Kiseiba Formation in the Libyan Desert to the south, the latter considered Campanian-Maastrichtian (Ezzat 1974; Hendriks *et al.* 1987) or Lower Maastrichtian (= Early Maastrichtian age) in Dakhleh and Kharga (Awad and Ghobrial 1966; Hermina 1967; Hermina *et al.* 1961; Issawi *et al.* 1978; Mansour *et al.* 1982; and Said 1962). Issawi (1972) correlated the Hufhuf Formation at Baharia Oasis with the Qusseir or Variegated Shales and considered them equivalent to El-Nakkady's (1951) Nubian Phosphate Bed. Fay and Hermann-Degen (1984) erected the Nubia Series or Group, of which the Duwi Fm is the latest unit and the last of three cyclothems. The Duwi Fm is generally considered to be Late Campanian or Early Maastrichtian in age, separates the lower and middle Nubia members from the Dakhla Formation, and forms a useful marker for both age and stratigraphy because of its fauna, mineralogy, and ease of recognition in the field.

The Duwi Fm conformably overlies and generally intergrades into the Qusseir Fm which in turn overlies the Taref Fm. The Taref Fm contains sandstone layers which resist erosion and form low hills or ridges along the southern boundary of the oasis and a highland separating the eastern inhabited area with Balat and Teneida from the more extensive western region with the chief towns of Mut and Qasr. There are extensive deposits of dark red muds or claystones which alternate with the sandstones; less extensive deposits of grey to grey-green shales also occur within this unit. These softer deposits are more readily eroded by wind and usually allow the formation of basins by the wind blown sands between the sandstone ridges. Occasional hills that are capped by a harder sandstone or Pleistocene marl caps exist near Bashendi and Ismant.

The Nubia Series' or Group's Maghrabi Formation lies unconformably upon a Precambrian basement complex which is found at a depth of about 100 m on the Abu Ballas divide, south of Dakhleh Oasis. The contact dips to the northwest to about 600 and 1300 m to the southeast and northwest of the oasis, respectively.

Fay and Hermann-Degen (1984) consider that their Nubia Series represents three cyclothems, the first of which they term the Maghrabi Formation with a pro-deltaic sand-

Fig. 2.4. Nubia Series' Taref Formation sandstone remnant in the form of a sitting griffon and hill in background. Part of the southern sandstone rim of the oasis, ca. 5 km southeast of Teneida on road to Kharga.

Fig. 2.5. Duwi Formation above Qusseir Formation. The Duwi Fm is represented by the multiple bands forming the bench; it extends upwards to the single band to the right and downwards to the minor band in the middle of the footslope. The Qusseir Fm is the lower gray shale slope in the left foreground. Surface blocks and debris are derived from the Tarawan Fm chalks.

Fig. 2.6. Exposure of Qusseir Formation variegated shale at Bee's Friday Site fossil locality. Tarawan chalk caps the escarpment on the far horizon to the north (left) and Duwi Fm caps the conical hill in the left middle distance.

mud-sand sequence, the second is the Taref Formation with a sandy floodplain and fluvial channel sequence, and the third is the Mut Formation (= Qusseir Fm) with a pro-deltaic sand and mud regime.

The upper Nubia shales and mudstones comprise Fay and Hermann-Degen's (1984) Taref Fm, which they diagnose as deposits in a deltaic floodplain and channel sands of Late Cenomanian age: Hendriks *et al.* (1987) give its age as Turonian. The delta deposited sandstones that show the swirls and pointbars typical of channel sands, red muds and claystones from overbank deposition in lagoons between the distributaries, and shales in the more open shallower environments. Brookes (1986, fig. 31) has identified nested meander formations in aerial photographs of the upper Nubia (= Taref Fm) sandstones, some of which may be between 50 and 100 m wide, and demonstrate the fluviatile nature and scope of this delta. The sandstones are coarse to medium grained, with angular to subangular quartz grains in mainly tabular foreset beds between 0.5 and 1.0 m thick and, when dissected, form bedrock yardangs or small gebels, often of weird aspect. These sandstones are apparently barren of fossils, often severely eroded by aeolian processes (Fig. 2.4), although extensive cross-bedding and coarse clasts are common, suggestive of an environment in which preservation of large saurian bones might be expected.

The contact between the Qusseir (= Mut) and Nubia Fms appears to have extensive but minor relief or to intergrade as the delta was flooded by a prograding sea (Fig. 2.5). This may reflect the minor unconformity between the two formations accepted by many authors (Hendriks *et al.* 1987). The shales that comprise the Qusseir Fm vary from dark and papery to greenish or brownish, angular blocky shales, and lack much gypsum intrusion in the joints (Fig. 2.6). They are more extensive in Kharga Oasis and appear thinner in Dakhleh Oasis near Maohoub, where they are unrecognisable in places and the Duwi Fm lies directly upon Nubia claystones.

The Qusseir red clays and shales contain occasional lag deposits of weathered bones and teeth of terrestrial and aquatic origin, representing terrestrial, fluviatile and marine reptiles and fishes. These fossiliferous concentrations appear to result from localised swirls or gyres in currents, with the heavier bone and tooth fragments coming to rest in minor depressions in a surface of fine-grained mud (Fig. 2.7). The shales generally represent deposition of fine sediments in still waters either between termini of deltaic distributaries or off-shore from them. Occasional lodged or hanging boulders within the shales (Fig. 2.8) indicate transportation of large clasts, possibly entangled in the roots of trees dislodged by floods.

The red claystones represent overbank deposition between the distributaries. They show little bedding but there is evidence of channel and current action in the underwater lags of disarticulated, rolled and broken bones of larger vertebrates present in the deposits near Bashendi or Teneida, and lungfish toothplates in the reentrant of

Fig. 2.7. Dyrosaurus *vertebra in fossiliferous lag at Bee's Friday Site. Matrix is paper shale with gypsum in partings. Knife is 10 cm long.*

Fig. 2.8. *Dropped or hanging boulder in Qusseir Formation, northeast of Teneida, on Military Road up the Libyan Escarpment. Note foreset beds and distortion caused by the boulder's impact.*

Fig. 2.9. *Contact between overlying Duwi and underlying Qusseir Formations at southeast entrance to Wadi el-Batikh. The Duwi Fm shows its characteristic resistent phosphoritic layers and the Qusseir shale forms the slope at the foot of the section. Toothplates of* Ceratodus humei *and teeth of* Scapanorhynchus rapax *have been recovered from the Qusseir deposits. The Libyan Escarpment is visible on the far horizon with the piedmont of Duwi Fm phosphoritic bands and chalk mantled residual hills of Dakhla Fm shale visible across the wadi floored with Tarawan Fm. chalk debris.*

the Wadi el-Batikh (Fig. 2.9). No sandstone deposits have been observed in this formation although sandy shales are present. Limey algal beds and heads are present in some places within the shales, e.g., west side of the entrance to the Wadi el-Ueb. Fragments of turtle carapaces, teeth and vertebrae of crocodilians, and bones and teeth of terrestrial sauropods, carnosaurs and other reptiles have been found mixed with shark, saw-fish and ray teeth, fish bones, garpike scales, fish peloids, clay balls, fruits, nuts and carbonised plant matter, plesiosaur and mosasaur remains.

Coeval and similar deposits in the south of Kharga Oasis and referred also to the Qusseir Fm or Variegated Shales (= Baris Fm of Fay and Hermann-Degen 1984) have yielded a similarly mixed terrestrial and fluviatile fauna. Taxa recorded are a chelonian, probably wrongly assigned to ?*Podocnemis* (Pause 1979), others with more deeply arched carapaces, a sauropod (probably the titanosaurid *Aegyptosaurus*, also reported by Pause), the longirostrine crocodile *Dyrosaurus* (Churcher and Russell 1992), and the giant lungfish *Neoceratodus tuberculatus* (Churcher 1995). Fruit, nuts and wood fragments are also present, but no microfaunal elements nor marine taxa.

The Duwi Fm phosphorites vary from about 10 to 15 m thick in Dakhleh Oasis (Fig. 2.10). In the central and eastern parts of the oasis, from Budkulu to Teneida, the Duwi Fm piedmont has 2 to 4 main phosphoritic layers at the top of the formation and often a shelly limestone at its base. In the western part, between Qasr and Gebel Edmonstone, the phosphoritic layers are fewer and the limestone may be poorly formed. Interspersed between these harder layers are light grey to greenish paper shales. The phosphoritic layers are brown to dark grey, usually coarsely granular. Teeth, bones and peloids may resist weathering and may stand out from the rock face or be found among the debris below. Gypsum is sparsely present in the phosphoritic layers.

The lower surfaces of the phosphoritic layers show numerous chambers and tunnels in the muds that form the shales (Fig. 2.11; see also Kleindienst *et al.*, this volume, Chapter 1, Fig. 1.3, Top). These were probably formed by crabs or small crustaceans that burrowed into the muds and were later infilled by a storm surge depositing phosphoritic debris. No invertebrate remains have been noted within these excavations. The mass of fish and reptile bones, teeth, peloids and excrement that provided the raw material for the phosphorites was washed over and into these burrows and chambers. It has formed casts of the burrows in a brown granular phosphoritic limestone that contrasts with the surrounding grey-green shale matrix. Gypsum is frequently present at the shale-phosphorite contact.

Above the Duwi Fm the Late Cretaceous and Early Eocene Dakhla Fm shales give most of the height to the Libyan Escarpment (Figs 2.3 and 2.12). The Duwi-Dakhla contact is generally distinct and without transition (Fig. 2.5), suggestive of a sudden lowering of the deposit or change in depositional environment from one where near-

Fig. 2.10. Exposure of Duwi Formation forming the piedmont shelf between Qasr and Maohoub, looking east. Note northwards dip of about 5°.

Fig. 2.13. Dakhla Formation black shales with marl horizons exposed in the Upper Wadi el-Tawil. The Tarawan Formation chalk cliffs and the Exogyra Overwegi Bench are visible in the far valley wall, as are falling sand glaciers.

Fig. 2.11. Lower surface of Duwi Formation phosphoritic layer showing chamber (left centre) and network of burrows attributed to crabs (Crustacea, Decapoda) filled by phosphoritic matrix. The chamber's diameter is ca.10 cm.

Fig. 2.12. Dakhla Formation black shales overlain by Tarawan Formation chalk in Upper Wadi el-Tawil. The main shelf in the distance and foreground is formed by the Exogyra Overwegi Bench's shell deposit. Surficial deposits of white wind blown sand and Tarawan Fm chalk debris mantle the gullies and shale surfaces unless scoured by wind. Skyline shows bedrock yardangs on surface of el-Battikh Promontory.

shore underwater swales accumulate debris to a deeper and stiller anoxic environment where deposition was slow and biological material scarce.

The Dakhla Fm shales are the thickest unit in the escarpment and represent about 230 m of deposit. These shales vary from light grey or greenish to almost black, from thin papery, through blocky, to almost limey clays or claystones, with reddish-brown areas where algal reefs, mats or heads are present. The sequence of deposition was neither continuous nor uniform. The major interruption is represented by the Exogyra Overwegi Limestone Bench formed by a shelly limestone chiefly composed of the oyster *Exogyra overwegi*. This bench lies about two-thirds the way above the contact with the Duwi Fm and probably represents the geographically extensive Maastrichtian-Palaeocene hiatus noted by Hendricks *et al.* (1987) and which may obliterate the K-T boundary locally.

The Overwegi Bench effectively divides the Dakhla Fm shales into thinner upper and thicker lower units. The capping Tarawan limestone fails as discrete blocks and forms a strong scarp wherever it is exposed (e.g., Wadi el-Tawil), and may form a bench on which debris from higher units, e.g., Tarawan Fm chalk, lies. The Dakhla shales also include a number of variably extensive marl or marly-limestone beds which are more numerous in the lower levels and also form minor scarps in the bare erosional topography (Fig. 2.13). Three associated beds extend over much of the lower levels of the upper part of the Wadi el-Tawil and are used to distinguish the lowest level of a middle shale unit. Unfortunately, the thickness of the Overwegi Bench and occurrences of the marl beds vary unsystematically along the face of the Dakhleh portion of the Libyan Escarpment and elsewhere, and thus they may only be used as local markers.

In the region of Gebel Edmonstone, the upper Dakhla shale unit grades through a number of limestone, limey shale and dark shale bands into the overlying Tarawan chalk, suggesting that, at least near Maohoub and in the

Fig. 2.14. Mosasaur jaw specimen weathering from a marl bed, upper Wadi el-Tawil. Undulations represent tooth attachments and sockets. Knife is 10 cm long.

Fig. 2.15. Cluster of mosasaur vertebrae deposited by a local current swirl near base of the Dakhla Formation black shale. Note heavy gypsum layers enveloping vertebrae and in shale partings. Knife is 10 cm long.

Upper Wadi el-Tawil, the transition from Dakhla to Tarawan deposition was not a clear change. This may represent a latest Cretacous downwarping of the area between Dakhleh and Kharga oases. In the Kharga Basin, the Overwegi Bench is not easily identified, and does not provide the notable stratigraphic marker present in Dakhleh.

Throughout the Dakhla shales the horizontal bedding planes and oblique or vertical partings may be filled with gypsum sheets, which may also wrap around included fossil vertebrate bones or teeth. Fossil vertebrate elements may also occur within the marl beds where they are usually undistorted and lack gypsum crystalization (Fig. 2.14). Fossils within the shales, especially bones, teeth and arthropod exoskeletons, are usually encased in a coat of gypsum (Fig. 2.15) and may be 'exploded' by expansion of gypsum crystals within their cavities. Teleost remains are compressed when in the shale (see Kleindienst et al., this volume, Chapter 1, Fig. 1.3, Bottom).

The Cretaceous-Tertiary contact (K/T Boundary) has not been located in either the upper levels of the Dakhla shales or the Overwegi Bench and is considered missing. Hendriks et al. (1987, fig. 2) show two hiatus in the middle of the Dakhla Formation and between it and the overlying Tarawan Fm chalk in the El-Kharga-Baris area that could mask the K/T zone, and it is likely that similar hiatus are present in the section exposed at Dakhleh. They also suggest that the Overwegi Bench represents a more widespread hiatus and may obscure the K/T Boundary over much of Egypt. However, in the Dakhleh Oasis section of the Libyan Escarpment, mosasaurs are found above this bench, both near Qasr and in the upper Wadi el-Tawil, and the recovered vertebrate fauna, although sparse, apparently does not differ from that present in the lower levels of the formation. Thus it appears more likely that the K/T Boundary lies at the base of the Tarawan Fm, possibly hidden within an erosional unconformity.

The Tarawan Fm chalks stand as a 20 to 25 m high cliff along most of the escarpment rim and lie apparently conformably over the upper Dakhla shales (Fig. 2.16). The Tarawan Fm lithology varies from massive chalk, through chalky bands with irregular concretionary horizons, to limestone or limey chalks. Chert concretions as geodes or vugs occur in restricted exposures, e.g., at the head of the Wadi el-Ueb, and probably represent minor facies changes. No vertebrate fossils have been noted in these chalks but a varied fauna of red ferruginised invertebrate fossils is present (e.g., bryozoa, corals, gastropods, bivalves, belemnites, nautiloids, ammonites and crabs).

The division of the Tarawan Fm into the older Tarawan and Kurkur Fms underlying the Garra Fm is hard to accept (Fay and Herman-Degen 1984), as no older formation appears to underlie the Garra Fm in the middle of the Dakhleh Escarpment (see Kleindienst et al., this volume, Chapter 1). If their lithologies differ as reported, then the three divisions should perhaps be considered as facies of a single formation and the suggested asynchrony ignored.

Fig. 2.16. Scarp face of Tarawan Formation chalk on south margin of upper valley of the Wadi el-Tawil, looking southeast. Note sand dunes piled against Tarawan Fm scarp by the prevalent north wind, the family of separated blocks descended below Tarawan surface and clefts indicating cliff sapping in the main present face.

CRETACEOUS VERTEBRATES FROM THE LIBYAN ESCARPMENT AT DAKHLEH OASIS

Collection of vertebrate fossils from the formations comprising the Dakhleh portion of the Libyan Escarpment is dependent on often widely separated, scattered, or poorly preserved specimens weathering out or lying on the surface. Some specimens, e.g., bony fish, turtles, isolated reptilian bones, have been found *in situ*. In a few instances a number of water sorted elements, sometimes weathered and water worn, are found as a lag deposit in an ancient aquatic swale or drift (Fig. 2.6). Materials are recovered after considerable searching, may be damaged by gypsum infiltration, sand-blasting or weathering on the surface, and elements are seldom associated or in articulation. Table 2.2 gives a tentative list of taxa from the fossiliferous horizons.

a. Nubia Formation sandstones, claystones and shales

No fossils have been observed in this formation. The claystones and shales appear not to differ markedly from those in the overlying Qusseir Fm and perhaps fossils will be located here in due course. The sandstones are coarse, sometimes crudely sorted with large shale, mud or other clasts, and are laid in thick, foreset beds ranging from 1 to 3 m thick. Their fabric suggests that large terrestrial saurians might be preserved somewhere within them.

b. Qusseir (=Mut) Formation shales

Fossils from the Qusseir Fm shales in the Dakhleh exposures are not common. Churcher (1988, 1989) erroneously reported a crocodilian vertebra as champsosaurian.

Three localities are known where drift deposits of weathered and water concentrated fragmentary bones, teeth and scales are found. In one, Bee's Friday Site (Fig. 2.6), a varied fauna of large terrestrial and marine vertebrates is mixed with microfaunal taxa that derived from the deltaic environment (Churcher and Russell 1992). Taxa identified are the sharks *Squalicorax*, *Scapanorhynchus*, a ray cf. *Onchosaurus*, small and large mosasaurs and a crocodile cf. *Dyrosaurus*, together with bones of teleosts, e.g. *Enchodus*, and fish peloids. Subsequently specimens assignable to *Spinosaurus* and *Carcharodontosaurus* were obtained.

The second comprises water rolled skeletal elements of marine chelonians and crocodilians, with few terrestrial or pelagic taxa included and no microvertebrates. The third comprises a mixed terrestrial assemblage in which marine aquatic taxa are sparse. Another site yielded only isolated lungfish (*Ceratodus humei*: Churcher and De Iuliis, In press) toothplates and turtle bone fragments. One terrestrial site probably representing a swale has yielded parts of a large skull, vertebral and longbone elements from the crocodilian *Dyrosaurus* and the shaft of a titanosaur longbone.

Fossilised tree trunks up to 4 m long and 30 cm in diameter occur at two localities, and fragments of fossil wood are widespread but sparse. Small cones, 70–90 mm long, probably from a cycad (U. Thanheiser, 1996, *pers. comm.*) occur near a locality with many chert concretions east of Teneida (see Kleindienst *et al.*, this volume, Chapter 1, Fig. 1.37, Bottom). Other fruits are known from synchronous deposits in Kharga Oasis.

c. Duwi Formation phosphorites and shales

Seven earlier reports of taxa from this formation (Churcher 1980, 1981, 1982, 1983, 1986, 1988, 1989) have outlined the marine vertebrates from this nearshore deposit.

The fauna from the Duwi Fm comprises marine elasmobranchs, teleosts and reptiles, of Late Campanian to Early Maastrictian age, that lived in the southern gulf of the Tethys Sea that inundated the rejuvenated Palaeozoic Dakhla Basin (Hendriks *et al.* 1987). I here revise this list in the light of more recent field work and identifications.

Nine species of Elasmobranchii, provisionally identified as the selachian sharks *Squalocorax pristodontus*, *Sq. kaupi*, *Scapanorhynchus rapax* and probably *Sc. raphiodon*, *Cretolamna appendiculata* var. *lata*, the sawfish *Schizorhiza stromeri* and *Onchosaurus (Ischyriza)* sp., possibly *O. pharao* or *O. maroccanus*, and the rays *Rhombodus binkhorsti* and *Parpalaeobates atlanticus* are known. Teleosts are fewer but include six or more taxa: the salmonids *Enchodus libycus* and *E. bursauxi*, two tetraodonts *Stephanodus libycus* and *Stephanodus* sp., two ichthyodectids *Ichthyodectes* and *Xiphactinus* and some as yet identified large fishes. Reptilia are Chelonia, represented by a large cryptodire with a thick complete shell up to 1 m long, a pelomedusid resembling the '*Podocnemis*' reported from Kharga by Pause (1979) and a small baenid-like form, Crocodilia by the marine gavial-like *Dyrosaurus* and an unidentified crocodile, Plesiosauria by *Elasmosaurus* sp., and Mosasauria by *Mosasaurus beaugei*, *M.* cf. *anceps*, a large form identified only to *Mosasaurus* sp., a small *Clidastes* sp., and *Globidens aegyptiacus*.

d. Dakhla Formation shales and marls

Vertebrate fossils are relatively common in the Dakhla Fm shales and marls but not observed in the Overwegi Bench. Elasmobranchs represented are *Squalicorax pristodontus*, *Scapanorhynchus* sp., two *Cretolamna* spp., one large and one small, and *Rhombodus binkhorsti*; teleosts identified are *Enchodus* sp., possibly larger than *E. bursauxi*, a large armoured teleost, and other unidentified large teleosts; Reptilia are represented by the pelomedusid chelonian referred to '*Podocnemis*' by Pause (1978), a large thick carapaced turtle up to 1 m long, and a baenid-like form; Crocodilia by *Dyrosaurus* sp.; Plesio-

Table 2.2. Preliminary list of fossil vertebrates from the Qusseir (=Mut), Duwi and Dakhla formations exposed in the Libyan escarpment at Dakhleh Oasis

	QUSSEIR (=MUT) FM	DUWI FM PHOSPHORITES	DAKHLA FM SHALES		
			LOWER	MIDDLE	UPPER
ELASMOBRANCHII					
Squalicorax					
S. *pristodontus*	?	x			
S. *kaupi*		x			
Squalicorax. sp.	x		x	x	x
Scapanorhynchus					
S. *rapax*			x	x	
S. *raphiodon*		x			
S. *tenuis*		x	x	x	x
Scapanorhynchus sp.	x	x			
Cretolamna					
C. *appendiculata* var. *lata*	x	x			
C. cf. *biauriculata*		x			
Cretolamna sp. small			x	x	x
Physogaleus sp.		?			
Schizorhiza					
S. *stromeri*		*x*			
Onchosaurus					
O. *maroccanus*		x			
O. *pharao*		x			
Onchosaurus sp.	x				
Parapalaeobates					
P. cf. *atlanticus*	x	x	x		
Rhombodus					
R. cf. *binkhorsti*		x			
TELEOSTEI					
Enchodus					
E. *libycus*		x	x	?	
E. *bursauxi*		x	x	x	
Enchodus sp.		x			
Stephanodus					
S. *libycus*		x			
Stratodus					
S. *apicalis*		?	?	?	?
Saurodontus			x		
Protosphyraene			x		
Cimolichthys				x	
Anogmius				x	
DIPNOI					
Ceratodus					
C. *humei*	x				
Neoceratodus					
N. *africanus*	x				
'N'. *tuberculatus*	x				
CHELONIA					
Large chelonian sp.	x	x	x	x	
?*Podocnemis*					
?P. cf. *aegyptiacus*	x				
?*Podocnemis* sp.		x			
Chelonia Indet.	x	x	x	x	x
MOSASAURIA					
Tylosaurus sp.		x	x		
Mosasaurus					
M. *beaugei*				?	
M. cf. *anceps*	x	x		?	

	QUSSEIR (=MUT) FM	DUWI FM PHOSPHORITES	DAKHLA FM SHALES LOWER	DAKHLA FM SHALES MIDDLE	DAKHLA FM SHALES UPPER
M. cf. *maximus*		x			
M. cf. *hoffmanni*		*x*			
M. cf. *conodon*	*x*	*x*			
Mosasaurus sp.		x	x	x	x
Halisaurus sp.	x	x			x
Plotosaurus sp.				x	
Prognathodon sp.		x	x		x
Platecarpus sp.	x			x	x
Clidastes sp.	x	x	x	x	x
Globidens					
G. aegyptiacus	x	x	x		
PLESIOSAURIA					
Elasmosaurus	?	x	x	x	
ARCHOSAURIA					
Spinosaurus	x				
Carcharodontosaurus	x				
'*Aegyptosaurus*'	x				
CROCODILIA					
Dyrosaurus	x	x	x	x	
'*Crocodilus*'		x			

sauria by *Elasmosaurus* sp., and Mosasauria by *Mosasaurus beaugei, Mosasaurus* sp., *Clidastes* sp., and *Globidens aegyptiacus.*

Vertebrate fossils are slightly more common below the Overwegi Bench. Teeth of *Scapanorhynchus raphiodon*, a large *Cretolamna*, and *Parapalaeobates sp.,* jaw fragments of *Enchodus* sp. and ?*Anogmius* sp., a vertebra of an unidentified ichthodectid, and fragments of a shoulder girdle of *Clidastes* sp., have been recovered.

e. Tarawan Formation chalks

No vertebrate fossils have been observed in these chalks, although wood, algal and invertebrate, mainly molluscan and crustacean, remains are common.

DISCUSSION

This prelimininary note extends reports by Zittel (1883) and Beadnell (1901) in which notices of the fish remains were first published, and by Domnik and Schaal (1984) who give a general account of the fauna of the Duwi Fm and its stratigraphic equivalents in Egypt, founded on samples obtained for assesssing the phosphate levels within the Duwi Fm for its economic potential. It also summarises my interim reports published in the Journal of the Society for the Study of Egyptian Antiquities over 1980 to 1989, with some minor additions.

The Late Campanian Tethyian 'Gulf of Egypt' was undoubtedly highly salty on the evidence of its deposits of gypsum and halite, as is the modern Red Sea or Persian Gulf, and lay within 5–7° North latitude of the Late Cretaceous equator. It was rich in nutrients and provided an ideal habitat for a varied and numerous fauna. From the aspect of the Dakhleh Oasis' late Cretaceous exposures, the gulf was probably most productive during Duwi Fm times as, with gradual and continuing subsidence or transgression of the area by Tethys Ocean, the sequence goes from terrestrial through deltaic and littoral to deep anoxic marine.

The environment of the region during the deposition of the Duwi Formation in the area now known as Dakhleh Oasis is suggested by the known or suspected habitat requirements or tolerances of the taxa so far recognised as fossil. Free ranging and predatory species such as the sharks *Squalicorax* and *Scaphanorhynchus* that preyed on animals larger than could be easily swallowed whole or after a few bites, suggest that they may have preyed on large teleosts such as *Enchodus*, or sharks such as *Cretolamna* that take their prey more or less whole. These forms are generally open water or coastal forms, but not pelagic, and a gulf environment would be eminently suitable. Sawfish such as *Schizorhiza* and *Onchosaurus* and rays such as *Rhombodus* or *Parapalaeobates* are bottom feeders or hunt near the bottom of shallow waters, deltaic channels, or even in rivers, for their food, which is often invertebrates or small fishes. Smaller predators such as the juveniles of the sharks or teleosts may have formed the middle of the food chain and would consume smaller algal eaters or detritivores such as *Stephanodus*. The smaller fishes would in turn be preyed upon by the sea turtles, who would also scavenge any large carcasses, and inshore by the smaller '*Podocnemis*'.

The larger predatory mosasaurs, *Tylosaurus, M. beaugei* and *M.* cf. *anceps,* have teeth adapted for feeding on larger fishes, such as *Enchodus, Scapanorhynchus, Squalicorax, Ichthyodectes*, or free-swimming ammonites or cephalopods. These dominant large predators reflect a more open sea environment and were probably rarer in the inshore habitats. The large toothed mosasaurs, presently only determined to *Tylosaurus* sp. and *M.* cf. *anceps,* appear to have been the top predators in the food web as, with teeth >40 mm high, they could prey on other mosasaurs, *Elasmosaurus* and large teleosts and elasmobranchs. The smallest *Clidastes*-like mosasaurs presumably inhabited the nearer shore zones and those within the delta's distributaries and marginal brackish lakes. There appears to have been a triangular food column in which the larger mosasaurs were at the pinnacle, the medium sized mosasaurs and larger sharks and teleosts formed the middle, and the smaller mosasaurs such as *Clidastes* and lesser sharks and teleosts the bottomm of the predatory guilds, with all of them battening on the smaller invertebrate and algal eating fishes.

The mosasaur *Globidens* ate molluscs, such as the ammonite index fossil *Bostrychoceras polyplocum*, or bottom dwelling molluscs, such as *Exogyra overwegi* that is present in large numbers in the Overwegi Bench of the Dakhla Fm, and whose hard shells required a specialised dentition for crushing them. The plesiosaur *Elasmosaurus* was probably also an open gulf dweller and fed on smaller fishes or the young of *Enchodus*, etc.

The large variety of mosasaurs at all levels of the marine section suggest an open sea, either nearby in the lower units or present in the upper units, inhabited by wide-ranging predators. These predators would come inshore to escape storms or to find smaller food animals or perhaps to breed. At such times they would be found associated with *Elasmosaurus* and the near shore denizens, as preserved in the Duwi Fm deposits. Occasional ventures into the deltaic environment allows them to be sparsely represented in the Qusseir Fm deposits where they are associated with terrestrial archosaurs.

Acknowledgements
The collection or location of many of the less numerous or better specimens noted in this report was often due to the sharp eyes of members of the Dakhleh Oasis Project when in the field engaged on other research. I am particularly indebted to R.A. Frey, A.F. Hollett, M.R. Kleindienst, J.E. Knudstad, A.J. Mills, and P.G. Sheldrick for their interest and acuity. I also thank my field assistants over the seasons, A. Armstrong, S.A. Churcher, H.N. Bryant, J. Hewetson, G.R. Hurlburt, and G. De Iullis for walking many miles in my shoes, carrying specimens, and labelling and curating them. D.A. Russell, then of the Canadian Museum of Nature, Ottawa, worked with me in the field in 1993 and assisted in the identifications: I am most grateful for his advice and knowledge. My wife Bee acted as field assistant and photographer during many seasons and endured the harsh conditions. We all owe a great debt to A.J. Mills for organising well-run home bases in different villages and maintaining transport with marginal facilities, and to all the others who assisted in making the fieldwork possible. The fieldwork was supported by National Science and Reseach Council Grant GP001704 over the years.

Address for Author
C.S. Churcher, Department of Zoology, University of Toronto, Toronto, Ontario, Canada M5S 1A1 *and* Department of Palaeobiology, Royal Ontario Museum, Toronto, Ontario, Canada M5S 2C6. Present address R.R.1, Site 42, Box 12, Gabriola Island, British Columbia, Canada V0R 1X0

REFERENCES

Awad, G.H. and M.G. Ghobrial. 1966. Zonal stratigraphy of the Kharga Oasis. *Geological Survey of Egypt*, Paper **34**, 1–77.

Ball, J. and H.J.L. Beadnell. 1903. Baharia Oasis: its topography and geology. *Geological Survey of Egypt*, 84p.

Beadnell, H.J.F. 1901. Dakhla Oasis: its topography and geology. *Geological Survey of Egypt Report*, **1899**, part IV, 1–107.

Bisewski, H. 1982. Zur Geologie des Dakhla-Beckens (Südwest-Ägypten): sedimentologie und geochemie de Nubischen Gruppe. *Berliner Geowissenschaftliche Abhandlungen (A)* **40**: 1–86.

Blanckenhorn, M. 1921. *Ägypten. Handbuch der Regionalen Geologie* **7** (9). Heidelberg: Winter Verlag, 244p.

Brookes, I.A. 1986. *Quaternary Geology and geomorphology of Dakhleh Oasis Region and Environs, south-central Egypt: Reconnaissance findings*. York University, Toronto: Department of Geography, Discussion paper no. 32, 90p.

Brookes, I.A. 1989. Early Holocene basinal sediments of the Dakhla Oasis region, south central Egypt. *Quaternary Research* **32**: 139–152.

Brookes, I.A. 1994. Geomorphology and Quaternary geology of the Dakhla Oasis region, Egypt. *Quaternary Science Reviews* **12**: 529–552.

Churcher, C.S. 1980. Dakhleh Oasis Project: Preliminary observations on the geology and vertebrate palaeontology of northwestern Dakhleh Oasis: a report on the 1979 fieldwork. *Journal for the Study of Egyptian Antiquities* **10**: 379–395.

Churcher, C.S. 1981. Dakhleh Oasis Project: Geology and Paleontology: Interim a report on the 1980 field season. *Journal for the Study of Egyptian Antiquities* **11**: 194-212.

Churcher, C.S. 1982. Dakhleh Oasis Project – Geology and Palaeontology: Interim report on the 1981 field season. *Journal for the Study of Egyptian Antiquities* **12**: 103–114.

Churcher, C.S. 1983. Dakhleh Oasis Project: Palaeontology: Interim report on the 1982 field season. *Journal for the Study of Egyptian Antiquities* **13**: 178–187.

Churcher, C.S. 1986. Dakhleh Oasis Project: Palaeontology: Interim report on the 1985 field season. *Journal for the Study of Egyptian Antiquities* **16**: 114–118.

Churcher, C.S. 1987. Dakhleh Oasis Project: Palaeontology: Interim report on the 1988 field season. *Journal for the Study of Egyptian Antiquities* **17**: 177–181.

Churcher, C.S. 1986. Dakhleh Oasis Project: Palaeontology: Interim report on the 1987 field season. *Journal for the Study of Egyptian Antiquities* **16**: 114–118.

Churcher, C.S. 1995. Giant Cretaceous lungfish *Neoceratodus tuberculatus* from a deltaic environment in the Quseir (=Baris)

Formation of Kharga Oasis, Western Desert of Egypt. *Journal of Vertebrate Paleontology 15: 845–849.*

Churcher, C.S. and G. De Iuliis. In press. A new species of *Protopterus* and a revision of *Ceratodus humei* (Dipnoi: Ceratodontiformes) from the Mut Formation of Eastern Dakhleh Oasis, Western Desert of Egypt. *Journal of Palaeontology.*

Churcher, C.S. and D.A. Russell. 1992. Terrestrial vertebrates from Campanian strata in Wadi el-Gedid (Kharga and Dakhleh Oases), Western Desert of Egypt. *Journal of Vertebrate Paleontology, Abstract 35,* **12** (Supplement to no 3): 23A.

Domnik, W. and S. Schaal. 1984. Notes on the stratigraphy of the Upper Cretaceous phosphates (Campanian) of the Western Desert, Egypt. *Berliner Geowissenschaftliche Abhandlungen (A)* **50**: 153–175.

Ezzat, M.A. 1974. Exploitation of ground water in El-Wadi El-Gedid Project Area (New Valley). Part II. Hydrogeologic Conditions in the Dakhleh-Kharga Area. *Ground Water Series in the Arab Republic of Egypt. Cairo: Ministry of Agriculture and Land Reclamation.*

El Kammar, A.M., A.M. Abdallah and G.I. Abdel Gawad. 1982. Petrography and lithofacies studies on the Upper Cretaceous [to] Lower Tertiary sediments of the Abu Tartur plateau, Western Desert, Egypt. *Annals of the Geological Survey of Egypt* **12**: 213–236.

El-Nakkady, S.E. 1951. Stratigraphical Study of the Mahamid District. *Bulletin of the Faculty of Science, Alexandria University* **1**: 17–43.

Fay, M. and W. Hermann-Degen. 1984. Mineralogy of Campanian/Maastrichtian sand deposits and a model of basin development for the Nubian Group of the Dakhla Basin (southwest Egypt). *Berliner Geowissenschaftliche Abhandlungen (A)* **50**: 99–105.

Germann, K., W.-D. Bock and T. Schröter. 1984. Facies development of Upper Cretaceous phosphorites in Egypt: sedimentological and geochemical aspects. *Berliner Geowissenschaftliche Abhandlungen (A)* **50**: 345–361.

Hendriks, F., P. Luger, J. Bowitz and H. Kallenbach. 1987. Evolution of the depositional environments of SE-Egypt during the Cretaceous and Lower Tertiary. *Berliner Geowissenschaftliche Abhandlungen (A)* **75**: 49–82.

Hermina, M.H. 1967. Geology of the north-western approaches of Kharga. Geological Survey of Egypt, Paper 44, 1–87.

Hermina, M. 1990. The surroundings of Kharga, Dakhla and Farafra Oases, 259–292. *In* Said, R., ed., *The Geology of Egypt.* Rotterdam/Brookfield: A.A. Balkema, 734p.

Hermina, M.H., M.G. Ghobrial and B. Issawi. 1961. *The Geology of the Dakhla Area.* Cairo: Geological Survey of Egypt and Mining Research Department, 33p.

Hermina, M.H. and B. Issawi. 1971. Rock-stratigraphic classification of the Upper Cretaceous-Lower Tertiary exposures in southern Egypt, 147–154. *In* Gray, C., ed., *Symposium on the Geology of Libya, Tripoli, 1969.* Tripoli: University of Libya, Faculty of Science, 522p.

Hume, W.F. 1925. *Geology of Egypt* (3 vols). Cairo: Survey of Egypt, Ministry of Finance.

Issawi, B. 1972. Review of the Upper Cretaceous-Lower Tertiary stratigraphy in central southern Egypt. *Bulletin of the American Association of Petroleum Geologists* **56**: 1448–1463.

Issawi, B., M.Y. Hassan and A.N. Attia Said. 1978. Geology of the Abu Tartur Plateau, Western Desert, Egypt. *Annals of the Geological Survey of Egypt* **8**: 91–127.

Klitzsch, E., J.C. Harms, A. Lejal-Nicol and F.K. List. 1979. Major subdivisions and depositional environments of Nubia strata, southwestern Egypt. *Bulletin of the American Association of Petroleum Geologists* **63**: 967–974.

Mansour, H.H., B. Issawi and M.M. Askalany. 1982. Contribution to the geology of west Dakhla oasis area, Western Desert, Egypt. *Annals of the Geological Survey of Egypt* **12**: 255–281.

Pause, M. 1979. Über eine fossile Schildkröte (*Podocnemis*) aus der mittleren Kreide der südlichen Kharga-Oasen (SW-Ägypten). *Diplom-Arbeit, Institut für Geologie und Paläontologie der Technischen Universität Berlin,* 42p.

Said, R. 1962. *Geology of Egypt.* Amsterdam/New York: Elsevier, 377p.

Stromer, E. von and W. Weiler. 1930. Ergebnisse der Forschungsreisen Prof. E. Stromers in den Wüsten Ägyptens, VI. Beschreibung von Wirbeltier-Resten aus dem nubischen Sandstein Oberäegyptens und aus ägyptischen Phosphaten nebst Bermerkungen über die Geologie der Umgegend von Mahmîd in Oberägypten. *Abhandlungen der Bayerischen Akademie der Wissenschaften, Mathematisch-Naturwissenschaftliche Abteilung, Neue Folge* **7**: 1–42.

Zittel, K.A. von 1883. Beitrage zur Geologie und Palaeontologie der Libyschen Wüste und der Angrenzenden Gebiete von Aegypten. I. Geologischer Theil. *Palaeontographica* **30**: 1–147.

3

SOIL FUNGI FROM EASTERN DAKHLEH OASIS

John C. Krug and R. Shah Khan

Samples of soil were collected by Alan F. Hollett from the sides of irrigation furrows and an ancient agricultural area, in the neighbourhood of 'Ein Birbiyeh, on February 5th., 1987. These were plated and cultured for fungal spores on modified Leonian's agar medium (Malloch 1981), using the soil dilution plate technique (Warcup 1950) modified by pretreatment for about 5 minutes with 50% ethanol. The following taxa of Ascomycetes, Coelomycetes and Hyphomycetes were isolated, which probably represent only a very small percentage of the total population of terricolous fungi present at these sites. In order to place the results in perspective, Khan and Krug (1994) reported 241 taxa of coprophilous Ascomycetes in an extensive study from East Africa, while Faurel and Schotter (1964a, 1964b, 1965a, 1965b), in more restricted studies, recorded 70 species of coprophilous fungi from Algeria and 111 species from the central Sahara. Although these studies are based on a different substrate, comparable numbers of terricolous fungi would be expected in similar samplings.

Ascomycetes
  Discomycetes
  Ascobolus cf. *xylophilus* Seaver
    Pyrenomycetes
  Areolospora bosensis (Das) D. Hawksworth
  Byssochlamys nivea Westling
  Chaetomium bostrychodes Zopf
  Chaetomium caprinum Bainier
  Chaetomium convolutum Chivers
  Chaetomium globosum Kunze: Fr.
  Chaetomium murorum Corda
  Chaetomium subspirale Chivers

Emericella nidulans (Eidam) Vuill.
Eupenicillium javanicum (van Beyma) Stolk & Scott var. *javanicum*
Eupenicillium javanicum (van Beyma) Stolk & Scott var. *levitum (Raper & Fennell) Stolk & Samson*
Eurotium amstelodami Mangin
Eurotium chevalieri Mangin
Gelasinospora hippopotama Krug, Khan & Jeng
Neosartorya fischeri (Wehmer) Malloch & Cain
Neosartorya spinosa (Raper & Fennell) Kozakiewicz
Talaromyces flavus (Klöcker) Stolk & Samson var. *flavus*
Talaromyces helicus (Raper & Fennell) C.R. Benj. var. *helicus*
Talaromyces stipitatus (Thom) C.R. Benj.
Talaromyces wortmannii (Klöcker) C.R. Benj. var. *wortmannii*
Thielavia terricola (Gilman & Abbott) Emmons
  Loculoascomycetes
Aporospora terricola Krug & Jeng
Preussia minimoides (Ahmed & Cain) Valldosera & Guarro

Coelomycetes
  Phoma exigua Desm.

Hyphomycetes
  Acremonium strictum W. Gams
  Aspergillus niger van Tieghem
  Gilmaniella humicola Barron
  Nigrospora sphaerica (Sacc.) Mason

'Reports from the Survey of Dakhleh Oasis, Western Desert of Egypt, 1977–1987', edited by C.S. Churcher and A.J. Mills. Dakhleh Oasis Project: Monograph 2. Oxbow Monograph 99.

COMMENTS

Ascobolus cf. *xylophilus* was described from the U.S.A. (Seaver 1911) and a revised description was provided by Brummelen (1967). The fungus subsequently was reported from France (Brummelen and Candoussau 1981). Both collections were obtained from decaying coniferous wood at high elevations. Our collection differs from the extant material in possessing a yellowish apothecium with cylindrical asci and broader, yellow-brown ascospores measuring 26–32 × (14–) 16–20 μm. As pointed out by Brummelen and Candoussau (1981) the large spore size and clearly warted to punctate ornamentation are very characteristic. Since our material is very scanty, the collection is tentatively referred to *A. xylophilus* in spite of the differences in substrate and elevation. This is the first report from Africa.

Areolospora bosensis is considered to have a pantropical distribution and this record further supports this hypothesis. The taxonomy and distribution of this fungus are discussed by Krug, Khan and Udagawa (1994). It is known from Colombia, India, Nepal, Pakistan, the Phillipines, Sri Lanka (Ceylon), Thailand, United States of America and Venezuela outside Africa, and only from Nigeria and the Sudan elsewhere in Africa. This Egyptian record is interesting as it represents a further xeric occurrence similar to the fungi from dry, sandy soil from Illinois, USA reported by Wicklow and Wilson (1990).

Eupenicillium javanicum var. *levitum* has only been reported occasionally but the anamorph, which is associated with both this variety and the typical variety, is widespread. This appears to be the first report of the teleomorph from Africa.

Gelasinospora hippopotama is unique in having ascospores with a combination of multiple germ pores and very small circular pits (Krug, Khan and Jeng 1994), although a number of other species have been described with multiple germ pores (Cailleux 1971). Typical members of this genus have spores with one or two germ pores and several types of pits are known in different species (Arx 1982). *G. hippopotama* differs in that its pits vary from wide and shallow to narrow and deep within one species. It is known from Malawi and the Sudan elsewhere in Africa and the only extralimital record is from Venezuela.

Talaromyces helicus is known from a number of isolates from temperate latitudes but has been isolated less frequently from tropical countries. It is known only from Zambia elsewhere in Africa and our isolate represents the first report for Egypt.

Talaromyces wortmannii var. *wortmanii* is unusual for this genus in producing reddish coloured ascocarps. This strain is also known from the Sudan, Malawi, and Zimbabwe in Africa and extralimitally from Hawaii, Indonesia, India and Pakistan. On the basis of this evidence it probably represents another case of a pantropical distribution.

Aporospora terricola was described by Krug and Jeng (1999) who discuss fully the taxonomy and possible phylogenetic relationships. It differs from similar genera with thick-walled, cylindrical asci lacking an apical structure, by possessing biapiculate, pigmented, smooth, two-celled ascospores without germ pores. This fungus also is known from Malawi and Tunisia, but these isolates are considered to represent a separate population.

Preussia minimoides was described by Ahmed and Cain (1972) as *Sporormiella minimoides*, from Canada and Mexico, but subsequently was reported from East Africa (Khan and Cain 1979) and Spain (Valldosera and Guarro 1990). The original collections were from dung of mammals but isolations were obtained from arid soils from both Morocco and Namibia. This is the first record from Egypt and only the third from soil, with all such isolations being from Africa.

Phoma exigua is usually recorded as a wound parasite or leaf spot. Several isolates have been obtained from underground tubers but the fungus also has a wide distribution in soil itself (Domsch *et al.*, 1980). The identification of soil isolates of *Phoma* is difficult as most of the taxonomy of the genus is related to the host plant. Many of the previous isolates of this species have been from temperate latitudes although it has been recorded from both India and Libya.

Most of the other records represent widely distributed soil fungi, occurring in temperate as well as tropical latitudes. Several of the taxa probably represent new records for Egypt, which is not surprising as very little work has been done on terricolous fungi in that country.

Acknowledgements
We thank Alan F. Hollett of the Egyptian Department, Royal Ontario Museum, for collecting the soil samples during his field work for the Dakhleh Oasis Project in Dakhleh Oasis during winter and spring, 1987. Our appreciation also is extended to Dr. C.S. Churcher, Department of Zoology, University of Toronto for his interest and helpful comments; and to Dr. S. Udagawa, Nodai Research Institute, Tokyo University of Agiculture for assistance with several identifications.

This research was supported by grants from the Natural Sciences and Engineering Research Council, National Research Council of Canada.

Addresses for Authors
John C. Krug: Department of Botany, University of Toronto, 25 Willcocks Street, Toronto, Ontario, Canada M5S 3B2 *and* Centre for Biodiversity and Conservation Biology, Royal Ontario Museum, 100 Queen's Park, Toronto, Ontario, Canada M5S 2C6.
R. Shah Khan: Department of Botany, University of Toronto, 25 Willcocks Street, Toronto, Ontario, Canada M5S 3B2. *Present address*: Department of Zoology, University of Toronto, 25 Harbord Street, Toronto, Ontario, Canada M5S 3G5.

REFERENCES

Ahmed, I. and R.F. Cain. 1972. Revision of the genera *Sporormia* and *Sporormiella*. Canadian Journal of Botany **50**: 419–477.

Arx, J.A. von. 1982. A key to the species of *Gelasinospora*. *Persoonia* **11**: 443–449.

Brummelen, J. van. 1967. A world-monograph of the genera *Ascobolus* and *Saccobolus* (Ascomycetes, Pezizales). *Persoonia* **1** (Supplement): 1–260.

Brummelen, J. van and F. Candoussau. 1981. *Ascobolus xylophilus* redescribed from France with remarks on its taxonomic position. *Persoonia* **11**: 377–394.

Cailleux, R. 1971. Recherches sur la Mycoflore coprophile Centrafricaine. Les genres *Sordaria, Gelasinospora, Bombardia* (Biologie, Morphologie, Systématique); Écologie. Bulletin trimestriel de la Société Mycologique de France **87**: 461–567.

Domsch, K.H., W. Gams and T.-H. Anderson. 1980. *Compendium of soil fungi, I.* New York: Academic Press, 859p.

Faurel, L. and G. Schotter. 1964a. Notes Mycologiques, II. Quelques champignons coprophiles des environs d'Alger. *Revue de Mycologie* (Paris) **29**: 267–283.

Faurel, L. and G. Schotter. 1964b. Notes Mycologiques, III. Quelques champignons coprophiles des environs du Sud-algérois. *Revue de Mycologie* (Paris) **29**: 284–295.

Faurel, L. and G. Schotter. 1965a. Notes Mycologiques, IV. Champignons coprophiles du Sahara central et notamment de la Tefedest. *Revue de Mycologie* (Paris) **30**: 141–165.

Faurel, L. and G. Schotter. 1965b. Notes Mycologiques, V. Champignons coprophiles du Tibesti. *Revue de Mycologie* (Paris) **30**: 330–351.

Khan, R.S. and R.F. Cain. 1979. The genera *Sporormiella* and *Sporormia* in east Africa. *Canadian Journal of Botany* **57**: 1174–1186.

Khan, R.S. and J.C. Krug. 1994. A synopsis of the coprophilous Ascomycetes of East Africa, 755–772. *In* J.H. Seyani and A.C. Chikuni, eds, *Proceedings of the XIIIth Plenary Meeting of AETFAT, Zomba, Malawi, 2–11 April, 1991 vol.* **1**.

Krug, J.C. and R.S Jeng. 1999. *Aporospora*, a new genus of terricolous Ascomycetes. *Mycoscience* **40**: (In press).

Krug, J.C., R.S. Khan and R.S. Jeng. 1994. A new species of *Gelasinospora* with multiple germ pores. *Mycologia* **86**: 250–253.

Krug, J.C., R.S. Khan and S. Udagawa. 1994. A reappraisal of *Areolospora bosensis*. *Mycologia* **86**: 581–585.

Malloch, D. 1981. *Moulds: their isolation, cultivation and identification.* Toronto: University of Toronto Press, 97p.

Seaver, F.J. 1911. Studies in Colorado fungi – I. Discomycetes. *Mycologia* **3**: 57–66.

Valldosera, M. and J. Guarro. 1990. Estudios sobre hongos coprófilos aislados en España. XV. El género *Preussia (Sporormiella). Boletin Sociedad Micologica de Madrid* **14**: 81–94.

Warcup, J.H. 1950. The soil-plate method for isolation of fungi from soil. *Nature* **166**: 117–118.

Wicklow, D.T. and D.M. Wilson. 1990. *Paecilomyces lilacinus*, a colonist of *Aspergillus flavus* sclerotia buried in soil in Illinois and Georgia. *Mycologia 82: 393–395*.

4

FLORA, VEGETATION AND PALAEOBOTANY
OF THE DAKHLEH OASIS

J. C. Ritchie

INTRODUCTION

The primary aim of the botanical part of the Dakhleh Oasis Project was to reconstruct the past vegetation and environment, on the basis of plant macrofossil and pollen data. However, until 1996, no Holocene or other Quaternary sediments had been discovered that contain adequately preserved remains. As others have found elsewhere in this hyperarid core of the Sahara, the prevailing processes of deflation, wind-scour and desiccation appear to have removed and degraded unconsolidated, potentially fossiliferous sediments. Our investigations at Dakhleh, and those of colleagues at adjacent archaeological sites in the eastern Sahara (Wendorf and Hassan 1980; Wendorf and Schild 1980), have shown that playas and yardangs, the most common types of water-laid deposits in the area are devoid of adequately preserved pollen. Recent findings from sites in the northern Sudan suggest that primary lacustrine sediments that have remained buried and moist will yield a reliable pollen record, but it appears that such a geomorphological circumstance is rare (Haynes 1987; Haynes *et al.* 1979, 1989; Ritchie *et al.* 1985). Indeed, until the preliminary analyses of these recent discoveries came to light, the Quaternary vegetational history of the eastern Sahara was based entirely on indirect, albeit well-informed speculation, "since there are virtually no factual data available regarding plant species present in the past" (Wickens 1982, 31).

Despite the failure to find suitable sediments for biostratigraphic analyses (and the search continues), useful botanical data have been collected. They are reported here under the headings of Modern Flora and Vegetation, and Modern Pollen Deposition. Both topics, besides their intrinsic interest, are pertinent to the interpretation of fossil pollen data from desert environments. The former is an amplification of an earlier, preliminary account (Ritchie 1980) and the latter is a summary version of an article addressed to a more specialised, palynological readership (Ritchie 1986). The paper concludes with a brief review of recent evidence for Holocene vegetation change in the eastern Sahara, and an Appendix presenting the record of plant remains found in archaeological and other samples collected by members of the project.

MODERN FLORA AND VEGETATION

Modern Flora

The vascular plant flora of the oasis is meagre, due no doubt to the hyperarid climate of the region and the highly specialized soil conditions produced in cultivated areas. In particular the highly salinised and erratically watered soils in the precincts of cultivation provide an environment within the tolerance of relatively few plants. In addition, populations of native species, particularly woody taxa, have been severely depleted by exploitation, particularly for firewood.

So far I have recorded 67 taxa of native or naturalised species, and in addition, of course, there is a set of cultivars that make up most of the green cover of the settled parts of the oasis.

The Dakhleh flora is tentatively grouped by phytogeographical elements in Table 4.1, but one should view such grouping with caution. Quézel (1978, 481) provides a comprehensive review of African phytogeography, and

'Reports from the Survey of Dakhleh Oasis, Western Desert of Egypt, 1977–1987', edited by C.S. Churcher and A.J. Mills. Dakhleh Oasis Project: Monograph 2. Oxbow Monograph 99.

makes the point that it is difficult to assign Saharan taxa to particular geographical elements because of "...the large climatic fluctuations that took place in the Sahara during the entire Quaternary ... and brought with them vast floristic mixing". I have grouped the flora into the broad geographical categories recognized by the main authorities on the region (see Lebrun 1976, 1977, 1979; Ozenda 1983; Quézel 1978; Täckholm 1974; Wickens 1976). Saharo-Arabian taxa have their main centre of distribution in the Sahara and extend eastward into the Arabian desert; two sub-categories of this group have extensions northward into the Mediterranean in one case and southward into the Sahelian zone in the other. A small group is centred on the Mediterranean with extensions into the Sahara. The remainder are cosmopolitan, Saharan endemics, weeds, or naturalised introductions. A rough numerical breakdown of these groups is given in Table 4.1.

The following list describes the 67 species found in Dakhleh Oasis. Taxa in brackets are those reported for the oasis but which I have so far failed to find. I am certain that the list is not complete, particularly in such families as Cruciferae and Compositae and I anticipate that up to 25 species will be added by future investigators. My primary aim, of course, has been palaeoecological and not floristic. The species are described in alphabetical order and I have abstracted the distribution notes from the floristic sources cited above; habitat and other notes have been culled from my field observations and the literature. I have not attempted a comprehensive review of weed species, but interested readers can find detailed treatments in Kosinova (1975) and Boulos and el-Hadidi (1984). Zahran and Willis' (1992) recent book on the vegetation of Egypt provides full accounts of the flora and vegetation of all the oases, including Dakhleh, with a comprehensive bibliography, and the recent report of Kehl and Bornhamm (1993) is accompanied by a vegetation map of southwestern Egypt, including the Dakhleh and Kharga oases.

Table 4.1. Phytogeographical elements in the native and naturalised flora of Dakhleh Oasis: an approximate quantitative summary by floral geographic regions.

Grouping	No. of Taxa	% of Flora
1. Saharo-Arabian	17	24
2. Saharo-Arabian with Mediterranean extensions	2	3
3. Saharo-Arabian with Sahelian extensions	7	10
4. Mediterranean with Saharan extensions	3	4
5. Tropical with Saharan extensions	9	13
6. Saharan endemic	1	1
7. Cosmopolitan	22	31
8. Weeds & naturalised introductions	10+	14
TOTALS	71+	100%

Acacia is a large genus of trees and shrubs which is represented in North Africa by about a dozen species and varieties, depending on which authority is followed. The taxa are differentiated both geographically and ecologically, and as the polyad pollen grains are very large and therefore not dispersed over large distances, this genus is of particular value and interest to palynologists. Not all species can be distinguished palynologically but several groups can be separated that yield useful palaeoecological insights (Bonnefille and Riollet 1980; Guinet and Lugardon 1976). Two species are common in Dakhleh and one is rare.

1. *Acacia raddiana* Savi (= *A. tortilis partim*) forms large trees (Fig. 4.1) locally, where the ground water is high, and in the absence of human depredations.
2. *Acacia nilotica* (L.) Willd. ex Del. is the common small tree along irrigation ditches and at the margins of cultivations.
3. *Acacia ehrenbergiana* Haynes is a shrubby taxon, rare in Dakhleh where it is near its northern limit. The last two species have tropical centres with extensions north into the Sahara.
4. *Aerva javanica* (Burm. f.) Spreng. (Amaranthaceae) is a common desert semi-shrub in silty sands. It is a Saharo-Arabian taxon with extensions into tropical Africa and is of particular interest to palaeoecologists because its pollen, unusually in this family, can be distinguished specifically.
5. *Alhagi maurorum* Medic. is a Saharo-Arabian taxon, very common in the eastern Sahara; it is a low spiny shrub that spreads actively into abandoned cultivation and also forms minor dunes in shallow sand expanses (Fig. 4.2).
6. *Ammania auriculata* (Chenopodiaceae) is a common desert shrub found in wadi channels and stony depressions. I have found it at only three localities in Dakhleh, all in the vicinity of Maohoub.

Asphodelus sp. This genus has a Mediterranean centre of distribution, with extensions into the Sahara. The specimen collected was in vegetative condition and could not be identified to species at The Natural History Museum, London, but is probably

7. *A. fistulosus*, noted by Kosinova (1975) as a characteristic weed of winter crops in Dakhleh and Kharga oases.
8. (*Balanites aegyptiaca* Del.) is an important tree, significant also because its pollen is distinguishable and has been recorded in Holocene sediments from the Sahara (Maley 1981; Ritchie *et al.* 1985). It has a tropical centre of distribution, being a Sahelian species extending into the Sahara. Täckholm (1974) recorded this species in Dakhleh.
9. *Boerhavia coccinea* Mill. is a common Saharan annual, but recorded only once by me in Dakhleh, in an abandoned field near Maohoub.
10. *Brassica nigra* (L.) Koch. is a widespread, cosmopolitan weed, apparently naturalised in the oasis.
11. *Calligonum comosum* Her. is a common Saharan shrub, but rare in Dakhleh. It occurs on stony, alluvial soils.
12. *Calotropis procera* Ait. (Asclepiadaceae) is a common shrubby member of the milkweed family found scattered throughout the oasis and often within settlements. It

Fig. 4.1. A grove of mature Acacia raddiana *trees in Dakhleh Oasis.*

Fig. 4.2. Alhagi maurorum *forms low coppice dunes. A line of* Acacia *trees is visible in the background.*

survives possibly because it is toxic to cattle. It is a tropical species with northern extensions into the Sahara.

13. *Capparis aegyptia* Lam. (Capparidaeceae) is a Saharo-Mediterranean low shrub, recorded by me only twice in the oasis.

14. *Capparis decidua* (Forssk.) Edgew. is a tall shrub or tree (*tondob*) with a widespread distribution in the Saharo-Arabian and Sahelian zones, often found as individual specimens many kilometres from any other plants, presumably supported by local pockets of ground water accessible to its long root system. Only one specimen has been reported in the Dakhleh area, south of Teneida, but beyond the oasis depression. In common with other important genera in its family (*Boscia, Maerua, Cadaba*), *Capparis* is of interest to the palaeoecologist as its pollen is distinguishable at the generic level.

15. (*Cardiospermum halicacabum* [L.]) has not been found, but it is reported in Dakhleh by Täckholm (1974).

16. *Cassia italica* (Miller) Lam. is a widespread shrub of the tropical Sahelian element with extensions into the Sahara. It is common in Dakhleh at margins of irrigated fields.

17. *Chenopodium album* L., a common perennial on saline flats, is present throughout the oasis.

18. *Citrullus colocynthis* (L.) Schrad. is a Saharan species, common as a weed in cultivated areas.

19. *Convolvulus arvensis* L. is a cosmopolitan creeper, apparently naturalised in Dakhleh.

20. *Corchorus olitorius* L. is a weedy annual that is sometimes cultivated for its fibres, though not in Dakhleh. It is a widespread, tropical species.

21. *Cornulaca monacantha* Del. is an important shrub member of desert and steppe vegetation throughout North Africa, Arabian zones and Afghanistan. It forms miniature dunes in the central Saharan region, forming communities in flat, low areas after episodic rains. During dry periods the plant dries up but persists, retaining the low dune features for many years. Such desiccated specimens were recorded in shallow pans and washes on top of the Libyan Escarpment to the north of Dakhleh.

22. *Cyperus laevigatus* L. is an important, widespread tropical sedge, characteristic of wet, saline habitats. It is common along irrigation ditches throughout the oasis.

23. *Desmostachya bipinnata* (L.) Stapf is one of the most important desert grasses of the Sahara. It spreads by long, deep rhizomes (Fig. 4.3) both laterally and vertically. It is particularly common in flat expanses of shallow sand over silty soil with a high water-table in areas southeast from Mut (Fig. 4.4), where it forms extensive miniature dunes (see also Kleindienst et al., Chapter 1, this volume, Figs 1.50, Top & 1.51, Top).

24. *Dichanthium annulatum* (Forssk.) Stapf is a perennial grass, local in Dakhleh in sand dune areas. It is a Saharo-Arabian species with tropical extensions.

25. *Echinochloa crus-galli* (L.) P. Beauv. is a common weedy grass around settlements and fields.

26. *Emex spinosus* (L.) Campd. is a naturalised weed species, associated with cultivation.

27. *Erodium neuradifolium* Del. is a Saharan species, locally common in the oasis on marginal dune soils.

28. *Erucaria pinnata* (Viv.) Täckh. et Boulos is a weedy, Saharan species, locally common on sandy soils.

29. *Euphorbia peplus* L. is a cosmopolitan weedy herb of local occurrence in Dakhleh.

30. *Fagonia arabica* L. is locally common throughout the oasis; this spiny low shrub occurs on heavy textured silty soils. It is an eastern Saharo-Arabian species, and belongs to a small group of shrubs and herbs that establish quickly after episodic rains and then persist during dry periods as dried, dead remnants, sometimes retaining seed (Haynes 1983).

31. *Gnaphalium luteo-album* L. is a common weed, associated with cultivation.

32. *Hammada elegans* (Bunge) Botsch. is a common halo-phytic perennial herb, confined to wet saline soils. It is a Saharan species.

33. *Haplophyllum tuberculatum* (Forssk.) A. Juss. is a Saharan species, found by me at one site near Mut, in sandy soil at the margin of an abandoned field.

34. *Hibiscus trionum* L. One specimen of this weed species was observed by me near Bashendi.

35. *Hyoscyamus muticus* L. is a weedy Saharan species, common near cultivation and villages.

36. *Hyphaene thebaica* (L.) Mart. is reported in the oasis by members of the project (living and dead clumps northwest

Fig. 4.3. Desmostachya bipinnata *spreads by underground rhizomes.*

Fig. 4.4. Desmostachya bipinnata *may form low dunes in areas with a high water table, as in this area immediately south of Sheikh Mabrouk. Living clumps show leaves and seed heads; dead clumps have been sheared by wind driven sand.*

of Bashendi), but I have not seen it in Dakhleh. This African tropical and subtropical palm species is scattered in the eastern Sahara and has been introduced in many localities from early times.

37. *Imperata cylindrica* (L.) Beauv., common along irrigation ditches in sandy soils, and often forming an imposing palisade, is the true Halfa grass, sometimes confused in name and identity with *Desmostachya* sp. It is a cosmopolitan species.

38. *Indigofera hochstetteri* Baker (Leguminosae). This annual member of a large Saharan genus is locally common in sandy soils near Mut; its main area of distribution is Soudanian-Sahelian with extensions into the Sahara.

39. *Lagonychium farctum* (Banks and Sol.) Bobr. is a common, low, spiny shrub with conspicuous dark brown woody legumes and commonly colonises abandoned and marginal dune areas. It is a Saharo-Arabian taxon.

40. *Maerua crassifolia* Forssk. is a tree or tall shrub. This tropical Sahelian-Saharan species grows often as isolated individuals on sand, apparently tapping some deep water-table. It produces small edible fruits and its pollen, abundantly produced, can be identified to genus. Its leaves are eaten by camels. A specimen occurs west of Maohoub.

41. *Malva parviflora* L. is a small annual of Mediterranean distribution, and is recorded once in abandoned cultivation south of Mut.

42. *Medicago polymorpha* L. is a common cosmopolitan weed associated with cultivation.

43. *Melilotus indica* (L.) All. is a common weed associated with cultivation.

44. *Paronychia arabica* L. A widespread Saharan species, locally common in sandy soils on the margins of cultivation in Dakhleh, this species has been recorded from pollen in both Holocene sediments and modern samples (see below).

45. *Phoenix dactylifera* is the familiar date palm, abundantly cultivated throughout the oasis for its high quality fruit; introduced at some unknown but distant time past.

46. *Phragmites australis* (Cav.) Trin. ex Steud. is a common, highly variable grass that forms dense cover at springs and along large irrigation ditches, and whose aggressive rhizomes even spread out into marginal dune sands. It is a cosmopolitan species par excellence.

47. *Polygonum lanigerum* R. Br. is a cosmopolitan weedy grass, common in rice cultivation.

48. *Polypogon* sp. A specimen of this weedy grass genus was collected in the winter of 1978 but could not be identified to species because of the absence of reproductive structures.

49. *Portulaca oleraceae* L. is a common, cosmopolitan, annual weed, locally abundant near fields and villages.

50. *Potamogeton crispus* L. is locally common as a weedy aquatic in larger irrigation ditches.

51. *Rumex aegyptiacus* L. One specimen was found by me along an irrigation ditch. It appears to be endemic to Egypt.

52. *Rumex dentatus* L. occurs locally in abandoned sandy fields. This cosmopolitan species is widely naturalised.

53. *Salicornia fruticosa* (L.) L. This Saharo-Arabian species is a locally common halophytic perennial confined to poorly drained, saline soils.

54. *Salix subserrata* Willd. This tropical species extends into the Sahara at many localities, apparently having been widely introduced. Only one small stand was originally seen in Dakhleh; since 1988 it has been planted near water channels in the Balat-Teneida area and elsewhere.

55. *Salsola baryosma* (Schult.) Dandy is a common desert shrub. This tropical species extends north into the Sahara, occupying sandy soils with relatively high water-tables and locally saline conditions.

56. *Salvadora persica* L. This tropical tree has been found at only one station in Dakhleh (Fig. 4.5), near Bashendi, but it is scattered throughout the tropical Sahelian zone, extending into the Sahara and eastward into Arabia, Iran and India. Its old woody stems are collected for firewood, the young shoots are reported to serve as toothbrushes, the leaves are favoured by camels, and the fruits are collected for human consumption. It produces relatively abundant pollen, and the small grains are well dispersed and regularly

Fig. 4.5. Salvadora persica *is a rare tree in Dakhleh Oasis. This specimen is found near Bashendi and shows roots exposed by migrating sand.*

Fig. 4.6. Zygophyllum album *may form dense stands on abandoned cultivated areas where the salinity is high, as in the general vicinity of Teneida.*

recorded in both modern and fossil samples. Thus it serves as an effective palaeoecological indicator.

57. *Saponaria vaccaria* L. is an infrequent plant in Dakhleh. It is a cosmopolitan herb of disturbed, sandy soils.

58. *Schouwia thebaica.* A Saharo-Arabian perennial common in the deserts of the Negev and Arabia, the only specimen from the oasis was a dead relic of some past episode of rainfall, collected from the crest of Gebel Edmonstone. The plant had retained seed, presumably viable, in the characteristic way of such desert species adapted to a climate of sporadic rainfall in an otherwise arid regime. Other specimens have been seen by members of the project in the Wadi el-Tawil, on the Libyan Plateau above the Escarpment, between Balat and Teneida, near Bab el Jasmund above Qasr, and north of Bashendi.

59. *Scirpus tuberosus* Desf. is a common Saharan rush, abundant in the oasis along irrigation channels and at the margins of ponds and artificial lakes.

60. *Stellaria media* (L.) Vill. is a cosmopolitan weed species, common in waste land near villages and cultivation.

61. *Stipagrostis scoparia* (Trin. et Rupr.) De Winter. This species is locally common in the eastern Sahara, forming miniature dunes in areas with periodic rainfall or moderately high, though local, water-tables. I found only one patch in Dakhleh, in a dune area southeast of Mut.

62. *Sueda vermiculata* Forssk. A common Saharan halophytic shrub, found only locally here, in damp saline soils adjacent to abandoned cultivation.

63. *Tamarix aphylla* (L.) Karst. I found a single specimen of this small tree at the oasis, although it is possible that it was previously overlooked by confusing it with the following taxon. It is a Saharan species, widespread and highly drought resistant.

64. *Tamarix nilotica* (Ehren.) Bge. is a small tree, often of shrub size, effective in stabilizing mobile sand into dunes, and the chief species to form 'coppice dunes'. Its remarkable halophytic adaptations are well known. It is a widespread Saharan species with extensions into the Mediterranean region.

65. *Typha australis* Schum. et Thonn. An abundant semi-aquatic, cosmopolitan plant, it forms dense stands in older, larger irrigation ditches, at spring mounds, and at the margins of ponds.

66. *Ziziphus spina-christi* (L.) Willd. A Saharan tree, local in the oasis, between Qasr and Maohoub, but scattered throughout the Eastern Desert.

67. *Zygophyllum album* L. is a succulent semi-shrub. This Saharan endemic forms locally dense communities (Fig. 4.6) on abandoned cultivation, tolerant of apparently high salinity levels.

Modern Vegetation

Extensive uplands of rock outcrop, dunes and sand sheet are essentially plantless (the 'absolute desert' of White 1983), due no doubt to the lack of rainfall or the low moisture retaining capacity of the soils. The vegetation that does occur is limited in both space and time by the extreme aridity and the high variability of the precipitation. Recent tracking of storms by satellite (Haynes 1983; Haynes *et al.* 1987) has amplified the early records showing that rainstorms lasting 1 to 3 days can occur in the region, with completely dry intervening periods of one or two decades (Beadnell 1909; Goudie and Wilkinson 1977). Two main categories of vegetational response characterise such a regime and determine the structure and occurrence of vegetation.

One response is the evolution in certain desert plants of the capacity "to regulate the timing of seed dispersal and germination within a given year, and to spread the germination of one year's seed production over a number of years following the death of the mother plant" (Ellner and Shmida 1981, 138). A large proportion of the annual and perennial species that dominate the Saharo-Arabian deserts display this effective adaptation to a very variable, arid climate (Stebbins 1971; Venables and Lawlor 1980; Zohary 1973). The second ecological response involves trees and shrubs with highly efficient root systems that can exploit localised, deep ground water sources.

The vegetational expression of these adaptations is the occurrence of scattered more or less permanent plant communities or individuals of trees and shrubs in topographic lows where, apparently, ground water is accessible, and transient communities of annuals and perennials flourish in wet episodes and either disappear or remain as dead skeletons in the intervening droughts. The former are highly fragmentary in Dakhleh, probably in part because of human exploitation of the wood and in part because of the extreme aridity of the area. They represent the limit of the tropical savannah vegetation, that becomes continuous in areas to the south with annual precipitation >50 mm (White 1983; Wickens 1976). Characteristic species are various *Acacia* species, *Capparis decidua*, *Maerua crassifolea*, *Salvadora persica*, *Zizyphus spinichristi*, *Calotropis procera* and *Tamarix* species.

The transient communities can be found in Dakhleh Oasis in both 'natural' environments and those influenced by cultural activities. Observations made during the first field season of remnant communities and associated soils on the Libyan Plateau, have been amplified in subsequent seasons. Depressions varying in size from 20–50 m in diameter to a few hectares were seen on the plateau immediately north of the escarpment with many dried plants of *Fagonia arabica*, *Cornulaca monacantha* and *Desmostachya bipinnata*. Elsewhere patches of dried *Stipagrostis* (sp. indet.) have been noted forming miniature dunes in shallow sand sheets over silty soil. Plant skeletons are common on the escarpment plateau north of the oasis, confined to dry depressions that show evidence of transient ponding. It is likely that these events were related to intense storms, possibly including that of December, 1977 which caused germination and temporary establishment of plants in the Kiseiba-Nabta area 250 km south of Dakhleh

(Haynes *et al.* 1987). Similar responses to soil moisture increases are seen in the extensive flat areas southeast of Mut where adjacent well drilling has, apparently, raised the water-table. Extensive flat areas are occupied by a relatively continuous community dominated by *Desmostachya bipinnata* and *Alhagi maurorum* (Fig. 4.7).

It is likely that a slight change in climate causing more frequent rainstorms and a measurable annual precipitation of >25 mm might produce extensive vegetated tracts in low situations in and around Dakhleh Oasis, similar in plant community structure and composition to what is found today, for example in the western Omdurman Desert (Kassas 1956).

MODERN POLLEN DEPOSITION

A survey of modern pollen spectra in Dakhleh was undertaken to provide data essential to adequate interpretation of any fossil spectra that might be produced. A detailed report has been published separately (Ritchie 1986) where interested readers can find the particulars of methods, results and conclusions.

Pollen analysis in desert environments involves several acute difficulties. I have already referred to the problem of poorly preserved grains in most desert sediments, due apparently to excessive oxidation. But when adequate spectra are available, from either modern or fossil samples, their interpretation poses difficulties. As Maley (1981), Schulz (1976) and Van Campo (1975) have shown from sites elsewhere in the Sahara, that with few exceptions the plants that dominate the local and regional vegetation make up a very small proportion, usually less than 10%, of the total pollen sum. The reason is that most of these taxa either produce small amounts of pollen and/or the pollen grains are large and are dispersed very small distances from the parent plant. By contrast, the taxa that dominate the pollen spectra (grasses, sedges, Chenopodiaceae and Amaranthaceae) produce copious pollen usually adapted to dispersal over long distances.

In Dakhleh Oasis the indigenous taxa directly indicative of desert vegetation (*Acacia, Tamarix, Calligonum, Fagonia, Maerua* and *Paronychia*) constitute <10% of the pollen sum while the ubiquitous taxa (Chenopodiaceae-Amaranthaceae, Gramineae, Cyperaceae, etc.) comprise >50%. The influences of cultivation are registered variably in the spectra, with small proportions of palm and olive pollen and large percentages of the relatively recently introduced trees *Casuarina* and *Eucalyptus*. These results, corroborative of earlier investigations elsewhere, are of value when Holocene and older spectra are interpreted.

Fig. 4.7. Continuous cover of Desmostachya bipinnata *and* Alhagi maurorum *over sand sheets or low dune fields in the general vicinity of Teneida.*

PALAEOECOLOGY

While lacustrine, playa, and sand sheet sediments have provided evidence of past Holocene environments in the

Dakhleh region (Brookes 1989; Kröpelin 1993), we still lack direct biostratigraphic data from the oasis. However, recent finds from adjacent areas of the eastern Sahara have provided palaeoenvironmental reconstructions that might have been regional in extent.

In particular, several lake basins in northwest Sudan and adjacent southern Egypt have been investigated, with well preserved Holocene sediments of finely laminated sapropels, marls, and diatomites, reported by Haynes (1987) Haynes *et al.* (1979, 1989), Pachur and Hoelzmann (1991) and others. These lacustrine sediments have been shown to contain abundant, excellently preserved pollen, and preliminary results from one of the sites (the Oyo Depression, roughly 700 km south-southwest of Dakhleh) provide the first secure evidence from the entire eastern Sahara for vegetational and climatic change (Ritchie 1994; Ritchie *et al.* 1985).

One of the sites, in Selima Oasis, indicates a humid period in the early Holocene (10,000 to 8,500 years BP) followed by a brief dry episode and a second humid period from 8,500 to roughly 4,500 years BP (Haynes *et al.* 1989). At all these sites the sedimentological evidence suggests clearly that deep and, in some cases, extensive lakes must have occupied these depressions; and the pollen evidence suggests that a woodland savanna vegetation covered the adjacent land surfaces, analogous floristically to communities found today in such areas as central Sudan (Wickens 1982) and the Ennedi Massif in Chad (Gillet 1968). Palaeoclimatic reconstructions based on these findings are difficult, because, as today, it is not always possible to separate the role of ground water, in controlling both the extent of vegetation cover and the presence of water bodies, from the influence of precipitation. Further, Maley (1981) has demonstrated that precipitation regimes of different origins and types can be suggested from different sedimentological and biostratigraphic data.

Recent investigations of radiocarbon-dated charcoal samples from the eastern Sahara provide important corroboration of the palynological findings from the lacustrine sites referred to above, demonstrating in particular that many of the Sahelian and Soudanian woody taxa recorded in the pollen record were present locally (Neumann 1989, 1991).

In summary, the growing body of palaeobotanical data from sites surrounding Dakhleh, primarily to the south, indicates that, during the period between 9,000 and 5,000 radiocarbon years BP, wooded savannas and shrubby desert communities occupied landforms with raised water tables. Palaeoenvironmental inferences from other lines of evidence, particularly limnological, that deep, ground-water-supported lakes occurred in scattered localities, and faunal and archaeological evidence (Haynes and Mead 1987; Kröpelin and Soulié-Märsche 1991; Street-Perrott and Perrott 1993), support the notion that a less arid climate prevailed. Recently Petit-Maire *et al.* (1993) have published an excellent 1:5,000,000 map summarizing all known palaeogeographic evidence for the Saharan Holo-cene. The broad agreement of these interpretations with palaeoclimatic simulations based on GCM output (COHMAP Members 1988), supports the Milankovitch-based propositions of an intensified African monsoon in response to seasonal shifts of solar radiation.

Acknowledgements
I am most grateful to Mr. A.J. Mills for inviting me to join this project, and for his continued support and encouragement. The following colleagues have provided invaluable advice and assistance in the field or laboratory: Drs. M. Van Campo, Ian Brookes, C.S. Churcher, C.V. Haynes, Jean Maley and N.K.B. Robson. I am particularly indebted to Dr. Churcher for his constructive and careful editorial contributions.

Address for Author
J.C. Ritchie, Department of Botany, University of Toronto, Scarborough, Ontario, CANADA M1C 1A4 *and* 'Pebbledash Cottage', Corfe, Taunton, Somerset, ENGLAND TA3 7AJ for all correspondence. E-mail: jcr@eclipse.co.uk

REFERENCES

Beadnell, H.J.L. 1909. *An Egyptian oasis.* London, John Murray, 248p.

Bonnefille, R. and G. Riollet. 1980. *Pollens des savanes d'Afrique orientale.* Paris, Centre Nationale de la Recherche Scientifique, 140p.

Boulos, L. and M.N. el-Hadidi. 1984. *The weed flora of Egypt.* Cairo, The American University in Cairo Press, 178p.

Brookes, I.A. 1989. Early Holocene basinal sediments of the Dahhleh Oasis region, south central Egypt. *Quaternary Research* **32**: 139–152.

COHMAP Members. 1988. Climatic changes of the last 18,000 years: observations and model simulations. *Science* **241**: 1043–1052.

Ellner, S. and A. Shmida. 1981. Why are adaptations for long-range seed dispersal rare in desert plants? *Oecologia* **51**: 133–144.

Gillet, H. 1968. Le peuplement végétal du massif de l'Ennedi (Tchad). *Mémoires du Muséum national d'histoire naturelle, série B (Botanie)* **7**: 1–206.

Goudie, A. and J. Wilkinson. 1977. *The warm desert environment.* Cambridge, Cambridge University Press, 88p.

Guinet, P. and B. Lugardon. 1976. Diversité des structures de l'exine dans le genre *Acacia* (Mimosaceae). *Pollen et Spores* **18**: 483–511.

Haynes, C.V. 1983. Quaternary studies, Western Desert, Egypt and Sudan, 1975–1978. *National Geographic Society Research Reports* **15**: 257–293.

Haynes, C.V. 1987. Holocene migration rates of the Sudano-Sahelian wetting front, Arba'in Desert, eastern Sahara, 69–84. *In* Close, A.E., ed., *Prehistory of arid North Africa: essays in honor of Fred Wendorf.* Dallas, Southern Methodist University Press, 347p.

Haynes, C.V., P.J. Mehringer Jr. and S.A. Zaghloul. 1979. Pluvial lakes of northwest Sudan. *Geographical Journal* **145**: 437–445.

Haynes, C.V. Jr. and A.R. Mead. 1987. Radiocarbon dating and paleoclimatic significance of subfossil *Limicolaria* in north-western Sudan. *Quaternary Research* **28**: 86–99.

Haynes, C.V. Jr., P.J. Mehringer Jr., D.L. Johnson, H. Haas, A.B. Muller, El S. Zaghloul, A. Swedan and T.A. Wyerman. 1987. Evidence for the First Nuclear-age recharge of shallow ground-water, Arba'in Desert, Egypt. *National Geographic Research* **3**: 431–438.

Haynes, C.V., C.H. Eyles, L.A. Pavlish, J.C. Ritchie and M. Rybak. 1989. Holocene palaeoecology of the eastern Sahara: Selima Oasis. *Quaternary Science Reviews* **8**: 109–136.

Kassas, M. 1956. Landforms and plant cover in the Omdurman Desert, Sudan. *Bulletin de la Société géographique d'Egypte* **24**: 43–58.

Kehl, H. and R. Bornkamm. 1993. Landscape ecology and vegetation units of the Western Desert of Egypt. *Catena Supplement* **26**: 155–178.

Kleindienst, M.R., C.S. Churcher, M.M.A. McDonald and H.P. Schwarcz. This volume, Chapter 1. Geography, Geology, Geochronology and Geoarchaeology of the Dakhleh Oasis Region: An interim report, 1–54.

Kosinova, J. 1975. Weed communities of winter crop in Egypt. *Preslia* **47**: 58–74.

Kröpelin, S. 1993. Geomorphology, Landscape Evolution and Paleoclimates of Southwest Egypt. *Catena Supplement* **26**: 31–65.

Kröpelin, S. and I. Soulié-Märsche. 1991. Charophyte remains from Wadi Howar as evidence for deep Mid-Holocene lakes in the eastern Sahara or northwest Sudan. *Quaternary Research* **36**: 210–223.

Lebrun, J.-P. 1976. *Catalogue des plantes vasculaires du Niger. Etude Botanique 3.* Institut d'Elevage et de Médecine vétérinaire des Pays tropicaux, Maisons Alfort, 433p.

Lebrun, J.-P. 1977. *Eléments pour un atlas des plantes vasculaires de l'Afrique seché, vol. 1. Etude Botanique 4.* Institut d'Elevage et de Médecine vétérinaire des Pays tropicaux, Maisons Alfort, 259p.

Lebrun, J.-P. 1979. *Eléments pour un atlas des plantes vasculaires de l'Afrique seché, vol. 2. Etude Botanique 6.* Institut d'Elevage et de Médecine vétérinaire des Pays tropicaux, Maisons Alfort, 254p.

Maley, J. 1981. Etudes palynologiques dans le bassin du Tchad et paléoclimatologie de l'Afrique nord-tropicale de 30,000 ans a l'époque actuelle. *Travaux et documents de l'Office de la recherche scientifique et technique outre-mer,* no. 129, Paris, 1–586.

Neumann, K. 1989. Holocene vegetation of the eastern Sahara – charcoal from prehistoric sites. *African Archaeological Review* **7**: 97–116.

Neumann, K. 1991. In search for the green Sahara: palynology and botanical macro-remains. *Palaeoecology of Africa and the surrounding islands* **22**: 201–212.

Ozenda, P. 1983. *Flore du Sahara, edit. 2.* Paris, Centre National de la Recherche Scientifique, 622p.

Pachur, H.-J. and P. Hoelzmann. 1991. Palaeoclimatic implications of Late Quaternary lacustrine sediments in western Nubia, Sudan. *Quaternary Research* **36**: 257–276.

Petit-Maire, N., N. Page and J. Marchand. 1993. The Sahara in the Holocene: map at 1:5,000,000. *UNESCO-CGMW Publication* 252, Aix-en-Provence.

Quézel, P. 1978. Analysis of the flora of Mediterranean and Saharan Africa. *Annals of the Missouri Botanical Garden* **65** (2): 479–534.

Renfrew, J.M. 1973. *Palaeoethnobotany: the prehistoric food plants of the Near East and Europe.* New York, Columbia University Press, 248p.

Ritchie, J.C. 1980. Preliminary observations on the botany of the Dakhleh Oasis. *Journal of the Society for the Study of Egyptian Antiquities* **10**: 397–422.

Ritchie, J.C. 1986. Modern pollen spectra from Dakhleh Oasis, Western Egyptian Desert. *Grana* **25**: 177–182.

Ritchie, J.C. 1994. Holocene pollen spectra from Oyo, northwestern Sudan: problems of interpretation in a hyperarid environment. *The Holocene* **4**: 9–15.

Ritchie, J.C., C.H. Eyles and C.V. Haynes. 1985. Sediment and pollen evidence for an early to mid-Holocene humid period in the eastern Sahara. *Nature* **314**: 352–355.

Schulz, E. 1976. Aktueller Pollenniederschlag in der zentralen Sahara und Interpretationsmöglichkeiten quartärer Pollenspektren. *Palaeoecology of Africa and the surrrounding islands* **9**: 8–14.

Stebbins, G.L. 1971. Adaptive radiation of reproductive characteristics in angiosperms. II. Seeds and seedlings. *Annual Review of Ecology and Systematics* **2**: 237–260.

Street-Perrott, F.A. and A. Perrott. 1993. Holocene vegetation, lake levels, and climate of Africa, 318–356. *In* Wright, H.E. Jr., J.E. Kutzbach, T. Webb III, W.F. Ruddiman, F.A. Street-Perrott and P.J. Bartlein (eds), *Global climates since the Last Glacial Maximum.* University of Minnesota Press, Minneapolis, 544p.

Täckholm, V. 1974. *Students' Flora of Egypt, edit. 2.* Cairo, Cairo University, 888p.

Van Campo, M. 1975. Pollen analyses in the Sahara, 45–64. *In* Wendorf, F. and A.E. Marks, eds., *Problems in prehistory: North Africa and the Levant.* Dallas, Southern Methodist University Press, 462p.

Venables, D.L. and L. Lawlor. 1980. Delayed germination and dispersal in desert annuals: escape in space and time. *Oecologia* **46**: 272–282.

Wendorf, F. and F. Hassan. 1980. Holocene ecology and prehistory in the Egyptian Sahara, 407–420. *In* Williams, M.A.J. and H. Faure, eds, *The Sahara and the Nile.* Rotterdam, Balkema Press, 607p.

Wendorf, F. and R. Schild. 1980. *Prehistory of the eastern Sahara.* New York, Academic Press, 414p.

White, F. 1983. *The vegetation of Africa - a descriptive memoir to accompany the Unesco/AETFAT/UNSO vegetation map of Africa.* Paris, United Nations Economic and Scientific Cooperative Organisation, 356p.

Wickens, G.E. 1976. *The flora of Jebel Marra (Sudan Republic) and its geographical affinities.* London, Her Majesty's Stationery Office, 368p.

Wickens, G.E. 1982. Palaeobotanical speculations and Quaternary environments in the Sudan, 23–50. *In* Williams, M.A.J. and D.A. Adamson, eds, *A land between two Niles.* Rotterdam, Balkema Press, 246p.

Zahran, M.A. and A.J. Willis. 1992. *The vegetation of Egypt.* London, Chapman and Hall, 432p.

Zohary, M. 1973. *Geobotanical foundations of the Middle East,* 2 vols. Berwyn, Pennsylvania, Swets North America, 762p.

APPENDIX A

Plant remains identified from site collections made by Dakhleh Oasis Project members.

Site: 30/405–M1–1/1
Under Body 2 (Dec. 3/80)
Myrtus sp. Many leaf and twig fragments. This taxon is absent from the modern flora.

Site: 31/405–L4–2
Temple infilling
Vitis vinifera. This sample contained 37.5 g. of carbonised grape pits. The identification was based on metric measurements obtained from Renfrew (1973). Although several of the pits fell into the *Vitis silvestris* range I would discount this identification as the pits were carbonised, and their morphology differed.
Triticum sp. (possibly *T. monocarpum*). This sample contains fragments from at least 5 grains.

Site: 32/390–D1–1
Roman Period Site (fill)
Phoenix dactylifera. This unit contained 8 uncharred date pits. Specimen (h) still has part of the shriveled fruit on it. Lengths and diameters (mm) are: (a) 16.5 × 8.4, (b) 19.5 × 7.5, (c) 18.8 × 7.7, (d) 15.0 × 8.85, (e) 19.5 × 8.1, (f) 18.3 × 8.1, (g) 20.0 × 7.3, and (h) 23.0 × 10.04: Max 23.0 – min 15.0 (mean 18.8) × max 10.0 – min 7.3 (mean 8.3); N = 8.
Olea europea. 1 uncarbonised olive stone. (a) 15.03 × 10.8 × 9.91 mm.

Site: 32/390–E1–1 Test 1
Near Oven 1. Level 1. Roman Period Site.
Tamarix sp. Large pieces of charcoal, total weight 260 g.

Site: 32/390–E1–1
Near Oven 2. Roman Period Site.
This sample contains some sediment and unidentified stems.

Site: 32/390–E1–1 Test 1
Around Oven 2/Storage Bin. Roman Period Site.
Tamarix sp. and *Salix* sp. charcoal.

Site: 32/390–E9–2/2
Roman Cemetery (fill)
Phoenix dactylifera. 11 uncharred and 9 charred date pits. Lengths and diameters (mm) are: (a) 21.4 × 7.15, (b) 24.8 × 9.43, (c) 15.36 × 7.28, (d) 20.43 × 9.3, (e) 20.05 × 8.6, (f) 21.45 × 7.25, (g) 15.35 × 9.6, (h) 15.31 × 7.8, (i) 16.0 × 8.4, (j) 17.0 × 7.45, and (k) 18.2 × 7.2: Max 24.8 – min 15.3 (mean 18.7) × max 9.6 – min 7.2 (mean 8.1); N = 11.

Site: 32/390–K4–1/1/1
Fill
Phoenix dactylifera. 1 uncharred date pit; length 22.1 × diameter 9.4 mm.

Site: 33/390–D8–1
Kiln Layer 1. Roman Period Site.
This sample comprises a fragment of rope 80 mm long, consisting of 2 twisted strands, each composed of some 25 twisted vegetable fibres.

Site: 33/390–D8–1
Kiln. On kiln floor.
Unidentified dried grass, and a single uncharred twig of unknown wood.

Site: 33/390–D8–1
Kiln. On Ash Layer 2.
Tamarix sp. Two small uncharred twigs (1.5 g.).

Site: 33/390–E9–2
Grave 1 (fill). Roman Period Site.
Myrtus sp. Leaf fragments (0.6 g).

Site: 33/390–F6–2
Surface
Several unidentifiable mineralised roots.

Site: 33/390–F8–1/B
Roman Period Farmhouse (fill)
Tamarix sp. One small twig, partially charred.

Site: 33/390–F9–1
Kiln 1. Outside draught hole of kiln. Roman Period.
Tamarix sp. Uncharred wood (23 g).

Site: 33/390–F9–1
Kiln 3. From dump surface.
Tamarix sp. and *Sesbania* sp. charcoal.
Monocot indet. charcoal forms the major part of the sample.

Site: 33/390–F9–1
Kiln 1. North side, 60 cm below grade. Roman Period.
Charcoal. Carbonised plant stem with monocotyledonous internal structure. Triangular cross section suggests Typhaceae or Cyperaceae probably *Typha* sp.

Site: 33/390–F9–1
Kiln 1. On stone against N side, E half, Level 2.
Typha sp. Charcoal.

Site: 33/390–F9–1
Kiln 3. In sand fill. Roman Period Site.
Prunus sp. 15 pits. Lengths, and greater and lesser diameters (mm) are: (a) 24.6 × 13.2 × 6.8, (b) 23.7 × 12.4 × 6.9, (c) 25.8 × 13.05 × 7.75, (d) 21.5 × 12.55 × 7.0, (e) 24.2 × 13.2 × 7.05, (f) 23.3 × 11.9 × 6.7, (g) 23.5 × 12.3 × 6.95, (h) 21.8 × 12.2 × 6.4, (i) 22.0 × 12.7 × 7.1, (j) 23.25 × 11.45 × 6.7, (k) 21.7 × 12.55 × 6.25, (l) 21.45 × 13.0 × 7.1, (m) 22.8 × 12.05 × 6.92, (n) 19.95 × 11.6 × 6.0, (o) 21.45 × 12.6 × 6.3 (seed broken): Max 25.8 – min 19.95 (mean 22.83) × max 13.2 – min 11.45 (mean 12.45) × max 7.75 – min 6.00 (mean 6.79); N = 15.

Site: 33/390–F10–2
Grave 1. Late Christian Period.
Myrtus sp. Leaves.

Site: 33/390–F10–2
Grave 2. Late Christian Period.
Myrtus sp. Leaf and stem fragments.

Site: 33/390–F10–2
Grave 4. Late Christian Period.
Myrtus sp. Leaf and stem sections.

Site: 33/390–H6–2/7
Roman Period Site (fill)
Phoenix dactylifera. 4 date pits. Lengths, greater and lesser diameters (mm) are: (a) 20.75 × 9.1 × 8.45, (b) 22.75 × 8.87 × 7.85, (c) 22.0 × 8.5 × 7.85, and (d) 23.0 × 9.2 × 8.6: Max 23.0 – min 22.0 (mean 22.1) × max 9.2 – min 8.5 (mean 8.9) × max 8.6 – min 7.85 (mean 8.2); N = 4.
Punica granatum. Two pieces from the fruit wall. One was almost complete, from a fruit 27 mm in diameter; the other was much larger, from a fruit estimated to be about 55 mm in diameter.
Olea europaea. 5 olive pits. Lengths, greater and lesser diameters (mm) of 3 measurable pits are: (a) 17.5 × 7.45 × 6.9, (b) 15.45 × 7.7 × 7.6, and (c) 14.1 × 9.4 × 9.45: Means 15.7 × 8.2 × 8.0; N = 3.
Phoenix dactylifera. A woody piece of a leaf sheath approximately 10 × 8 cm.

Site: 33/390–M5–1/1
Phoenix dactylifera. 2 date pits, one charred. Lengths, greater and lesser diameters (mm) are: (a) 19.97 × 9.43 × 7.5, and (b) 18.35 × 10.02 × 8.7.
Olea europaea. 1 olive pit. Length, greater and lesser diameters are: 17.45 × 9.0 × 8.4 mm.

5

PLEISTOCENE ARCHAEOLOGY AND GEOARCHAEOLOGY OF THE DAKHLEH OASIS: A STATUS REPORT

M. R. Kleindienst

"It is clear that any regional geographic study would be considered incomplete if it ignored the historic past. We wish to show that it would be equally defective if it ignored the prehistoric past" (Caton-Thompson and Gardner 1932, 369).

INTRODUCTION

Background

Having acted as consultant to the Dakhleh Oasis Project (DOP) since 1979 to advise on Pleistocene prehistory, "... that strange compound of archaeology and geology ..." (Caton-Thompson and Gardner 1932, 369), I joined DOP as Co-Investigator for Pleistocene archaeology and geo-archaeology in 1983. Field investigations were initiated by a three-week reconnaissance survey in January, 1986 (22 field days), followed by further preliminary survey and the first sets of systematic sampling from piedmont gravel terraces in eastern Dakhleh during January–March, 1987 (61 field days), and three weeks in 1988 (26 field days) (Fig 1.1, this volume).

For logistical reasons while based in Ezbet Bashendi, the initial work on Dakhleh Pleistocene archaeology has concentrated on eastern Dakhleh, with reconnaissance visits to terrace remnants and areas of artesian spring deposition in central and western Dakhleh. A protocol for detailed field recording of morphological and technological attributes of Pleistocene lithic artifacts was developed in 1987, which provides data for analyses in Toronto; artifacts are not removed from Dakhleh. Unfortunately, in 1989, illness prevented the projected study of artifacts recovered from systematically collected areas in 1987–1988. Therefore, this report is based mainly upon field observations, and preliminary artifact sorting and analyses, from 1978 to 1988.

History of Research

Pleistocene artifacts were first collected in Dakhleh by Winlock in 1908, but were not published until 1936. Caton-Thompson (1952) noted these finds in passing, and equated one illustrated retouched specialised flake from western Dakhleh, found about 1.5 km southeast of Deir el-Hagar, with her 'Khargan Aterian' (Winlock 1936, pl. II.6, cited in Caton-Thompson 1952). Caton-Thompson viewed Dakhleh and southern Kharga only from the air (1952, 1983).

As part of an extended reconnaissance from Kharga on the east to Abu Mingar on the west, and south into the desert, a limited survey "... in the vicinity of Dakhla Oasis, including the fringe of the Eocene Plateau just north of the village of Balat ..." and excavations were carried out by R.E. Schild, F. Wendorf, and B. Issawi during the Combined Prehistoric Expedition 2 (CPE) to Dakhleh Oasis in 1972 (Schild and Wendorf 1977; cf. 1975; Wendorf and Schild 1980). They considered that their survey

'Reports from the Survey of Dakhleh Oasis, Western Desert of Egypt, 1977–1987', edited by C.S. Churcher and A.J. Mills. Dakhleh Oasis Project: Monograph 2. Oxbow Monograph 99.

"... failed to disclose any important sites, except near Kharga. All of the sites which were found had been derived or completely deflated, and as consequence the prospects looked very bleak. Eventually, however, an area just west of the village of Balat furnished our first signficant sites, ..." (Schild and Wendorf 1977, 8).

The two published excavated Pleistocene spring vents west of Balat were designated E-72–1 and E-72–2 (DOP index numbers 31/420–N4–1 and N4–2, and Prehistoric Locality 147). These are designated as the reference locality for the 'Balat Unit' (Kleindienst 1985; see below). It is noted that the term 'Industry' was used in Kleindienst (1985). Despite disclaimers (Clark and Kleindienst 1974), the term 'Industry' continues to connote some intrinsic relationship of archaeological aggregates within designated units with 'a group of prehistoric people' or ethnicity. Therefore, in DOP investigations McDonald and Kleindienst apply the term 'Unit' to refer ONLY to the known cultural content of defined, named cultural stratigraphic units. For the Pleistocene Stone Age, this is at present restricted to stone artifacts.

Little information is available about any other localities which might have been noted by the Combined Prehistoric Expedition in Dakhleh. They record that southwest of Balat:

"More than fifty of the spring vents and tufa hills were closely examined, but only a few yielded any traces of occupation, none associated with tufas. On the other hand, the floor of the wadi and wind-eroded deflational concavities contained numerous stone artifacts in a typical lag situation. Most of these appeared to be of Aterian and possibly Mousterian affiliations. Numerous Levallois pieces, Mousterian and Levallois points, and rare Aterian pedunculates were noted scattered on the surface. These entirely destroyed and mixed occupations did not seem to be suitable for further work" (Schild and Wendorf 1975, 67).

Wendorf and Schild (1980, 170–171) recorded that nothing was found *in situ* in the Pleistocene laminated silts below the escarpment (Kleindienst *et al.*, this volume, Chapter 1 [PLS]); and that no artifacts were "associated with [the] gravel bed" below the escarpment on the north (Piedmont Terrace Gravels [P-I, P-II]), or with the 'tufa' (Calcareous Silty Sediments [CSS]) to the southwest of Balat. Artifacts associated with old spring vents were "of Acheulian and Middle Palaeolithic ages, and in most cases limited to only a few pieces". In 1981, Roubet (1981) noted artifacts in northeastern Dakhleh, which she described as 'Middle Palaeolithic', corresponding to a 'Mousterian facies'.

Other DOP investigators have noted Pleistocene localities in the course of their surveys since 1978, mainly in the central and southern sectors of the oasis, beginning with finds by Bard, Hollett and Mills in the first field season (Churcher 1980, 1981, 1982, 1983, 1986; McDonald 1980, 1981, 1982, 1983, 1986, 1987, 1990a, 1990b, 1990c, 1991a, 1991b; Mills 1979, 1980, 1981, 1982, 1983). McDonald recorded occurrences of

Acheulian, and of at least two units of 'Middle Palaeolithic', including the presence of tanged 'Aterian' points found as isolated specimens. However, a systematic survey for Pleistocene evidence could not proceed until the geological/geomorphological framework had been established by Brookes (1983, 1986). Hence, this aspect of DOP investigation has barely begun.

Geoarchaeological investigations in 1986–1987 were in collaboration with Brookes; those on lithic raw material sourcing are with McDonald. The location of Pleistocene evidence reported here results as much from the keen eyes of other members of the Project – Brookes, Churcher, McDonald, Sheldrick and Wiseman – as from my own fieldwork; this report incorporates their data, as well as the contributions of all the other DOP staff who have ranged over the oasis and dutifully carried home their finds to be recorded and catalogued. I gratefully acknowledge the contributions to the Pleistocene data base by all these colleagues. The assistance of M. Wiseman greatly expedited both fieldwork and recording after 1988.

Mapping of Pleistocene deposits (see Kleindienst *et al.*, this volume, Chapter 1) has established a sequence of depositional and erosional episodes, leaving dissected elevated remnants of three alluvial gravels on pediment surfaces ('pedisediments' [P-I, P-II, P-III]), a sequence of ?lacustrine laminated sediments falling between P-II and P-III in time (Pleistocene Laminated Sediments [PLS]), and evidence for several episodes of water-deposited sediments (elevated terrace remnants of Ferruginous Sandy Sediments [FSS] and Calcareous Silty Sediments [CSS]); and 'spring mounds' marking the locations of ancient spring conduits or vents. Other, bedrock surfaces in the oasis also carry lag gravels and/or Pleistocene artifacts. The survey has occasionally extended onto the Libyan Plateau to the north, and into the desert south of the oasis proper.

METHODS

Research Design

The nature of Dakhleh Pleistocene archaeological occurrences as recorded by McDonald (1980, 1981, 1982, 1983) and others (e.g., Schild and Wendorf 1975, 1977; Wendorf and Schild 1980; Wendorf *et al.* 1976) prior to 1986, and results of 1986–87 fieldwork by Kleindienst (1985, 1987) and Brookes (1983, 1986) predicated an approach to changing oasis environments different from that of a survey to locate 'archaeological sites' (Kleindienst 1987, 1988). Lithic artifacts of probable Pleistocene age are differentially distributed across the landscape, mainly as surface finds. While the potential for obtaining localised, short timespan, excavated samples is high in some spring mound deposits, these pose unique and difficult problems for excavation. Other *in situ* occurrences are rare: until 1989, only a few artifacts had come from fluvial gravels on

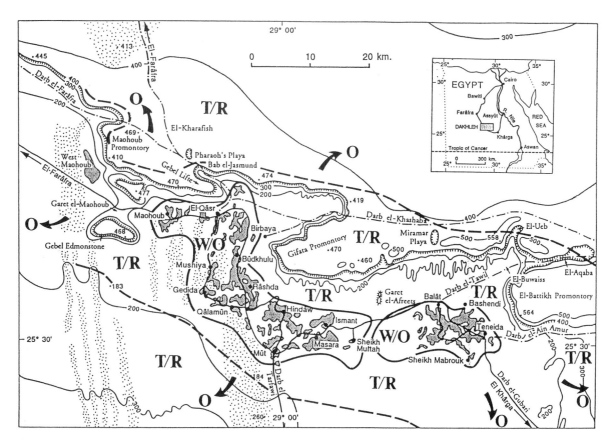

Fig. 5.1. Idealised model of landuse in the Pleistocene 'Palaeoasis' at Dakhleh Oasis. Basemap showing topography, major settlements, main roads, cultivated areas (hatched) and dune belts (stippled). The surveyed palaeoasis lies between the broken lines. Key: W/O – Watered Areas with ancient springs and modern wells, hypothesized as foci for occupation; T/R – Transit and/or Resource Extraction Zones; O – Zones of distant occupation loci away from the oasis, on Libyan Plateau or in the desert.

pediment surfaces (P-II, Loc. 84; P-III, Loc. 233), or terraced sediments (FSS - 2 occurrences – Loc. 155; CSS – Loc. 151; and 31/420–F9–4 recorded as '31/420–F9–2' – Loc. 362 [Churcher 1982, fig. 1; 1983]). All visited outcrops of Pleistocene Laminated Sediments have continued to prove sterile (Table 5.1). See comments in Kleindienst *et al.* (this volume, Chapter 1).

Archaeologists, particularly those concerned with the earlier time ranges, have been criticised for their pre-occupation with locating 'sites' rather than with the sampling of evidence for human uses of a landscape (Dunnell and Dancey 1983; Foley 1981a, 1981b; Isaac 1981). Desert landscapes present particularly severe sampling problems for Pleistocene 'site' surveys because of deflation and possible redistribution of remains, in addition to masking by later sediment deposition; however, they do provide an ideal laboratory for testing aspects of 'off-site' (Foley 1981b) or 'scatters-and-patches' archaeology (Isaac 1981).

Work in the Dakhleh Oasis has consequently been directed first at *ascertaining the distributions, kinds and frequencies of lithic artifacts* within the oasis and 'palaeoasis' environs; and at *relating these to geomorphic*

units, changing palaeoenvironments, and potential resources. Using such an approach, negative evidence may be as meaningful as positive evidence. The outer boundaries of the palaeoasis (Kleindienst 1987) are envisaged as extending ca. 50 km from known reliable oasis water-sources, a conservative estimate of 'two-day's march' east, south, or west into a desert or dry savanna, or north onto the plateau (Fig. 5.1).

Observations during the 15 weeks of field research have provided a model for Pleistocene human behaviour. Given (1) that entirely resource-extraction-based Pleistocene societies were mobile; (2) that the limiting ecological factor in the Western Desert has always been water availability; and (3) that the Dakhleh area provided perennial artesian water sources, at least during protracted periods of Pleistocene time: the hypothesis to be tested is that *"The areas with more-or-less reliable artesian water supplies in the central-western and central to central-eastern Dakhleh palaeoasis would have been the foci for Pleistocene human occupation"* (Fig. 5.1). These are the areas of natural artesian spring venting, now marked by spring mounds and spring terrace deposits (Kleindienst *et al.*, this volume, Chapter 1). It is possible that seepage springs occurred along the scarp face. No evidence of Pleistocene occupation related to scarp-face water supplies has yet been found, although large blocks of spring tufa are incorporated as components of the fluvial P-I, P-II and P-III gravels. The central 'occupation zone(s)' of the palaeoasis would have been surrounded by a 'transit zone', which would have been utilised for resource extraction (organic and inorganic), or simply traversed. Beyond that zone, at distances of one to two day's marches one would again find archaeological occurrences representing habitation, the stopping-points used when people moved out of or into the better-watered area of the palaeoasis.

One would expect to find a greater incidence of transported 'finished' or 'worked-out' stone tools in the occupied watered zone than in the transit-extraction zone. There, one would expect to find workshop/quarry debris, and partially-worked tools ('roughouts' or 'rejects'), near sources of raw materials. One might also expect small, repeatedly used 'outlook' sites would be preserved on prominences. Other, casual or short-term uses of the area in the Pleistocene are less likely to be archaeologically visible, although rare lost or discarded 'finished' tools would occur as isolated finds. The outer zone of desert or desert-plateau stop-over localities would, again, produce a higher incidence of transported and curated objects and materials, rather than strictly workshop/quarry materials. If survey extended even further from Dakhleh, one might find a network of more distant stopping places, in terms of 'day's march' distances (± 25 km). The projected survey transects (see below), and excavations where possible, will be directed at testing and refining the model for Pleistocene regional land use in the Dakhleh area.

In 1987, a single exploratory traverse south, to test whether archaeological occurrences could be found at one to two days' march distances from the central, spring mound area in eastern Dakhleh, easily located an occurrence with Middle Stone Age (MSA) occupation debris near an isolated gebel in the desert about 30 km southeast of Teneida (Loc. 225) as predicted in the model (Kleindienst 1988). A systematically surveyed traverse south of Loc. 228 (southern 'Southeast Basin') by McDonald and Sheldrick in 1989 discovered Pleistocene, as well as Holocene localities nearby (Locs 245–249). In the 11 km from the Holocene playa to the southern gebels, only scattered isolated MSA flakes and one 'Aterian' point (Loc. 255) were found (McDonald 1990a).

General Observations and Methodology

Another problem in addressing the Pleistocene remains in the eastern Sahara and the Nile Valley, or in northeastern Africa in general, is that, due to historical accidents of academic training, most researchers have seen the Sahara as the hinterland of Europe, or of the Near East, rather than as the northward extension of prehistoric Africa. This mindset is reflected in their choice of nomenclature (e.g., Caton-Thompson 1952 [partim]; McBurney 1960; Schild

and Wendorf 1975; Simmons and Mandel 1985, 1986; Wendorf 1965, 1968; Wendorf and Schild 1980). Without denying the possibilities for interactions with the north and east, recent palaeoenvironmental reconstructions (e.g., Churcher, this volume, Chapter 8; Gautier 1980, 1988, 1993; Kröpelin 1987; Neumann 1989; Pachur and Kröpelin 1987; Pachur et al. 1987) and archaeological evidence (McHugh et al. 1988, 1989; also Allsworth-Jones 1986; Clark 1980: 548) indicate patterns that link Saharan with sub-Saharan Africa; such linkages confirm Caton-Thompson's (1946, 28, 32) perceptions of 'equatorial stimuli'. In consequence, an African rather than an European or Near Eastern nomenclature is employed at Dakhleh. The cultural evidence from Pleistocene localities is designated as 'Earlier Stone Age' (ESA) or 'Middle Stone Age' (MSA); and named cultural stratigraphic units are designated when defined. Indeterminate aggregates are designated as 'Pleistocene Stone Age' (PSA).

Prehistoric sites are listed here by locality number, in addition to the Dakhleh Site Index number (see Appendix II, this volume). The nature of prehistoric evidence in many cases makes the assignment of a 'site' number difficult – when several archaeological occurrences are closely grouped, when defining the number of occurrences would require detailed sampling, or when localities are far outside the mapped Dakhleh grid. Areal and aerial photographs were not available prior to 1986, which made precise location of many prehistoric sites found in the early years problematic. Although most localities can now be located on the gridded basemap, the DOP prehistorians (Kleindienst and McDonald) have usually found it preferable to refer to the running count of locality numbers (which may refer to one artifact at one extreme, or to broad diffuse scatters at the other), rather than to the more cumbersome and perhaps misleading DOP grid-designated indexed 'sites'. Pleistocene locality (Loc.) numbers between 001 and 145 were designated by McDonald, higher numbers by Kleindienst, Brookes or Wiseman unless otherwise noted.

Collections made between 1978 and 1986 are generally highly selected, small 'grab samples', as indeed are many collected since. In a few instances all recognized artifacts were collected: e.g., at 312/420–H6–2, Loc. 091; 31/420–L1–1, Loc. 082; 31/420–L3–1, Loc. 081. Because the geomorphological framework was not established until 1986, although most of the earlier collections sampled a limited area on one geomorphic unit, those which resulted from several kilometre-long traverses probably include material from two or more geomorphic contexts. These appear to cover combinations such as P-III, dissected P-III, and modern wadi (?31/420–A5–1, Loc. 058), or hillslope and surrounding surface (?31/420–M3–2, Loc. 034). The high terrace remnants to the north below the escarpment (P-I, P-II) received little attention before 1986.

In several instances, ESA or MSA artifacts were found on the surface of spring mounds disturbed by excavations for burial pits or other historic uses (e.g., 31/405–F9–6,

Loc. 040; 30/405–L1–3, Loc. 054; and 31/405–E8–2 are all spring mounds used as cemeteries; and 31/405–D7–3, Loc. 007, was breached on the north, with the removal of conduit sediments, in historic times.) These historic diggings undoubtedly helped to expose the Pleistocene artifacts. A number of the historic sites are located on gravel terraces (P-III, or ?low-lying P-II) (e.g., 31/420–D6–1 Ismant el-Kharab/Kellis; 31/420–G6–2 Qasr el-Halakeh; 31/435–D5–2 'Ein Tirghi cemetery; 33/390–L9–1 Amheida). Pleistocene artifacts have been collected from time to time off the gravel surfaces at these sites, including two by Winlock at Ismant el-Kharab in 1908 (1936, pl. II.14, 15).

Systematic surface collecting involves either gridded areas or 'Sets' of transects. Grids employ 2 × 2 m or smaller grid squares, depending upon the size of the material to be collected. Transect 'Sets' employ a 100 m long central line, with perpendicular lines to either side spaced at 20 m intervals; side lines extend 100 m from the central line, or end before that at a precipice. The lines are walked twice, collecting all artifacts lying within 1 m to either side of the line. A complete Set collection represents approximately 2,575 m² of surveyed surface area. This method has proved a practical means of gathering randomised surface collections, and for sampling fairly large areas with limited time and effort. The chert (or rock) densities on the surface in the area of each Set are counted within one square metre 'density squares.' The starting points for central lines, and of density squares, are determined by hammer-throws.

OBSERVATIONS

Sources of Lithic Raw Materials Used in Prehistoric Dakhleh

Sampling and recording of geological sources for lithic raw materials have been undertaken within the geo-archaeological survey. The locations of outcrops or surface scatters of materials suitable for knapping, for making ground stone artifacts, or for other uses have been recorded in the course of fieldwork. These observations also provide information regarding activity patterning during the Pleistocene (and Holocene), based upon the distribution of raw materials. More systematic work, and compositional analyses, remain to be done in the future.

The coarser-grained, upper members (now formations) of the Nubia sandstones (Taref, Maghrabi, Sabaya [Klitsch *et al.* 1987, cf. Egyptian Geological Survey and Mining Authority 1982) include predominantly grey to tan and fine-grained quartzites, grading to quartz-cemented or 'silicious' sandstones of varying friability. Within the oasis, heavily ferruginised quartzites (sometimes called 'ironstone') occur mainly as joint fillings, or along fault lines. In the outlying gebels to the south of Teneida, in the desert, there are massive outcrops of yellowish quartzites,

ferruginised quartzites, and fine-gravel conglomerates with 3–4 mm pebble inclusions. Some areas around outcrops yield PSA knapping debris. Cobbles of these rocks are included in gravel spreads and inverted-wadi gravels; these are associated with MSA workshop debris. Based upon hand examination (no petrographic work has yet been done), the Nubia quartzites were knapped from Upper Acheulian times, but were only occasionally used in the oasis during the MSA occupations. Those who dropped artifacts found on the southern margins of the oasis, and to the south, relied more heavily upon these types of Upper Nubia Group (Series) rocks (e.g., 30/420–E2–1, Loc. 214, 36%; 30/420–E2–2, Loc. 215, 14%); and those in the desert proper used them almost exclusively for raw materials (cf. Loc. 225, 94%). In the Nubia sandstone area of deflation pans south and southwest of Sheikh Muftah (cf. Brookes 1989), weathered chunks of white chalcedony to 20 cm size are found in the surface lag; these were used by MSA and Holocene peoples; no bedrock source has been found. (A similar significant component of white chalcedony has been noted in the lag in southern Kharga Oasis near Baris).

Coarser-grained conglomerates within the Upper Nubia Group Formations have left rare quartz pebbles in the surface lag, although few outcrops of conglomerates have been noted. These quartz pebbles were used by Pleistocene and Holocene inhabitants in the oasis. Barite crystals, some of large size and including 'roses', and gypsum crystals and 'roses' are found in the desert between Dakhleh and Kharga (Beadnell 1901); wind-abraded crystals of barite and gypsum can be found on the desert surface, and in surface lags on the Nubia Group rocks. Barite and calcite were sculpted into forms for personal adornment by Bashendi peoples (Loc. 228, McDonald 1990b).

Small nodules of grey-brown chert (most <50 mm long), favoured as a raw material in mid- to late Holocene localities, weather out of the Mut (= Qusseir) Formation claystone (e.g., 31/420–P5–2, Loc. 148), and can be found in the surface lag where the red/green claystone has disappeared. The nodules are also incorporated into spring deposits where the conduits penetrated the Mut Formation, and are found in the CSS. (Churcher found larger nodules in the Mut or Quessir Formation near Tenida in 1994, pers. comm.) Small clusters of rose quartz crystals are found in places in and on the surface of the claystone.

The Duwi Formation again provides outcrops of quartzites, mainly tan to light brown, with a range of grain sizes. These quartzites are often 'impure', with a coarse granular consistency and, when the less resistant minerals weather-out, have a distinctive pisolithic surface texture. The more friable Duwi Formation quartzites seem to have been among the favoured raw materials for making grinding slabs and handstones. Other potentially knappable raw materials (e.g., silicified limestone) occur locally. The Duwi Formation requires additional survey; fragments of well silicified petrified wood, a rarely knapped material, may originate here.

The Dakhla Formation outcrops lie outside the usual areas of the archaeological survey, and have received less attention (Kleindienst *et al.*, this volume, Chapter 1). However, they include haematite/limonite nodules useful for pigments and dolomitic limestones (Churcher, pers. comm., 25/II/1988), pebbles of which are among the most resistant of the rock types on the surface of any gravel lag, and which still remain as small pebbles far to the south of the oasis, where other limestone has been destroyed. This pink to pale yellow material was occasionally knapped (e.g., Loc. 204 in the Upper Wadi el-Tawil). Fossils from these beds, or from the Duwi Formation, were also collected and worked in antiquity. A labret, probably made from a silicified internal cast of a fossil gastropod, was found by Kleindienst on the surface at 31/420–P6–1, Loc. 100, and McDonald found an unworked fossil shell nearby. Abundant haematite nodules are a potential source for pigments.

The major source of raw materials for knapping in the oasis are the limestone formations capping the Libyan Plateau escarpment to the north. (Recent partitioning of the 'Tarawan Formation' (Egyptian Geological Survey and Mining Authority 1982, Hermina 1990, Klitzsch *et al.* 1987) is ignored for the purposes of this report; see Kleindienst *et al.*, this volume, Chapter 1.) Chert nodules, some over 40 cm in greatest dimension, can be observed outcropping at different horizons in the limestones along the scarp rim, and can also be obtained from large fallen blocks in the colluvium mantling the northern scarp. Spot checks show that the colour ranges from browns through tans to greys, sometimes banded or mottled (greys seem more common in the west), with a wide range in homogeneity or 'grain', and hence in knapping quality. Judging from the incidence of chert nodules and fragments in the high terrace gravels overlying pediment surfaces, the limestones include virtually no chert at the promontory west of the entrance to the Wadi el-Battikh (el-Battikh Promontory), northeast or east of Teneida. The surface of the plateau and the cliffs south of the upper Wadi el-Tawil bear almost no chert, but surface lag occurs on the north rim and on the promontory between el-Ueb and the Wadi el-Tawil (el-Tawil Promontory). Further northwest, chert has been seen outcropping on the north rim of the northern Wadi el-Ueb or 'North Wadi' – the northern valley joining the Wadi el-Tawil drainage northeast of Bashendi – although P-I and P-II gravels below the escarpment to the west of the confluence of these drainages include less chert than do those to the north and northwest of Balat. There, above 32/420–L6–1 and L7–1 (Locs 187 & 188) the limestones also include abundant nodules (Brookes, pers. comm., Jan. 18, 1987). Chert colours here are predominantly browns. Even in the gravels on the most southerly central terrace remnant (31/420–L1–1 and L2–1, Loc. 216), chert pieces >15 cm in greatest dimension can be found in the poorly-sorted boulder gravels. One distinctive type is 'wood-grained chert' (DeCelles and Gutschick 1983). To the northeast of el-Qasr, the cherts

are greyer, and are abundant in the gravels; but a short distance further west, north of Maohoub, the gravels are almost devoid of cherts, as apparently are those north of Gebel Edmonstone, and below the escarpment there. Grab samples of chert from gravels north of Edmonstone are yellow-tan in colour, and include vugs of quartz crystals. These are difficult to knap with precision, and highly variable in quality, although small worked pieces can be found on the pans southwest of Edmonstone. The gravels north of West Dakhleh have not been explored.

On the surface of the Libyan Plateau, north of Balat, an outcrop of homogeneous, translucent dark brown chert (which would qualify as 'flint') was located in the southeast rim of a large deflation basin (named 'Miramar'). This chert had been utilised for some Holocene artifacts there. Churcher has noted similar material on the plateau northwest of el-Qasr (pers. comm., 3/V/1991). This quality of material has rarely been seen on the high gravel terrace remnants, or on the oasis floor.

It should be noted that both at outcrops, and on weathering from the fluvial terrace gravels, the chert breaks up naturally into sharp-edged fragments of all sizes. 'Pot lids' are easily recognised as natural fractures; but, particularly after abrasion and/or weathering, other fragments easily produce a wide range of 'pseudo-cores' and 'pseudo-flakes' which may closely mimic some products of human knapping. (An excellent description of the phenomenon can be found in de Morgan 1896.) Our identification of surface artifacts is, in consequence, extremely conservative.

Tarawan cherts were the raw materials mainly used by the Balat unit stoneworkers, and almost exclusively by MSA knappers in Dakhleh. Tarawan cherts were not as favoured during the Holocene, except by Masara Unit Variant A stoneworkers (McDonald 1986). However, recycling of highly selected PSA artifacts by the Holocene inhabitants of Dakhleh is frequently observed (McDonald 1981; cf. 1986, fig. 1a). In the central-south sector, in Masara Variant B, the aggregate is "based largely on old worn lithics" and their systematic reduction (McDonald 1986, 104, 108, pl. VII; 1987, 1991a, 1991b). 'Holoports', PSA artifacts recycled during the Holocene, include large well-finished lanceolate and tanged points of Dakhleh Unit type, Levallois points, specialised cores, and Balat and/or Upper Acheulian-type bifaces. Either Holocene rockhounds recovered these 'finished' tools from the surfaces of nearby springmounds; or these artifacts represent isolated lost or discarded tools. Alternatively, PSA occupation sites remain to be discovered south of Ezbet Sheikh Muftah. (Some were located in 1991, 1992 and 1993 by Kleindienst, Wiseman and O'Carroll.)

Large, clear or varicoloured calcite crystals are found along joints, or lining fissures and cavities in the Tarawan Formation limestones. These are a potential source for decorative ornamental stone. One find by Churcher of a limestone Upper-Acheulian type biface on a P-II surface northeast of Teneida (32/435–M5–1, Loc. 159) indicates that artifacts of this raw material may be missing from the archaeological record because of weathering and aeolisation. The escarpment caprock limestones are not highly resistant to erosion. Based upon the usual preferences for raw materials with which to make large cutting-edged tools, limestone may even have been a raw material of choice during Upper Acheulian times. Where other raw materials were available, chert was *not* the preferred raw material for Acheulian bifaces elsewhere in Africa (Clark 1975; Kleindienst 1959, 1962). Limestone was also occasionally knapped during the Holocene (McDonald 1991a).

Eocene Esna Formation shales, and Thebes Formation limestones (now Thebes Group, Hermina 1990), which outcrop above and well north of the escarpment, have not yet been surveyed for raw materials. Caton-Thompson (1952) cited the Thebes Formation [now the El Rufuf Formation of the Thebes Group, Hermina 1990) as the major source for chert at Kharga Oasis. At least below the Refuf Pass, some of the Thebes chert in the Upper Sheet Gravels fractures into thin tabular pieces, and is of a 'caramel' or yellow-orange colour, as described by Caton-Thompson (1952). Nodules of darker coloured chert are also present, to ±12 cm in greatest dimension. (Brookes and Kleindienst transected along the abandoned Western Oases Railway Line to Kharga as far as the Upper Sheet Gravel surfaces below the Refuf Pass on February 12, 1987 and noted no chert in outcrops of the Tarawan Formation.) Habitual use of a distinctive tabular type of 'caramel' chert has been noted by McDonald (1982, 1983, 1985, 1986) at Dakhleh within Sheikh Muftah and Bashendi aggregates, and continuing into Old Kingdom times. The source may actually have been the 'flint mines' at Kharga (Caton-Thompson 1952, pl. 127); or a source closer to Dakhleh in the Thebes limestones that still remains to be found. Although PSA stoneworkers at Kharga utilised the nodular and tabular 'caramel' chert, few PSA artifacts of this material have been found at Dakhleh. (Caton-Thompson [1952, 100] recorded two handaxes of 'tough silicified limestone' at Kharga [Refuf Pass, Upper Sheet Gravels, Locus I, II]. This is probably not Tarawan limestone, but possibly from the Thebes Group formations.)

Within the Pleistocene sediments, the chert nodules and pieces incorporated into the P-I, P-II, and P-III gravels were undoubtedly, in themselves, an important source of raw materials. Sizeable pieces can be found 10–15 km from the escarpment, for instance at Locality 216, where the cherts from the gravels must have provided the raw materials for the 'Aterian' Dakhleh Unit knappers. Masara blade knappers used a 'honey-coloured coarse-grained' chert at 31/420–G4–1, Loc. 83, (McDonald 1982, 123; 1986) on P-III gravels, near Duwi Formation outcrops. The immediate local source is the gravels. The P-II gravels, or P-II gravels let-down onto P-III, probably furnished the chert nodules used in the Balat Unit aggregates at Loc. 147 (Schild and Wendorf 1977).

A distinctive, localised raw material source, nicknamed

'chert-balls', is found north of Bashendi (McDonald 1983), from northeast on the surface of gravels in a recent, beheaded wadi (once the eastward drainage from Wadi el-Tawil), and extending southward in P-II/P-III gravels and lags to the north of the 'Bashendi Rock Art Basin' (BRAB, Locs 161, 283), and adjacent deflation basins. The lag and nodules are let down between the sandstone gebels in BRAB, and are again abundant south of the basin rims on the lag gravel-covered sandstone surface. They occur in P-II inverted wadi gravels and in/on P-II/P-III gravels as far south as Teneida. Occasional pieces can be found to the west of Balat, although these may be holoports. These large (20 to >50 cm diameter) botryoidal or bulbous nodules are unusually large 'geodes' (Pettijohn 1957) or unusual 'paramandoura' (Bromley and Ekdale 1986; Clayton 1986). No bedrock source has yet been found for these large nodules, which characteristically have a reticulated rind, and variable but often distinctively banded internal structure, with a tough 'core material' resembling an orthoquartzite.

'Fields' of large nodules have long been reported from the top of the Libyan Plateau, and are abundant northeast of Kharga, possibly in the Thebes Fm, and are termed 'battikh' or 'melons' (Cailliaud 1826; Caton-Thompson 1952; Caton-Thompson and Gardner 1932; Hume 1925). These are generally poorly silicified. However, if the Dakhleh specimens are comparable, some may represent the most resistant component of long-eroded Thebes limestones, which once capped the area. Others may have a more local provenance. (In 1994, Churcher found an extensive field of geodes weathering out of Mut (Qusseir) Formation shales, northeast of Teneida, Loc. 347.)

Only one other localised cluster of similar nodules has been noted, by Sheldrick and McDonald in 1987, ca. 5 km south of el-Masara cultivation. These are associated with the area of a shallow basin in the Taref sandstone (Locs 207, 340). The nodules here, reaching ca. 20 cm diameter, lack all or most of their outer rinds, are heavily battered, and appear to be lag residuals from long-eroded gravels in which they were transported to their present location. Many retain only their 'cores'. Artifacts in the surface lags indicate that they have been knapped from Middle Pleistocene through Holocene times.

The raw material(s) of the nodules from the Bashendi area, especially the unweathered medulla, is easily recognisable from colour and/or surface texture. It was used by Balat Unit knappers for hammerstones and bifaces (e.g., Loc. 007, 187E; or 31/435–M2–1, Loc. 128, where McDonald discovered four nodules which had been worked in ESA/MSA times), and by MSA peoples (cf. 32/420–L7–1, Loc. 188B, where a spheroid of core material had been carried onto a high P-I remnant for use as a hammerstone; or Loc. 225, over 30 km southeast of Teneida, where flakes were struck from a biconical core). Examples of their use for artifacts have also been variously noted 40–50 km to the south and west of Bashendi, and in a Holocene basin on the Libyan Plateau, by Kleindienst,

McDonald, Sheldrick or Brookes. It seems that occasionally the larger nodules themselves were transported, when they are found in isolation several km to the south of Ezbet Sheikh Muftah or on the Taref sandstone rim ca. 12 km south. In the main source area it is easier today to find nodules larger than 20 cm in diameter; probably smaller nodules were selected for use long ago.

Except where removed by erosion, Pleistocene spring mounds are usually capped by a lithified ferruginised sand grading to quartz-cemented sandstone, with variable grain size, the aptly termed 'sand-rock' of Caton-Thompson (1952, 54, 155; Caton-Thompson and Gardner 1932). When sufficiently indurated, these deposits were used for handstones and grinding slabs. (Two small Balat bifaces at Loc. 007 are of this material, or of the 'ironstone' capping Nubia Formation sandstone mesas.) Spring mounds also include other lithic materials (Beadnell 1901) such as nodules of iron sulphide found in western Dakhleh (33/390– I9–5, Loc. 208), or chalcedony. They also include fine-grained sediments coloured by iron oxides (yellow-red-brown shades), or other minerals (black, white, sulphate yellow) which have been successfully used as pigments by DOP artists (O'Carroll, Leimert, Howell, pers. comms., 1986). Many spring mounds have been extensively quarried, presumably in Holocene times, perhaps to obtain pigments, clays, or building materials, such as sandstone slabs, or for fertilizer.

Localities on Alluvial Pleistocene Terrace Gravels (P-I, P-II, P-III) and Recent Wadi Gravels) (Table 5.1)

Systematic transect sampling of the geomorphic surfaces is providing information on the intensity of human activity in various parts of the oasis at various times, as well as on regional chronology (Kleindienst 1988). In 1987, intensively sampled fluvial gravel surfaces (P-II, Loc. 187A, northwest of Balat below the highest point ['Balat Point', 519 m asl] on the scarp rim, Fig. 5.1) yielded scattered implements of Upper Acheulian type, as well as those of the Balat Unit (final ESA/early MSA), comparable to those excavated by Schild and Wendorf from spring conduits near Balat (Loc. 147). A diffuse 'cluster' was found on the southern end of the western P-II terrace (Loc. 187E) in 1988. The Locality 187A surface also bears spatially separated occurrences of workshop materials belonging to at least two MSA units utilising the Levallois method of chert nodule reduction. Finds of conjoining cores and flakes in close proximity (≤2 m) indicate less post-depositional disturbance than is usually assumed for such surfaces, and emphasize the need for testing geological models of desert pavement development on these surfaces (McFadden et al. 1987). The conjoining pieces also allow fairly precise estimation of the amount of material removed from artifact edges in various stages of aeolisation and weathering. Material on the surface ranges from slightly weathered/abraded, with reddish

patina, through heavily weathered/abraded artifacts which are dark brown (patina and/or 'desert varnish'), and pock-marked, sometimes on both faces. Usually, the condition of the 'up' face differs from that of the 'down' face, indicating that the piece has probably not been transported or disturbed for a long period of time, if ever, since exposure.

The surfaces of the high terrace remnants (Kleindienst et al., this volume, Chapter 1) are veneered by chert and/or limestone fragments of varying size and angularity; the surface scatter ranges from 'sparse' to 'dense'. 'Sparse', as counted at Loc. 187A, includes 550–750 fragments >20 mm long/m² (chert, 45–335 fragments; 0.9–1.7 kg/m²); 'dense' contains 1,600 pieces/m² (chert, 180–1,000 fragments; 7.5–7.6 kg/m²). Low relief, mainly developed by small drainage channels which may follow the relief of the underlying gravel surface, is from 0.5–1.5 m. Except where stripped by wind and/or water erosion, the veneer is underlain by a variable thickness of fine sediment (soil profile), which overlies silica- and calcite-cemented fluvial gravels. Occasionally, an artifact is found newly exposed in situ in the fine sediment; these are in fresh or mint condition, compared with the slightly to heavily abraded artifacts on the surface. The patina is light grey to tan, and may be matte or glossy. These observations confirm the liklihood of the 'accretion hypothesis' for desert dust deposition below the surface desert pavement (Breed et al. 1980; Cooke et al. 1993). Attempts at test-pitting at Locs 187A in 1987 showed that heavily cemented gravels are unlikely to yield to any excavation method short of dynamite, jackhammers, or very slowly, by hammer and chisel. No in situ artifacts have been found.

The surface sampling method, satisfactorily tested in 1987–88, utilises Sets of transects covering up to 2,575 m² and spaced ca. 0.5 km apart along the north-south axes of P-II remnants and along the axes of isolated P-I remnants. The north-south transect sampling, initiated northwest of Balat, will continue south across P-III and younger dissected surfaces to the spring mound/spring terrace area west of the Balat cultivation. Unfortunately, removal of gravel from these surfaces for industrial purposes in Historic times, which has increased in effect since 1978, has stripped much of the original lag and any contained artifacts from the central part of the oasis. Five additional complete transects are projected, originating on pediment gravel surfaces northeast of Teneida, northeast of Bashendi, north of Mut, northeast of el-Qasr, and north of Maohoub, avoiding the most cultivated areas. The preliminary work indicates that while the incidence of Pleistocene artifacts directly correlates with the incidence of cherts incorporated in P-II gravels and adjacent scarp colluvium and limestones, the correlation does not hold for P-I surfaces, and appears unlikely to characterise P-III surfaces. The Libyan Plateau surfaces above the oasis also require surveying.

Localised workshop areas situated near the northerly or southerly edges characterise the isolated P-I remnants

Table 5.1. Recovery contexts of Pleistocene Stone Age artifacts, Dakhleh Oasis, 1978–1989, with estimated ages. Key: Sectors: W – west, N – north, E – east, S – south, C – central. Locations of sections of sectors shown in Figure 5.2.

Cultural Stratigraphic Units	IN SITU Finds	Surface Finds & Distribution	Geological/Geomorphological Contexts (Cf. Kleindienst *et al.*, this volume, Chapter 1.
[ca. 10,000 BP]			
Indeterminate		Scatter, small bifaces	Spring rejuvenation conduits: W-C Dak.
'Small-sized' MSA		Workshop scatters	P-III gravels, young surfaces: C-S & E-S Dak. Spring mounds: C-C & C-S Dak. Terraced ferrunginous and calcareous deposits (FSS & CSS): C-S Dak.
[ca. 40,000 BP]			
Indeterminate	Levallois debitage	Workshop	P-I surface: E-N Dak. Spring mounds: C-S Dak.
'Aterian' (Dakhleh Unit)	1 core		P-III gravel: C-N Dak.
'Aterian' (Dakhleh Unit)		Workshop	P-II gravels: C-C & C-N Dak.
		Special activity scatters	Basin surface: SW of Edmonstone (W-C)
		Scattered, isolated, tanged pieces	Desert surface: E-S; P-III gravels: C & E-C Dak.; Spring mound area: C-C & C-S Dak.; P-II gravels: C-N Dak.
'Aterian' surface: (cf. Dakhleh Unit)		Occupation Defined clusters, shaped tools	Deflated basin E-C dak. Deflated sandstone surface: E-C Dak. Deflated ferruginous terraced surface (FSS): C-S Dak. Desert surface: E-S
		Scattered finds	Plateau: C-N. P-II gravels and colluvium: E-N Dak. P-III gravels: E-C & E-N Dak.
[ca. 100,000 BP]			
MSA ('medium-sized'-provisional)		Lookout sites	P-I gravels: C-N Dak.
		Diffuse scatters	?P-II, P-III gravels: C-N, W-N Dak.
		?special activity scatters	basin rims: C-S desert.
[ca. 200,000 BP]			
'Large-sized' MSA		Diffuse workshop scatters; small work stations, bifacial points	P-II gravels: N Dak.; P-I gravels: N Dak. ?spring mounds: C-S Dak.
[ca. 300,000 BP]			
Indeterminate	2 flakes 1 core	Levallois debitage	Calcareous terraced deposits (CSS): C-C & C-S Dak.
Indeterminate		Scattered flakes	Calcareous terraced (CSS): E-C Dak.
Balat Unit	Numerous, in spring conduits	Spring mound surfaces, rare to numerous bifaces; ?Levallois-associated	Spring mounds: C-C, C-S, E-C Dak.
		Diffuse clusters bifaces	Bedrock: C-C Dak. P-II gravels: C-N Dak.
Balat Unit?	1 biface, 2 flakes		Gravel remnant, ?P-II: C-C Dak.
		Isolated finds, bifaces, ?Levallois-associated	P-III gravels: C-C & C-S Dak.; P-II gravels: E-W Dak. P-I gravels: E-W Dak.
	1 core, 1 biface 1 hammerstone		Ferruginous terraced deposits (FSS): C-S Dak.
[?ca. 400,000 BP]			
Upper Acheulian		Scattered, isolated bifaces	P-II gravels: E-W & C-N Dak. Spring mound associated: W-C Dak.

Table 5.2. Artifact densities obtained by transect Set sampling from Pleistocene alluvial terrace gravels in Dakhleh Oasis, 1987 & 1988.

Terrace & Locality Numbers	Artifacts				Area	Density
	Cores	Flakes	Tools	N	m² Collected	Artifacts/m²
P-I: 188B						
Set I	10	17	1	28	1,186	.02
P-II: 187A (north to south)						
Set VI >sᵃ	31	138	3	172	1,087	.16
Set V	46	161	2	209	1,613	.13
V/WKSᵇ	74	334	1	409	540	.76
Set IV	56	192	8	256	2,054	.12
Set III	7	29	2	38	2,042	.02
Set II	15	61	2	78	2,464	.03
Set I	7	49	7	63	1,344	.05
10 density squares	–	11	–	11	10	1.10
Dissected P-II:						
Set VI <sᶜ	35	277	2	314	798	.39
P-II: 216						
Set I	159	262	3	424	768	.55
2 density squares	–	6	–	6	2	3.00

ᵃ – VI >s, P-II gravel surface, above rim of remnant.
ᵇ – V/WKS, workshop cluster south of Set V; total collection.
ᶜ – VI <s, dissected P-II gravel surface, below rim of remnant.

northwest of Balat (Locs 188A, 188B, just south of 187), in contrast to the general scatter of artifacts on P-II remnants near the scarp, where densities vary from 0.02 to 0.16 artifacts/m² over collected transects, and reach 0.76/m² in a 'dense' workshop area (Table 5.2). In the randomly-sited density squares for counting chert incidence in surface veneer, artifact densities on Loc. 187A range from 0 to 3/m²; 10 squares give an average density of 1.1 artifacts/m² for chert-bearing areas. (All flakes <50 mm are unlikely to be collected in the surface transects, which also cover areas with little or no chert in the veneer. Artifacts are not restricted to chert-bearing areas, however.)

'Aterian' (Dakhleh Unit) workshops, including tanged tool forms and points with ventral basal retouch, were located on a southerly P-II remnant in 1988 (Loc. 216); here the transect density is 0.55 artifacts/m² on the P-II gravel surface, and over 30 artifacts/m² in the defined workshop area collected by 1 m grid squares on the north end of the remnant (Table 5.2, unanalysed). The 'Aterian' prepared cores and flakes can be distinguished, typologically and metrically, from those analyzed from the P-II surface scatter (Table 5.3). They are also usually in

fresher condition, with a lighter reddish-brown patina. This is the first confirmation from elsewhere in the western oases for Caton-Thompson's (1946, 1952) 'Kharga Aterian' unit. 'Aterian' has been reported from further south, at Dungul Oasis (Hester and Hobler 1969; Hobler and Hester 1969).

On Loc. 216's isolated P-II remnant, defined workshop areas are also found near the edges of the gebel-top suggesting that the isolated remnants of both P-I and P-II had reached approximately their present topographic expression at the time of the human stone-working activities, which would then fall within or post-date the downcutting phase that resulted in the P-III surfaces. This evidence for the human use of the gravels on topographic highs independently confirms Brookes' (1986) reasoning on the development of the P-I/P-II/P-III sequence.

The only *in situ* find from gravels presently correlated with P-II on the basis of topographic expression is from 31/420– E5–1 (Loc. 084). One handaxe and one flake were found by Sheldrick in 1981 (Churcher 1982; McDonald 1982), eroding from a small isolated remnant of small-sized gravels. The biface is tentatively assigned to the Balat Unit, because of its small size (McDonald

Table 5.3. *Dimensions of selected artifact classes from Pleistocene alluvial terrace surfaces, P-II and dissected P-II, Dakhleh Oasis, 1987 and 1988.*

Locality Number	Set	Artifacts N	Dimensions Chart Length (mm) Range	Mode	Mean
			Specialised struck cores (Levallois – last stage rejects): MSA		
P-II: 187A	VI >s[a]	11	60–100	80–90	83
	V	17	50–110	90–100	80
	V/WKS[b]	25	50–120	80–90	81
	IV	19	60–120	70–90	89
	I, II, III	14	50–140	80–90	86
	correction[c] for rounding, 03–06 (05) = range 83–95 (lightly to heavily abraded/weathered):				
	Total	86	50–140	80–90	84 = ca. 89+
Dissected P-II: 187A	VI <s[d]	16	60–130	60–70	80
	VI <s–G[e]	21	60–130	70–90	88
	correction[c] for rounding, 01–06 (04) = range 81–92 (fresh to heavily abraded/weathered):				
	Total	37	60–130	70–90	85=ca. 89+
216	I	64	40–100	70–80	71
	BC-G[f]	89	50–100	60–70	72
	correction[c] for rounding: 0–03 (1.5) = range 71–75 (fresh to lightly abraded/weathered):				
	Total	153	40–100	70–80	72=ca. 73.5-
			Specialised flakes ('Levallois' rejects): MSA		
P-II: 187A	VI >s[a]	29	40–120	50–60	72
	V	45	40–120	70–80	69
	V/WKS[b]	44	40–110	70–80	64
	IV	31	40–120	60–70/90–100	81
	I, II, III	31	30–130	70–80/100–110	77
	correction[c] for rounding, 03–06 (05) = range 67–87 (lightly to heavily abraded/weathered):				
	Total	180	30–130	70–80	76=ca. 81+
Dissected P-II: 187A	VI <s[d]	64	40–120	60–70/80–90	75
	VI <s-G[e]	88	40–150	60–70	81
	correction[c] for rounding, 01–06 (04) = range 76–87 (fresh to heavily abraded/weathered):				
	Total	152	40–150	60–70	78.5 = ca. 82+
P-II: 216	I	33	40–100	60–70	66
	BC-G[f]	62	40–110	60–70	70
	correction[c] for rounding, 0–03 (1.5) = range 66–73 (fresh to lightly abraded/weathered):				
	Total	95	40–110	60–70	69 = ca. 70.5-
			Specialised flake scars on struck cores (Levallois, last stage strikes): MSA		
P-II: 187A	VI >s[a]	12	50–100	50–60	67
	V	16	40–90	50–60	61
	V/WKS[b]	24	30–80	60–70	49
	IV	19	50–110	50–60	69
	I, II, III	11	30–80	60–70	67
	correction[c] for rounding, 0–03 (1.5) = range 61–72 (lightly to heavily abraded/weathered):				
	Total	82	30–110	60–70	63 = ca. 64.5+
Dissected P-II: 187A	VI <s[d]	14	30–100	70–90	71
	VI <s-G[e]	21	40–110	60–70	68
	correction[c] for rounding, 0–03 (1.5) = range 68–74 (lightly to heavily abraded/weathered):				
	Total	35	30–110	60–70/80–90	69 = ca. 70.5+
P-II: 216	I	62	30–90	60–70	58
	BC-G[f]	78	30–90	50–60	56
	correctionc for rounding, 0–01 (0.5) = range 56-59 (fresh to lightly abraded/weathered):				
	Total	140	30–90	50–60	56

[a] – VI >s, P-II gravels, above rim of remnant.   [b] – V/WKS, workshop cluster south of Set V; total collection   [c] – estimates, based upon conjoining pieces
[d] – VI <s, dissected P-II gravels, below rim of remnant: lag from P-II surface; possibly smaller material derived from north, upstream
[e] – VI <s-G, all specialised cores and flakes seen in area bounded by Set VI O1 and 100 lines collected
[f] – General collection, selected pieces, outside grid-collected area

1982, fig. 1), and the nature of the trimming which can be matched on specimens found at Locality 147 by DOP and by Schild and Wendorf (1977, pls. XV.2, XVIII, XXXVII.1). The raw material and condition, however, are anomalous. The biface is made in a light tan-coloured, translucent chert not noted elsewhere at Dakhleh, with a porcelaneous white patina, also not noted elsewhere at Dakhleh (but similar to the patina described for excavated spring mound bifaces of Thebes cherts at KO10, Kharga Oasis [Caton-Thompson 1952, 64, 'condition 3']). On a second visit in 1982, a battered chert nodule and another flake of tan chert were found by McDonald. A relatively fresh biface was found on the talus below the remnant. About 30 m to the north, on the surface below another isolated small gravel remnant at about the same elevation, two small ovates of Acheulian type were noted by McDonald, and collected by Brookes in 1982 (1986, fig. 12); both are of ferruginous quartzite in relatively fresh conditon. Other cores and flakes found on the talus or bedrock surfaces around the remnants may have weathered-out of the gravels; a few are white patinated. Despite the present elevation of the deposits (ca. 145 m asl), given the limited size of the exposures, the small size of the components, and less consolidation than other P-II gravels, it is not impossible that the gravels at Loc. 084 belong to the post-P-II downcutting phase rather than to the deposition of P-II gravels. Possibly they represent an inverted wadi deposit.

On the south end of the P-II remnant at Loc. 187E, one biface of quartz-cemented sandstone (possibly from the Duwi Formation) found in a solution pipe might have come from the gravels: this raw material is unlikely to have withstood the abrasion/weathering shown by the chert or quartzite specimens from the gravel surface. A chert biface-trimming flake with the tan patina of chert pieces found in the gravels was found on the talus of the remnant. A chert biface and a large trimming flake with similar patina were found resting on the eroded gravel face. However, the physical correlation of Balat Unit artifacts with P- II gravel deposition has *not* been demonstrated by *in situ* finds. Wendorf and Schild (1980) suggest that the excavated spring vents originally surfaced at the level of the P-II gravels on the remnant to the north (Loc. 147, Occur. 3, elev. ca. 145 m asl). If so, the Balat Unit artisans were using the P-II surface as at other localities to the west and north, except perhaps for Loc. 084. It is, however, puzzling that a range of Balat artifacts, in a similar range of conditions to those excavated from spring vents, can be found on the P-II remnant and talus to the north of the eroded vents at Loc. 147. The Balat Unit inhabitants of Dakhleh may already have been using a landscape where dissection of P-II gravels and equivalent surfaces was well advanced, or the Balat occupation coincided with the erosional period.

No systematic sampling on P-III gravels has yet been done. However, most samples collected from surfaces north of the cultivated areas in western and central Dakhleh are P-III-related (P-III gravel surface, dissected P-III gravel surface, or P-III lag). Based upon these collections, McDonald (1981, 226–230; 1982) identified a larger-sized 'northern' variant of the MSA. (31/405–N1-1, Loc. 033, with mean length of flakes and blades = 75 mm; 31/405–M3-2, Loc. 034, mean length = 69 mm.) Isolated finds of 8 tanged 'Aterian' points were mainly from P-III-related gravels between Ismant and Balat, south to Sheikh Muftah (McDonald 1982). The only *in situ* find from P-III gravels is a fresh, well-worked, triangular specialised chert core found by Kleindienst and Churcher in 1988, eroding from a small terrace remnant north of Esbet el-Sheikh Wali (31/405–M2-1, Loc. 233). Further work is needed to determine whether the various P-III surface finds of MSA in the 60 to 70 mm average size range are related to the 'Aterian' Dakhleh Unit represented by the workshops at Loc. 216, or on the dissected area north of Loc. 187A, where the first tanged blade in Dakhleh was found. The P-III gravels are slightly less indurated than the older P-I and P-II gravels, and are planned to be excavated.

Archaeological Occurrences Associated with Water Deposited Sediments (Spring Mounds, FSS, CSS) (Table 5.1)

Rapid survey in 1986 and 1987 indicates that different spring mounds appear to contain different artifacts, which relates to the geologically brief eruptive span of any spring vent (Haldemann 1962). Judging from isolated *in situ* artifacts (31/420–E10-3, Loc. 146, four small specialised flakes; 31/420–L9-1, Loc. 149, one struck core; 31/420–M9-3B, Loc. 152, one specialised flake) and from surface finds, included artifacts range from Balat Unit bifaces to debitage which suggests the presence of several MSA industries utilising Levallois cores and flakes. This confirms the observations of Schild and Wendorf (1975), but does not agree with Brookes' (1986, 1993) suggestion of a single major episode of Pleistocene spring mound formation. It is tempting to speculate, however, that the spring deposits may encompass the crucial time range during which 'hominids' became 'humans': when the long-established equilibrium systems of *Homo erectus* gave way to the disequilibrium systems introduced by *Homo sapiens sapiens*, during the terminal Middle Pleistocene through to the early Late Pleistocene (Table 5.1).

Spring mounds in Dakhleh vary in their degree of topographic expression, depending upon the combined effects of the surface expression of the originally-deposited sediments, their degree of erosion, and the degree of erosion of sediments surrounding the conduit(s). Thus, the most reduced conduits are not necessarily the oldest. Rejuvenation of older eroded conduits has only been noted at one locality in western Dakhleh (32/390–I3-1, Loc. 162). Here, an indeterminate PSA lithic aggregate is associated with the later vents. Detailed mapping of spring localities is required in both eastern and western Dakhleh, followed by testing to devise adequate excavation methodology, and then by large scale excavation. Previous workers at Kharga and Dakhleh (Caton-Thompson 1952; Schild and Wendorf 1977) concentrated on removing sediments from the feeder conduit ('spring eye'), without excavating the surrounding deposits of the mound super-structure. At Dakhleh, many spring vents have been preserved as isolated mounds. This will allow more extensive work on the superstructures than has been possible before. Such excavations may indicate why the thousands of artifacts found previously were incorporated within the feeder conduits of artesian springs.

A few *in situ* artifacts have come from the CSS (31/420–L10–1, Loc. 151, 2 tan quartzite trimming flakes; 31/420–F9–4, Loc. 362, 1 core), and the FSS (31/420–I6–2, Loc. 155, Occur. 2, 1 struck Levallois core). These can only be classed as PSA. (One biface was found in the FSS in 1992 at Loc. 323, Occ. 1, of Balat Unit type, similar to that from Loc. 084.)

Archaeological Occurrences and Associated Surfaces on the Dakhleh Oasis' Southern Desert Margins, or in the Desert to the South (Table 5.1)

McDonald (1981, 226–230; 1982) identified a smaller 'southern' variant of the MSA from several localities on the southern desert margin of the oasis, from south of Mut (30/405–I2–2, Loc. 043, mean length of flakes and blades = 44 mm; 30/405–L2–3, Loc. 051, mean length = 50 mm), to the northeast and south of Sheikh Muftah (31/420–H6–1, Loc. 090, mean length = 54 mm), and extending to south of Teneida (30/435–M2–2, Loc. 121, mean length of flakes and blades = 49 mm). (Some spring mound occurrences were also assigned to this variant: e.g., 31/405–F9–6, Loc. 040.) She tentatively compared these collections to the 'Khargan' as defined by Caton-Thompson (1952, 29–30, 132–137). No further archae-ological work has been done in these areas, although additional localities below or on spring terrace (FSS) remnants have been noted by Brookes in the course of geological survey (30/420–E1–1, 2 occurrences at Loc. 203; 30/420–E2–1 and E2–2, Locs 214, 215). My brief observations of collections and field relationships suggest that this 'southern MSA variant' may represent more than one cultural stratigraphic unit, and/or a special activity variant. (Wiseman [1993] began more detailed work on these aggregates in 1992.)

One locality in the desert south of Mut, collected in 1980 (31/405–M1–2, Loc. 60), was assigned by McDonald (1981) to her larger-sized 'northern' MSA variant. The artifacts suggest that the locality may belong instead to the still 'larger sized MSA' unit from the P-II at Locality 187A; these also may represent a special activity variant belonging to some more recent MSA unit. Loc. 225, in the desert south of Teneida, provided evidence of 'Aterian' affiliations in 1991 (see below).

Cultural Stratigraphic Units (Fig. 5.2, Tables 5.1 and 5.4)

A simplified distribution of designated localities is given in Figure 5.2 and Table 5.4. The oasis has been subdivided into nine sectors: the missing 'west-south' has never been surveyed; and desert-south transects have only been undertaken in the east. While the subdivisions presented here are somewhat arbitrary, they do give an idea of the frequency of occurrence of Pleistocene Stone Age artifacts (147 archaeological occurrences at 95 designated localities). The gross numerical distribution is similar to that found by Simmons and Mandel (1985, 1986) in a three-week survey of northern Kharga Oasis.

'Earlier Stone Age': Upper Acheulian Unit (5 occurrences)

Isolated bifaces of Upper Acheulian type have been found associated with spring mounds in west-central Dakhleh (33/390–I9–1, Loc. 002; 31/405–D7–3, Loc. 007), and on the high terrace gravels in central-north and east-north Dakhleh (Locs 159, 187A, 187C).

K. Bard noted a group of three large 'quartzite' handaxes on the slope of a low spring mound (Loc. 002) in 1978; and a fourth on top of the mound. One, an elongated ovate with linguate tip, was collected (Bard's fieldnotes 25/XI/1978; Kleindienst 1985; McDonald 1980) and deposited in The Museum of Egyptian Antiquities, Cairo. It was unavailable for study. Measurements from Bard's outline sketch are 218 × 136 × 50 mm. (Note that these measurements would require correction for the removal of material by abrasion/weathering for comparison with specimens in mint condition.)

Hope and Howell collected four 'oversized lithics' during a sandstorm on December 10, 1980, in the 33/390–I9–1, Loc. 002, area: an asymmetrical ovate, 173 × 106 × 40 mm; a cordiform, 140 × 115 × 40 mm; an elongated ovate with linguate point, 183 × 110 × 59 mm, with the same form as the larger specimen sketched by Bard; these are all handaxes of Upper Acheulian type. The fourth specimen, a cordiform with an abruptly truncated thick butt and a heavily battered tip, 140 × 110 × 59 mm, would fit the definition of a 'core axe' and could even be a Historic Period 'maul' (examples are found in this area). The three handaxes may be the three specimens recorded by Bard, as she noted that one of those left on the surface was similar in outline to the collected specimen (pers. comm., 9/VI/1987). I could locate neither the original find spot nor additional specimens during two brief visits to the area with Brookes in 1986.

Except for the 'heavy duty' cordiform, these handaxes are worked around all or most of the circumference; the material is a light-coloured quartzite or quartz-cemented sandstone (probably from the upper Nubia Group Forma-tions, but possibly from the Duwi Formation). The pieces are fresh, to slightly rounded, with light tan patina.

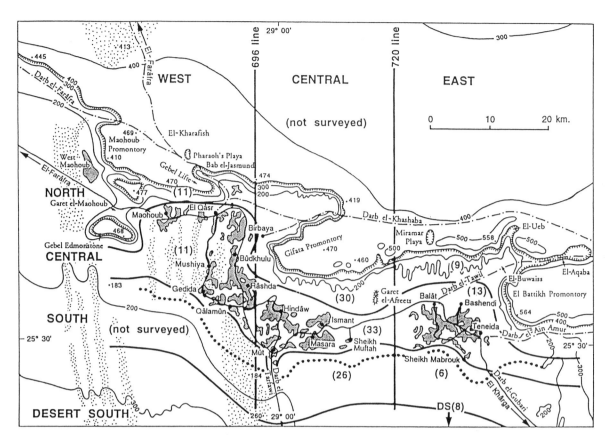

Fig. 5.2. Distribution of designated Pleistocene localities within tentative geoarchaeological zones, 1978–1991, Dakhleh Oasis. Basemap showing topography, major settlements, main roads, cultivated areas (hatched) and dune belts (stippled). Numbers of presently recognised Pleistocene localities per sector given in parentheses. The boundary between North and Central zones approximates the Duwi Cuesta or S'ioh Ridge at the foot of the Libyan Escarpment and that between Central and South zones approximates the southern margin of the modern oasis depression, indicated by the dotted line. The southern boundary approximates the sandstone margins f the Darb el-Arbai'n Desert sandsheet.

Assymetrical biconvex sections suggest that the primary forms were large end-struck or side-struck flakes.

On the P-II gravel surface at Locs 187C and 187A, two isolated handaxes of Upper Acheulian type and made of chert, were found in 1987. In a transect at Loc. 187A, Set I/0–East line, an ovate acuminate in abraded/weathered condition (pocking on both faces), with heavy yellow-brown patina and point heavily damaged, was recovered. It measures 127+ × 97 × 50 mm; the original length was ca. 190 mm. At Loc. 187C, an elongate ovate or ovate acuminate, heavily abraded/weathered with pockmarking on both faces, and heavy brown patina, the point heavily damaged, was also recovered. It measures 155+ × 110 × 40 mm; the original length was ca. 195 mm. The primary forms of the raw material cannot be determined. A limestone biface from the P-II gravel surface at Locality 159 is an extremely eroded limande, or a cleaver-edged biface with a flake struck off the bit; it measures 153 × 84 × 34 mm.

These specimens are assigned to the Upper Acheulian on the basis of form and a qualitative assessment of trimming technique. The use of raw materials other than chert for handaxes is also consistent with Middle Pleisto-

cene Acheulian preferences elsewhere in Africa (e.g., Kalambo Falls Prehistoric Site, Zambia; Isimila Prehistoric Site, Tanzania; Kleindienst 1959, 1962). The conditions of the chert specimens are consistent with their having been exposed longer than Balat Unit or MSA artifacts on Loc. 187 surfaces. These are rare finds, only sufficient to indicate a possibly mid-Middle Pleistocene occupation in Dakhleh. At present, it is difficult to distinguish any isolated finds of small-sized Upper Acheulian bifaces from those of the Balat Unit, except on the basis of condition and morphology. As yet, detailed analyses of shaped tools have not been completed.

A small surface aggregate was recovered from the spring mound Loc. 007, in west-central Dakhleh. This is tentatively assigned to the final or Upper Acheulian unit, although the 11 bifaces are small sized (length range 78 to 160 mm; thickness/ length [T/L] ratio 0.26; mean width/ thickness [W/T] ratio 2.6 compared with 2.4 for the 8 large Upper Acheulian bifaces). Use is made of raw materials other than chert (44%, including 9% of 'chert ball' geode materials). Further work is needed to establish whether a Levallois technique was used.

The artifacts in fresh or mint condition at Loc. 007

Table 5.4. Archaeological occurrences at 95 designated Pleistocene localities in Dakhleh Oasis, 1978–1989. Key: Sectors: W – west, N – north, E – east, S – south, C – central, DS – desert south. Locations of sectors shown in Fig. 5.2.

Cultural Stratigraphic Unit Assignment (1989)	Sector									Total Number	%
	W-N	C-N	E-N	W-C	C-C	E-C	C-S	E-S	E-DS		
'MSA': 'small sized'	–	–	–	1	2	1	12	6	–	22	15.0
Dakhleh Unit	–	1	–	(1)[a]	6[b]	1	–	–	2	10	6.8
'MSA': undifferentiated	9	19	6	3	12	6	10	–	5	70	47.6
'MSA': 'large sized'	–	5	–	–	–	–	–	–	–	5	3.4
'ESA' isolates	2	1	1	2	5	1	2	–	–	14	9.5
Balat Unit	–	2	–	–	5	3	1	–	–	11	7.5
'Upper Acheulian'	–	2	1	2	–	–	–	–	–	5	3.4
'PSA': indeterminate	–	–	1	3	3	1	1	–	1	10	6.8
TOTAL NUMBER	11	30	9	11	33	13	26	6	8	147	99.5
PERCENTAGE	7.5	20.4	6.1	7.5	22.5	8.8	17.7	4.1	5.4		100
DESIGNATED LOCALITIES											
Number	6	14	9	8	19	7	19	6	7	95	
Percentage	6.3	14.7	9.5	8.4	20.0	7.4	20.0	6.3	7.4		

[a] Isolate recorded by Winlock (1936).   [b] Plus 8 isolates, c-c.

appear to derive from the 'backdirt' produced by historic removal of the spring conduit sediments; many show ferruginous staining. Others, more weathered/abraded, were found on the upper slopes of the mound. Together with easily identified Holocene pieces (confirmed by McDonald, pers. comm., 26/II/1987), six fresh, lightly patinated specialised cores and flakes, two in abraded condition, and a reworked abraded Aterian point are in the surface collection. The point is a typical holoport, and these may all be holoports. The mound was located in 1979 by Mills, who made a small collection. He excavated a small Roman settlement and cemetery at its base. McDonald made a small collection in 1980. Kleindienst and Brookes, in 1987, collected all artifacts found on the summit and upper slopes of the mound, excluding obvious Holocene pieces and clusters.

The Acheulian aggregate includes cores, trimming flakes, hammerstones and small light-duty scrapers as well as the 11 bifaces. It can be compared with Locus VIIA, below the Refuf Pass, Kharga, where *in situ* handaxes occurred with discoidal cores, classed as 'Evolved Acheulian' (lengths from 51 to >137 mm; Caton-Thompson 1952, 95–96).

'Earlier Sone Age': Balat Unit (11 occurrences)
The Balat Unit, designated in 1986 (Kleindienst 1985), was defined by Schild and Wendorf (1977; Wendorf and Schild 1980) from large aggregates recovered from excavated spring vents west of Balat, at Loc. 147. Although there is some use of quartzite, most artifacts are of chert, probably from nodules taken from the surrounding gravels (?P-II, preserved on remnant to the north) (Wendorf and Schild 1980, percentage not published; Schild and Wendorf 1975, 69, record 'more than 99%' chert; also

Wendorf *et al.* 1976). Among the 5,729 *in situ* artifacts in Occurrence E-72–1, and 1,201 in Occurrence E-72–2 (Wendorf and Schild 1980; cf. 5,725 for E-72–1 in Schild and Wendorf 1977), only two crude 'Levallois flake cores' (Schild and Wendorf 1977,23) were recovered which "... can be classified within the proto-Levallois category ..." (Schild and Wendorf 1975, 70). Most shaped tools are bifaces (n = 677, 42%), varying in plan form, but mainly with 'thick, unworked butts' (Schild and Wendorf 1975, 70), and of small size (for 428 bifaces from both *in situ* and surface contexts at E-72–1, lengths range from 46 to 156 mm, and mean = 97 mm [Schild and Wendorf 1977]). The emphasis in trimming is at the tip and along one or both laterals. The W/T ratio ranges from 1.1 to 3.9 for the same sample, with means for various form categories ranging from 1.8 to 2.6, and mean of total = 1.96 (Schild and Wendorf 1977). Most of the 147 other 'retouched tools' are light-duty scrapers, including a considerable number of denticulated and notched edges (Schild and Wendorf 1977, 23, 44).

The Balat Unit bifaces are smaller than those from the 'Evolved Acheulian' in spring mound KO10 at Kharga (Caton-Thompson 1952, 59, 63) with which they were compared (Schild and Wendorf 1977: McDonald 1982: KO10, 367 handaxes, lengths range from 40 to 212 mm, mean recalculated = 148 mm). However, the KO10 handaxes show a similar choice of raw material (non-chert = 0.6%) and in trimming patterns to those of the Balat Unit. Large-sized raw material is not available at or near the KO10 spring mound, and may have been transported for some distance (Caton-Thompson 1952).

Isolated small bifaces have been reported by DOP investigators since 1978, from diverse contexts, and distributed from eastern to western Dakhleh in all sectors except the east-south. Some may actually be well-prepared unstruck specialised (Levallois) cores; some may belong with earlier or, more likely, later cultural stratigraphic units than the Balat Unit. The central sector includes more designated Balat localities (5/11) than any other sector. Designated finds of isolated bifaces are also more frequent here (5/14, although not all finds recorded in field notes have been included), suggesting that many are, in fact, Balat Unit products. (Some bifaces/core-axes were found in MSA contexts in 1991 and 1992.)

Bifaces similar to those from Loc. 147, and assigned to the Balat Unit, have been found on spring mounds to the southwest of that locality (31/420–H6–3, Loc. 155, Occurs 1 and 6; 31/420–L9–2, Loc. 150, the most southerly Balat occurrence), or below spring mounds (31/420–H6–1, Loc. 091). Artifacts exhibiting Levallois technique are found in some surface associations or rarely *in situ* in nearby spring deposits. However, the association of bifaces with specialised cores or flakes remains to be demonstrated in excavated contexts. The evidence from Loc. 147 suggests that the use of Levallois techniques was minimal; the two cores classed as 'proto-Levallois' (Schild and Wendorf 1977, 23) could be accidental and within the range of discoidal core preparation. Surface finds by Schild and Wendorf on dissected P-II (= P-III) gravels around the excavated spring vents may well be younger than the *in situ* artifacts. This equivocal association is repeated in the 'Acheulio-Levalloisian' at Kharga (Caton-Thompson 1952, 26–27, 99–102). Small *in situ* aggregates from four occurrences in the Upper Sheet Gravels below Refuf Pass yielded 61 artifacts in fresh to abraded condition: 11 bifaces; one lanceolate biface/point; various unspecialised cores interpreted as specialised core roughouts; unspecialised flakes; and only two possible specialised pieces – a flake blade (Caton-Thompson 1952, pl. 59.5) and one small ?struck 'shapely discoidal core' (Caton-Thompson 1952, 101–102, unillustrated, cf. pl. 65.3). This might well be similar to the two cores found by Schild and Wendorf (1977). In my brief observations in 1987 of the surface of the Upper Sheet Gravels near the Kharga railway right-of-way at ca. Km 157, I noted few artifacts, but a greater incidence of bifaces than is seen on the P-II gravels at Loc. 187 in Dakhleh, and few specialised cores or flakes (estimated density ≤1 artifact per 20 metres, over a 400 m transect of ca. 2 m width).

No definitive evidence yet exists at *either* Dakhleh *or* Kharga for an 'Acheulio-Levalloisian' unit in which handaxes are clearly associated with a significant incidence of specialised flake production techniques. Restudy of the Khargan evidence and contexts is badly needed, particularly because the spring tufas at Kharga provide the best possibilities for chronometric dating, if associated archaeological units at Kharga can be correlated with those at Dakhleh (see Kleindienst *et al.*, this volume, Chapter 1).

The single biface, and flakes, found *in situ* at Loc. 084 are tentatively assigned to the Balat Unit (discussion above). Diffuse 'clusters' (apparently associated con-

centrations) of bifaces have been found on the central Taref sandstone ridge (Kleindienst *et al.*, this volume, Chapter 1, fig. 1.2) at an elevation of 142 m (31/420– L3– 1, Loc. 081, McDonald 1982), similar to the elevations of the gravels at Locs 084 and 147, and on P-II gravel at Loc. 187E. In both cases, the artifacts are dominantly of Tarawan chert, with some usage of other rocks (quartz-cemented sandstone, quartzite, or 'chert ball' material; 7% at Loc. 187E). The bifaces are small (n = 33, lengths range from 51 to 139 mm at Loc. 081; n = 15, lengths range from 88 to 160 mm, mean = 128 mm at Loc. 187E); and are noticeably thick-butted with emphasis upon tip and edge trimming (Loc. 187E: T/L ratios range from 0.18 to 0.40; mean = 0.31; W/T ratios range from 1.4 to 3.2, mean = 2.0). The association of the two specialised cores found in the Loc. 081 'cluster' is doubtful (McDonald 1982). The concentration at Loc. 187E included no cores, and no specialised flakes, nor were any found in the immediate vicinity of the dispersed 'cluster' (approximately 50 m in diameter) on the southern edge of the terrace. Isolated bifaces and unspecialised discoidal flake cores occur, together with a few isolated specialised cores and flakes, and two bifacial points (MSA), in the markedly sparse scatter of chert on the ca. 20,000 m² of the mapped southwest portion of the remnant. The discoidal flake cores appear to fit the category of 'subdiscoidal core' at Loc. 147 (Schild and Wendorf 1977, pl. VI).

The Balat Unit has been considered 'Upper Acheulian' (Schild and Wendorf 1977), 'Late Acheulian' (Wendorf and Schild 1980), or 'final Acheulian' (Kleindienst 1985); it might also be considered to be 'early Middle Stone Age'. In attempting to make comparisons with archaeological occurrences found at great distances from Dakhleh and Kharga, Schild noted that:

"It seems ... resemblances could be better explained by the nature of limited abilities of morphological evolution of bifaces, some of which were undoubtedly changing toward more functionally adapted cutting tools or knives" (Schild and Wendorf 1977, 100; also see 1975).

Although the stratigraphic evidence is still unsatisfactory Africa-wide, several different patterns can be discerned in the shift from ESA to MSA industries during the late Middle to early Late Pleistocene, which must represent experiments with new materials, new technologies, and new lifeways (Clark 1982). Of immediate interest here, is the pattern in eastern and central Africa which results in the elusive 'Sangoan' techno-complex. The changes can be observed at Kalambo Falls, Zambia, one of the few stratified sequences to cover the shift from ESA to MSA. There, the uppermost Acheulian bifaces (handaxes and cleavers) are replaced in part by heavy-butted bifaces in which trimming is restricted to the tips and one or both laterals ('core axes'); the shift can be demonstrated most easily in the changed width/thickness index (W/T) for bifacial tools (Sheppard and Kleindienst 1986, 1988, 1996). There is also a shift in the choice of the kind and form of raw materials, which becomes more pronounced later in the Late Pleistocene, accompanied by size diminution in some tool forms. Evidence for a similar pattern was noted in the Nubian Nile Valley (e.g., Chmielewski 1968; Guichard and Guichard 1968; Kleindienst 1972), as well as at Kharga (KO10, Caton-Thompson 1952; Clark 1982).

The Balat Unit is not 'Sangoan'. However, from an African viewpoint, the pattern of technological change is analogous. Perhaps the term 'Intermediate' should be resurrected (cf. Bar-Yosef 1982) to apply to periods when long-established typo-technical traditions are in process of change through experimentation with materials and techniques. This results in highly variable archaeological aggregates, even from occurrences within relatively restricted areas and time ranges. Interestingly, Caton-Thompson (1983) was instrumental in introducing the concept at the 1955 Pan-African Congress on Prehistory.

Change in the material cultural system can only be by addition, subtraction, or replacement. Prehistorians are misguided in seeking 'transitions' between periods of relatively stable cultural patterning. When people *choose* to solve old, or new, problems in a new way, there is no 'transition' in their actions: on one occasion they do it one way, and the next they do it another: they may experiment with doing it several different ways before choosing the one which best suits their purposes. They may change only some aspects of their stone tool production system (McBrearty 1991), or they may change different aspects at different times. The result of individual choices is abrupt. The *illusion* of transition is created because not everyone chooses to do the same thing at the same time, and because our control of events is imprecise.

The Balat Unit, utilising mainly chert, succeeds the Upper Acheulian in which completely trimmed, cutting-edged tools are made of diverse, coarser-grained raw materials; in some cases these are of large size. Material treatment shifts from the use of large flakes (or perhaps split chert nodules/cobbles) as primary forms to the use of entire nodules/cobbles, with trimming restricted to bits and laterals, retaining a heavy butt. The size range of bifacially-worked artifacts is reduced, and the average size may be much reduced. The dynamics of the design problems, and of the solutions which may result in widely-separated analogies in lithic aggregates, which are represented in the observed changes from 'Upper Acheulian' to 'something else', have yet to be understood throughout Europe and Africa. However, I agree with Schild (Schild and Wendorf 1975) that the technical choices made by the Balat Unit artisans show such change: they no longer follow the patterns of the Acheulian inhabitants of Dakhleh.

'Middle Stone Age': Undifferentiated (70 occurrences)

Most of the 70 designated PSA localities yielding aggregates emphasising specialised flake production techniques can only be classed as 'Middle Stone Age'. More specific assignments await further systematic studies and detailed analyses. The distribution of localities reflects the ubiquitous occurrence of relatively large-sized specialised cores and flakes in the central (12) and central-north (19) sectors. Those in the central-south sector are associated with spring deposits (9/10). Fewer localities were noted in the west (9 north, 3 central) or east (7 north, 7 central). None occur in the east-south sector; 5 are in the east-desert-south.

Some of these localities on the high piedmont terrace surfaces undoubtedly belong in the 'large-sized' MSA unit, but have not yet been adequately sampled. The P-III aggregates from which McDonald identified a 'northern' MSA unit (1981, 1982) also require further study. These, and a few other aggregates suggest that a 'medium-sized' pre-'Aterian' MSA unit occurs at Dakhleh, and/or that there is a larger-sized, and earlier phase of the 'Aterian' (see below).

'Middle Stone Age': 'Large-sized' unit (5 occurrences)

Systematic sampling at Locality 187A, on the P-II gravel surface (Tabs 5.2 and 5.3) has established the existence of an MSA unit in which final-stage specialised cores average ca. 89 mm in greatest dimension, and final stage flakes ca. 81 mm (corrected values, Table 5.3). Such artifacts recovered from workshops reflect the reject stage of specialised flake production and represent what the artisans left behind, as too small, or otherwise unsuitable for use and transport. The thin scatter on the P-II surface appears to represent the cumulative effect of slow surface processes on many individual small work areas where Tarawan chert nodules were reduced. Maximum surface processes is estimated as 1 m at Loc. 187A (Kleindienst *et al.*, this volume, Chapter 1). Small individual knapping stations are preserved on gravel surfaces in other situations, e.g., on the P-III at Loc. 201. Only one denser 'cluster' has been located on the Loc. 187A gravel surface (Loc. 187/V-WKS), lying in a hollow near the eastern edge of the remnant, and surrounded by areas with 'sparse' concentrations of chert fragments. The workshop aggregate includes 46 specialised cores, 28 unspecialised/ initial trim cores, 85 specialised flakes and fragments, and 333 unspecialised flakes and fragments. The only 'tool' is a hammerstone. Embedded in the silt, below the veneer, was a single specialised core rough-out in fresh condition with grey, slightly glossy patina (190 × 155 × 50 mm), which indicates the original size of chert nodules worked, and the potential size of some early-stage specialised flake removals which were not found on the remnant. The fine silts require excavation. The core size in the workshop cluster is comparable to that found in the Set samples; but mean specialised flake and flake scar lengths are smaller (Table 5.3). This may be a sampling anomaly or the workshop cluster may represent another MSA unit.

Few shaped tools have been found, either in Loc. 187A transect Sets, or by deliberate searching. It should be noted, however, that the condition of the material makes identification of fine retouched tools problematic to impossible. Almost all pieces in the veneer show some edge damage, and only those certainly retouched are recorded as shaped 'tool' forms.

Bifaces of Balat type, some of which could be MSA, were found only on the southeastern portion of the Loc. 187A remnant, opposite the southwestern portion of Loc. 187E where they also occur. In two instances, the bifaces were reworked after they had already been abraded/weathered; the 'double-patinated' specimens suggest that the MSA artisans saw them as part of the available raw material, and that they predate the MSA. Alternatively, the reworked pieces may indicate the existence of a Balat variant using specialised techniques, which cannot yet be distinguished from the larger-sized MSA unit.

Long, lanceolate bifacial 'points', with cortex or talon retained on a truncated butt, also appear to belong to this MSA aggregate. These are reminiscent of Guichard and Guichard's 'Nubian Middle Paleolithic bifacial foliates', but are distinctive. They (1965, 86–98, fig. 21.1; 1968) figure one possible example, termed a 'Mousterian point with bifacial retouches', which appears to be reworked. At Dakhleh, one was found isolated at Loc. 187E (142+5 [tip damaged] × 69 × 25 mm); another was found ca. 8 km to the south, at Loc. 148 (155+8 × 67 × 30 mm), on P-III gravels. A third point, more refined in workmanship, and snapped in antiquity, lay in a small workshop 'outlook' area on the southeastern edge of P-I remnant at Loc. 188A (135 × 35 × 12 mm). Two partially-worked examples, in different stages of production, were found in Loc. 187A transects.

Near Kharga, Brookes found a similar point (130 × 62 × 23 mm) on a high remnant above the Upper Sheet Gravels, south of the Refuf Pass ('Pre-Upper Sheet Gravels', Caton-Thompson 1952, 5, fig. 1). Simmons and Mandel (1985, fig. 26.B, KUDWE 6, 'biface') figure a possible example, only partially bifacially-worked, from a 'cluster' on the slope of a spring mound southwest of Gebel et Teir. Caton-Thompson (1952) apparently found no similar bifaces in Kharga (none are illustrated), or else assigned all bifacial 'points' to the 'Aterian'. She (1952, 27) stated: "No hand-axes or other bifacial tools have been found which could be attributed to the Levalloisan." Wendorf *et al.* (1987) at Bir Tarfawi also followed this practice and illustrated no 'bifacial foliates'; Close (1988; 1993) later suggested that some belonged with units earlier than 'Aterian'; and subsequently the ascription to 'Aterian' has been withdrawn for most Bir Tarfawi/Bir Sahara MSA finds (Wendorf *et al.* 1990, 1993). Wendorf and Schild (1980, fig. 2.50 a,c) illustrated two points from BT-14, Areas A and C, both of which are smaller and less refined than the Dakhleh specimens: identified as an 'atypical Quinson point', and an 'elongated bifacial Mousterian point'.

With regard to Saharan MSA points in general, in the original definition of unifacial/bifacial/normal/elongated 'Mousterian points', Bordes (1961, 22) specified: "Ce sont des pièces triangulaires, subtriangulaires, parfois losangiques, plus ou moins allongées, à extrémité acuminée, obtenues par *retouches importante* à partir d'un éclat *de type quelconque*, Levallois ou non" [original emphases].

The term 'Mousterian point' has never been closely defined (cf. Brèzillon 1968). Bordes (1961, 21) also noted: "Nous avons donné sous un mode plaisant une définition de la pointe d'ordre pratique, quand on hésite sur la qualification 'pointe' ou 'racloir convergent': dans ce cas, on se demande si vraiment on emmancherait l'outil au bout d'un bâton pour aller chasser l'ours. Si oui, c'est indiscutablement une pointe! Et nous ajoutions en note que ce critere plaisant était uniquement d'ordre pratique, et ne présupposait rien quant au veritable emploi des pointes moustériennes." This qualification to the contrary, given a total absence of bears in Egypt, I would also argue for the total absence of 'Mousterian points'.

It is unlikely that the illustrated specimens mentioned are 'typical' finds, and the varied designations support that inference. The combination of partial or complete bifacial working (possibly to straighten the longitudinal profile) and truncated butt have implications for hafting techniques and use. Rare and isolated finds suggest curation. I suggest that this point form be studied in its Saharan contexts, and named from a Saharan reference locality. At Loc. 187, end and side scrapers, one retrimmed bifacial scraper, one bifacial 'ovate' point, and a few minimally-retouched flakes, some with ventral bulbar thinning, complete the retouched tool inventory. In addition, a few 'naturally-backed couteau' and 'Levallois points' can be sorted out of the unretouched flakes.

Reworking of older, already abraded/weathered cores as well as of Balat type bifaces, suggests a protracted period of MSA usage of the P-II surface at Loc. 187. The obvious cognate for this 'large-sized' Dakhleh MSA unit is the Kharga 'Levalloisian' unit of Caton-Thompson (1952, 27–29). She discovered nine localities with *in situ* materials, stratigraphically from deposits below the Thebes limestone escarpment, in the Refuf Pass (four occurrences), the Abu Sighawal Pass (three occurrences), and the Bulaq and Mantana Passes (one occurrence each). These small aggregates were designated as 'Lower Levalloisian'. Combined, they include 20 specialised cores with a length range from 59 to 133 mm, mean = 83 mm, and 16 specialised flakes, length range from 56 to 133 mm, mean = 80 mm. For the four Refuf Pass occurrences, the mean length for 13 cores is 94 mm, and for 11 flakes, 92 mm (recalculated from Caton-Thompson 1952: 103–105, 108–109, 115–116, 144). Based upon size, and geomorphic associations, it appears that the Loc. 187 'large-sized' MSA unit is cognate to the 'Lower Levalloisian' at Kharga.

(For recalculation of the mean length dimensions from Caton-Thompson [1952], I have simplified her typology to fit the gross classes at Dakhleh. Caton-Thompson gives N and means of length for her categories, so that totals can be obtained by N × Mean; the totals for her classes can then be added according to the simplified typology, and new means calculated. One cannot find the standard deviation [SD], however, because her original measurements are not given. It must be emphasised that Caton-Thompson was well ahead of her time in providing metric information which allows for such comparisons!)

'Middle Stone Age': 'Medium-sized' Unit (provisional): included within 'undifferentiated MSA'

The occurrence at Dakhleh of a cognate for the medium-sized 'Upper' and 'Indeterminate Levalloisian', found above the Tarawan escarpment and at spring mounds KO8A and KO10 in Kharga (Caton-Thompson 1952, 28), is suggested by McDonald's (1981) recognition of a 'northern' MSA variant. Recalculated values for the Kharga 'Upper' and 'Indeterminate Levalloisian' give mean length values between 61–71 mm for specialised cores, and 68–83 mm for specialised flakes. Samples are small except at KO8A, where 155 specialised cores average 65 mm in length, and 138 specialised flakes average 68 mm (no weathering/abrasion correction needed) (Caton-Thompson 1952, 95, 143, 80). The 'northern' variant samples fall within this size range; some may belong to the Dakhleh Unit (mean artifact lengths between 69 to 75 mm, not corrected for condition).

The small samples from the 'outlook' occurrences on the high P-I surfaced remnants (elevations >235 m a.s.l.) may belong here as well. At Locs 188A and 188B, corrected mean specialised core and flake lengths average ca. 80 mm, somwhat less than in the Loc. 187A 'large-sized' unit (total, 17 cores, length range from 52 to 98 mm, uncorrected mean = 77 mm; 11 flakes, length range from 50 to 113 mm, uncorrected mean = 77 mm). These lightly abraded to abraded aggregates are less standardised/refined than those in the Dakhleh Unit; the condition of these artifacts on isolated high remnants suggests longer surface exposure than does the condition of the Dakhleh Unit artifacts. No tanged pieces were found.

'Middle Stone Age' – 'Aterian': Dakhleh Unit or cf. Dakhleh Unit (10 designated occurrences, plus isolates, and 'holoports')

Caton-Thompson (1946, 1952) established no unit name for the 'Aterian' at Kharga. Because the first diagnostic PSA artifact reported from Dakhleh (Winlock 1936) – a point with distinctive ventral bulb thinning – established the 'Aterian presence' at Dakhleh and in the western oases (McDonald 1980), this unit is here designated as the 'Dakhleh Unit'. Until 1987, it was known mainly from isolated finds by Bard, McDonald, or Sheldrick of diagnostic bifacial lanceolates and tanged or 'pedunculated' artifacts, distributed from west to east in the central sectors of the oasis, mainly from P-III-related contexts. Two workshop areas were located in 1987, where smaller-sized specialised cores and flakes, many in fresh to lightly abraded or weathered condition, are associated

with partially-worked tanged objects, and points with bulbar thinning: Loc. 334, on the dissected area north of the head of the P-II gravel-surfaced remnants of Loc. 187 (grid collected 1997); and 31/420–I1–1 & I2–1, Loc. 216, on a P-II remnant (grid-collected in 1988; excavations into underlying silty soil projected). At Loc. 216, struck cores range in length from 40 to 100 mm, mean = ca. 74 mm, and lengths of specialised flakes range from 40 to 110mm, with a mean of ca. 71 mm (condition corrected values, Table 5.3). The values for aggregates recorded for the Kharga 'Aterian' are remarkably similar: Bulaq Pass, A Site, 7 m terrace *in situ* and surface finds, 19 specialised cores, length range from 51 to 120 mm, mean = 73 mm, and 36 specialised flakes, range from 51 to 101 mm, mean = 71 mm; spring mound KO6E, *in situ* and surface finds, 155 specialised cores, length range from 45 to 103 mm, mean = 68 mm, and 71 specialised flakes, length range from 46 to 128 mm, mean = 71 mm (recalculated from Caton-Thompson 1952, 119, 88; not corrected for condition).

Additional tanged and lanceolate points are holoports found by McDonald and Sheldrick, which extend the Dakhleh Unit distribution to the southern sectors of the oasis. One isolated tanged point was noted in the 1989 desert traverse by McDonald and Sheldrick (McDonald 1990a, Loc. 255).

Locality 225, discovered in 1987 in the desert southeast of Teneida and Ein el-Sheikh Mabrouk Badr, and surface collected in 1991, can probably be assigned to the Dakhleh Unit. Lying at the southeast base and on the lower slopes of a small eroded Nubia Group quartzite gebel, it provides an occupation aggregate rather than only workshop material. The collection includes one tanged point, unifacial and bifacial points, Levallois points, and various scraper forms, as well as unretouched flakes and worked-out core 'nubbins'. The length range of eight tools made on specialised flakes is 63 to 160 mm, mean length 112 mm, which suggests that this locality represents a different and probably earlier phase of the Dakhleh Unit than does Loc. 216. Further work is projected for this site and neighboring localities.

The Dakhleh Unit material awaits detailed analysis. The inventory is known to include tanged points, ranging from those with ventral retouch only at the tang to fully bifacial forms (McDonald 1982, fig. 3), untanged bifacial 'lanceolate' points of varying size, tanged blades, tanged flakes, and tanged scrapers, and burins, plus points with bulbar thinning, and scrapers on flakes. An unusual use of raw material form is a 'gouge' for which the 'handle' is supplied by a natural conical rod-form struck-off a chert nodule (Loc. 187A), possibly a pseudomorph for a haft normally made of a perishable material. The Levallois technique is refined, and the single core found *in situ* in P-III gravels at Loc. 233 is of this type. (Surveys in 1991 and 1992 established that Dakhleh Unit artifacts are associated with the surface of P-III gravels, and associated planed-off sandstone surfaces north, east and northeast of Bashendi.)

'Middle Stone Age': 'Small-sized' Unit (provisional) (22 occurrences)

The 'small-sized' MSA material was characterised by McDonald (1981, 1982) from localities in the central-central and central-south sectors. A few additional occurrences have been surface-collected by Brookes (Locs 203, 214, 215). The specialised (Levallois technique) cores and flakes are smaller than in the Dakhleh Unit, and no tanged objects have yet been found in association, although bifacial working is present. More than one cultural stratigraphic unit may be represented in these occurrences, which come mainly from the southern margins of the central-south and east-south sectors, as surface finds on the Nubia sandstone cuesta/plain. A few spring mound occurrences are recognised (31/405–F9–6, Loc. 040; 30/405–L1–3, Loc. 054; 31/420–N2–1, Loc. 080, in the central sector; and 31/420–E10–3, Loc. 146; 31/420–M10–1, Loc. 153, in the central-south sector); and some of the central-south occurrences found by Brookes appear to be associated with surfaces of terraced FSS or CSS deposits.

If the cognates for the 'small-sized' MSA unit at Kharga are the 'Levalloiso-Khargan' and/or the 'Khargan' (Caton-Thompson 1952), as suggested by McDonald (1981), some or all of the assigned localities may predate rather than postdate the Dakhleh Unit as is indicated in Table 5.1. Caton-Thompson and Gardner (Caton-Thompson 1952, 117–118) found Kharga 'Aterian' stratigraphically above 'Levalloiso-Khargan' at Bulaq Pass (A Site). Unfortunately, the 'Levalloiso-Khargan' was defined from small aggregates of abraded artifacts, which come from contexts in which the aggregates could have resulted from natural sorting. The validity of the unit is doubtful. The 'Khargan' (Caton-Thompson 1952, 132–133) came mainly from surface occurrences in 'solution pans' in the Plateau Tufa below the Thebes escarpment at Bulaq Pass: those at low altitudes contained 'Aterian'; those at middle altitudes contined a 'mix' of 'Aterian' and 'Khargan'; and those at the highest altitudes contained 'Khargan'. McBurney (1960) questioned the validity of many 'tools', though not the existence of small-sized specialised cores and flakes. (Length values recalculated for Bulaq Pass, solution pans F, G, H [Caton-Thompson 1952]: for 48 specialised cores, range from 36 to 91 mm, mean = 52 mm; for 71 specialised flakes, range from 21 to 102 mm, mean = 56 mm.) On this evidence, a pre-'Aterian' age is doubtful. Caton-Thompson (1952, 151) also recorded a small-sized "Epi-Levalloisian" aggregate with specialised flaking technique from a spring mound context (KO5B).

Hester and Hobler (1969; Hobler and Hester 1969) found 'Khargan' at both Kurkur (four localities) and Dungul oases (16 localities), on the Plateau or on pediment-terrace remnants, in some cases associated with slab structures. These are still the only other recorded occurrences of 'Khargan'. At Dungul, the 'Khargan' overlies a tufa radiocarbon dated 20,950 BC ± 600, and is therefore, *contra* Hester and Hobler, almost certainly post-'Aterian', if, indeed, they are different units. Caton-

Thompson (1952), and Hester and Hobler (1969) note difficulties in typological differentiation. (The date can also be questioned.) Tillet (1989) has asked where the central Saharan 'Aterian' populations went during the hyperarid phase beginning ca. 19,000/19,500 BP.

Size diminution of specialised elements is a time trend in Africa, but is not a certain indicator of stratigraphic position if different kinds of localities/activities are being considered. (The provisional Dakhleh chronology is based upon material from workshop localities to provide control for activity differentials.) Definition within the 'small sized' MSA aggregates is a problem requiring attention in both Dakhleh and Kharga. One factor that may make unit definition difficult in Dakhleh is that any attractive and diagnostic artifacts are likely to have been preferentially collected by Holocene peoples. (See Wiseman 1993; this volume, Chapter 6.)

Cultural Stratigraphic Unit: 'Indeterminate' (10 occurrences)

Included as 'indeterminate' are a number of workshop areas, without diagnostic attributes, some small collections without diagnostics, and one occurrence (32/390–I3–1, Loc. 162), where a distinctive aggregate of flakes with small triangular ?MSA bifaces was collected in west-central Dakhleh, in 1986. This is associated with spring rejuvenation vents, and may be late in the Pleistocene sequence. No additional work has yet been done in western Dakhleh except for one reconnaissance southwest of Gebel Edmonstone in 1992.

SUMMARY

Status of Pleistocene Archaeological Research in Dakhleh Oasis: 1978–1989

In assessing the status of research on Pleistocene archaeology and geoarchaeology at Dakhleh, I must re-emphasize that this report is based upon reconnaissance and pilot studies. Substantial progress has been made in determining the associations of various cultural stratigraphic units with geomorphic units, and with the geological stratigraphy, although *in situ* finds have been rare except in spring deposits, and these may be misleading. Progress in the characterisation of some cultural stratigraphic units will allow future work in eastern Dakhleh to concentrate upon specific problem areas.

The find of a previously unrecorded aggregate in 1986, however, serves to underline the fact that the Pleistocene evidence at Dakhleh is still incompletely surveyed, and that new PSA units as well as the refinement of knowledge about the units already defined can be expected in the future. In addition to the projected transects, the areas west of Gebel Edmonstone and from Gebel Edmonstone to Ismant require further survey for PSA localities, and to determine the geomorphic settings and the nature of the aggregates present in the localities noted during the earlier years of DOP survey. Laboratory analysis alone will require a major investment of time and effort. The results to date, however, illustrate that significant information can be obtained from intensive, systematic, regionally-directed study of the surface aggregates, and their distributions. The work at Dakhleh is at that stage of archaeological research which logically develops from the regional studies pioneered by G. Caton-Thompson and E.W. Gardner in Kharga Oasis and the Fayum Depression.

Endnotes on Pleistocene Archaeological Chronology: 1994

The Pleistocene stratigraphic framework has been provided mainly by Brookes (1986, see Kleindienst et al., this volume, Chapter 1). Because the most feasible chronometric dating method for Pleistocene archaeology appeared to be uranium-series dating, a few samples were submitted to H.P. Schwarcz (McMaster University) in order to ascertain whether any Dakhleh sediments were satisfactory for dating. These include samples of large spring-tufa boulders found in or on Pleistocene alluvial gravels or colluvium. The boulders derived from scarp sources that have either been completely destroyed by subsequent erosion, or which remain undiscovered. The tufas are amenable to U/Th dating, although some samples of CSS and the matrix of P-II gravels (Loc. 084) are not. Many more determinations are required from different sedimentary units to establish a valid chronometric framework. Samples were obtained from Caton-Thompson's and Gardner's 'Tufa 4' and 'Tufa 3' in the Refuf Pass at Kharga in 1992, for comparative dating.

At present, three Dakhleh boulders have been successfully dated (Kleindienst et al., this volume, Chapter 1), and each appears to represent a different period of tufa formation. These can only be used as indicators for conditions that produced significant groundwater discharge from the Libyan Plateau escarpment face and which deposited tufas below spring localities: one boulder from central-north Dakhleh is beyond dating range, but appears to represent a period early in the Middle Pleistocene; a second, from west-north Dakhleh, dates to the later Middle Pleistocene; and a third, from the east-north sector, falls near the beginning of the Late Pleistocene. It is tempting to correlate even these sparse results with the now-recognised stages of the Pleistocene recorded in deep-sea cores, or with the hypothetical climatic forcing schemes for Africa (Bernard 1962; Brookes 1993; Rognon 1989; Short et al. 1991). However, as noted by Deacon and Lancaster (1988), independent, land-based sequences are needed to test such models. Africanists have learned to be wary of fitting their sequences into preconceived models, when experience teaches that often local conditions significantly modify the effects of gross climatic changes (Fontes and Gasse 1991).

Water, of course, is the key to all habitation in Dakhleh.

It should be noted that conditions which could have produced groundwater discharge from the Libyan Plateau scarp need not coincide with conditions that produced artesian discharge from spring eyes in the Nubia Group terrain. The artesian springs would drain aquifers which are presumably recharged from the south, perhaps far to the south for the deeper aquifers, or more locally for near-surface aquifers, while the Plateau scarp springs drain higher aquifers that would be charged locally, or from the north and east. Thus, changes in Pleistocene precipitation patterns in either the north or south may ultimately water Dakhleh Oasis, but through different sources. Even today, dug wells on the Plateau recently produced water (C. Bergman, pers. comm. 1992), and two scarp springs recorded as active during Historic times are still active: Ain Amur on the northeast face of Gebel abu Tartur, northeast of Dakhleh, and Ain Tafnis, on the west face of Gebel el-Tafnis in southern Kharga Oasis (Ball 1900; Cailliaud 1826; Vivian 1990), both of which discharge where shales overlie the 'Overwegi Bed(s)'. 'Qanawat', or underground aqueducts dug in Historic times, drain from the Libyan Escarpment in northern Kharga and still carry water when cleared (B. Baghat, pers. comm., 8/II/1992; Haynes 1983).

No scarp springs and only a few discharging artesian springs are known today in Dakhleh. However, it is likely that the scarcity of natural artesian springs is effected by the large numbers of dug wells and boreholes. Beadnell (1901) reported that the number of dug wells in 1896 had resulted in significant drawdown of the near-surface Nubian aquifers. A few hamlets are still dependent upon near-surface flowing wells, some as shallow as 1 to 2 m excavations into the surface sandstones. In some cases the water may come from leakage from the deep boreholes. However, we cannot be certain that even under conditions as arid as those of today that scarp and/or artesian water would not have been available at Dakhleh. Even local rainfall may be significant.

> "Quite a small rainfall would have allowed man to wander over the limestone plateau during the winter, as at the present time the rare thunderstorms that occur farther north sometimes provide pools of drinking water which last for months. In December 1932 a pool was formed between Bahariya Oasis and Sittra, which was originally about a kilometer and a half long by half a kilometer wide, and this provided the water supply for the members of Mr. Walpole's survey expedition and fifty camels for over five months" (Little 1933: 527).

Further, given that animals as diverse as elephants, rhinos and baboons dig for water, it seems incongruous that prehistorians rarely allow our prehistoric ancestors the wit to improve their water supplies by digging into spring sources, or aquifers, as do the Namibian San or other arid zone dwellers. Caton-Thompson reported two instances of Holocene digging at Kharga (1952: 186); MSA dug-waterholes have recently been reported from Bir Sahara, BS-12 (Campbell 1992; 1993). I have, therefore, taken as my null hypothesis the proposition that with topographic conditions approximating those of the present, Dakhleh was habitable throughout the Late Pleistocene, and perhaps for the the past 300,000 to >400,000 years (Thurston 1987).

The specific 'guesstimate' dates given in Table 5.1 are based upon long-distance typological and technological correlations, and should be treated as such. Large bifaces of Upper Acheulian type have been found in spring mound contexts and as isolates lying *on* P-II alluvial gravels. The Upper Acheulian pattern in eastern Africa breaks up between 350,000 and 200,000 years ago, so that 'typical' Upper Acheulian artifacts can be regarded as dating from at least 350,000–400,000 BP. (e.g., Cornelissen 1989; 1992; Cornelissen *et al.* 1990; Howell *et al.* 1972; Kleindienst *et al.* 1977; Lee *et al.* 1976; Mehlman 1987, 1989, 1991). (This also occurs in the Levant [Goren-Inbar 1995, 97, fig. 3].) McHugh (McHugh *et al.* 1988, 1989; Szabo *et al.* 1989) accepted similar dates in southern Egypt. The Upper Acheulian at Bir Tarfawi dates to >350,000 BP (Wendorf *et al.* 1991, 1993). Either the palaeosprings associated with the Dakhleh Upper Acheulian (Locs. 002, 007) broke surface at the P-I/P-II levels, or they post-date P-II surface gravels and their dissection. The rarity of Upper Acheulian finds may explain why no artifacts have been found *in* P-I gravels, and why so few artifacts have been found *in* P-II gravels (Loc. 084, discussed above). I, therefore, postulate that P-I and P-II gravel deposition predates 350,000 BP, and that initiation of the P-II dissection probably predates 200,000 BP.

As noted above, I consider that the Balat Unit postdates the Acheulian *sensu stricto*, and that it falls within the period between 'typical' ESA and 'typical' MSA aggregates. Again, on eastern African evidence, this would be between ca. 300,000 and 150,000 BP (Cornelissen *et al.* 1990; McBrearty 1991; Mehlman 1987, 1989, 1991). Balat Unit localities are spring mound-associated in central-south Dakhleh, or lie *on* P-II gravels to the north, but these may postdate the P-II dissection.

Provisional seriation in the MSA is based upon the prevalent African trend of size diminution in lithic artifacts from the Middle Pleistocene through the terminal Late Pleistocene. Hence, the generalised MSA is provisionally dated from late Middle Pleistocene to the beginning of the Late Pleistocene, after ca. 250,000 BP (e.g., Laury and Albritton 1975; Wendorf *et al.* 1975, 1991, 1993). The much smaller sized Dakhleh Unit aggregate from Locality 216 is provisionally placed between 50,000 and 20,000 BP, later than the 'medium-sized' MSA unit (Tillet 1985). (Chronometric U-series dates obtained in 1994, after this paragraph was written, give some confirmation for these estimates; see Kleindienst *et al.*, this volume, Chapter 1.)

Additional information has been gathered in 1991 and 1992, which is not discussed here except where directly relevant to localities discovered previously. Several localities now support the existence of one or more larger-sized, earlier phase(s) of the Dakhleh Unit, and the correlation of the Dakhleh Unit with the P-III gravel surfaces. These are 'guesstimated' at >70,000 to 50,000 BP. There are several new localities containing aggregates which cannot be assigned to any defined or provisonally defined cultural stratigraphic unit. Some are typo-techno-logically early in the MSA; others are probably as late as or later than the Loc. 216 Dakhleh Unit. It will come as no surprise to the Pleistocene archaeologists (Kleindienst, Wiseman) if we ultimately discover and date several units that fall within the 30,000 to 10,000 BP period to link with the Masara Holocene Unit (McDonald 1991a, this volume, Chapter 6; Wiseman 1997).

Acknowledgements
Work in 1986 and 1988 was funded by SSHRCC grant 410–85–1146; that in 1987 and 1988 by SSHRCC grant 410–87–1414, and, in 1987, a University of Toronto Research Leave Grant. A grant from the Humanities and Social Sciences Committee of the Research Board, University of Toronto, facilitated attendance at the ICLPNA Conference at Dymaczewo, near Poznan, Poland, in September 5–10, 1988. Work at Dakhleh was made possible by the organisational skills of Edwin C. Brock, and Hisham S. Higazy of the Canadian Institute in Egypt; and depended upon the superb logistical and camp organisation of A.J. Mills and R.A. Frey. I am indebted to all members of the Project who brought interesting occurrences to my notice, especially Michelle Berry, Rufus Churcher, Alan Hollett, Colin Hope, Jonathan Howell, Jim Knudstad, Karla Kroeper, Lech Krzyzaniak, Jenny Leimert, Mary McDonald, John O'Carroll, Peter Sheldrick and Marcia Wiseman. A.F. Hollett has provided essential technical assistance. I am much indebted to Mr. G. Freeman, whose foresight and constant support sustained the Dakhleh Oasis Project until ill-health forced his retirement from DOP in 1988. We miss him. Above all, I am indebted to Joan Davies who has endured the stress of winters at home alone in Toronto.

Address for Author
M.R. Kleindienst: Department of Anthropology, Erindale College, University of Toronto at Mississauga, Ontario, Canada L5L 1C6 *and* Research Associate, Department of Near Eastern and Asian Civilizations, Royal Ontario Museum, 100 Queen's Park North, Toronto, Ontario, Canada M5S 2C6; *also* Research Associate, Department of Anthropology, Field Museum of Natural History, Chicago, Illinois, USA 60605.

REFERENCES

Allsworth-Jones, P. 1986. Middle Stone Age and Middle Palaeo-lithic: the evidence from Nigeria and Cameroun, 153–168. *In* Bailey, G.N. and P. Callow, eds, *Stone Age prehistory. Studies in memory of Charles McBurney.* Cambridge: Cambridge University Press, 265p.

Ball, J. 1900. *Kharga Oasis: its topography and geology*. Cairo, Survey Department, Public Works Ministry. Geological Survey Report 1899, Part II, 116p.

Bar-Yosef, O. 1982. Some remarks on the nature of transitions in prehistory, 29–33. *In* A. Ronen, ed., *The Transition from Lower to Middle Palaeolithic and the Origin of Modern Man*. Oxford: British Archaeological Reports, International Series 151, 329p.

Beadnell, H.J.L. 1901. *Dakhla Oasis: its topography and geology*. Cairo: Survey Department, Public Works Ministry Geological Survey Report, 1899, part IV, 107p.

Bernard, E.A. 1962. Interprétation astronomique des pluviaux et interpluviaux du Quaternaire africain, 67–95. *In* Mortlemans, G. and J. Nenquin, eds., *Actes du IVᵉ Congrès Panafricain du Préhistoire et de l'Étude du Quaternaire, Section II*. Tervuren, *Musée Royale de l'Afrique Centrale, Annales, série in-8°, Sciences Humaines* 40, 373p.

Bordes, F. 1961. *Typologie du Paléolithique ancien et moyen*. Bordeaux: L'Institute de Préhistoire de l'Université de Bordeaux, Mémoire 1, 85p.

Breed, C.S., N.S. Embabi, H.A. El-Etr and M.J. Grolier. 1980. X. Wind deposits in the Western Desert. *Geographical Journal* **146**: 88–90.

Brèzillon, M.N. 1968. La dénomination des objets de pierre taillée. Matériaux pour un vocabulaire des préhistoriens de langue française. *Gallia Préhistoire IVe supplément*. Paris: Editions du Centre National de la Recherche Scientifique, 411p.

Bromley, R.G. and M.A. Ekdale. 1986. Flint and fabric in European chalks, 71–82. *In* Sieveking, G. de G., and M.B. Hart, eds, *The Scientific Study of Flint and Chert. Proceedings of the 4th International Flint Symposium held at Brighton Polytechnic 10–15 April 1983*. Cambridge: Cambridge University Press, 290p.

Brookes, I.A. 1983. Dakhleh Oasis Project. Dakhleh Oasis – a geoarchaeological reconnaissance. *Journal of the Society for the Study of Egyptian Antiquities* **13**: 167–177.

Brookes, I.A. 1986. *Quaternary geology and geomorphology of the Dakhleh Oasis region and its environs, south-central Egypt. Reconnaissance findings*. North York, Toronto: York University, Department of Geography, Discussion Paper Series 32, 90p.

Brookes, I.A. 1989. Early Holocene basinal sediments of the Dakhleh Oasis region, south-central Egypt. *Quaternary Research* **32** 139–152.

Brookes, I.A. 1993. Geomorphology and Quaternary geology of the Dakhla Oasis Region, Egypt. *Quaternary Science Reviews* **12**: 529–552.

Cailliaud, F. 1826. *Voyage a Méroé, au fleuve Blanc, au-delà de Fazoql dans le midi du Royaume de Sennâr, a Syouah et dans cing autres oasis, fait dans les années 1819, 1820, 1821, et 1822*. Paris, L'Imprimérie Royale [1972, facsimile edition, Farnborough, Hampshire: Gregg International Publishers, vol. I], 429p.

Campbell, A.L. 1992. The significance of Middle Paleolithic water holes at Bir Sahara in the Western Desert of Egypt, 207–216. *In* H. L. Dibble and P. Mellars, eds., *The Middle Paleolithic: Adaptation, Behavior and Variability*. Philadelphia: University of Pennsylvania Museum, Monograph no. 72, 232p.

Campbell, A.L. 1993. 35. BS-12: A site associated with West Lake 2 (1988 excavations), 519–527. *In* F. Wendorf, R. Schild, A. E. Close and Associates eds, *Egypt during the Last Interglacial. The Middle Paleolithic of Bir Tarfawi and Bir Sahara East*. New York/London: Plenum Press, 596p.

Caton-Thompson, G. 1946. The Aterian Industry: its place and significance in the Palaeolithic world. *Journal of the Royal Anthropological Institute* **76**: 1–44.

Caton-Thompson, G. 1952. *Kharga Oasis in Prehistory*. London: Athlone Press, 213p.

Caton-Thompson, G. 1983. *Mixed Memoires*. Gateshead, Tyne and Wear: Paradigm Press, 346p.

Caton-Thompson, G. and E.W. Gardner. 1932. The prehistoric geography of Kharga Oasis. *The Geographical Journal* **80**: 369–406.

Chmielewski, W. 1968. Early and Middle Paleolithic sites near Arkin, Sudan, 110–147. *In* Wendorf, F., ed., *The Prehistory of Nubia*, vol. 1. Dallas: Burgwin Research Center and Southern Methodist University Press, 531p.

Churcher, C.S. 1980. Dakhleh Oasis Project. Preliminary observations on the geology and vertebrate palaeontology of north-western Dakhleh Oasis: a report on the 1979 field work. *Journal of the Society for the Study of Egyptian Antiquities* **10**: 370–396.

Churcher, C.S. 1981. Dakhleh Oasis Project. Geology and palaeontology: interim report on the 1980 field season. *Journal of the Society for the Study of Egyptian Antiquities* **11**: 194–212.

Churcher, C.S. 1982. Dakhleh Oasis Project. Geology and palaeontology: interim report on the 1981 field season. *Journal of the Society for the Study of Egyptian Antiquities* **12**: 108–114.

Churcher, C.S. 1983. Dakhleh Oasis Project. Palaeontology. Interim report on the 1982 field season. *Journal of the Society for the Study of Egyptian Antiquities* **13**: 178–187.

Churcher, C.S. 1986. Dakhleh Oasis Project. Palaeontology. Interim report on the 1985 field season. *Journal of the Society for the Study of Egyptian Antiquities* **16**: 1–4.

Churcher, C.S. This volume. Chapter 8. Holocene faunas of the Dakhleh Oasis, 133–151.

Clark, J.D. 1975. A comparison of the Late Acheulian industries of Africa and the Middle East, 605–659. *In* Butzer, K.W. and G.Ll. Isaac, eds, *After the Australopithecines. Stratigraphy, Ecology, and Culture Change in the Middle Pleistocene*. The Hague: Mouton, 911p.

Clark, J.D. 1980. Human populations and cultural adaptations in the Sahara and Nile during prehistoric times, 527–582. *In* Williams, M.A.J. and H. Faure, ed., *The Sahara and the Nile*. Rotterdam: A.A. Balkema, 607p.

Clark, J.D. 1982. The transition from the Lower to Middle Palaeolithic in the African Continent, 235–255. *In* A. Ronen, ed., *The Transition from Lower to Middle Palaeolithic and the Origin of Modern Man*. Oxford: British Archaeological Reports, International Series no. 151, 329p.

Clark, J.D., ed. 1991. *Cultural Beginnings. Approaches to Understanding Early Hominid Life-Ways in the African Savanna*. Bonn: Dr. Rudolf Habelt GMBH, 208p.

Clark, J.D. and M.R. Kleindienst. 1974. The Stone Age cultural sequence: terminology, typology and raw material, 71–106. *In* Clark, J.D., ed., *Kalambo Falls Prehistoric Site, II*. Cambridge: Cambridge University Press, 420p.

Clayton, C.J. 1986. The chemical environment of flint formation in Upper Cretaceous chalks, 43–54. *In* Sievking, G. de G., and M.B. Hart, eds, *The Scientific Study of Flint and Chert. Proceedings of the 4th International Flint Symposium held at Brighton Polytechnic, 10–15 April, 1983*. Cambridge: Cambridge University Press, 290p.

Close, A.E. 1988. BT-14, a stratified Middle Palaeolithic site at Bir Tarfawi. *Paper presented at International Commission of the Later Prehistory of North-eastern Africa Symposium, Dymaczewo, Poland, September 5–10*.

Close, A.E. 1993. BT-14, A stratified Middle Palaeolithic site at Bir Tarfawi, Western Desert of Egypt, 113–122. *In* Krzyzaniak, L., M. Kobusiewicz and J. Alexander, eds, *Environmental Change and Human Culture in the Nile Basin and Northern Africa until the Second Millenium BC*. Poznan: Poznan Archaeological Museum, 494p.

Cooke, R., A. Warren and A. Goudie. 1993. *Desert Geomorphology*. London: UCL Press Limited, 526p.

Cornelissen, E. 1989. *De Mogelijkheid van de Midden-Kapthurin-formatie (Baringo, Kenya) voor een etnografische Benadering van het Laat-Acheuleaan*. Deel 1, II. Ph.D. Thesis, Departement Archologie en Kunstwetenschap, Afdeling Oudheid, Faculteit van Letteren de Woksbegeerte, Katholieke Universiteit Leuven, 418p.

Cornelissen, E. 1992. *Site GNJH-17 and its implications for the archaeology of the Middle Kapthurin Formation, Baringo, Kenya.* Tervuren, Belgium: Musée Royale de l'Afrique Centrale, 192p.

Cornelissen, E., A. Boven, A. Dabi, J. Hus, K. Ju Wong, E. Keppens, R. Lanhohr, J. Moeyersons, P. Pasteels, H. Pieters, H. Uytterschaut, F. van Noten and H. Workineh. 1990. The Kapthurin Formation revisited. *The African Archaeological Review* **8**: 23–75.

DeCelles, P.G., and R.C. Gutschick. 1983. Mississippian woodgrained chert and its significance in the western interior United States. *Journal of Sedimentary Petrology* **53**: 1175–1191.

de Morgan, J. 1896. *Recherches sur les origins de l'Egypte. L'Age de la Pierre et les Métaux.* Ernest Leroux, ed. Paris: 282p.

Deacon, J. and N. Lancaster. 1988. *Late Quaternary Palaeoenvironments of Southern Africa.* Oxford: Clarendon Press, 225p.

Dunnell, R.C. and W.S. Dancey. 1983. The siteless survey: a regional scale data collection strategy, 267–287. *In* Schiffer, M.B., ed., *Advances in Archaeological Method and Theory* **6**. New York: Academic Press, 359p.

Egyptian Geological Survey and Mining Authority. 1982. *Geological Map Sheet NG-35 Dakhla, 1:1,000,000.* Cairo: Geological Survey of Egypt.

Foley, R. 1981a. Off-site archaeology: an alternative for the shortsited, 157–183. *In* Hodder, I., G. Ll. Isaac, and N. Hammond, eds, *Pattern of the Past. Studies in Honour of David Clark.* Cambridge: Cambridge University Press, 164p.

Foley, R. 1981b. *Off-site Archaeology and Human Adaptation in Eastern Africa.* Oxford: British Archaeological Reports, International Series no. 97, 265p.

Fontes, J.C., and F. Gasse. 1991. PALHYDAF (Palaeohydrology in Africa) program: Objectives, methods, major results. *Palaeogeography, Palaeoclimatology, Palaeoecology* **84**: 191–215.

Gautier, A. 1980. Contributions to the archaeozoology of Egypt, 317–344. *In* Wendorf, F. and R. Schild, eds, *Prehistory of the Eastern Sahara.* New York: Academic Press, 414p.

Gautier, A. 1988. The Middle Palaeolithic game fauna of Bir Sahara and Bir Tarfawi (Western Desert). *Paper presented at International Commission of the Later Prehistory of North-Eastern Africa Sympopsium. Dymaczewo, Poland, September 5–10.*

Gautier, A. 1993. The faunal spectrum of the Middle Palaeolithic in Bir Tarfawi, Western Desert, 123–127. *In* Krzyzaniak, L., M. Kobusiewicz and J. Alexander, eds, *Environmental Change and Human Culture in the Nile Basin and Northern Africa until the Second Millenium BC. Poznan: Poznan Archaeological Museum,* 494p.

Goren-Inbar, N. 1995. The Lower Paleolithic of Israel, 93–109. *In* Levy, T.E., ed., *The Archaeology of Society in the Holy Land.* London: Leicester University Press, 624p.

Guichard, J. and G. Guichard. 1965. Contributions to the Prehistory of Nubia, no. 3. The Early and Middle Paleolithic of Nubia: a preliminary report, 57–116. *In* Wendorf, F., ed., *Contributions to the Prehistory of Nubia.* Dallas: Fort Burgwin Research Center and Southern Methodist University Press, 164p.

Guichard, J. and G. Guichard. 1968. Contributions to the study of the Early and Middle Paleolithic of Nubia, 148–193. *In* Wendorf, F., ed., *The Prehistory of Nubia, I.* Dallas: Fort Burgwin Research Center and Southern Methodist University Press, 531p.

Haldemann, E.G. 1962. Mud-Volcanoes in the Sekenke area (with note on archaeology by Maxine R. Kleindienst). *Tanganyika Notes and Records* **58–59**: 242–257.

Haynes, C.V. 1983. Quaternary studies, Western Desert, Egypt and Sudan, 1975–1978. *National Geographic Society Research Reports* **15**: 257–293.

Hermina, M. 1990. The surroundings of Kharga, Dakhla and Farafra oases, 259–292. *In* Said, R., ed., *The Geology of Egypt.* Rotterdam/Brookfield: A.A. Balkema, 734p.

Hester, J.J. and P.M. Hobler. 1969. Prehistoric Settlement Patterns in the Libyan Desert. *University of Utah Anthropological Papers 92, Nubian Series 4*, 174p.

Hobler, P.M. and J.J. Hester. 1969. Prehistory and environment in the Libyan Desert. *South African Archaeological Bulletin* **23**: 120–130.

Howell, F.C., G.H. Cole, M.R. Kleindienst, B.J. Szabo and K.P. Oakely. 1972. Uranium-series dating of bone from the Isimila Prehistoric Site, Tanzania. *Nature* **237**: 51–52.

Hume, W.F. 1925. *Geology of Egypt, vol. 1. The Surface Features of Egypt, their Determining Causes and Relation to Geological Structure.* Cairo: Government Press, 408 pp.

Isaac, G. Ll. 1981. Stone Age visiting cards: approaches to the study of early land use patterns, 131–155. *In* Hodder, I., G. Ll. Isaac, and N. Hammond, eds, *Pattern of the Past.* Cambridge: Cambridge University Press, 443p.

Kleindienst, M.R. 1959. *Composition and Significance of a Late Acheulian Assemblage, Based upon an Analysis of East African Occupation Sites.* Ph.D. Thesis, Department of Anthropology, University of Chicago, 342p.

Kleindienst, M.R. 1962. Components of the East African Acheulian assemblage: an analytic approach, 81–111. *In* Mortelmans, G. and J. Nenquin, eds, Actes du IVe *Congrès Panafricain de Préhistoire et de l'Étude du Quaternaire, Section III.* Tervuren: *Annales du Musée Royal de l'Afrique Centrale, serie in-8°, Sciences Humaines* **40**: 505p.

Kleindienst, M.R. 1972. Brief observations on some Stone Age sites recorded by the Yale University Prehistoric Expedition to Nubia, 1964–1965, 111–112. *In* Hugot, H.J., ed., *Actes de VIe Session, Congrès Panafricain de Préhistoire, Dakar 1967.* Chambéry: Les Imprimeries Réunies de Chambéry, 598p.

Kleindienst, M.R. 1985. Dakhleh Oasis Project. Pleistocene archaeology. Report on the 1986 season. *Journal of the Society for the Study of Egyptian Antiquities* **15**: 136–137.

Kleindienst, M.R. 1987. Pleistocene archaeology of the Dakhleh Oasis, Egypt: background to the Holocene adaptations, Abstract. *Program and Abstracts, Society for American Archaeology, 52nd Annual Meeting, Toronto*, 88.

Kleindienst, M.R. 1988. Off-site archaeology at the Dakhleh Oasis: a contribution to the Pleistocene archaeology of Egypt. *Paper presented at International Commission of the Later Prehistory of North-eastern Africa Symposium, Dymaczewo, Poland, September 5–10.*

Kleindienst, M.R., J.D. Clark, C.Lee and J.L. Bada. 1977. Amino acids in fossil woods. Nature **267**: 468.

Kleindienst, M.R., C.S. Churcher, M.M.A. McDonald and H.P. Schwarcz. This volume. Chapter 1. Geography, Geology, Geochronology and Geoarchaeology of the Dakhleh Oasis region: An interim report, 1–54.

Klitzsch, E., F.K. List and G. Pöhlmann. 1987. *Geological Map of Egypt NG 35 SE Dakhla, 1:500,000.* Cairo: The Egyptian General Petroleum Corporation.

Kröpelin, S. 1987. Palaeoclimatic evidence from early to mid-Holocene playas in the Gilf Kebir (southwest Egypt). *Palaeoecology of Africa* **18**: 189–208.

Laury, R.L. and C.C. Albritton. 1975. Geology of the Middle Stone Age archeological sites in the main Ethiopian Rift Valley. *Bulletin of the Geological Society of America* **86**: 999–1011.

Little, O.H. 1933. Further remarks on the Kharga Oasis. I. *Geograpical Journal* **81**: 526–528.

Lee, C, J.L. Bada and E. Peterson. 1976. Amino acids in modern and fossil woods. *Nature* **259**: 183–186.

McBrearty, S. 1991. Recent research in western Kenya and its implications for the status of the Sangoan industry, 159–176. *In* J.D. Clark, ed., *Cultural Beginnings*. Bonn: Dr. Rudolf Habelt GMBH, 208p.

McBurney, C.B.M. 1960. *The Stone Age of Northern Africa*. Harmondsworth, Middlesex, Penguin Books, 288p.

McDonald, M.M.A. 1980. Dakhleh Oasis Project. Preliminary report on lithic industries in the Dakhleh Oasis. *Journal of the Society for the Study of Egyptian Antiquities* 10: 315–329.

McDonald, M.M.A. 1981. Dakhleh Oasis Project. Second preliminary report on lithic industries in the Dakhleh Oasis. *Journal of the Society for the Study of Egyptian Antiquities* 11: 225–231.

McDonald, M.M.A. 1982. Dakhleh Oasis Project. Third preliminary report on the lithic industries in the Dakhleh Oasis. *Journal of the Society for the Study of Egyptian Antiquities* 12: 115–138.

McDonald, M.M.A. 1983. Dakhleh Oasis Project. Fourth preliminary report on the lithic industries in the Dakhleh Oasis. *Journal of the Society for the Study of Egyptian Antiquities* 13: 158–166.

McDonald, M.M.A. 1986. Dakhleh Oasis Project. Holocene prehistory: interim report on the 1987 season. *Journal of the Society for the Study of Egyptian Antiquities* 16: 103–113.

McDonald, M.M.A. 1987. Adaptations in Dakhleh Oasis in the early- to mid-Holocene. *Abstract. Program and Abstracts, Society for American Archaeology, 52nd Annual Meeting, Toronto*, 98.

McDonald, M.M.A. 1990a. Dakhleh Oasis Project. Holocene prehistory: interim report on the 1988 and 1989 seasons. *Journal of the Society for the Study of Egyptian Antiquities* 20: 24–53.

McDonald, M.M.A. 1990b. The Dakhleh Oasis Project. Holocene Prehistory: interim report on the 1990 season. *Journal of the Society for the Study of Egyptian Antiquities* 20: 54–64.

McDonald, M.M.A. 1990c. The Dakhleh Oasis Project. Holocene Prehistory: interim report on the 1991 season. *Journal of the Society for the Study of Egyptian Antiquities* 20: 65–74.

McDonald, M.M.A. 1991a. Technological organization and sedentism in the Epipalaeolithic of Dakhleh Oasis, Egypt. *The African Archaeological Review* 9: 81–109.

McDonald, M.M.A. 1991b. Systematic reworking of lithics from earlier cultures in the early Holocene of Dakhleh Oasis, Egypt. *Journal of Field Archaeology* 18: 269–273.

McDonald, M.M.A. This volume. Chapter 7. Neolithic cultural units and adaptations in Dakhleh Oasis, Egypt, 117–132.

McFadden, L.D., S.G. Wells and M.J. Jercinovich. 1987. Influence of eolian and pedogenic processes on the origin and evolution of desert pavements. *Geology* 15: 504–508.

McHugh, W.P., J.F. McCauley, C.V. Haynes, C.S. Breed and G.G. Schaber. 1988. Paleorivers and geoarchaeology in the southern Egyptian Sahara. *Geoarchaeology: an International Journal* 3: 1–40.

McHugh, W.P., C.S. Breed, G.G. Shaber, J.F. McCauley and B.J. Szabo. 1989. Acheulian sites along the "Radar Rivers," southern Egyptian Sahara. *Journal of Field Archaeology* 15: 361–379.

Mehlman, M.J. 1987. Provenience, age, and associations of archaic *Homo sapiens* crania from Lake Eyasi, Tanzania. *Journal of Archaeological Science* 14: 133–162.

Mehlman, M.J. 1989. *Later Quaternary archaeological sequences in northern Tanzania*. Ph.D thesis. Department of Anthropology, University of Illinois at Urbana-Champaign, 756p.

Mehlman, M.J. 1991. Context for emergence of modern man in eastern Africa: some new Tanzanian evidence, 177–196. *In* J.D. Clark, ed., *Cultural Beginnings*. Bonn: Dr. Rudolf Habelt GMBH, 208p.

Mills, A.J. 1979. Dakhleh Oasis Project. Report on the first season of survey, October-December, 1978. *Journal of the Society for the Study of Egyptian Antiquities* 9: 163–185.

Mills, A.J. 1980. Dakhleh Oasis Project. Report on the second season of survey, September-December, 1979. *Journal of the Society for the Study of Egyptian Antiquities* 10: 251–282.

Mills, A.J. 1981. Dakhleh Oasis Project. Report on the third season of survey, September-December, 1980. *Journal of the Society for the Study of Egyptian Antiquities* 11: 175–192.

Mills, A.J. 1982. Dakhleh Oasis Project. Report on the fourth season of survey, September-December, 1981. *Journal of the Society for the Study of Egyptian Antiquities* 12: 93–101.

Mills, A.J. 1983. Dakhleh Oasis Project. Report on the fifth season of survey, September-December, 1982. *Journal of the Society for the Study of Egyptian Antiquities* 13: 121–141.

Neumann, K. 1989. Holocene vegetation of the eastern Sahara: charcoal from prehistoric sites. *The African Archaeological Review* 7: 97–116.

Pachur, H.-J. and S. Kröpelin. 1987. Wadi Howar: paleoclimatic evidence from an extinct river system in the southeastern Sahara. *Science* 237: 298–300.

Pachur, H.-J., H.-P. Röper, S. Kröpelin, and K. Goschin. 1987. Late Quaternary hydrography of the eastern Sahara. *Berliner geowissenschaftliche Abhandlungen (A)* 75.2: 331–384.

Pettijohn, F.J. 1957. *Sedimentary Rocks* (edit. 2). New York: Harper and Row, 718p.

Rognon, P. 1989. Variations de l'aridité au Sahara depuis 125 000 B.P. en relation avec les 'contraintes' orbitales et glaciares. *Bulletin de la Société Géologique de France, Séries 8*, 5: 13–20.

Roubet, C. 1981. La préhistoire des environs de Balat. Prospection de Janvier 1981. *Bulletin de l'Institute Français d'Archéologie Orientale* 81: 223–226.

Schild, R.F. and F. Wendorf. 1975. New explorations in the Egyptian Sahara, 65–112. *In* Wendorf, F. and A.E. Marks, eds, *Problems in Prehistory: North Africa and the Levant*. Dallas: Southern Methodist University Press, 462p.

Schild, R.F. and F. Wendorf. 1977. *The prehistory of the Dakhla Oasis and adjacent desert*. Warsaw: Polish Academy of Sciences, Institute for the History of Material Culture, 259p.

Sheppard, P.J. and M.R. Kleindienst. 1986. Technological change in the Early and Middle Stone Age at Kalambo Falls (Abstract). The longest record: the human career in Africa. *A Conference in Honour of J. Desmond Clark, 12–16 April, Berkeley, California, Abstract Volume*, 82.

Sheppard, P.J. and M.R. Kleindienst. 1988. Technical change in the Earlier and Middle Stone Age of Kalambo Falls. *Paper presented at Annual Meetings, Canadian Archaeological Association, Whistler, B.C., May 13–16, 1988*.

Sheppard, P.J. and M.R. Kleindienst. 1996. Technological change in the Earlier and Middle Stone Age of Kalambo Falls, Zambia. *African Archaeological Review* 13(3): 171–196.

Short, D.A., J.G. Mengel, T.J. Crowley, W.T. Hyde and G.R. North. 1991. Filtering of Milankovich cycles by earth's geography. *Quaternary Research* 35: 157–173.

Simmons, A.H. and R.D. Mandel. 1985. *Human Occupation of a Marginal Environment: an Archaeological Survey near Kharga Oasis, Egypt*. Lawrence: University of Kansas, Museum of Anthropology Project Report Series 57, 243p.

Simmons, A.H. and R.D. Mandel. 1986. *Prehistoric occupation of a marginal environment: an archaeological survey near Kharga Oasis in the Western Desert of Egypt*. Oxford: British Archaeological Reports, International Series 303: 242p.

Szabo, B.J., W.P. McHugh, G.G. Schaber, C.V. Haynes and C.S. Breed. 1989. Uranium-series dated authigenic carbonates and Acheulian sites in southern Egypt. *Science* 24: 1053–1056.

Tillet, T. 1985. The Palaeolithic and its environment in the northern part of the Chad basin. *The African Archaeological Review* 3: 163–177.

Tillet, T. 1989. L'Atérien saharien: essai sur l'comportement d'une civilisation paléolithique face à l'accroissement de l'aridité.

Bulletin de la Société Géologique de France Séries 8, **5**: 91–97.

Thurston, H. 1987. Everlasting oasis. *Equinox* **35**: 30–43.

Vivian, C. 1990. *Islands of the Blest. A Guide to the Oases and Western Desert of Egypt*. Ma'adi, Egypt: Trade Route Enterprises, 309p.

Wendorf, F., ed. 1965. *Contributions to the Prehistory of Nubia*. Dallas: Fort Burgwin Research Center and Southern Methodist University Press, 164p.

Wendorf, F., ed. 1968. *The Prehistory of Nubia*. Dallas: Fort Burgwin Research Center and Southern Methodist University Press, 1084p.

Wendorf, F., A.E. Close, and R. Schild. 1987. Recent work on the Middle Palaeolithic of the eastern Sahara. *The African Archaeological Review* **5**: 49–63.

Wendorf, F., A.E. Close, R. Schild, A. Gautier, H.P. Schwarcz, G.H. Miller, K. Kowalski, H. Krolik, A. Bluszcz, D. Robins and R. Grün. 1990. Le dernier interglaciare dans le Sahara oriental. *L'Anthropologie (Paris)* **94**: 361–391.

Wendorf, F., A.E. Close, R. Schild, A. Gautier, H.P. Schwarcz, G.H. Miller, K. Kowalski, H. Królik, A. Bluszcz, D. Robins, R. Grün and C. McKinney. 1991. Chronology and stratigraphy of the Middle Paleolithic at Bir Tarfawi, Egypt, 197–208. *In* J.D. Clark, ed., *Cultural Beginnings*. Bonn: Dr. Rudolf Habelt GMBH, 208p.

Wendorf, F., R.L. Laury, C.C. Albritton, R. Schild, C.V. Haynes, P.E. Damon, M. Sahafiqullah and R. Scarborough. 1975. Dates for the Middle Stone Age of East Africa. *Science* **187**: 740–742.

Wendorf, F. and R. Schild. 1980. *Prehistory of the Eastern Sahara*. New York: Academic Press, 414p.

Wendorf, F., R. Schild, A. E. Close and Associates. 1993. *Egypt during the Last Interglacial. The Middle Paleolithic of Bir Tarfawi and Bir Sahara East*. New York/London: Plenum Press, 596p.

Wendorf, F., R. Schild, R. Said, C.V. Haynes, A. Gautier, and M. Kobusiewicz. 1976. The prehistory of the Egyptian Sahara. *Science* **193**: 103–114.

Winlock, H.E. 1936. *Ed-Dakhleh Oasis: Journal of a Camel Trip made in 1908*. New York: Metropolitan Museum of Art, 61p.

Wiseman, M.F. 1993. The Dakhleh Oasis during the terminal Pleistocene: Is anybody home?, 283–285. *In* R.W. Jamieson, S. Abonyi and N.A. Mirau, eds, *Culture and Environment: A Fragile Coexistence. Proceedings of the Twenty-Fourth Annual Conference of the Archaeological Association of the University of Calgary*. Calgary: University of Calgary Archaeological Association, 444p.

Wiseman, M.F. This volume. Chapter 6. Late Pleistocene prehistory in the Dakhleh Oasis, 109–115.

6

LATE PLEISTOCENE PREHISTORY
IN THE DAKHLEH OASIS

Marcia F. Wiseman

ABSTRACT

The period between approximately 60,000 and 11,000 BP is thought to be one of progressive desiccation in the Saharan Western Desert. Some scholars believe that such climatic deterioration prompted a withdrawal of human habitation from the area. This paper adopts a dissenting view. Although secure dates remain elusive, technological and stylistic attributes of the lithic artifacts found in and around Dakhleh Oasis support the opinion that humans were indeed present during this time-span.

INTRODUCTION

The 1993 field-season marked the first season to be devoted exclusively to testing the proposition that the Western Desert was devoid of human habitation during a hyperarid period which began ca. 60,000 BP, and lasted until the onset of the Holocene wet period ca. 11,000 years ago (Close and Wendorf 1992: 63; Schild 1987: 21). Although there is a strong likelihood of an occupational hiatus in the hyperarid southern regions of the Sahara during the latter part of the Late Pleistocene (= Würm maximum), there is increasing evidence to suggest that such was not the case everywhere within this vast area, nor throughout the whole extended time-period cited above. For example:

1. At least two of the non-climatic factors which influence the availability of water during arid phases, i.e., variation in the available water at the foot of a scarp and the presence of major artesian aquifers (Rognon 1980: 49–50, 59), are operative in and around Dakhleh Oasis. The presence of tufas indicate that springs were active along the Libyan Escarpment at different times, perhaps inclusive of the last 30,000 or 40,000 years (Kleindienst pers. com., 1993); samples of these tufas collected by M.R. Kleindienst, H.P. Schwarcz and myself since the 1992 season are in the process of being uranium/thorium dated by H.P. Schwarcz at McMaster University.

2. Elsewhere in the Western Desert, radiocarbon dates of ca. 26,000 BP from the base of a Bir Tarfawi water-hole and from the base of a shallow lake near Bahariya indicate that, within this postulated arid period, there was at least one moister phase of unknown duration (Pachur and Röper 1984: 251). Paulissen and Vermeersch (1987: 62) suggest another moist phase ca. 23,000–21,000 BP.

3. Radiocarbon dates on samples of Saharan groundwater indicate that the extreme dry period was restricted to between 20,000 and 14,000 BP, whereas dates on deep groundwater for the period of >50,000 to 20,000 BP are relatively abundant (Sonntag et al. 1980: 160; see also Thorwiehe et al. 1984: 211). These data are supported by mineralogical studies of deposits in the Nile delta which reflect the differential contribution of the combined Blue Nile and Atbara Nile during periods of increased or decreased humidity (Foucault and Stanley 1989: 46).

4. An increasing number of 'Upper Palaeolithic' occurrences in ecologically comparable areas have been reported recently, e.g., the Abu Noshra sites in Sinai (Phillips 1988).

'Reports from the Survey of Dakhleh Oasis, Western Desert of Egypt, 1977–1987', edited by C.S. Churcher and A.J. Mills. Dakhleh Oasis Project: Monograph 2. Oxbow Monograph 99.

Major difficulties in attempting to establish a Late Pleistocene presence in the oasis, i.e., between ca. 40,000–30,000 and 12,000 BP, include:

1. The expectation that this time-period will be sparsely represented in the archaeological record because it coincides in part with the Würm glacial maximum, a period of global climatic stress;
2. A lack of reliable chronological control, either by radiometrically-datable material or stratigraphic context; and
3. The absence of regional prototypes for this time-span.

According to Paulissen and Vermeersch (1987: 62), the only well-dated sites in the Nile Valley to fall within the 40,000 to 20,000 BP gap in the Egyptian prehistoric record are characterized by a fully developed blade technology. Reconnaissance during previous seasons' work with the Dakhleh Oasis Project (in 1988, 1991 and 1992), although not focused specifically on later Late Pleistocene material, yielded relatively few blade-cores attributable to this time-range. Two of the most convincing cores were found during the 1992 season on Pediment 2 gravels (Kleindienst *et al.*, Chapter 1, this volume) north of Bashendi, and quite close to the escarpment (Loc. 316E, 32/435–I4–1). Found in association with these cores were two end-scrapers and a burin on a truncated blade. On typological grounds alone this locality might fall into the later Late Pleistocene time-range and, as such, appears worthy of further investigation.

A more fruitful prototype, however, has been suggested by the small-sized, Levallois-related material previously identified by McDonald (1981: 227–230; 1982: 118–121) as a 'Southern Middle Palaeolithic', i.e., a southern variant of the Middle Stone Age (MSA). McDonald (1982: 230), moreover, has pointed out a potential relationship between this material and Caton-Thompson's 'Khargan Industry' (Caton-Thompson 1946: 61, 113–114; 1952: 132–139). Similar small-sized, Levallois-related materials recovered from Nubia and the Nile Valley have been reported as 'Halfan' by Marks (1968) and 'Halfan-Levallois' by Van Peer and Vermeersch (1990). Comparisons have been made by Van Peer and Vermeersch (1990: 139,145) to Caton-Thompson's 'Epi-Levalloisian', a term she used in one sense to subsume the 'Khargan' (Caton-Thompson 1952: xi) and, in another, to refer to material she believed to be derived from the 'Khargan' (Caton-Thompson 1952: 157).

Caton-Thompson (1946: 59) used the term 'Epi-Levalloisian' to "... denote comprehensively those varied regional industries of Levalloisian technique ... which anachronistically occupy the Upper Palaeolithic period." Paulissen and Vermeersch (1987: 62) have questioned the dates of all these Levallois-related occurrences, inclusive of the 'Sebilian' (Vignard 1923) and the 'Levallois-Idfuan' (Wendorf and Schild 1976), claiming that the suggested dates are too young. Material identified as 'Khargan' at Dungul Oasis overlies, and consequently

is assumed to post-date, a tufa dated by radiocarbon analysis to 22,900 ± 600 BP (WSU-256) (Hester and Hobler 1969: 14). This date, however, is based on samples formed mainly of carbonates (Hester and Hobler 1969: 11), and therefore may also be too young.

OBSERVATIONS

Several older collections from the southern margins of the Dakhleh Oasis which were noted to contain 'small MSA' [i.e., Loc. 054 (30/405–L1–3) collected by A. Von Gernet in 1980, Loc. 120 (30/435–L3–1) collected by M.M.A. McDonald in 1982, and Locs 203A and 203B (30/420–E1–1) collected by I.A. Brookes in 1987] have been studied. These are mixed collections of largely indeterminate flake-blanks, some larger MSA material and a few pieces of smaller-sized, Levallois-derived material. These few pieces, however, as well as McDonald's (1981: figs 2–i, j & 3–k) illustrations of notched flakes and a piercer from Loc. 043 (30/405–I2–2) which appear to be 'Khargan'-related, prompted reconnaissance along the southern margins of the oasis on the last field-day of the 1992 season.

These efforts were rewarded: 51 artifacts (26 flakes and flake fragments, seven cores and 18 retouched 'tools') were collected from the surface of a deflated sandstone hollow southeast of the village of Sheikh Muftah on the east side of the Sheikh Muftah Valley (Loc. 324, 41/420–F10–4). This material appeared unlike any earlier MSA encountered; moreover, the collection appeared to be discrete, with little or no admixture of technologically earlier MSA or Holocene cultural materials. The lithic artifacts were identified as 'Khargan'-related on their unmistakable resemblance to those from Kharga Oasis illustrated by Caton-Thompson (1946: fig. 5; 1952: pls 76–80).

The fact that this small collection appeared to be from a rarely found, discrete context dictated field strategy for the 1993 season. It was considered of prime importance that Loc. 324 (31/420–F10–4) be revisited, in order to enlarge the sample, and thereby begin the process of defining this cultural unit at Dakhleh. In addition, it was decided to employ the method of transect sampling developed by M.R. Kleindienst (Chapter 5, this volume), to establish 'background counts'; in this case, particular note was taken of 'Khargan'-related material in proportion to the general scatter of artifacts of other cultural affiliation, as well as to unworked, naturally-occurring stone. Finally, it was hoped that time would permit a reconnaissance survey of the east side of the Sheikh Muftah Valley and the perimeter of the pan to the south, in order to locate other potential concentrations of 'Khargan'-related materials.

The first objective met with considerable success. The sample of 'Khargan'-related lithic artifacts from the discrete concentration at Loc. 324 (31/420–F10–4) was increased to 161. Many of these artifacts were found in two adjoining deflation hollows, approximately 6 by 1.5 m and 5 by 2 m, respectively. These basins were surrounded by standing sandstone slabs which were higher on the west and north sides. In contrast to the slab 'structures' found by Hobler and Hester (1969: 122) at Dungul Oasis, however, those at Loc. 324 appeared to be completely natural in origin.

The transect lines (i.e., a 100 m line, with 100 m cross-lines intersecting the original line at 20 m intervals) were set out in an area adjacent to Loc. 324, but in a more open setting, and therefore an area likely to have been more heavily traversed in the past. (Collectively, these transect lines comprise Loc. 324/I, 31/420–F10–4). Collections of all the cultural material along these lines further enlarged the total sample of 'Khargan'-related specimens. Of the 728 artifacts collected, however, only some were found to relate unequivocally to the 'Khargan Industry'.

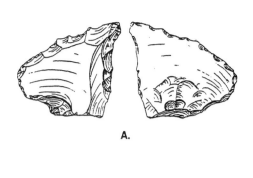

A.

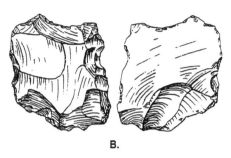

B.

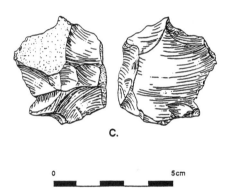

C.

0   5cm

Fig. 6.1. 'Khargan'-related Artifacts. A. Borer. B. Notch. C. Perforator.

Table 6.1. Number and Percent of 'Khargan'-related Artifacts from Locality 324 (31/420–F10–4) by Type.

Artifact Type	Number	Percent
Flakes	24	14.9
Flake fragments	22	13.7
Levallois cores	22	13.7
– struck	(18)	
– unstruck	(2)	
– bipolar*	(2)	
Core fragments	2	1.2
Chips and chunks	18	11.2
Retouched 'tools'	73	45.3
TOTALS	161	100.0

* *cf.* 'Hawarian' (see Debono 1973: 54, 77, pl. 283)

Table 6.2. Number and Percent of 'Khargan'-related Tools from Locality 324 (31/420–F10–4) by Type.

'Tool' Type	Number	Percent
Abruptly retouched, intentionally fractured (snapped) flakes	21	28.8
Retouched flakes	14	19.2
Retouched blades	4	5.5
Scrapers	8	10.9
– end	(1)	
– side	(3)	
– end & side	(1)	
– nosed or steep	(3)	
Denticulates	7	9.6
Notches	6	8.2
Basally notched, retouched flakes	4	5.5
Borers	4	5.5
Perforators	3	4.1
Burins	2	2.7
TOTALS	73	100.0

Analyses of the artifacts from Locs 324 and 324/I (41/420–F10–4) were completed in the field. Preliminary frequency counts for the artifact classes and 'tool'-types found in Loc. 324 are presented in Tables 6.1 and 6.2. The mean dimensions of the flakes from Loc. 324 are: length 42 mm, width 31 mm, and thickness 9 mm. The mean dimensions for cores from this same locality are: length 49 mm, width 47 mm, thickness for struck cores 19 mm, and thickness for unstruck cores 24 mm. More detailed quantitative work on the specimens from this locality and analysis of the quantitative data from the transect are in progress. Several cores and 'tools' from Loc. 324 are shown in Figures 6.1–6.6.

Reconnaissance along the east side of the Sheikh Muftah Valley failed to locate additional 'Khargan'-related occurrences. Concentrations of cultural material attributable to both the 'Khargan' and the 'Aterian', however, were noted on a terrace remnant to the west (Loc. 328, 30/420–E1–3). Surveys of the perimeter of the pan to the

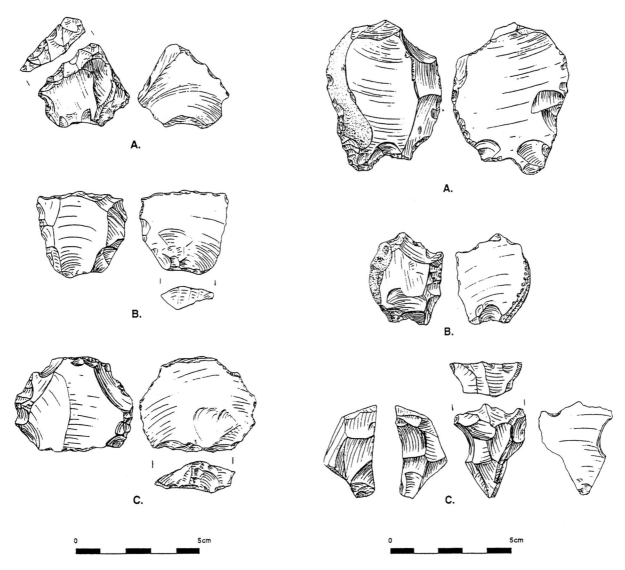

Fig. 6.2. 'Khargan'-related Artifacts. A-C. Abruptly re-touched, intentionally fragmented flakes.

Fig. 6.3. 'Khargan'-related Artifacts. A. & B. Basally notched, retouched flakes. C. Denticulated end-scraper.

south located at least two concentrations of mixed cultural materials, inclusive of a substantial representation of 'Khargan'-related artifacts, on the east side of the pan (Locs 329, 30/420–E1–4 & 330, 30/420–E2–4). These localities appear promising, and deserve future systematic work.

DISCUSSION AND CONCLUSIONS

The increased sample-size of lithic artifacts retrieved from Loc. 324 (31/420–F10–4) permitted confirmation of their identification as 'Khargan'-related. First impressions regarding the technological characteristics of this collection are summarized as:

1. Flakes, both unretouched blanks and those which have been modified into tools, tend to be small (mean length 42 and mean width 31 mm), quite thick (mean

thickness 9 mm), and relatively amorphous in shape, giving an overall 'chunky' appearance to the collection.

2. Many of the tools are made on flake fragments which seem to have been produced by intentional fracture (Fig. 6.2A, B, C); (cf. 'mutilated flakes' in Caton-Thompson 1952: 135; pls 77, 78).

3. Proximal ends of flakes are sometimes 'thinned' by the inverse removal of relatively large flakes (Fig. 6.1B). Proximal truncations are common, occurring on 36 (22.4%) of the 161 specimens from this locality (Fig. 6.4B). Distal truncations are also present, but appear to be less frequent, occurring on 25 (15.5%) of the 161 artifacts. The question arises as to whether the high incidence of intentional fracture provided a less labour-intensive technique for removal of the bulbar (and distal) ends. Other techniques applied to the proximal ends are basal notching (Fig. 6.3A, B),

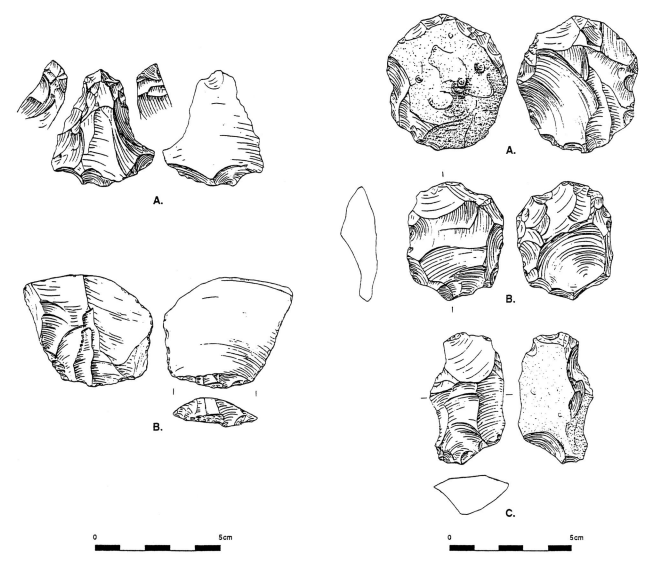

Fig. 6.4. 'Khargan'-related Artifacts. A. Nosed or steep scraper. B. Flake with basal truncation.

Fig. 6.5. 'Khargan'-related Artifacts. A. & B. Levallois flake-cores – struck. C. Levallois blade-core – struck.

and flaking the proximal end to a 'V' (Fig. 6.3C). It is presumed that both techniques would facilitate hafting.

4. Retouch is steep, no doubt because of the thickness of the initial blank, and frequently consists of relatively large flakes removed from the thick margins of a blank, thereby producing at best a denticulated appearance and, at worst, a very informal, coarse, and at times almost careless, *ad hoc* look to the 'retouched' pieces (Figs 6.2A, B, C; 6.3C; 6.4A). Although finer retouch is present, it is not common, and therefore not characteristic of this collection.

5. The struck cores are relatively thin (mean thickness 19 mm), in addition to being small (mean length 49 and mean width 47 mm). Most are 'flat-backed' (Figs 6.5A, B, C; 6.6A, B), and it is possible that some larger (?older) flakes are being recycled as cores. It seems that the major differentiating factor for these

cores is not size *per se*, since some, but not all, are very small (e.g., Fig. 6.6B), but their very flat appearance. Almost no platform remains on those cores which have been struck. Unstruck cores, on the other hand, tend to have thick platforms (Fig. 6.6C); most of the platform is apparently 'struck off' with the flake. It is of interest to note two opposed-platform Levallois cores (='Hawarian' according to Debono 1973: 54, 77; pl. 283) included in the collection from Loc. 324 (31/420–F10–4).

6. The predominant tool-type is the abruptly retouched, intentionally fragmented (i.e., snapped) flake, which forms 45.3% of the entire tool repertoire (Table 6.2; Fig. 6.2A, B, C). Also prevalent are borers (Fig. 6.1A), notches (Fig. 6.1B), perforators (Fig. 6.1C), flakes which have been basally notched, presumably for hafting (Fig. 6.3A, B), denticulates (Fig. 6.3C), and scrapers (Fig. 6.4A).

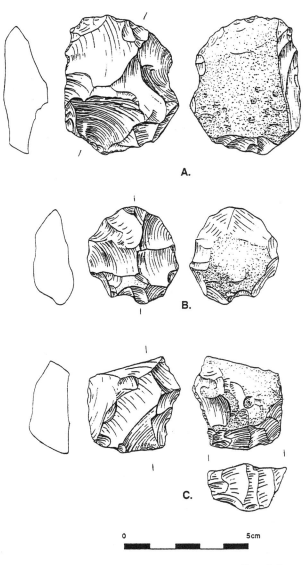

Fig. 6.6. 'Khargan'-related Artifacts. A. Levallois flake-core – struck. B. Levallois "button"-core – unstruck. C. Levallois core – unstruck.

In view of the rather *ad hoc* appearance of many of the 'retouched' pieces (see #4 above), it is hardly surprising to note that the validity of the 'Khargan Industry' as a discrete archaeological entity has been questioned by McBurney (1960: 155–158), who suggested that much of the observed retouch "... wears a singularly haphazard appearance", and therefore should be attributed to accidental or natural agencies. McBurney's observations, however, do not negate the existence of small-sized Levallois cores and flakes as reported and illustrated by Caton-Thompson (1946, 1952), among others. It is

significant, moreover, that researchers such as Hester and Hobler (1969: 123) and Debono (1973: 54), all of whom have had abundant, first-hand experience with similar material, believe the 'Khargan' to be a valid designation which should be retained in the archaeological literature. This latter view is supported at Dakhleh by the distinctive characteristics (e.g., abrupt retouch, numerous truncations, intentional snapping of thick flakes, *ad hoc* appearance of retouch, 'chunky' appearance of the thick, amorphous flakes and 'tools') observed in the surface collections from the discrete clusters found at Loc. 324 (41/420–F10–4).

A more complex issue to be investigated is the relationship between the 'Khargan' and 'Aterian'. In the absence of stratigraphic context and datable material, it is difficult to assess whether the 'overlap' first noted by Caton-Thompson (1946: 61) is spatial, resulting from the same group of *Homo sapiens* performing different tasks within a given region, or if it is temporal, as a result of different groups occupying roughly the same area at different periods of time. The former hypothesis suggests that the 'Khargan' may be an activity variant of the late 'Aterian'. This first hypothesis, however, seems less likely in view of the marked technological contrasts observed in the lithic repertoire: contrast the very fine, inverse retouch which characterizes 'Aterian' bulbar thinning with the apparent 'Khargan' preference for either notching the base with a single blow (Fig. 6.3A, B) or, even more drastically, removing the entire proximal end by intentional fracture (Figs 6.1A; 6.2A, B, C).

The alternative hypothesis, that 'Khargan'-related material comprises a distinct unit, is dependent upon a degree of chronological control which eludes us at present. By her own admission, Caton-Thompson's (1946: 113) chronological placement of the 'Khargan Industry' before the 'Aterian' is "... less conclusive than one would wish owing to the rarity of material *in situ*." Hobler and Hester (1969: 122) also acknowledge that "... irrefutable stratigraphic evidence of the relative age of the two industries is lacking", but, on the basis of their seriation of the cultural material, suggest that the 'Aterian' is younger. Kleindienst (Chapter 5, this volume), however, noting that the 'Khargan' post-dates a tufa with an age of $22,900 \pm 600$ BP at Dungul Oasis (Hester and Hobler 1969: 14), suggests that it is almost certain that the 'Khargan' is post-'Aterian', a view endorsed here on the basis of technological characteristics alone.[1]

The similarities between the material retrieved from Loc. 324 (31/420–F10–4) and the 'Khargan Industry' artifacts from the type-sites at Kharga, supported by the *terminus ante quem* date provided by the tufa at Dungul Oasis, appear to negate the hypothesis of an occupational

[1] Continued reconnaissance south of Sheikh Muftah during the 1994/95 field-season located a concentration of 'Khargan'-related artifacts overlying deposits of calcrete which cap calcareous silty sediments (CSS). An Isochron date of ca. $40,000 \pm 10^3$ BP has been obtained by H.P. Schwarcz using uranium/thorium on three samples of CSS from this area (Kleindienst *et al.*, Chap. 1, this volume), thereby providing a limiting date for the overlying cultural material. This cultural material has since been incorporated within the 'Sheikh Mabrouk Cultural Unit' at Dakhleh Oasis.

hiatus in Dakhleh Oasis, at least during part of the later Late Pleistocene. It seems clear that only further work, preferably on subsurface material in fresher condition, and ideally, the recovery of datable material will provide a firmer definition of the 'Khargan'-related unit at Dakhleh in both a cultural and a temporal sense.

Acknowledgements

I would like to acknowledge with thanks the contributions of Maxine Kleindienst, who has guided my interest in this study from its inception; Mary McDonald for her continuing encouragement; Rufus Churcher for his editorial guidance and assistance; Henry Schwarcz for his continuing efforts in squeezing dates from stone and last, but always first, Tony Mills for his unfailing and good-humoured support. Thanks are also due to John O'Carroll, who turned his keen eye and talented hand to the lithic illustrations presented in these pages.

Address for Author

Marcia F. Wiseman, Department of Anthropology, University of Toronto at Scarborough.

REFERENCES

Caton-Thompson, G. 1946. The Levalloisian Industries of Egypt. *Proceedings of the Prehistoric Society* 12(4): 57–120.

Caton-Thompson, G. 1952. *Kharga Oasis in Prehistory*. London: Athlone Press, 213p.

Close, A.E. and F. Wendorf. 1992. The beginnings of food production in the Eastern Sahara, 63–72. *In* Gebauer, A.B., and T.D. Price, eds, *Transitions to Agriculture in Prehistory*. Madison, Wisconsin: Prehistory Press, 180p.

Debono, F. 1973. Prospection préhistorique (campagnes 1972–1973). Le Ouadi Rimeila et le Ouadi Bariya: Etude complémentaire. La Vallée des Reines et la Vallée des Pelérins d'Espagne. *Graffiti de la Montagne Thébaine* 1(4): 35–85.

Foucault, A. and D. J. Stanley. 1989. Late Quaternary palaeoclimatic oscillations in East Africa recorded by heavy minerals in the Nile delta. *Nature* 339: 44–46.

Hester, J. J. and P. M. Hobler. 1969. *Prehistoric Settlement Patterns in the Libyan Desert*. Salt Lake City: University of Utah Anthropological Papers no. 92, Nubian Series no. 4, 174p.

Hobler, P. M. and J. J. Hester. 1969. Prehistory and environment in the Libyan Desert. *South African Archaeological Bulletin* 23(4): 120–130.

Kleindienst, M. R. This volume. Chapter 5. Pleistocene archaeology and geoarchaeology of Dakhleh Oasis: A status report, 83–108.

Kleindienst, M.R., C.S. Churcher, M.M.A. McDonald and H.P. Schwarcz. This volume, Chapter 1. Geography, geology, geochronology and geoarchaeology of the Dakhleh Oasis Region: An interim report, 1–54.

Marks, A. E. 1968. The Halfan Industry, 392–460. *In* Wendorf, F., ed., *The Prehistory of Nubia*, Vol. 1. Dallas: Fort Burgwin Research Center and Southern Methodist University Press, 531p.

McBurney, C.B.M. 1960. *The Stone Age of Northern Africa*. Harmondsworth, Middlesex: Penguin Books, 288p.

McDonald, M.M.A. 1981. Dakhleh Oasis Project: Second preliminary report on the lithic industries in the Dakhleh Oasis. *Journal of the Society for the Study of Egyptian Antiquities* 11(4): 225–231.

McDonald, M.M.A. 1982. The Dakhleh Oasis Project: Report on the fourth season of survey, October 1981 – January 1982. *Journal of the Society for the Study of Egyptian Antiquities* 12(3): 93–101.

Pachur, H.-J. and H.-P. Röper. 1984. The Libyan (Western) Desert and the Northern Sudan during the Late Pleistocene and Holocene. *Berliner Geowissenschaftliche Abhandlungen*, 50(A): 249–284.

Paulissen, E. and P.M. Vermeersch. 1987. Earth, man and climate in the Egyptian Nile Valley during the Pleistocene, 29–67. *In* Close, A.E., ed., *Prehistory of Arid North Africa: Essays in honor of Fred Wendorf*. Dallas: Southern Methodist University Press, 357p.

Phillips, J.L. 1988. The Upper Paleolithic of the Wadi Feiran, Southern Sinai. *Paléorient* 14(2): 183–200.

Rognon, P. 1980. Pluvial and arid phases in the Sahara: the role of non-climatic factors. *Palaeoecology of Africa and the Surrounding Islands* 12: 45–62.

Schild, R. 1987. Unchanging contrast? The Late Pleistocene Nile and Eastern Sahara, 12–27. *In* Close, A.E., ed., *Prehistory of Arid North Africa: Essays in Honor of Fred Wendorf*. Dallas: Southern Methodist University Press, 357p.

Sonntag, C., V. Thorweihe, J. Rudolph, E.P. Löhnert, C. Junghans, K.O. Münnich, E. Klitzsch, E.M. Shazly and F.M. Swailem. 1980. Isotopic identification of Saharian groundwaters, groundwater formation in the past. *Palaeoecology of Africa and the Surrounding Islands* 12: 159–171.

Thorweihe, U., M. Schneider and C. Sonntag. 1984. New aspects of hydrogeology in Southern Egypt. *Berliner Geowissenschaftliche Abhandlungen* 50(A): 209–216.

Van Peer, P. and P.M. Vermeersch. 1990. Middle to Upper Palaeolithic Transition: the evidence from the Nile Valley, 139–159. *In* Mellars, P., ed., *The Emergence of Modern Humans*. Edinburgh: Edinburgh University Press, 555p.

Vignard, E. 1923. Une nouvelle industrie lithique, Le Sébilien. *Bulletin de l'Institut Français d'Archéologie Orientale* 22: 1–76.

Wendorf, F. and R. Schild. 1976. *Prehistory of the Nile Valley*. New York: Academic Press, 404p.

7

NEOLITHIC CULTURAL UNITS AND ADAPTATIONS IN THE DAKHLEH OASIS

Mary M. A. McDonald

INTRODUCTION

Three distinct prehistoric industries from the Holocene epoch have been identified to date in Dakhleh Oasis. These industries, termed Epipalaeolithic, Aceramic Neolithic, and Ceramic Neolithic, each represented by a number of sites, have been distinguished on the basis of preferred lithic raw material, chipped stone tool kits, other categories of artifacts including pottery, and settlement patterns (McDonald 1982, 1983). Since this sequence was published, however, much new information has been generated through further archaeological field seasons in Dakhleh, geomorphological investigations of the oasis, and from elsewhere in the eastern Sahara, and through the publication of detailed sequences from two locations in Southern Egypt (Banks 1984; Wendorf *et al.* 1984) and new information on mid-Holocene climates (Haynes 1982; Ritchie *et al.* 1985).

This paper is thus a revision and elaboration of the Dakhleh Holocene cultural sequence in light of this new information. Except for a brief review of the Epipalaeolithic, the focus will be on the latter part of the sequence, the Neolithic, the portion to which most of the new information pertains. In brief, the new data support the subdivision of the Neolithic into two units and point to sometimes striking differences between the two in artifact assemblages and site locations. This paper reviews evidence from lithic assemblages, associated artifacts, and site distributions of the two cultural units, and discusses implications for subsistence, sedentism, group composition, and related matters.

One fact that has emerged from recent fieldwork is that the old terms for the units, 'Aceramic' and 'Ceramic' Neolithic, are inappropriate, as pottery is present in both. Because relative dates for the two are not yet secure, here

they will be named after present-day communities located near significant localities, the 'Aceramic Neolithic' becoming the Bashendi Unit, and the 'Ceramic Neolithic' the Sheikh Muftah Unit.

EPIPALAEOLITHIC

A brief description of the only other Holocene prehistoric unit so far defined in the oasis, the Epipalaeolithic, will set the stage for the discussion of the Neolithic.

The terms 'Epipalaeolithic', 'Terminal Palaeolithic', 'Late Palaeolithic', 'Post Palaeolithic' and 'Early Neolithic', have all been applied to roughly similar early Holocene sites scattered across the Western Desert and in the Nile Valley (e.g., Vermeersch 1984; Wendorf and Schild 1976; Wendorf *et al.* 1984). The term Epipalaeolithic is used for the Dakhleh Oasis region, in the absence of firm evidence for such important 'Neolithic' traits as food production and pottery making.

The lithic industry is characterised by blades with edges steeply, usually directly, retouched to form denticulates, notches, or sometimes piercers. Burins are present but rare. Bladelets occur commonly in the débitage but are not often modified into tools, exceptions being a few points with proximal stems produced by steep, direct retouch (Ounan points) and a few drill bits (*mèches de foret*). On the other hand, backed bladelets, scalene triangles, segments, or other geometric microliths, are rare to absent. The majority of cores are blade or bladelet cores, usually with a single platform or, less frequently, opposed platforms. Raw materials include a variety of cherts, usually quite fine-grained, but blades are produced

'*Reports from the Survey of Dakhleh Oasis, Western Desert of Egypt, 1977–1987*', edited by C.S. Churcher and A.J. Mills. Dakhleh Oasis Project: Monograph 2. Oxbow Monograph 99.

from other materials such as ferruginous sandstone, and even limestone.

In addition to the chipped stone, Epipalaeolithic sites yield grinding stones, both handstones and milling slabs, the largest recorded so far measuring 700 × 340 × 40 mm. Eggshell fragments, and clusters of sandstone cobbles – possible hearths – are found on those sites, but as yet no pottery, and only scraps of mammalian bone.

Most of the located Epipalaeolithic sites are not within Dakhleh Oasis itself, but atop the Libyan Plateau bordering it to the north, or on Gebel Edmonstone at its west end. On Gebel Edmonstone, sites consist of small clusters thinly sprinkled over the flat surface of that tableland, but on the plateau to the north they occur on much rougher ground. They have been found at both ends of the Oasis, above Maohoub to the west and Balat to the east, in the narrow corridors between bedrock yardangs, or as more extensive scatters on slope-foot muddy pans and on eroded lake sediments in broader basins within yardang fields (Kleindienst *et al.*, Chapter 1, this volume). Within the oasis itself only one or two possible sites have been located, with a third in the desert beyond, about a kilometre south of the modern cultivation.

There are so far no firm dates for the Dakhleh Epipalaeolithic. No absolute dates are available, nor does the Dakhleh industry, with its emphasis on retouched blades and lack of geometric microliths, closely resemble more securely dated Early Holocene industries elsewhere in the eastern Sahara (Wendorf *et al.* 1984). General parallels with these industries, with late Capsian material to the west, and the El Kabian of the Nile Valley, suggest a date of perhaps 8000 BP for the Dakhleh Epipalaeolithic.

BASHENDI UNIT

While there are some similarities in artifact classes and site location, material of the Bashendi Unit is on the whole strikingly different from that of the Epipalaeolithic.

Chipped Stone

The Bashendi industry is predominantly a flake industry made on small nodules of chert or quartzite. Within the débitage from different sites, flakes outnumber blades by from 2:1 to 30:1. In one sample, 60% of flakes are less than 30 mm long. Cores are much more varied than in the Epipalaeolithic and include single platform, and opposed platform and ninety-degree cores, as well as disk-shaped and amorphous cores. Bashendi tool assemblages, however, are often more varied, with numerous blades, and with larger implements on average than this picture suggests, as blanks are also drawn from other sources. These sources include worn Middle Palaeolithic material that litters parts of the oasis, a fine-grained, grey, tabular chert which is usually worked bifacially and, especially on plateau sites, large biconvex fragments that have

spalled off big chert nodules and that are also worked bifacially. Other raw materials knapped on Bashendi sites include limestone, ferruginous sandstone, agate, petrified wood, and a fairly coarse-grained chert used for heavy-duty tools.

The largest Bashendi tool collection to date comes from site 30/450–F8–3 (174), where a 570 m², mapped area yielded 200 tools. In this collection, points or arrowheads constitute the largest tool class (27%). Within this class are seven types (Fig. 7.1a, top). These include, in descending order of importance, points made on bladelets with well-defined, bifacially retouched tangs but otherwise modified, at most, by unifacial edge retouch; small triangular points with some edge retouch and proximal concave truncation (Bou Saâda points; see Tixier 1963); tanged points with retouch covering most or all of both surfaces; asymmetrical points shaped by edge retouch; bipoints made on bladelets with some bifacial edge retouch at one or both ends; bipoints with fine rippled retouch covering much of one or both faces; and tanged, winged, bifacially retouched points. This is a relatively homogeneous collection in terms both of raw material and size: few points exceed 30 mm long and more than 50% are <20 mm long. In addition, one other point was found on this site, a bifacially retouched, hollow-based point, 47 mm long.

Other tool classes in the 30/450–F8–3 collection are listed in Table 7.1. The bifaces include three foliates ranging in length from 43 to 91 mm, and an asymmetrical item which may be a rough knife. Grouped with the piercers are nine drill bits. The *varia* class includes a plane, a possible burin, and a heavy-duty cutting implement 200 mm long.

While the 30/450–F8–3 lithics collection is fairly representative of the Bashendi Unit, material from other sites indicates that proportions of tools vary and a few other types may be present. Thus, some sites have higher proportions of drill bits, or bifaces other than arrowheads, or of heavy-duty tools – picks, scrapers, or cutting implements. Similarly, proportions of points can vary

Table 7.1. Bashendi Unit, Site 30/450-F8–3. Classes of Retouched Tools. Percentages to nearest whole number.

Class	No.	%
Points	54	27
Denticulates	27	14
Notches	27	14
Piercers	22	11
Combinations	12	6
Scrapers	11	6
End scrapers	2	1
Bifaces	7	3
Retouched tools	33	17
Varia	4	2
	---	---
	199	101

Fig. 7.1. Artifacts from Bashendi Unit sites.

TOP, Site 30/450-F8-3. Seven types of arrowheads.

BOTTOM, Various sites. Small artifacts in ground stone and shell. Top to bottom: top – ground stone palette; central row – Two stone labrets or ear plugs (left), unfinished(?) pierced ostrich egg-shell bead (centre), bobbin-shaped labret or ear stud (centre right), section of shell bangle or bracelet (right); bottom – pierced flat stone item, possibly a toggle. Scale in centimetres.

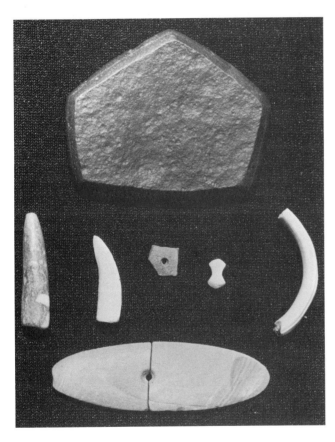

Associated Artifacts

Aside from the chipped stone, Bashendi Unit sites yield grinding stones, hammerstones, a variety of small ground-stone items, pottery, bone points and worked eggshell.

Grinding stones, both handstones and milling slabs, abound on Bashendi Unit sites. The 570 m² mapped area at 30/450–F8-3 yielded 14 handstones or fragments thereof, and over 60 fragments of milling stones, mostly of sandstone. Two intact milling stones found near 30/450–F8-3 measured 420 × 330 × + 40 mm, and 620 × 460 × 25–34 mm. A total of ten hammerstones, most converted from chert or quartzite cores, were also recovered from the mapped area at 30/450–F8-3.

A variety of small ground and/or polished stone items have been found on Bashendi Unit sites (Fig. 7.1b). From 30/450–F8-3 came a five-sided palette in a fine-grained, dark grey stone; two items, 45 and 34 mm long, round in section and tapering at one end, one possibly in barite; and a five-sided bead (Fig. 7.1b, top; centre row, left and middle). Other sites have yielded a conch-shell bracelet fragment (Fig. 7.1b, centre row, right), a flat toggle-shaped item 80 mm long in a veined, buff-coloured, fine-grained rock (Fig. 7.1b, bottom), a small waisted cylinder or bobbin (Fig. 7.1b, centre row, middle right), and several circular beads in agate and other stone. Finally, a fragment of a diorite disk macehead from a mixed surface scatter in the Sheikh Muftah area (31/420–C10–4:142) *might* pertain to the Bashendi Unit.

Until recently there was no proof that Bashendi sites had pottery. In 1986, however, handmade pottery was found on a number of Bashendi sites in an area entirely devoid of Sheikh Muftah Unit material and lacking debris from most subsequent periods, making the association relatively secure. The sherds from this area, on and around site 30/450–F8-3 (McDonald 1985), are small, few in number (only a half-dozen came from the mapped area of 30/450–F8-3), and sometimes highly wind eroded. They are all of Handmade Fine 1 ware (C. Hope, pers. comm., 1986), sand-tempered, thin-walled (3.2–5.6 mm thick) and

from site to site. For example, bifacial bipoints predominate at some sites, while types not found at 30/450–F8-3 are featured at others: diamond-shaped bifacial points at 30/450–F8-5 (178) for instance, or bifaces with a three-pointed tang at 31/420–P5-1 (101) (McDonald 1983, pl. XIII.a). Finally, as the Bashendi and Sheikh Muftah Units are redefined in the light of new evidence, it appears that side-blow flakes, heretofore listed as a Sheikh Muftah trait (McDonald 1982, 1983), in fact are confined largely to Bashendi Unit sites.

fired brown, dark grey or pinkish. Surfaces seem smoothed or compacted, and some bear a horizontal dashed pattern. The only evidence on shape comes from a pointed base sherd.

Several possible bone tools, including two awls and four points, highly eroded, came from 30/450–F8–3. Another point, somewhat better preserved, 21 mm long, came from the nearby site 30/450–F7–1 (176). The bone points from 31/435–A6–3 (116) (McDonald 1983, pl. XIV.c) may also pertain to the Bashendi Unit (see below).

Finally, worked ostrich eggshell is a feature of many Bashendi sites. The mapped portion of 30/450–F8–3 yielded 108 shell beads or fragments, either round, square, polygonal or, rarely, triangular in shape. Some have the central hole incompletely drilled through, and were clearly in the process of manufacture. The majority of Bashendi sites bear similar evidence of ostrich eggshell bead manufacture. In addition to beads, a dozen fragments of decorated ostrich shell were found at 30/450–F7–5 (184). The most common motif is a hatched band. A single decorated fragment was found at one other Dakhleh site, 31/420–M9–2 (104).

Site List for Bashendi Unit

At least 28 sites bearing some or all of the artifacts and traits listed above have been identified so far in Dakhleh and its environs. Ten of these sites, then identified as Aceramic Neolithic sites, are listed in earlier reports (McDonald 1982, 1983). To these should be added the 'aceramic' scatter at 32/390–D2–2 (006) at the west end of the oasis (McDonald 1980), site 30/450–A4–1 (137) at the east end, and four plateau sites above the eastern part of Dakhleh. The other six sites and five smaller scatters are all in the vicinity of 30/450–F8–3 in the southeast corner of the present oasis.

In addition to these 28 sites, another four, 31/420–D10–3 (069) Cluster 5, 31/420–C10–2 (074), 31/420–M9–2, and 31/435–A6–3, previously classed as 'Ceramic Neolithic' because they have pottery (McDonald 1982, 1983), may in fact be Bashendi Unit sites. The pottery on 31/420–M9–2 and 31/435–A6–3, like that on 30/450–F8–3, is fine-tempered, thin-walled, and has a smoothed surface. Similar pottery, some of it decorated (Hope 1983, fig. 1), came from one portion of 31/420–C10–2 (a site which also yields Sheikh Muftah Unit material). Pottery aside, these resemble Bashendi Unit sites in their choice of lithic raw materials, in the tool classes and specific types represented (side blow flakes at 31/420–D10–3 and 31/420–M9–2, heavy-duty tools in grey chert at 31/420–C10–2 and 31/435–A6–3, a bifacial, bipointed arrowhead at 31/420–C10–2), and in the working of ostrich eggshell and bone (31/420–M9–2 and 31/435–A6–3). The collection from one other site, 31/420–C10–4 (see above), like that from nearby 31/420–C10–2, appears to be a mixture of Bashendi and Sheikh Muftah Unit materials.

Subsistence and Settlement Patterns

Information on subsistence at Bashendi sites is limited by the fact that they are largely or completely deflated. One of the more promising sites (31/435–L1–1:125), with large pieces of bone as well as lithics on its surface, retained over the several square metres that were excavated at most 100–120 mm of soft, grey, virtually sterile material above a hard, reddish-coloured, ancient spring deposit. The only bone or fresh chipped stone from the excavation was lodged after deflation in desiccation cracks. Likewise, at the rich surface site 30/450–F8–3, the presence in some spots of lithics vertically embedded in the ground suggested that some intact deposit might be preserved. Again, however, virtually nothing was recovered from below the surface. The only exception so far is charcoal, which is preserved under some of the rock clusters, presumed to be hearth mounds, found at 30/450–F8–3 and other sites.

Despite this problem, some information on subsistence at Bashendi Unit sites is available. While no plant food remains have been recovered, the use of cereals or other vegetable food can be inferred from the presence of grinding stones at practically all sites. Animal bones were recovered from a number of sites, and those from eight locations have been analysed (Churcher, this volume, Chapter 8). Cattle were found at virtually all these sites, and hartebeest and gazelle at most of them. Other faunal elements found on or near sites of this unit include Cape buffalo, Grevy zebra, elephant, goat and possible sheep. Given the apparent omnipresence of cattle on Bashendi sites and the fact that domesticated cattle appear to have been present elsewhere in the eastern Sahara by the early Holocene (Wendorf et al. 1984), it seems likely that the Bashendi cattle were herded. The status of the caprovids is unclear, as horncores only of goat have been recovered, and the evidence for sheep is unconfirmed and at best uncertain. Hartebeest and gazelle seem to have been routinely hunted, while the larger game animals in the assemblage may occasionally have been hunted, or at least scavenged. On the subject of animal carcass processing at Bashendi sites, while long bones are split to expose the marrow cavity, Churcher (1983, 181) observed that "... bone fragments are large, and small elements such as phalanges, carpals or teeth are often entire. Materials are clustered with apparently associated elements in one cluster."

The 17 measurable Bashendi sites range in size from about 80–8000 m². Within this range, three groups are detectable: seven are under 500 m², six are between 1200–2500 m², while three fall between 7000–8000 m². The anomaly, 30/450–F8–3, has an area of 4100 m². No evidence of structures was found on these sites, but many have one or more clusters of sandstone or other cobbles covering a sometimes mounded deposit often containing charcoal. Seven of these possible hearth-mounds occur on the mapped area of 30/450–F8–3. They are circular or oval, with diameters from about 1.75–4.0 m.

Bashendi Unit material is located both within the oasis

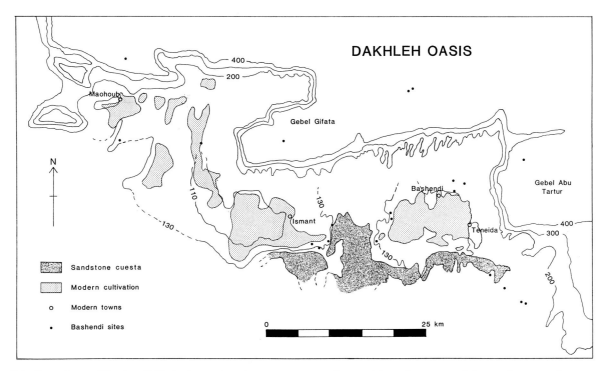

Fig. 7.2. Locations of Bashendi Unit sites related to contours, modern cultivated areas and the southern sandstone cuesta in eastern Dakhleh Oasis. (Note: Gebel Abu Tartur is named el-Battikh Promontory elsewhere in this volume.)

and in the now-desolate areas beyond its borders (Fig. 7.2). It occurs on the plateau above Dakhleh, the settlement pattern coinciding in part with that of the Epipalaeolithic, but apparently more extensive. Indeed, of the half-dozen points on the plateau surveyed so far, only the smooth surfaces of the southern and western edges of Gifata Promontory above modern Ismant, and of Gebel Edmonstone, lack Bashendi material. It occurs in the same broad deflation hollows within yardang fields, above Maohoub and Balat, that also contain Epipalaeolithic sites, although within the basins the two kinds of sites do not overlap. Another small Bashendi site is located on the edge of muddy pan sediments in a basin near the northwest corner of el-Battikh Promontory at the east end of the oasis. Finally, a fairly continuous scatter of hearths and artifacts runs for over 2 km along the base of a low scarp on Gebel Gifata Promontory north of Ismant. Abundant Bashendi Unit material has also been found in an area of the desert well to the southeast of the present borders of the oasis. Thin scatters of this material occur in one part of a 10 km² plain covered with Pleistocene Laminated Sediments (PLS) (Kleindienst *et al.*, Chapter 1, this volume), near the piedmont zone north of the Kharga road, 10 km southeast of Teneida. Site 30/450–F8–3 is located another 3–4 km to the south. It is one of a dozen sites and small clusters of Bashendi material within a PLS-filled basin (Kleindienst *et al.*, Chapter 1, this volume) surrounded by sandstone gebels, some of them bearing petroglyphs.

Unlike the Epipalaeolithic, Bashendi Unit material is commonly found also in certain environments within the oasis itself. Over a dozen sites are known, most of them in the eastern half of the oasis, the only portion systematically surveyed so far for prehistoric sites. Sites are often in the vicinity of, but never immediately adjacent to, areas now under cultivation. They are found in the Central Lowland on deflated tabular dune deposits (e.g., 31/420–P5–1 west of Balat, or 32/405–A2–3 [022] at Budkhulu), or on spring terraces, such as a cluster of sites to the south and southeast of Ezbet Sheikh Muftah, or site 31/420–M9–2 in Holocene wetland sediments southwest of Balat. Northeast of Ezbet Bashendi is a string of three sites, one near a spring-line, the other two in basins among sandstone gebels beyond it. It is possible that additional Bashendi sites within the oasis are now obscured by the debris from later occupations.

Dating of Bashendi Unit

With very few absolute dates available so far, the Bashendi Unit must be dated largely through comparison with more securely-dated material elsewhere in the region.

One radiocarbon date of 5745 ± 80 yr BP (S-2415), was obtained on ostrich eggshell from 31/420–M9–2. A comparable date, 5800 ± 60 yr BP (Beta-6873), comes from eggshell on a Neolithic cluster at 32/390–D2–2, but whether this is a Bashendi cluster is unknown. Both dates were calculated using a ^{14}C half-life of 5568 years and are 'uncorrected' for ^{13}C variations from the standard.

As for relative dating, the best sequence for the eastern Sahara is that based on work done in the south of Egypt and in Kharga Oasis by the Combined Prehistoric Expedition (CPE) (Wendorf *et al.* 1984). The majority of parallels for Bashendi material in that sequence are with the 'Middle Neolithic', dating from 7700 to 6200 BP. Parallels include such general traits as a new emphasis on flake production, the appearance of ground stone items, and the predominance of varied projectile points as a tool class (Banks 1984). Other shared traits include Ounan and Bou Saâda points, rare hollow-based points (Wendorf *et al.* 1984, fig 10.5.e), and decorated eggshell (Banks 1984, fig. V.22).

At the same time, the presence of other traits in the Bashendi collections suggests that this material falls towards the end of Wendorf *et al.*'s (1984) Middle Neolithic, or even post-dates it. Bifacially worked tools and side-blow flakes for example, important components in some Bashendi assemblages, are rare to absent in the Middle Neolithic, but do occur in Wendorf *et al.*'s (1984) Late Neolithic.

Some of the best parallels for the Bashendi material in fact are not in the south but with the 'Bedouin Microlithic' in neighbouring Kharga Oasis (Caton-Thompson 1952), and with the 'Fayum A' in the Fayum Depression (Caton-Thompson and Gardner 1934). The Kharga lithic industry differs in some respects – it includes more blades and features some elements such as transverse arrowheads that are absent from the Bashendi assemblage. Otherwise it resembles the Bashendi Unit closely in the variety of raw materials, and production of bifacially retouched knives as well as a similar range of unifacial and bifacially retouched points (Caton-Thompson 1952, pls 97, 99, 100). Pottery is scarce or absent. Ostrich eggshell is decorated or used for bead production (Caton-Thompson 1952, pl. 111.11). Finally, site distribution seems very similar, with sites located in the oasis itself, atop the local plateau, and well out in the desert (Caton-Thompson 1952). Unfortunately however, no dates are available for the Kharga Bedouin Microlithic.

The Fayum A industry (Caton-Thompson and Gardner 1934) shares with the Bashendi assemblage a variety of bifacial items such as knives, 'daggers', and several types of arrowheads. Also found are side-blow flakes, and numerous notches and denticulates. Fayum A sites are dated from 6400 to 5600 BP (Wendorf *et al.* 1984).

Dating evidence from further afield is more ambiguous. In the Nile Valley such 'Bashendi' traits as bifacial knives, side blow flakes, hollow-based points and bone points occur on Predynastic sites, which now appear to be considerably younger than 6000 BP (Baumgartel 1960; Clark *et al.* 1974, fig. 9.E6; Hassan 1984; Hays 1984). In the central Sahara, these same traits and others such as bifacial flakes and drills, are found on such VI Millennium BP sites as Adrar Bous III and the upper layers of Ti-n-Torha North (Banks 1984; Camps 1974).

To sum up the evidence for dating the Bashendi Unit, the weight of the comparative evidence (bone points, eggshell beads, etc.) suggests dates approaching 6000 BP and even younger. It is likely in fact that a considerable span of time, perhaps centuries, is represented by these

sites. If that is the case, the radiocarbon date of 5745 ± 80 yr BP (S-2415) for 31/420–M9–2 may be correct, especially if, as the relative abundance of pottery on its surface and other evidence suggests, the site was occupied well on in the Bashendi sequence.

SHEIKH MUFTAH UNIT

Sheikh Muftah Unit sites differ substantially from those of the Bashendi Unit in assemblages and site locations.

Chipped Stone

A characteristic feature of Sheikh Muftah sites is the presence in the chipped stone assemblages of a fine-grained, golden brown, tabular chert that is frequently burned or heat-treated to a deep wine colour. On average about 40% of Sheikh Muftah tools are knapped from this raw material, while on some sites the figure can rise to 65% or more. There is, however, relatively little débitage in this material and most of it consists of small trimming flakes or fragments, reflecting the ease and economy of fashioning tools from thin sheets of chert. For example, 31/420–P6–1 (100) yielded a sample of 3550 pieces of débitage, of which only 26% were of tabular chert. In the same collection, 65% of the 164 tools were of tabular chert.

The other major raw material category for Sheikh Muftah sites is a grey nodular chert similar to that found on Bashendi sites. Cores are small and quite irregular, reflecting the quality of the parent nodules. In a sample of 196 'cores' from 31/420–P6–1, fully half have only one or two flakes removed. Of the 34 cores with five or more flakes removed, 13 are single-platform cores, 11 are changed orientation, 7 amorphous and 3 are opposed platform cores. Unused flakes in this material are small (81% <30 mm), while only 1% are 'blade-like'.

In the 31/420–P6–1 collection the tabular and grey nodular cherts are the only raw materials represented except for quartzite which constitutes about 1% of the débitage. Larger proportions of quartzite are found on sites elsewhere in the oasis, but other materials found in Bashendi collections are either present in reduced quantities (grey tabular chert, agate, worn Palaeolithic material), or, as in the case of petrified wood, absent from Sheikh Muftah sites.

Tool collections also differ from those of the Bashendi Unit. Table 7.2 lists tool classes represented in a collection of 164 tools from a 265 m² mapped area on 31/420–P6–1. In this collection the majority of scrapers, denticulates and composite tools, and nearly half of the piercers, are of tabular chert. A wide variety of shapes are represented, and tools in tabular chert can be quite large, often exceeding 100 or even 150 mm in their greatest dimension. Among the piercers there are no *mèches de foret*. The *varia* class includes three serrated blade segments in

Table 7.2. Sheikh Muftah Unit, Site 31/420-P6–1. Classes of Retouched Tools. Percentages to nearest whole number.

Class	No.	%
Denticulates	44	27
Piercers	21	13
Scrapers	57	35
End scrapers	2	1
Notches	1	1
Combinations	35	21
Varia	4	2
	—	—
	164	100

fine-grained chert; one excavated from a hearth bears some sheen. The fourth item in the class is a biface, a probable knife fragment in the yellow-brown tabular chert.

A few additional classes and tool types can be added to this short list from collections of other Sheikh Muftah sites. Projectile points are present on some sites but are usually rare, never more than 10% of the tools. In contrast to the variety on Bashendi sites, only two types are present here. Most common is a carefully bifacially retouched, tanged point which may also be winged or serrated. These vary in size and shape, ranging in length from 25 to 67 mm and in plan form from triangular to rod-like. The other type is a larger point, usually bipointed *lanceolate* in shape, with rough bifacial retouch. Similar points are found on some Bashendi sites.

Side-blow flakes, characteristic of Bashendi sites, are at best rare in the Sheikh Muftah Unit. They have been found on four or five sites, usually as single finds. Other tool types found on some Sheikh Muftah sites include planes, picks, 'massive scrapers' or 'hoes' (cf. Wendorf and Schild 1980, 193), and sickle elements (McDonald 1982, 1983).

Associated Artifacts

Artifact categories found on Sheikh Muftah sites include grinding stones, ground stone items, pottery, worked bone, and copper.

Both handstones and milling slabs occur on virtually all Sheikh Muftah sites, although less densely than they do on some Bashendi sites. An exception to this generality is 31/420–F9–3 (092), where a scatter 30 m in diameter yielded eight milling slabs or fragments and eight handstones, both in either sandstone or ferruginous sandstone. In addition to the flat slabs, grinding stone fragments with thicker sections and a circular depression, possible mortars, were found on 30/435–C3–1 (111) and 30/435–K3–1 (119).

Ground and/or polished stone items on Sheikh Muftah sites include palettes, spheroids, maceheads, and other fragments that might be axes or similar implements. A palette fragment similar to that from Bashendi site 30/

450–F8–3, in the same fine-grained, dark grey stone, came from 31/420–N6–1 (145) to the west of the Balat cultivation. Two other possible palettes, one in diorite, the other a fragment in an unidentified whitish rock, were found on two spring mounds near Mut. Site 31/420–D9–1 (072), near Ezbet Sheikh Muftah, yielded a small sandstone pestle-like object, 45 mm long and 24 mm in diameter. A grooved sandstone spheroid with a diameter of about 42.5 mm, a possible *bola*, came from 30/435–B3–1 (107), near the southern boundary of the oasis. A disk macehead fragment of diorite from 31/420–C10–4, as mentioned above could, on the basis of surrounding surface material, be assigned to either the Bashendi or the Sheikh Muftah Unit. Another fragment of diorite, with a sharp but battered edge (a possible axe or celt) came from 30/450–B3–2 (136) in the southeast corner of the oasis. Stone beads seem rare on these sites: one of agate was recovered from 30/435–B6–1 (143) on the southern boundary.

Worked bone is found only rarely, even on sites strewn with unworked bone fragments. So far, no bone projectile points have been recovered from Sheikh Muftah sites. Piercing implements have been found, such as an awl from 30/435–B3–1, and a blackened awl or needle fragment from 31/405–G6–2 (064).

Other classes of artifacts, while prominent on Bashendi sites, are rare or absent in the Sheikh Muftah Unit. Examples are hammerstones, and worked ostrich eggshell – either beads or decorated fragments – even though sites often bear scatters of eggshell fragments.

Pottery, on the other hand, is much more plentiful and varied. All of it is handmade, but a variety of wares, surface treatments, wall thicknesses, forms, and sizes are present (Hope 1980, 1981, 1983, Chapter 14, this volume). Forms include jars of various sizes, restricted bowls, and deep open bowls, while bases can be flat, rounded or pointed. Vessel rim diameters range from 100 to at least 320 mm. Mending or suspension holes have been drilled into some, and large sherds are often modified into discs with diameters from 50 to >90 mm. The only other ceramic object recovered is a small, elongated vessel, the shape of the bowl of a spoon, and measuring 89 × 62 × 29 mm. It comes from 30/450–B4–1 (135) in the southeast corner of the oasis.

It remains unclear whether incised pottery decoration is a trait of the Bashendi or the Sheikh Muftah Unit, or of both. The decoration – incised lines, punctate designs, and rim ticking (Hope 1983, fig. 1) – usually occurs on fine-tempered, thin-walled pottery somewhat similar to the plain ware of the Bashendi Unit. The largest collections all come from contexts that may be mixed – 31/420–C10–2 (see above) and two of the Mut spring mounds. The small collections from these Mut sites (31/405–G6–1:035, 31/405–G6–2) include good Sheikh Muftah materials such as brown tabular chert and tanged arrowheads, but also such Bashendi traits as diamond-shaped bifacial points and sizeable proportions of knives in grey tabular chert, with material from Old Kingdom and Roman times mixed in.

Occasionally, Sheikh Muftah sites yield sherds reminiscent of early Nile Valley material. From 31/405–G6–1 came fragments of a red-coated, possible black-topped jar that could date from the Egyptian Predynastic Period (Hope 1981). Site 30/435–C3–1, near the oasis southern boundary, with an otherwise pure Sheikh Muftah assemblage, yielded the rim and neck of a late Predynastic or Dynasty I large storage jar (C.A. Hope, pers. comm., 1986).

Other than this possibly intrusive material, Sheikh Muftah pottery seems to be the product of a local tradition. No close parallels have been found with pottery from elsewhere in the Western Desert, even from nearby Kharga Oasis (Banks, 1984; C.A. Hope, pers. comm., 1986; Wendorf and Schild 1980).

Copper fragments and small tools are often found on sites of the Sheikh Muftah Unit. To date a total of 22 pieces of copper and two fragments of malachite have been recovered from 14 sites scattered throughout the oasis. Items include small rods, usually pointed at one end and square in cross section, wire, and various flat pieces, usually fragmentary (McDonald 1983, fig. 1). The largest object so far weighs 60 gm. One fragment, on analysis by U.M. Franklin (Metallurgy and Materials Science Department, University of Toronto), proved to be completely mineralised, consisting now of copper chloride, with a thin coating of copper carbonate. The mineralised microstructure suggests the material might have been smelted (U.M. Franklin, pers. comm., 1983).

Subsistence and Settlement Patterns

As with the Bashendi Unit, many Sheikh Muftah sites are largely or completely deflated. Some, however, retain remnants of intact deposits, as in the hearth mounds and fire pits at sites 31/420–N6–1 and 31/405–G6–2, in the more extensive ashy layers of 30/420–P1–1 (105) or 31/420–C10–3, or within tabular dune layers as at 31/420–P6–1, or playa sediments at 30/435–B6–1. Aside from small test pits, no Sheikh Muftah Unit sites have yet been excavated.

Information on subsistence at Sheikh Muftah sites accordingly is somewhat limited. As with Bashendi sites, there is only indirect evidence from grinding stones and sickle blades for the use of plant foods. Faunal remains from 18 sites have been identified. Cattle, hartebeest, and gazelle are present on almost all sites (respectively, 14, 14, and 13 sites), goat (and possibly sheep) on at least six, and ass and 'large bird' on three sites each. Grevy zebra and Cape buffalo were found on two or three sites. Of these mammals, it appears that at least goat and ass have joined cattle on the list of domesticates, unless these materials are intrusive. Marine shells, including a cowrie, have been recovered from three sites, including 31/420–P6–1. Concerning butchering techniques at these sites, Churcher (1983) observed that bones are broken into smaller fragments than they are on Bashendi sites, perhaps to fit more easily into pots for boiling.

Sheikh Muftah sites appear to be smaller on average than Bashendi sites. Aside from an anomalously large one, the 33 measurable sites range from 20 to 3500 m², with three sub-groups detectable: 10 are very small, ranging between 20 and 150 m²; 15 between 500 and about 800 m²; and 5 between 2000 and 3500 m². Two other sites measure 250 m², while the large site 31/420–P6–1 covers 14,400 m². As with Bashendi sites, no evidence of structures has been detected, but many clusters include one or more hearths. Others, such as 30/420–P1–1, have extensive ashy deposits. In some areas, as in the vicinity of Esbet Sheikh Muftah, surface scatters appear to blend into each other or overlap, suggesting repeated occupations.

Sheikh Muftah Unit site distribution is quite different from that of the Bashendi Unit (Fig. 7.3). Of the approximately 70 sites discovered so far, virtually all are located within the bounds of the oasis itself. Only two, with a total of three clusters, were found on the Libyan Plateau above Dakhleh. These are all on el-Battikh Promontory at the east end, on the edge of pan muds in two separate basins lying along an old route from the oasis to the Nile, the Darb el-Tawil.

Within Dakhleh itself, 61 Sheikh Muftah sites have been recorded in the intensively-surveyed portion of the oasis running eastward from Mut and Hindaw. As with Bashendi sites, none is located in the piedmont zone. Within the cultivated lowlands, the only traces of the Neolithic are artifact clusters on the flanks of spring vents above the modern fields. Ten vent mounds north of Mut and two near the western boundary of the Balat cultivated area bear Neolithic material. The remainder lie outside the modern cultivation, but either never far removed (usually ≤1 km), or close to areas moist enough to support extant stands of the false 'halfa' grass (probably *Desmostachya bipinnata*), tamarisk (*Tamarix*) or similar hardy vegetation (see Ritchie, Chapter 4, this volume).

A single Sheikh Muftah site has been recorded to the north of the cultivation. It lies at the end of a line of springs running northeastward from Ezbet Bashendi. Traces of Neolithic material elsewhere along this line may represent other Sheikh Muftah sites now obscured by intensive occupation in Pharaonic and Roman times.

All other Sheikh Muftah sites in the eastern oasis lie well to the south. The majority trace a discontinuous line along the 130 m contour south of the cultivated areas. Eighteen sites occupy valleys dissecting the spring terraces just south of the Mut-Sheikh Muftah cultivated lands, while further east, many sites lie to the west and south of the Balat-Teneida cultivation. Nine of these latter sites lie between 'Ein Duma and Sheikh Mabrouk and border not the modern cultivation itself but the zone of salt-impregnated crusted land south of it, designated as low-slope wetland or possibly a large playa by Kleindienst *et al.* (Chapter 1, this volume). The sites lie along the southern boundary of this crusted land, where it abuts a sandstone cuesta running eastward about 20 km to the piedmont of

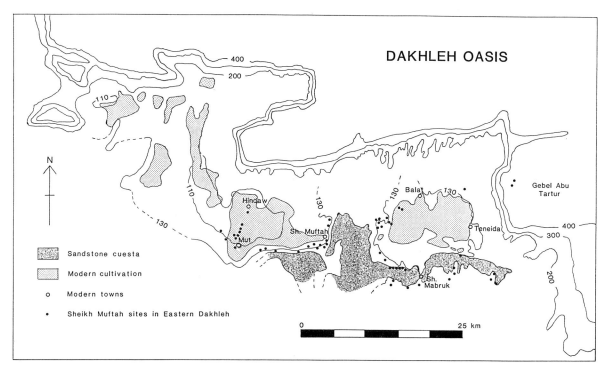

Fig. 7.3. Locations of Sheikh Muftah Unit sites related to contours, modern cultivated areas and the southern sandstone cuesta in eastern Dakhleh Oasis. (Note: Gebel Abu Tartur is named el-Battikh Promontory elsewhere in this volume.)

Gebel Abu Tartur. This cuesta in turn is bordered to the south by several partly contiguous bodies of playa sediment 1–2 km wide and dotted, like that to the north, with patches of false halfa and similar grasses. Sheikh Mabrouk, the southernmost modern oasis settlement, lies within this band. Associated with this southern belt of former playas are an additional eight Sheikh Muftah sites including 30/ 450–B4–1, a series of clusters stretching over 1.3 km along the edge of the crust beyond the Teneida-Kharga road in the extreme southeast.

So far no Sheikh Muftah sites have been found in the desert beyond these southern playas, suggesting that they marked the southern limit of Sheikh Muftah settlement around Dakhleh. Whether these sites are actually confined to the edges of playa sediment or whether others are now buried under it, remains unclear. A few of the clusters actually run under the sediment for a short distance, but on the other hand no trace of Neolithic material has been found on the crusted surfaces inside their margins.

The playa deposits appear to consist of two members produced under different climatic regimes (see below, and Churcher 1983, 181; Kleindienst *et al.*, Chapter 1, this volume). Most Sheikh Muftah scatters around the crusted former wetlands lie on the surface of the lower member. In one or two cases, however, scatters of typical Sheikh Muftah pottery and chipped stone are actually embedded in the higher member. Therefore, it is most likely that these sites are associated with the higher true playa member, while scatters on the lower one have been let down from the higher by deflationary processes.

Dating of Sheikh Muftah Unit

It has already been suggested both that the Sheikh Muftah Unit ('Ceramic Neolithic') is younger than the Bashendi Unit, and that it may span well over a millennium (McDonald 1982, 1983). Both suggestions still seem correct, but dating evidence for the Sheikh Muftah Unit remains poor.

In the Combined Prehistoric Expedition sequence for the eastern Sahara, the best parallels for the Sheikh Muftah material are with the Late Neolithic from Kharga Oasis. Late Neolithic collections from southern Egypt are not very similar technologically or typologically and, in some respects, they more closely resemble Bashendi than Sheikh Muftah materials from Dakhleh (Banks 1984; Wendorf *et al.* 1984; see above). The Kharga Late Neolithic, on the other hand, like the Dakhleh Sheikh Muftah Unit, emphasizes the working of tabular chert as well as a simple flake core technology on nodular chert. Important tool categories include scrapers, denticulates, and perforators in a variety of shapes and sizes, and often made of tabular chert. Planes, picks, and 'hoes' are also present (Caton-Thompson 1952; Wendorf and Schild 1980). The Late Neolithic seems to occur later in Kharga than in Nabta Playa or the Bir Kiseiba area; two dates, 5450 ± 80 yr BP (SMU-741) and 4650 ± 60 yr BP (SMU-412), have been published (Wendorf and Schild 1980).

On present evidence, these dates also seem reasonable for the Dakhleh Sheikh Muftah Unit. In fact, the cross-dating of a few individual finds, artifact types, and similar evidence, indicate the Sheikh Muftah may span a long period including much of the Old Kingdom. First, certain finds suggest there might be some overlap with, or continuity from, Bashendi Unit material. Both units share such artifact types as bifacial knives, bipointed projectile points with rough bifacial retouch and, perhaps, the thin-walled pottery. In addition, identical palettes made of the same dark-grey stone were found on sites from both units. Otherwise, two items, the disk macehead from 31/420–C10–4, and the red-coated jar from 31/405–G6–1, resemble Predynastic Nile Valley material. The large storage jar from 30/435–C3–1 suggests a Dynasty I date. Suites of radiocarbon dates from new excavations now suggest the Predynastic in Upper Egypt ranges from 5200 to 4500 BP (Hassan 1984; Hays 1984), while Dynasty I spans approximately 4440 to 4220 BP (= 3150 to 2900 BC) in calibrated dendrochronological years (Hassan 1980).

Finally, there is evidence, including stratigraphic evidence, that the Sheikh Muftah persisted into Old Kingdom times in Dakhleh. Sheikh Muftah material occurs adjacent to Old Kingdom sites, as at 33/390–I9–1 (002) near the Sheikh Mubaris tombs in the western half of Dakhleh. Sheikh Muftah pottery has been found on the 'Ain Aseel townsite near Balat (C.A. Hope, pers. comm., 1986) and Old Kingdom sherds on some Sheikh Muftah sites. Furthermore at Mut, Sheikh Muftah sherds were associated with Old Kingdom pottery and some tabular chert in an undisturbed stratum just above virgin soil beneath the ruins of the temple at Mut el-Kharab (Hope 1981). This indicates that some Sheikh Muftah sites are contemporaneous with the Late Old Kingdom occupation of Dakhleh, and so date from 2220 BC or later.

To sum up, then, available evidence suggests the Sheikh Muftah Unit appeared in Dakhleh sometime after the middle of the VI Millennium BP, and persisted well past 5000 BP. In this light, the Bashendi Unit might have survived beyond 5500 BP, if the features it shares with the Sheikh Muftah and the Nile Valley Predynastic imply some contemporaneity with these latter units rather than, for instance, a simple ancestral relationship to them.

Finally, the long time span here suggested for the Sheikh Muftah Unit may provide a partial explanation, that of internal development through time, for the variation among Sheikh Muftah assemblages. Thus sites with copper, and with high proportions of tools on tabular chert, including scrapers and sickle elements, characteristics also of Old Kingdom assemblages, may fall relatively late in the sequence. Likewise, sites with high proportions of tools on nodular chert and double patinated tools, with arrowheads and perhaps knives, may be early (McDonald 1982; 1983, table 1). On this scale a site like 31/420–P6–1, with its emphasis on tabular chert for tools, its use of copper and an absence of arrowheads, would be late.

MID-HOLOCENE CLIMATIC SEQUENCE FOR THE EASTERN SAHARA

Two cultural units, the Bashendi and the Sheikh Muftah, distinguishable on the basis of artifact assemblages and site distribution, have been defined for Dakhleh Oasis in the mid-Holocene. Differences in material culture and site distribution, in turn, have implications concerning subsistence, seasonality, sedentism, group composition, and external contacts in the two periods. Before these problems are addressed, the cultural patterns documented here must be considered in the light of data on mid-Holocene climates of the eastern Sahara. A growing body of evidence points to a change towards drier conditions that seems roughly to coincide with, and thus may have played a role in, the cultural changes described above.

Environmental evidence of several kinds indicates there was a humid episode in the eastern Sahara in the early to mid-Holocene. So far only one site has been discovered in the eastern Sahara with sediment and pollen evidence for the earlier Holocene, but the sequence from this site accords well with palaeoclimatic evidence from elsewhere in the Sahara and from northeast Africa in general (Ritchie et al. 1985). The material is from lake sediments in the Oyo Depression, some 700 km south-southwest of Dakhleh, in an area that today is only slightly less arid than Dakhleh itself. The evidence suggests, for the period 8500 to 6100 BP, a moister regime than today, supporting a lake surrounded by savanna vegetation. After 6100 BP it became progressively drier until, by 4500 BP, the lake was completely dry and all vegetation had disappeared, except in oases or wadis.

This picture is generally supported by other kinds of palaeoenvironmental evidence from several locations scattered throughout the Egyptian Western Desert and generated by members of the Combined Prehistoric Expedition and other workers (Banks 1984; Haynes 1982; Wendorf and Schild 1980; Wendorf et al. 1984). The evidence at Nabta Playa, Bir Kiseiba and other oases and wells in the south, Gebel Uweinat and Gilf el-Kebir, Kharga Oasis and the Great Sand Sea, and at Siwa and Garra Oases in the north, comes from the lithostratigraphy of playas, sequences of dune formation and stability, archaeological site locations, and faunal and sparse botanical evidence from archaeological sites. These various lines of evidence point to a period of increased humidity beginning, for the eastern Sahara, about 10,000 BP and persisting, with fluctuations, for about 5000 years (Banks 1984, fig. III.3). In most sequences a brief period of aridity or of oscillating conditions intervenes at or shortly after 7000 BP. The drying trend marking the end of the humid episode starts by about 6000 BP in Nabta, Kiseiba, and Kharga, at least, and is well under way in most places by 5000 BP.

This early to mid-Holocene climatic picture appears to be reflected in the archaeological record of the eastern Sahara. In Wendorf et al's (1984) sequence, the Early

Neolithic appears in Nabta and Kiseiba by 9800 BP, and persists through several stages of development for about 2000 years. The Middle Neolithic, dated from 7700 to 6200 BP, seems to be a period of cultural florescence in the southern part of the Western Desert. The numerous sites vary in size but include extensive ones with deep deposits suggesting a degree of sedentism (Banks 1984). The Late Neolithic in this area, in contrast, is represented by relatively few sites, tending to be small and shallow, and may not persist beyond 5800 BP (Banks 1984; Wendorf *et al*. 1984). The Late Neolithic does continue in what were perhaps better-favoured locations such as Gilf el-Kebir and some of the large oases to the north. Late Neolithic sites in Wadi el-Akhdar in Gilf el-Kebir are dated 5800 to 5060 BP (Wendorf *et al*. 1984) while occupation of Kharga and Dakhleh Oases continues well beyond 5000 BP.

A generally similar picture emerges from studies of sites well away from the oases or highlands, in what is today empty desert. Here, numerous 'stone places' or rock clusters have been interpreted as the campsites of Neolithic cattle herders (Gabriel 1984, 1986). On the basis of over 50 radiocarbon dates from sites in both the central and eastern Sahara, the Neolithic occupation has been divided into three stages, starting at 8500 BP, with the densest occupation occurring between 5800 and 5300 or 5000 BP. Frequency subsequently drops off, and by 3800 BP, such sites have disappeared entirely, apparently because of increasing aridity.

In summary, it appears that the drying trend terminating the early Holocene humid episode is reflected in the archaeological record for the eastern Sahara by a reduction in the number of sites and their disappearance from many regions by about 5000 BP.

Evidence bearing on the mid-Holocene environment in Dakhleh, while presently limited and somewhat equivocal, seems generally to support this picture. It is likely that the area around Dakhleh was drier during the humid episode than that around Nabta and Kiseiba, due to a rainfall gradient from south to north (Banks 1984; Wendorf and Schild 1980). At the same time, the relatively rich faunal assemblages from Bashendi and Sheikh Muftah sites suggest that Dakhleh itself by mid-Holocene times was somewhat wetter than the smaller oases to the south, where the wild fauna was dominated by hare and gazelle.

Dates relating Neolithic sites securely to geological contexts are not yet available. It is therefore possible only to say at this time that geoarchaeological work strongly points to the coexistence of at least seasonal water bodies and Neolithic occupations, at least in eastern Dakhleh where this work has concentrated. Further, geological and archaeological evidence points to a trend towards aridity, beginning about 5500 BP.

As for cultural associations, most of the Dakhleh Neolithic sites lie on the deflated surfaces of former pans, or on the deflated surface of the lower playa member. In a few cases, though, archaeological material from Bashendi and Sheikh Muftah Units is actually embedded in tabular dune deposits. In addition, there are at least two locations where Sheikh Muftah artifacts are embedded in the Upper Playa Member.

ADAPTATION TO DAKHLEH OASIS BY BASHENDI AND SHEIKH MUFTAH GROUPS

The evidence presented here for two distinct cultural units in mid-Holocene Dakhleh, considered in light of climatic data and archaeological evidence from elsewhere in the eastern Sahara, suggests that Bashendi and Sheikh Muftah Units represent quite different adaptations to the oasis environment.

Bashendi Adaptive Patterns

It can be argued that Bashendi Unit groups were not oasis dwellers, but rather the local version of the nomadic pastoralists whose campsites are scattered across the central and eastern Sahara. This is suggested in part by the Bashendi site distribution. Sites are found not only within the oasis, but at almost every location visited on the now-desolate plateau, as well as on plains and basins on the desert floor well south of the oasis. While site location, size, and numbers suggest habitual occupation of areas well away from the oasis, aspects of the material culture point to some degree of nomadism. The absence of structures or features other than hearths is suggestive, but hardly conclusive evidence, given the deflated state of these sites and the scarcity of such evidence on most sites, short-term or otherwise, for this era in the eastern Sahara. On the other hand, the scarcity of pottery, at a time when it had already been used in the area for thousands of years, conforms with the pattern for non-sedentary societies worldwide (Rafferty 1985), and specifically for North African pastoral groups such as the Kel Tamasheq of Mali. This group uses very little pottery, because of its fragility (Smith 1980). The heavy grinding stones of the Bashendi Unit would probably not normally encumber a mobile group, as evidence suggests they were left behind when a site was abandoned.

There is a little evidence from elsewhere in the Western Desert to suggest the mid-Holocene pastoral nomads may have had a Bashendi-like material culture. While few details are yet available on assemblages associated with the desert 'stone places', they include numerous arrowheads, grinding stones, and ostrich eggshell clusters, but very little pottery (Gabriel 1984). Similar material is reported by members of the 1938 Bagnold expedition for sites lying on mud deposits or near scarps in the area between Dakhleh and Kharga Oases and Gilf el-Kebir and Gebel Uweinat to the southwest. Assemblages include chipped stone, grinding stones, rare ground stone items, and ostrich eggshell, sometimes decorated or made into beads. Pottery is, however rare on sites located northeast of Gilf el-Kebir (Bagnold *et al.* 1939). More details on the chipped stone industry are available for sites discovered by Caton-Thompson and Gardner (Caton-Thompson 1931) in the desert between Abydos on the Nile and Kharga Oasis. One such site, 75 km into the desert, near an outcrop of tabular chert, yielded a side-blow flake and bifacially retouched bipoints similar to Bashendi points. Ostrich eggshell fragments were present, but no pottery (Caton-Thompson 1931, fig. 1).

If, as this evidence suggests, the Bashendi Unit is a product of nomadic pastoralists who may have ranged well beyond the limits of Dakhleh, several additional questions arise concerning the groups involved, their migration patterns and their relationship to Dakhleh Oasis.

At least three models of migration patterns have been proposed for the central and eastern Sahara in the mid-Holocene. One involves movements of up to several hundred kilometres between ecological zones such as massifs and lowlands, the massifs serving as refuges during the dry season (Banks 1984; McHugh 1974). Another involves year-round wandering within the lowlands (Gabriel 1984, 1986). A third, proposed for Nabta and Kiseiba, is a 'tethered strategy' with herding units ranging away from a settled core group in the oasis, and aggregating again during the wet season (Banks 1984).

While evidence on this subject is still very scarce for the Bashendi Unit, a version of the first model may apply, with the oasis serving as the annual refuge or aggregation point for mobile cattle-herders. As yet, there is no equivalent in Dakhleh of the extensive stratified sites which in Nabta Playa are interpreted as permanent settlements anchoring mobile groups (Banks 1984). On the other hand, there is some evidence for aggregation, a process found commonly among hunter-gatherers, and occasionally among herders (Smith 1980), in which several otherwise dispersed, small groups come together regularly for feasting, ritual, courtship, and similar activities. Researchers are now defining criteria for identifying aggregation sites in the archaeological record (Conkey 1980). Also, intriguing parallels to finds on Bashendi sites in Dakhleh come from the Southern African ethnographic and archaeological record on aggregation (Wadley 1986). During the aggregation phase of the Kalahari San, *hxaro* or gift exchange helps promote friendly social contact. The favourite *hxaro* gifts are arrows and ostrich eggshell beads manufactured, by men and women respectively, only in the aggregation camps. The arrows are quite varied, bearing stylistic information on group and even individual identity (Wadley 1986; Weissner 1983). In addition to the ethnographic material, Wadley cites archaeological evidence for similar behaviour at some mid-Holocene sites in Southern Africa.

Assuming the analogy holds in the Dakhleh area, so far removed from the Kalahari, the above evidence suggests that some Bashendi sites – sizeable ones such as 30/450–F8–3 and 31/420–P6–1, with varied projectile points and evidence of knapping and bead manufacture – might be aggregation sites. Interestingly, within the mapped area of 30/450–F8–3, the several point types cluster to some extent around different hearth mounds. This could reflect the disposition of family units of an aggregated group within the camp, assuming of course that the hearths are contemporaneous.

Postulated aggregation sites in Dakhleh are located both within and beyond the present borders of the oasis, although those borders may have expanded and been less distinct during the Holocene humid episode. Dispersal sites, then, in this postulated pattern, may have included some of the smaller, less richly littered Bashendi sites within Dakhleh (although some of these could be special-purpose camps used during the aggregation season), as well as others far out in what is now the desert. While Bagnold *et al.*'s (1939) and Gabriel's (1984, 1986) evidence suggests such desert sites exist, more must be known of their location, size, and assemblages before some could be fitted with confidence into the postulated Dakhleh pattern. There may of course have been aggregation sites in the desert as well, but the large oases of Dakhleh and probably Kharga would have become increasingly attractive for this purpose as the wider region began to dry out by the VI Millennium BP.

One other kind of evidence that might reflect on the mobility of Bashendi groups is the presence of tool types such as bifacial foliates, sideblow flakes, and hollow-based points, which are widely distributed from the central Sahara to the Nile Valley. Scarce pottery is of little help in defining cultural boundaries and external ties of this unit, the only exception, providing it pertains to the Bashendi rather than Sheikh Muftah Unit, being the incised wares. These are generally dissimilar to decorated wares elsewhere in the eastern Sahara, except for possible parallels with material from Wadi el-Bakht in the Gilf el-Kebir (Hope 1983).

If the postulated link between Neolithic desert sites and the Bashendi Unit is sound, it may be that some of the petroglyphs found in eastern Dakhleh and in the desert between Dakhleh and Kharga (Winkler 1939), particularly those depicting Ethiopian elements such as giraffe, ostrich, and several large antelopes (Churcher 1983), are products of the Bashendi Unit or related groups. There is as yet no firm proof of this tie from Dakhleh itself. Bashendi material is nevertheless found frequently enough around petroglyph sites to suggest it. Site 32/435–L10–2 (124), for instance, consists of small clusters of Bashendi chipped stone at the bases of the three hills constituting petroglyph site 32/435–L10–1. The clusters occur at the foot of rock faces decorated with giraffes, long-horned cattle, and other animals and birds (Churcher 1983; Mills 1983). Likewise, to the southeast of Dakhleh, 30/450–F8–3 and the other Bashendi sites nearby are virtually the only cultural remains of any period found in the vicinity of a petroglyph site with inscribed giraffes and similar fauna (30/450–F9–1) (180).

Sheikh Muftah Adaptive Patterns

Site distribution and certain features of the assemblages suggest the Sheikh Muftah Unit represents a quite different adaptation from the Bashendi Unit. In short, it appears that it was much more tightly focussed on the oasis proper.

Thus, unlike Bashendi sites which are scattered within and beyond the oasis, virtually all Sheikh Muftah sites are well within it. The only exceptions are the two sites on Gebel Abu Tartur. Their location on the Darb el-Tawil to the Nile suggests they likely served as way-stations rather than desert habitation sites. Likewise, there is no evidence for Sheikh Muftah sites farther out in the desert. Localities reported by Gabriel (1986), as stated above, more closely resemble Bashendi than Sheikh Muftah sites, yielding very little pottery, or none at all. Similarly, O.H. Myers, for instance, reports pottery with Nubian C-Group affiliations on sites at Uweinat, Gilf el-Kebir and points south, but he found no pottery on sites to the northeast, on the road to Dakhleh and Kharga (Bagnold *et al.* 1939).

The Sheikh Muftah Unit then seems very much an oasis-oriented culture. Sites tend to concentrate along contours or they hug the edges of former wetlands. Bashendi sites show little such alignment, and no affinity for the crusted wetland. Bashendi site 30/450–A4–1, for instance, is located near site 30/450–B4–1 (135), a string over 1 km long of Sheikh Muftah clusters bordering a playa. Site 30/450–A4–1, however, is situated about 200 m outside the playa border, at the foot of a sandstone hill.

While there is no indication that Sheikh Muftah groups were settled permanently in one spot, they do seem to have stayed year-round in the oasis. Evidence pointing to a pattern of aggregation and dispersal for the Bashendi Unit is absent from Sheikh Muftah sites. Not only are shell beads and a variety of point types no longer being manufactured; Sheikh Muftah sites are generally smaller with a smaller range than Bashendi sites. Sheikh Muftah evidence suggests habitation sites and smaller special purpose sites all within the oasis, rather than a pattern in which relatively large groups converge on a particular site seasonally.

The Sheikh Muftah pottery corpus appears to corroborate this. The quantity present on sites and the large size of some vessels suggests a people considerably more settled than the Bashendi groups. Further, the fact that the corpus has no close parallels with other collections from the eastern Sahara, reinforces the impression that Sheikh Muftah groups had an adaptive pattern tightly focussed on Dakhleh Oasis.

This is not to say they were completely isolated. The presence of a little pottery from the Nile Valley, marine shells, exotic stone such as diorite, and perhaps copper, points to some contact with groups beyond the Western Desert. The sites atop el-Battikh Promontory on the Darb el-Tawil suggest there might have been occasional direct contact with the Nile, a distinct possibility if these people had the domesticated ass.

All this suggests that Sheikh Muftah groups subsisted mainly on oasis resources. This switch from the postulated Bashendi pattern of exploitation of both the oasis and the surrounding desert, can probably largely be explained by the drying trend under way by 5000 BP, which would have left the desert uninhabitable. While subsistence details remain scanty, there is a little evidence to suggest that even within the oasis Sheikh Muftah groups may have been under some stress. The location of so many sites along the same contour may indicate a relationship to the oasis water table. The fact that Sheikh Muftah animal bones are broken into very small pieces could reflect in part a need to extract all possible food value from them, another sign of economic stress (cf. Hodder 1979).

Last, as mentioned above, certain features of the artifact assemblages suggest there may have been some overlap between Bashendi and Sheikh Muftah occupations of Dakhleh. If this was the case, the two modes of adaptation probably could have coexisted, with Bashendi groups continuing to aggregate in the oasis after other groups began occupying it full-time. Groups from the two units would have to adjust to or accommodate each other, perhaps by entering into some kind of symbiotic relationship and/or, in the case of Bashendi groups, by aggregating at sites beyond Sheikh Muftah occupation.

SUMMARY AND CONCLUSIONS

Two cultural units have been defined for Dakhleh Oasis in the mid-Holocene, sharing such broad 'Neolithic' features as ceramics, grinding stones, ground stone items, relatively limited, simple, chipped stone toolkits and, in addition, the exploitation of cereals or other plants and of a range of animal species, wild and domesticated. Beyond these broad similarities, the two units are distinguishable on the basis of a variety of traits: 1) preferred lithic raw material, 2) the overall structure of the lithic industry as well as specific tool types, 3) the relative abundance and variety of pottery, and 4) certain changes in other artifact classes – the disappearance of worked eggshell after the Bashendi, for instance, or the later introduction of copper implements. In addition, there is a marked change in site distribution, from an extensive pattern of Bashendi sites both within and beyond the oasis, to a Sheikh Muftah pattern tightly focused on the oasis.

Environmental and archaeological data from various locations in the eastern Sahara indicate both these occupations coincided with a period of climatic change in the Western Desert – a drying trend marking the end of the early to mid-Holocene humid episode. Neolithic groups seem to have come late to Dakhleh, compared with their record in Bir Kiseiba and Nabta Playa to the south. It is suggested, by analogy with mobile groups producing similar classes of artifacts in present-day Southern Africa, that the earliest Neolithic groups, those of the Bashendi Unit, were but seasonal visitors to Dakhleh. Small groups, otherwise pasturing their cattle in what is now empty desert, appear to have aggregated regularly in the relatively lush oasis. There they supported themselves with processed plant foods and wild game as well as the products of their herds, and engaged in group social activities facilitated by gift exchange.

During the 6th Millennium BP, in the face of continued regional desiccation, this pattern gave way to one in which groups remained year-round in the oasis. Through time, more sedentary Sheikh Muftah groups relied increasingly on produced foods; hunting seems to have declined in importance, for instance, and new domesticates were added to the list. Additionally, with copper, they acquired a new technology, or at least a significant new product. Otherwise, their mode of adaptation remained stable and successful enough to persist until new colonists arrived from the Nile Valley in late Old Kingdom times.

While some of this reconstruction remains tentative, based in part on analogy, the reconstruction at least suggests directions for further research to test some of these hypotheses. Locational analysis of scatters on well-preserved sites like 30/450–F8–3 could yield information on group size and composition and possibly even gender roles at postulated aggregation sites. Charcoal-filled hearth mounds may yield botanical evidence of plant foods used at these sites, as well as seasons of occupation. More information can come from comparative studies of chipped stone assemblages and associated artifacts from Dakhleh sites of different sizes and locations, with these problems in mind. Finally, more information on the assemblages from some of the recently-discovered desert 'stone places' might help us assess the relationships of the two Neolithic units defined here to the desert beyond Dakhleh Oasis.

ENDNOTE

Since this chapter was completed in 1986, eight additional seasons of fieldwork have produced much new information on Dakhleh's late prehistory, including nearly 50 additional radiocarbon dates. Most of this new information is already published in the Dakhleh Oasis Project's Annual Reports in the Journal of the Society for the Study of Egyptian Antiquities and elsewhere, and much of it is alluded to in Chapter 1 (Kleindienst *et al.*, Chapter 1, this volume). I have decided not to alter this paper on the Holocene prehistory, however, as any attempt to update it by incorporating new information would result in a completely rewritten account in which the thrust of the paper – the definition of the three major units, never fully developed in other articles – would be submerged or lost.

This endnote is intended both as a bridge to the information in the geomorphological section and to reinforce two themes implicit in the chapter. One is that there appears to be a changing pattern of occupation, through early to mid-Holocene, from the periphery downslope towards the centre of the oasis. The other

concerns the apparent episodic nature of the late prehistoric record. While the geomorphic evidence might suggest a single pluvial event during the Holocene until about 4500 BP (Brookes 1993, 549), archaeological and dating evidence points to possibly many and sometimes prolonged interruptions in occupation of the oasis during this timespan. These themes are developed more fully in McDonald (in press).

A suite of 67 radiocarbon dates for late prehisoric Dakhleh shows two major breaks, one between the Epipalaeolithic (now termed Masara) and Bashendi Cultural Units, and one falling within the Bashendi Cultural Unit, which is therefore subdivided it into Phases A and B (McDonald 1990).

The first major occupation episode in the Holocene falls in the first half of the IX Millenium BP. The sites of the Masara occupation are found in locations marginal to the present oasis – on the Libyan Plateau, notably in the Miramar Basin, and to the south of the oasis, on the sandstone ridges to the southwest of Sheikh Muftah, and beyond the Southeast Basin on the Kharga Road.

Following a prolonged break, Bashendi A sites are occupied from the last half of the VIII into the VII Millenium, from about 7600 to 6850 BP. The most intensive occupation in the eastern Dakhleh region occurs within the Southeast Basin, outside the present oasis, on the road to Kharga. After a hiatus of several centuries in the list of radiocarbon dates, 24 dates from Bashendi B sites attest to an occupation for that subunit of over a millenium, beginning about 6500 BP. More than half of the Bashendi B dates occur before 6100 BP. Most are from the Southeast Basin, and one comes from a site on top of the Plateau. Of the 11 dates of 6100 BP or later, most are from the Southeast Basin, but four come from within the oasis proper, where they are associated with ancient tabular sand-sheets, either southwest of the present Balat cultivation areas or in Western Dakhleh.

Sites of the Sheikh Muftah Unit are associated with the same tabular sand sheets, as well as with salt-encrusted playa deposits in various basins, and with other Central Lowland contexts, as outlined in this chapter. Dating the Sheikh Muftah sites remains problematical but, for reasons discussed in this chapter, and in Chapter 1 on the geomorphology (Kleindienst *et al.*, Chapter 1, this volume), it seems likely that most Sheikh Muftah sites are later than about 5500 BP, and some are coeval with the Old Kingdom presence in the oasis.

Acknowledgements

I wish to thank A.J. Mills who, as director, invited me to participate in the Dakhleh Oasis Project and, in the field each season, provided invaluable assistance. My thanks also go to G. Freeman, of the Society for the Study of Egyptian Antiquities, who organised flights to Cairo and generally facilitated matters from Toronto. Each season I have enjoyed the friendly collegiality of all expedition members, and benefitted particularly from the help and insights provided by C.S. Churcher, C.A. Hope, M.R. Kleindienst, I.A. Brookes and J.C. Ritchie. Various members have helped me with fieldwork from time to time, notably P.G. Sheldrick, A.F. Hollett, and R.A. Frey who assisted over a number of seasons, and those who helped during single seasons – A. von Gernet (1980), M. MacKellar (1988),G. Mumford (1990), D. Tangri (1990), and K. Walker (1992). I wish to thank the Egyptian Antiquities Organisation for its support and assistance over the years. I also thank Ian Brookes for arranging for the original word processing of this manuscript.

Address for Author
Mary M.A. McDonald, Department of Archaeology, University of Calgary, Calgary, Alberta, Canada T2N 1N4

REFERENCES

Bagnold, R.A., R.F. Peel, O.H. Myers, and H.A. Winkler. 1939. An expedition to the Gilf Kebir and 'Uweinat, 1938. *The Geographical Journal* **93**: 281–313.

Banks, K.M. 1984. *Climates, cultures and cattle: the Holocene archaeology of the eastern Sahara*. Dallas: Department of Anthropology, Institute for the Study of Earth and Man, Southern Methodist University, 259p.

Baumgartel, E.J. 1960. *The cultures of prehistoric Egypt*, vol. II. London: Oxford University Press, 164p.

Brookes, I.A. 1993. Geomorphology and Quaternary Geology of the Dakhla Oasis Region, Egypt. *Quaternary Science Reviews* 12: 529–552.

Camps, G. 1974. *Les civilisations préhistoriques de l'Afrique du nord et du Sahara*. Paris: Doin, 373p.

Caton-Thompson, G. 1931. Royal Anthropological Institute's Prehistoric Research Expedition to Kharga Oasis, Egypt. Preliminary outline of the season's work. *Man* **31**: 77–84.

Caton-Thompson, G. 1952. *Kharga Oasis in prehistory*. London: Athlone Press, 213p.

Caton-Thompson, G. and E.W. Gardner. 1934. *The Desert Fayum*. London: Royal Anthropological Institute, 167p.

Churcher, C.S. 1983. Dakhleh Oasis Project – Palaeontology: interim report on the 1982 field season. *Journal of the Society for the Study of Egyptian Antiquities* **13**: 178–187.

Churcher, C.S. This volume. Chapter 8. Holocene faunas of the Dakhleh Oasis, 133–152.

Clark, J.D., J.L. Philips, and P.S. Staley. 1974. Interpretations of prehistoric technology from ancient Egyptian and other sources; Part 1: Ancient Egyptian bows and arrows and their relevance for African prehistory. *Paleorient* 2: 323–388.

Conkey, M.W. 1980. The identification of prehistoric hunter-gatherer aggregation sites: the case of Altamira. *Current Anthropology* **21**: 609–630.

Gabriel, B. 1984. Great plains and mountain areas as habitats for the Neolithic man in the Sahara, 391–398. *In* Krzyzaniak, L. and M. Kobusiewicz, eds, *Origin and early development of food-producing cultures in north-eastern Africa*. Poznan: Polish Academy of Sciences, 503p.

Gabriel, B. 1986. Paleoecological evidence from Neolithic fireplaces in the Sahara, Abstract. *In 'The Longest Record: The Human Career in Africa'*, *A Conference in Honour of J. Desmond Clark*, University of California, Berkeley, California, April 12–16, 1986, 105p.

Hassan, F.A. 1980. Radiocarbon chronology of Archaic Egypt. *Journal of Near Eastern Studies* **39**: 203–207.

Hassan, F.A. 1984. Radiocarbon chronology of Predynastic Nagada settlements, Upper Egypt. *Current Anthropology* **25**: 681–683.

Haynes, C.V., Jr. 1982. Great Sand Sea and Selima Sand Sheet, eastern Sahara: geochronology of desertification. *Science* **217**: 629–633.

Hays, T.R. 1984. Predynastic development in Upper Egypt, 211–219. *In* Krzyzaniak, L. and M. Kobusiewicz, eds, *Origin and early development of food producing cultures in north-eastern Africa*. Poznan: Polish Academy of Sciences, 503p.

Hodder, I. 1979. Economic and social stress and material culture patterning. *American Antiquity* **44**: 446–454.

Hope, C.A. 1980. Dakhleh Oasis Project – Report on the study of the pottery and kilns. *Journal of the Society for the Study of Egyptian Antiquities* **10**: 283–313.

Hope, C.A. 1981. Dakhleh Oasis Project: Report on the study of the pottery and kilns: Third season – 1980. *Journal of the Society for the Study of Egyptian Antiquities* **11**: 233–241.

Hope, C.A. 1983. Dakhleh Oasis Project – Preliminary report on the study of the pottery – Fifth season, 1982. *Journal of the Society for the Study of Egyptian Antiquities* **13**: 142–157.

Hope, C.A. This volume. Chapter 14. Pottery manufacture in the Dakhleh Oasis, 215–243.

Kleindienst, M.R., C.S. Churcher, M.M.A. McDonald, and H.P Schwarcz. This volume. Chapter 1. Geography, Geology, Geochronology and Geoarchaeology of the Dakhleh Oasis Region: An interim report, 1–54.

McDonald, M.M.A. 1980. Dakhleh Oasis Project – Preliminary report on lithic industries in the Dakhleh Oasis. *Journal of the Society for the Study of Egyptian Antiquities* **10**: 315–329.

McDonald, M.M.A. 1982. Dakhleh Oasis Project – Third preliminary report on the lithic industries in the Dakhleh Oasis. *Journal of the Society for the Study of Egyptian Antiquities* **12**: 115–138.

McDonald, M.M.A. 1983. Dakhleh Oasis Project – Fourth preliminary report on the lithic industries in the Dakhleh Oasis. *Journal of the Society for the Study of Egyptian Antiquities* **13**: 158–166.

McDonald, M.M.A. 1985. Dakhleh Oasis Project – Holocene Prehistory: Interim report on the 1984 and 1986 seasons. *Journal of the Society for the Study of Egyptian Antiquities* **15**: 126–135.

McDonald, M.M.A. 1990. The Dakhleh Oasis Project: Holocene Prehistory: Interim report on the 1991 season. *Journal of the Society for the Study of Egyptian Antiquities* **20**: 65–76.

McDonald, M.M.A. In press. The late prehistoric radiocarbon chronology for Dakhleh Oasis within the wider environmental and cultural settings of the Egyptian Western Desert [tentative title]. *In* Marlow, C.A., ed., *Proceedings of the First Dakhleh Oasis Project Seminar, held at the Department of Anthropology, Durham University, July 5–9, 1994*. Oxford: Oxbow Books.

McHugh, W.P. 1974. Cattle pastoralism in Africa – a model for interpreting archaeological evidence from the eastern Sahara Desert. *Arctic Anthropology* **11**, Supplement, 236–244.

Mills, A.J. 1983. Dakhleh Oasis Project – Report on the fifth season of survey: October, 1982 – January, 1983. *Journal of the Society for the Study of Egyptian Antiquities* **13**: 121–141.

Rafferty, J.E. 1985. The archaeological record on sedentariness: recognition, development, and implications, 113–156. *In* Schiffer, M.B., ed., *Advances in Archaeological Method and Theory*, vol. 8. New York: Academic Press, 306p.

Ritchie, J.C., C.H. Eyles, and C.V. Haynes, Jr. 1985. Sediment and pollen evidence for an early to mid-Holocene humid period in the eastern Sahara. *Nature* **314**: 352–355.

Ritchie, J.C. This volume. Chapter 4. Flora, vegetation and palaeobotany of the Dakhleh Oasis, 73–81.

Smith, S.E. 1980. The environmental adaptation of nomads in the West African Sahel: a key to understanding prehistoric pastoralists, 467–487. *In* Williams, M.A.J. and H. Faure, eds, *The Sahara and the Nile*. Rotterdam: A.A. Balkema, 607p.

Tixier, J. 1963. Typologie de l'Epipaléolithique du Maghreb. *Mémoires du Centre des Recherches Anthropologiques, Préhistoriques et Ethnographiques*, no. 2. Paris, Arts et Metiers Graphiques, 209p.

Vermeersch, P.M. 1984. Subsistence activities on the Late Palaeolithic sites of Elkab (Upper Egypt), 137–142. *In* Krzyzaniak, L. and M. Kobusiewicz, eds, *Origin and early development of food-producing cultures in north-eastern Africa*. Poznan: Polish Academy of Sciences, 503p.

Wadley, L. 1986. Private lives and public lives: a social interpretation for the Stone Age in southern Africa, Abstract. *In 'The Longest Record: The Human Career in Africa', A Conference in Honour of J. Desmond Clark*, University of California, Berkeley, California, April 12–16, 1986, 105p.

Weissner, P. 1983. Style and social information in Kalahari San projectile points. *American Antiquity* **48**: 253–276.

Wendorf, F. and R. Schild. 1976. *Prehistory of the Nile Valley*. New York: Academic Press, 404p.

Wendorf, F. and Schild. 1980. *The prehistory of the eastern Sahara*. New York: Academic Press, 414p.

Wendorf, F., R. Schild, and A.E. Close. 1984. *Cattle-keepers of the eastern Sahara: the Neolithic of Bir Kiseiba*. Dallas: Department of Anthropology, Institute for the Study of Earth and Man, Southern Methodist University, 452p.

Winkler, H.A. 1939. *Rock drawings of southern Upper Egypt*, vol. II. London: Egypt Exploration Society, 40p.

8

HOLOCENE FAUNAS OF THE DAKHLEH OASIS

C. S. Churcher

ABSTRACT

Animal remains were collected from surface lag-gravel deposits at 18 sites, usually associated with Neolithic artifacts. Taxa identified to genus and species are Mollusca (4 taxa); *Pila ovata*, *Gyraulus costulatus*, *Etheria elliptica*, *Melanoides tuberculata*: Reptilia (1 taxon); *Geochelone sulcata*: Aves (1 taxon); *Struthio camelus*: Mammalia (15 taxa);*Lepus capensis*, *Felis* sp., *Canis aureus lupaster*, *Loxodonta africana*, *Hippopotamus amphibius*, *Alcephalus buselaphus*, *Gazella dorcas*, *G. leptoceros*, *Capra hircus* (domestic?), *Syncerus caffer* cf. *aequinoctialis*, *Pelorovis antiquus*, *Bos primigenius*, *B. taurus* (domestic?), *Equus grevyi*, *?E. quagga* (= *E. burchelli*), *E. asinus* (domestic?).

These animals show a typical African savanna facies similar to that present today in East Africa or the southern Sudan. Animals locally extinct in Egypt are assumed to have been extirpated by man. Domestic stock is present mixed with the wild taxa, and remains of Pharaonic, Roman or later times have been let down into the sample by deflationary erosion.

INTRODUCTION

The surficial, visible and easily recorded features, archaeological, palaeontological and geological deposits, and settlement and land use patterns of the Dakhleh Oasis were surveyed by teams of specialists during field seasons in the years 1977–1987. This paper records the observed Holocene zooarchaeological evidence in the context of the surficial Quaternary geology. Surveys were made and collections of selected specimens assembled during field seasons of 1979 (Nov 22–Dec 10), 1980 (Nov 14–Dec 1), 1981 (Jan 15–30, 1982), 1982 (Nov 17–Dec 13), 1985 (Jan 19–Jan 30), 1986 (Jan 1–28), and 1987 (Jan 10–28). All but two have been briefly recorded (Churcher, 1980, 1981, 1982, 1983, 1988).

Dakhleh Oasis lies in the Western Desert of Egypt, ·centred at about lat. 25° 50′N and long. 29° 00′E, and about 300 km southwest of the Nile River at Assiyut and at about the latitiude of Luxor (see Kleindienst *et al.*, this volume, Chapter 1, Fig. 1.1). It lies at the base of part of the escarpment that limits the Libyan Plateau in the south and west, in a depression that is at present suffering aeolian erosion and topographical lowering. Dakhleh Oasis is some 80 km long east-west and 25 km north-south and lies between and around the embayments between three spurs of the escarpment – Gebel Edmonstone and Maohoub Promontory in the west, Gifata Promontory in the centre, and the western buttress of el-Battikh Promontory in the east (Fig. 8.1). The inhabited areas are discontinuous, with the eastern part of the oasis centred on Balat and separated from the western by 8 km of rocky desert. Most of the settlements and farmed areas lie between rocky, stoney, sandy or 'regh' areas, with occasional 'seif'-dune ridges and 'barchan' or crescent dunes overiding cultivable soils in the west (Beadnell 1901; Brookes 1983; Churcher 1980, 1981, 1982; Kleindienst *et al.*, this volume, Chapter 1). The cultivable areas lie toward the bottoms of the depression and the preserved Palaeolithic, Neolithic and Old Kingdom sites lie outside or on the fringes of the cultivated areas.

The cultivation is interspersed with areas of salinated flats, aeolian deflated soils or claystone bedrock of Late

---

'Reports from the Survey of Dakhleh Oasis, Western Desert of Egypt, 1977–1987', edited by C.S. Churcher and A.J. Mills. Dakhleh Oasis Project: Monograph 2. Oxbow Monograph 99.

Cretaceous age (Mut Formation.), ridges of linear seif dunes that trend from west of north to east of south (350°–170°), and scattered spring mounds (Kleindienst et al., this volume, Chapter 1). The oasis occurs because aeolian deflation at the foot of the Libyan Plateau (partly by adiabatically energised north winds) has lowered the land surface so it is close to or intersects the water table provided by aquifers in the Nubia Series sandstones immediately beneath the Qusseir (= Mut) Formation shales and Taref Formation red clays. The area has been inhabited by man since Palaeolithic times, although climatic fluctuations may have caused him to abandon the oasis between Palaeolithic and Neolithic times. Evidences of Old Kingdom, Roman, Byzantine and Islamic occupation are numerous.

Investigation of the Neolithic and other faunal assemblages (reconstructed in Figs 8.2 & 8.3) formed part of the archaeological, palaeontological and ecological survey of the oasis. It was hoped that faunal assemblages from Palaeolithic levels might also be recovered but, although Palaeolithic artifact assemblages were located (Kleindienst, this volume, Chapter 5), their conditions of preservation show that all vestiges of the original entombing soils have been removed, presumably by aeolian erosion. The tools made of perishable materials and left on the scoured surface, and thus any animal materials that might have been present, were also presumably removed by a combination of harsh insolation and scouring winds. However, a single palaeolithic horizon with Early Middle Stone Age tools and vertebrate remains was located in 1996.

Faunal remains from later Pharaonic, Ptolemaic or Romano-Byzantine times are scarce and no faunally rich midden deposit has been located. Such deposits, when present, represent refuse fill within the older towns such as Qasr or Ismant el-Kharab (= Kellis).

These collections representing the Neolithic, Old Kingdom and, less abundantly, Romano-Byzantine faunas allow reconstructions and interpretations of their changes through time, deductions as to past ecologies, and speculations on the geomorphological evolution and ecological sequence in the oasis.

MATERIALS AND METHODS

The oasis was surveyed on foot by members of the project, including trained archaeologists, geological and biological specialists, 'guftis', and surveyors. Whenever a site was located – in this instance sites in which bones, teeth or shells were noted – it was mapped, described, and a representative collection of fragments assembled. As many of these sites also included human artifacts, the examination and sampling was often carried out in conjunction with M.M.A. McDonald who made collections of the lithic assemblage, artifacts such as ostrich egg shell beads, pottery, needles and copper metal objects. Most materials were collected from among those lying on the surface, where they formed a composite stone, bone and tooth lag

after exposure by aeolian erosion. In a few instances specimens that were partly still within the matrix were recovered and, in even fewer cases, small sample test pits sunk. These latter were chiefly to test whether the apparent lag represented more than a surface covering and, in fact, was the top of a deeper deposit, and to sample the stratigraphy and thus gain insights on the modes of accumulation of the specimens and deposition of the matrix.

The recovered specimens were transported to the expedition's base house where each specimen was labelled, stabilised, and given a field identification.

The conditions of the materials range from complete to fragmentary, with few elements in association except for tooth rows either in bone or in the matrix after dissolution of the bone. Most large elements show green breaks brought about when the bone was fresh and before the element was entombed. Some were charred or calcined from fire. Some had been eroded to form ventifacts after aeolian exhumation had taken place. Such specimens preserved the harder cortical matrix and had lost much of the softer cancellous bone.

Preservation of the elements is variable. Some bones, mostly from the Bashendi Unit, have suffered mineralisation, mainly by iron oxides, manganese dioxide, calcium carbonate or by gypsum. In the latter case, the bones are often exploded due to crystal formation within the bone microstructure, and thus comprise specimens that cannot be conserved. All the others are heavier and sturdier than in life, and comprise excellent, if incomplete, specimens. Other bones have lost material by leaching, and these, if they have not been so eroded by aeolian sand blasting as to become mere lattices of the original bone, require extensive perfusing and hardening with chemical stabilisers such as 'Glyptal', 'Household Cement' diluted in acetone, polyvinal acetate (PVA) beads dissolved in acetone or ethyl alcohol, or PVA Glue (white carpenters' glue) diluted with water. Specimens that have been subjected to heat within a hearth often require such care.

After preservation the materials were further conserved in the laboratory, and a catalogue of all materials assembled. The information thus gained allows the larger faunal picture to be reconstructed and interpretations of ecology and human activities to be proposed.

SITE DESCRIPTIONS

Locations and Identifications

The sites are located in Figure 8.1. Each is identified by a map sheet number (e.g. '31/420') of the Egypt 1:25,000 series, and by a grid reference (e.g. 'F9–3') which indicates the square (F9) on the sheet and that it is the third (3) site identified in the square (see Introduction and this volume, Appendix II). The squares are located by 15 alphabetical abscissae (A-N, P) and a numerical ordinate (1–10). Each square has a one kilometre side and each map sheet covers an area 10 by 15 km. Numerical site identifiers given in reports in the Journal of the Society for the Study of Egyptian Antiquities may be inaccurate. A general map of Dakhleh Oasis is given in Kleindienst *et al.*, this volume, Chapter 1, Fig. 1.1.

The sites considered here are only those that are fossiliferous or contain abundant faunal remains (see Appendices 2 and 3, this volume). Palaeolithic sites and those earlier than ca. 5000 BC, excepting that discovered in 1996 after the end of the survey, have preserved no biological materials and are therefore not considered.

Neolithic sites with zooarchaeological deposits are located close to the 130 m contour of the oasis basin and are divisible into two categories, those without or with very sparse pottery (Bashendi Cultural Unit) and those usually with pottery (Sheikh Muftah Cultural Unit). The Masara Cultural Unit sites generally lack zooarchaeological materials. The Bashendi Unit deposits generally lie stratigraphically below Sheikh Muftah Unit deposits when both are present in a limited geographical area (e.g. 32/390–D2–2, Loc. 006), and bone fragments from Bashendi sites or levels are usually larger, more darkly stained, and from more massive mammals than those from Sheikh Muftah sites or levels.

Old Kingdom sites are often farther towards the centre of the oasis depressions than are the Neolithic sites but, when found in conjunction with Sheikh Muftah Unit deposits, are higher stratigraphically than the older cultural levels.

No section has yet been identified in which a clear progression through the Neolithic into the Old Kingdom or later deposits is present. Such a site appears unlikely if progressive dessiccation of the oasis area resulted in a contracting ring of occupation with the older Neolithic situated outside the younger Neolithic and Pharaonic sites. Palaeolithic sites are situated in sites well outside the present oasis, often on higher remnant land surfaces along the Libyan Escarpment (see this volume, Kleindienst *et al.*, Chapter 1 and Kleindienst, Chapter 5.) Ptolemaic, Roman and Byzantine sites have been identified, and in some cases are associated with vestiges of classical Pharaonic occupation. Contact or mixed layers between classical Graeco-Roman and ancient Egyptian occupation are few, and probably exist only at Mut el-Kharab (Mills, this volume, Chapter 10).

Neolithic Sites

The Neolithic deposits are often exposed as a surface lag or still in place within the surrounding matrix, either within more or less horizontally laid clayey silts for the early deposits, or within sandy silty-sands probably laid down as coppice dunes or dune sheets in which root casts of anchoring vegetation are visible (McDonald, this volume, Chapter 7). The recovered materials were generally exposed on the surface and mixed with more recent debris as surficial lags. At some sites the older materials, e.g., of Bashendi or Sheikh Muftah age, exist *in situ* in a lower

stratum and are covered by a lag that contains eroded Sheikh Muftah, Old Kingdom or Roman materials. The earliest Masara Cultural Unit has yielded no associated faunal remains.

Only five localities are known where the Bashendi Unit contains faunal remains. These are two sites where Bashendi is not mixed or associated with either Sheikh Muftah or Old Kingdom materials (31/420–M9–2, Loc. 104; 31/435–L1–1, Loc. 125), two sites where Bashendi and Sheikh Muftah Neolithic materials are stratigraphically separate and geographically proximate (31/420–D9–1, Loc. 072; 31/420–F9–3, Loc 092), and one site where Bashendi, Sheikh Muftah, and Old Kingdom materials are associated in a broad area with both stratigraphic and geographic discontinuous separation (32/390–D2–2, Loc. 006).

Sheikh Muftah Unit materials are recorded from three of the sites just mentioned (31/420–D9–1, 31/420–F9–3, 32/390–D2–2), and from six other sites. Four sites contain only Sheikh Muftah materials (30/420–P1–1, Loc. 105, 30/435–B3–2, Loc. 108; 31/420–F9–3, Loc. 092; 31/420–P6–1, Loc. 100) and all lie in the southeast sector of the oasis. Site 33/390–I9–1/2 shows Sheikh Muftah faunal materials near to but geographically separate from Old Kingdom deposits, and Site 31/420–E10–1, Loc. 071 contains a possible mixture of Sheikh Muftah and Old Kingdom remains.

The middle Neolithic 'Bashendi Cultural Unit' deposits yield stone tools, hearths, and bones and teeth that are dense, often darkly mineralised with iron or manganese salts, and are dark brown, reddish brown, or black. No querns have been found *in situ* in the matrix, although surface specimens are more common on Bashendi than Sheikh Muftah sites. The lithics are made from a dark grey nodular chert also present in the Sheikh Muftah Unit, but are larger and coarser, and comprise projectile points, scrapers, knives, drills and denticulates.

The faunal remains may be well preserved and mineralised, consist of teeth or complete ankle, wrist or toe bones and large fragments of long bones and skulls. Specimens are oriented randomly within the matrix, as though they had sunk into it when it was soft or had been trampled in by other animals' feet. Bones from this unit were broken green and appear to reflect crude percussion butchery to extract marrow by either roasting or boiling within skin bags heated by stones. The bone fragments are large, often as long as 200 mm, represent large mammals, and a few show charred or calcined areas.

The later Neolithic 'Sheikh Muftah Cultural Unit' deposits contain stone artifacts, querns (metates and manos), coarse pottery shards or occasional vessel, hearths, ostrich egg shell fragments, teeth and fragments of bones. The lithic materials are characterised by a golden brown tabular chert, which is fashioned into small points, denticulates and scrapers. The dark grey chert, characteristic of the Bashendi Unit, was also used (McDonald, this volume, Chapter 7). These materials may occur as small,

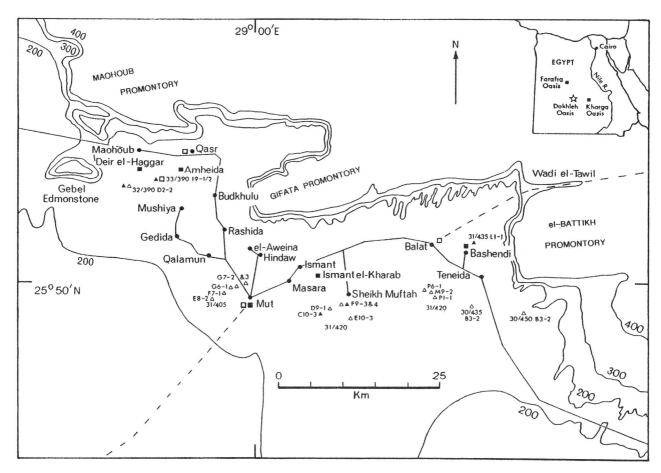

Fig. 8.1. Dakhleh Oasis showing locations of major Holocene fossiliferous sites, and historic and modern settlements and roads. Modern towns and villages – solid dots (●), Roman towns – solid squares (■), Old Kingdom Pharaonic sites – hollow squares (□), Sheikh Muftah Neolithic sites – hollow triangles (△), and Bashendi Neolithic sites – solid triangles (▲). Fossiliferous sites are identified by map sheet and Grid Index Identifiers (Appendix II). Straight lines show modern roads; dashed lines indicate main caravan routes. Contours in metres.

isolated scatters, with or without evidence of fire, or may occur as dense oval or circular concentrations ('living floors') of bones, teeth, flints, pottery, ostrich egg shell and ash. The tooth, bone or shell fragments are light, apparently slightly demineralised, and vary from creamy white or light brown to bleached ash blonde, except when discoloured by fire. They are more abundant but smaller than bones in the earlier Bashendi Unit. The bones are usually broken to expose marrow cavities and fragments are generally less than 100 mm in greatest dimension, and may have been broken to fit within the pottery vessels which are usually ca. 250–350 mm in diameter and 400 mm high.

Old Kingdom sites are characterised by the large, tabular nature of the lithic artifacts made in a caramel or buff chert, by smaller tools in a grey nodular chert, and by polished pottery, copper points, ground stone objects, querns, and plentiful bone and tooth materials (McDonald, this volume, Chapter 7). Sites with combined aggregations of Sheikh Muftah and Old Kingdom tools exist and, although the tools are distinctive, the bones and teeth are usually similar in both colour and preservation.

These bones are light cream to white, light and slightly denatured, brittle, and broken as are the Sheikh Muftah remains. It is often impossible to determine the age of the bone fragments from Sheikh Muftah or Old Kingdom levels without reference to the associated lithic and pottery artifacts.

31/420–P1–1 (Loc. 105) 'Ein Duma (Fig. 8.1)
Sheikh Muftah Unit (Churcher 1988)

This site lies southeast of Bir Yosuf and southwest of the wells of 'Ein Duma and 'Ein Tauwabit (see below), in an area of calcreted and salinated salt crust, and the better specimens come from exposures at the edge of the crust (Churcher 1983, fig. 1). The fauna includes hartebeest (*Alcelaphus buselaphus*), gazelle (*Gazella dorcas*), and cattle (possibly *Bos taurus*).

Two main clusters have been observed, one discovered in 1982 and another in 1987 (Churcher 1983, 1988) The first cluster comprised a hearth in which an upturned Neolithic pot, lacking its bottom, contained some bone fragments and, on the fringes, a charred split hartebeest tibia. The second cluster comprised a blow-out in which lay remains of gazelle and cattle.

The sediments at 'Ein Duma represent a wet environment that may have been a marsh, playa pan or seasonal shallow lake (see this volume, Chapter 1, Fig. 1.46, Top). They may be divided into four units or layers: a basal Taref or Mut Fm. clay penetrated by tree root casts and small vertical root or stem casts; a clay sediment with plant remains that is stratigraphically divisible into a lower level with much small plant remains without orientation and an upper level in which plant remains are sparse and some inclined or level bedding is visible; above these lies a clay soil with the Sheikh Muftah Unit hearths (with bones, teeth, pottery and artifacts) and fine horizontal plant remains; the top is a salt crust that is more recent as it passes through the Neolithic deposits and incorporates some bones, lithics and ashes.

Roots of large trees, up to 100 mm in diameter and 3 m long, run horizontally in the uppermost level of the clays and fan out from centres of stumps, although no evidences of the stumps remain, and indicate that trees grew in the area during Neolithic times. Elsewhere, the clays are marbled or swirled as from loading of water-logged sediment. Nearby are a few low but old spring mounds. The association of the ancient spring mounds, water-logged sediments and areas with hearths suggests that Neolithic man camped near water and trees, in an environment where animals would seek shelter or forage, and drink.

30/435–B3–2 (Loc. 108) 'Ein Tauwabit (Fig. 8.1)
Sheikh Muftah Unit (Churcher 1983)

This Late Neolithic site lies within north-south trending re-entrants in the sandstone ridge that forms the southern boundary of the oasis between Mut and 'Ein el-Sheikh Mabrouk Badr, and southeast of Esbet Marzouk. Similar sites (30/435–B3–3, Loc. 108) exist in other re-entrants but yield few artifacts or faunal remains. Only fragments of ostrich egg shell *Struthio camelus*), mammalian long bones (possibly *Bos* or *Alcelaphus*) and hind foot of ass (*Equus asinus*) have been recovered, but the latter is more likely historic than Neolithic.

30/450–B3–2 (Loc. 136) Camel Grass Plain (Fig. 8.1)
Sheikh Muftah Unit (Churcher 1986, 1988)

This is an oval of bare earth about 60 by 40 m, lying near the northern margin of a large level depression in which camel or halfa grasses (*Andropogon distadryos, Imperata cylindrica*, or *Desmostachya bipinnata*) or shoak (*Alhagi maurorum*) are the major vegetation. Sparse *tamarisk (Tamarix* sp.) bushes rooted in small coppice dunes are scattered in the area and sandstone bluffs and islets border or are present in the depression (see Kleindienst *et al.*, this volume, Chapter 1, Fig. 1.50, Bottom). The site comprises many scattered fragments of bones, teeth, pottery and flints, with a few larger stones (possibly hearth stones) but no grindstones or querns. Faunal elements include *Struthio camelus, Bos* sp. (or another large bovid), *Alcelaphus, Gazella* cf. *dorcas, Capra hircus* and *Equus asinus. E. asinus* is represented by associated lumbar vertebrae, sacrum, pelvis, and left hind limb elements, and other pieces, of a single animal, all buried intrusively in the sediments, and thus probably an historic burial.

Five Spring Mounds to the North of Mut

31/405–E8–2 (Loc. 367) Spring Mound West of Mut-Qasr Road (Fig. 8.1)
Sheikh Mabruk and Old Kingdom Units (Churcher 1981)

This large spring mound lies southwest of F7–1 (see below)

and within areas 2 and 3 of E8. It has lost most of its summit from excavation during Roman times and has a few Roman burials in the western and southern slopes.

Both Neolithic and Old Kingdom faunal remains are recognised on the basis of grey chert and caramel coloured cherts associated respectively with dark brown or creamy white bone remains.

The Neolithic fauna comprises ostrich (*Struthio camelus*) on the evidence of egg shell fragments, Dorcas gazelle (*Gazella dorcas*), large bovid (*Syncerus caffer, Bos primigenius* or *Bos taurus*) and goat (*Capra hircus*). The Old Kingdom fauna also comprises cattle (*Bos taurus*) and Dorcas gazelle, also hartebeest (*Alcelaphus buselaphus*), possibly rhim, white or Loder's gazelle (*Gazella leptoceros*), goat (*Capra hircus*), a small cat (*Felis* sp., either *F. sylvestris, F. chaus* or *F. domesticus*, a rat-size rodent, and an unidentified large bird.

31/405–F7–1 (Loc. 038) Spring Mound on Mut-Qasr Road (Fig. 8.1)
Sheikh Muftah Unit (Churcher 1981)

This spring mound lies east of the main road as it leaves Mut in a northwesterly direction. It is extensive and lies in squares F7, F8 and F9.

Bone fragments were located about 3 m above the surrounding base level on the east side. Churcher (1981, 200) recorded "Aves (long bone shaft), juvenile *Alcelaphus buselaphus* (tibia, distal end), and either *Capra ibex* or a large *Gazella* sp. (vertebrae, innominate and calcaneum)." The bird specimen remains unidentified, the hartebeest *A. buselaphus* is confirmed, and the *Capra* is probably not *C. ibex* but *C. hircus*, as no ibex has been recognised throughout the oasis during subsequent years, and the large gazelle may be *G. leptoceros*, which has been identified at Sheikh Muftah South (31/420–E10–3, Loc. 146) in 1987.

These materials are associated with possible Neolithic flake fragments and derive from a level above the modern field level corresponding to that of the Neolithic deposits at Sheikh Muftah South or East, and elsewhere.

31/405–G6–1 (Loc. 035) (Fig. 8.1)
Sheikh Muftah Unit (Churcher 1981)

This is a low, linear spring mound that trends northwest to southeast and is situated in squares F6, G6 and G7, to the northeast of F7–1. It lies approximately parallel to the Mut-Qasr road. A scattering of fragmentary bones assigned to the Neolithic include "aurochs (*Bos primigenius*), hartebeest (*Alcelaphus buselaphus*), sheep (*Ovis aries*), Dorcus [*sic*] gazelle (*Gazella dorcas*), and a large *Gazella* sp." (Churcher 1981, 201). These identifications should be modified to large bovid (*Syncerus caffer, Bos primigenius* or *B. taurus*), sheep replaced by caprovine (probably *Capra* sp.), with hartebeest, Dorcas gazelle and the large gazelle, probably *G. leptoceros*, confirmed.

31/405–G7–2 (Loc. 036) Spring Mound between Hindau and Mut-Qasr Roads: east of drainage ditch (Fig. 8.1)
Sheikh Muftah Unit (Churcher 1981)

This small, low spring mound lies east of the southern end of G6–1 and in parts of G7. It yielded a few small clusters of Neolithic tools, pottery and bone debris. The Neolithic bones are stained red or yellow with iron oxides and are mixed with creamy bone fragments probably derived from later human chamber burials within the crest of the mound.

The fauna includes "aurochs (*Bos primigenius*), hartebeest

(*Alcelaphus buselaphus*), and ibex (*Capra ibex*) and fragments of ostrich egg shell (*Struthio camelus*)" (Churcher 1981, 201–202). These identifications are modified to large bovid (*Syncerus caffer*, *Bos primigenius* or *B. taurus*) and caprovine (probably *Capra* sp.), with hartebeest and ostrich confirmed.

31/405–G7–3 (Loc. 037) Spring Mound between Hindau and Mut-Qasr Roads: west of drainage ditch (Fig. 8.1)
Sheikh Muftah unit (Churcher 1981)

This small spring mound lies east of F7–1 and between the areas F7 and G7. Only unidentifiable mammalian bone fragments have been observed.

31/420–C10–3 (Loc. 118) West Dune Hill (Fig. 8.1)
Sheikh Muftah units (Churcher 1988)

This site lies southwest of Sheikh Muftah West (31/420–D9–1) and northeast of the Roman Tombs (31/420–B10–1) south of Ismant el-Kharab (= Kellis).

Scattered iron-stained bones, some *in situ*, of Bashendi age, are revealed in an aeolian deflation depression, associated with hearths, light slag and a surface scattering of Sheikh Muftah and Old Kingdom flint tools mixed with wind eroded and freed Bashendi materials.

Molars of the zebra (*Equus grevyi*) and fragments of bones and teeth of large bovid (either *Bos* or *Syncerus*), caprovin (*Capra* sp. or *Ovis* sp.), antelopes (*Gazella* and *Alcelaphus*) and a dentition of ass (*Equus asinus*) have been recovered. The bones are scattered overall but clustered in association with hearths, pottery and Neolithic flint implements. The zebra, large bovid and some antelope materials are probably of Bashendi age, and the ass Roman, with the caprovin materials of Sheikh Muftah or Roman ages.

31/420–D9–1 (Loc. 072) Sheikh Muftah West (Fig. 8.1)
Balat and Sheikh Muftah Units (Churcher 1982, 1986, 1988, 1988)

The Neolithic site to the southwest of Esbet el-Sheikh Muftah, here referred to as Sheikh Muftah West, is a diffuse concentration or series of clusters and isolated occurrences of Neolithic tools and fragmented bone and tooth debris in a poorly developed yardang field between remnants of Roman hydraulic works associated with a number of wells. Almost all the bone material is highly reduced by splitting and by removal of articular ends.

Molluscan material comprises the amphibious snail *Pila ovata* and the water snail *Gyraulus costulatus* which have been found between the low yardangs and are presumed to derive from the Neolithic sediments. However, these snails could derive from the Roman material dredged from wells, but only *P. ovata* has been seen *in situ* in dredged material. The only identified avian material is ostrich egg shell (*Struthio camelus*). Mammalian taxa include gazelle (of a size that suggests *Gazella dorcas*), bubal hartebeest (*Alcelaphus buselaphus*), Cape hare (*Lepus capensis*), cattle, either aurochs (*Bos primigenius*) or Cape buffalo (*Syncerus caffer*), probably goat (*Capra hircus*), ass (*Equus asinus*), and a small carnivore. No horn cores of any artiodactyl have been recovered, so the identities of the goat, cattle and gazelle are not confirmed, although teeth, tooth rows and postcranial elements provide a reasonably secure identification. The ass is identified from a calcaneum from a hearth associated with goat and pottery.

31/420–E10–1 (Loc. 071) Sheikh Muftah South (Fig. 8.1)
Sheikh Muftah Unit (Churcher 1987, 1988)

This is an extensive later Neolithic site that follows the 130 m contour south of 31/420 F9–3 (Sheikh Muftah East) in a westerly convex arc between the valley floor and a higher terrace of salt-crusted valley floor. Some Old Kingdom lithic material lies on its surface. The lithic and osseous materials are frequently grouped together with ash and may represent the accumulated debris of many short-lived occupations of an extensive and desirable campsite. The area has many small (±1.0 m high) yardangs, many of which have small spring eyes at their northern ends (see Kleindienst *et al.*, this volume, Chapter 1, Fig. 1.40, Top), and four Neolithic burials occur on the western fringes of the area, which suggests that the campsite may have been desirable because of its proximity to available water.

The bone fragments in this area are finely broken with punctate marks, as at 31/420–D9–1 (Loc. 072) and, except for the occasional small artiodactyl jaw with teeth or small podials and epipodials, all elements are separated and broken spirally or longitudinally to expose the marrow cavity.

The taxa identified are large bovid (*Bos* or *Syncerus*), hartebeest (*Alcelaphus buselaphus*), goat (*Capra hircus*), Dorcas gazelle (*Gazella dorcas*), and rhim or white gazelle (*Gazella leptoceros*). Ostrich egg shell (*Struthio camelus*) is present, as are a few thin walled long bone fragments that may derive from large birds. (Fragments of warthog [*Phacochoerus aethiopicus*] and extinct zebra [*Equus grevyi*] were recovered in 1998.)

31/420–F9–4 'Bone Butte' Hillock East of Ezbet Sheikh Muftah (Fig. 8.1)
?Epipalaeolithic (Churcher 1982)

This is a north-south trending flat-topped hillock capped with a caliche layer between 0.3 and 0.75 m thick (Churcher 1982, fig. 1; Brookes 1983, pl. 23a). It has yielded a diagnostic biface core from a lens of gravel in the basal layer of angular clay debris with gravel stringers. A large bone, originally thought to be a pelvic bone but now considered likely a scapula, of a large ungulate, was found *in situ* but in fragmentary condition at the contact between the Nubia clays and the calcareous spring sediments, which are older than the Late Acheulian spring mounds (Churcher 1983; Kleindienst *et al.*, this volume, Figs 1.37, top; 1.38, Top and 1.31–1.33). It has been dated by radiocarbon analysis at 15,755 ± 380 yr BP (S-2499) (Brookes 1986). This date is suspect because contamination with younger carbon may have reduced the apparent age to <16,000 years BP. Unfortunately carbonate analysis had to be relied upon, as the Saharan temperatures effectively destroy all collagen (see Kleindienst *et al.*, this volume, Chapter 1, for further discussion).

The presence of a biface that cannot be confidently determined as Neolithic, with the remains of a large mammal, suggests that a Bashendi unit age or earlier is probable. However, the biface derives from the basal gravelly sand and may thus represent a Palaeolithic origin, which would suggest that the bone was not Neolithic and possibly Palaeolithic or Middle Stone Age, and thus not conformable with the radiocarbon date.

31/420–F9–3 (Loc. 092) Sheikh Muftah East (Fig. 8.1)
Bashendi and Sheikh Muftah Units (Churcher 1982, 1986, 1987, 1988)

This site lies due south of the village of Ezbet el-Sheikh Muftah, at the edge of the present cultivation, and occupies a lower and well deflated eastern area that has little or no pristine pottery on the surface. It lies 3–5 m below the higher and more concentrated area that appears to represent the roots of a very old spring mound and to hold a concentrated litter of Neolithic tools and bone and tooth fragments.

The lower Bashendi horizon at this site yield larger bone fragments and has produced teeth of zebra (*Equus grevyi*) and bone fragments of buffalo (*Syncerus caffer*). The stratigraphically higher Sheikh Muftah level has produced remains of gazelles assigned to Dorcas gazelle (*G. dorcas*) on their small size, bubal hartebeest (*Alcelaphus buselaphus*), cattle (*Bos primigenius* or *Syncerus caffer*), canid, either jackal or fox (*Canis aureus lupaster* or *Vulpes* sp.), small equid of the size of a small Burchell's zebra (*Equus quagga*) or large ass (*E. asinus*), and egg shell fragments of ostrich (*Struthio camelus*). A single partial proximal phalanx of a large equid was recovered from this level in 1987, and may also represent Grevy's zebra (*E. grevyi*).

31/420–M9–2 (Loc. 104) Bir Yosuf (Fig 8.1)
Bashendi 'B' Unit (Churcher 1983)

This site lies west of the limits of cultivation approximately due west of the well of Bir Yosuf. All specimens are associated with small hearths, and sometimes with pottery and lithics. As is usual for the Dakhleh Neolithic, all specimens are fragmented. The site is assigned to the Bashendi Unit on its lithics and pottery. Only the mollusc *Melanoides tuberculata*, a hardy freshwater gasteropod that inhabits the sides of irrigation ditches, is known. This snail is also known from Roman and recent times, and so may be less ancient. The vertebrate fauna includes ostrich (*Struthio camelus*), represented by close concentrations or isolated fragments of egg shells, cattle (*Bos* or *Syncerus*), and gazelle (*Gazella dorcas*).

31/420–P6–1 (Loc. 100) Marzouk West (Fig. 8.1)
Sheikh Muftah Unit (Churcher 1983)

This site is named from and lies due west of Ezbet Marzouk, in a north-south trending deflation hollow bounded on the west by sand dunes and on the east by a low ridge of sand stabilised by dead halfa grass (*Imperata cylindrica* or *Desmostachya bipinnata*). The area has a surface litter of Neolithic flint tools, some pottery, and scattered hearths, with ostrich egg shell, bone and tooth remnants scattered and clustered throughout. A heavily deflated burial of a Neolithic child was observed. By 1993 this area had been overtaken by cultivation.

The molluscan fauna comprises a few fragmentary shells of the large snail (*Pila ovata*) and scattered fragments of the Nile oyster (*Etheria elliptica*). The *Pila* fragments probably date from the Roman period, as extensive hydraulic works from that time exist to the southwest, and the area in all probability held ditches that irrigated the Roman period field system. Roman pottery is present but is not extensive in the area. The *Etheria* remains were introduced, as this genus requires permanent or running sweet water, both of which were absent in the area during historic times.

The vertebrate fauna includes large bovid (*Bos taurus* or less likely *Syncerus caffer*), gazelle (*Gazella dorcas*), goat (*Capra hircus*), large antelope (probably *Alcelaphus buselaphus*), and ostrich (*Struthio camelus*). The mammalian taxa are represented by isolated teeth or tooth rows, fragmented skeletal elements, and a few complete pieces. As with all the

Neolithic animal food remains known in the oasis, all but a few bones have been reduced to splinters and the articular ends removed or destroyed. However, the tip of a horn core confirms *Capra* rather than *Ovis*, and a dentary with the milk lower fourth premolar in process of replacement represents a subadult *Bos taurus* that may have been a domesticate killed purposefully at that stage in its development.

31/435–L1–1 (Loc. 125) Bashendi (Fig. 8.1)
Bashendi Unit (Churcher 1986)

This site lies northeast of Esbet Bashendi in a deflation depression just north of the line of spring mounds and excavated *saqias* that mark the former northern limit of cultivation. All faunal elements are stained red or dark brown with haematite; the fragments are large, and many small elements such as phalanges, carpals or teeth are often entire. Some association of clustered elements is also evident. Taxa represented are large bovid (*Bos* or *Syncerus*), possibly hartebeest (*Alcelaphus*) and a smaller bovid, possibly goat (*Capra hircus*) or gazelle (*Gazella* sp.).

32/390–D2–2 (Loc. 006) Bir Talata el-Maohoub (Fig. 8.1)
Bashendi and Sheikh Muftah Units (Churcher 1981, 1982, 1986)

This extensive site lies southwest of Deir el-Haggar, south of Ezbet el-Sheikh Maohoub and about 1 km east of the abandoned village from which it takes its name. It is located at the southern edge of the northwest extremity of the oasis depression, where the valley slope meets the bottom plain, and comprises an area of 4 m high yardangs eroded in historic irrigation deposits, linear and isolated oval to scalloped dunes on its eastern limits and interspersed with deflated areas that penetrate to a level above the Mut red clay but seldom have reached that member. (See Kleindienst *et al.*, this volume, Chapter 1, Fig. 1.44.)

Concentrations of Sheikh Muftah Neolithic artifacts and faunal remains occur in two places, with small isolated clusters scattered elsewhere. At least two Neolithic burials with scattered remnants of skeletons, possibly of Sheikh Muftah age, have been observed. Roman hydraulic engineering in ancient spring mounds has disturbed parts of the area and introduced Roman era potsherds and food remains. All these materials are scattered as an aeolian lag on the surface. The Bashendi Neolithic materials are exposed along the northern edge of the site, just above the present level of the basin floor, in shallow deflation basins approximately 25 m in diameter. The Bashendi materials lie stratigraphically about 1.0–1.5 m or more below the level on which Sheikh Muftah remains are found.

Animals identified from Bir Talata el-Maohoub are:

REPTILIA: *Geochelone sulcata* – Sheikh Muftah Unit.

AVES: *Struthio camelus* – Sheikh Muftah Unit and Old Kingdom.

MAMMALIA: Carnivora; *Canis aureus lupaster* – Sheikh Muftah Unit: Proboscidea;*Loxodonta africana* – Bashendi Unit: Artiodactyla; *Hippopotamus amphibius* – Bashendi Unit, ?*Alcelaphus buselaphus* – Sheikh Muftah Unit, *Gazella dorcas* – Sheikh Muftah Unit and Old Kingdom, ?*Capra hircus* – Sheikh Muftah Unit and Old Kingdom, *Bos primigenius* – Bashendi Unit, *B. taurus* – Sheikh Muftah Unit and Old Kingdom, *Syncerus caffer* cf. *aequinoctialis* – Bashendi Unit, *Pelorovis antiquus* – Bashendi Unit. Perissodactyla; *Equus asinus* – Roman.

(Fieldwork in 1997–1998 raised the possibility that the oldest level may contain a Pleistocene age fauna.)

An area in the southwest of the site consists of a series of some 50 small mounds that contain fossilised wood. Each of these represents one tree, with the central root stock and radiating main roots shown by fragmentary fossilised remnants of the ligneous root system. Measurements of the 20 best preserved mounds give diameters of 50–300 mm (mean 199 mm) for the preserved central trunk areas. The mounds are spaced between 4.5 and 1.8 m apart (mean 3.1 m) and vary from 0.7 to 2.1 m in diameter (mean 1.2 m). These data suggest a woodland composed of trees 6 or 7 m high, spaced about 3 m apart, and occupying a gentle slope on the edge of the oasis.

Isolated fragments of fossil wood, mounds or root systems are sparsely scattered elsewhere over this site and suggest that much of the plain bordering the bottom of the oasis was wooded in Neolithic times.

Associated with all these fragments of fossil wood are teeth and bones of *Bos primigenius*, *Alcelaphus buselaphus*, *Gazella dorcas* and *Capra hircus*, and sparse Sheikh Muftah Unit chert tools. However, the most eloquent deposits of Sheikh Muftah Unit and Old Kingdom materials are present as two extensive clusters or living floors in which the debris of human occupation is so dense that many pieces touch one another. No organised sampling by test excavation has been attempted in these floors.

The yardangs represent remnant deposits of historic Roman or later irrigation deposits, and show many evidences of root casts, buried surfaces, and rhizomes. One yardang near to the exposures of Bashendi Unit deposits shows the cast of a branching tree that was overwhelmed by irrigation deposits (see Kleindienst *et al.*, this volume, Chapter 1, Fig. 1.45). The limbs were between 200 and 300 mm in diameter, the branches at angles of about 30°, and the form typical of *Acacia* sp. The mold of the trunk has within it long abandoned termite galleries and no wood fragments, indicating that the sand engulfed the tree at a time when water was available to these insects.

In another yardang, the articulated skeleton of the left hind foot of a donkey (*E. asinus*) was revealed. It lay approximately horizontally within poorly stratified irrigation deposits and, because of its evident isolation, lack of tooth marks, or evidence of damage before entombment, was probably carried to its resting place by a dog, fox or jackal, as happens in the oasis today. Because these elements lay above the horizon that yields Sheikh Muftah Unit or Old Kingdom age deposits, the ass is considered to be of Roman age.

33/390–I9–1/2 Sheikh Mubaris' Tombs (Fig. 8.1)
Bashendi and Sheikh Muftah Units (Churcher 1981, 1982)

This compound site takes its name from the three tombs named for Sheikh Mubaris, and extends from immediately east of the tombs eastwards to an area of ancient spring mounds mantled with sand dunes. The area is a slightly undulating plain covered with a stoney lag gravel with many bone fragments and lithic tools.

Immediately east and northeast of Sheikh Mubaris' tombs an area has yielded some large, darkly red-stained bones and teeth of large bovid (?*Bos taurus*, *B. primigenius* or *Syncerus caffer*), gazelle, possibly both Dorcas and whitefronted or rhim (*Gazella dorcas* and *G. leptoceros*), hartebeest (*Alcelaphus buselaphus*), and ostrich egg shell (*Struthio camelus*). The bones are generally black, dark brown, mottled black and grey, or creamy white. The darker specimens are frequently mineralised and are assumed to derive from Sheikh Muftah times on the basis of the cultural material. The creamy white bones are more localised, smaller and more broken, and less mineralised, and are considered to represent an Old Kingdom component. The darkly stained specimens are present only in the area near Sheikh Mubaris' tombs (33/390–I9–1) but the creamy white materials are scattered over the greater portion of the site (33/390–I9–2).

DISCUSSION

The recognised faunal elements comprise Mollusca, Reptilia, Aves and Mammalia. No evidence of Pisces in ancient sediments has been found and only the introduced tilapia (*Oreochromis nilotica*) is present in the oasis today (Hollett and Churcher, this volume, Chapter 9). Amphibia are also absent from the fossil record, although adults of the African toad (*Bufo regularis*) have been seen each year and tadpoles in 1979 and adults of a frog (*Ptychadena mascareniensis* or *Rana ridibunda*) were heard calling during March 1988 and observed in 1992 (Hollett and Churcher, this volume, Chapter 9) near Bashendi. The palaeofaunal elements will be discussed by major taxon (phylum or class) and by genus and/or species.

Phylum Mollusca

Four genera of aquatic Mollusca considered indigenous to the oasis are recognised: *Pila ovata*, *Melanoides tuberculata*, *Gyraulus costulatus* and *Corbicula fluminalis vara*.

Pila ovata, (Ampullariidae)
This large land snail is known from four fossiliferous sites, and is associated mainly with Roman hydraulic works where it is found embedded in the dredged spoil. Shell fragments and almost complete shells lying on surfaces of Neolithic or Old Kingdom sites may derive from sediments of those ages but in all cases there are nearby hydraulic works of Roman age from which they may have been derived. No living population of *Pila* has been located in Dakhleh Oasis.

Bell (1966) reviewed the species of *Pila* present in the Sudan and concluded that they were part of a single morphologically variable species. A round morph was called *Ampullaria kordofana*, an elongate morph *A. ovata*, and a giant morph *A. wernei*. The correct genus for *Ampullaria wernei* is *Pila* Röding 1798, which has priority over *Ampullaria* Lamarck 1799. Bell suggested that *Pila ovata* varied its shell form in response to environmental effects and that the species is morphologically variable. Thus he considered *Pila* monotypic as *P. ovata* (Olivier) 1804 has priority over *P. wernei* (Phillippi) 1851 and *P. kordofana* (Phillippi) 1851 (*non* Parreyss). *P. ovata* buries itself in mud to avoid drought conditions and this is confirmed by specimens in which the opercula were in the closed position, excavated from the Roman and Islamic dredgate near Sheikh Mubaris' Tombs, 'Ein Duma and

'Ein Tauwabit. Although no living individuals have been located, some shells appear 'fresh' and its presence in dug wells may yet be observed.

It is possible that *P. ovata* was introduced by the Roman settlers in the oasis to provide an alternative source of protein as no specimens have been recovered from Neolithic levels. However, it was present in Holocene sites in lower Wadi Howar (5640 + 70, Hv 14434 and 7260 + 70, Hv 14438) of equivalent age (Pachur and Kröpelin 1987). Gautier (1980, 1981) does not record it from Palaeolithic levels in either Nabta Playa or Kharga, nor from Bir Sahara and Bir Tarfawi, although he (1983) does record it from the early Neolithic at both Saggai 1 and Geili in the Sudan. No escargotieres similar to those at Mechta-el-Arbi, Algeria (Baker 1935; Lubell *et al.* 1976) composed of *Helix melanostoma*, or concentrations on Neolithic living floors, or in house middens of Roman or Islamic age, similar to that in the cave of Haua Fteh (Hey 1967), have so far been located. *H. melanostoma* is as varied in form as *P. ovata* (Baker 1935) and occupied similar habitats.

Melanoides tuberculata (Melaniidae)

Melanoides tuberculata may be found today in clefts in the rocks below Locality 278 at the Second Cataract on the Nile, or on sandbanks below Abd el-Qadir in Sudanese Nubia (Martin 1968). Fossil *M. tuberculata* is reported from inactive pond sediments (carbonaceous silts) at Bir Tarfawi in the southern Egyptian Desert (Wendorf *et al.* 1977), about 300 km south of Dakhleh. It is also known from an evaporite limestone silt at Bir Sahara, about 30 km southwest of Bir Tarfawi, and from Greco-Roman playa sediments at Kharga Oasis (Gautier 1980).

In Dakhleh, this tall, coiled shell with tuberculate ornamentations is often found in massive concentrations in the silts associated with abandoned irrigation channels of Roman and Islamic age, and scattered in clusters on the surfaces of Neolithic and possibly Old Kingdom sites. Living *M. tuberculata* has been collected from a drainage/irrigation ditch at Teneida in the eastern oasis in 1982, but it is not commonly observed in such ditches.

Today this snail lives on the edges of wet ditches, usually well shaded by vegetation and is an indicator of stable water courses with flowing water. Local extinction is possible in the environment of controlled irrigation in an oasis. However, reintroduction from neighbouring populations is possible through the agency of water birds carrying eggs or larvae in the mud on their feet, or from the permanent water sources.

Gyraulus costulatus or G. ehrenbergi (Planorbidae)

This spiral snail is known from modern sandy banks of the Nile below the Second Cataract at Locality 278, and as a fossil from Localities 81, 516 and 3400 in Sudanese Nubia (Martin 1968). *Gyraulus* sp. is also reported as a fossil by Wendorf *et al.* (1977) from presently inactive pond sediments (carbonaceous silt) at the oasis of Bir

Tarfawi in the southern Western Desert, and *G. costulatus* from an evaporite limestone silt at Bir Sahara, some 30 km southwest of Bir Tarfawi.

Records in the oasis span from the Sheikh Muftah Unit at Sheikh Muftah West (31/420 D10–3, Loc. 069) through the Old Kingdom at Sheikh Mubaris' (33/390 I9–1) to Roman times at Bir Yosuf (31/420 M9–2), although only at Sheikh Muftah West is the age considered reliable because the specimens were *in situ*.

Corbicula fluminalis vara (Corbiculidae)

The modern bivalve *Corbicula consorbina* is recorded from a silty beach between rocks and in clefts in rocks on sandy banks below the Second Cataract on the Nile at Locality 278, and on sandy banks at Abd el-Qadir in Sudanese Nubia (Martin 1968). Martin records no modern *C. (fluminalis) vara s.l.* from Egypt or the Nile, but recognises it as fossil from Localities 81, 501, 502, 34, D-5, 319, 504, 235, 201, 1027 and 278 in Sudanese Nubia. Wendorf *et al.* (1977) recorded fossil *C. consorbina* from a later cycle of ponding at Bir Sahara in the Western Desert of Egypt. Martin (1968) considered *C. (fluminalis) vara* distinct from *C. consorbina* on a number of characters, including a diagnostic larger umbo. However, Leigh and Butzer (1968) considered "all the Corbiculae of Africa and southwestern Asia [to be] identical at the specific level", following Llabador (1962).

C. fluminalis vara (*sensu* Llabador 1962) has been found subfossil associated with Old Kingdom specimens at Sheikh Mubaris' Tombs (33/390 I9–1). This site is of low relief and in no way resembles or could have provided environments similar to those in which Martin (1968) observed it. It probably derives from silts laid down under ponded or marshy conditions, but no evidence of such deposits remains at this site.

Environmental Implications of the Mollusca Recovered from Holocene Sites in Dakhleh Oasis

Melanoides tuberculata lives in the damp, shady, vegetated margins of distributory channels leading from wells and, as well as being recorded from Teneida in Dakhleh, has been recovered from Kurkur Oasis (Leigh 1968). *Gyraulus* "is characteristic of decaying vegetation" (Leigh and Butzer 1968; 514) and *Corbicula fluminalis vara* is "primarily associated with muddy habitats or with stagnant or slowly moving waters such as canals, pools or marshy tracts" (Leigh and Butzer 1968, 509). *Pila ovata* lives in marshy, muddy vegetated areas, such as flooded areas marginal to irrigation ditches or overflow areas, and buries itself in the mud under threat of drought (Bell 1966). In the ancient oasis the marginal vegetation around flowing spring mounds would have provided habitats suited to all these snails and also possibly to the bivalve *Corbicula*. During subsequent Neolithic to Roman times the distribution channels, natural ponds and marshes, and the water sources themselves would all have provided similarly suitable habitats. The molluscs attest constantly flowing water, vegetation, marginal marshy habitats, and shady areas with rotting plant matter.

Class Reptilia

A land tortoise, *Geochelone* sp., probably *G. sulcata*, is reported from Bir Talata el-Maohoub (32/390–D2–2) on the evidence of a fragmentary section of the plastron (Churcher 1981). When reconstructed the plate is about 95 mm long by 67.5 mm wide by 5 mm thick. As the plastron plates run transversely across the body and form the ventral shield, the individual probably had a minimal diameter of 190 mm and, as carapace length is about four times the width of a plate, its length was about 370 mm.

The specimen is identified as *Geochelone* because "when the sulcus (joints between the horny plates on the plastron) is viewed in cross-section or in raking light, ... the edges appear to be raised ... If so, this would almost surely indicate a tortoise, probably *Geochelone sulcata* or *G. pardalis*, ..." (J.H. Hutchison, pers. comm., 1981). Villiers (1958) noted that *G. sulcata* inhabits the Sahel and Sudan regions of western and central Africa north of the equator. It lives in very dry areas where rain is extremely rare and fresh water is lacking. It consumes mainly grasses and succulent plants, often of the genus *Ipomaea*, a genus that is still present in Dakhleh Oasis (Ritchie, this volume, Chapter 4). Neither *G. pardalis* nor *G. sulcata* has been reliably reported from Egypt, and the northernmost record for *G. sulcata* is Dongola in the northern Sudan, and for *G. pardalis* Mongalla, southern Sudan. Thus, *G. sulcata* appears to be the more likely identification (Loveridge and Williams 1957).

The environment indicated by *G. sulcata* is one of infrequent rains, desertic conditions generally, with vegetation, including grasses and succulents. With the presence of flowing spring mounds and patches of grass and other herbs among trees as the likely ecotone of the oasis during the Neolithic-Old Kingdom transition, and the whole surrounded by desert or semidesert savannas, the presence of a tortoise such as *G. sulcata* is not unexpected.

No evidence of other reptiles, such as *Crocodylus* (Crocodilia), *Varanus* (Lacertilia), or *Cerastes* (Ophidia) has been recovered, although lizards and snakes are present in the oasis and the surrounding desert today (Hollett and Churcher, this volume, Chapter 9).

Class Aves

Little evidence of birds other than ostrich (*Struthio camelus*) is available at any site. Ostrich egg shell fragments and beads are common from almost all sites of Neolithic age, whether containing Masara, Bashendi or Sheikh Muftah unit lithics.

Evidence from bones of birds is very scarce. The few fragments of long bones are nearly unidentifiable: they may represent storks, vultures, geese, ducks, bustards and smaller birds (Churcher 1981). Since the end of the survey, two ostrich vertebrae have been recovered by M.M.A. McDonald from 30/450–A9–1 (Loc. 228) to the southeast of Teneida. This is a Bashendi Unit site and these bones are the first evidence that ostrich was physically present in the oasis at that period, about 7500 BP (average of four dates) (Churcher, 1992). Ostrich is also reported from near Abu Ballas, about 200 km southwest of Dakhleh, and in the Wadi el-Akhdar in Gilf el-Kebir (Van Neer and Uerpmann 1989). The Abu Ballas occurrences are dated at about 7500 or 6500 BP, which is coeval with the Dakhleh occurrence. Many of the fragments of 'ungulate' long bones may derive from ostrich but are not large enough to be diagnostic.

Class Mammalia

Remains of at least 13 taxa of mammals have been recovered from the Neolithic or levels associated with Neolithic sites or remains and may be presumed to have formed part of the Neolithic fauna of the present Dakhleh Oasis local area. They represent wild (11 taxa) and domestic (3 taxa) animals. Some additional wild taxa are only tentatively identified (3 taxa) and a few may be confused (e.g. *Equus quagga* and *E. asinus*; *Vulpes v. aegyptiaca*, *V. r. rueppelli* and *Canis aureus lupaster*; *Felis chaus* and *F. sylvestris lybica*). Small rodent remains are uncommon, except in debitage and midden deposits of Roman age.

Hare (*Lepus capensis*) has been recovered from the Bashendi Unit site at Sheikh Muftah West (31/420–D9–1), with scattered elements recovered without context and suspected to be recent.

No rodent remains are known from Neolithic sites, although isolated elements from mixed Old Kingdom and Neolithic scatters east of Sheikh Mubaris' Tombs (32/390–I9–1/2) may include Neolithic elements. These remains are mainly postcranial and identification to taxon is probably not possible.

Carnivores are also under-represented in the Neolithic deposits, although jackal (*Canis aureus lupaster*) and fox (either *Vulpes v. aegyptiaca* or *V. r. rueppelli*) have been recognised from the Sheikh Muftah level at Bir Talata el-Maohoub (32/390–D2–2), and fox from the mixed Old Kingdom and Sheikh Muftah level at Sheikh Mubaris' Tombs (32/390–I9–1/2). The fox remains constitute a few isolated teeth and small postcranial elements. Because remains of recent foxes may be seen in the oasis today, these isolated elements, even though associated with recognisable Neolithic or Old Kingdom artifacts and surface debris, may represent later dissynchronous additions to the assemblage.

Small cats (*Felis chaus* or *F. c. nilotica*) are also represented by a few fragments from the mixed Old Kingdom and Sheikh Muftah level at Sheikh Mubaris' Tombs and at the Mut Spring Mounds.

Elephant (*Loxodonta africana*) was first recognised from the Bashendi level at Bir Talata el-Maohoub on the evidence of many fragments from a single molar, later substantiated by ivory tusk fragments. Subsequent to the end of the survey, M.M.A. McDonald recovered remnants of another elephant tooth at 30/450–A9–1 (Loc. 228), southeast of Teneida, also from the Bashendi Unit. Fragments from large bones are common in Bashendi levels elsewhere in the oasis and may represent elephant at those localities (e.g. Sheikh Muftah East, Bashendi). Alternatively, they may represent large mammals such as buffalo or hippopotamus known from the same levels, or giraffe (*Giraffa camelopardalis*), known only from petroglyphs.

Hippotamus (*Hippopotamus amphibius*) is known from a partial atlas from the Bashendi level at Bir Talata el-Mahoub. Fragments of longbones and skull, including part of a nasal, are also assigned to this species.

Bovids provide the majority of faunal remains from the Neolithic sites and are generally widely distributed between sites. The long horned extinct buffalo (*Pelorovis antiquus*) and the locally extinct Cape buffalo (*Syncerus caffer*) are recognised only from Bashendi levels at Bir Talata el-Maohoub, Sheikh Muftah East and Bashendi. However, cheek teeth of large wild cattle such as *Pelorovis*, *Syncerus* and *Bos primigenius* (aurochs) are difficult to separate with confidence, and large molar teeth may derive from any of these cattle (Churcher 1972). *Pelorovis* is identified on the presence of large upper molars with central fossettes and triangular interlophar endostyles and on associated navicular-cuboid and calcaneum, and *Syncerus* on a partial horn core from Bir Talata el-Maohoub. *Bos primigenius* is also recorded from there on the evidence of a conical, twisted horn core with a basal cross-section of about 100 mm. Unfortunately this specimen was destroyed.

The bubal hartebeest (*Alcelaphus buselaphus*) is common in both Bashendi and Sheikh Muftah levels at sites throughout the oasis. It is well represented by teeth and postcranial elements but horn cores are absent, unlike at Kom Ombo (Churcher 1972). It was probably still prevalent in the oasis during the 19th century and Osborn and Helmy (1980, fig. 152) show its 'previous distribution' to include Dakhleh Oasis.

The gazelle common in the present oasis is the Dorcas gazelle (*Gazella d. dorcas*). It is known from most Neolithic sites which have produced reasonable quantities of bones. The rhim or white gazelle (*G. leptoceros*) is probably equally widely distributed in the deposits but, unlike *G. dorcas* which is easily identifiable by its small size and for which a number of both male and female horn cores have been recovered, can be confirmed only from an isolated male horn core from Sheikh Muftah South of probable Sheikh Muftah age, and from another horn core from 30/450–A9–1 (Loc. 228), southeast of Teneida, of Bashendi age.

Domestic bovids (cattle, sheep and goats) are chiefly represented by goats (*Capra hircus*) by many postcranial elements, upper and lower molar rows, and by the typically flattened and twisted horn cores. *C. hircus* is present in both later Neolithic levels. No evidence of sheep (*Ovis aries*) has been recorded. The presence of many recognisable elements of *Capra* and the absence of evidence of *Ovis* suggests that the latter was truly absent in the Neolithic of the oasis.

Equids are represented by two and possibly three species – Grevy's zebra (*Equus grevyi*), the domestic ass (*E. asinus*), and possibly Burchell's or common zebra (*E. quagga = E. burchelli*). *E. grevyi* is known mainly from the Bashendi level at Sheikh Muftah East and West, and at West Dune Hill in both the Bashendi and Sheikh Muftah levels. It is represented by isolated teeth and a few postcranial elements. *E. asinus* is widely reported from Old Kingdom and Roman levels, intrusive burials of asses of unknown but probably historic ages occur on many sites, e.g., Camel Grass Plain (30/450–B3–2), and remains of recent individuals occur widely in the oasis today. A few fragments, including a maxillary tooth row, have been obtained from an ash pit of presumed Sheikh Muftah age at West Dune Hill and from among the surface debris at Sheikh Muftah East. Among the remains from Sheikh Muftah are a few of an intermediate-size equid that could represent either *E. quagga* or a large male jackass.

Provenance

The survey of the Neolithic bone-bearing sites of Dakhleh Oasis has resulted in the classification of such sites not only by their lithic technologies (Masara, Bashendi, and Sheikh Muftah Units; McDonald, this volume, Chapter 7), but by the lack of faunal remains, the presence of larger bone fragments, with the inclusion of large and now locally extinct Ethiopian taxa, and the presence of numerous smaller bone fragments, together with the exclusion of the larger Ethiopian taxa and the inclusion of more numerous domestic taxa (Table 8.1).

The fossiliferous sites may be classified thus:

1. Bashendi Unit Neolithic Sites. Bone fragments are large, often stained black or dark brown by iron oxides, sometimes calcined or charred, and may derive from locally extinct or now extinct taxa such as elephant, zebra, hippopotamus or buffalo. The specimens are often isolated or in clusters of fragments of bones and teeth, but seldom with associated elements, and may be associated with fire cracked stones. Only teeth and the smallest bones are intact, and all long bones are split to expose marrow cavities. Specimens have been recovered from within wet sediments, or burnt or charred in hearths, and without any consistent horizontal orientation. Pottery and lithic fragments are very sparse or absent. Meat was presumably roasted in fires, bones split to obtain marrow, and roasted or boiled in skin bags with heated stones.

2. Sheikh Muftah Unit Neolithic Sites. Bone fragments are small, split longitudinally, almost always less than 100 mm

Table 8.1. Schematic relationships of fossiliferous sites with cultures and surficial geology.

AGE/PERIOD	CULTURE	GEOLOGY
Roman	Isolated pottery clusters with food debris and sparse animal remains outside clusters	Disturbed deposits for clusters as associated with dredged spring eyes. Remainders in coarse sandy 'dune' deposits.
Old Kingdom – Pharaonic	Scattered bone and tooth fragments, ostrich egg shell frags and beads, copper, tabular lithic tools.	Matrix sandy and specimens not *in situ* – all exposed by erosion and left as a suface lag.
Sheikh Muftah Unit – Neolithic	Scattered bone and tooth fragments, ostrich egg shell beads, lithic burins, scrapers, knives and projectile points, pottery common. Also concentrated in living floors with hearths. Burials present.	Soils developed in silty sands of lake and playa beds. Some stones or pebbles. Dry.
Bashendi Unit – Neolithic	Sparse, scattered large bone fragments, teeth, lithic blades, scrapers and projectile points, pottery sparse, with hearths.	Soils developed in silty sands of lake and playa beds. Possibly wet or marshy.
Masara Unit – Epipalaeolithic	No fossils recovered, except ostrich egg shell.	Basinal lake and playa sediments and sand sheet
	EROSIONAL UNCONFORMITY	
Palaeolithic	Handaxes, blades, etc., vertically concentrated by deflation.	Lag gravel between Holocene and Cretaceous. Transported handaxes in pediment gravels
	EROSIONAL UNCONFORMITY	
Cretaceous	None	Nubia Group, Taref Formation: red clays and sandstones within Dakhleh Oasis.

long, usually stained light brown or bleached creamy white, occasionally burnt but seemingly only secondarily within ashes or within a rekindled fire. Few articulations are preserved (e.g., tibial ends with tarsal elements). Taxa include wild gazelles and hartebeest, and domestic goat and cattle, and possibly ass. Pottery is always present in at least moderate quantities and grey and caramel coloured lithics are often associated with smaller hearths and always with extensive concentrations of materials. The bone fragments are without cancellous ends and most fragments fit within the usual Neolithic cooking pot (about 200 mm diameter by 300 mm high) for boiling to produce soup.

Some sites are extensive and may include areas of great concentration where bone, teeth, potsherds, and lithics may cover more than 50% of the surface. Neolithic sites southwest of Sheikh Muftah include a number of ash concentrations, in which pottery fragments, a few bones or teeth, but no charcoal or lithics are present. These deposits are interpreted as remains of fires ignited to 'burn' pottery, as the ash areas are too extensive, and thus the fires too hot, for them to be used for cooking or heating. In other areas smaller ash circles (less than 1 m in diameter), often contain bone fragments, teeth, or pottery

fragments, and have occasionally yielded nearly complete pots or bones. These smaller fireplaces are interpreted, therefore, as campfires.

The more extensive sites may represent an accumulation of debris over many years of short, seasonal visits, or the site of an annual clan meeting. The small sites may denote one or a few nights' camps by family groups.

3. Old Kingdom Sites. Bone fragments are small as in the Sheikh Muftah age sites, often a light cream or milky white and lighter coloured, but fragments from both sites may be confused as to origin and the sites may yield small rodent and carnivore elements. Goats, cattle and probably asses constitute the domestic taxa, and gazelle and hartebeest the wild taxa. Lithics, common at the site, are characteristically a light caramel brown, finely worked from laminar blanks. Lithics made of grey nodular chert and ostrich egg-shell beads are present.

Evidence from Petroglyphs

Rock carvings of animals and symbols are common on the sandstone faces of many smaller gebels cut from the

Taref Formation sandstone lenses (Krzyzaniak and Kroeper 1985).

To date animals identifiable are ostrich (*Struthio camelus*), large birds, possibly geese (*?Anser* sp.) or ducks (*Anas* sp.), and bustards (*?Otis* sp.), lion (*Felis leo*), leopard or cheetah (*Felis pardus* or *Acinonyx jubatus*), dog (*Canis familiaris* similar to a hunting dog), elephant (*Loxodonta africana*), zebra (*Equus* sp. – *E. quagga* or *E. grevyi*), wild pig (*Sus* sp.), giraffe (*Giraffa camelopardalis*), gazelle (*Gazella* sp.), oryx (*Oryx ?dammah*), hartebeest (*Alcelaphus buselaphus*), goats (*Capra hircus*), and long-horned cattle (*Bos ?taurus*) are recognisable. They are depicted in a number of styles and at present cannot be associated with cultural units. Later depictions of men on horse or camels, and of laden camels, may be confidently assigned to later and historic times. However, these depictions independently confirm the presence of the identified faunal elements and suggest that remains of giraffe, oryx, lion, leopard and wild pig may be expected in the Neolithic Masara, Bashendi or Sheikh Muftah Unit levels.

The presence of goat in these depictions substantiates the certain identification of this domesticate in the faunal evidence. However, no petroglyphs suggest either Barbary or domestic sheep, and this supports the absence of identifed *Ovis* materials among the bones and teeth. The question is raised, therefore, that sheep were not part of the Neolithic herds in the Dakhleh area during the period 6000 to 2500 BC.

Faunal Interpretation

The recovered fauna of Neolithic age in the Dakhleh region suggests an ecology in which water, forage and shade were not scarce, and in which an Ethiopian facies was paramount (Figs 8.2 & 8.3). Man was present and is represented by Neolithic sites scattered throughout the oasis and surrounding terrain. As the area's climate became more xeric his activities were increasingly restricted to the oasis and its available water, at least during the drier seasons. Consequently, the Bashendi age sites and earlier Masara age sites are found further from the centres of the oasis and scattered over much of the surrounding land. The later Sheikh Muftah sites lie either closer to the oasis centres or in deposits that overlie the Bashendi deposits. There is thus an apparent withdrawal of human occupation sites from the surrounding areas into the oasis as the desiccation of the environment progressed.

The main changes have involved the increasing climatic aridity, increasingly xeric floristic elements, and replacement of endemic Ethiopian vertebrates by introduced domestic stock (Fig. 8.3). As the bases for comparisons involve skeletal remains left by man as the major selective taphonomic agent, no basic fauna is recognised as representative of that present in the Egyptian Western Desert below the Libyan Escarpment during early Neolithic times.

Small animals are generally better indicators of ecological conditions than large, as they are unable to travel appreciable distances to escape inclement climates. In the Dakhleh deposits, the molluscs best illustrate this and indicate shady, marshy areas with slow-flowing streams of fresh water. Thus, available water was plentiful for ungulate megafauna. While it is true that some animals may be able to travel long distances between water and forage, and may not need water more frequently than once every three or four days, e.g. elephants, or may be able to exist in a dry, harsh environment, e.g. gazelles or hartebeest. The presence of hippopotamus, cattle (buffaloes or aurochs) and equids (zebras and possibly asses) in the Neolithic indicates the presence of year-round available standing water. The domestic goats, asses and cattle also regularly require twice daily waterings.

Thorn trees (*Acacia* sp.) were probably a dominant element of the environment, with palms such as the wild date (*Phoenix dactylifera*) or doum (*Hyphene thebaica*), tamarisk (*Tamarix* sp.) and buffalo thorn, jujube or zizouf (*Zizyphus spina-christi*) widely distributed. These would provide browse, fuel and shade for animals and man. The surrounding areas would be at least seasonally grassed, with occasional trees along water courses or near standing water, and would provide grazing for the large ungulates and the habitat for ostrich, gazelles and hartebeest.

The Neolithic fauna so far represented in the Dakhleh Oasis deposits lacks any significant large carnivores and many large ungulates. No remains of lion (*Felis leo*), leopard (*F. pardalis*), cheetah (*Acinonyx jubatus*), wild dog (*Lycaon pictus*), or other viverrid, canid, felid or mustelid carnivores have been recovered. Large ungulates not represented by skeletal materials include giraffe (*Giraffa camelopardalis*), oryx (*Oryx dammah*), addax (*Addax nasomaculatus*), eland (*Taurotragus oryx*), roan or sable antelope (*Hippotragus equinus* or *H. niger*), and rhinoceros (*Diceros bicornis* or *Ceratotherium simum*), as have been reported from sites to the south and southeast (Gautier 1980, 1981, 1984a, b). (In 1998, remains of *Hyaena* and a suid, possibly warthog, *Phacochoerus aethiopicus*), have been obtained from the Sheikh Muftah level.) If the sites from which faunal evidence has so far been obtained represent the remains of living floors of transient nomads rather than middens of settled groups, then carnivore remains would be scarce as scavenging of the bones after boiling provides little nutrition and the proximity to humans, their fires and stock would inhibit their predation. Humans may well have scavenged occasional kills of lions or other carnivores, and the presence of elephant, hippopotamus and giant buffalo may attest to this activity. The absence of giraffe, oryx, rhinoceros and other large ungulates may reflect chance exclusion of animals that were only available when stolen from other predators.

Three large bovines are present in the Neolithic and Old Kingdom deposits. Long-horned cattle similar to the aurochs (*Bos primigenius*) and Cape buffalo (*Syncerus*

Fig. 8.2. Reconstruction of landscape and megafauna of Dakhleh Oasis in Bashendi Cultural Unit times. The scene is set at a spring in the Libyan Escarpment piedmont. Plants shown are Acacia *(Nile thorn),* Hyphaene *(doum palm),* Phoenix *(wild date palm),* Scirpus *(rush) and* Typha *(reed). Animals are* Struthio *(ostrich),* Loxodonta *(elephant),* Hippopotamus *(hippopotamus),* Pelorovis *(giant buffalo),* Syncerus *(Cape buffalo),* Alcelaphus *1(hartebeest),* Gazella *(gazelle),* Giraffa *(giraffe),* Equus *(zebra),* Homo *(man) and other birds.*

Fig. 8.3. Reconstruction of landscape and megafauna of Dakhleh Oasis in Sheikh Muftah Cultural Unit times. The scene is located as in Figure 2, but with advancing desiccation of the Escarpment, and with man having occupied the spring area. Plants shown are Acacia *(Nile thorn),* Hyphaene *(doum palm),* Phoenix *(wild date palm),* Scirpus *(rush) and* Typha *(reed). Animals are* Struthio *(ostrich),* Alcelaphus *(hartebeest),* Gazella *(gazelle),* Bos *(cow),* Capra *(goat),* Equus *(zebra or ass),* Homo *(man) and other birds.*

caffer) are identified on the certain evidence of horn cores (Churcher 1980, 1982), and the giant long-horned buffalo (*Pelorovis antiquus*), on the evidence of dental and postcranial elements, from the Bashendi levels at a number of sites. No certain evidence of these bovines exists from later levels, although large molar teeth are present in Sheikh Muftah levels and smaller molar teeth similar to those of domestic cattle (*Bos taurus)* are present throughout later levels.

Grevy's zebra (*Equus grevyi*) is certainly known only from Bashendi levels at Sheikh Muftah South and East and West Dune Hill, but may be present in the Sheikh Muftah levels. Ass or donkey (*Equus asinus*) is present throughout the oasis in all surface scatters, but probably is of more recent origin. No *in situ* ass materials have been dated to Old Kingdom or earlier ages and thus all specimens are probably intrusive. An intermediate sized equid, possibly Burchell's zebra (*E. quagga = E. burchelli*) or a large jackass, may also be present at Sheikh Muftah East.

Goat (*Capra hircus*) is probably present in all levels and at all sites, but here is only confirmed by its typically compressed and twisted horn cores from the Sheikh Muftah levels at Bir Talata el-Maohoub, Marzouk West and North, Sheikh Muftah West and South, West Dune Hill, and Old Kingdom levels at Sheikh Mubaris' Tombs. Unidentified materials are assigned to caprovine.

The temporal distribution of these taxa and the placement of later sites nearer to the water resources of the oasis attest to the progressive dehydration of the environment. The Neolithic occupants herded cattle and goats, and possibly asses, at the same time that the wild fauna included elephant, zebra, hippopotamus, hartebeest, gazelles, buffaloes and ostrich. While many of these animals require little water, the presence of man and his herds of animals pre-empting available grazing and preventing wild animals from reaching the available water sources during excessively dry periods could have combined to cause the more sensitive wild fauna to be reduced and eventually eliminated from the area.

Comparisons with Neolithic Faunas from the Western Deserts of Egypt and Sudan

The Late Quaternary faunas of Egypt and the Sudan were reviewed by Churcher (1981, 1982, 1983). Gautier (1980) discussed the faunal elements from Neolithic levels at Kharga Oasis to the east of Dakhleh and noted a single ruminant tooth. Caton-Thompson (1952) reported gazelle horn cores that Gautier believed originated from the Wadi Tufa, but their provenance is unproven. The Neolithic spring mounds described by Caton-Thompson (1952) yielded gazelle (*Gazella dorcas*), hyaena (*Hyaena* cf. *striata*), sheep and/or goat, and cattle, similar to but smaller than aurochs (*Bos primigenius*), according to Gautier (1980).

Wendorf *et al.* (1977) and Gautier (1980) described the molluscs and vertebrates from Nabta Playa, about 200

km south-southeast of Dakhleh. The fauna includes fish, turtle, birds and mammals and is dated at 9370 ± 70 and 7580 ± 80 yr BP but, except for 'large bovid/cattle' and 'large gazelle', is composed of smaller animals and lacks any of the larger and now locally extinct mammals. The domestic stock was recognised as probably sheep (*Ovis ammon* f. *aries*), possibly goat (*Capra aegagrus* f. *hircus*) (Muzzolini 1984) and bovines that could be small aurochsen, large cattle or even Cape buffalo, chiefly on size. The rest of the fauna includes hedgehog (Erinaceidae), mongoose (?*Herpestes ichneumon* or *Mungos mungos* [Gautier 1984b]), wild cat (*Felis libyca? = F. sylvestris?*), jackal or dog (*Canis* sp.), hare (*Lepus capensis*), porcupine (*Hystrix cristata?*) and gazelles (*Gazella rufifrons?* or *G. dama?*), many of which were probably extant in the smaller oases in recent times.

Gautier (1984c, 1987) reported on the fauna from fourteen sites associated with the Kiseiba Scarp in southern Egypt, about 200 km west of Lake Nasser at Lat. 23°N. This comprises 25 taxa and includes three Mollusca – *Aspatheria rubeus*, *Corbicula consorbina* (redeposited) and *Zootecus insularis*, one Amphibia – large frog or toad, two or more Reptilia – *Testudo* sp. and Lacertilia spp., three Aves – *Struthio camelus*, *Ammoperdrix heyi*, and *Otis tarda* or *Choriotis arabs*, and 16 Mammalia – *Paraechinus aethiopicus*, *Lepus capensis*, *Gerbillus gerbillus*, *Euxerus erythropus*, *Arvicanthis niloticus*, *Jaculus jaculus*, *Hystrix cristata*, *Canis aureus*, *Vulpes rueppelli*, ?*Mungos mungos*, *Hyaena hyaena*, *Felis silvestris* or *F. margarita*, *Loxodonta africana*, *Gazella dama*, *G. dorcas*, and *Bos primigenius* f. *taurus*. Dates for the sites containing this compound fauna range from 9220 ± 140 yr BP (SMU 925) to 6330 ± 100 (Gd 926), with most dates between 8210 ± 70 (SMU 739) and 7170 ± 80 (SMU 749).

Hassan and Gross (1987) speculate on the probable mid-Holocene fauna of Siwa Oasis and surrounding area and conclude that it must have been similar to that known from sites in Dakhleh, Kharga and oases to the south dating from the same period. No osseous or other evidence of vertebrate taxa is recorded, apart from ostrich egg shell.

Gautier (1980) also reported on the Neolithic mammals from Wadi el-Bakht, Gilf el-Kebir in the southwest corner of Egypt and 340 km southwest of Dakhleh. This fauna included dog (*Canis lupus* f. *familiaris*), Dorcas gazelle (*Gazella dorcas*), sheep and/or goat, and cattle (*Bos primigenius* f. *taurus*), collected by Gautier, in a fauna with elephant (*Loxodonta africana*, noted as ?*Elephas* sp.), addax (*Addax* cf. *nasomaculatus*), hartebeest (*Damaliscus* sp., = *Alcelaphus* sp.), gazelle (*Gazella* sp.), goat? (?*Capra* sp.), jackal? (*Canis* cf. *anthus*), ass (*Equus asinus*), and ostrich (*Struthio camelus*), on a collection obtained in 1938 by O.H. Myers (Bagnold *et al.* 1939) and tentatively identified by D.M.A. Bate (Clutton-Brock, pers. comm., in Gautier, 1980). Van Neer and Uerpmann (1989) report ostrich from site 65/50–1 at about 6500 BP and from site 85/56 at about 7500 BP near Abu Ballas, midway between Dakhleh Oasis and Gilf el-Kebir, and at Wadi el-Akhdar in Gilf el-Kebir (undated). Identification of the hartebeest taxa *Alcelaphus*, *Damaliscus* and *Beatragus* is difficult except on horn cores, upper molars or lower dentitions containing P_2–P_4 (Churcher 1989; Gentry and Gentry 1978); thus the hartebeest may be a species of either *Alcelaphus* or, less likely, *Damaliscus*.

Gautier (1968) listed the late Pleistocene and Holocene faunas from Nubia (northern Sudan and southern Egypt) and included aurochs (*Bos primigenius*), possibly eland (*Taurotragus oryx*) and ass (*Equus asinus*) in the Quaternary faunas. Both aurochs and ass were recognised from the Epipalaeolithic (15,000–10,000 BC) site of Kom Ombo on the Nile (Churcher 1972). Wendorf *et al.* (1977) listed and Gautier (1981) described the molluscs and vertebrates from the wells of Bir Sahara and Bir Tarfawi, ca. 300 km south of Dakhleh, and identified warthog (*Phacochoerus aethiopicus*, extinct camel (*Camelus thomasi*), giant buffalo (*Homoioceras [=Pelorovis] antiquus*), large antelope, white rhinoceros (*Ceratotherium simum*), and ass, with ages greater than 41,450 yrs BP for Bir Sahara and 44,190 ± 1380 yrs BP for Bir Tarfawi.

Gautier (1984a) listed molluscs and mammals from Kadero in the central Sudan. These included Mollusca – *Pila ovata*, *Etheria elliptica*, *Corbicula consorbina* (probably intrusive); wild Mammalia – *Lepus capensis*, *Syncerus caffer* and four smaller bovids; domestic Mammalia – *Canis lupus* f. *familiaris*, *Bos primigenius* f. *taurus*, *Ovis ammon* f. *aries*, and *Capra aegagrus* f. *hircus*. Kadero lies some 6 km east of the Nile and 18 km north of Khartoum, and is situated on an erosional remnant of an ancient alluvial plain. The site is dated on three radiocarbon analyses at 5280 ± 90 (SMU-482), 5260 ± 90 (T-2188) and 5030 ± 70 yrs BP (T-2189), median 5155 ± 83 yrs BP (Krzyzaniak 1984).

Pachur and Kröpelin (1987) listed the fauna from Wadi Howar, northern Sudan, dated at between 9,200 and 4,500 years BP. The fauna comprised Ostracoda; Mollusca – including *Pila wernei*, *Melanoides tuberculatus*, *Gyraulus costulatus* and *Mutela nilotica*; Reptilia – *Geochelone pardalis*; Aves – *Struthio camelus*; wild Mammalia – *Bubalus bubalis* (=*Pelorovis antiquus*), *Alcelaphus buselaphus*, *Gazella dorcas*, *?Equus (Hippotigris) quagga*, *Loxodonta* sp., *?Diceros bicornis* (7370 ± 80 yrs BP, HV 13566), *Giraffa camelopardalis* (3825 ± 115, HV 14433), *Hippopotamus amphibius* (4720 ± 110, UZ 2168), *Hippotragus equinus*, *Phacochoerus aethiopicus*, *Tragelaphus* sp., *Addax nasomaculatus* and *Arvicanthis niloticus* (radiocarbon dates associated with taxa are included in parentheses); and domestic Mammalia – *Bos* sp. and *Equus africanus* (=*asinus*). These materials were obtained from lake deposits in what is now a dry wadi system leading into the Nile and reflect better watered conditions than found anywhere in the northern Sudan today.

Wet phases that lasted twice or thrice as long as the alternating dry phases characterised the climate of the

eastern Sahara between 10,300 and 4,500 years BP, after which the climate became increasingly arid and the wet periods less marked and of shorter duration (Butzer and Hansen 1968; Hassan 1986). The Neolithic fauna of the Western Desert, away from the Nile Valley and between 8,000 and 6,000 years BP, reflects easily available grass able to support a flourishing pastoral economy (El-Yahky 1985). Siwa Oasis was occupied by hunter gatherers during Early Holocene times, between 10,000 and 7,000 BP (Hassan and Gross 1987). This change from an environment in which a pastoral and hunting/gathering way of life was possible, and even well-adapted, gave way to one where the natural resources of plants and animals were reduced, and both the faunal diversity and human population must have contracted.

The original savanna grasslands and woodlands probably extended from the southern Sudan almost to the Mediterranean coast. Ritchie *et al.* (1985), on the basis of pollen samples, infer a savannah woodland between 8,500 and 6,000 years BP and *Acacia* bushveld and scrub grass between 6,000 and 4,500 years BP in the region of Oyo, Sudan. The common mammals, as compiled from the scattered fossiliferous sites, are wild cattle (including Bos primigenius, *Syncerus caffer* and *Pelorovis antiquus*), large antelope such as hartebeest (*Alcelaphus buselaphus*), addax (*Addax nasomaculatus*), or roan (*Hippotragus equinus*), camel (*Camelus thomasi*), white and ?black rhinoceros (*Ceratotherium simum* and *?Diceros* sp.), zebra (*Equus grevyi* and possibly *E. quagga*), warthog (*Phacochoerus aethiopicus*), elephant (*Loxodonta africana*), gazelles (*Gazella dorcas*, *G. dama*, *G. rufifrons*, and/or *G. leptoceros*), giraffe (*Giraffa camelopardalis*), and smaller mammals such as Cape hare (*Lepus capensis*), golden jackal (*Canis aureus*), sand fox (*Vulpes rueppelli*), porcupine (*Hystrix cristata*), wild cat (*Felis silvestris* or *F. margarita*), mongoose (*Herpestes ichneumon* or *Mungos mungos*) and striped hyaena (*Hyaena hyaena*). Ostrich (*Struthio camelus*) appears to have been widespread on the evidence of egg shell fragments and beads, but skeletal evidence is sparse. These animals reflect a mixed thorn bush and scrub grassveld environment, such as that reported by Ritchie *et al.* (1985).

The extensive epipalaeolithic fauna from Kom Ombo in the Nile Valley (Churcher 1972) provides a sample of the animals that might have been present in a well-watered savanna environment from about 15,000 to 10,000 BC (17,000 to 12,000 BP) and which may have represented a faunal base from which the Neolithic Holocene peoples in the Dakhleh area might have selected prey or commensals. The Kom Ombo fauna includes Pisces (3), Reptilia (1), Aves (22) and Mammalia (14), total 40 taxa. In Dakhleh the presence of indigenous fish is unknown, the only Neolithic reptile recorded is a tortoise, and birds other than ostrich, especially water birds, are unrecorded. Thus the Kom Ombo fauna is only comparable to the Neolithic Dakhleh fauna in mammalian taxa. The common species are man (*Homo sapiens*), a medium sized canid (*Canis* cf.

lupaster), Cape hare (*Lepus capensis*), ass (*Equus asinus*, probably instrusive), hippopotamus (*Hippopotamus amphibius*), hartebeest (*Alcelaphus buselaphus*), Dorcas gazelle (*Gazella dorcas*), and wild cattle (*Bos primigenius*). Neither mammalian sample is taxonomically diverse and both apparently display a constant human selectivity for similar larger game. The presence of hyaena, jackal, fox or dog, and small cats records the commensal scavengers at the camp sites. The extinct forms, at least for Egypt, of wild cattle and hippopotamus apparently reflect similar hunting abilities, and the hare, hartebeest and gazelle, a reliance on perhaps the most common and easily obtainable herbivores. Churcher's (1972) identification of a gazelle horncore to *Gazella leptoceros* was reviewed by Gautier and Van Neer (1989) and reassigned to *G. dorcas*. Peters (1990) reviewed Gaillard's (1934) large bovid materials assigned to '*Bubalus vignardi*' (= *Homoioceras vignardi* of Bate 1951 and Churcher 1972) and showed them to be within the variation expected in *Bos primigenius*.

Few records exist of faunas from Predynastic sites in which a broad sample of wild taxa is included. A typical fauna is that recorded from Hierakonopolis by McArdle (1982) in which *Capra* and/or *Ovis* is the most numerous taxon with 451 individuals and *Bos* a close second with 375 animals. *Sus* (66), *Canis* (7) and *Equus ?asinus* (1) are the other domesticates and *Gazella* (2) and *Hippopotamus* (2) the wild taxa. It is noteworthy that McArdle remarks that no evidence of horncores from the 'sheep' or caprovines was recovered, and that *Capra* was more numerous than *Ovis* by approximately 3 to 1. He speculates that the Predynastic sheep were hornless to explain this anomaly, similar to that observed in the Dakhleh Neolithic samples, but horned sheep and rams are depicted in early friezes which indicates that horns were was probably the normal condition.

As most of the sites from which faunal evidence has been recovered are probably remnants of human encampments, it is natural that the remains available for recovery are for the most part the result of human selection from the surrounding fauna, with a few items representing scavengers or commensals that were incorporated into the deposit by chance. The remains of hares, gazelles and hartebeests are numerous and represent many individuals. Although the remains of large cattle are prevalent, these bones last well and a single skeleton provides many fragments, so they may appear over-represented. Large mammals, such as rhinoceros, elephant, hippopotamus, and giraffe are infrequently part of the deposits, and their scarcity may represent scavenging by man of kills made by lion, hyaenas or wild dog, or infrequent hunting successes.

Rodent remains are also scarce, probably mainly because small bones are often able to be eaten by man or his commensal scavengers and, if buried, usually do not preserve well and are hard to recover. Thus the faunal evidence only provides a view of the actual fauna through a 'window' created by man's interaction with the fauna. This interaction is limited by man's abilities to kill only those animals that were within his power, and these provide the most numerous samples. Scavenging activities may then provide evidence of the larger animals outside his abilities to kill; although, if a large animal were to be killed, it is likely that man would move his encampment to near the carcass so as to use it and protect it from other carnivores. However, no elephant, buffalo or rhinoceros-kill site has been located to date. It is also likely that the Neolithic hunter/gatherers collected small birds and mammals, as do modern Kalahari peoples, and that these comprised a steady and significant portion of their diet. In this case, the ease of destruction of bird and rodent bones permits little evidence of their presence to be preserved in the food debris, and thus only the larger hare, porcupine and grass rat have been identified.

As the climate became drier, the influence of man and his flocks and herds would be increasingly felt by the wild fauna. Man would camp by the available and diminishing water holes, and thus prevent wild fauna from gaining access. Grazing and browse would also be used by man's domestic animals and less would be available for wild herbivores. Thus, man would reduce the wild fauna, not necessarily by actually exterminating taxa, but by excluding the larger and water-dependent forms from the basic resources. Man would not worry at the absence of rhinoceros, giraffe or buffalo, as these were not major food items. In fact, hartebeest and gazelle are present unabated throughout the Neolithic and into Old Kingdom deposits, suggesting that those grazers and browsers adapted to semi-arid conditions were able to sustain themselves in competition with man's herds of cattle and goats.

The domestic animals introduced by man into the eastern Sahara or Western Desert were mainly cattle and goats, possibly with asses and sheep.

Dakhleh has produced evidence of Cape buffalo (*Syncerus*), giant or long-horned buffalo (*Pelorovis*) and wild cattle or aurochs (*Bos primigenius*), as well as of domestic cattle (*Bos taurus*). Evidence for *Syncerus* and *Pelorovis* represents some of the most northern records for these taxa in Africa. Aurochsen are not found further south than Egypt – in Dakhleh and Wadi el-Bakht, Gilf el-Kebir (Gautier 1980) – although evidence for aurochsen has to be 'proven' by horn cores, as dentitions are not completely reliable (Gentry 1967). Thus it appears that aurochsen were either introduced by man into the eastern Sahara or were at the southern limit of their natural range and were replaced by buffaloes to the south. Man's herds of cattle would then take over the grazing of the aurochs and buffaloes to their eventual exclusion and local extinction during desertic cycles. The absence of large wild bovines from Old Kingdom sites and the presence of only domestic cattle sustains this deduction. Goats (*Capra aegagrus*) are present in the latest Neolithic deposits, with many teeth and postcranial elements attributable to them. They are confirmed by the recovery of horn cores from Neolithic sites, as these cannot be confused with those of either sheep or gazelles.

Note added in proof

This chapter was compiled in 1990. Consequently it has become progressively more inaccurate in parts with each new discovery over the intervening years. Comments inserted in the text inform the reader of recent major discoveries but cannot provide all new details. The most significant discovery is of a late Middle Pleistocene horizon containing early Middle Stone Age tools and a varied fauna of vertebrates and a snail. A report on this has been submitted to Palaeogeography, Palaeoclimatology, Palaeocology (Churcher *et al.*, submitted). This fauna does not differ significantly from that observed in the Holocene wild assemblages recorded here. A recent status report on the Holocene fauna will appear in *Archaeologia* (Churcher, In press).

Address for Author

Department of Zoology, University of Toronto, Ontario, CANADA M5S 3G5, *and* Department of Palaeobiology, Royal Ontario Museum, Queen's Park, Toronto, Ontario, CANADA M5S 2C6, *and* R.R.1, Site 42, Box 12, Gabriola Island, British Columbia, CANADA V0R 1X0 (mailing address).

REFERENCES

Bagnold, R.A., O.H. Myers, R.F. Peel, and M.A. Winkler. 1939. An expedition to the Gilf Kebir and Uweinat, 1938. *Geographical Journal* 93: 287–313.

Baker, F.C. 1935. Part III. The Mollusca of the shell heaps or escargotieres of northern Algeria, 185–225. *In* Pond, A.W., L. Chapuis, A.S. Romer and F.C. Baker, eds, *Prehistoric habitation sites in the Sahara and North Africa*. Beloit, Wisconsin: Logan Museum Bulletin No. 5, 244p.

Bate, D.M.A. 1951. The mammals from Singa and Abu Hugar. *British Museum (Natural History), Fossil Mammals of Africa* 2: 1–28.

Beadnell, H.J.L. 1901. Dakhleh Oasis: its topography and geology. *Geological Survey of Egypt*, 1899 4: 1–107.

Bell, S.V. 1966. The species of *Pila* Roding occurring in the Sudan. *Sudan Notes and Records* 17: 161–164.

Brookes, I. 1983. Dakhleh Oasis – A geoarchaeological reconnaisance. *Journal of the Society for the Study of Egyptian Antiquities* 8: 167–177.

Brookes, I.A. 1986. *Quaternary Geology and Geomorphology of Dakhleh Oasis Region and Environs, South-central Egypt: Reconnaissance findings*. York University, Toronto: Department of Geography, Discussion Paper No. 32, 90p.

Butzer, K.W. and C.L. Hansen. 1968. *Desert and river in Nubia*. Madison: University of Wisconsin Press, 562p.

Caton-Thompson, G. 1952. *Kharga Oasis in prehistory*. London: Athlone Press, 213p.

Churcher, C.S. 1972. Late Pleistocene vertebrates from archaeological sites in the plain of Kom Ombo, Upper Egypt. *Royal Ontario Museum, Life Sciences Contributions* No. 82, 1–172.

Churcher, C.S. 1980. Dakhleh Oasis Project: Preliminary observations on the geology and vertebrate palaeontology of northwestern Dakhleh Oasis. *Journal of the Society for the Study of Egyptian Antiquities* 10: 379–395.

Churcher, C.S. 1981. Dakhleh Oasis Project: Geology and Paleontology: Interim report on the 1980 field season. *Journal of the Society for the Study of Egyptian Antiquities* 11: 194–212.

Churcher, C.S. 1982. Dakhleh Oasis Project: Geology and Paleontology: Interim report on the 1981 field season. *Journal of the Society for the Study of Egyptian Antiquities* 12: 103–114.

Churcher, C.S. 1983. Dakhleh Oasis Project: Palaeontology: Interim report on the 1982 field season. *Journal of the Society for the Study of Egyptian Antiquities* 13: 178–187.

Churcher, C.S. 1986. Equid remains from Neolithic horizons at Dakhleh Oasis, Western Desert of Egypt, 413–421. *In* Meadow, R.H. and H.-P. Uerpmann, eds, *Equids in the Ancient World. Tübinger Atlas des Vorderen Orients, A (Naturwissenschaften)* 19: 1–423.

Churcher, C.S. 1987. Dakhleh Oasis Project: Palaeontology: Interim report on the 1988 field season. *Journal of the Society for the Study of Egyptian Antiquities* 17: 177–181.

Churcher, C.S. 1988. Palaeontology: Interim report on the 1987 field season. *Journal of the Society for the Study of Egyptian Antiquities* 16: 114–118.

Churcher, C.S. 1989. Fossil vertebrates from near Naro Moru, Western Foothill Zone, Mount Kenya, 175–188. *In* Mahaney, W.C., ed., *Quaternary and environmental research on East African mountains*. Rotterdam, Balkema, 483p.

Churcher, C.S. 1992. Ostrich bones from the Neolithic of Dakhleh Oasis, Western Desert of Egypt. *Palaeoecology of Africa and Surrounding Islands* 23: 67–71.

Churcher, C.S. In press. The Neolithic fauna from archaeological contexts in Dakhleh Oasis, Egypt. *Archaeologia*.

Churcher, C.S., M.R. Kleindienst and H.P. Schwarez. In press. Faunal remains from a Middle Pleistocene lacustrine marl in Dakhleh Oasis, Egypt: palaeoenvironmental reconstructions. *Palaeogeography, Palaeoclimatology, Palaeoecology*.

El-Yahky, F. 1985. The Sahara and Predynastic Egypt: an overview. *Journal of the Society for the Study of Egyptian Antiquities* 15: 81–85.

Gaillard, C. 1934. Contribution à l'étude de la faune préhistorique de l'Egypte. *Archives du Muséum d'Histoire naturelle de Lyon* 14: 1–125.

Gautier, A. 1968. Mammalian remains of the northern Sudan and southern Egypt, 80–99. *In* Wendorf, F. ed., *The prehistory of Nubia*, vol. 1. Dallas: Fort Burgwin Research Center and Southern Methodist University Press, 1084p.

Gautier, A. 1980. Appendix 4. Contributions to the archaeozoology of Egypt, 317–344. *In* Wendorf, F. and R. Schild, eds, *Prehistory of the eastern Sahara*. New York: Academic Press, 414p.

Gautier, A. 1981. Non-marine molluscs and vertebrate remains from Upper Pleistocene deposits and Middle Paleolithic sites at Bir Sahara and Bir Tarfawi, Western Desert of Egypt, 126–145. *In* Schild, R. and F. Wendorf, eds, *The prehistory of an Egyptian oasis*. Warsaw: Institute of the History of Material Culture, Polish Academy of Sciences, 155p.

Gautier, A. 1983. Animal life along the prehistoric Nile: the evidence from Saggai 1 and Geili (Sudan). *Origini* 12: 50–115.

Gautier, A. 1984a. Quaternary mammals and archaeozoology of Egypt and the Sudan: a survey, 43–56. *In* Krzyzaniak, L. and M. Kobusiewicz, eds, *Origin and early development of food-producing cultures in North-Eastern Africa*. Poznan: Polish Academy of Sciences, 503p.

Gautier, A. 1984b. The fauna of the Neolithic site of Kadero (central Sudan), 317–319. *In* Krzyzaniak, L. and M. Kobusiewicz, eds, *Origin and early development of food-producing cultures in North-Eastern Africa*. Poznan: Polish Academy of Sciences, 503p.

Gautier, A. 1984c. Archaeology of the Bir Kiseiba region, eastern Sahara, 49–72. *In* Wendorf, F., R. Schild and A.E. Close, eds, *Cattle-keepers of the eastern Sahara: the Neolithic of Bir Kiseiba*. Dallas: Department of Anthropology, Southern Methodist University Press, 438p.

Gautier, A. 1987. Prehistoric men and cattle in North Africa: A dearth of data and a surfeit of models, 163–187. *In* Close, A.E., ed., *Arid North Africa. Essays in Honor of Fred Wendorf.* Dallas: Department of Anthropology, Southern Methodist University Press, 357p.

Gautier, A. and W. Van Neer. 1989. Animal remains from the Late Palaeolithic Sequence at Wadi Kubbaniya, 119–161. *In* Wendorf, F., R. Schild, A.E. and Close, eds, *The Prehistory of Wadi Kubbaniya. Vol. 2. Stratigraphy, Paleoeconomy and Environment.* 2 vols. Dallas: Southern Methodist Press, 960p.

Gentry, A.W. 1967. *Pelorovis oldowayensis* Reck, an extinct bovid from East Africa. *Fossil Mammals of Africa*, No. 22. *Bulletin of the British Museum (Natural History), Geology series* **14**: 245–299.

Gentry, A.W. and A. Gentry. 1978. Fossil Bovidae (Mammalia) of Olduvai Gorge, Tanzania, Part I. *Bulletin of the British Museum (Natural History), Geology Series* **29**: 289–446.

Hassan, F.A. 1986. Desert environment and origins of agriculture in Egypt. *Norwegian Archaeological Review* **19**: 63–76.

Hassan, F.A. and G.T. Gross. 1987. Resources and subsistence during the Early Holocene at Siwa Oasis, northern Egypt, 85–103. *In* Close, A.E., ed., *Prehistory of arid North Africa: essays in honor of Fred Wendorf.* Dallas: Southern Methodist University Press, 357p.

Hey, R.W. 1967. Appendix 4A. Land snails, 358. *In* McBurney, C.B.M., ed., *The Haua Fteah (Cyrenaica) and the Stone Age of the south-east Mediterranean.* Cambridge: Cambridge University Press, 380p.

Hollett, A.F. and C.S. Churcher. This volume. Chapter 9. Notes on the Recent fauna of the Dakhleh Oasis, 153–170.

Kleindienst, M.R, C.S. Churcher, M.M.A. McDonald, and H.P. Schwarcz. This volume. Chapter 1. Geography, Geology, Geochronology and Geoarchaeology of the Dakhleh Oasis Region: An interim report, 1–54.

Kleindienst, M.R. This volume. Chapter 5. Pleistocene archaeology and geoarchaeology of the Dakhleh Oasis: A status report, 83–108.

Krzyzaniak, L. 1984. The Neolithic habitation at Kadero (central Sudan), 309–316. *In* Krzyzaniak, L. and M. Kobusiewicz, eds, *Origin and early development of food-producing cultures in North-Eastern Africa.* Poznan: Polish Academy of Sciences, 503p.

Krzyzaniak, L. and K. Kroeper. 1985. Report on the reconnaissance season of the recording of petroglyphs, December 1985. *Journal of the Society for the Study of Egyptian Antiquities* **15**: 138–139.

Leigh, E.G. 1968. Mollusca from the Kurkur Oasis, 513–514. *In* Butzer, K.W. and C.L. Hansen, eds, *Desert and river in Nubia.* Madison: University of Wisconsin Press, 562p.

Leigh, E.G. and K.W. Butzer. 1968. Fossil Mollusca from the Kom Ombo plain, 509–511. *In* Butzer, K.W. and C.L. Hansen, eds, *Desert and river in Nubia.* Madison: University of Wisconsin Press, 562p.

Llabador, F. 1962. Résultats malacologiques de la mission scientifique du Ténéré. *Missions Berliet, Ténéré-Tchad, Documents Scientifique, Arts et Métier Graphiques,* 237–270.

Loveridge, A. and E.E. Williams. 1957. Revision of the African tortoises and turtles of the suborder Cryptodira. *Bulletin of the Museum of Comparative Zoology* **115**: 163–557.

Lubell, D., F.A. Hassan, A. Gautier and J.L. Ballais. 1976. The Capsian escargotieres. *Science* **191**: 910–920.

Martin, F. 1968. Pleistocene molluscs from Sudanese Nubia, 57–59. *In* Wendorf, F. ed., *The prehistory of Nubia,* vol. 1. Dallas: Fort Burgwin Research Center and Southern Methodist University Press, 1084p.

McArdle, J. 1982. Preliminary report on the Predynastic fauna of the Hierakonopolis Project, 116–121. *In* Hoffman, M.A., ed., *The Predynastic of Hierakonopolis.* Egyptian Studies Association, No. 1, 154p.

McDonald, M.M.A. This volume. Chapter 7. Neolithic cultural units and adaptations in the Dakhleh Oasis, 117–132.

Mills, A.J. This volume. Chapter 10. Pharaonic Egyptians in the Dakhleh Oasis, 171–178.

Muzzolini, A. 1984. Les premiers ovicaprines domestiques au Sahara. Nabta Playa, les figurations d'Ouenat et les "Steinplatze". Actes du deuxieme Colloque Euro-africain, "Le passe du Sahara et des zones limitrophes de l'epoque des Garamantes au Moyen Age". *L'Universo* **64** (5): 150–157.

Osborn, D.J. and I. Helmy. 1980. The contemporary land mammals of Egypt (including Sinai). *Fieldiana (Zoology), n.s.,* No. 5 (Publ. No. 1309), 1–597p.

Pachur, H.-J. and S. Kröpelin. 1987. Wadi Howar: paleoclimatic evidence from an extinct river system in the southeastern Sahara. *Science* **237**: 298–300.

Peters, J. 1990. Late Palaeolithic ungulate fauna and landscape in the Plain of Kom Ombo. *Sahara* **3**: 45–52.

Ritchie, J.C. This volume. Chapter 4. Flora, vegetation and palaeobotany of the Dakhleh Oasis, 73–81.

Ritchie, J.C., C.H. Eyles and C.V. Haynes. 1985. Sediment and pollen evidence for an early to mid-Holocene humid period in the eastern Sahara. *Nature* **314**: 352–355.

Van Neer, W. and H.-P. Uerpmann. 1989. Palaeoecological significance of the Holocene faunal remains of the B.O.S. Missions, 308–341. *In* Kuper, R., ed., *Forschungen zur Umweltgeschichte der Ostsahara.* Köln: Heinrich-Barth-Institute, Africa Praehistorica, 341p.

Villiers, A. 1958. Tortues et crocodiles de l'Afrique noire française. *Institut Français d'Afrique Noire, Initiations Africaines* **15**: 1–354.

Wendorf, F. and Members of the Combined Prehistoric Expedition. 1977. Late Pleistocene and Recent climatic changes in the Egyptian Sahara. *The Geographical Journal* **143**: 211–234.

9

NOTES ON THE RECENT FAUNA OF THE DAKHLEH OASIS

Alan F. Hollett and Charles S. Churcher

INTRODUCTION

Observations on the birds and mammals and limited collection of invertebrate and vertebrate specimens were undertaken as a minor aspect of the activities of the Dakhleh Oasis Project, chiefly during the years 1978 to 1987. Significant new or confirmatory observations made in later years are also included. Hollett was in the oasis throughout all field seasons, which spanned the months from late October to late March. Churcher's visits were generally restricted to three to five weeks in any one season. Ornithological observations, mainly field records of individuals seen during the course of other work throughout the oasis, at Lake Mut, and in the surrounding desert, with a few specimens acquired from road kills, have resulted in publication of selected avian records by Goodman *et al.* (1986).

Mammalogical observations involved fewer sightings, since most mammals in the oasis are either nocturnal, cryptic, or both, probably due to the effect of man's presence, and are based mainly on trapped specimens, spoor identification, scat recognition and analysis, and random skeletal elements found in the surrounding desert. Herpetological observations derive from a few specimens found during field work or excavation, some of which were preserved as pickled museum specimens. Ichthyological remains are normally absent, but tilapia (*Onychromis niloticus*) was introduced into Lake Mut about 1980. Specimens were randomly collected: selected specimens are deposited in the appropriate departments of the Royal Ontario Museum, Toronto.

Taxa are included in these lists that are considered in already published lists to be present in the oasis. Remarks or observations are only included if we have noted evidence of presence or possible presence. No comment by us indicates status only based on others' records.

ZOOGEOGRAPHY AND ENVIRONMENT

The environment and available habitat for fauna in Dakhleh Oasis have been characterised by Migahid *et al.* (1960). Ritchie (this volume, Chapter 4) reviews the major vegetation observed by him in the oasis. The oasis itself is some 70 km long, 20 km broad at its maximum north-south diameter, and between 5 and 10 km wide at its wider cultivated parts (Fig. 9.1). It comprises a more or less interconnecting network of discontinuous cultivated areas separated by sand dune garbs, rock areas, salinated or calcreted ancient field systems, and uncultivated fallow areas of soils or sandy laminar dunes. It is bounded on the north by the edge of the Libyan Plateau as the Libyan Escarpment and to the south by a sandstone ridge of the Nubia Group Taref Formation. To the east the oasis pinches out between the Taref Fm. sandstone ridge and the limestone lag-armored surface of the Qusseir (= Mut) Formation shale piedmont. To the west it ends at Gebel Edmonstone, where the Duwi Formation extends south-westerly to meet the Nubian sandstone ridge and pinches out the cultivable areas. A western extension of the cultivation exists northwest of Gebel Edmonstone, but is not part of the old oasis and represents part of the extensions of cultivation using deep artesian water to irrigate unused soils. Two low points exist in the oasis, in the separated main Mut and eastern Teneida basins, at 122 m and 92 m a.m.s.l. respectively.

Migahid *et al.* (1960) characterise the land forms and habitats into six categories:

'Reports from the Survey of Dakhleh Oasis, Western Desert of Egypt, 1977–1987', edited by C.S. Churcher and A.J. Mills. Dakhleh Oasis Project: Monograph 2. Oxbow Monograph 99.

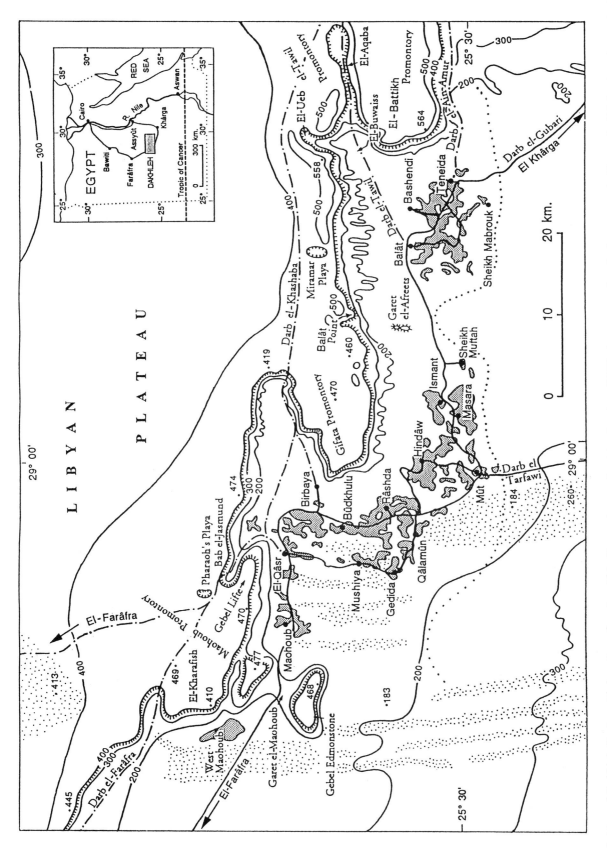

Fig. 9.1. Map of Dakhleh Oasis, with location of oasis within Egypt. Areas of cultivation (ca. 1970) shown cross hatched, towns and villages (solid dots), main roads (heavy lines), caravan roads (dot-dash lines), Libyan Escarpment (parallel contours topped by scarp symbol), and linear sand dunes (dotted). The oasis depression is bounded by the Libyan Escarpment to the north and a low sandstone ridge (dotted line) to the south. Names are derived from the 'Egypt 1:25,000' series of maps, from local residents, explorers' notes and from usage developed by members of the Dakhleh Oasis Project. Contours and spot heights in metres.

1. *Sand Plains*. Sand sheets occur throughout the oasis. Vegetation is mainly *Tamarix aphylla*, *Alhagi maurorum*, and the xerophytes *Calotropis procera* and *Hyoscyamus muticus* on stable areas.

2. *Sand dunes*. Mainly in the west of the oasis, although small dunes occur throughout. Barchan dunes are unstable and move at between 10 and 20 metres/yr (Beadnell 1909; Embabi 1970–71). Elongate dunes are also present with their morphologically permanent form but mobile granular surface as grains move along the crests. Stable dunes may grow *Tamarix aphylla*, *T. nilotica* or *T. tetragyna* var. *deserti* and *Alhagi maurorum*. In basins between dunes *Cressa cretica*, *A. maurorum* and *Stipagrostis scoparia* may grow. Windbreaks of *Tamarix* spp., *Acacia nilotica*, *Lagonychium farcatum* and *Saccharum* sp. or introduced *Eucalyptus globosus* or *Casuarina equisetifolia* may be planted for dune control.

3. *Wastelands*. These are usually salt-encrusted or calcrete cemented soils on old agricultural lands, and develop when irrigation brings too much salts to the surface without adequate flushing and causes cementation of the soil particles. Salty *sebakha* areas develop on the surface and cementation forms within the soil below. Plant cover may comprise xerophytes such as *Zygophyllum album*, *Hyoscyamus muticus*, *Sporobolus spicatus*, *Astragalus trigonus* and in wetter areas *Cyperus laevigatus*.

4. *Cultivated Lands*. Major crops are vegetables, oranges, dates, olives, figs, bananas and prickly pear and, in winter, wheat, barley, and alfalfa and, in summer, maize and rice. These lands are all irrigated from nearby wells through a system of small irrigation channels. Date palms (*Phoenix dactylifera*) and shelter trees (*Acacia nilotica* or *A. raddiana*, *Eucalyptus globosus* and *Casuarina equiseti-folia*) are planted on the edges of the fields and channels.

5. *Salt Marshes*. Small marshes are scattered throughout the oasis and in many residual drainage ditches. Extensive marshes are located near Lake Mut, Lake Qalamun and other small overflow lakes or ponds. There is usually a rich algal flora in such wet habitats, whose margins are fringed by rushes (*Scirpus* sp.) when the water level is stable year-round, and by tamarisk (*Tamarix* sp.) when the water level fluctuates.

6. *Aquatic Habitats*. Well pools, irrigation canals and open surfaces of reservoirs often have floating masses of algae. However, no floating plants such as water hyacinth (*Eichornia* sp.) or deep rooting water plants such as water lilies (*Nymphaea* sp.) have been observed.

LOCATIONS OF FAUNAL OBSERVATIONS

Locations from which specimens were taken or at which observations were made are shown in Figure 9.1.

Locations within Dakhleh Oasis:

1.	Gharb el-Maohoub	25° 40′ N, 28° 45′ E
2.	Maohoub (Ezbet el-Sheikh Maohoub or Abar Meihub)	25° 47′ N, 28° 56′ E
3.	Deir el-Haggar, S of Maohoub	25° 45′ N, 28° 56′ E
4.	Bir Talata el-Maohoub	25° 38′ N, 28° 48′ E
5.	Bir el Nokta, NW of Maohoub	25° 47′ N, 28° 54′ E
6.	Sheikh Mubaris' Tombs	25° 41′ N, 28° 52′ E
7.	Qasr or El-Qasr al-Dakhl	25° 47′ N, 28° 52′ E
8.	Dinaria	25° 44′ N, 28° 54′ E
9.	Umar Seraya	25° 42′ N, 28° 54′ E
10.	Rashda (= Rashida)	25° 35′ N, 28° 56′ E
11.	Gedida (= Ezbet Gedida)	25° 35′ N, 28° 53′ E
12.	Qalamun or El Qalamun	25° 33′ N, 28° 54′ E
13.	Lake Qalamun	25° 32′ N, 28° 55′ E
14.	Lake Mut (includes Bir Talata al-Mut, Pumping Station 4, and 4 km N of Mut)	25° 31′ N, 28° 58′ E
15.	Aweina or Ezbet Sheikh el-Aweina	25° 33′ N, 28° 58′ E
16.	Mut	25° 29′ N, 28° 59′ E
17.	Masara	25° 31′ N, 29° 02′ E
18.	Sheikh Wali (el-Sheikh Waly)	25° 31′ N, 29° 01′ E
19.	Ismant (Asmant)	25° 32′ N, 29° 04′ E
20.	Smint or Ismant el-Kharab	25° 31′ N, 29° 05′ E
21.	Sheikh Muftah	25° 30′ N, 29° 06′ E
22.	Balat	25° 34′ N, 29° 16′ E
23.	'Ein Duma	25° 29′ N, 29° 14′ E
24.	Ezbet Bashendi (Bashendi)	25° 33′ N, 29° 18′ E
25.	'Ein Tirghi	25° 33′ N, 29° 15′ E
26.	'Ein Birbiyeh	25° 32′ N, 29° 20′ E
27.	Teneida	25° 31′ N, 29° 21′ E
28.	Sheikh Mabrouk	25° 26′ N, 29° 15′ E

Locations not in Dakhleh Oasis:

29.	Ezbet Zayat (= Abou-al-Oql'), midway between Dakhleh and Kharga oases	25° 14′ N, 29° 44′ E
30.	Ain Amur	25° 39′ N, 30° 00′ E
31.	Kharga	26° 26′ N, 30° 33′ E
32.	Ain Umm Dabadib	25° 46′ N, 30° 25′ E
33.	Abu Minquar, 175 km NW of Maohoub towards Farafra Oasis	26° 30′ N, 27° 36′ E
34.	Farafra Oasis	27° 03′ N, 27° 58′ E
35.	Bahariya Oasis (Qasr Bawiti)	28° 21′ N, 28° 52′ E
36.	Siwa Oasis	29° 12′ N, 25° 31′ E
37.	Bir Tarfawi, 300 km S of Dakhleh	22° 55′ N, 28° 53′ E
38.	El-Sherg el-Uweinat	21° 54′ N, 24° 58′ E

FAUNAL OBSERVATIONS

Records are arranged with numbers in the left hand column indicating the order of species recorded and, if in parentheses, that the taxon has not been observed by us. Numbers in parentheses after the scientific name indicate the number of specimens obtained by us.

Mollusca

Four taxa of freshwater Mollusca are known from shells that have been recovered from the Neolithic levels of the oasis. These taxa are represented by many specimens or by whole specimens and thus do not appear to have been imported, as may be the case for fragments of shells of the Nile oyster (*Etheria elliptica*). The three snails considered to be endemic are – *Pila ovata, Melanoides tuberculata*, and *Gyraulus ehrenbergi* – and one bivalve – *Corbicula luminalis vara*. Remains of only *Pila ovata*, a large pulmonate land snail probably eaten as escargot, and the helical *Melanoides tuberculata* have been recovered from Roman period levels, the former as a land snail inhabiting wetlands or at least areas with available moisture, such as the enlarged wells or spring mounds, and the latter probably in the irrigation ditches with which its remains are often associated.

During the survey of the oasis, only living specimens of *M. tuberculata* were found in an irrigation canal at Teneida on October 20th, 1982. It is probable that the waters now are too saline or contain too much solute that is detrimental to the molluscs' life cycle or metabolism, and that the progressive reduction in recorded species is due to this rather than to a lack of moisture, as wells and irrigation canals have always been available. Further, migrant water birds would continually carry eggs to reintroduce the species to the oasis.

Fragments of the valves of *Etheria elliptica* have been recovered from Neolithic sites in the eastern end of the oasis near Teneida and Sheikh Muftah. These are considered to represent imported specimens as the valves are large, fairly thick, and could have served as palettes or tools. However, no signs of working or modification other than breakage and edge wear due to use as scrapers are visible. These fragments appear to represent a morphotype intermediate between the elongate morph typical of fast-running streams and the rounded or spiny morphs typical of slow or still waters (Gautier 1983). No living *E. elliptica* is known (or expected) for either Dakhleh or Kharga oases.

Pisces

Only one introduced fish is present in the oasis.

Cichlidae – cichlids

1. Tilapia – *Oreochromis nilotica*.

Dead immature and subadult individuals up to 25 cm head-tail length, have been observed in the shallows of Lake Mut since 1982. It probably provides a good food source for fishing ducks, herons and cormorants. Small tilapia persist in the main irrigation ditches, near to the wells or springs (e.g., 'Ein Tirghi), consume mosquito larvae, and are used for food.

Amphibia

Two amphibians have been observed in the oasis.

Bufonidae – Toads

1. Common African Toad – *Bufo regularis*.

Adult individuals of this toad have been found in wet places near irrigated lands, along ditches or near wells from 1979 to present, where they advertised their presence by calling. In 1986 an occurrence of tadpoles was noted in a shallow pond formed from overflow irrigation water, indicating that breeding

takes place adventitiously. Marx (1968) gave no breeding record of toads from any of the western oases, except of *Bufo viridis* from Siwa. Goodman (pers. comm. to Hollett, 1988) obtained three specimens of *B. viridis* (UMMZ 172127–9) from northeast of Bawiti, Bahariya Oasis, on 28 April, 1981.

Ranidae – Frogs

2. A medium-sized green frog, probably either *Ptychadena mascariensis* (Mascarena frog) or *Rana ridibunda* (Lake frog), was observed calling and in numbers near a well about half a kilometre southeast of Bashendi during warm weather between March 1 and 6, 1988. No frogs are recorded from any of the western oases (Marx 1968).

Reptilia

A few reptiles have been recorded and collected from the oasis. As most of our fieldwork was carried out during the winter months, October-March, most reptiles were quiescent. However, lizard and snake tracks were frequently seen, attesting to their presence and activity when the temperatures were high enough. One snake track exhibited the side-winder mode of locomotion used to cross hot sand or to move over substrate that provides little traction. This track may be from *Cerastes*.

Gekkonidae – Gekkos

1. Elegant or Spotted Gekko – *Stenodactylus stenodactylus* (1).

Specimens of spotted gekkos are found under stones, often abandoned Neolithic lower querns or metates, in deflated areas peripheral to the oasis. Marx (1968) gives no record of this species in the western oases except in Siwa.

Agamidae – Agama Lizards

(2.) Sinai Agama – *Agama sinaita*.

Ten specimens (BMNH 1909.F.28–37) were collected by W.J. Harding-King from 'Belat' (=Balat) (S.M. Goodman, pers. comm. to Hollett, 1988), but the species is not certainly *A. sinaita* and may be *A. mutabilis*. Marx (1968) lists no agamids from the oases.

Lacertidae – Lizards

(3.) Bosc's Lizard – *Acanthodactylus boskianus*.

Two specimens (BMNH 1909.F.28, 38–39) were collected by W.J. Harding-King from Balat and one (UMMZ) on March 22, 1984 (S.M. Goodman, pers. comm. to Hollett, 1988) from Pumping Station No. 4 at Lake Mut by S.M. Goodman. Marx (1968) does not list this lizard from any of the oases.

(4.) Red-spotted Lizard – *Eremias rubropunctata*.

Four specimens (BMNH 97.10.28.356–9) were collected by J. Anderson from Kharga Oasis (S.M. Goodman, pers. comm.to Hollett, 1988). Marx (1968) does not list this lizard from any of the oases.

Varanidae – Monitors

(5.) Desert Monitor – *Varanus griseus*.

Jarvis (1936) records an episode when a monitor lizard entered his wife's tent while they were encamped in the oasis. No specimens of monitors were seen by us, although tracks of a lizard at least 45 cm long were observed and were assumed to be made by such a lizard because of its size, long tail, and distance between foot-prints. Marx (1968) lists no specimens from the western oases. Dorsal vertebrae and chewed limb bones were collected in February, 1988 southwest of Sheikh Muftah by Churcher.

Scincidae – Skinks

6. Eyed or Ocellated Skink – *Chalcides ocellatus* (2).

Skinks were observed within cultivated areas and often close to old walls or stone piles. One specimen (BMNH 97.10.28.403) was collected by J. Anderson from Kharga Oasis (S.M. Goodman, pers. comm. to Hollett, 1988). Marx (1968) records this skink only from Siwa, El Bahrein and Bahariya oases.

Colubridae – Boas

7. Flowered Snake – *Coluber rhodorachis* (1).

A male specimen (16750) was obtained from near Ismant on January 21, 1987. Marx (1968) gives no record of this snake in the western oases but records exist for the Nile Valley, near Minya and at El Dakka, south of Aswan.

8. Saharan Sand-snake – *Psammophis schokari aegyptius* (2).

Two specimens (11546, M, 11547, F) were obtained on December 19, 1980. Marx (1968) records this snake from Siwa Oasis only.

Viperidae – vipers

9. Horned or Greater Cerastes Viper – *Cerastes cerastes* (1).

The head of a specimen (11549) was collected on December 19, 1980 at Lat. 25° 15′ N, Long. 29° 00′ E, in the desert south of Sheikh Wali. A small specimen from near ‘Ein Birbiyeh and a mummified partial specimen with an ingested gekko from Bashendi were obtained in February-March, 1987. Marx (1968) gives no record of this viper from the western oases, although it is known from the Nile Valley south of Assiyut.

10. Horned Viper? – *Cerastes vipera* (1).

A male specimen (16749) was collected at ‘Ein Birbiyeh on January 13, 1987.

ORNITHOLOGICAL OBSERVATIONS

Observations on the birds of Dakhleh Oasis have been made by R.E. Moreau (1927) who visited in 1925, from April 10 to 13; by H.J.L. Beadnell in 1927, from February 19 to April 11, who visited both the oasis and the area around Bir Tarfawi to the south, and whose observations were published by Moreau (1928). R.E. Meinertzhagen (1930) visited Dakhleh in late March, 1928, and donated specimens to the Department of Ornithology, British Museum (Natural History), London, now at Tring, Hertfordshire, but not all his published records are substantiated by museum specimens, *et vice versa*. Al Hussaini (1959) visited Dakhleh during the winter of 1958–59 and also deposited specimens in the British Museum (Natural History). Scharlau (1963) visited the oasis from October 2 to 4, 1962, and reported observing 55 species. Kiepenheuer and Linsenmair (1965) observed and collected birds in Dakhleh between August 12 and 13, 1963. Researchers from the Palearctic Migrant Survey visited Dakhleh between January 15 and 20, 1972: the specimens collected by them are deposited in the United States

National Museum, Washington, D.C., U.S.A. Our observations until 1985 have been published in the main by Goodman *et al.* (1986) and this paper comprises these and subsequent observations.

AVES: Annotated List of Wild Species

Observations and specimens based on those published by Goodman *et al.* (1986) for Dakhleh Oasis, and those submitted by Hollett to Goodman *et al.*, with selected new observations from 1985 to 1996. Abbreviations: FB = former breeder, RB = resident breeder, WV = winter visitor, AV = accidental vagrant, and PV = passage visitor.

(1.) Ostrich – *Struthio camelus*. FB

Last recorded at Abou-al-Oql’(= Ezbet Zayat) in 1935, about midway between Kharga and Dakhleh (Al Hussaini 1959). Many fragments of ostrich egg shell may be found in the areas around the oasis, but these are generally attributable to Old Kingdom or Neolithic deposits (see McDonald and Churcher’s papers, this volume, Chapters 7 and 8). Two vertebrae, one cervical and one thoracic, were recovered in February, 1990, *in situ* within Holocene (ca. 7500 BP) deposits among Bashendi Unit Neolithic cultural remains from about 15 km southeast of Teneida (Loc. 228, this volume, Appendix III) (Churcher 1992). No certainly recent fragments have been observed. Moreau (1934) attributes the ostrich of the Libyan Desert to *S. c. massaicus*, present still in the Sudan.

2. Great Crested Grebe – *Podiceps cristatus*. AV or WV

One bird was seen at Lake Mut on February 21, 1986. This is the first record of this species in the Western Desert.

3. Little Grebe – *Tachybaptus ruficollis capensis*. RB, WV?

Little grebes are commonly present on Lake Mut each winter since 1980, with at least 200 birds seen during the winter of 1982–83. The 1987 population was considerably reduced, perhaps to as few as 100, and on March 10, 1988 only some 20 individuals were observed. Little grebes are also common on Lake Qalamun, and may represent either new immigrants or individuals that were earlier on Lake Mut.

4. Great Cormorant – *Phalacrocorax carbo*. AV or WV

The first two individuals were seen on Lake Mut on January 19, 1985. During the winters of 1985–86, eight individuals, and 1986–88, seven individuals were noted. The availability of tilapia (*Oreochromys*, see above) is obviously important for this piscivorous species.

5. Little Bittern – *Ixobrychus minutus minutus*. ?PV or RB

Three or four were seen in reeds fringing an overflow pond between Qalamun and Beit el-Arab by A.J. and L.F. Mills on January 24, 1996. One was hit by their Landrover and, upon examination, found to be a male approaching breeding conditon. The species is recorded from Wadi Natrun and Farafra (Goodman *et al.*, 1986) and as breeding in Dakhleh Oasis in 1995 (Riad, 1995a). Thus, this species appears to be newly breeding in the oasis.

(6.) Night Heron – *Nycticorax nycticorax*. PV

Scharlau (1963) saw nine individuals between October 2 and 4, 1962.

(7.) Squacco Heron – *Ardeola ralloides.* PV

Goodman *et al.* (1986) collected one female from 14 km north of Mut on 22 March, 1984.

8. Cattle Egret – *Bubulcus ibis* (4). PV, WV, RB?

Common throughout the oasis on all cultivated lands. Local residents tell us that the species nests in the oasis but no nesting colony has been located. A skin and three skeletons were collected as roadkills in 1986–88 west of Teneida. Al Hussaini (1959) first observed this species in the oasis and Scharlau (1963) recorded several hundred individuals between October 2–4, 1962. Present numbers may be between two and three thousand. Breeding seems likely as the two roadkill individuals, one male and one female, recovered from a small drainage pond by the side of the main Teneida-Balat road, near 'Ein Birbiyeh, were apparently a pair, which supports the local information.

9. Little Egret – *Egretta garzetta garzetta* PV

On April 25, 1981, 25 birds were seen; in mid-October, 1982, about 12; on March 22, 1984, at least 15, and on March 8, 1987, six were seen at Lake Mut. Scharlau (1963) reported about six birds between October 2 and 4, 1962. This species seems to be consistently present in the oasis but not abundant.

10. Grey Heron – *Ardea cinerea.* PV, WV

First noted by us in February, 1982 and annually since. The numbers appear to be increasing with six seen in February, 1982; 25 on October 13, 1982; 15 in February, 1985; 50 in February, 1986; and 200 in February, 1987. On January 23, 1987, at least 200 individuals were observed around the margins of Lake Mut, with at least 65 standing on a section of bare sand dune, some 20 to 100 m from the shore, in full sun, presumably warming themselves, at about 10.30 am. This heron was first recorded for the oasis by Meinertzhagen (1930) in March, 1930, and later by Schlarlau (1963) who saw four between October 2–4, 1962. With the creation of lakes Mut and Qalamun, and the provision of a food source when the lakes were stocked with tilapia, this bird appears to have become a regular winter visitor. The population appears to have left the oasis by March 10, 1988, as only two were seen on that date.

11. Purple Heron – *Ardea purpurea purpurea.* PV

One bird seen among a flock of Grey Herons at Lake Mut in 1986. Schlarlau (1963) observed a single bird between October 2 and 4, 1962.

12. Black stork – *Ciconia nigra.* ?AV

One bird seen in flight between Bashendi and Balat on December 11, 1992. This is the first record of this species in the oasis. One bird shot but not recovered on May 18, 1975, in Quattara Oasis (Goodman *et al.,* 1986).

13. White Stork – *Ciconia ciconia ciconia* (1). PV

A single bird was seen at Lake Mut on February 21, 1986. Goodman *et al.* (1986) saw two birds on April 24, 1981 at Mut. Previous records of this species are of six birds from 90 km east of the oasis near a salt lake (Kiepenheuer and Linsenmair 1965) and "one dead in the desert halfway between Dakhla and 'Uweinat at 26° 30′ N, 27° 28′ E" (Moreau 1934, cited in Goodman *et al.* 1986, 26). Another dead bird was found on the Darb el-Amur in the western part of the Wadi el-Batikh, approximately 20 km east of Teneida at the foot of the Libyan Escarpment, on February 27, 1991.

14. Spoonbill – *Platalea leucorodia leucorodia.* PV

One bird seen roosting with Cattle Egrets at Ezbet Bashendi in early October, 1982; and eight at Lake Mut on February 21, 1986. Scharlau (1963) saw single adult and immature birds between October 2 and 4, 1962.

15. Egyptian Goose – *Alopochen aegyptiacus.* AV?

Six birds, probably belonging to this species, were seen on Lake Mut on January 25, 1982.

16. Shelduck – *Tadorna tadorna.* AV

Two birds, probably a pair, of this species, seen on Lake Mut on January 23, 1987, probably constitute the first record of this species for Dakhleh Oasis. Meininger and Mullié (1981) counted about 130 birds at Wadi Natrun in January, 1979. Goodman *et al.* (1986) record 11 birds on January 6, 1982, also at Wadi Natrun. Flocks of thousands occur every year on Wadi Natrun (Goodman *et al.* 1986: 3,000–5,000) so the Lake Mut pair may represent strays that have penetrated further into the Western Desert.

(17.) Wigeon – *Anas penelope.* PV

Listed by Meinertzhagen (1930) and Jarvis (1936) as occurring in Dakhleh, but without details.

(18.) Gadwall – *Anas strepera.* PV

Jarvis (1936) recorded this duck as present in the oasis but without details.

19. Teal – *Anas crecca.* PV, WV

On January 26, 1982, 150 birds and in November, 1982, about 50 birds were noted on Lake Mut. On February 10, 1984, 250 birds were noted; in February, 1985 a large number (uncounted); and on February 21, 1986, 200 seen. On January 23, 1987, more than 200 individuals were seen on Lake Mut, and again on February 15, 1987. Moreau (1927) saw a few at Umar Seraya between April 10 and 13, 1925. Presumably Lake Mut is attractive to this species and provides a suitable wintering place.

20. Mallard – *Anas platyrhynchos platyrhynchos.* PV, WV, CB?

Seen on Lake Mut on January 23, 1987, when four (two pairs) were observed flying. Meinertzhagen (1930, 467) records that "A female, shot at Dakhla Oasis on 25/iii/1928, had huge ovaries and appeared to be about [to] lay." Goodman *et al.* (1986) report four at Abu Minqar on March 21, 1984.

21. Pintail – *Anas acuta acuta.* PV, WV

About 200 birds were seen on January 26, 1982; about 250 on February 21, 1986; and about 25 birds on January 23, 1987, all on Lake Mut. Scharlau (1983) noted its presence between October 2–4, 1962.

(22.) Garganey – *Anas querquedula.* PV

Goodman *et al.* (1986) observed three individuals on April 24 and four on April 25, 1981 at Lake Mut. Moreau (1927, 240) saw 'at least a score' (20) at Umar Seraya and many more at Dinaria on April 12, 1925. Scharlau (1963) noted about 40 birds between October 2–4, 1962.

23. Shoveler – *Anas clypeata.* PV, WV

About 12 individuals were seen in mid-October to mid-November 1982 on Lake Mut. This species has been seen there every year since, with 200 on February 21, 1986; 150+ on January 23, 1987; and 200+ on March 10, 1988. Goodman *et al.* (1986) observed six to 10 on Lake Mut between April 24–25, 1981. Beadnell (1909) and Jarvis (1936) record them for Dakhleh, but without details.

(24.) Marbled Duck – *Marmaronetta angustirostris*. FB
Goodman *et al.* (1986) observed a few near Mut on September 7, 1984. Jarvis (1936) shot this species in the oasis and Moreau (1927) saw two birds at Umar Seraya between April 10–13, 1925. Meinertzhagen (1930) records this species as breeding in the oasis, but there is no recent evidence for this and the record is ambiguous.

25. Pochard – *Aythya ferina*. WV
Six birds (three pairs) were seen at Lake Mut on March 8, 1987. Jarvis (1936) listed this species for Dakhleh.

26. Ferruginous Duck – *Aythya nyroca*. WV
Seen near Lake Mut, Lake Qalamun and Ezbet Bashendi during November, 1982, and January and February, 1984.

(27.) Tufted Duck – *Aythya fuligula*. WV
Jarvis (1936) saw this species in Dakhleh.

(28.) Honey Buzzard – *Pernis apivorus*. PV
Scharlau (1963) observed two birds on October 2, 1962, in Mut.

29. Black Kite – *Milvus migrans*. PV, WV
Seen on January 14, 1982; in mid-January, 1983; on February 21, 1986; and February 15, 1987.

30. Egyptian Vulture – *Neophron percnopterus*. PV
Observed on November 1, 1978; October 22, 1979; and October 6, 1980. Moreau (1927) noted it as uncommon from April 10–13, 1925. On April 26, 1981, Goodman *et al.* (1986) saw an adult in the desert midway between Dakhleh and Farafra oases. Meinertzhagen (1930) records it as breeding in Dakhleh, but this lacks documentation and all records fall within migratory periods of the species (Bijlsma 1983; Cramp and Simmons 1980).

(31.) Griffon Vulture – *Gyps fulvus*. PV?
Meinertzhagen (1930) gives unsubstantiated records for this species at Dakhleh.

32. Short-Toed Eagle – *Circaetus gallicus*. PV
One bird seen on March 1 and 3, 1987 at about 100 m through binoculars. Meinertzhagen (1930) saw a few individuals in late March, 1928.

33. Marsh Harrier – *Circus aeruginosus aeruginosus*. PV, WV
Seen near Mut and Qalamun in early October, 1982, and during January and February, 1985, near Mut. Four birds were seen on March 6, 1986, and one on February 15, 1987. Moreau (1927) saw one near Rashida on April 11, 1925, and Scharlau (1963) saw a female on October 3, 1962.

(34.) Hen Harrier – *Circus cyaneus cyaneus*. WV
Schlarlau (1963) saw a male on October 2, 1962.

(35.) Pallid Harrier – *Circus macrourus*. PV
Moreau (1927) frequently saw this bird between April 10–13, 1925. One was found at Bir Tarfawi, in winter or early spring, 1927 (Moreau 1928).

36. Buzzard – *Buteo buteo*. PV
Individuals have been seen regularly in January and February, 1984–1988. Goodman *et al.* (1986) report one bird on March 22, 1984, 4 km north of Mut.

37. Long-legged Buzzard – *Buteo rufinus*. PV, WV
One individual seen on January 21, 1982 and another at 'Ein Birbiyeh on February 4 and 27, 1987. One bird inhabited the area around Teneida and was regularly observed at 'Ein Birbiyeh during January and February, 1988.

(38.) Lesser Spotted Eagle – *Aquila pomarina*. PV
Goodman *et al.* (1986) report one bird on April 24, 1981 at Lake Mut. Reports of this species and/or *A. clanga* are between April 10–13, 1925, near Qasr (Moreau 1927) and between October 2 and 4, 1962 (Scharlau 1963).

(39.) Steppe Eagle – *Aquila rapax*. PV
Goodman *et al.* (1986) record two birds on February 2, 1983 near Qasr and one on March 23, 1984, 21 km north of Mut (near Rashida?).

(40.) Booted Eagle – *Hieraetus pennatus*. PV
Goodman *et al.* (1986) record one bird on October 19, 1980 and Scharlau (1963) a dark-phase individual on October 3, 1962 in the oasis.

41. Kestrel – *Falco tinnuculus*. RB, PV, WV
This species was been consistently observed between late September, 1982 and mid-January, 1983, and regularly every season since 1978. Goodman *et al.* (1986) observed Kestrels during March, 1980 and on April 25, 1981. Meinertzhagen (1930) found birds sitting on eggs in mid-March, 1928, and an immature male was collected on January 17, 1973 (S.M. Goodman, pers. comm. to Hollett, May 7, 1987).

(42.) Red-footed Falcon – *Falco vespertinus vespertinus*. PV
Two males were taken on March 25, 1928 by Meinertzhagen (1930).

(43.) Sooty Falcon – *Falco concolor*. MB
Moreau (1934) reported that the Bagnold Expedition shot one bird 'flying over its natural roosting place' on October 2, 1932 in desert about 110 km south of Dakhleh, 24° 30′ N, 28° 58′ E.

44. Lanner Falcon – *Falco biarmicus tanypterus*. RB
This species was observed during October-December 1978–1980; in January 1982; between late September, 1982 to mid-January, 1983; and every season to 1987. Goodman *et al.* (1986) observed two at Ezbet Zayat, on March 24, 1984. Also, it is probably resident at Bir Tarfawi, where it was observed between February 19 and April 11, 1927 (Moreau 1928).

In 1987, Hollett saw one immature bird captured and caged just south of Masara, for eventual resale to Saudis. A nesting pair, NE of Bashendi, was observed agressively defending their nest on February 23, 1988 and again observed in February, 1992.

45. Saker – *Falco cherrug*. AV
One possible sighting of two birds on November 28, 1980.

(46.) Barbary Falcon – *Falco pelegrinoides*. AV?
Meinertzhagen (1930, 370) records that "Falcons, probably [*F. peregrinus pelegrinoides*] were seen in Dakhla Oasis, where they are said to be resident." No details are given and the birds may well have been Lanner Falcons.

47. Quail – *Coturnix coturnix* (1). PV
Three birds seen on January 15, 1987 near Ezbet Bashendi, three on March 1, 1987 near Balat, and two on March 10, 1988 at Lake Mut. Moreau (1927) noted occasional birds at Umar Seraya and near Mut between April 10 and 13, 1925. Moreau (1927–28, tab. I) noted 'a few' birds at both 'Dakhleh' and

'Baharia' and, with C.S. Davis, that they were abundant in Kharga, and that H.J.L. Beadnell had noted 'a number including many dead' at 'Bir Tarfawi, 150 Miles (240 km) S. W. of Kharga' during the spring. During the autumn he noted 'a few' at 'Baharia', reported by Abdel Gawad Eff Adel Samad, and 'a few' at Kharga reported by the local inhabitants. A single male road kill was obtained on March 2, 1989, near Oulad Abdullah, southwest of Teneida. Goodman *et al.* (1986) record six to eight birds at Ezbet Zayat on March 24, 1984.

(48.) Water Rail – *Rallus aquaticus aquaticus*. PV

Scharlau (1963) recorded this species between October 2 and 4, 1962.

49. Moorhen – *Gallinula chloropus chloropus*. WV, RB

First recorded on January 26, 1982, when at least 200 birds were seen, and between late September, 1982 and mid-January, 1983, when they were numerous, all on Lake Mut. Goodman *et al.* (1986) record at least ten individuals on April 24, 1981, that may have been breeding on Lake Mut. It is likely that, as for the Little Grebe, their numbers have declined since 1982, but it appears to be a regular winter visitor to the oasis.

50. Purple Gallinule – *Porphyrio porphyrio*. AV

One bird observed dead in desert 25 km south of Teneida in 1987.

51. Coot – *Fulica atra atra*. WV, RB?

At least 1500 Coots were present on Lake Mut on January 26, 1982; and between late September, 1982, and mid-January, 1983, about 1000 were observed on Lakes Mut and Qalamun. More than 200 were observed on Lake Mut on February 21, 1986. Only 12 birds were seen on Lake Mut on January 23, 1987. Goodman *et al.* (1986) saw ten birds on Lake Mut on April 24, 1981. Meinertzhagen (1930) saw birds with nesting material during March. The recent reduction in numbers from 1000–1500 to less than 100 may parallel that of Little Grebe and Moorhen, with a permanent winter population numbering in the tens being established. On March 10, 1988, no coots were observed at Lake Mut, possibly because the wintering population had already departed.

52. Crane – *Grus grus grus*. PV

Large numbers of cranes were seen heading north during March, 1986. More than 150 were seen flying south in October, 1978 (Goodman *et al.* 1986, erroneously place this sighting in Kharga). One flock of 110 birds was seen flying north on February 28, 1987 and a second uncounted flock on March 1, 1987. Five or six flocks of between 15 and 35 birds were observed crossing the oasis depression west of Teneida and east of Ismant during early March, 1988. Moreau (1927, 241) noted that "immense numbers pass by way of Dakhleh in the spring, flying due north" and that "Jarvis has seen the sky `practically grey with them' and a thousand more walking about the bare desert." Moreau (1928) further reported a flock of several hundred west of Bir Tarfawi on March 8, 1927. O.C. Wingate (1934, 305) reported on 3 March, 1933, about 80 miles (128 km) west of Dakhla, "birds, flying in a perfect wedge-shaped formation about 20′ [6 m] above the surface of the desert. [By the] heavy flapping of great wings I knew them for crested cranes ... The direction of their flight ... was almost exactly that of 'Uweinat, continued to the north it meets the west branch of the Nile Delta at the coast [at Alexandria]. ... They had certainly not come from the Nile Valley." Moreau

(1967) also reported several hundred seen in the spring of 1927, 320 km west of Dakhleh.

(53.) Demoiselle Crane – *Anthropoides virgo*. PV

Moreau (1927) reports that D. Wallace saw this species in the oasis, and later (1967) reported a flock passing overhead during the spring of 1965.

(54.) Houbara Bustard – *Chlamydotis undulata undulata*. RB?

Meinertzhagen (1930) reported that this bird was absent from Dakhleh during the winter, reappeared in the spring, and apparently bred on the desert fringe. This is unconfirmed.

55. Black-winged Stilt – *Himantopus himantopus himantopus*. FB

Seen at Lake Mut in early October, 1982, and again about 20 on March 10, 1988. Goodman *et al.* (1986) saw six to eight birds on Lake Mut between March 22 and 23, 1984, and 20 on Lake Mut on September 7, 1984. Moreau (1927) saw six birds south of Umar Seraya on April 12, 1925.

56. Avocet – *Recurvirostra avosetta*. PV, WV

Three birds were seen on Lake Mut on October 27, 1980, and five in mid-October, 1982. Moreau (1927) cited D. Wallace who reported winter records from Umar Seraya.

(57.) Collared Pratincole – *Glareola pratincola pratincola*. PV

Goodman *et al.* (1986) saw a group of eight birds near Ezbet Zayat, and about 40 at Lake Mut on April 24, 1981.

58. Little-Ringed Plover – *Charadrius dubius curonicus*. PV, WV

Two birds were seen at Lake Mut on February 21, 1986 and another two on March 8, 1987. Goodman *et al.* (1986) observed one bird on April 24, 1981, at Lake Mut; several more were seen in mid-October,1982. Single immature female and male birds were taken on January 20, 1972 by the Palearctic Migrant Survey (Goodman *et al.* 1986).

59. Ringed Plover – *Charadrius hiaticula*. PV, WV

Occasionally observed in January and February, 1985, and in mid-October, 1982, at Lake Mut. Also on March 22, 1984, at Lake Qalamun (Goodman *et al.* 1986).

(60.) Kentish Plover – *Charadrius alexandrinus alexandrinus*. RB?, PV

Goodman *et al.* (1986) record five to ten birds at Lake Mut on March 22, 1984.

(61.) Caspian Plover – *Charadrius asiaticus*. AV

Goodman *et al.* (1986) observed two birds at Lake Mut on April 24, 1981, one in breeding and one in winter plumage. It is an occasional visitor to Egypt (Goodman and Watson 1983).

62. Spur-Winged Plover – *Hoplopterus spinosus*. RB?, (PV)

Three birds seen on October 20, 1980 at Mut.

63. White-Tailed Plover – *Chattusia leucura*. WV?, (PV)

Nine birds seen at lake Mut on December 2, 1992 and probably 20 seen flying in a flock over this lake. This is the first record of this species in the Western Desert. Riad (1995a) records seeing six birds in Dakhleh Oasis on March 23–24, 1993 and 15 in March, 1995.

64. Lapwing – *Vanellus vanellus*. PV, WV

One bird seen at Teneida in late December, 1982 and six in mid-January, 1983, near Lake Mut.

(65.) Little Stint – *Calidris minuta*. PV

Goodman *et al.* (1986) observed 30 birds on April 24 and 25, 1981, and collected one bird from a flock of 40 on Lake Mut on March 22, 1984. Scharlau (1963) recorded about 250 birds between October 2 and 4, 1962.

(66.) Temminck's Stint – *Calidris temmincki*. PV

Goodman *et al.* (1986) saw at least 15 birds on April 24, 1981. Scharlau (1963) noted about 30 birds between October 2–4, 1962.

(67.) Curlew Sandpiper – *Calidris ferruginea*. PV

Goodman *et al.* (1986) saw five birds at Lake Mut on April 24, 1981, and Scharlau (1963) saw one between October 2 and 4, 1962.

(68.) Dunlin – *Calidris alpina*. PV

Goodman *et al.* (1986) record it on September 7, 1984, near Lake Mut.

(69.) Ruff – *Philomachus pugnax*. PV

Goodman *et al.* (1986) saw six birds on April 5, 1981, and Scharlau (1963) observed about 15 between April 2–4, 1961.

(70.) Jack Snipe – *Lymnocryptes minimus*. PV

Meinertzhagen (1930) records this species for Dakhleh during March, but without details.

(71.) Snipe – *Gallinago gallinago gallinago*. PV

Meinertzhagen (1930) records many hundreds in mid-March and Scharlau (1963) saw about eight between October 2–4, 1962.

(72.) Black-tailed Godwit – *Limosa limosa limosa*. PV

A dehydrated specimen was found at Bir Tarfawi (Moreau 1928).

73. Spotted Redshank – *Tringa erythropus*. PV, WV

Three were observed on January 25, 1982, and Goodman *et al.* (1986) saw ten on April 24, 1981, and others on September 7, 1984.

74. Redshank – *Tringa totanus*. PV, WV

Two birds were seen on January 22, 1982, and others between mid-October, 1982, and late January, 1983, near lakes Mut and Qalamun, and regularly at Lake Mut from 1984–1988. Goodman *et al.* (1986) noted two birds on April 24, 1981. Five birds were seen at Lake Mut on March 10, 1988.

75. Marsh Sandpiper – *Tringa stagnatilis*. PV, WV

One bird seen at Lake Mut on December 1, 1978; others in mid-October, 1982. Goodman *et al.* (1986) saw three near Qalamun on March 22, 1984.

76. Greenshank – *Tringa nebularia*. PV, WV

Seen during late September, 1982, to late January, 1983. Goodman *et al.* (1986) saw five birds on April 24, 1981.

(77.) Green Sandpiper – *Tringa ochropus*. PV, WV

Al Hussaini (1959) considered this species a winter visitor to the oasis, Scharlau (1963) recorded about ten birds between October 2–4, 1962, and Goodman *et al.* (1986) saw 12–14 on March 22, 1984 at Lake Mut.

(78.) Wood Sandpiper – *Tringa glareola*. PV

Scharlau (1963) saw about ten birds between October 2–4, 1962. Goodman *et al.* (1986) saw five birds on April 28, 1981.

79. Common Sandpiper – *Actitis hypoleucos*. PV, WV

Two birds were seen on January 26, 1982, at Lake Mut, and six at Lake Mut on February 21, 1986. Goodman *et al.* (1986) record about 30 on April 24, 1981, at Lake Mut.

80. Black-headed Gull – *Larus ridibundus*. PV, WV

Four birds were seen on November 6, 1981; 15 on January 16, 1982; six between late September, 1982, and mid-January, 1983; 15 on January 23, 1987; 10 on February 15, 1987; and 20+ on March 10, 1988, all at Lake Mut. Some of the last were in breeding plumage. Another in winter plumage was seen on January 23, 1986, at Lake Mut. Goodman *et al.* (1986) record two birds on April 25, 1981.

81. Common Tern – *Sterna hirundo*. AV

Five birds were seen at Lake Mut on January 23, 1987. Goodman *et al.* (1986) saw 20 on September 7, 1984, at Lake Mut.

(82.) Whiskered Tern – *Chlidonias hybridus hybridus*. PV

Scharlau (1963) saw three birds between October 2–4, 1962, and Goodman *et al.* (1986) saw 12 on April 24, 1981.

(83.) White-winged Black Tern – *Chlidonias leucopterus*. PV

Scharlau (1963) observed three between October 2–4, 1962. Goodman *et al.* (1986) saw about 80 at Lake Mut on April 25, 1981.

84. Spotted Sandgrouse – *Pterocles senegallus*. RB

This bird was fairly common during the winters of 1978–88. An uncatalogued pair, collected on January 30, 1959, is deposited at Ain Shams University, and a female was collected on January 17, 1972 (USNM 551083) (Goodman *et al.* 1986). Goodman *et al.* (1986) saw six at Ezbet Zayat, where Meinertzhagen (1930, 518) stated that they 'can always be met with.' It may be considered resident in the area.

85. Rock Pigeon – *Columba livia dakhlae*. RB

From October-December, 1978–82, and January to March, 1983–88, this species was observed daily, and numbers seemed to increase towards the middle of March, 1987. Goodman *et al.* (1986) examined four specimens (USNM 551084–551087), all with very pale plumage typical of the subspecies. Interbreeding with local domestic pigeons appears minimal. Meinertzhagen (1930) restricts *C. l. dakhlae* to Dakhla and Kharga oases, but those at Farafra and Barhariya oases are subspecifically undetermined. Observed roosting on the crests of the escarpment above Maohoub in winter, 1980, above el-Aweina in winter, 1982, and north of Bashendi in winter, 1986. The latter flock of about 30 birds was uniformly coloured with dark outer wings and tail fans, and light grey to almost white, bodies and inner wings.

86. Turtle Dove – *Streptopelia turtur*. MB, PV, WV

This bird has been observed throughout the oasis from 1978 to 1988. They seemed commoner in 1987 and could be observed daily around Bashendi. Goodman *et al.* (1986) noted it as common on October 18, 1980; saw a few on April 24, 1981; and on March 24, 1984. Eight birds were seen on March 24, 1984 at Ezbet Zayat, including USNM 206927. Adult males with enlarged testes were collected on January 16, 1972 (USNM 551092) and March 24, 1984 (USNM 206927) from Ezbet Zayat and are referrable to *S. t. rufescens*.

87. Palm or Laughing Dove – *Streptopelia senegalensis aegyptiaca*. RB

Seen nesting at el-Aweina on January 13, 1981, and frequently observed between late September, 1982, and mid-January, 1983. It is a common breeding resident and nests were found around Bashendi on January 30, February 4 and 6, 1987. Meinertzhagen (1930) located two nests in March, 1928. Goodman *et al.* (1986) consider the subspecies *dakhlae* synonymous with *aegyptiaca*, following Vaurie (1965).

(88.) Barn Owl – *Tyto alba alba.* RB?

Meinertzhagen (1930) regarded this bird as resident in the oasis, but no substantiation then or since is known. Its occurrence in the Western Desert requires verification.

(89.) Eagle Owl – *Bubo bubo ascalaphus.* RB?

Meinertzhagen collected two specimens (BMNH 1965. M.5057–8) taken on March 25 and 27, 1928 (Goodman *et al.* 1986).

90. Little Owl – *Athene noctua.* RB

Regularly seen or heard from mid-September to mid-March 1978–98, and breeding in late February to early March. Goodman *et al.* (1986) observed at least five at different localities and collected a specimen (USNM 551131) on January 15, 1972.

91. Egyptian Nightjar – *Caprimulgus aegyptius.* MB?

Individuals seen on October 18, 1978 and in late January, 1984. Scharlau (1963) saw about 60 between October 2–4, 1962. The subspecies in Dakhleh may be either *aegyptius* or *saharae*.

92. Pallid Swift – *Apus pallidus.* PV, RB

Regularly seen between late September, 1982 and mid-January, 1983 and during January-March, 1984 to 1988. Scharlau (1963) saw about 100 birds between October 2–4, 1962, and Goodman *et al.* (1986) saw several on April 25, 1981. Goodmann and Watson (1983) identified a female taken on January 16, 1972 as *A. p. brehmorum*. Meinertzhagen (1930) considered this species resident and breeding in earth cliffs.

93. Blue-cheeked Bee-eater–*Merops superciliosus persicus.* PV

Observed in flocks of more than 100 on March 10 and 11, 1986, and a smaller flock on March 15, 1987 at Bashendi. Moreau (1927) observed several between April 10 and 13, 1925.

94. Bee-eater – *Merops apiaster.* PV

Schlarlau (1963) saw two birds between October 2–4, 1962, and Goodman *et al.* (1986) saw several flocks on April 24 and 25, 1981. A. J. Mills has noted flocks every year (1979–1996) in March, which do not stay long in the oasis.

(95.) Roller – *Coracias garrulus garrulus.* PV

Meinertzhagen collected a specimen (BMNH 1965.M.5998) on March 25, 1928, Scharlau (1963) saw a bird between October 2 and 4, 1962, and Goodman *et al.* (1986) another on April 25, 1981.

96. Hoopoe – *Upupa epops.* RB, PV

Commonly observed daily during November-December, 1978 to 1982, and January-March, 1983 to 1998. One bird was seen at Bashendi carrying nesting materials on February 6, 1987. Goodman *et al.* (1986) saw several pairs on April 25, 1981. *U. e. epops* is a passage migrant throughout the Western Desert and *U. e. major* is the presumed resident in the oasis (Goodman *et al.* 1986).

(97.) Wryneck – *Jynx torquilla torquilla.* PV

Moreau (1927) saw several at 'Abar Meihub' (= Maohoub) between April 10 and 13, 1925.

(98.) Bar-tailed Desert Lark – *Ammomanes cincturus arenicolor.* RB?

Meinertzhagen (1930) noted that it had been observed in the desert between Dakhleh and Kharga oases, but gives no confirmatory information.

99. Desert Lark – *Ammomanes deserti.* RB

Seen on October 18, 1978, and six were seen at Sheikh Mabrouk on February 9, 1987. Goodman *et al.* (1986) reported this species on October 18, 1980. Meinertzhagen (1930) stated that it was abundant, but Goodman *et al.* (1986) failed to find it in 1981.

100. Hoopoe Lark – *Alaemon alaudipes alaudipes.* RB

Common throughout the oasis from late September to mid-January, 1978–98. Goodman *et al.* (1986) saw five, three of which were singing and presumably males on breeding territories.

(101.) Short-toed Lark – *Calandrella brachydactyla.* PV

Meinertzhagen (1930) noted it as a passage migrant through the oasis and Goodman *et al.* (1986) saw five resting in the desert, halfway between 'Asyut' (= Assiyut) and Kharga on April 22, 1981.

(102.) Crested Lark – *Galerida cristata altirostris.* RB?

Goodman *et al.* (1986) noted it on September 7, 1985.

103. Sand Martin – *Riparia riparia.* PV

Frequently seen in late autumn 1982, but seen infrequently in 1987 and 1988. Moreau (1927) noted 'numbers' at 'Abar Meihub' (= Maohoub) between April 10–13, 1925 and Goodman *et al.* (1986) saw a few in April 24–25, 1981. Many nesting holes are visible in old coppice dunes, tabular dune sections and yardangs, and in other cut-bank deposits suitable for its nesting burrows.

104. Pale Crag or Rock Martin – *Ptyonoprogne obsoleta obsoleta.* RB

Observed on January 23, 1982. Moreau (1927) found a few breeding birds at Mut and Qasr in mid-April, 1925, Scharlau (1963) saw it between October 2–4, 1962, and Goodman *et al.* (1986) saw it on April 25, 1981.

105. Swallow – *Hirundo rustica.* PV, WV

Regularly seen during October-December, 1978–80, but only a few birds present in January, 1982. One bird seen on March 15, 1987 at Bashendi, and two on March 10, 1988 at Lake Mut. Goodman *et al.* (1986) saw small numbers on April 24, 1981. The form recorded in Dakhleh is light-breasted, either *H. r. rustica* or *H. r. transitiva*.

(106.) Red-rumped Swallow – *Hirundo daurica rufola.* PV

Meinertzhagen (1930) recorded many hundreds within mixed flocks of Swallows and House Martins in late March, 1928.

(107) House Martin – *Delichon urbica urbica.* PV

Meinertzhagen (1930) noted it as very common in late March, 1928, in mixed flocks of Swallows and House Martins, and Goodman *et al.* (1986) saw small numbers on April 24, 1981.

108. Tawny Pipit – *Anthus campestris campestris.* PV

Two birds were observed on February 8, 1987, at Bashendi, and again on March 1, 1987, near Balat. Goodman *et al.* (1986) saw eight at Ezbet Zayat on March 24, 1984, and collected one (UMMZ 206884).

109. Meadow Pipit – *Anthus pratensis pratensis*. WV
Two birds were seen on January 15, 1982 near Aweina; 25 on January 30, 1987, in Bashendi; a single bird on March 3, 1987, in Balat; and another on March 10, 1988 at Lake Mut.

110. Red-throated Pipit – *Anthus cervinus*. PV, WV
One bird observed on November 28, 1981 at Aweina. Goodman *et al*. (1986) saw about 15 on April 26, 1981, along the Dakhleh-Farafra Road, and a flock of about 40 at Qalamun on March 22, 1984. Male and female specimens (USNM 551762–3) were taken on January 16, 1972 (Goodman *et al*. 1986).

111. Wagtail – *Motacilla flava pygmaea*. RB?
Two birds seen at Lake Qalamun on February 17, 1984.

112. Yellow Wagtail – *Motacilla flava feldegg*. PV
A single bird of this Balkan and Black Sea subspecies was seen at close range at Lake Mut on March 3, 1987. Either six or seven birds or a single bird followed us on March 10, 1988 at Lake Mut. Scharlau (1963) reported about 100 birds each day for October 2 to 4, 1962. Subspecies of *M. flava* are migrant in the Western Desert, except *pygmaea* (Meinertzhagen 1930), and Scharlau's records may refer to *M. f. flava*, *thunbergi*, or *feldegg* (Vaurie 1959).

113. White Wagtail – *Motacilla alba alba*. PV, WV
Seen frequently throughout the oasis from late September to December, 1978–1982, and from January to March, 1983–1988. Scharlau (1963) saw one bird on October 2, ten on October 3, and 15 on October 4, 1962. Goodman *et al*. (1986) noted small numbers on April 24 and 25, 1981.

114. Rufous Bush Robin or Bush Chat – *Cercotrichas galactotes galactotes*. MB, PV, (WV)
One bird was seen on January 16, 1982 and two on March 8, 1987 at Lake Mut. Meinertzhagen (1930) considered it a common summer visitor, Kiepenheuer and Linsenmair (1965) saw many between August 10–14, 1963, and Goodman *et al*. (1986) noted single birds on March 22, 1984, at Lake Mut, and others singing near Mushiya, and at Ezbet Zayat on March 24, 1984.

(115.) Nightingale – *Luscinia megarhynchos megarhynchos*. PV
Moreau (1927) noted individuals on April 10 and 11, 1925.

116. Bluethroat – *Luscinia svecica*. PV, WV
One male seen on January 14 and 15, 1982, and another in mid-January, 1983; one female was seen on March 8, 1987 at Mut. Two males (USNM 551493–551494) collected on January 19, 1972 cannot be assigned to subspecies, either *L. sveccia volgae* (=*occidentalis* of Meinertzhagen 1930) or *cyanecula* (Goodman *et al*. 1986).

117. Black Redstart – *Phoenicurus ochrurus*. WV
One male seen almost daily from January 9 to 17, 1985 and another on February 6, 1987 at Bashendi.

(118.) Redstart – *Phoenicurus phoenicurus*. PV
Scharlau (1963) saw six birds on October 2 and a pair on October 3, 1962. Goodman *et al*. (1986) saw a bird on April 15, 1981.

(119.) Whinchat – *Saxicola rubetra*. PV
Scharlau (1963) saw one bird on October 3 and 12 on October 4, 1962.

120. Stonechat – *Saxicola torquata torquata*. WV
One bird was seen on January 14, 1982, near Aweina. Al Hussaini (1959) collected specimens from the oasis.

121. Isabelline Wheatear – *Oenanthe isabellina*. PV, WV
Two birds were seen on February 19, 1986, at Bashendi. Goodman *et al*. (1986) noted it on October 19, 1980, reported a female (USNM 551409) taken on January 19, 1972, and an unsexed bird (UMMZ 206881) on March 22, 1984.

122. Wheatear – *Oenanthe oenanthe oenanthe*. PV
Recorded on February 19 and 25, 1986, a single male seen at Bashendi on January 16, 1987, and another on January 19, 1988 between Bashendi and Teneida. Moreau (1934) reported that the Bagnold Expedition shot one bird from a flock about 160 km southwest of Dakhleh, 24° 20′ N, 28° 45′ E, on October 3, 1932, and Goodman *et al*. (1986) saw several individuals on April 25, 1981.

(123.) Black-eared Wheatear – *Oenanthe hispanica melanoleuca*. PV
Moreau (1927) saw several between April 10–12, 1925, and Scharlau (1963) saw a male between October 2–4, 1962. Goodman *et al*. (1986) saw one at Ezbet Zayat on March 24, 1984.

124. Desert Wheatear – *Oenanthe deserti deserti*. PV, WV, RB?
Not uncommon between late September, 1982 and mid-January, 1983. It was seen regularly during January-March, 1987, at Bashendi, when it seemed to be much more common than in previous years. Goodman *et al*. (1986) saw two on April 25, 1981. Meinertzhagen (1930) collected two males and a female (BMNH M.11935–11937) on March 27, 1928, that he assigned to *O. d. atrogularis*, but Goodman *et al*. (1986), using size and plumage colour characters (Vaurie 1959) assigned them to *O. d. deserti*.

125. White-crowned Black Wheatear – *Oenanthe leucopyga leucopyga*. RB
Regularly observed between late September and mid-January, 1978–98. Birds seen nesting at 'Ein Tirghi and at Ismant el-Kharab in late March, 1987. Meinertzhagen (1930) found eggs in late March, 1928, and Goodman *et al*. (1986) noted a few birds on April 25, 1981.

126. Sedge Warbler – *Acrocephalus schoenobaenus schoenbaenus*. PV
One bird was seen at Lake Qalamun on March 5, 1986. A male (UMMZ 206865) was taken at Lake Mut on March 22, 1984 (Goodman *et al*. 1986).

(127.) Reed Warbler – *Acrocephalus scirpaceus scirpaceus*. PV
Goodman *et al*. (1986) observed a small number on April 24, 1981.

128. Clamorous Reed Warbler – *Acrocephalus stentoreus stentoreus*. RB
Frequently observed in the reeds fringing Lake Mut, between 1982–1988, and is apparently ever more numerous since 1982. Goodman *et al*. (1986) found at least ten breeding birds on April 25, 1981, in reeds at Lake Mut near Bir Talata al-Mut. A singing male (UMMZ 206940) with enlarged testes was collected on March 22, 1984 (Goodman *et al*. 1986).

(129.) Olivaceous Warbler – *Hippolais pallida*. MB?, PV
Scharlau (1963) saw two birds between October 2–4, 1962. Goodman *et al.* (1986) record this species as not uncommon and possibly breeding on April 24, 1981. A male (UMMZ 206944), collected on March 22, 1984, is referred to *H. p. elaeica* (Goodman *et al.* 1986).

(130.) Icterine Warbler – *Hippolais icterina*. PV
Scharlau (1963) saw six between October 2–4, 1962. A male (BMNH 1965.M.13678) was collected on March 26, 1928, by R.E. Meinertzhagen (Goodman *et al.* 1986).

(131.) Subalpine Warbler – *Sylvia cantillans albistriata*. PV
Goodman *et al.* (1986) saw a group of seven at Lake Mut on March 22, 1984, and collected a male (UMMZ 206854).

(132.) Sardinian Warbler – *Sylvia melanocephala*. PV, WV
A dead specimen was recovered in December, 1979, and the species has been regularly recorded from reed-beds and tamarisk in the oasis during the winters of 1980–1988, and subsequently.

(133.) Rüppell's Warbler – *Sylvia rueppelli*. PV
Scharlau (1963) saw one bird between October 2–4, 1962, and Goodman *et al.* (1986) saw six on March 22, 1984 at Lake Mut.

134. Lesser Whitethroat – *Sylvia curruca curruca*. PV, WV
Six birds were seen on January 15, 1982. Goodman *et al.* (1986) saw one at Ezbet Zayat on March 24, 1984.

135. Common Whitethroat – *Sylvia communis communis*. PV
Recorded in early October 1982 and by Goodman *et al.* (1986) on March 22, 1984.

(136.) Bonelli's Warbler – *Phylloscopus bonelli orientalis*. PV
Moreau (1927) reported several seen at 'Abar Meihub' (= Maohoub) between April 10 and 13, 1925.

(137.) Wood Warbler – *Phylloscopus sibilatrix*. PV
Moreau (1934) reported that the Bagnold Expedition collected this species on October 2, 1932, at 25° 15′ N, 30° 10′ E, between Dakhleh and Kharga oases, and at 24° 20′ N, 29° 30′ E, 96 km south of Dakhleh. Goodman *et al.* (1986) saw one bird in Dakhleh on April 24, 1981.

138. Chiffchaff – *Phylloscopus collybita*. PV, WV
Seen on November 28, 1980; in January 1982; regularly between late September, 1982, and mid-January 1983; and January-March, 1984–1988. The subspecies *collybita* and *abietinus* are both winter visitors to Egypt from late September to late April or early May (Meinertzhagen 1930).

(139.) Willow Warbler – *Phylloscopus trochilus trochilus*. PV,
A specimen collected between Kharga and Dakhleh on August 13, 1963 was identified by Steinbacher (1965) as *P. t. trochilus*. Goodman *et al.* (1986) saw this species in the oasis on October 19, 1980.

(140.) Spotted Flycatcher – *Muscicapa striata*. PV
Moreau (1934) records one collected on October 3, (1932?) about 160 km south of Dakhleh, 24° 20′ N, 28° 45′ E and Goodman *et al.* (1986) note the species in the oasis in early October, 1982.

(141.) Pied Flycatcher – *Ficedula hypoleuca hypoleuca*. PV
Moreau (1927) saw a male at 'Abar Meihub' (= Maohoub) between April 10 and 13, 1925.

(142.) Golden Oriole – *Oriolus oriolus oriolus*. PV
Scharlau (1963) saw a male between October 2–4, 1962.

(143.) Isabelline Shrike – *Lanius collurio isabellinus*. AV
Moreau (1934) reported a specimen 'shot from a party' at 25° 06′ N, 29° 30′ E, about 96 km south of Dakhleh, on October 2, 1932 and another on October 3, 1932, at 25° 50′ N, 27° 41′ E, between Gebel Uweinat and Dakhleh, both by the Bagnold Expedition.

(144.) Red-backed Shrike – *Lanius collurio collurio*. PV
Scharlau (1963) saw three birds between October 2–4, 1962.

(145.) Great Grey Shrike – *Lanius excubitor*. RB?, WV?
Moreau (1927) recorded a bird at Rashda during April 10–13, 1925.

146. Woodchat Shrike – *Lanius senator*. PV
Seen at 'Ein Birbiyeh on March 5, 1986. Goodman *et al.* (1986) record a bird on March 24, 1984, at Ezbet Zayat, and Meinertzhagen (1930) records the species as a spring migrant.

(147.) Masked Shrike – *Lanius nubicus*. PV
Goodman *et al.* (1986) saw a male on April 24, 1981.

148. Brown-necked Raven – *Corvus ruficollis ruficollis*. RB
Seen daily and sometimes in fairly large numbers between late September, 1982, and mid-January, 1983. A single flock of about 30 was seen between Balat and Bashendi on January 30, 1988. Also a pair was seen regularly collecting nesting materials at 'Ein Birbeyeh during March, 1987. Meinertzhagen (1930) stated that it nests in palm trees in the oasis and in nearby cliffs.

149. House Sparrow – *Passer domesticus niloticus*. RB
One seen at Bashendi on January 17, 1985, and 20 at Balat on March 5, 1986. Goodman *et al.* (1986) record small numbers on October 18, 1980, and April 24, 1981.

(150.) Spanish Sparrow – *Passer hispaniolensis hispaniolensis*. PV, WV
Meinertzhagen (1930) noted that several had been observed at Dinaria during March 1928 and Al Hussaini (1959) considered it a winter visitor to the oasis.

151. Goldfinch – *Carduelis carduelis niediecki*. RB
A flock of nine was seen between Bashendi and Teneida on January 11, 1984, 12–15 on January 17, 1985, eight on January 12, 1987, and four on January 19, 1988, all in the same area. One bird was seen at 'Ein Birbiyeh on February 26, 1987.

152. Linnet – *Carduelis cannabina*. PV
A flock of about 30 was observed feeding near Balat on March 1, 1987, and about 50 birds, seen at the same locality on March 3, 1987.

153. Trumpeter Finch – *Bucanetes githagineus*. RB
First seen at 'Ein Tirghi on February 3, 1987, and seen regularly until early March. Six were seen on February 5, 1987, with one carrying nesting material. A single male was seen at Balat on March 1, 1987. Breeding pairs have been observed annually nesting in the small rocky outcrops in the desert areas peripheral to the eastern oasis. Moreau (1927) observed one bird between April 10 and 13, 1925, at Teneida and Meinertzhagen (1930) listed it as resident.

Domestic Fowl

1. White-fronted Goose – *Anser albifrons*.

Domestic geese are common in all villages in the oasis. They resemble in many details and size those depicted as early as Old Kingdom Pharaonic times, e.g mural from the tomb of Nofermaat and Itet at Meidum (Wilkinson 1983, fig. 1) which was on display in the Cairo Museum (CG 1742)(see also Houlihan 1986). The birds have orange-red bills, with the males having a white band at the base of the bill that extends slightly more towards the top of the head than below. The eyes are dark and not outlined. The neck is brown and lined above body level and speckled at the base. The breast is transversely barred with variably arranged bars of brown, white and black. The wing coverts and secondaries are uniform mauvey-grey, with black pinions. The venter and underside of the tail are white and the dorsum of the tail is grey in males and light or medium brown in females. The legs are orange-red, similar to the bills, with dark brown or black claws.

2. Duck – *Anas platyrhynchos*.

Domestic ducks are not as common as geese, perhaps because geese are better able to care for themselves and ward off the local village dogs or wild foxes and jackals. Those that have been noted are generally splotched black and white, with the black predominantly on the dorsal areas. There is a carbuncular red base to the bill around the upper nostrils.

3. Chicken – *Gallus gallus*.

Common even in the smallest and poorest villages, and usually free-ranging, although chicken-farms are presently operated at Balat and Mut for eggs and meat for sale. Roman age fowls are smaller than any normal modern European breed of chicken and similar in size to the medieval European hens except that they differ in the shape of the rostrum, on evidence from Roman 3rd Century midden remains from Ismant el-Kharab (= Kellis). The free-ranging chickens of the oasis are similar in size to those of Roman times.

4. Turkey – *Meleagris gallopavo*.

Present in most villages. Large, grey or mottled birds, similar to the Mexican wild type.

5. Pigeon – *Columba livia*.

Commonly free ranging within villages and farm lands, and nesting in niches in walls or on house roofs. Colouration highly variable, from pure white to almost entirely black, with varied patterns.

Discussion of Ornithological Observations

Scharlau (1963) noted 55 species of birds in Dakhleh Oasis in 1962. Goodman *et al.* (1986) listed 144 species as possible visitors, migrants, winter residents or breeding residents in the oasis. Of these, most are passage or winter visitors and only 28 breed there regularly. The record of 152 species in this list reflects the longer periods that both of us were able to remain in the oasis: probably a full record will only be possible when a year-round observations are possible but, even then, vagrant birds will obscure the true migrants and visitors.

The gradual extension of cultivation, reclamation of shifting dune land and other land suitable for irrigation because of increased water supplies from deep-drilled wells has extended all habitats, especially the rupestrine, marsh and lakeside biomes, and this is reflected in the increased number of species of waterbirds and great increases in the numbers of individuals. As these numbers may increase because of continued expansion of the water supplies and the ecologically available resources, it may be reflected in increased numbers of predators to prey on the increased avian population.

The single most important ecological change was the creation of Lake Mut, followed by Lake Qalamun nearby, with the resultant increase in water fowl to feed on the algal and littoral plant food and on the introduced tilapia. In March, 1988, the presence of brine shrimp (*Artemia salina*) was noted in large numbers in the sheltered shallows of the lake, and this may allow greater flamingo (*Phoenicopterus ruber*) to visit the oasis for short periods. Subsequent visits to Lake Mut have recorded the continuing presence of the shrimp, but in much reduced numbers.

MAMMALOGICAL OBSERVATIONS

Osborn and Helmy (1980) list the present terrestrial mammalian fauna of Egypt and Sinai and Qumsiyeh (1985) the Chiroptera as far is known from present records and specimens. We have obtained specimens by trapping, recorded sightings of small mammals, and noted trackways present in the areas in which we have resided, e.g., Maohoub, Gedida, Aweina and Bashendi. Most specimens comprise skins and skulls, although depredations by ants reduced some individuals to damaged skeletons and skeletons collected from the surrounding desert are incomplete. All specimens are deposited in the Royal Ontario Museum, Collection of Mammals, Toronto.

MAMMALIA: Annotated List of Wild Species

Insectivora

No records of either hedgehogs (*Hemiechinus auritus* or *Parechinus* spp.) or shrews (*Crocidura* spp. or *Suncus* spp.) are known from the Wadi el-Gedid (Osborn and Helmy 1980), of which Dakhleh Oasis is a part, nor have we any evidence for them in Dakhleh specifically. However, Wassif (1959a) noted that De Beaux (1932) obtained nine specimens of *Paraechinus deserti* from 'Cufra' Oasis. This is the only record of hedgehogs in an oasis.

Chiroptera

Large and a small bats have been observed flying at dusk over courtyards and open water tanks in the oasis.

Megachiroptera

1. Egyptian Fruit Bat – *Rousettus aegyptiacus*.

Two roosts of this megachiropteran were located in Qasr and one in Bashendi in 1989. One roost in Qasr was visited during February, 1990, and two male specimens obtained: both specimens are deposited in the Collection of Mammals, Royal Ontario Museum as ROM.M 97602 (skin and skeleton) and 97603 (alcoholic). One male (97602) was in breeding condition, and the other (97603) was possibly immature. These specimens are grey rather than reddish, as are most rousettine bats, including those in the Nile Valley and delta, but measurements on the skins of both and of the skull of the older male (97602) fit within ranges given by Qumsiyeh (1985) for males from the Nile populations (Churcher 1991). These specimens constitute the first records of megachiropteran bats in the oases of the Western Desert.

Microchiroptera

2. Trident Horseshoe or Leaf-Nosed Bat – *Asellia tridens tridens*

A single mandible of this bat was recovered from wall fill at locus 31/405 M5–1. Sightings of a small bat assumed to be *A. t. tridens* are common over water and courtyards in warm weather but no live specimens have been obtained.

Hoogstraal (1962) considers the Northeast African Trident Leaf-Nosed Bat (*Asellia t. tridens*) to be highly adapted to desert conditions, records it from Dakhleh, and states that it roosts in caves, tombs and behind the leaves of date palms. Gaisler *et al.* (1972) reviewed the bats recorded from Egypt and noted only *A. tridens* from Mut (Wassif 1949).

Other Microcheiropterans

The City of the Dead at Kharga Oasis has yielded *Otonycteris hemprichi* and *Rhinopoma hardwickei* is 'very common' (Wassif 1949). *O. hemprichi* was recorded from Siwa by Anderson (1902). Gaisler *et al.* (1972) note that *Rhinolophus mehelyi* and *Plecotus austriacus christei* are also found in the Western Desert.

Lagomorpha

3. Cape Hare – *Lepus capensis*.

A single sighting of a hare occurred at night in 1979 near Balat. Hoogstraal (1963) and Osborn and Helmy (1980) list no record of hare from the Wadi el-Gedid and the latter assign all hares in the Western Desert to *L. c. rothschildi*. Scattered and sparse remains of *Lepus* have been recovered from within the oasis. Some of these are undoubtedly more recent than those from archaeological sites, and derive from areas not associated with fossil vertebrate remains, suggesting that hares are widespread in the oasis, but probably not numerous.

Rodentia

4. Greater Gerbil – *Gerbillus pyramidium gedeedus*.

Nine specimens were obtained from cultivated lands and garden edges at Maohoub (82845 M; 1978), northwest of Gedida (84038 M; 1979), Bashendi (88168 M, 88169 M, 88170 F, 88173 M, 88175 F; 1982) and Aweina (87687 M, 87690 ?; 1982). Osborn and Helmy (1980) describe the greater gerbil in Wadi el-Gedid as a new subspecies, distinct from *G. p. pyramidium* of the Nile Valley, and recovered specimens from Maohoub in Dakhleh Oasis.

5. Large North African Dipodil – *Dipodillus campestris haymani*.

No specimen of this species has been obtained from Dakhleh Oasis, although dipodils with light, sandy pelage and little inflation of the anterodorsal margin of the meatus have been noted but assigned to *Dipodillus a. amoenus*. Osborn and Helmy (1980, fig. 45) plot one locality for *D. c. haymani* near Mut, but list (p. 153) Batras, in Farafra Oasis, as the only site in Wadi el-Gedid which has yielded specimens.

6. Charming Dipodil – *Dipodillus amoenus* amoenus.

Thirteen specimens have been obtained from sand dunes

with low vegetation at Maohoub (82844 M, 82847 F, 82848 M; 1979), in desert at Deir el-Haggar, south of Maohoub (82843 M; 1979), from garden edges at Gedida (84021 F, 84023 M, 84024 M, 84039 M, 84040 M; 1979), at Bir Talata on the south shore of Lake Mut, northwest of Mut (86151 M, 86153 M, 86155 M; 1980) and garden edges at Bashendi (88171 M; 1982). Osborn and Helmy (1980) record three localities for this subspecies in Dakhleh Oasis – south of Mut, and Gharb el-Maohoub and Bir el-Nokta, between Maohoub and Qasr.

(7.) Silky, Pallid or Sundevall's Jird – *Meriones crassus perpallidus*.

A single skull (93872; 1986) of this jird was recovered from Roman age deposits at Ismant el-Kharab, but is probably modern and intrusive. This is the first record of this species from Dakhleh Oasis, as Osborn and Helmy (1980) record it only from Abu Minqar, 170 km northwest of Maohoub on the Farafra road, and not within the Dakhleh Oasis Depression.

8. Grass or Field Rat, Nile Kusu – *Arvicanthis niloticus niloticus*.

One specimen (82849 M; 1978) of this rat was obtained from a garden edge near Maohoub. Osborn and Helmy (1980) record 13 specimens from Mut and one from Kharga.

(9.) Black or House Rat – *Rattus rattus*.

Osborn and Helmy (1980) record this species from Bulaq in Kharga Oasis and Abu Minqar. Because Dakhleh lies between these two localities, it may already be present in Dakhleh and its eventual detection is probable.

10. House Mouse – *Mus musculus praetextus*.

Nineteen specimens have been obtained from within dwellings and garden edges: Maohoub (88172 M; 1978: 82850 M; 1979), northwest of Gedida (84022 M; 1979), southeast of Qalamun (84033 F, 84034 M, 84035 M, 84036 M, 84037 F; 1979), Bir Talata on south shore of Lake Mut (86152 M, 86154 M, 86156 M; 1980), Aweina (87686 F, 87688 F, 87689 M; 1981), and Bashendi (88172 M, 88177 M, 88178 F, 88179 M, 88180 F; 1982). Osborn and Helmy (1980) record this subspecies from north of Mut, Bir el-Nokta, Gharb el-Maohoub, and also from Abu Minqar. This mouse is also present in Baharia and Kharga (Wassif 1959a, b) and Siwa (Hoogstraal 1963).

11. Egyptian Spiny Mouse – *Acomys cahirinus helmyi*.

Twenty-two specimens have been obtained from cultivated areas, garden edges and fence lines throughout the oasis: near Maohoub (82846 M, 82851 M, 82852 M; 1978), southeast of Qalamun (84025 M, 84026 F, 84027 M, 84028 M, 84029 M, 84030 F, 84031 F, 84032 M; 1979), Aweina (87680 F, 87681 F, 87682 M, 87683 M, 87684 M, 87685 M, 87686 F, 87687 M;1981) and Bashendi (88167 F, 88174 M, 88176 M; 1982). Wassif (1959b) first recorded this mouse from Mut as *A. c. cahirinus*. Osborn and Helmy (1980) described specimens from south of Mut as *A. c. helmyi* n. subsp., presumably distinguishing it from *A. c. cahirinus* of Wassif (1959b) by its lighter colouring.

12. Lesser Jerboa – *Jaculus jaculus jaculus*.

A skull (101849, 1993) of this jerboa has been recovered from Romano-Byzantine deposits at Ismant el-Kharab (31/420 D6–1) where it is probably intrusive. Osborn and Helmy (1980) record this species from both Kharga and Dakhleh (Balat) oases but Hoogstraal (1963, 30) stated "Small scattered populations exist in oases of the Western Desert as far west as Siwa." This record confirms its occurence in central Dakhleh Oasis.

Carnivora

(13.) Egyptian Jackal – *Canis aureus lupaster*.

No specimens have been collected from the desert areas around the oasis, although sightings, scats and night-time vocalisations have been recorded, both within the oasis depression and on the Libyan Escarpment north of Balat. An individual was seen on February 15, 1987 on the south shore of Lake Mut. Osborn and Helmy (1980, 369) record the species from Dakhleh and note published records for Rashda and Mut. Inhabitants of the oasis refer to 'deeb' (wolf) and aver that such animals exist in the surrounding desert. No evidence of a canid the size of even the smallest true wolf has been observed in the region; this Arabic name for wolf is locally taken to refer to this animal, which is also called the wolf-jackal.

14. Egyptian Fox – *Vulpes vulpes aeqyptiaca*.

Fragmentary remains of this fox have been recovered from the barren areas near Maohoub (skull, jaw and partial postcranial, 94368; 1978), in the eastern portion of the oasis at 'Ein Duma, near Bashendi (skull, jaws and partial postcranial, 94354; 1987) and dead animals recovered as road kills from between Balat and Teneida in 1992. Foxes are commonly sighted throughout the oasis, usually on barren lands or near edges of cultivation in early morning or late evening, when they may be coming in to forage or for water. Records of sightings include Maohoub, Gedida, Aweina, Sheikh Muftah, between Ismant and the western margin of the eastern portion, Bashendi, Teneida and Sheikh Mabrouk. Osborn and Helmy (1980) record this fox at Mut, 'Asment' (= Ismant), Sheikh Wali (= El Sheikh Waly) and Balat. Hoogstraal (1964) gave no record of this fox for any oasis. This fox is common in Dakhleh and constitutes a widely distributed population, as witnessed by the numerous scats seen throughout the oasis and its surrounding desert.

(15.) Rüppell's Sand Fox – *Vulpes rueppelli rueppelli*.

Some of the remains, scats or sightings attributed to jackal or fox may represent this species. Osborn and Helmy (1980) record this fox only from Mut.

16. Fennec Fox – *Fennecus zerda*.

Fragmentary remains of a very small canid have been recovered from southeast of Maohoub, near Sheikh Mubaris' Tombs (32/390 I9–1/2 an isolated dentary from a lair about 2 km northeast of Bashendi on February 5, 1991, a damaged skull with longbones from Bir Talata el-Maohoub (32/390 D2–2) on March 4, 1993, and a complete dehydrated female from Bashendi on February 5, 1993. Osborn and Helmy (1980) record a specimen from Mut, a sighting at Qasr, and note a published record from Mut. Flower (1932) collated records of this fox from Dakhleh and Kharga oases.

(17.) Hyaena – *Hyaena hyaena dubbah*.

Osborn and Helmy (1980) cited a sighting from Mut, with observed tracks and a published record for Dakhleh Oasis. Another record, for Kharga, for which a £E 50.00 bounty was paid in 1981, was reported by Helmy to Osborn (pers. comm. to Churcher, 1988). However, extensive walking and climbing over the desert areas around the oasis, the Libyan Escarpment and the edge of the Libyan Plateau, investigations of rock shelters, clefts in the cliffs, and lairs have yielded few evidences (phosphate rich scats, bones, food remains, tracks, etc.) to substantiate this claim. Two probable hyaena lairs, one with much broken bone, were noted about 15 km southwest of Balat by M.R. Kleindienst and Churcher on February 1998. One of these yielded ass bones broken in the manner typical of hyaenas (A.J. Sutcliffe, 1998, pers. comm.) Inhabitants of the oasis continue to use 'dubbah', sometimes confused with 'deeb', to describe a large carnivore inhabiting the desert surrounding the oasis.

18. Jungle or Swamp Cat – *Felis chaus nilotica*.

Osborn and Helmy (1980) report two specimens obtained near Mut, indicate sightings near Balat and Abu Minqar, and note a published record for the oasis. Tracks of a cat the size of a large house cat were noted on the south shore of Lake Mut on January 23, 1987, and in subsequent years to 1991, and may represent this animal, as the abundance of birds and dead fish may have attracted it.

(19.) Wild Cat – *Felis sylvestris libyca*.

Osborn and Helmy (1980) record a single specimen from Mut. A small tabby cat, with a broad head, was sighted about 1 km south of the village of Oualad Mohammed, southwest of Teneida in eastern Dakhleh Oasis, on March 1, 1993 at the margin of cultivation away from habitation but near water. It is identified to this taxon. Spoor of small cats are common around most inhabited or cultivated areas, and may represent this or the previous taxon, or domestic cats.

20. Caracal – *Caracal caracal schmitzi*.

Osborn and Helmy (1980) record caracal only for Egypt east of the Nile. A mounted specimen of a caracal of unknown provenance was displayed during the 1980's on the coping of a house at Ezbet el-Arab, north of Mut. A night sighting of a large short-tailed self-coloured cat occurred on November 21, 1979. A dehydrated skull and neck with skin was recovered from the top of a gebel near the road camp east of the oasis on February 20, 1996 and constitutes the first authenticated record of a large cat in the Wadi el-Gedid. The specimen has the attenuate nasal processes of the premaxilla and subequal rostral and postorbital widths noted by Osborn and Helmy (1980) but its bullae are small, the superior postorbital processes long and almost meet the inferior processes, and the protocone on the upper carnassial is well developed. As *F. chaus* can attain sizes comparable to both *Caracal* and *F. serval*, this identification needs to be confirmed.

Artiodactyla

(21.) White or Scimitar Horned Oryx – *Oryx dammah*.

Osborn and Helmy (1980) indicate that this antelope was present in the oasis at least until about 1874 (Schweinfurth 1874). No bones or teeth of a large antelope have been noted among the many ass, cow, or camel remains found in areas surrounding the oasis, nor have any elements attributable to this animal been certainly recognised in the Neolithic fauna. Local residents refer to a large antelope – 'meha', 'Abu Herab', or 'Begra el-Ouash' – as present in the surrounding desert, but we consider this to represent memories of oryx, addax or hartebeest in the region during the last century.

(22.) Addax – *Addax nasomaculatus*.

Osborn and Helmy (1980) indicate that addax was present in the oasis, probably as late as the middle of the 19th Century. As for oryx, no skeletal evidence of this antelope has been recognised nor has it yet been noted in the Neolithic fauna. Local residents refer to a large antelope – 'meha', 'Abu Herab', or 'Begra el-Ouash' – as present in the surrounding desert, but again we consider this to represent memories of oryx, addax or hartebeest in the region during the last century.

(23.) Bubal Hartebeest – *Alcelaphus buselaphus*.

Osborn and Helmy (1980) indicate that this hartebeest once inhabited the oasis. The last records of this taxon in Egypt are in or about 1935 in Siwa Oasis (Osborn and Helmy 1980) and west of the Fayum about 1900 (Anderson 1902). No skeletal evidence of this animal has been noted among the large ungulate remains in the surrounding desert, although Neolithic remains are recognized.

(24.) White or Slender-Horned Gazelle, or Rhim – *Gazella leptoceros*.

Osborn and Helmy (1980) record a sighting of a rhim on the escarpment of the Libyan Plateau northeast of Kharga on the Assiyut road, but give no details. A horn core of this species has been recovered from Neolithic deposits at Sheikh Muftah, teeth have been recovered from other Neolithic levels, and a sawn horncore from surface debris of Roman age at Ismant el-Kharab.

25. Dorcas Gazelle – *Gazella dorcas*.

Small herds of a male and two to four females or young or single males have been seen in sand-sheet areas between dunes where halfa grass (*Imperata cylindrica*) is the main cover. Sightings have occurred southeast of Teneida near Sheikh Mabrouk (1986), and southwest of Balat near 'Ein Duma (1985–6). Gazelle tracks have been noted in many areas on the periphery of the oasis, both on the Libyan Plateau and south into the desert, usually associated with xerophytic natural vegetation or made when moving between such patches. Isolated skeletal elements, chiefly horns, horncores and partial longbones, have been recovered from sites around the oasis. The population is resident, not numerous and migratory around sites in the oasis, with small 'family' groups or isolated males usually observed. Remnants of *G. dorcas* have been recovered from Neolithic, Pharaonic and Roman age deposits.

Osborn and Helmy (1980) report sightings of a single individual at Mut in 1969, a small herd in the eastern portion of the oasis, 60 km from Mut, in 1966 (possibly that observed by us south of Sheikh Mabrouk in 1986), and at Bir el-Shab, 150 km south of Kharga in 1967.

(26.) Barbary or Maned Sheep, or Aoudad – *Ammotragus lervia ornatus*.

Osborn and Helmy (1980) report a single weathered skull from Ain Amur, northwest of Kharga and a sighting at Ain Umm Dabadib, north-northeast of Kharga, as the sole evidence of this species on the Libyan Escarpment near Dakhleh. They also note the examination by Helmy in February, 1972, of the head of a recently killed specimen from Bir El-Obeid, northwest of Farafra, which is evidence of a continued if sparse population on the northern arm of the escarpment. No fragmentary evidence of this sheep has been noted among the many recent skeletal elements seen by the authors, nor is there any evidence of it among the Neolithic or Roman age faunal remains.

Domestic Mammals

Lagomorpha

1. Rabbit – *Oryctolagus cuniculus*.

Rabbits are bred and kept by many inhabitants for meat, in the same manner as in Roman times, in 'cunicularia' with nesting in tubular pottery earths. Their coloration is of the wild type.

Carnivora

2. Dog – *Canis familiaris*.

Dogs run loose in the oasis, forming well organised social packs in each village, and some members appear to be owned by villagers while others are scavengers. During the day, when the sun is not too hot, the village dogs aggregate in social groups and lie around sunning themselves on south facing slopes of small hills or mounds. Some animals accompany their owners into the fields daily, and it is not unusual to see dogs with asses, goats, sheep and even camels or water buffalo gathered in a farmer's field. The dogs are generally off-white or cream coloured, although how much of the reddish colour is due to the red soils staining their coat is unclear. Their noses are usually black, ears are short (possibly due to damage from fighting, i.e. dog-eared!) and pricked, and tails moderately long, bushy, and curled over the back, and a short coat. The coat is mediumly short, with stiff guard hairs and a light underfur, even in winter. Dogs' ears are often clipped short by their owners in the local belief that the animals will then not wander away from home. A.J. Mills noticed this on puppies in the Project's landlord's house in 1996 and also in the Sudan. There appears to be little difference between the ancient dogs of the oasis and the modern population (Churcher, 1993). The introduction of exotic breeds of dogs shows in few individuals, mainly in Mut, where traces of Alsatian, collie and terrier are occasionally observed.

3. Cat – *Felis domesticus*.

The domestic cats of the oasis are the slim, small-headed, gracile Egyptian form, with short coats. Colours and patterns vary from self-coloured to blotchy or tabby, and from white to grey, brown, black or marmalade. Cats appear to be active mainly at night, as they are seldom seen during the day, but may be encountered at any hour of the night stalking across the roofs of the houses, or investigating kitchens. No evidence of recent introductions or modern breeds has been observed.

Perissodactyla

4. Horse – *Equus caballus*.

A few horses have been observed in or around Mut, and less frequently in outlying places. They are brown, chestnut or roan, lightly built, with 'Arab' features. They may have been more numerous before the advent of motorised transport. Remains of large equids are present in Roman deposits.

5. Ass or Donkey – *Equus asinus*.

Asses are common throughout the oasis, as in the Nile Valley, and are used for all forms of transport. They stand from 1.0 – 1.3 m at the shoulder, although the males may be larger, up to 1.5 m. They range in colour from white to black, with countershaded, piebald, skewbald, roan and other colours, and many of the white or grey individuals have one or two shoulder stripes.

6. Mule – *Equus asinus* x *Equus caballus*.

Few mules have been seen in the oasis, and they are as scarce as horses. All have been typically long-eared, long-legged, rangy, large, and self-coloured light to dark grey.

Artiodactyla

7. Pig – *Sus scrofa*.

Pigs are kept in the oasis according to local reports, but we have never seen or heard them. Remains of pig have been commonly recovered from Roman levels at Qasr, Mut, Ismant el-Kharab and elsewhere.

8. Dromedary – *Camelus dromedarius*.

Dromedaries are found throughout the oasis but are not numerous as they are usually grazed for long periods away from the oasis, perhaps because their Arab owners own little land there. It is also said that there is a parasite or disease which attacks camels when kept for lengthy periods in the oasis (A.J. Mills, pers.comm., 1996). They are often seen near villages originally settled by Arabs (e.g., Ezbet el-Arab or Sheikh Maohoub). Droppings are found throughout the oasis, especially in the surrounding desert fringe, and may represent animals that were once in the area or may be dispersed widely by wind. Remains of camels are common in the surrounding desert areas, especially along the ancient caravan routes to Kharga, Ain Amur, Farafra or Gebel Uweinat. Camel is sparsely known from Roman age deposits, but not in Dynastic levels, although *Camelus thomasi* is known fossil from Bir Sahara and Bir Tarfawi (Gautier 1981), and Dakhleh Oasis (Churcher *et al.* 1997, In press).

9. Goat – *Capra hircus*.

Goats are common throughout the oasis, and occur in mixed herds with sheep. They are generally coloured brown or black, with short or long coats. Remains of goats are recognised from Old Kingdom, Roman, Islamic, and possibly Neolithic deposits.

10. Sheep – *Ovis aries*.

Sheep are numerous throughout the oasis, and occur in mixed herds with goats. They are generally dark brown or black, with longer, woolier coats than goats. Remains of sheep have been hard to confirm in Neolithic or Old Kingdom times because no horn cores have been recovered, but they were present in the oasis in Roman and Islamic times.

11. Asiatic Water Buffalo – *Bubalus bubalis*.

No water buffalo was seen in the oasis until 1985, when a small herd of about five was observed north of Ismant el-Kharab and north of the main road between Masara and Ismant. Since then individuals have been seen in other villages, e.g., a breeding cow in Bashendi from 1988 onwards. A fragment from a horncore has been recovered from Roman levels at Ismant el-Kharab.

CONCLUSIONS

The animals listed and commented on in this report require little discussion. The new records of occurrence, breeding or or residence speak for themselves for the avifauna. The mammalian fauna is similarly self expressive, with comments on the evidence for the present occurrence or absence of animals alleged to be in the oasis relating to faunal lists of other authors. The record of the mega-chiropteran *Rousettus aegyptiacus* is the only new record of a mammal in the oasis.

Because of the harsh conditions of the Western Desert of Egypt, even within an oasis, the resident mammals are either sparse and widely distributed, or small, cryptic and usually nocturnal. The most obvious mammals are the foxes, which can be seen most early mornings or evenings, as they enter the oasis from the surrounding desert to scavenge over the cultivated areas. The resident birds may be numerous, although their populations may fluctuate widely, and migratory species are present in the oasis for only short periods when transiting the oasis. Winter residents are present for periods of a few months, but again their populations appear to peak rapidly and then fall off to a much lower level, depending on available food and their discovery of the oasis' lakes and expanding cultivation. Raptors are generally few, being represented by single individuals or pairs, and apparently visit the oasis for a period before returning to the Nile Valley. Thus the collection of specimens and the recording of sightings are restricted by infrequent opportunities and the full extent of the the faunal spectrum can only be documented by persistent efforts throughout all periods of the year.

Acknowledgements

We thank Dr. Steven M. Goodman of the Museum of Zoology, University of Michigan, and Peter L. Meininger of the Birds of Egypt Project, Grevelingenstraat 127, Middelburg, The Netherlands, for assisting us with the records of birds known from the Western Oases, and Dr. Dale J. Osborn of Ladova 7, 128 00 Prague 2, Czecho-slovakia, for assistance with the occurrence and distribution of recent mammals in Egypt. The paper was read in draft by Dr. Goodman, Dr. Osborn and Dr. Achilles Gautier of the Laboratorium voor Paleontologie, Rijksuniversiteit, Gent, Belgium and their constructive comments on many aspects of the records and distributions appreciated. We also thank Anthony J. Mills, Field Director of the Dakhleh Oasis Project, for his willingness to make it possible for us to carry on these studies while so many other activities were in progress, and the members of the Dakhleh Oasis Project mainly over the years 1978 to 1987, who drew our attentions to occurrences of animals, their remains or scats, and for adding to the breadth of information contained in the report. Support for the work was through the Social Sciences and Humanities Research Council of Canada Grants to the Project and through National Sciences and Engineering Research Council Grant A-1704 to Churcher for his field and laboratory work. Additional support was given to the Project by the Royal Ontario Museum, its Egyptian Department, and the Society for the Study of Egyptian Antiquities, Toronto.

Addresses for Authors

Alan F. Hollett, Egyptian Department, Royal Ontario Museum, 100 Queen's Park North, Toronto, Ontario, CANADA M5S 2C6 *and* Box 512, 51, Fox St., Lunenburg, Nova Scotia, CANADA B0J 2C0.

Charles S. Churcher, Department of Zoology, University of Toronto, Ontario, CANADA M5S 1A1; Department of Vertebrate Palaeontology, Royal Ontario Museum, 100 Queen's Park North, Toronto, Ontario, CANADA M5S 2C6, *and* R.R.1, Site 42, Box 12, Gabriola Island, British Columbia, CANADA V0R 1X0.

REFERENCES

Anderson, J. 1902. *Zoology of Egypt: Mammalia* (Revised and completed by W.E. De Winton). London: Hugh Rees, 374p.

Al Hussaini, A.H. 1959. The avifauna of Al-Wadi Al-Gedid in the Libyan Desert. *Bulletin of the Zoological Society of Egypt* **14**: 1–14.

Beadnell, H.J.L. 1909. *An Egyptian Oasis.* London: John Murray, 248p.

Bijlsma, R.G. 1983. The migration of raptors near Suez, Egypt, autumn 1981. *Sandgrouse* **5**: 19–44.

Churcher, C.S. 1991. Egyptian fruit bat from Dakhleh Oasis, Western Desert of Egypt. *Mammalia* **55**: 139–143.

Churcher, C.S. 1992. Ostrich bones from the Neolithic of Dakhleh Oasis, Western Desert of Egypt. *Palaeoecology of Africa and the Surrounding Islands* **23**: 67–71.

Churcher, C.S. 1993. Dogs from Ein Tirghi Cemetery, Balat, Dakhleh Oasis, Western Desert of Egypt, 39–60. *In* Clason, A., S. Payne and H.-P. Uerpmann, eds, *Skeletons in her Cupboard: Festschrift for Juliet Clutton-Brock.* Oxbow Monograph 34, 259p.

Churcher, C.S. This volume. Chapter 8. Holocene faunas of Dakhleh Oasis, 133–151.

Churcher, C.S., M.R. Kleindienst, M.F. Wiseman and M.M.A. McDonald 1997. The Quaternary faunas of Dakhleh Oasis, Western Desert of Egypt. The Second Dakhleh Oasis Research Project Seminar, June 16–20, Royal Ontario Museum and University of Toronto, Toronto, Ontario, Canada.

Churcher, C.S., M.R. Kleindienst and H.P. Schwarcz. In press. Faunal remains from a Middle Pleistocene lacustrine marl in Egypt. *Palaeogeography, Palaeoclimatology, Palaeoecology.*

Cramp, S. and K.E.L. Simmons, eds. 1980. *Handbook of the Birds of Europe, the Middle East and Africa. The Birds of the Western Palearctic. Vol. 2. Birds of Prey to Bustards.* Oxford: Oxford University Press, 695p.

De Beaux, O. 1932. Spedizione scientifica all' Oasi di Cufra. Mammiferi. *Annali del Museo civico di Storia naturale Giacomo Doria, Genova,* **55**: 1–21.

Embabi, N.S. 1970–71. Structures of barchan dunes at the Kharga oases depressions, the Western Desert, Egypt. *Bulletin de la Société de géographie d'Egypte* **43**: 53–71.

Flower, S.S. 1932. Notes on the recent mammals of Egypt, with a list of the species recorded from that kingdom. *Proceedings of the Zoological Society, London,* **1932**: 368–450.

Gaisler, J., G. Madkour and J. Pelikan. 1972. On the bats (Chiroptera) of Egypt. *Acta scientiarum naturalium academiae scientiarum bohemslovacae Brno* **6** (8): 1–40.

Gautier, A. 1981. Non-marine molluscs and vertebrate remains from Upper Pleistocene deposits and Middle Paleolithic sites at Bir Sahara and Bir Tarfawi, Western Desert of Egypt, 126–145. *In* Schild, R. and F. Wendorf, eds, *The Prehistory of an Egyptian Oasis.* Wroclaw: Polish Academy of Sciences, 155p.

Gautier, A. 1983. Animal life along the prehistoric Nile: the evidence from Saggai 1 and Geili (Sudan). *Origini* **12**: 50–115.

Goodman, S.M., P.L. Meininger and W.C. Mullié. 1986. *The Birds of the Egyptian Western Desert.* University of Michigan, Miscellaneous Publications, Museum of Zoology, no. 172, 1–91.

Goodman, S.M. and G.E. Watson. 1983. Bird specimen records of some uncommon or previously unrecorded forms in Egypt. *Bulletin of the British Ornithologists' Club* **103**: 101–106.

Hoogstraal, H. 1962. A brief review of the contemporary land mammals of Egypt (including Sinai). 1. Insectivora and Chiroptera. *Journal of the Egyptian Public Health Association* **37**: 143–161.

Hoogstraal, H. 1963. A brief review of the contemporary land mammals of Egypt (including Sinai). 2. Lagomorpha and Rodentia. *Journal of the Egyptian Public Health Association* **38**: 1–35.

Hoogstraal, H. 1964. A brief review of the contemporary land mammals of Egypt (including Sinai). 3. Carnivora, Hyracoidea, Perissodactyla, and Artiodactyla. *Journal of the Egyptian Public Health Association* **39**: 205–239.

Houlihan, P.F. 1986. *The Birds of Ancient Egypt.* London: Aris and Phillips, 191p.

Jarvis, C.S. 1936. *Three Deserts.* London, John Murray / New York, Dutton, 313p.

Kiepenheuer, J. and K.E. Linsenmair. 1965. Vögelzug an der nordafrikanischen Küste von Tunisien bis Rôtes Meer nach Tag- und Nachtbeobachtungen 1963 und 1964. *Vögelwarte* **13**: 80–94.

Marx, H. 1968. Checklist of the reptiles and amphibia of Egypt. *Special Publication of the United States Naval Medical Research Unit, Cairo,* no. 3, 1–91.

McDonald, M.M.A. This volume. Chapter 7. Neolithic cultural units and adaptations in Dakhleh Oasis, 117–132.

Meinertzhagen, R.E. 1930. *Nicoll's Birds of Egypt, 2 vols.* London: Hugh Rees, 700p.

Meininger, P.L. and W.C. Mullié. 1981. Some interesting ornithological records from Egypt. *Bulletin of the Ornithological Society of the Middle East* **6**: 2–5.

Migahid, A.M., M. el Shafei Ali, A.A. Abd el Rahman and M.A. Hammouda. 1960. An ecological study of Kharga and Dakhla Oases. *Bulletin de la Société de géographie d'Egypte* **33**: 279–310.

Moreau, R.E. 1927. Some notes from the Egyptian Oases. *Ibis,* ser. 12: 210–245.

Moreau, R.E. 1927–28. Quail. *Bulletin of the Zoological Society of Egypt* **1**: 6–13.

Moreau, R.E. 1928. Some further notes from the Egyptian Deserts. *Ibis,* ser. 12: 453–475.

Moreau, R.E. 1934. A contribution to the ornithology of the Libyan Desert. *Ibis,* ser. 14: 595–632.

Moreau, R.E. 1967. Water-birds over the Sahara. *Ibis* **109**: 232–259.

Osborn, D.J. and I. Helmy. 1980. The contemporary land mammals of Egypt (including Sinai). *Fieldiana (Zoology),* n.s., no. 5, publ. no. 1309, 1–579.

Qumsiyeh, M.B. 1985. The bats of Egypt. *Texas Tech University, The Museum, Special Publication,* no. 23, 1–102.

Riad, A.M. 1995a. New information on the birds of the Western Desert of Egypt. *Ornithological Society of the Middle East, Bulletin* **35**: 32–35.

Riad, A.M. 1995b. The first breeding record of Sparrow *Passer hispaniolensis* in Egypt. *Ornithological Society of the Middle East, Bulletin* **35**: 38–39.

Ritchie, J.A. This volume. Chapter 4. Flora, Vegetation and palaeobotany of Dakhleh Oasis, 73–81.

Scharlau, W. 1963. Ornithologische beobachtungen in der ägyptischen Oase El-Dachla. *Ornithologische Mitteilungen* **15**: 246–248.

Schweinfurth, G. 1874. Notice sur la grande oases du Desert Libyque. *Bulletin de la Société de géographie, Paris* (ser. 7) **6**: 627–634.

Steinbacher, J. 1965. Zur vögelfauna nordafrikanischer Küstengebiete. *Senkenbergiana Biologica* **46**: 429–459.

Vaurie, C. 1959. *The Birds of the Palaearctic Fauna: a systematic reference, order Passiformes.* London: H.F. and G. Witherby, 762p.

Vaurie, C. 1965. *The Birds of the Palaearctic Fauna: a systematic reference, non-Passiformes.* London: H.F. and G. Witherby, 763p.

Wassif, K. 1949. Trident bat (*Asellia tridens*) in the Egyptian oasis of Kharga. *Bulletin of the Zoological Society of Egypt* **8**: 9–12.

Wassif, K. 1959a. On a collection of mammals from the Egyptian oases of Bahariya and Farafra. *Ain Shams Science Bulletin,* no. 4, 137–145.

Wassif, K. 1959b. Mammals from the Egyptian oases of Kharga, Dakhla, Bahariya and Farafra (Al-Wadi Al-Gadid). *Bulletin of the Zoological Society of Egypt* **14**: 15–17.

Wilkinson, C.K. 1983. Egyptian wall paintings: the Metropolitan Museum's collection of facsimiles, pp. 8–63. *In* Wilkinson, C.K. and M. Hill, *Egyptian Wall Paintings: the Metropolitan Museum of Art's Collections of Facsimiles.* New York: The Metropolitan Museum of Art, 165p.

Wingate, O.C. 1934. In search of Zerzura. *The Geographical Journal* **83**: 281–308.

10

PHARAONIC EGYPTIANS IN THE DAKHLEH OASIS

A. J. Mills

A considerable body of evidence for human occupation during historical periods in the Dakhleh Oasis has been gathered during the process of the archaeological survey of the Dakhleh Oasis Project. Summaries of the results of these seasons of survey are published as reports in the *Journal of the Society for the Study of Egyptian Antiquities* (1979, **9**[4]: 163–210; 1980, **10**[4]: 251–427; 1981, **11**[4]: 175–241; 1982, **12**[3]: 93–138; 1983, **13**[3]: 121–210). It is now apparent that since the late VI Dynasty there has been continuous habitation in the oasis and that traditionally there were close links with the Nile Valley. At the same time, local traditions and developments are displayed which are seen as the result of localised conditions and other, Saharan or sub-Saharan, influences. In a hyperarid region like the Dakhleh Oasis, environmental factors play a more obviously active role in influencing human activities.

The archaeological survey of the Dakhleh Oasis region was designed to produce data on the location of sites where evidence for human activity was present, on the date, nature, extent and preservation of those sites, and on the location of each relative to natural features and other sites. The survey was performed on foot and all parts of the oasis not under crops were investigated during the five seasons from 1978 to 1982. Evidence that the climate of the region has not significantly altered in the last 4,500 years is generally accepted (Butzer 1976), and it seems most improbable that permanent settlement has existed outside the present oasis area during and subsequent to the period of Pharaonic influence. There are, of course, routes to other parts of Egypt, with their graffiti, wayside camps and water holes; and lookout and hunting posts in isolated locations away from the oasis floor. While these form part of our evidence concerning the entire complexity of living in an isolated region, locating them is an on-going process, part of a wider survey in the 'palaeoasis' region for environmental and prehistoric data, and they will not form part of present considerations.

The oasis, today, is a large area, some 70 km from east to west and up to 30 km across from north to south (see Kleindienst *et al.*, this volume, Chapter 1, Fig. 1.1). The floor of the oasis is a lacustrine clay. It unconformably overlies the Qusseir (= Mut) Formation shales or the red muds and sandstone members of the Taref Formation, of the Nubia Group. The northern and eastern boundaries of the oasis are formed by a 350 m high limestone, phosphorite, shale, marl and chalk escarpment, of epicontinental marine origin, while the less distinct southern edge lies along the strikes of a rising set of Nubia Formation sandstone lenses, and grades into a stony, sandy Saharan waste. The oasis floor is generally flat, lying at about 120 m above sea level, with localised undulations. It is interrupted by outcrops of sandstone and by spring vent mounds. Within the oasis there are areas of land under crop, fallow or unused farmland, wadi bottoms, gravelled terraces, rocky outcrops and sand flows, all interspersed randomly. The climate of the region is hyperarid, with essentially only a trace of annual rainfall. Temperatures range from warm to hot, although December and January morning temperatures can sink to -1° or -2° Celsius. The water, so essential for life, is present in underground aquifers at various depths, and most is brought to the surface by artesian pressure. It seems that there is still plenty of water in reserve in Dakhleh although, at present, extraction is accelerating and the use of water appears profligate.

According to officials in Mut, the present (1987)

'Reports from the Survey of Dakhleh Oasis, Western Desert of Egypt, 1977–1987', edited by C.S. Churcher and A.J. Mills. Dakhleh Oasis Project: Monograph 2. Oxbow Monograph 99.

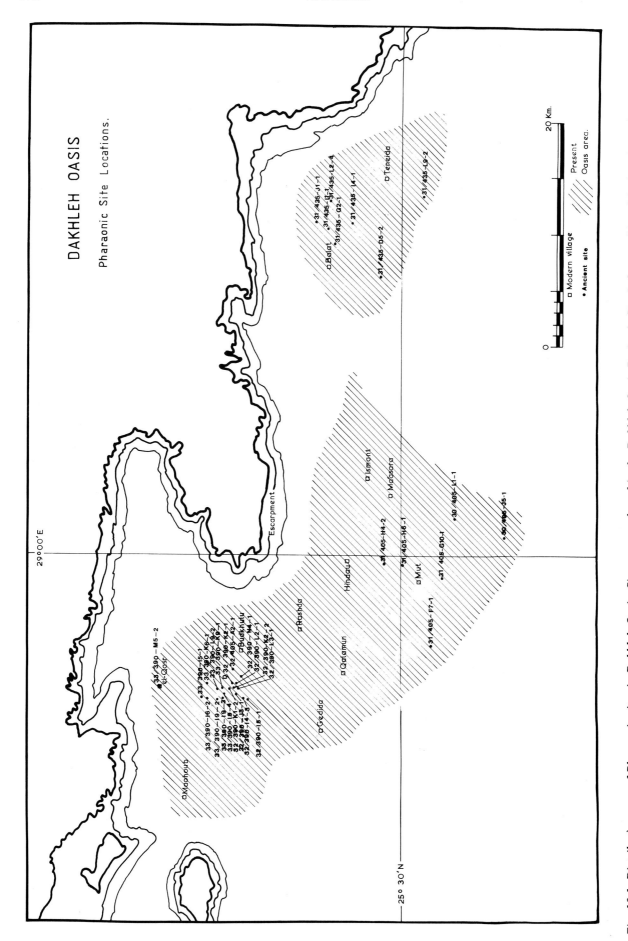

Fig. 10.1. *Distribution map of Pharaonic sites in Dakhleh Oasis. Sites are numbered in the Dakhleh Oasis Project's Site Index, see List of Archaeological Sites, this volume, Appendix II. Shaded areas represent those under shifting cultivation in the modern oasis.*

population is about 65,000 in Dakhleh Oasis, which is probably in excess of that of any former time. It is distributed in seventeen major settlements and a larger number of smaller communities. The largest, Mut, with about 15,000 people, is situated centrally and at the southern and southwesternmost point of Dakhleh. It is the capital town and contains local administrative offices, the largest market, the secondary school, and the various amenities useful to a rural population of this size. The remaining towns and villages are situated in the midst of the land farmed by their inhabitants. Generally, the only occupation of the resident population is farming, apart from a few who are traders. There are two factors that are having a major effect on society in the late 20th Century in Dakhleh. The building of a tarmacadamed road in the 1960's, linking the oasis with Kharga Oasis and Assiyut in the Nile Valley, on the allignment of the Darb el-Gubari, greatly facilitates travel where formerly it was difficult and expensive. The second is the advent of electricity and television in the 1980's, which allows a longer active day and introduces other cultural ways to all the oasis inhabitants and which, because of television's compelling nature, encourages people to remain awake until midnight, thereby altering the daily cycle of their activities.

The resources of the oasis are limited. There are no mineral deposits, apart from ochres and a sulphurous deposit in the region of Qasr, which was extracted, probably in Medieval times. Local stone sources are only used locally - sandstone for building, limestone for mortars and plasters, and flint and chert for hand tools. The clay soil is rich, however, and agriculture is the basis of the economy, as indeed it traditionally has been in the Nile Valley. Three cereal crops are grown each year: rice, which is harvested in November; wheat, which is harvested in April; and sorghum, the hot-weather crop. Fruit gardens and vegetable plots together with small mixed flocks of sheep and goats, and of poultry, and many donkeys and a few cattle provide the remainder of the output of the land, and the populace needs only to produce extra in order to obtain such commodities as cloth, tea, and sugar which are not locally produced. Little contribution is made to the national economy of Egypt but, to judge from the amount of fallow land in the oasis, little strain is put on the resources of the region by its traditional agricultural methods and crops.

Farming techniques are, to a large extent, the result of the irrigation system. Land is irrigated by flooding from time to time and an elaborate system of canals, channels and field levels has been developed which permits a high degree of control on the amount of water used and the specific location of the irrigated place. It is necessary to have relatively small field plots, seldom as large as half an acre, and often only three or four metres square, each bounded by a low earth dyke, so that the contained land can be levelled and the flooding accurately controlled. The sharper the contours, the smaller the size and greater the number of fields concerned. It is a labour-intensive

activity and, in fact, the preparation of the ground, planting, irrigating and harvesting are all principally done by hand. Generally, stubble grazing occurs following a harvest. Land ownership is a relatively minor matter, while the ownership and control of wells is of paramount importance and the wealthiest Dakhleh residents are those who have maintained control of the water sources. This power was largely assumed by the Egyptian national government during the land reforms of the 1950's. Today, most bore-holes in the oasis are sunk under government contract and the output sold at subsidised rates to the farmers, although occasionally private individuals still bore deep wells or excavate shallow *saqia* wells for themselves.

The establishment of the system of irrigation was one of the fundamental elements in the establishment of the Pharaonic Egyptian state. In the Nile Valley an annual regime was imposed on the agricultural cycle by the inundation of the bottom land by the river. Part of this flood water was trapped in basins at the edges of the valley for use during times of lower river levels. The basin water was led onto the land, when later required, by a system of canals and, as the basic elements of the technology required only a good eye for land levels and a simple mattock to create the earth retaining banks, the system developed early and quickly. Because it was precisely suited to the particular conditions of Egypt, it continued largely unaltered until the introduction of large-scale water-lifting devices, the *sanduk* (a vertical wheel driven by waterflow) and subsequently the *saqia* (a vertical ox-driven wheel) during the Ptolemaic and Roman periods, which meant that water could be lifted from wells or canals in practical quantities. Among the effects these machines had were to render obsolete the retaining basins and to bring into cultivation tracts of land that previously had been inaccessible.

Conditions in the Dakhleh Oasis are in part similar to those in the Nile Valley, but there are essential differences. The farmland itself is flat, or gently sloping, and the creation of the irrigation fields can be accomplished with equal facility in both regions. The soil, however, is different. In the Nile Valley it is predominantly a riverine overbank alluvium, whereas in Dakhleh Oasis, it is a lacustrine clay. Both are rich, although the natural annual flooding of the Nile River provides a more productive soil in the long run. A major result of the difference in soil composition is one of drainage, for the lighter alluvial soil permits water to percolate through it, while the Dakhleh clays have only evaporation as the means of dissipating irrigation water. The major difference, however, is that of the water sources for each region. Neither has any rainfall that could be useful for agriculture and both must rely on their surface and underground resources. The Nile Valley has, of course, the river and its network of canals and storage basins. The oasis has vast underground aquifers at various depths which hold water under pressure and which feed the surface of the ground via natural vents or bored wells.

In Dakhleh Oasis, once the water is on the surface it will collect in pools at low-lying points unless it is otherwise distributed. As the rate of evaporation must exceed a source's rate of production for such a pool to dry, it must follow that in an uncontrolled situation most production will result in standing surface water. Until the source ceases, such pools and swamps will continue to exist unless effective drainage is instituted – difficult if the water is in a low-lying area - or unless some lifting machinery is used to relocate the surface water. This must have been the case during the three millennia following the ending of the mid-Holocene humid phase, about 6,000 to 3,000 BC, the period of final settlement and subsequent disappearance of the Neolithic Sheikh Muftah Cultural Unit peoples in the area (McDonald, Chapter 7, this volume), and of the domination of the region by the Pharaonic Egyptians. One sees, then, a landscape somewhat similar to that of today, with areas of gravel and rock outcrop, areas covered by sand dunes, and areas of settlement and agriculture. The only addition would have been areas of standing surface water in many of the lower places, for evidence from the Nile Valley indicates that the ancient Egyptians possessed only the most primitive technology for lifting water. The earliest known mechanical device is the well-sweep (or *shaduf*), for which the earliest evidence is seen in depictions of the Amarna Period (1346–1334 BC), e.g., the tomb of Nefer-hotep at Thebes (No. 49) (Davies 1933). Other devices for water lifting includes a pair of buckets on a yoke, as in the XII Dynasty tomb of Khnum-hotep at Beni Hassan (Newberry 1893).

The earliest attestation of Egyptian connections with the oasis is found in the Archaic Period ceramics (ca. 2920–2650 BC) from Site 32/390–L2–1 (Hope 1980). However, the few objects found to date are insufficient to permit the conclusion that Egyptians were already resident in Dakhleh, when the alternative explanation that these are trade pieces can be supported.

By the time the Egyptians arrived in the oasis in any number, around 2300 BC, they had already had several hundred years of settled, agriculturally-based life in their valley homeland. Only if conditions were radically different, would they have been likely to change their successful system in major aspects. Certainly, there would have been no question of reversion to more primitive systems, such as those probably practiced by the resident Sheikh Muftah population. It seems that the farming landscape of today's oasis is largely the result of the imposition of Old Kingdom techniques imported from the Nile Valley.

The purpose that underlay the Egyptians' migration into Dakhleh is not yet understood, but it is evident that there was a serious attempt to colonise the region. Of the 50 Pharaonic sites located by the survey (see List of Archaeological Sites, this volume, Appendix II), 42 contain material dating to the period of the initial influx in the late Old Kingdom. They are distributed in three main concentrations, and it would seem that a capital was established at Ain Aseel (31/435–I1–1), northeast of the present town of Balat, where a sizeable town was built. This site was discovered by Ahmed Fakhry in 1947 and has been the subject of intensive excavation by the Institut Français d'Archéologie Orientale au Caire (Vercoutter 1986). A complex political organization and social stratification is evident from the large mastaba tombs and funerary stelae of the governors at nearby Kila' ed-Debba (31/435–G2–1) (Osing *et al.* 1982; Valloggia with Henein 1986). The fact of there being officials of the Egyptian central government resident in the oasis indicates some degree of planning and involvement on the part of the court, although no records have come to us from the inscriptions of the period. Such an extensive community as represented by the large number of sites and the great size of some – Site 33/390–I9–3 has a sherd scatter covering some 50 hectares - could not have been a simple outpost or entrepot, but must have been self-supporting and essentially independent of the Nile for its mundane requirements. This fact is borne out by the discovery of a number of sites of pottery kilns (e.g., 33/390–I9–3 and 33/390–K9–1) where ceramics of normal Egyptian form and finish were manufactured (Hope 1981). To judge from the large constructions at Ain Aseel, a long-term settlement was intended. In the event, it appears to have lasted for about a century, through the First Intermediate Period.

One basic problem for this early Pharaonic community in Dakhleh must have been the control of the water supply. The resident Neolithic population was, presumably, living in a symbiotic balance with the oasis environment. A large influx of Egyptians would have created an imbalance on the landscape through increased subsistence requirements. The upgrading of the region for their more highly developed technology would not have been a great problem for the newcomers. There were already similarities between their valley homeland and the new oasis - no rainfall, hot weather, and a generally flat landscape - and the same crops and animals could be husbanded. The main problem was that the water resource was irregular and uncontrolled, particularly when compared with that of the Nile. There is no seasonality to a spring that flows constantly, and there is a random location of spring vents across the landscape. Where a spring vent occurs on relatively high ground, it would be easy to control the distribution of its outflow, as at Gebel Gala in Kharga Oasis (Caton-Thompson 1952); however, many of the springs would have been located beside or in the pools where the outflow collected. The random location of springs would have meant that it was only possible to undertake irrigation in their vicinity, whatever the quality of the soil.

The control and distribution of irrigation water would have been a relatively simple matter for the Egyptians. They were accustomed to levelling land, constructing canals and aqueducts, and drainage patterns. However, without the technology to raise water mechanically or to dig deep wells, they were subject to the vagaries of spring location and their access to useful agricultural land would have been severely restricted and subsistence patterns thereby affected. An explanation occurs which can outline a solution to the Egyptians' dilemma in terms of the limitation of Pharaonic technology. If a coffer dam, or containment basin, were constructed around a spring vent, using the local clay soil as the basic material, water could then be raised to the maximum allowed by the artesian pressure. The resulting pool could then be tapped at the top of the basin and water led off in built channels. The system would have the additional advantage of drying up land below a hitherto uncontrolled spring. Thus land, much more extensive than formerly, would be made available to meet the new subsistence requirements of the increased populations. The dense cluster of sites towards the western end of the oasis is situated in an area where there is a large number of spring mounds. Dating the dredgeate on the sides of these may provide a better understanding of the realities of the situation.

Because no large-scale excavation has been performed on any of the sites bearing Old Kingdom remains, it is not yet possible to assess the quality of the community. However, it is possible to come to some preliminary conclusions and ideas from the survey information.

The commonest artifacts on all these sites are ceramics. These are treated as indicators for dating, cultural affinities, technology, style, use, and many other aspects of the occupation. Studies by Arnold (1982) and Ballet (1987), as well as the ongoing work of Hope (1980, 1981, Chapter 14, this volume), leave no doubt as to the dating of this material to the late VI Dynasty and First Intermediate Period, nor does their similarity to so much recorded from Nile Valley sites leave any question as to the producers of the material being a part of the same tradition. With the occurrence of similar lithics both on the sites of the Old Kingdom and those of the Sheikh Muftah indigenes and small amounts of ceramics of each on the sites of the other (McDonald, Chapter 7, this volume), a contemporaneity is probable, although the nature of the relationship between the two is not yet clear. It would seem that the two are not fully present, mixed, on one site, for sites of each occur adjacent to one another (e.g., 33/390–I9–3 and 33/390–I9–1). The discovery of sites with a number of pottery kilns (33/390–I9–3, 33/390–K9–1) not only provides new information on ceramics manufacture and pyrotechnology, but also gives an insight into the intended independence and longevity of the community. The range of forms indicates all the activities within the community that might be expected in a permanent settlement.

Testing in the cemetery sites (32/390–J3–1, 32/390–K2–1, 32/390–L2–1, 33/390–I9–2, 33/390–I9–4 and 33/390–L9–2) also provides information. The mud brick mastaba tombs of 32/390–J3–1 (Mills 1979, pl. XVI) are of a complexity and size to indicate both social stratification in the nearby community and give an indication of its relative prosperity. The site also confirms the idea that the community in the oasis was widespread and more than just the single important centre at Ain Aseel with satellite farming areas. Grave goods are not plentiful, but those recovered serve to demonstrate a close connection with the Nile Valley. The interesting series of pottery offering tables from 32/390–K2–1 (Mills 1979, pl. XV.1, 3, 5) and 33/390–L9–2 is in the tradition of the soul houses (Petrie 1907) and ceramic offering trays (Petrie 1900, pl. XIX) of the Nile Valley. Scarabs and a few other amulets and beads are most probably imported from Nile Valley production workshops. The only inscriptions of the period have been recovered from the Balat sites 31/435–I1–1 and 31/435–G2–1 (Osing et al. 1982; Valloggia with Henein 1986). They too serve to demonstrate the closeness of the cultural ties of the oasis community with the Nile Valley homeland.

The distribution of the Old Kingdom sites needs some consideration. The pattern is that there are three main areas of concentration (Fig. 10.1). The westernmost, situated between el-Qasr and Gedida, lies within several square kilometres. It is an area which is currently in the path of moving sand, a circumstance which masks the surface of the ground and may deprive us of some information. There are many spring mounds throughout the area and no doubt sufficient water would always have been available. While six of these sites are cemeteries, eleven bear the remains of occupation. Most of them have been heavily deflated and now consist principally of a scattering of sherds on the surface. Consequently, it becomes difficult to assess the real extent of the settlements they represent. Testing at 33/390–I9–3 has, however, revealed some remains of mud brick architecture (Mills 1979, pl. XV), and it is expected that the eventual excavation at this site will produce data on subsistence and related problems.

Of the sites in the central part of the oasis, in the vicinity of Mut, by far the most significant is 'Mut el-Kharab' (31/405–G10–1) (Mills 1981). The site, as it presently stands, towards the south side of the town, is the ruin of a Roman temple enclosure, with a heavy temenos wall of mud brick, the remains of brick buildings within, and the foundations of a temple structure. However, two indications reveal an earlier importance. The first is two hieratic stelae found by H.J. Lyons, and presented to the Ashmolean Museum (Porter and Moss 1952). The second indication is the ceramics from the site. Part of the testing of the site by the survey was the collection of a sample of sherd material from the surface (Hope 1981). A proportion of the material dates to the same late Old Kingdom period. Indeed, the beginnings of Mut would seem to date from the earliest Egyptian settlement in the oasis, for there are also sherds of the hand made local ceramics at the site (Hope 1981). Again, there are many spring mounds in the vicinity of Mut, including some inside the ruined enclosure.

The eastern group, centered on Ain Aseel (31/435–I1–1) is equally as early an establishment and was probably much more important that Mut. It would have been the administrative centre of the community in Dakhleh. Again, there is a line of spring mounds nearby, which would have supported agriculture. Apart from the Kila' ed-Debba burial ground (31/435–G2–1), the other Old Kingdom sites in the area (31/435–I4–1, 31/435–J1–1, 31/435–L2–4 and 31/435–L9–2) are either small or completely eroded with only a surface scattering of potsherds remaining.

The archaeological evidence suggests that after the First Intermediate Period, through the second and first millennia BC, there was never more than a small community in the oasis. The number of sites bearing material representing these centuries is small. In western Dakhleh, 33/390–M5–2, in the town of Qasr, has the remains of a Ptolemaic temple dedicated to 'Thoth, Twice Great of Hermopolis' (Mills 1980, 260); 32/405–A2–1, a mud brick temple with evidence from ceramics of use from Dynasty XXVI onwards (Mills 1981); and 32/390–K1–2, a small cemetery with Second Intermediate Period material. In the eastern part of Dakhleh the cemetery at 'Ein Tirghi, 31/435–D5–2, bears material remains of most of the period from the XII Dyanasty down to about the 5th Century AD (Mills 1983; Hope, Chapter 14, this volume), including ceramics, amulets, and coffins. The localities of the settlements associated with this latter, long-used cemetery remain undiscovered, but their existence must be inferred.

It is to Mut, and Site 31/405–G10–1, that one returns for what appears to have been the main permanent settlement in Dakhleh since the late Old Kingdom. The ruin, 'Mut el-Kharab', is at the southwest edge of the modern town of Mut. It is an enclosure, some 300 x 200 m, built on rising ground, with the remains of mud brick structures within and adjacent to it on the south and west. Sherd material collected from the enclosure yields dates in virtually all periods from the Old Kingdom and from the New Kingdom onwards. One must, in addition, take note of the two hieratic stelae that are stated to have come from the site.

One stela, Ashmolean Museum 1894.107.a (Gardiner 1933), dates to the 5th year of the reign of Shoshenk I (ca. 940 BC) and concerns a dispute over water rights. There is much important information contained in this document. The stela records the outcome of a petition by Nesubast to the oracle of the local deity, Setekh, and would have been placed in a prominent position in a public area of the local temple. The fact that this was a local cult centre signifies that there ought to have been a settlement of some size and permanence. The supplication of Nesubast concerns title to land irrigated by a certain well and the occasion of the oracular judgement was a visit of the governor, a relative of the Pharaoh. Part of the defense was historical, in that Nesubast claimed ownership back to his grandmother, in Dynasty XXI, which demonstrates a long-term community with written records of the usual administrative kind. It also shows that the resident population was a settled colony, rather than a temporary group that might have been regularly replaced. The document tells us that there was a plurality of wells, at least some of which were privately owned. In addition, it may provide us with the ancient name of Mut, as Sa-wahet. It is mentioned, in the introductory passage on the stela, that the governor, Wayheset, a royal relative, had been sent to the area "to

restore order in the Oasis-land, after he had found it in a state of war and turmoil" (Gardiner 1933, 22). Whether this phrase is an indication of the Libyans' occupation of Egyptian territory or whether it signals some local upheaval cannot be certainly stated.

The second stela, Ashmolean Museum 1894.107.b (Janssen 1968), again associated with a temple cult of Setekh, is the record of the donation of a daily offering of bread in the temple. The date of this text is given as year 24 of Py (726 BC), in Dynasty XXV. From the stela, Janssen identifies a Libyan tribe, the Shain Esdhuti, as being resident in the oasis, although he is uncertain whether it was very large or ever in touch with the Nile Valley. What we can see from this find is an apparent continuation of the same temple and settlement, although with the probable addition of Libyans to the community - perhaps as a result of policies of the XXII Dynasty.

What is absent, in these considerations of the continuity and quality of the settlement at Mut, is the confirming archaeological material. Even if the Roman temenos encloses the remains of the temple of Setekh, giving us the general location of the site, the size and archaeological history of the settlement have been lost, presumably beneath the buildings and pavements of the present town. Winlock (1936, 41) records that in 1908 Mut was a town 'built on an irregular hill of rock' (actually an old complex springmound). 'Old Mut' is about 3 km distant from Mut el-Kharab, and modern Mut now extends for some distance in all directions from the base of that hill across the flat surrounding plain, covering any traces of former settlement there may have been. The decline of the eastern oasis site, Ain Aseel, and the continuation of that at Mut may be linked by political or social causes, by environmental reasons or landscape changes, or may be a coincidence. One fact that may have some bearing on the matter is that Ain Aseel was established at the conjunction of both routes from Kharga Oasis and the direct route from the Nile Valley over the Libyan Plateau. Mut, on the other hand, is located centrally within the oasis, an administrative advantage, and is also at its southwesternmost point, an advantage for travelling into the southern desert along the Darb el-Tarfawi. However, the area of the oasis is so relatively small as to render significance of such advantages minimal. Neither, as well, appears to bear the remains of great defensive works, and cannot have been located for military reasons. On balance, it would seem that Ain Aseel was established in its location for reasons of communications to the Nile, but the situation for Mut was chosen for local reasons. Local inhabitants to-day assert that the best agricultural land in the oasis is in the vicinity of Mut.

It would also seem that the later Pharaonic oasis community was never restricted to the single centre at Mut; there are the sites located at some distance from Mut, and it should be supposed that the population never became so severely depleted. That it was considerably smaller than in its first surge in the late Old Kingdom is undoubted, but that it never disappeared is equally certain.

Such evidence as exists in the Nile Valley sources concerning this colony is equivocal, inasmuch as nowhere can the Dakhleh Oasis be specifically identified. We are left, principally, with the information that various administrators were responsible for the oases down through Egyptian history, and that the main produce from the oasis brought to the Nile Valley as tribute or for trade was agriculturally derived - wine, basketry, fruit, matting, and woven goods (see Redford 1976).

The advent of the Ptolemaic rulers in Egypt began a new prosperity and laid the foundations for the great Roman expansion and subsequent Byzantine consolidation that evolved into the Islamic community of to-day. The archaeological evidence in Dakhleh Oasis for these eras is overwhelmingly greater than for earlier, Pharaonic times and must form another study.

The problems that are the legacy of the archaeological survey are many. They will principally have to be solved on the ground in the oasis and several are already being investigated. It will be necessary to understand the nature of the resident community. It has the appearance of one directly related, culturally, to the Nile Valley, but whether there is a genetic relationship as well is uncertain. Current work at 'Ein Tirghi (31/435–D5–2) by J.E. Molto and others ought to present us with a population profile, based on human skeletal remains, which can then be compared with data from the Nile Valley to ascertain the closeness of this relationship (see Frey 1986; Molto 1986; Sha'aban 1988). In addition, work at this site is producing material remains of much of the period between the end of the Middle Kingdom and the Ptolemaic, a succession of historical periods not well represented on other sites in Dakhleh. Ceramics, decorated wooden coffins, and amulets are among the grave goods and will, when the material is fully analysed, give us important information on the types of goods manufactured in the oasis and those that were imported, which in turn should yield information on the trades represented in the oasis and the quality of the goods when compared with those manufactured in the Nile Valley.

A wide range of questions regarding the subsistence patterns of the oasis community also concerns us. Again, much information on nutrition is being gained from the work at 'Ein Tirghi, but much data can also be produced from a careful examination of midden and other occupation debris at sites such as 33/390–I9–3. It will also be important to attempt to restore the landscape levels to the Pharaonic periods, and associate these with water sources. Most springs leave a mineralised deposit, now seen in the form of a hill with a depressed eye in the centre and, if the suggestion that some were artificially formed or enhanced by the ancient Egyptians is correct, testing ought to enable us to pinpoint those springs which were active and used by those Egyptian farmers. The related questions concerning water and land use, subsistence and ecology will all bear heavily on our interpretations of the economy of the region. It will not be sufficient to rely on the Egyptian sources for information on the goods brought as tribute or

requested as luxuries, for these are not necessarily the stuff of everyday living.

The site of ancient Mut must command some of our attention, for it seems that only here has there been a permanent community in Dakhleh for the past few millennia. There are two strong factors in the oasis which cause settlements to cease. One is the movement of sand, which is inexorable. There has been no way of diverting a moving dune as a means of protecting farmland or settlement, and, for instance, we see the Roman period temple at 'Ein Birbiyeh (31/435–K5–1) as having been completely buried in a sand dune, and again, many of the present residents in Maohoub recently moved there, abandoning a hamlet south of Gedida when that became sanded up. The second factor is that a water source can dry up, an event which can be the result of a number of causes. The aquifer feeding the well can become depleted; sand will blow into the water head, gradually silting it up; suspended particles in the water can become deposited at the well mouth; and dissolved minerals can be deposited as evaporites at the well mouth. It seems that it is often easier to abandon such a well than it is to clear the eye (Beadnell 1909). Mut must have escaped both of these oasis evils for the settlement to have lasted for so many centuries in one place.

Another problem area that requires attention is that of the fluctuation of the population through time. The arrival of Egyptian settlers, around 2300 BC, saw the addition of the new migrants to an existing group of Sheikh Muftah inhabitants. This new grouping must have taxed the resources of the oasis until changes were effected by the newcomers. Nevertheless, the area supported both the indigenes and the migrants, who appear to have lived side by side for some decades. By the end of the First Intermediate Period, however, the Sheikh Muftah culture had disappeared and the size of the Egyptian community diminished. Some of the answer to this complicated change must be sought in sites that yield Sheikh Muftah Cultural Unit artifacts, but information must also come from environmental studies and from the few Pharaonic remains of the Middle Kingdom. It is possible to account for the disappearance of the Sheikh Muftah inhabitants from the archaeological record in several ways. It may be the case that the decline in size of the Egyptian community and the disappearance of the Sheikh Muftah people were related to the same natural or local event, or it may have been a fortuitous coincidence. As the two populations coexisted, apparently peacefully, for a century or more, military action by one on the other can probably be discounted. Similarly, as there is no noticeable adoption of Egyptian traits such as manufacturing technology, building techniques and architecture, or writing, it is improbable that the latter became 'Egyptianised' or assimilated to the point of disappearance from the archaeological record. Perhaps part of the explanation may be sought in the changes wrought to the Dakhleh landscape by the Old Kingdom farmers, who applied Nile Valley techniques and crops to the oasis, so altering it that the more primitive subsistence patterns could no longer be economically viable. Those Sheikh Muftah people, who would not change their own ways, possibly moved away from the oasis into more suitable grazing or hunting territory.

The matter of the external connections of the Egyptians living in the Dakhleh Oasis is not as simple as it would seem on the surface, for there were people living in the other great western oases and there must have been communication between them (Fakhry 1974; Porter and Moss 1952). In addition, there is the question of relationships with the desert areas further west and to the south. We know, from the smaller Dakhleh stela (Ashmolean 1894.107.b, Janssen 1968), that a tribe of Libyans was in the oasis in the XXV Dynasty; and possibly the great overland Egypt-Sudan trade route, the Darb el-Arba'in, which passes along the length of the Kharga Oasis, may also have been accessible to Dakhleh sites. El-Sherg el-Uweinat, a recent development scheme in the vicinity of the Sudan border, south of Bir Tarfawi, has a dual tarmacadamed road access, with one route from Mut, in Dakhleh, and the other from Baris, in southern Kharga. As often as not, modern pavements follow older routes across the desert. Some evidence should be recoverable in excavations to demonstrate such population movements. And, of course, a complete investigation of the nature, quality and incidence of the oasis dwellers' connection to the Nile Valley will have to be made. Again, archaeology has much to offer as a complement to the textual sources that we already have.

Address for Author

A.J. Mills, Egyptian Department, Royal Ontario Museum, 100 Queen's Park, Toronto, Ontario, Canada M5S 2C6, *and* The Barn, Above Town, Egloshayle, Wadebridge, Cornwall, England PL27 6HW.

REFERENCES

Arnold, Do. 1982. Keramikfunde aus Qila 'el-Dabba, 42–56. *In* Osing, J., M. Moursi, Do. Arnold, O. Neugebauer, R.A. Parker, D. Pingree and M.A. Nur-el-Din. 1982. *Denkmäler der Oase Dachla aus dem Nachlass von Ahmed Fakhry*. Deutsches Archäologisches Institut, Abteilung Kairo, Archäologische Veröffentlichungen 28, 117p.

Ballet, P. 1987. Essai de classification des coupes types Maidum-Bowl du sondage nord de 'Ayn-Asil (Oasis de Dakhla). Typologie et evolution. *Cahiers de la Céramique Egyptienne* 1: 1–16.

Butzer, K.W. 1976. *Early hydraulic civilization in Egypt*. Butzer, K.W. and L.G. Freeman, eds. Prehistoric Archeology and Ecology. Chicago: University of Chicago Press, 134p.

Beadnell, H.J.L. 1909. *An Egyptian oasis*. London: John Murray, 248p.

Caton-Thompson, G. 1952. *Kharga Oasis in Prehistory*. London: Athlone Press. 213p.

Davies, N. de G. 1933. *The tomb of Nefer-hotep at Thebes,* 2 vols. New York: Metropolitan Museum of Art, 81p.

Fakhry, A. 1972, The search for texts in the Western Desert. *Textes et langages de l'Égypte pharaonique II, Bibliothèque d'Etude,* Le Caire, 207–222.

Fakhry, A. 1974. *The oases of Egypt, II, Bahriyah and Farafra Oases*. Cairo: The American University in Cairo Press, 189p.

Frey, R.A. 1986. Dakhleh Oasis Project: Interim report on excavations at the 'Ein Tirghi cemetery. *Journal of the Society for the Study of Egyptian Antiquities* 16: 92–102.

Gardiner, A.H. 1933. The Dakhleh stela. *Journal of Egyptian Archaeology* 19: 19–30.

Hope, C.A. 1980. Dakhleh Oasis Project – Report on the study of the pottery and kilns. *Journal of the Society for the Study of Egyptian Antiquities* 10: 283–313.

Hope, C.A. 1981. Dakhleh Oasis Project: Report on the study of the pottery and kilns: Third season – 1980. *Journal of the Society for the Study of Egyptian Antiquities* 11: 233–241.

Hope, C.A. This volume. Chapter 14. Pottery manufacture in the Dakhleh Oasis, 215–243.

Janssen, J.J. 1968. The smaller Dakhla stela. *Journal of Egyptian Archaeology* 54: 165–172.

List of Archaeological Sites indexed by the Dakhleh Oasis Project. This volume. Appendix II, 251–266.

McDonald, M.M.A. This volume. Chapter 7. Neolithic cultural units and adaptations in Dakhleh Oasis, 117–132.

Mills, A.J. 1979. Dakhleh Oasis Project: Report on the first season of survey: October-December 1978. *Journal of the Society for the Study of Egyptian Antiquities* 9: 163–185.

Mills, A.J. 1980. Dakhleh Oasis Project: Report on the second season of survey, September-December, 1979. *Journal of the Society for the Study of Egyptian Antiquities* 10: 251–282.

Mills, A.J. 1981. Dakhleh Oasis Project: Report on the third season of survey: September-December, 1980. *Journal of the Society for the Study of Egyptian Antiquities* 11: 175–192.

Mills, A.J. 1983. Dakhleh Oasis Project: Report on the fifth season of survey: October, 1982 – January, 1983. *Journal of the Society for the Study of Egyptian Antiquities* 13: 121–141.

Molto, J.E. 1986. Dakhleh Oasis Project: Human skeletal remains from the Dakhleh Oasis, Egypt. *Journal of the Society for the Study of Egyptian Antiquities* 16: 119–127.

Newberry, P.E. 1893. *Beni Hasan, Part I*. Archaeological Survey of Egypt, Memoir no. 1, 1–85.

Osing, J., M. Moursi, Do. Arnold, O. Neugebauer, R.A. Parker, D. Pingree and M.A. Nur-el-Din, eds. 1982. *Denkmäler der Oase Dachla aus dem Nachlass von Ahmed Fakhry*. Deutsches Archäologisches Institut, Abteilung Kairo, Archäologische Veröffentlichungen 28, 117p.

Petrie, W.M.F. 1900. *Dendereh, 1898*. The Egyptian Exploration Fund, Memoir no. 17, 1–74.

Petrie, W.M.F. 1907. *Gizeh and Rifeh*. London: British School of Archaeology in Egypt and Egyptian Research Account, Thirteenth Year, 1907, 30p.

Porter, B. and R.L.B. Moss, eds. 1952. *Topographical bibliography of ancient Egyptian hieroglyphic texts, reliefs and paintings. VII. Nubia, the deserts, and outside Egypt*. Oxford: Oxford University Press, 433p.

Redford, D.B. 1976. The oases in Egyptian history to Classical times, Part I – to 2100 B.C. *Journal of the Society for the Study of Egyptian Antiquities* 7: 7–10.

Sha'aban, M.M. 1988. *Palaeodemography of a pre-Roman population from el-Dakhleh, Egypt: evidence from the skeletal remains at site 31/435–D5-2*. Toronto: University of Toronto, Ph.D. thesis, 369p.

Valloggia, M. with N.H. Henein. 1986. Balat I. Le mastaba de Medou-Nefer. *Fouilles de l'Institut Français d'Archéologie Orientale* 31: 1–239.

Vercoutter, J. 1986. Introduction, ix-xv. *In* Valloggia, M. with N.H. Henein, Balat I. Le mastaba de Medou-Nefer. *Fouilles de l'Institut Français d'Archéologie Orientale* 31: 1–239.

Winlock, H.E. 1936. *Ed Dakhleh Oasis. Journal of a camel trip made in 1908*. New York: Metropolitan Museum of Art, 77p.

11

PATHOLOGICALLY SLENDER HUMAN LONG BONES FROM THE DAKHLEH OASIS

P. G. Sheldrick, M.D.

INTRODUCTION

During the 1979 survey season of the Dakhleh Oasis Project several cemeteries were test excavated for the purpose of identifying and dating the sites. The remains of over 100 individuals were examined, many showing healed fractures, arthritis and other examples of pathology. Four skeletons showed a distinct bone abnormality whose cause is still uncertain. They were found in two cemeteries several kilometres apart, and probably date from the time of the Roman occupation of Egypt, i.e. from the 1st Century AD. One cemetery (32/390–I6–1) is located near the village of Mushiya and the other (31/405–D7–2) near Qâlamûn. The specimens were first reported in *Paleopathology Newsletter* (Sheldrick 1980).

DESCRIPTION

The striking feature of all the long bones of these four skeletons is the slenderness and fragility of their shafts. The cortex of each long bone is thin and brittle, and the marrow space is relatively enlarged, despite the reduced cross-sectional area. The trabeculae of the medulla are delicate and widely separated.

Three of the four individuals showing abnormalities of this description were found in Tomb 1 in the cemetery at Mushiya (32/390–I6–1). The pottery from the surface and the style of the tomb suggest a date from Roman times. In the burial chamber, a scarab was found bearing the cartouche of Psammetichus I of Dynasty XXVI (664–610 BC; Rose 1985), but this may have been an heirloom. Further study may produce a more accurate dating of the tomb. The remains of 20 individuals of varying ages and both sexes were also found in Tomb 1. Most bones are robust, well preserved and pathologically unremarkable. However, the three skeletons in question are unfortunately poorly preserved, mainly because of the fragile nature of their abnormal bones. The axial skeletons were osteoporotic and adhered to the soil which showed evidence of mineralisation or hardening from at least one inundation of salt-rich water. Few of the bones were retrieved intact.

The first skeleton, probably from a female in her late teens, was extended and supine. The right humerus is best preserved, has a length of 254 mm, and yet a minimum diameter of the diaphysis of only 8 mm at about mid-shaft. The cortex is very thin, about 2 mm thick in cross-section. Despite the obviously slender diaphysis, the epiphyses are of near normal size, which gives the bone a club-like appearance at both ends. Incidentally, the skull exhibited *cribra orbitalia*, but was otherwise normal.

Two other skeletons of young adults show the abnormality even more dramatically, although their preservation is poorer. Both skeletons were extended supine and placed one directly above the other so that it was difficult to distinguish the bones of one from the other. One left humerus is broken above the epicondyles, but is still 250 mm long from the fracture line to the superior surface of the humeral head (*caput humeris*). The proximal epiphysis is fully fused to the diaphysis, indicating adulthood. Remarkably, the minimum diameter at about diaphyseal mid-shaft is only 5 mm. The diaphyseal shafts of the long bones of these two individuals show the same slender construction with thin cortices and sparse spongiosa as in the teenaged female skeleton. The right femur (Fig. 11.1) of the lowermost skeleton appeared to be hyperflexed at the hip joint and was well enough preserved to be measured

'Reports from the Survey of Dakhleh Oasis, Western Desert of Egypt, 1977–1987', edited by C.S. Churcher and A.J. Mills. Dakhleh Oasis Project: Monograph 2. Oxbow Monograph 99.

in situ. The total length was 360 mm (the extremities distingrated during excavation, see Fig. 11.1A), allowing the individual's height in life to be estimated at 1.49 ± 0.394 m, or 4' 10" (Trotter and Gleser 1958). The femur has a minimum diameter of only 10 mm at about 65% of the length (or about 234 mm) from the proximal end. The maximum diameter at the mid-shaft is 12 mm. This dimension usually averages about 27.8 mm in normal femora excavated from the oasis.

Another interesting comparison with normal bones can be done using a 'robusticity index', based on the maximum subtrochanteric diameter (Bass 1971). In the right femur described above, this diameter is only 15 mm.

The formula for the Robusticity Index (RI) is:

$$\text{Robusticity Index} = \frac{\text{Maximum subtrochanteric diameter}}{\text{Maximum femoral length}} \times 100$$

Which, when applied to the femur, is:

$$= 15/360 \times 100$$
$$= 4.17$$

Table 11.1 gives normal RI's measured and calculated from normal femora excavated from the cemetry at 'Ein Tirghi (31/435–D5–2). If two standard deviations are subtracted from the smallest mean RI: 6.73 – (2 × 0.74), we get a smallest probable RI of 5.25. At 4.17, the RI of the abnormal femur is well below this figure. In other words, this example is far slenderer than any conceivably normal femur.

The shaft of the femur is so thin that one wonders if it could have supported the weight of even this short-statured adult (Fig. 11.1D). There is a remarkable paucity of markings for muscle attachments on the surfaces, e.g., the linea aspera is barely visible in contrast to the distinct ridge present on a normal human femur.

Both skulls have full adult dentitions showing some attrition, as in young adults, but the third molars appear to be congenitally absent. One skull also shows *cribra orbitalia*, bilateral chronic *mastoiditis* and an apical abscess of the left central incisor.

The fourth example was found in a similar tomb several kilometres away in Tomb 1 of the cemetery near Qâlamûn

(31/405–D7–2). The site also dates from Roman times, i.e., 1st Century AD. The 12 limb bones were recovered from a profusion of disturbed bones in the sand fill of the tomb chamber, so that it is impossible to say whether one or more individuals are represented. Although the bones are more robust and better preserved than those previously described, the same slender structure is evident. A right fibula is 288 mm long and only 8 mm in diameter at mid-shaft, and a right humerus is 269 mm long and 10 mm in diameter, also at mid-shaft. In all cases the long bone shafts are so altered that they exhibit none of the characteristic criteria of normal long bones. All the other human bones found in this tomb are of normal size and morphology and lack any significant pathology.

Strangely, no healed fractures nor any bowing deformities are found in any of the bones of all four examples. It is possible that some of the broken bones represent fracturing occurring shortly premortem, as opposed to postmortem damage. This is doubtful, however, because even a fracture that is only a few days old will show the first signs of healing, with a callus of new bone forming a bridge across the gap. A callus bridge is always bulkier than the original bone and forms a swelling that persists, in some bones, for years. Fractures without signs of healing occur either hours before death, during the laying out or interment, or from subsequent events, including excavation. The lack of any healed fracture suggests that the broken bones did not occur during the lives of these three individuals, at least before their deaths.

One possible diagnosis is *osteogenesis imperfecta*; however, the absence of fractures and angular deformities argues against this. Only one example of *osteogenesis imperfecta* has been previously reported from ancient Egypt (Gray 1969), and therefore it may be considered unlikely. Other possibilities are *osteoporosis* secondary to *hyperadrenocorticoidism*, *hyperparathyroidism*, etc., and disuse atrophy. Usually these conditions show a loss of bone mineralisation, but not the striking narrowing of the long bone shafts seen in these specimens. Perhaps a young growing person suffering from a paralysing disease such as polio could develop such attenuated bones. The shape of a normal growing bone is greatly influenced by mechanical stress. Stresses are applied by muscles and by weight bearing. The points of attachment of muscles are usually visible as distinct features, usually called tubercles, tuberosities, facets, lineae, etc. As muscles get stronger, these features become larger and more distinct. Similarly, muscular and weight-bearing stresses stimulate a bone to increase its mass and therefore its strength. This is manifest as an increase in shaft diameter and cortex thickness and is an example of Wolff's Law (Salter 1983). Even the cross-sectional shape of a bone is remodelled by mechanical use (Frost 1987). All of these features are lacking in the abnormal bones decribed here. Besides being slender, all the shafts are more or less circular in cross-section, so that it is impossible, for example, to distinguish a shaft fragment of humerus from one of fibula.

Table 11.1. Normal Robusticity Indices (RI) obtained from normal right and left femora excavated from the cemetry at 'Ein Tirghi (31/435–D5–2).

	Sample	Range of RI's	Mean	Standard Deviation
	N	Min.-Max.	RI	S.D.
Males, right	13	6.45–7.83	7.28	0.20
left	12	6.98–8.12	7.46	0.44
Females, right	11	5.06–7.50	6.73	0.74
left	11	5.69–7.62	6.79	0.56
Slender femur from Tomb 1	1	4.17	(4.17)	–

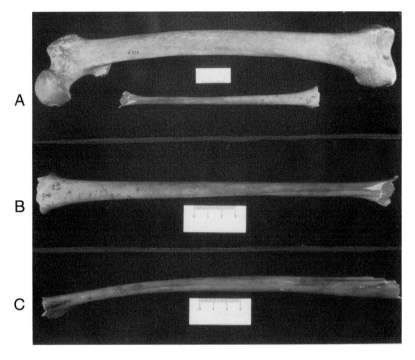

Fig. 11.1.

A. Pathologically slender adult right femur from Tomb 1 in Mushiya Cemetery (32/390–I6–1), lacking ends and with markedly slender diaphysis. Shown with normal adult femur (above) for comparison. Anterior views.

B. Enlarged anterior view of slender femur.

C. Enlarged lateral view of slender femur. Note almost isodiametric diaphyseal conformation in the slender femur.

D. Enlarged view of distal end of slender femur showing thin cortex and sparse trabeculae.
   Scales = 30 mm.

In 1988 two fragments of human long bones were found in the cemetery at 'Ein Tirghi (31/435–D5–2). Unfortunately, these were found in the fill of a badly disturbed tomb (Tomb 36), so that both dating and context are lacking. Because the fragments represent only short segments of diaphysis, it is impossible to identify from which bone(s) they originate. However, the specimens exhibit the exact same abnormality as described above, with a very slender shaft, thin cortex and proportionately enlarged marrow space.

One of these fragments is about 15 mm in diameter with a mean cortical thickness of about 1.5 mm. This was sectioned and examined microscopically by M. Cook at University Hospital, London, Ontario. The microscopic section shows woven, lamellar and circumferential lamellar bone with few osteons. This indicates an absence of new bone activity and no evidence of bone remodelling or turnover. Normal bone shows an abundance of osteons in response to mechanical loading, and to promote growth and remodelling. These abnormal bones, however, show no evidence of this ever having happened as histologically they resemble the bones of a newborn infant. In other words, this microscopic evidence strongly supports the theory that these individuals suffered from some sort of flaccid paralysis from an early age.

DISCUSSION

Recent unpublished work (J.E. Molto, pers. comm. 1990) on the other bones from the 'Ein Tirghi cemetery suggests there may be a high incidence of *spina bifida*, at least in that locale. This bone abnormality characteristically has a wide spectrum of manifestations in life. At worst, it is accompanied by a meningomyelocoele, in which parts of the spinal cord extrude into a thin sac that breaks open at the skin surface. In ancient times, all children having this condition certainly died. Conversely, the most benign form is *spina bifida occulta*, which is asymptomatic and evident only by the defect of the neural arch, commonly in the sacrum. This defect was found in greater-than-expected prevalence in tombs excavated at 'Ein Tirghi during the 1985 to 1990 seasons. Lying towards the middle of the spectrum of manifestations are individuals with *spina bifida* who have malformed elements of the spinal cord and nerve roots without the full meningomyelocoele. The trunk and limbs of these people are often paralysed and under-developed (Nelson *et al.* 1969). Under such circumstances, non-weight bearing, growing bones could form into the shape of the bones described above. It is conceivable that even in ancient times, such victims could have been cared for in bed even to young adulthood. If so, it would indicate a remarkable degree of nursing care and social support having been provided to these severly disabled people.

However, arguing against this theory is the fact that most *spina bifida* patients are paraplegic but not quadraplegic. A cervical (neck) lesion usually causes a very minimal or no neurological deficit, *fide* the modern medical literature (e.g., Behrman et al. 1992). In contrast to the four (or more) individuals described above, paraplegics have normally developed or overly developed upper limbs, because they use their arms for what locomotion they can accomplish, such as crawling, and this should manifest itself as more robust arm bones. This phenomenon has been termed 'work hypertrophy' and is another example of Wolff's Law (Salter 1983). However, such hypertrophy appears to be absent in these individuals and certainly in the presumed female skeleton first discussed. Thus *spina bifida* may be ruled out as the cause of this condition.

Unfortunately, the spinal columns of the individuals in this study did not survive, or are not identifiable, as all vertebrae found in these tombs appear normal. Most of the specimens described are deposited in the Department of Anthropology, University of Cairo, in the care of Dr. Moheb Sha'aban. It is hoped they will eventually be studied further. It is also hoped that future excavations will reveal more examples of this abnormality with better preservation, as well as associations of elements, and that consequently some of the questions raised above may be answered.

Acknowledgements

I wish to thank sincerely C.S. Churcher, M. Cook, A.J. Mills, J.E. Molto, M.H. Mychajlowycz and M.M. Sha'aban for their very generous assistance in preparing this work. I am also most grateful to Mrs. E. Cockburn and the *Paleopathology Newsletter* in which this material was first published for allowing me to use it as the basis for an expanded report.

Address for Author

P. G. Sheldrick, M.D., 209 Victoria Avenue, Chatham, Ontario, Canada N7L 3A7

REFERENCES

Bass, W.M. 1971. *Human Osteology: a laboratory and field manual of the human skeleton*, edit. 1. Columbia, Missouri: Missouri Archeological Society, 288p.

Behrman, R.E., R.M. Kliegman, W.E. Nelson and V.C. Vaughan III. 1992. *Nelson Textbook of Pediatrics*, edit. 14. Philadelphia, Pennsylvania: W.B. Saunders, 1965p.

Frost, H.M. 1987. Secondary osteon populations: an algorithm for determining mean bone tissue age. *Yearbook of Physical Anthropology* **30**: 221–238.

Gray, P.H. 1969. A case of osteogenesis imperfecta, associated with dentinogenesis imperfecta, dating from antiquity. *Clinical Radiology* 21: 106–108.

Nelson, W.E., V.C. Vaughan, III and R.J. McKay. 1969. *Textbook of Pediatrics*, edit. 9. Philadelphia: Pennsylvania, W.B. Saunders, 1589p.

Rose, J. 1985. *The sons of Re: cartouches of the kings of Egypt.* Warrington, Cheshire: JR-T, Croft, 175p.

Salter, R.B. 1983. *Textbook of disorders and injuries of the musculoskeletal system*, edit. 2. Baltimore, Maryland: Williams and Wilkins, 578p.

Sheldrick, P.G. 1980. "Skinny bones" from the Dakhleh Oasis. *Paleopathology Newsletter*, no. 30, 7–10.

Trotter, M. and G.C. Gleser. 1958. A re-evaluation of estimation of stature based on measurements of stature taken during life and on long bones after death. *American Journal of Physical Anthroplogy*, n.s., **16**: 79–124.

12

CONSERVATION, PRESERVATION AND PRESENTATION OF MONUMENTS AND OBJECTS IN THE DAKHLEH OASIS

Adam K. Zielinski

ARCHAEOLOGY AND CONSERVATION IN EGYPT

The number of finds and monuments illustrating the life of ancient Egypt can easily be estimated at millions of objects, thousands of structures, and an imposing volume of earthworks.

A smoothly functioning archaeological mission located anywhere in Egypt soon realises that the storage area required for its finds has to be several times bigger than that for its housing. The number of finds is constantly increasing, new sites are located and old sites analysed in more detail.

Egypt's concern to protect its heritage has resulted in an increasing number and importance of multidisciplinary projects in which conservation plays an important role. There is growing concern for protection of finds, for proper presentation of sites and for restrictions on the number of tourists allowed on sites. Today, an archaeologist applying for a concession to excavate a site will most likely be asked to protect the site when his work is completed, to preserve the finds, and often to present a proposal for reconstruction of the structure to be unearthed.

The harsh desert climate can be as aggressive as the most careless tourist or the most narrow minded developer, and an exposed site suffers serious damage if it is not left properly protected after excavation ceases. A few sandstorms can easily destroy a newly exposed fresco or wall surface, leaving only a limited and sometimes questionable photographic record.

A well conducted modern archaeological project requires fairly close daily cooperation between an archaeologist and a conservator. The need for such cooperation is still rejected by some archaeological projects, until circumstances force them to accept conservatorial assistance. This attitude represents an echo from the past, when the most important goals of a project were to expose a monument and to organise a staggering display of finds in some museum. Today many archaeological teams employ a professional conservator as one of their members. Such a liason has created the specialised discipline of 'archaeological conservation', and there is now a small group of conservators specialising in conservation carried out at the field site.

Modern archaeological conservation is concerned both with the site and with objects belonging to the site. The moment of excavation can be disastrous for archaeological remains. Their deterioration since being abandoned will have almost ceased, leaving them in near-equilibrium with their environment. When exposed by excavation, they are subject to reduced support from the surrounding matrix, to abrupt changes in temperature and relative humidity, to contact with light and air, and erosion by wind-borne mineral particles. The moment of excavation can also cause a conflict of priorities unless both conservator and excavator appreciate each other's concerns.

Although protective measures appear costly, the alternative is unacceptable – the irretrievable loss of information about partially excavated features through leaving them exposed to destructive agents from one season to the next. Measures designed for site protection between seasons should be employed as seriously as the preventive conservation of finds when work is resumed.

Sometimes neglected, post-excavation maintenance is more than 'passive conservation' because of the continuing need to use the site and its artefacts. Total

'Reports from the Survey of Dakhleh Oasis, Western Desert of Egypt, 1977–1987', edited by C.S. Churcher and A.J. Mills. Dakhleh Oasis Project: Monograph 2. Oxbow Monograph 99.

protection is incompatible with total use; if objects are to be handled for study and publication, and if the site is to be explored by visitors, maintenance will always be an active and demanding task.

Today, archaeology in Egypt is no longer the adventure it used to be, obscured by mystery, with the Pharaoh's Curse following the explorer, who wore a pith helmet and was accompanied by a mob of obedient servants. It is a science with a well established approach, often acting in close cooperation with other disciplines. In previous years, archaeologists were mainly interested in removing whatever objects could be moved to a museum for display. The site remained open and in most cases improperly maintained or guarded, and soon suffered damage. Some of the most spectacular sites at that time were reconstructed, and some reconstructed in conjectured form, and some were erased in order to expose even more spectacular material hidden beneath.

A desire to better understand the data revealed by the archaeological process led to the first efforts to preserve and protect the exposed sites for further investigations and analysis. The final result of such an evolving approach is a new discipline – the conservation of objects and monuments. The specific requirements of modern archaeology have resulted in further developments, creating a discipline of on-site archaeological conservation entirely devoted to the protection and preservation of archaeological finds in the field and for assisting archaeology.

CONSERVATION SERVICE ON SITE

The practice of conservation in general, and archaeological conservation in particular, is an activity which can be compared with a highly developed and sophisticated craft, where thorough professional education, manual ability, a decisive personality and an open mind are of greatest importance. In general terms the conservator has to deal with treatment consisting of three main activities:

1   an introductory site visit for observations, studies and general assessment of the site;
2   a development period for obtaining permits, paperwork, equipment, laboratory tests and experiments, and logistical planning for the field season; and
3   the on-site application of the conservation treatments.

The entire conservation operation can be broken down into a large number of small but essential actions, each of which should be well thought out in advance. This requires a good knowledge of local conditions and an experienced crew. The Egyptian reality also requires a good knowledge of local markets. We know from our experience in Egypt that one can locate all the necessary tradesmen and, that with proper doses of patience and encouragement, every order placed in a small workshop can be realised with surprising speed and efficiency. From the very beginning of our activity in the Dakhleh Oasis, profiting by our experience from previous projects in Egypt, we knew that all highly sophisticated laboratory equipment is much more useful in the laboratory than on site, and that laboratory tests are of great value when they supply us with required information before the beginning of the season. Harsh climate, ever present dust and sand, high temperatures, and voltage fluctuations in power supplied by local power stations are able to frustrate and discourage the most enthusiastic scientist.

The conservation team has to be able to weather all unexpected situations which, in practical terms means that several feasible solutions have to be planned for, each of which has to be practical in the local circumstances.

One matter never mentioned in publications concerning the practice of field conservation is the selection of team members. Quick decisions, imagination, manual ability and patience are among the most general requirements when selecting the team. A high level of professional education is (or should be) beyond discusssion. The idea of volunteer manpower, which has flourished in recent years, might cut down the expenses of the project but, on the other hand, may produce a final product of questionable quality. It is hard to expect that an enthusiast who works in an office eleven months of the year, and decides to spend his winter holiday in Egypt, can create a conservation miracle when a decorated stone piece is falling apart. Conservation in general is an expensive exercise and the manpower employed should be highly qualified in order to produce a product of the highest quality. The value of heritage is too high to make a monument a training centre. One of the requirements for a conservator is the ability to decide on the spot what to do, how to approach the problem, and to take responsibility for a decision. Professional experience eliminates panic on site, saves time, and ensures that the project can be completed.

The treatment when divided into daily tasks requires a well organised, dedicated and disciplined team. Delays should be expected and allowed for. Daily expectations of the amount of work or progress to be accomplished therefore should not be too ambitious. Such day by day hard work calls for good physical condition and determination from each member. Long term projects very often consist of repetitive operations and the danger is that boredom will divert attention, resulting in poor quality work and social tensions within the team. Inability to cope with new and unexpected conditions can considerably decrease productivity.

In sum, the conservation team should consist mainly of experienced members with good educational backgrounds who work well together. The person in charge should be able to count on the other members, and they in their turn should be able to observe, to judge and make wise decisions, and thus complete the task. As we know from experience, an unfinished project with the treatment left half done and the site unprotected during the off season, may result in much more serious damage to the monument than leaving it untouched.

The recent tendency to employ sophisticated tools often obliterates common sense, and the failure of the treatment is excused by the failure of the equipment. When undertaking an archaeological conservation project, we are dealing with the products of a simple technology, and we can be more successful by employing simple techniques once again. Often materials very similar to those used hundreds of years ago can be bought locally, and the correct decision can be undertaken by a person familiar with the technological history of the site, the properties of the materials offered, and the manner of their application. The conservation remedy may well involve a treatment similar to that which produced the original artifact or structure. One should not blindly follow the technical advice of prosperous chemical companies eagerly providing information, as such companies are mainly interested in their profits. One has to be able to predict the long term results if a new product is employed and the materials used should be proven by previous experience. However, there are no two identical situations and one should always be prepared to face new developments.

DETERIORATION OF MONUMENTS AND OBJECTS

Whatever the material of an object or structure which has been buried in the ground, the burial will have brought about profound physical and chemical alterations. An object is the material evidence of a message, either human, historical or technological, which it brings to us. In order to let the object retain its message as intact as possible it is essential from the moment of discovery to take a series of measures which will prevent the object, already altered by its stay underground, from being even more damaged by exposure. The 'on site' conservation deals with objects and monuments and, while an object can be moved when necessary and possible, the monument has to be treated at its location.

The problem of preserving and presenting *in situ* monuments and architectural remains is one of the most difficult tasks faced by conservators. The basic difficulty is that exposed and deteriorated structures are no longer able to withstand the elements, and that all man-made structures are in a state of dynamic change towards equilibrium with nature. The preservation of architectural surfaces decorated with paintings, stucco and mosaics, which come to light in the course of excavations, present particularly serious conservation problems. Their long term survival depends on their ambient environment and, being integral parts of an immovable architectural whole, they are always difficult to protect from the effects of deterioration caused by external agents.

Materials in nature continually deteriorate as a result of physical, chemical and biological processes. All construction materials, natural or artificial, without exception, are affected and their deterioration has be to

considered an important part of their existence. As one of the most widely accessible materials available to man, natural stone has been extensively used for many centuries. It is often a significant component, and in places the only one, of man-made structures the world over, and its properties, applications and behaviour over long periods of time constitute a story that is almost unbelievably complex.

The evolution and transformation of rocks is mainly the result of physico-chemical disparity between the initial formative environment of the rock and the new environments to which it becomes exposed in various ways. The changes produced by weathering in fresh rocks are governed by thermodynamic laws and can be ascribed to partial or complete migration of both major and minor chemical elements. Ultimately, the degree of alteration depends on the resistence to weathering of the minerals that constitute the rock, on their homogeneity, and on the specific areas exposed to disruptive agents. When used as building stones and free standing stones, rocks are subject to more influences in addition to those of natural weathering, such as man-made pollution, increased humidity, temperature fluctuations, or fire.

In other words, stone is as fragile and subject to exterior factors as other construction materials and, in spite of its hardness and weight, is as subject to decomposition as wood or mud brick. Like these materials, it should be protected against deterioration even if the protective measures can only arrest its decay temporarily.

DAKHLEH OASIS PROJECT AND ITS CONSERVATION UNIT

There are still some places in Egypt which have survived the march of contemporary civilisation and cheap development, and which remain unspoiled by modern man. As in the past, they remain remote, even desolate, with poor roads and lack of accommodation in terms of the expectations of a North American or European tourist. Dakhleh Oasis is one of these places. Only a few years ago tourists began to visit it as a new attraction, but the distance from Cairo and the modest accommodations discourage many. From a scientific point of view, the Oasis represents a place of great value, as it is almost untouched by modern civilisation, and contains undisturbed historical sites.

The establishment and development of what is today the Dakhleh Oasis Project reflect the needs and requirements of this enormous site. The civilisation and environmental complexity of the Oasis require close cooperation among the scholars who make up the Project's team. The number of monuments and objects even within one site, and awareness of the possiblity of their deterioration when being exposed, have resulted in the organisation of a permanent conservation unit to perform all necessary measures on site in order to prevent damage to the original fabric of the oasis.

The conservation unit was organised to carry out a variety of preservation, conservation and prevention treatments. Within a short time, its activities focussed on three main categories:

1   field conservation and preservation treatment on site;
2   collecting data, recording observations, and studies to obtain adequate information for understanding the processes of deterioration of the materials involved, and an understanding of the ancient technologies;
3   planning activity, including market research, for further seasons.

In the course of its work, the unit deals with the following materials: masonry (stone, mud brick, mortar, plaster); ceramics; organic materials; metals; and composite-material objects.

Members of the unit carry out inspection visits to sites being surveyed to study the present state of preservation of a given site, to understand its past and to observe its environmental phenomena. An inspection visit is always done in the presence of an archaeologist familiar with the site, and the ensuing conversation is of great importance for future plans for conservation or preservation. Such on site conversations are generally much more useful than those off-site, even when illustrated with slides. The presence of other scholars allows us to discuss problems arising on site and to answer questions on the spot. The Dakhleh Oasis Project's archaeological policy is discussed with the conservator, and the conservation treatment is subject to archaeological needs and requirements.

CONSERVATION PROBLEMS IN DAKHLEH OASIS: MATERIALS AND ENVIRONMENT

In terms of conservation-preservation problems, Dakhleh Oasis is a complicated interlocking system of natural and artificial phenomena. Climate changes as a result of human activity are beyond doubt. The quest for water has caused and continues to cause changes in settlement pattern. Limited areas of arable land have resulted in multiple occupations of a site. A contemporary small village is often located just beside or on top of an ancient settlement.

Increased demand for water in recent years has resulted in the large scale development of a net of deeply drilled wells which seriously disturbs the fragile environment of the oasis. Today the wells provide a constant stream of water rich in mineral salts, and the surplus water is deposited in evaporation ponds or is just allowed to drain into the soil. We noticed days with rapid changes in the relative humidity of the air, when the RH value would reach 70% in the morning and rapidly fall to 30% in the evening. Such a phenomenon poses a serious threat to more fragile archaeological finds, as increased moisture content in the air causes an increase in the volume of the hygroscopic salt crystals within an object. This increased volume of salt can 'explode' the affected object. Also,

many of the structures built in the Oasis are made of mud brick, and the increased volume of moisture in the air and adjacent soil can accelerate the deterioration of such structures.

So far, the Dakhleh Oasis Project has unearthed more mud brick than stone structures. The stone architecture consists of a Graeco-Roman necropolis in Ezbet Bashendi, with tombs built in local sandstone; an exposed late Roman temple at Deir el-Haggar (seriously damaged); and another late Roman temple buried in a large sand dune at 'Ein Birbiyeh. Stone as a construction material has been employed to a surprisingly modest degree throughout time in the oasis. Dakhleh Oasis is surrounded by vast deposits of sandstone and limestone, but most of the remaining structures are made of mud. The sandstone employed was not particularly carefully chosen and, as close inspection of one of the tombs has revealed, the blocks were often reused, being salvaged from earlier structures, as shown by the pattern of chisel marks on the blocks. These were originally of indifferent quality, which might suggest fairly primitive methods of quarrying. The stone structures in the oasis vary in their states of decay and disrepair from material deterioration, or by improper use of the adjacent supporting soil. Watering of the soil, often a heavy clay, results in its expansion, and later shrinkage when it dries. The movement of the subsoil, even if invisible to the naked eye, is the result of differential water content, and results in serious displacements within a structure. A major problem of conservation is how to achieve strict control of moisture within the subsoil supporting a structure.

Strong, almost constantly blowing winds create another serious problem, the movement of sand. A gale force wind may blow fine sand against an exposed structure and sand-blast its surface. As many sites being considered for future excavations are in long abandoned areas of the Oasis, any vegetation which could act as a wind break is at most modest and likely absent. Tree planting is one of the many preventive measures which must be undertaken before a site is exposed, but involves an adequate source of irrigation water.

A test examination at one of the many necropolises in the Oasis resulted in the exposure of rich deposits of decorated coffins and ritual funerary artefacts. The full excavations of other tombs or graves most likely will supply us with a large number of finds which will need to undergo conservation treatments.

PROJECTS OF THE CONSERVATION UNIT
Tomb of Kitinos

This tomb is one of a group of at least eight Graeco-Roman tombs at the north end of the village of Bashendi. It is built of local sandstone and consists of a square superstructure about 10×10 m standing above ground. Parts of the tomb are decorated with raised relief and with a minimum of preserved painting. In 1982 the Project was approached by the local office of the Egyptian Antiquities Organisation with a request to clean up the tomb and make it more attractive for visitors. Ahmed Fakhry records that the tomb was inhabited when he first discovered it in 1947. Nothing was done to the monument until 1972, when Fakhry cleared the sanctuary and built a pair of protective gate pillars and installed doors to safeguard the interior.

The condition of the tomb could be described as poor when we completed our inspection in 1984. All surfaces had been blackened by a coating of soot and other matter from cooking fires; the tomb was filled with debris and it had also been used as a cellar to stable a donkey; there was virtually no light inside to enable visitors to see the monument; and a modern village house was built on the tomb's roof. Also, much of the stone used in the tomb construction was of poor quality, and thus had deteriorated considerably.

The modern house was demolished, as well as parts of the west and north walls and the south-east corner, which had been rebuilt during the tomb's re-use as dwelling and storage space. The protective pillars built by Ahmed Fakhry as temporary structures were removed and the original surfaces exposed. The subfloor burial pits were investigated in each room. With the archaeological investigation completed, the restoration of the tomb could begin.

Restoration and conservation were based on results of tests carried out on samples of the deposits which covered the interior surfaces of the tomb.

The local sandstone used in the tomb had deteriorated both mechanically and chemically. Mechanical deterioration was exhibited by broken roofing slabs, wall blocks and other architectural elements, and by displacements within the walls. Chemical deterioration started with the high salt content of the original rock, exacerbated by rising salt-rich ground water, and resulted in extreme concentrations of salts within the stones of the tomb.

Structural repairs to the tomb and cleaning of the interior surfaces were carried out together during one field season. All materials used were Egyptian, purchased in Dakhleh Oasis or Cairo, and all were natural materials, apart from the iron doorway and glass skylights. These materials were chosen so that the natural balance of the tomb structure would be disturbed as little as possible and the original fabric maintained as much as possible. The rebuilding of the damaged parts of the walls, additional roofing, and installation of a door and skylights were done to enable the visitor to view the tomb as an entire structure and architectural unit.

A burial pit in the north-west room was left open to enable visitors to get an idea of the substructure of the tomb. All the other pits were refilled and the floors covering them rebuilt with a layer of rough stones buried in clean yellow sand. The floors are now easy to keep clean and blend in with local tradition. Some 50 cm of sand and debris were removed from the floor of the doorway, down to the original floor of the tomb. The

bottom two courses of the original door jambs were revealed and bear well cut decorations and inscriptions. Missing tomb walls were rebuilt with stone. A large quantity of stone, much of it deriving from the original structure, was recovered during the cleaning of the tomb. All of our stone repairs are pointed with regular lime mortar and can be easily distinguished from the original masonry, as this was built without mortar. The exterior walls were restored to the level of the cornice with mud bricks to prevent access to the roof of the tomb. These were plastered with mud-sand plaster to blend in with local tradition.

The tomb, of course, never had windows. Small skylights were installed in the newly rebuilt walls to provide some light for visitors as in Ezbet Bashendi, electricity is available only during restricted hours. None of the windows is visible from the outside of the tomb and all are too small to permit access. An iron door and frame were installed, in compliance with the Egyptian Antiquities Organisation's security regulations. The door opens inwards and was so fitted that vibrations from its opening and closing would not be transmitted to the fabric of the tomb.

The second part of the treatment was to clean the interior surfaces of the walls and ceiling of the tomb. This was accomplished by applying mixtures of organic solvents, and then mechanically removing the softened deposits.

The conservation unit completed the restoration over a six weeks period, and handed the completely restored tomb to the representative of the Egyptian Antiquities Organisation at the end of the 1984 field season.

In the 1985 field season the work in the tomb was confined to making latex moulds of the walls of the decorated chamber and its doorways. These have been cast and reconstructed in the new Egyptian galleries of the Royal Ontario Museum in Toronto by Gorgia Guenther. As in the previous season, all our supplies were purchased in Cairo or in the Dakhleh Oasis. The technology employed was developed under laboratory conditions in the Egyptian Department of the Royal Ontario Museum, and was entirely focussed on what was available in local Egyptian markets. This work was completed in five weeks by Alan Hollett, Rod Stewart and the author and the final product was 45 m² of latex mould of 6–8 mm thickness, reinforced with fine cloth and burlap.

Roman Temple at 'Ein Birbiyeh

The temple is named 'Ein Birbiyeh after a small spring nearby. Largely disregarded in the past because it was thought to be the ruins of a Roman stone fort, the site proved on testing in 1983 to be an almost complete Roman temple buried to the roof in a large sand dune. The present plan must be seen as a preliminary drawing because it only records the structure at the present ground level. From this it can be seen that the central temple building measures about 25 × 21 m, and seems to be situated within a mud brick *temenos*, which is entered at the east through a stone gateway. Inside the *temenos*, the temple is surrounded by a heavy stone wall which forms an ambulatory on three sides around the inner building.

The temple complex was built on a sand-clay-mud soil and is presently covered by an extensive deposit of irrigation and coppice dune deposits. Visible stone elements, that is roofing slabs and the tops of walls, are poorly preserved due to physical decomposition of the stone. The dune is littered with a large number of broken stone elements, many of which are misshapen and 'in most cases' beyond recognition.

The site is located in the midst of areas of abandoned cultivation. It sits across the path of the prevailing north winds blowing from the Libyan Escarpment which forms the northern boundary of the Oasis. These winds often blow at gale force and cause the build-up of a sand dune against any object in their path. Transects surveyed across the site suggest that the temple is probably built on top of a slight rise in the original grade surface. This slopes away from the temple in all directions. It lies well above the present water table.

The results of survey testing in 1983, test exposures in 1985 and laboratory research suggest that some parts of the temple will have to be dismantled, the damaged elements repaired where possible and then the structure reassembled. It is proposed that the excavation of this monument commence in the 1986 field season. An essential part of the excavation program will be to undertake conservation and preservation measures as the excavation proceeds. The poor quality of the stone on the surface of the site makes it imperative that the conservation program be developed prior to unearthing the temple. It is necessary to understand something of the structural nature of the masonry as opposed to just the material itself. To this end, two small test pits were dug in the sand fill adjacent to the walls of the temple. The pits were refilled immediately after examination.

A permanent windbreak to protect the exposed temple has been designed. It will be a strip of shrubs and trees planted some 100 m away from the site on the windward side. The plants will include tamarisk for a good ground cover, casuarina which grows quickly and acacia, which should remain in place for a century or more. These plants require little water, which is an important consideration in the Oasis.

With our existing knowledge of the state of preservation of the stone material and of site conditions, the main steps of the proposed treatment would be as follows:

- organising storage space and a working area,
- planting a protective windbreak around the site,
- removal of all stone elements presently on the surface to a proper storage area,
- dismantling the damaged or unsafe parts of the structure,
- repair of damaged stone elements,
- reassembling the structure.

The proposal is based on observations and conclusions drawn from site visits around Egypt, as well as from the present site. The proposed treatment has been discussed with the highest officials in the Egyptian Antiquities Organisation and our approach to the problem is fully supported by the Organisation. The procedure is based on supplies obtainable locally in Egypt, and is focused on natural materials which have proved durable and stable in local conditions and are able to survive the harsh climate of the Oasis.

ENDNOTE – added in 1996

The temple of 'Ein Birbiyeh's stone structure is so deteriorated that the decision has been made to excavate and record all the ornamentation and friezes as far as practicable, measure and interpret the building, remove all movable artifacts and infill from within the structure, and to rebury the whole building with clean sand to preserve the temple from immediate further deterioration.

Acknowledgements
The success of the conservation of the Tomb of Kitinos at Bashendi and the Roman temple at 'Ein Birbiyeh is in large measure due to the unstinting cooperation and efforts of A.J. Mills, the field director of the Dakhleh Oasis Project, whose efforts to smooth the way by obtaining materials and the willing assistance of the local Egyptian Antiquities authorities were essential to bringing the projects to successful conclusions. I should also like to acknowledge the assistance and help of others, both foreign and local, in the Project's field camp in Ezbet Bashendi for support in many ways, and especially that of Alan Hollett and Rod Stewart who assisted with the cleaning of Kitinos and took the latex squeezes; and Alan Hollett, Deborah Lebaron, Hisham Higazy, and Lesley Mills, all of whom have from time to time assisted with the on-going conservation of 'Ein Birbiyeh.

Address for Author
Adam K. Zielinski, P.O. Box 356, Wellington, Ontario, Canada
K0K 3L0

13

KELLIS: THE ARCHITECTURAL SURVEY OF THE ROMANO BYZANTINE TOWN AT ISMANT EL-KHARAB

James E. Knudstad and Rosa A. Frey

INTRODUCTION

In the 1981–82 winter field season of the Dakhleh Oasis Project, the authors initiated the first comprehensive examination of the known Romano-Byzantine townsite of Ismant el-Kharab or ancient Kellis. Prominent ruins on the site had been visited and described by early travellers, most notably J.G. Wilkinson (1843) and H.E. Winlock (1936). The present authors, in an initial period of two months in 1981–82, determined and mapped the extent of the site, its general topographical setting, its general surface features, sherd densities, possible industrial areas, middens, wells, canals, etc., and constructed fairly complete structural plans for large areas on the west and south of the site. During the following 1982–83 season, further exposure and mapping continued and specific tests to depth were carried out for the following: excavation of the pronaos and naos of the west temple, of the frontal entries to the main temple, the main east gate of Enclosure 1, the apse and south sacristy of the large east church, and the apse and sacristies of the small east church. This report treats primarily of the work carried out in these initial seasons. As a consequence of the rich architectural findings, detailed larger scaled excavations were initiated in 1985 by Colin A. Hope (1985), and have continued annually into 1998. (It should be noted that this report was originally prepared in 1985 and that subsequent excavations have added to the information available.)

Topography and Surface Features

The townsite of Ismant el-Kharab (Fig. 13.1) lies southeast of the modern town of Ismant and is designated as Site 31/420–D6–1 in the Dakhleh Oasis Project's Archaeological Sites Index (Appendix II, This volume; Mills 1982). The greater part of the site lies on a raised terrace of red Mut Formation clay bearing a mantle of gravel and flint and standing about 1 km distant from the nearest oasis bottom land to the south (Fig. 13.2). A broad flat wadi, about 200 m wide and flowing south-southwest, forms the northwest side of the terrace. Its intersection with another, about 150 m wide and cutting west-southwest through the terrace, outlines two sides of the site on an irregular tongue of land standing 4–6 m above the wadi bottoms. The northeast extent of the site appears delimited by gullies cut shallowly into the terrace. To the northwest, prominent rounded bluffs of exposed Mut Fm. clay bedrock flank the northwest side of the larger wadi. The terrace is slightly undulating, relatively free at present of moving sand and shows little sign of significant deflation in the vicinity of the site. Field systems and irrigation channels lying close by in both wadis appear to be relatively recent and associated with the sanded up depressions of three wells on the site and four others in the wadis. Those on the site appear to date from after the abandonment of the town, as they cut through standing architecture. The site measures about 1050 m northeast-southwest and 650 m northwest-southeast, with remains of a small subsidiary cemetery lying slightly detached to the north (Fig. 13.2.8). There are a few scattered tombs beyond the wadi to the south (Fig. 13.2.9), and others cut into the clay bluffs on the northwest side of the northwest wadi.

From surface remains it is clear that the town is essentially of mudbrick construction almost entirely roofed with skew vaults (Figs 13.3 and 13.4), but including a number of domes (Figs 13.5, 13.6, and 13.7). Exposed

'Reports from the Survey of Dakhleh Oasis, Western Desert of Egypt, 1977–1987', edited by C.S. Churcher and A.J. Mills. Dakhleh Oasis Project: Monograph 2. Oxbow Monograph 99.

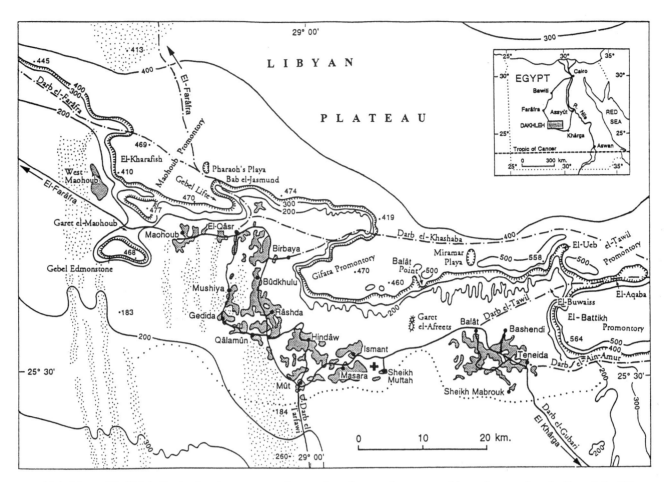

Fig. 13.1. Map of Dakhleh Oasis showing some modern and ancient settlements, cultivated areas (hatched),and the Libyan Escarpment to the north. Kellis or Ismant el-Kharab is situated between Ismant and Sheikh Muftah, shown by a ✚. Heights and contours in metres.

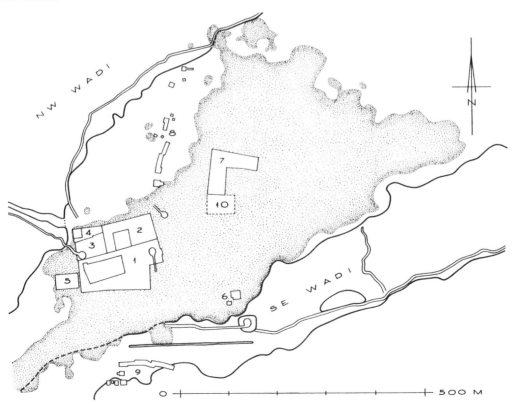

Fig. 13.2. Ismant el-Kharab or ancient Kellis: General Plan of Site. Key to main structures: 1. Enclosure 1 and Main Temple. 2. Enclosure 2. 3. Enclosure 3. 4. Enclosure 4 and West Church. 5. West Temple. 6. East Churches. 7. Large Unidentified Structure. 8. North Tombs. 9. South Tombs. 10. Private Houses in extensive residential area. Shaded area denotes extent of surface sherd scatter.

Figs 13.3–13.6

Fig. 13.3 (top left). View of Enclosure 1 from South Wadi. Fig. 13.4 (top right). Exposed wall tops and vaults. Fig. 13.5 (bottom left). Enclosure 2. Domed Room. Fig. 13.6 (bottom right). Enclosure 2. Pendentive in domed room (Fig. 13.5).

door lintel sockets, occasional roof beam emplacements and a few colonnades of broad span attest to some use of timber, while sandstone and limestone, available from exposures at a considerable distance to the north, are found only in limited formal contexts. Surface concentrations of stone chips in the areas of temple sanctuaries, gateways and some tombs indicate that stone was plundered for reuse. Such plundering has taken place in recent times. For example, Winlock (1936, 21) described North Tomb 1 as a chapel with a sandstone sanctuary, whitewashed and painted with offering scenes, and noted that "this sanctuary has been dug out recently". Nothing now remains of the decorated blocks which, fortunately, Winlock photographed (1936, Pl. XII).

An important surface feature of the townsite (as well as many others in the oasis) is the sherd scatter, which varies from light to dense and disappears abruptly beyond the periphery of occupation. The origin of the scatter on some sites was initially puzzling, as dense sherd layers are often found lying atop deep deposits of clean wind blown sand separating them from the occupational deposition which is

their usual context. To understand the origin and density of the scatter at Ismant it has been necessary to examine the erosional processes at work on the ruins.

The present condition of ancient Kellis appears to be the result of a particular sanding situation involving rapid burial followed by gradual deflation. Perched on its terrace on an otherwise open plain, the standing town would have acted as an obstruction and trap for wind blown sand. Evidence of repairs to major enclosure walls might suggest that the inhabitants may have been having trouble with sand accumulation during the town's life. Whether this contributed to the town's abandonment or not, present evidence makes it clear that abandonment was very quickly followed by filling and burial in wind blown sand to upper floor levels. This rapid burial appears to have been a critical factor in the town's remarkable preservation, generally to 2–4 m heights. Secondarily, and over more extended time, wind-blown sand then became the major erosional force at the site, slowly cutting away at the tops of walls in a process of deflation which continues to-day. The deflation in turn becomes a primary contributor to

Figs 13.7–13.10

Fig. 13.7 (top left). Enclosure 2. Pendentive in second domed room. Fig. 13.8 (top right). Eroding vault and surface sherd scatter. Fig. 13.9 (bottom left). Eroding walls showing heavy sherd admixture dropping to form sherd scatter. Fig. 13.10 (bottom right). Decorative use of mudbrick in Large Unidentified Structure (Fig. 13.2.7).

the density of the surface sherd scatter. It has been noted on many sites, particularly of the Roman period, that mudbricks were made with a varying admixture of sherds and that sherds in large amounts were used as chinking in mudbrick vault construction. As their mud matrix is literally blown away, the sherds remain as a growing mantle on the earlier accumulated sand in which the buildings are buried (Figs 13.8 and 13.9).

Another important factor in the dynamics of erosion is the angle at which an exposed wall stands relative to the direction of the prevailing wind. The effect can be readily illustrated by the tombs in the north group which still survive as standing structures. They were built on a line running south-southwest to north-northeast on a shallow diagonal to the northeast wind. Many of the tombs are well preserved to nearly full height, yet all of their windward walls, cut away at their bases, have collapsed into the wind. Their lightly built front porches have been deflated by the same process in most cases to one or two brick courses.

It is encouraging to observe in the surface remains of Kellis that most vaults and domes remain to a large extent preserved, indicating that much of the town is still in an early stage of erosion. This makes the site of particular

interest for, given the sequence of rapid burial followed by gradual deflation of upper levels, it is possible to recover a great deal of the town in plan with remarkable ease. Over most of the site, buried wall tops can be exposed simply by brushing aside surface sherds and a few centimetres of sand. Thus the method of recovery for the architectural survey presents little difficulty. Wall tops are traced, generally with trowel and brush, to a detail sufficient to establish features such as junctions, bondings, roofing, etc. This then allows for detailed sketching, notation and mapping, with the accuracy of the last across the site controlled by use of a theodolite and taping.

Kellis or Ismant el-Kharab proves to be a very useful model to study initially since there are other known Romano-Byzantine Period sites in the Dakhleh Oasis which may also lend themselves to similar examination. The larger town of Amheida near Q'asr or the settlement associated with the Deir el-Haggar temple in the northwest of the oasis were important local centres. However, they appear to have been less fortunate than Kellis in having suffered more severe post abandonment erosion. Their burial by sand would not appear to have been as swift, as many buildings are badly deflated or simply buried in their own

Fig. 13.11. Staircase in Large Unidentified Structure (Fig. 2.7).

rubble. These sites will require far more physical clearance preparatory to examination in plan and organization.

At Kellis this kind of collapse is fortunately limited. The large structure which lies along the main northwest wadi approach into the town (Fig. 13.2.7; Large Unidentifiable Structure, Fig. 13.12) initially posed such a problem, its plan obscured by collapsed walls and vaults. The plan is essentially L-shaped, measuring 92 m north-south by 95 m east-west. It is very well built, with parts standing several metres above present surface levels, with decorative brick work (Fig. 13.10), winding staircases (Fig. 13.11) and painted plaster decoration. Given its prominent location and its visible quality and scale of construction, it offers the possibility of a governor's palace or official residence. Indeed, subsequent examination has revealed a complex comprising a minimum of 216 rooms, courts and corridors constructed in four phases.

General Town Composition

The following major elements of the town have been readily traced by surface examination: a large walled enclosure containing a temple plus a probable administrative/commercial complex at the high west end of the site (Fig. 13.2.1–4), a smaller temple within an enclosure immediately west of the main temple (Fig. 13.2.5), a bath building to the southeast of the main temple complex, a walled ecclesiastical complex including two churches at the south centre of the site (Fig. 13.2.6), a small church built into the northwest corner of the expanded formal town enclosure (Fig. 13.2.4), lengths of several major streets and adjoining lanes, the residential town (including houses at Fig. 13.2.10), peripheral areas of industrial and/

or dumping grounds, two tomb groups to the north and south of the town (Fig. 13.2.8 & 9), and the smaller settlement plus cemetery slightly removed to the north, in the northwest wadi.

Although these elements conform generally to a common and very loosely rectangular north-south and east-west orientation Fig. 13.12), their positions are partially influenced by topography and their overall arrangement indicates no preconceived or obvious formal geometric planning for the town. The town centre occupies the terrace's southwest height and comprises the major temple complex and probable administrative/commercial area found in close association with it. This enclosed formal area exhibits an axial development and angle of approach lying between west and west-southwest and was altered and enlarged in at least five phases. The west temple is immediately to the west of the main complex at nearly the extreme west extent of the terrace. The greater part of the residential town is spread over the widening terrace width to the northeast and east with an overflow into a northern part of the southeast wadi. This is likely to describe an overall direction of growth over time, since the less dense, lightly built habitation lies to the northeast and two of the churches lie to the east, halfway down the slope into the southeast wadi. The streets so far traced assert essentially random growth within blocks of buildings.

FORMAL BUILDING ENCLOSURES

Main Temple and Administrative/Commercial Complex

The high ground at the southwest of the terrace bears a succession of large enclosures defined by relatively substantial walls separating the area from the rest of the town (Figs 13.3 and 13.12). The whole complex is roughly rectangular, covering an area approximately 150 m north-south by at least 200 m east-west. An examination of the characteristics of the plan as well as wall jointings and abuttments reveals an initial enclosure 175 m long, itself having evolved over time, and three successive smaller additions to its north side (Fig. 13.13). Enclosure 1 is distinguished by an axial but not symmetrical composition based on an axial street flanked by buildings leading from the main temple temenos gateway on the west to a main enclosure gateway on the east. Enclosure 2, smaller than the first, was added to the north side of Enclosure 1, in an alignment with its northeast corner. It appears to be divided into two blocks: a large assemblage of possible storerooms to the east and formal buildings to the west. Enclosure 3, fitted against the north temenos wall of the temple and the west wall of Enclosure 2, in the northwest angle, was obscured by the more recent digging of a well in its southwest corner. Enclosure 4 was added to the north of Enclosure 3 to complete the northwest corner of the whole complex. It contains two large stone built tombs and a small church complex in its west end. A subsequent fifth

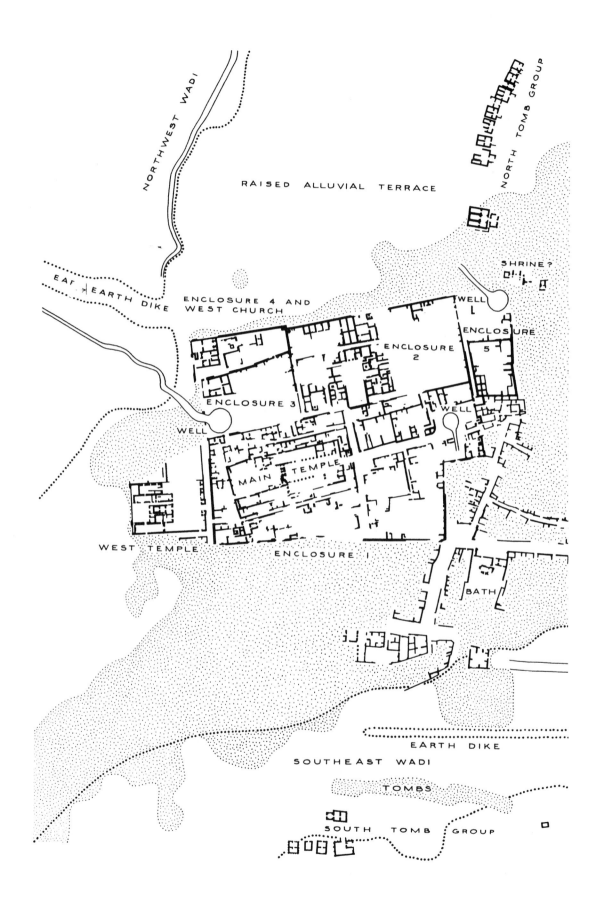

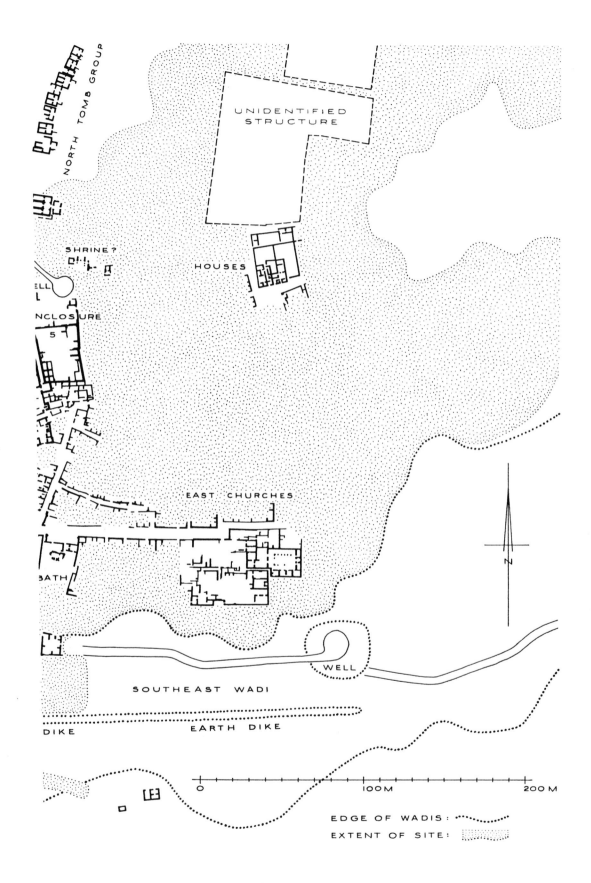

Fig. 13.12. Plan of site, showing principal features. Note median overlap of ± 60 m between west and east halves.

Fig. 13.13. Plan of Enclosures 1–4, including Main Temple and small West Church, and of West Temple.

enclosure, also damaged by later well digging and roughly 30 × 65 m, has been partially traced adjoining the east side of Enclosure 2.

The mudbrick enclosure walls, the heaviest such walls found on the site, vary from 1.0–1.5 m in thickness at the base. One section still stands about 8 m above its base. The walls were constructed in separate unbonded segments of irregular length and, wherever traced, their exterior faces continue straight without interruption, while interior faces often bear small buttresses of varying size and spacing (Figs 13.3 and 13.14). With few exceptions the enclosure walls appear to be unbonded to, and to have been built prior to, all inner and abutting walls. Their relatively slender construction, devoid of exterior battlements or towers, clearly served the purpose of monumentality, enclosing and defining formal precincts, rather than defense.

Only three entrances through the enclosure walls have been located; any others necessary for communication remain buried. The main east gateway into Enclosure 1 is incompletely traced but appears to be framed by two projecting towers, one or both containing rectangular stairwells. The south tower also appears to be integral

with a two-storey gatehouse. In addition, Enclosure 1 has an entry through its rear west wall near the south end, buried nearly to the top of its intact arch, giving access to a lane separating the enclosure from the west temple complex. A simple doorway has also been traced through the north wall of Enclosure 3 next to its northwest corner.

Enclosure 1: Main Temple Complex

An examination of wall jointings and abutments reveals that the plan of Enclosure 1 is itself the product of a sequence of developments and additions (Fig. 13.13).

The main temple precinct is the largest single element within the enclosure, with its temenos measuring about 40 × 80 m overall. It proves to have had a structural evolution of its own, including both expansion and major repair, for which some reasonable duration must be postulated. Upon reaching its full extent, it and those buildings that frame its axial approach would appear to have been free-standing prior to the erection of the Enclosure 1 wall. The latter, in plan, appears to have been 'wrapped' around these major elements in a somewhat irregular and accomodating fashion.

Figs 13.14–13.17

Fig. 13.14 (top left). Exterior face of Enclosure 1 wall, SE corner. Fig. 13.15 (top right). 'Pylon' elements in Main Temple complex: axial (L) and secondary (R) doorways. Fig. 13.16 (bottom left). Procession of priests. Main Temple, south chapel, painted plaster on north wall of entrance hall. Fig. 13.17 (bottom right). Procession of Gods on painted plaster. Main Temple, south chapel, south wall, middle register (Figs 13.2.6 & 13.13).

Of the temple itself virtually nothing remained on the surface except numerous fragments of cut sandstone blocks obviously discarded in the looting of the building for stone. The temple area was buried in wind-laid sand to estimated depths of 1–3 m. Both the temple and a small forecourt occupied most of an area measuring about 10 × 29 m, surrounded and defined by subsidiary mudbrick structures. A number of fragmentary pie-shaped baked brick column drum segments littering the surface attest to a columned forecourt. Wilkinson (1843, 364) was probably describing this temple when he wrote, "the most remarkable remains are a sandstone building, measuring 19 paces by 9, consisting of 2 chambers in a very dilapidated state."

In a need to substantiate the depth of deposition and degree of stratification to be found on the site a number of loci were chosen for initial tests through the overburden of sand. In one such sondage located in front of the presumed stone temple and forecourt, the stone and mudbrick elements of a pylon-like facade perhaps 13 m wide by 4 m thick were found, representing the front wall of an immediate temple temenos built essentially of mudbrick.

Limited clearance to floor level at the 'pylon' proves it to be preserved from 0.9–1.3 m in height and composed of three features: two stone-built doorways and a large frontal niche of lime-plastered mudbrick. Although the doorways are side by side and virtually identical in size and plan, the southernmost lies on the temple temenos axis, has jambs bearing the lower portions of a scene in carved relief, and must be considered the main inner doorway to the temple precinct proper, while the undecorated doorway to the north is secondary in importance (Fig. 13.15). The presence of axial and side doorways in the front facade is duplicated in the mudbrick chapel immediately to the south of the main sanctuary, as well as in the West Temple. Such paired doorways are a feature noted in other temples in the oasis. Both doorways have stone outer sills bearing recesses and wood sockets for double-leaved wooden doors. The north door sill also bears the swing scars of a later single-leaf door. Packed clay accumulations about 20 cm thick remain on both sills and the exterior doorjambs are heavily encrusted with black lamp oil residue, all of which suggest a late phase of ritual use.

The niche occupying the southern third of the facade, only partly exposed and examined in 1983, is rectangular, about 2 m wide by 2 m deep, and is framed by jambs bearing vertical lime plaster mouldings. A construction joint in the mudbrick masonry between the main doorway and the niche suggests that the latter may have been a later insertion. A fragmentary torus-and-cavetto moulding is found set a little more than 1.5 m high on its back wall. The plastered surface below the moulding is painted black and both the moulding and the centre of the wall are heavily encrusted with oil residue originating from a higher and now destroyed source.

An area of plastered facade to the south of the niche, protected by a later abutting mudbrick wall, bears polychrome painted decoration of distinctly Roman style affecting recessed moulded rectangular panelling with simple floral elements crossing the centres diagonally.

The rubble burying the doorways and niche was filled with architectural fragments of carved sandstone, baked brick and lime plaster. Included with the numerous fragments of cut stone relief were pieces of a carved and painted torus-and-cavetto moulded door lintel bearing outstretched wings and uraeii. Pie-shaped baked bricks, six to a circle, would have formed columns at least 70 cm in diameter. A mass of lime plaster fragments included elements for a type of small Corinthian capital surmounting a column of only 15 cm diameter. One such column fragment was found, painted olive green, composed of a build-up of two plasterings over a mud and straw under-body strengthened with a wood core. One capital, reconstructed from pieces, was similarly built up in plaster on a mud body and decorated with plaster scrolls, acanthus leaves and tendrils applied while wet, to a total height of 26 cm. The original placement of such purely decorative columns and capitals is not yet determined.

To the east of this 'pylon' is a forecourt 35 × 11 m, framed on the north and south by two colonnades of mudbrick columns and side courts 7 m wide. Each side court in turn acts as forecourt for smaller decorated chambers built of mudbrick flanking the stone temple and probably serving as side chapels.

The chapel to the south proves to be an excellent example of the potential for preservation on the site. The thick-walled east facade is pierced by both an axial doorway and a smaller north doorway, giving access to a hall or court 18 m long, leading to a vaulted chamber 5 × 12 m. Both hall and chamber inner wall surfaces preserve polychrome painted scenes on lime plaster over a thick mud plaster containing a high admixture of coarse straw. Originally, only limited exposures of these were made and then reburied in clean sand following documentation, as the plaster is extremely delicate. (In 1995 and 1996, these decorated scenes were exposed, recorded and fallen parts retrieved and conserved.)

In the entrance hall a 1.5 m length was cleared to 60 cm depth against the north wall, revealing the legs of five male figures, possibly priests, walking west toward the inner chamber. They wear yellow knee-length kilts with green tails. They walk on a red ground line over even bands of yellow, green and yellow. Below these bands is a Classical (Roman) motif of grape clusters and vines on a blue ground, with large rectangular panels imitating recessing in yellow, white and red (Fig. 13.16).

The southwest corner of the inner chamber was exposed for 2.5 m of the south wall and 70 cm of the west wall to a maximum depth of 1.3 m under preserved vaulting. Two registers of Egyptian deities are preserved above the spring of the vault, the upper register extremely faded from past exposure to sun and wind. Only a small part of a lower register was exposed because of the delicate condition of the plaster. The best preserved middle register measures 74 cm in height, and includes three male figures on the west wall facing north and, on the south wall, ten figures – seven males and one female facing west towards a male and female who face the group. All are late manifestations of Egyptian deities with elaborate garments and para-phernalia including individual composite crowns. All have suffered from vandalism, particularly in the faces (Figs 13.17 and 13.18). Damaged registers of hieroglyphs above and between the figures identify them further.

The opposing east ends of both side courts bear additional secondary chambers, presumably chapels. That in the northeast corner is clearly an insertion abutting the north colonnade. A plastered niche is partly preserved high in the centre of the north wall of the large central

Fig. 13.18. Gods on painted plaster. Main Temple, south chapel, south wall, middle register (figs 1 and 2).

chamber which is flanked by smaller rooms, one on the east and two on the west. The chapel in the southeast corner is more substantially built, with an axial doorway on the west opening to what may be a roughly square court with entries to three small unconnected chambers on the east.

The first temenos wall enclosing the forecourts and temple measures approximately 27 × 70 m and is constructed in segments of irregular length. Most of its west end wall has collapsed inward. The east gateway, probably stone framed, has been destroyed. A 13 m length of the north side, at the west end, is at an angle askew with the rest of the wall but parallel to and seemingly respecting a small lightly walled building immediately to the north. The full form and nature of this building, which appears to predate the temenos, remain unclear.

At some later time a further temenos was erected outside the first, enlarging the precinct by 5–6 m on its north, south and east sides and about 2 m on the west side. This enlargement also respects the small building standing within its northwest corner. Surface evidence suggests that the enlargement was concurrent with or subsequent to replacement of the collapsed inner west wall with the heavier, buttressed wall that is found standing outside it. The later temenos wall was provided with a new east gateway just outside the first framed by slightly projecting wall panels and one or two stair towers within. Again, the dressed stone which would have framed this opening has been removed, but scraps remain on the surface. On all sides the space between these inner and outer walls was subdivided into a number of small casually arranged rooms with additional stairwells: some of these rooms may be preserved at upper floor levels.

The later temenos is in turn surrounded by a broad street 4.5 m wide on the east and two narrower lanes 2 m wide on the north and south, presumably entered through doorways at their east ends where they join the north-south street. No free access is apparent along the west wall exterior. The north-south street east of the temenos appears to extend right across the whole of Enclosure 1, dividing the interior into two distinct areas. The east area is further divided north and south by the main axial street, 5–6 m wide, which leads from what appears to be an open plaza roughly 20 m square just inside the main east gate of the main enclosure, past four blocks of sizeable mudbrick buildings, to intersect with the main north-south street directly before the east gate of the temple temenos. The blocks of buildings to the southeast measure 26 m square and approximately 20 × 30 m respectively, while those to the northeast measure 19 × 23 m and 20 × 26 m. Several additional lanes and lesser buildings have been partially traced, but the detailed tracing and functional identification of all of these buildings awaits further work.

The skew vault is the most common roofing device throughout this and later enclosures, but the occasional dome or sockets for timber roof beams have been found. Numerous stairwells rising out of the sand attest to many

Figs 13.19 and 13.20

Fig. 13.19 (top). Test 4, Enclosure 1 gateway: domestic level with bread oven and vessels in mudbrick bins. Fig. 13.20 (bottom). Vessels in Feature 3, bin or manger.

of the buildings having stood, and perhaps still surviving, to upper floor levels.

In pursuit of areas likely to have seen maximum deposition, the main enclosure gateway and its street were chosen for testing to bottom. This test area, approximately 3 m square, was placed against the outer face of the north tower block of the main gate of Enclosure I, where two light mudbrick walls were seen to abut the tower at right angles and define part of a late secondary building extending right across the gateway. In wind deposited sand at a depth of 1 m, parts of the collapsed palm and mud roof of this structure were found, under which stood a virtually intact domed ceramic bread oven on a packed mud floor, at 1.65 m depth (Fig. 13.19). In use with the oven, but originating on a lower surface, was a mudbrick-walled bin, Feature 3, which on excavation yielded five intact vessels and miscellaneous sherds (Figs 13.20 and 13.21, Top). Floor 2, reached at 1.8 m depth, yielded another group of four complete pots and a pit containing another four (Fig. 13.21, Bottom). These examples of intact domestic wares and the wealth of sherds recovered in association with them proved extremely valuable when compared to sherds recovered from tests in the large east church (see below) where sherds could be dated by close association with coins and sherds of imported North

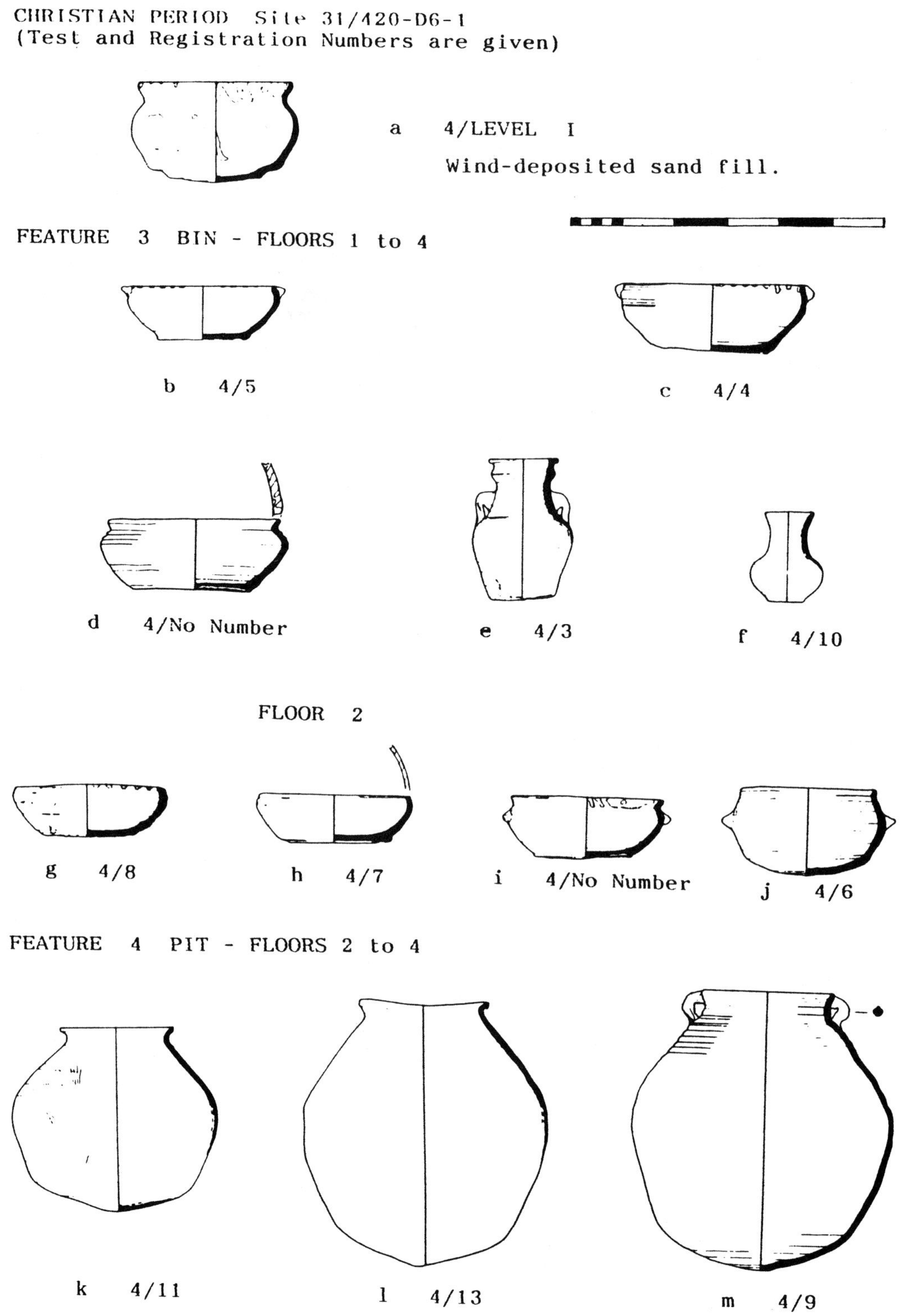

CHRISTIAN PERIOD Site 31/420-D6-1
(Test and Registration Numbers are given)

a   4/LEVEL   I

Wind-deposited sand fill.

FEATURE 3 BIN - FLOORS 1 to 4

b   4/5

c   4/4

d   4/No Number

e   4/3

f   4/10

FLOOR   2

g   4/8

h   4/7

i   4/No Number

j   4/6

FEATURE   4   PIT - FLOORS 2 to 4

k   4/11

l   4/13

m   4/9

Fig. 13.21. Pottery vessels from Test 4, East Gateway of Enclosure 1 (redrawn from Hope 1983, fig. 8, from an original by S.C. Munro-Hay). Scale = 30 cm.

African Red slipped ware. The tests complemented each other, as some shapes and wares were duplicated and the dated sherds from the church could be correlated with whole vessels from the gateway. As a result the range of dated pottery of the Christian Period in the Dakhleh Oasis was expanded and a partial framework was established for more precise dating of local wares (Hope 1983).

Further excavation below Floor 2 revealed that the oven and vessels associated with Floors 1 and 2 and Levels VII and VIII represent a late domestic use of the structure and that the so-called bin, Feature 3, was in fact constructed on Floor 4 together with a partition wall for use as a manger in a stable area. Levels IX and X, between Floors 3 and 4, consisted of compact layers of straw and dung. Floor 4/Level XI was a 3–8 cm thick layer of compacted clay lumps, sherds and mudbrick fragments, purposely laid down to form a surface on which to build the stable partitions. Below this in Level XII another similar arrangement of partitions was found, preserved as only one or two courses of bricks, constructed on another hard-packed surface at 2.45 m depth. This packed surface proved to be the top of a thick platform on which the gate tower and the secondary walls abutting it were built. Further testing to a depth of 3.7 m from surface into the platform revealed a homogeneous mass of wet-laid mud, extremely hard and compact, with almost no sherd or straw admixture, apparently forming a massive foundation for the construction of the gateway.

Enclosure 2

The second enclosure is a major addition measuring 56 × 107 m. Its northwest corner appears to have had a projecting exterior tower perhaps 4 m square. The northeast corner is only partly exposed and remains ill-defined. No entrances to the enclosure have yet been located, but these are presumably intact and obscured by the preserved height of the walls above them.

Surface evidence for the east half of the enclosure is limited to little more than the abutments of untraced inner walls and vaults with the exterior wall. Their regularity along the east wall suggests that the area was filled with blocks of large vaulted chambers, possibly arranged around a central open court now indicated by a sand-filled depression.

The west part of the enclosure is well-preserved and its plan has been traced in some detail. The central feature is a large formal building measuring 32 × 36 m, originally standing two storeys high. It is arranged as a U on the east, north and west sides of an 11 × 28 m court oriented on a north-south axis. The south end of the court abuts the exterior of Enclosure 1 (with a presumed entrance lower in the wall) and its north end terminates at the double-piered portico of a Classical megaron. The megaron is lime plastered, with a niche in the back wall flanked by engaged colonettes. This chamber and two smaller flanking rooms with entries from the open court frame the court on the

north. They are part of a range of rooms forming the north side of the block and seemingly segregated from the remaining east and west groups of rooms by passages. Each of the latter has a stairwell. The west group is remarkable for two ground floor rooms domed in decorative mud and lime-plastered mudbrick of exceptional technique (Figs 13.5, 13.6 and 13.7). Fragments of the upper floor are also preserved above these.

To the east of this block and adjoining its east wall stands another only partly traced group of rooms including a stairwell to a second floor. Most of the rooms are lime plastered, and are possibly the west portion of another such block.

To the west of the main block, in the 19 m wide distance to the enclosure's west wall, stands another block of rooms and stairwell, measuring 14 × 18 m, arranged around the south, west and north sides of a small court. A large semicircular niche against the east wall of the court gives the plan near symmetry on its east-west axis and would appear to have been the focal point of the building. The niche is large enough to have accomodated a life-size statue and is of Classical form, flanked by engaged columns supporting a half dome and with its base raised above floor level. A corridor 2.5 m wide, originally vaulted, surrounds the block - except possibly around the enclosed northern half which remains largely unexplored.

Enclosure 3

The third enclosure, an irregular parallelogram measuring 40 × 59 m, is an obvious addition to the west wall of Enclosure 2. No entry from either earlier enclosure is apparent, but a doorway at its northwest corner connects it with Enclosure 4 and there is vague evidence for a second doorway near the east end of the north wall. The north wall is characterised by regular and substantial buttressing. Various minor walls abutting the north and east enclosing walls have been traced, but only one building in the northwest corner consisting of five rooms around an open court has been traced in detail. The surface of the enclosure appears to dip markedly to the north. A later well dug in recent time into its southwest corner includes a canal cut through the west wall to now derelict fields in the wadi beyond.

Enclosure 4

This addition abuts the tower at the northwest corner of E closure 2. Its junction with the northwest corner of Enclosure 3 is very eroded and remains unclear. Four structures were found within: a small, two roomed building to the east abutting the north wall, a pair of squarish stone built tomb structures near the centre, and a small church complex in the northwest corner.

The two stone tombs, both measuring about 9 × 10 m, are built of coursed cut stone dressed to the exterior faces only, and have been dismantled to their first two courses.

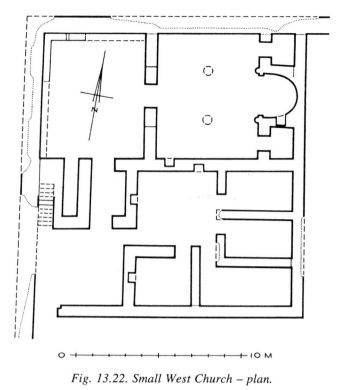

Fig. 13.22. Small West Church – plan.

Both bear fragments of stone paving or other construction within, and the northern example, built abutting the earlier southern one, retains what appear to be base courses for one side of a small forecourt or porch on its east side. Their alignment with the north wall of Enclosure 3, rather than with any other features of Enclosure 4, suggests that their construction predates the north walls of Enclosure 3. They bear resemblance in their size to the domed stone tombs in the village of Ezbet Bashendi (Osing *et al.* 1982, pl. 12.b, c), yet their location on the site, removed from other prominent tombs and sharing proximity with the church, remains intriguing.

The west church complex, built of mudbrick, abuts and utilises the northwest corner of Enclosure 4 (Fig. 13.13). The complex measures 16 × 17 m overall and is divided equally into a church on the north side and a block of rooms plus two courts on the south (Fig. 13.22). A single entry on the south leads to the first open court or room giving access to a second court and four rooms, to stairs and, via a passage, to an open court or roofed narthex on the west axis of the church. The nave is entered via a west axial doorway and the semicircular apse is flanked by engaged columns and doorways to small sacristies on each side. The body of the church, less apse, sacristies and possible narthex, measures 6 m long and >7 m broad. In the absence of any sign of vaulting, it must be assumed that the body was timber roofed, the span of which must have have been supported by one or possibly two pairs of columns effectively dividing it into nave and side aisles. Remains of columns or their bases have yet to be sought. The whole interior of the church was simply mud plastered,

and a small test in the much deflated northwest corner revealed a narrow mudbrick bench against the walls, a mud floor, and walls preserved to 1–2 m heights throughout the complex.

West Temple Complex

The west temple was found within its own temenos situated on lower ground behind the main temple, separated from the back wall of Enclosure 1, to which it is aligned, by a 4 m wide lane between (Fig. 13.13). The temples share a similar orientation to the east but in no way share similar axes. A west 'back' doorway into Enclosure 1, intact to its arch, was located 9 m south along the lane from the main axial gateway of the west temple temenos, so communication between the two complexes was possible,. if also indirect. A 3 m wide lane runs along the south side of the temenos and additional blocks of unexplored buildings lie to the northwest, north and south of the west temple, at this west edge of the town site.

The temple complex measures 31 × 17 m overall. Its plan was traced almost in its entirety and, although it shows a degree of axial symmetry and appears largely preconceived, it also shows a number of phases of construction, alteration, and later repair (Fig. 13.23).

The pronaos and naos, in this instance fully excavated during the program of selective testing across the town, were built as an initial and free standing rectangle, 5.1 × 8.2 m, in coursed cut sandstone complete with square sectioned vertical corner mouldings, each with an axial double-leaved doorway and outer jambs bearing scenes of inscribed relief (Fig. 13.24). It is probably one of these chambers that was mentioned by Winlock (1936, 21): "At the extreme west of the site there are the outlines of a small sandstone chamber, rectangular, perhaps 4 by 6 m., oriented east and west." There is also a side doorway in the pronaos' south wall. North, west and south exterior walls are of a slightly battered 52 cm thickness. The two cross walls bearing the axial doorways are 82 cm thick. A curious double thickness of the naos' north and south side walls appears to be the result of lining an outer wall of 53 cm thickness in each case with an additional 57–60 cm thick wall and differing course height against already largely finished inner faces. The resulting doubled thickness of about 1.1 m produced a narrowed north-south span across the naos closely matching that across the pronaos east-west. This provided the traditional narrowing of space towards the sanctuary, but may also reflect the mason's concern for minimising the distance to be spanned by single sandstone roofing slabs. Whether the double thickness was planned or improvised cannot easily be ascertained as all the walls rest on several courses of rough stone foundations and some dismantling would be necessary to determine whether the foundations under the doubled walls were similarly doubled or not.

The dressed stone walls are preserved only to the fourth course. Except for the lining in the naos, stone coursing is

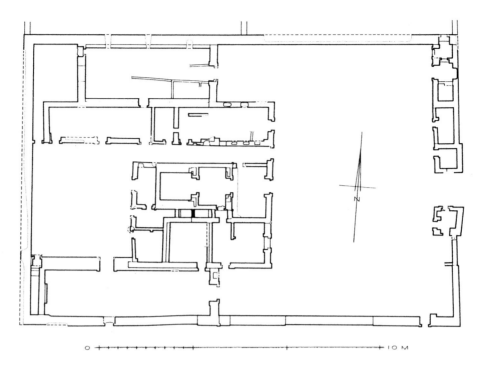

Fig. 13.23. West Temple – plan.

Fig. 13.24–13.26

Fig. 13.24 (top). West Temple. Sandstone pronaos and naos. Fig. 13.25 (bottom left). West Temple. Pronaos doorway, north jamb – decoration. Fig. 13.26 (bottom right). West Temple. Naos doorway, south jamb – decoration.

continuous throughout, varying from 25–46 cm in height. All blocks, including those of the topmost foundation course, are set in lime cement with thin wood shims occasionally added for levelling. Where robbers' pits dug to below foundations in the naos reveal it, it is clear that the underlying red clay was trenched or levelled to accept up to three or four courses of rough hewn stones set in loose sand. These support a final course of finished stones supporting walls and doorsills. Within the naos the faces of the stones of the lowest wall course were trimmed to a consistent level above their bases leaving a continuous inner projection indicating the original floor level. The floor itself, whether consisting of stone paving or some other finished surface, has been completely removed. Subfloor fill consisted of sand and stone debris and some ash. The charred right arm of a painted plaster statue, almost life size and constructed on an armature of wood, was found in the debris. The statue was of Classical form, the arm draped in the modelled folds of a toga.

Of the original doorsills only eroded fragments for the pronaos main door remain, showing that it had an inner rabbet in section. The remains of wood pivots in socket holes in the foundation stones under both axial doorways, as well as grooves worn into the jambs by door posts, indicate the use of double leaved doors in each.

The only intact carved reliefs are those on the outer jambs of both axial doorways. The outer jambs of the pronaos doorway bear opposing figures of a king in sunken relief with traces of paint. The figure on the right, preserved to full height, stands 70 cm tall wearing a red crown, white kilt, blue belt, ceremonial tail and collar (Fig. 13.25).

The two broken cartouches before the face and the vertical band of hieroglyphs in front of the figure are obscured by the thick black encrustation already noted in the main temple. The king strides forward, his right hand raised, palm upward, in an offering gesture and his left hand holding a staff and mace. The figure of the king on the opposite jamb has lost its crown but enough survives, with traces of white paint, to suggest the white crown. The broken cartouches on this side are legible, the lower part of the right one preserving the $^c3$ sign of Pr-$^c3$ (= 'pharaoh'), while the left preserves the group $^cnh\ dt$ (= 'given life'), most probably from a generic cartouche for 'Caesar'. (These figures and cartouches are being cleaned and studied.)

The jambs of the naos doorway bear decoration in raised relief, also encrusted. The main panel on each side shows a female figure, 48 cm tall without the crown, wearing a tight sheath dress decorated with fine blue painted diagonal stripes, an armband, long hair swept back to a curl behind the shoulder, a vulture head-dress and a lotus crown. She raises both arms together in offering to a goddess wearing a sheath, plain collar, straight lappet hairstyle and vulture headdress, holding a lotus staff in the right hand and an *ankh* sign in the left (Fig. 13.26). The goddess on the right jamb wears a composite red crown, while that on the left jamb wears a composite crown with sundisk, plumes and Hathor horns. There are five raised blue painted panels between the figures on each jamb, but of the hieroglyphs within, executed in black paint, only faint traces remain. Part of an upper register is preserved showing smaller female figures, 12 cm in height from preserved feet to thighs only. One figure is apparently offering to two goddesses carrying staffs and facing her. Again the hieroglyphic panels are too indistinct to be read.

In addition over 30 fragments of painted relief were found in the fill of both chambers, probably pieces of a smashed door lintel, the theme of which is at present not determined.

Prior to the finished dressing of the exterior surfaces of pronaos and naos, the walls of a larger mudbrick composition, measuring 14 × 24 m, were erected to enclose it. Where these walls abut each corner of the rear wall of the naos and for the whole length of the south wall including the projecting pronaos' side door jambs, the blocks bear only drafted joints and roughly chiselled surfaces. The addition of this mudbrick construction before the final dressing of the stone walls suggests that the whole plan was preconceived.

A small mudbrick forecourt with axial doorway was added to the front of the sandstone sanctuary, flanked by roughly balanced side chapels having frontal doorways and additional side entrances. Positioned between the forecourt and the north side chapel is a fourth doorway. This leads to a passage along the north wall of the stone built sanctuary and provides access to a rear court and subsidiary rooms in the complex. A chamber or 'contra temple' with axial and south doorways is built against the rear of the sanctuary, and rooms to the north and south include a long three-doored room completing the east-west length of the block on its north side. A southwest portion of this phase was not cleared and is presumed buried in part under the later final expansion described below. Much of the interior and exterior mudbrick wall surfaces retain a lime plaster finish with traces of Roman style painted panel decoration on maroon and yellow fields.

The outer temenos was added in a last major construction phase. The forward half of this enclosure provides a broad court between the earlier facade and the main east gateway. The possibility of a colonnade in the court is suggested by the recovery of a single pie-shaped baked brick of the type used in column construction. Sandstone fragments littering the vicinity of the main gateway were noticed by Wilkinson (1843) and are possibly the remains of a destroyed stone entrance. The gateway is flanked by projecting towers or gaterooms, with small rooms of slightly less width incorporated in the east temenos wall. To the west, two larger and fairly symmetrically balanced side chapels were created between the existing chapels of the earlier phase and the new temenos north and south side walls. The front walls of these chapels, with central doorways, are set 6 m to the rear of the earlier facade and are built integral with the temenos. A stairwell is present in the southwest corner of the temenos.

Alterations to the temple complex are numerous. In the stone sanctuary, niches were cut into the forward inner corners of the naos and pronaos, now surviving only as plaster-edged outlines of a dark oil crust on the upper face of the fourth course of sandstone. Ritual activities requiring the insertion of the niches and such liberal use of oil are not understood, but a need for both has left similar traces on other mudbrick temples in the oasis. A peculiar erosion or deterioration of the inner base course of the pronaos' south wall received crude repair and, similarly, the expected stone doorsill to the naos has been entirely replaced by the insertion, under eroded door jambs, of two heavy wood beams laid flat on one another. An oil saturated earth floor, replacing the missing stone paving of both rooms, bears a 9–14 cm thickness of accumulated oil crust over much of its area. A small column drum, 50 cm in diameter, and a molded base or capital of sandstone, 41 cm in diameter, were found set axially on this floor, seemingly as podia, in front of the naos doorway. Both are heavily coated with oil crust and sealed by it to the floor. The outer jambs of both axial doorways are also heavily coated. Crude mudbrick and mud blocking the pronaos' south doorway and partitioning of the narrow passage between the stone sanctuary and south side chapel appear to be much later modifications.

Both adjacent side chapels also show considerable alteration, in the form of blocked doorways, secondary niches and doorways cut into exisiting walls, and rooms subdivided by partitions. The north outer chapel was finally partitioned and later reused as a stable.

Bath Building

At an intersection of streets close to the southeast corner of the major temple complex, Enclosure 1, a major east-west street is fronted along its south side by an expanded bay 18 m long and 4–5 m in depth. It is defined by a mudbrick back wall bearing two doorways in its length and by engaged columns at the outer corners of both end walls (Fig. 13.27). This appears to be the remains of a colonnaded loggia with the intervening columns between engaged ends still buried or missing. One street entry passes through a mudbrick domed and lime plastered antechamber to a rectangular mudbrick enclosure about 20 × 30 m. A lime plastered wall bearing decorative vaulted and half domed niches appears to frame the east side of the enclosure. A structure in the centre of this enclosure, only partly traced, presents the partially dismantled fragments of three rooms of a once vaulted building solidly built of lime-and-ash-cemented baked brick. The ends of two of the rooms bear semicircular niches, one of them supporting a half dome in baked brick and both presumably fitted with tubs. All of these features, including the vertical flues of ceramic pipe found built into the walls, commonly distinguish bath houses throughout the Roman world. The sorry state of this central building is due entirely to the relative scarcity and value for reuse of baked brick recently robbed from the site. Lower levels and foundations of the ruin should, when thoroughly cleared of sand, reveal considerably more of its original extent and plan than has been recovered from initial surface examination.

East Church Complex

About 100 m along the street running east from the southeast corner of Enclosure 1, past the baths, another enclosed complex was found occupying an area sloping from the terrace height down to the southeast wadi (Fig. 13.28). Outer walls on the north and south clearly define a space 47 m wide, but the east-west length has been only sketchily traced for about 60 m. A small church built within the east outer wall and a much larger one added against the exterior of this same wall define the nature of the complex as ecclesiastical. With the exception of the churches, the inner spaces are divided into large and smaller courts, rooms and corridors which show no overall scheme, but considerable alteration. At least one stairwell has been located. A major gateway is placed at the side of a bay or loggia let into the south wall, but circulation within the complex itself is obscured by the heights of walls, many of which are preserved unbroken over still buried doorways.

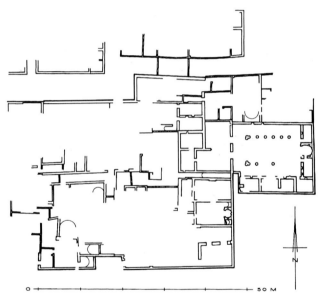

Fig. 13.28. East Churches complex – plan. Vaults indicated by arcs

Small East Church

This small church measures 5.5 × 8.5 m and is composed of an apse, flanking sacristies and a nave (Fig. 13.29), the latter probably subdivided into central and side aisles by columns or piers not yet found. At the east end the church stands 2.5 m high to the eroded stumps of arches over entries to the apse and sacristies (Fig. 13.30). At the northwest corner the walls are preserved to >4 m, with no signs of roof emplacements or vaulting. The interior is entirely filled with clean, wind blown sand, so doorways are buried and it remains unclear which of the adjacent chambers may be directly associated with the church. An attempt was made to clear sufficient sand from the east

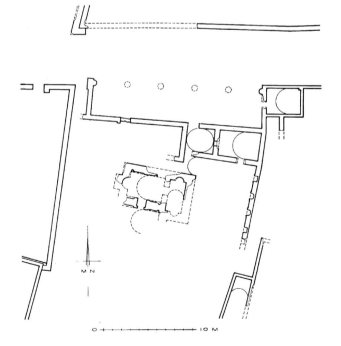

Fig. 13.27. Bath Building complex – plan. Vaults indicated by arcs.

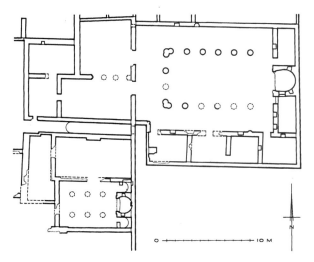

Fig. 13.29. The Small and Large East Churches – plan.

end of the buiding to reveal at least its apse and sacristies, but floor level was only reached in the apse.

The apse is virtually a three-quarter circle in plan, covered by a skew vault in the form of a half dome behind a frontal arch. A nearby parallel is found over the apse in the chapel at Qasr Ain Mustafa Kashef in Kharga Oasis. The half dome over the apse was a standard feature of early churches of the basilica plan. Commonly, in small native Egyptian churches, the apse was flanked with side chambers, wooden roofs were favoured and a narthex was formed by returning columns across the west end of the nave (Davies 1952; Krautheimer 1965). The curve of the apse is cut into the thickness of the outer east wall. It is clear at the intersection of faces, and at other jointings, that the east wall stood, lime-plastered, prior to the construction of the church against it. The apse has a small arched niche on either side and is decorated at the back with a deeply engaged short column, complete with capital, set slightly off centre (Fig. 13.31). The capital of moulded

Figs 13.30–13.33

Fig. 13.30 (top left). Small East Church – apse and north sacristry. Fig. 13.31 (top right). Small East Church – apse. Fig. 13.32 (bottom left). Large East Church – apse and south sacristry. Fig. 13.33 (bottom right). Large East Church – apse floor.

plaster consists of a row of three pointed leaves rising and spreading from a horizontal band. The sacristies are simple, small, three-sided cubicles with vaults opening directly to the nave. Both were only partly cleared of sand. The north sacristy has a niche built into the north wall with intact mudbrick and wooden shelves. The entrance to the south sacristy was at some later time reduced by the insertion of a small mudbrick wall. A torus and rabbet moulding of plaster on projecting mudbrick rings outlines and defines the arches over the apse and sacristies, those over the latter being simply the profiles of the skew vaults which roofed them. Shallow pilasters framing the apse are capped with a similar moulding to give the illusion of supporting the true arch crowning the apse.

With no evidence for vaulting surviving in the extant 4 m height of the outer walls, the church is presumed to have been roofed in timber. The roof must have been supported in part on pairs of columns or a double arcade on piers. The underside height of such a roof in this case must have been above the 4 m preserved wall heights, as no sign of beam holes is evident in the walls. The whole church interior appears to have been lime plastered. In addition, painted decoration is found to each side of the apse pilasters and throughout the apse interior. Under the arch mouldings to each side of these pilasters are faded traces of painted yellow capitals outlined in purple, bearing purple acanthus leaves and supporting a purple block above. The opposing pilaster or doorjamb faces are each divided into four or five decorative rectangular panels of geometric designs, outlined and partly filled with dark maroon and yellow on a red, or partly white field. The curve of the apse is divided vertically into four equal areas by the engaged central column and a painted column to each side. The columns and capitals are painted dark maroon, set on yellow bases, with a red base line at floor level between them. The niche arches, slightly recessed in plaster, are painted yellow outlined in dark maroon, as are also the front edges of the wooden shelves set into the niches. Between the bottom of each niche and the base line is a decorative painted square composed of a small cross within a small square within opposed pairs of trapezoids inside a narrow frame of parallel lines. The dark maroon and yellow colours used are reversed for like features on the two opposing squares. Two panelled, double-leaved shutters are painted to fill the spaces between the three columns. Most of the detail is rendered in dark maroon, yellow and some red, the shutter frames on a light red or pink field and the shutters on white with a heavy infilling of dark maroon. Shutter panel centres feature a freely painted branch motif. All the line work is clearly wrought in deft freehand fashion.

Large East Church

This large church, measuring over 17 × 20 m, is thought to be a later addition to the complex as it abuts, and uses for its west wall, the same east enclosure wall into which

the apse of the small church is cut. Although over four times the size of the small church, it shares in plan many of the same features (Fig. 13.32). A nearly three-quarter circular apse is framed by slight pilasters and the doorways to flanking sacristies. A mudbrick colonnade divides the main body of the church, 12.5 × 16.5 m, into a nave with a 6 m span, side aisles and narthex. Entry is through double doorways cut through the west wall/east enclosure wall. A row of four rooms is built integral with the church along its full south side. The body of the church and the apse are lime plastered.

Directly to the north of both churches is a partly traced block of lightly constructed buildings, 11 × 20 m overall. The two doorways from the large church open onto an L-shaped space divided in part by a short wall bearing an engaged column at its end. A gap in the plaster on the wall face directly opposite indicates that a corresponding short wall or pilaster bearing another engaged column is missing. This missing element and a restored colonnade of one or two columns in between engaged ones would offer a central area possibly divided into a court on the north and a roofed loggia on the south. Again, because of preserved wall heights above door lintels, means of access to this court and the churches from the rest of the complex remains unclear.

There are two peculiarities in the plan of the larger church. One is a short passage outside its southwest corner which creates an angled wall protruding into the body of the church. Within the church, this corner is modified with an inset and engaged quarter column preserving a fragment of flaring capital at its eroded top. The north end of this cornering passage coincides with the east end of a long vaulted passage leading from the east enclosure wall into the complex. The presence of a buried doorway connecting the two passages would prove conclusively that the church is a later addition modified in plan to allow continued use of the long passage. Another peculiarity is a deeply engaged column on the church's inner south wall. Its position is opposite that of a missing easternmost column in the south colonnade. Its purpose and asymmetry are not yet understood.

In a subsequent sondage within the apse to floor level, the sand was found to include much fallen mudbrick debris. The apse wall stands about 1.4 m above floor level and bears two arched niches and a doorway to the south sacristy. The wall faces around the niches bear sockets and impressions for missing rectangular wood frames probably supporting small hinged doors closing the niches. The doorway to the south sacristy bears similar impressions of a missing wooden door frame let into the wall face (Fig. 13.32). The apse floor is partially paved with pie-shaped mudbricks laid on a subfloor fill of red clay mixed heavily with wood ash. The pie-shaped mudbricks are one-sixth segments of column drums appropriate for columns of the same 330–350 mm radius as those still standing in the nave (Fig. 13.33). An important discovery was five coins on the floor of the apse. Unfortunately, only two are well enough preserved to be identified and dated. One of them has been tentatively dated to the reign of Carus or Numerianus, 282–284 AD, and the other to the reigns of Gratianus, Valentianus II or Theodosius I, 367–395 AD (A. Easson, *pers. comm.*, 1985).

Decoration of the wall of the apse consists of a 40 cm high painted dado with three painted columns on exaggerated bases standing upon it. The central column is painted grey with black horizontal lines across its base and the two flanking it are painted yellow. A large fragment of the arch framing the apse, found fallen in debris directly below its original position, provides a soffit profile 36 cm wide, with a bevelled back face rising >4 cm to the original crown of the apse's half dome. Its flat front face bears a 25 cm wide band of dark maroon paint with yellow above. The soffit is decorated with four circumferential rows of four-petalled flowers in buff, orange and yellow on a dark maroon field.

Within the body of the church are numerous niches, some of them arched. Ten standing mudbrick columns, including two triple-engaged corner piers at northwest and southwest, were traced at surface level, as well as the remains of three fallen columns and capitals. All are lime plastered and the northwest corner pier stands intact perhaps to halfway up capital. In this best preserved example, three columns are engaged to form an L-shaped corner pier with a capital consisting of a horizontal plaster band with tapering, slightly flaring plaster leaves rising from it. The capitals are assumed to have supported a light timber roof.

The south sacristy was also cleared as a part of the test and on its clay floor a scatter of 45 coins was found. Most were badly corroded, but the majority of the legible coins date to the reigns of Constantine the Great, 307–337 AD and Constantine II, 337–340 AD (A. Easson, *pers. comm.*, 1985). Pottery sherds also recovered date from a late Roman, early Christian time, with several sherds of imported North African red-slipped ware of a type known from mid-4th Century AD (Hope 1983). The room is mud plastered throughout, with the addition of a band of lime plaster based 1.15 m above floor level, running partially round the south end of the room. The clay floor rests on a subfloor and the east and west wall foundations below take the form of a slightly projecting footing made up of two courses of mudbrick laid flat atop one course of vertically laid rollock bond. The south wall and south ends of the east and west walls were found to rest on an earlier mudbrick wall fragment running parallel to the south wall. Only its north face was exposed. This earlier wall was probably reduced to its present height of four to seven courses when the church foundations were being prepared and it, in turn, rests directly on an 8–10 cm thick level platform of dense mud and straw, laid on levelled virgin soil.

North Tomb Group

The north tomb group stands in relative isolation on open terrace ground to the northwest of the town site (Figs 13.12 and 13.34). The tombs clearly form an intermittent line running south-southwest to north-northeast, with all entries facing approximately east-southeast. This line of tombs and the northwest edge of the site frame an open stretch of ground roughly 40 × 300 m running southward from the northwest wadi bottom up its slope and across the terrace on an alignment towards the northeast corner of Enclosure 1 and, further on, the main east gateway of Enclosure 1. The tombs, thus, would appear to be a grouping along a major approach route to the town, standing in positions best facing both roadway and town. Their presence here, possibly early in the town's development, could also offer an explanation for the total lack of town growth over the high ground in their vicinity and to their rear.

The deflated fragments of a small building in the vicinity of the tombs (Fig. 13.35), found standing about 30 m east of the northeast corner of Enclosure 1, are situated and allligned directly on the axis of this hypothesised approach road. Both the plan of this building and its placement are intriguing, but its south extent has unfortunately been largely destroyed and buried by an intrusive well. Its

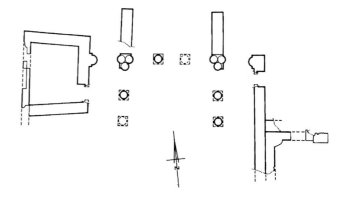

Fig. 13.34. North Tomb Group: Tomb 1 in foreground.

Fig. 13.35. North Tomb Group: shrine?

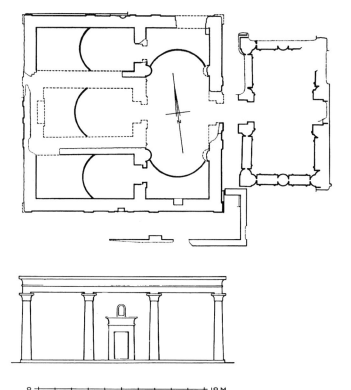

Fig. 13.36. North Tomb Group: Tomb 1 – plan and restored south elevation. Vaults indicated by arcs.

surviving north front presents a 9 m wide columned entry portico of a kind generally associated with a shrine or propylaeum. Engaged columns at side walls frame a pair of triple engaged columns acting as corner piers, which in turn frame two central columns to complete the colonnade. A short wall projects forward, northward, from each corner pier and fragmentary colonnades running south from the piers divide the interior into a 4.5 m wide central hall or court and two side aisles. Only fragments of the rest of the building are readily traceable on the surface.

Nineteen tombs still stand exposed above ground on the terrace surface on a line set parallel to and west of the axis of the above building. Traces of three more possible tombs are found at the north end, the final one on the wadi bottom. Three small heaps of unexamined mudbrick debris lying slightly to the west of the group may also be ruined tombs. The better preserved 19 tombs have been numbered northeastward from the southerly one standing about 40 m north of the northeast corner of Enclosure 1. Most of the tombs form two distinct clusters. Tomb 1 is the largest and most elaborate (Fig. 13.36), standing alone 25 m apart from its nearest neighbour. Tombs 2 to 11 form an almost continuous line (Figs 13.37 and 13.38), as do Tombs 13 to 16 (Fig. 13.39). Tomb 12 stands alone in the gap between these clusters. Tomb 19 stands 65 m to the north, closer to the scanty traces of the three farther possible tombs.

An examination of tomb size, plan, spatial distribution and juxtaposition provides clues to the sequence of erection. Tomb 1, in its prominent position closest to the formal town centre, is surely the earliest in the group. Its size and elaborate decorative treatment set it apart from the others and its relative importance may have discouraged the erection of others in close proximity (Figs 13.12 & 13.36). Tombs 2, 5, 7, 9 and 11 enjoyed comfortable spacing and possibly formed a simple linear sequence. Tomb 3 may be included in this sequence, except that it is rather close to the large Tomb 2, less than 2 m from it, and may more likely have been inserted at about the time of Tomb 4. Tomb 4 is too close to Tomb 5 to have allowed for construction of the false door found on the south wall of Tomb 5 and is obviously a later insertion. Tombs 6, 8 and 10 were also insertions, fitted in to incorporate the walls of adjacent tombs as side walls. The builders of Tomb 8 had some difficulty, as the alignment and length of tombs Tomb 7 and 9 are at odds, and Tomb 8's north side wall thus only partly engaged the skewed side wall of Tomb 9 (Figs 13.12 & 13.38).

The second cluster, Tombs 13 to 18, is not as closely spaced. Tombs 13, 14 and 16 enjoyed even spacing until

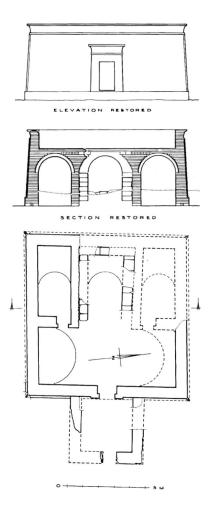

ELEVATION RESTORED

SECTION RESTORED

Fig. 13.37. North Tomb Group: Tomb 2, plan, section and elevation. Vaults indicated on plan by arcs and dotted line in section level of fill.

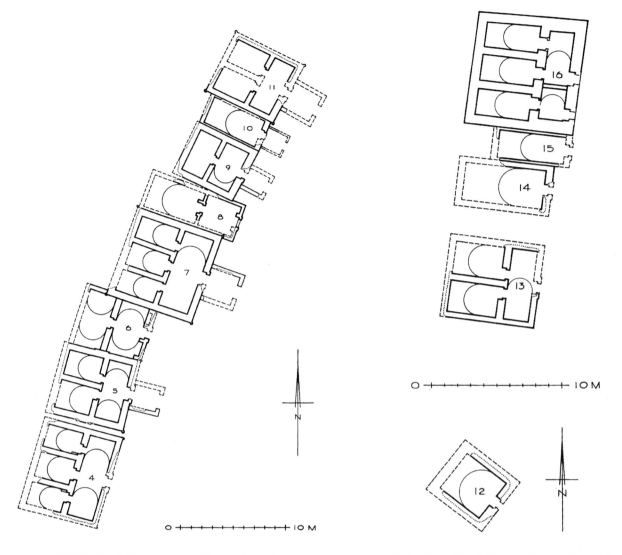

Fig. 13.38. North Tomb Group: Tombs 4 to 11 – plan.

Fig. 13.39. North Tomb Group: Tombs 12 to 16 – plan.

the insertion of Tomb 15 (Fig. 12.39). Tombs 17 and 18, less well preserved, are found out of line, presumably forced eastward by a drop in the terrace height to the northwest just behind Tombs 16 and 18.

The tombs vary in size and plan, but collectively represent a basic structural type, as well as a burial tradition common to a relatively affluent social group. Their variety and juxtaposition invite speculation as to their original relationships. If, for instance, each individual tomb represents a family or extended family group, the subsequent infilling with other tombs may reflect the desire of later generations to be associated either with ancestors or perhaps with unrelated higher status families.

Although all of the North Tombs have been essentially emptied, their structural preservation is surprisingly good, with most damage attributable to scouring of wall bases by wind driven sand or to vandalism ancient and modern. All these tombs are single-storeyed and vaulted mudbrick structures having plans that fall easily into five types:

Table 13.1. Categories and forms of tombs in the North Tomb Group.

Category of Tomb	Description and Layout	Tombs in Category
I	single chamber	Tombs 10, 12, 14, 15, 17
II	two chambers each front entry	Tomb 18
III	anteroom and single inner chamber	Tombs 6, 8, 9
IV	anteroom and two inner chambers	Tombs 3, 5, 11, 13, 19
Va	anteroom and three inner chambers	Tombs 4, 7, 16
Vb	anteroom and three inner chambers, the central chamber stone-lined	Tombs 1, 2

Tombs 1, 2, 5 and 7 show a definite batter to their outer wall faces. Tombs 1, 2, 3, 4, 5 and 7 were lime plastered on their exteriors and in part on their interiors. False doors occur on three sides of Tomb 1, on the north and south sides of Tomb 5 and possibly on Tomb 13. Roofing was with skew vaults of a single ring thickness throughout, and some of the vaulting supported a brick infilling to provide flat finished tops. Where preserved, doorways are topped with flat wooden lintels rather than with arches or short vaults. Door heights in some cases interrupt vaults springing from lower levels, forcing alternative brick arrangements within the body of the vaults in these areas. In the majority of the smaller tombs the interior mud plaster and mudbrick fabric is distinctly reddened, probably the result of intentional burning.

Seven tombs (2, 3, 5, 7, 9, 10 and 11) have the remains of thin and paired L-shaped walls projecting from their front faces, enclosing a small 'court' in front of their doorways. These were probably abbreviated forecourts standing to less height than the tombs themselves and, although the absence of door sockets indicates that they did not have doors, their purpose would seem to have been to offer the actual sealed entrances some segregation from open public ground. Most of the examples recovered are either deflated to present surface level or to only a few brick courses above. It is quite possible that most of the tombs were graced with such forecourts, but that some have completely disappeared.

Tomb 1 is the largest and most striking example on the site (Fig. 13.36). The main structure is 12 m square overall and stands 5 m high to nearly intact parapets. All four exterior faces are slightly battered and virtually identical in decorative detail. Four evenly spaced, tapered pilasters frame a central false door on three sides and a badly damaged true doorway on the east side. The doorways have torus-and-cavetto moulded lintels with an arched niche above each. The pilasters support cavetto moulded capitals, plain architraves, and torus-and-cavetto moulded parapets. The pilasters and door frames stand on a projecting sill or outer footing on all sides and the whole exterior was lime plastered. One exposed stone of the south door jamb shows that the east doorway had been framed in stone. Within, a vaulted transverse hall preserves a niche high at its south end, and was divided into unequal thirds by opposed engaged columns on its side walls. These columns may have supported arches dividing the vaulting above. The interior was lime plastered and painted in reds and yellows. The hall gives access to three chambers, the central one of cut sandstone blocks (now virtually destroyed, but described and photographed by Winlock (1936, 21, pl. XI)), flanked by parallel vaulted mudbrick side chambers. Winlock also observed that the rear of the sandstone chamber had a niche above floor level and that the mudbrick side chambers were painted yellow to the vault springs and the vaults painted white.

The tomb has an elaborate free-standing forecourt consisting of ten columns with intervening screen walls forming a rectangle with axial doorways centred on its broad sides. The columns flanking doorways are engaged with piers forming jambs and those at corners are double-engaged with piers to form the corners. The whole of the forecourt was also plastered and painted in reds and yellows. Fragments of a free-standing, lightly constructed outer enclosure wall, with buttresses on its inner faces, were also traced at the southeast corner and running parallel to and about 1.7 m from, the south side of the tomb. This low wall, along with the forecourt, is presumed to have enclosed the whole of the tomb.

Tomb 2 is about 10 m square and stands just under 5 m high to its parapets (Fig. 13.37). Its exterior is more simply decorated and more strongly battered than that of Tomb 1, with plain sides raised on a prominent step or footing all around and topped with torus-and-cavetto moulded parapets. The torus moulding extends down each exterior corner. The doorway in the east wall is badly damaged but evidence remains for its having been framed with projecting mudbrick jambs. The exterior, including the roof top, had been lime plastered. The interior is similar to that of Tomb 1 but lacks the niche and engaged columns in the transverse hall. The north, west and south walls of the central, stone-lined chamber were traced in part, but no decoration was uncovered. These walls are probably preserved to six or seven courses of cut and finished sandstone, but the doorway of the chamber, if preserved, remains buried in debris. A mass of high standing mudbrick in the wall between the stone chamber and the south side chamber preserves a curved, corbelled profile in section, indicating that this north projecting brickwork had originally rested upon a vault spanning the stone chamber below. A fragment of lime plaster on the roof above the extant south mudbrick vault shows that the outer parapets rose over a metre above a roof height level with the crown of the vaults.

Of the three possible tombs to the north, the first is 20 m down the wadi slope northeast of Tomb 19 and consists of the half-buried remains of a mudbrick rectangular construction recessed into the slope. Twenty-five metres further north are the level surface impressions, possibly of foundations, of a cemented masonry structure about 10 m square, with similar impressions of an axial projection measuring roughly 3 × 12 m extending from its east side. Forty metres beyond this, on the wadi bottom, a small but distinct scatter of sandstone chips, 8 m in diameter, may mark the site of a thoroughly dismantled stone structure.

South Tomb Group

To the south of the town, along the south bottom and slopes of the wadi, is another group of tombs in two distinct clusters as well as a dispersed scatter (Fig. 13.12). The first cluster of five tombs includes some of the larger, better preserved examples (Fig. 13.40). Tombs 1 to 4 stand in an evenly spaced row facing north at the base of the wadi slope, at a point where the wadi turns southwest.

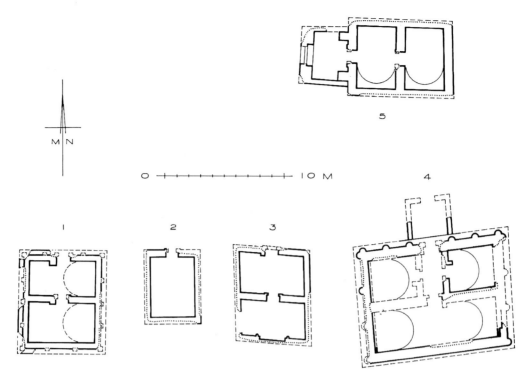

Fig. 13.40. South Tomb Group: first cluster of 5 tombs – plan.

Tomb 5 is about 10 m north of Tombs 3 and 4, and is unique in facing west. The second cluster of tombs lies 7 m north of Tomb 5 and takes the form of an 80 m long row of tightly juxtaposed tombs on a roughly east-west alignment. All but the easternmost of these tombs stand on the wadi bottom and it is their position on low ground which may explain their poor condition. They stand only 1.0–1.5 m high as sanded up heaps of collapsed mudbrick, congealed and mineralised into a hard mass by exposure to water subsequent to their collapse. There appears to be a maximum of ten tombs, but their forms are indistinguishable and it can only be assumed that they faced north across the wadi towards the town. In addition, there are about ten more tombs and possible tombs scattered along the wadi's south slopes for about 170 m to the east beyond the second cluster, with the furthest one more than 270 m distant. All are deflated and very fragmentary.

In none of the tombs was any use of stone noted. Lime plaster is only preserved on the interiors of the better preserved examples, but no paint was noted.

Due to the poor preservation of most of these tombs, a description of tomb types and plans can only be undertaken for the tombs in the first cluster. Only two categories of tombs seen in the North Tomb Group (Table 13.1) are present in the South Tomb Group. Category I is represented by Tomb 2 and category III by tombs 1, 3, 4 and 5. Of these, Tombs 1, 3 and 5 have a common arrangement of two vaulted transverse chambers entered and connected by axial doorways in their broad sides, as in Tombs 6, 8 and 9 of the North Group. Tomb 5 has, in addition, a forecourt with an axial doorway in its west facade. Tomb

Fig. 13.41. South Tomb Group: exterior of Tomb 4 showing engaged columns.

2 is a simple rectangular chamber with centred doorway. Tomb 4, measuring 9.5 × 12 m overall, is the largest and best preserved in the group. It is arranged within as two vaulted transverse chambers connected by axial doorways, but the first chamber is partitioned into unequal thirds to create a small central antechamber (Figs 13.40 & 13.41). It also has traces of a thin amd low-walled forecourt shielding its entrance.

All of the tombs are badly wind scoured on their exterior, but some decorative features are still visible. Overall, Tombs 1, 4 and 5 present features not found on any of the tombs of the north group, but it is not clear whether these reflect a significant temporal difference between the two groups. The outer wall faces of Tombs 1 and 4 preserve engaged pilasters and columns respectively. The pilasters of Tomb 1 are small and very poorly preserved, arranged four to the north and south sides and five to the east and west sides. The engaged columns of Tomb 4 are arranged four to the east and west sides and six to the north side (Fig. 12.41). They stand 2.3 m high on a raised projecting sill and support cavetto moulded capitals. Columns at the northwest and northeast corners form double-engaged pairs. The use of engaged columns in this example makes it the only one bearing possible comparison with the numerous standing tombs of el-Bagawat in Kharga Oasis (Fakhry 1951), which are similarly adorned. However, no evidence for the arches spanning from column to column, as on the el-Bagawat facades, is preserved on Tomb 4. If Tomb 5 had similarly engaged pilasters or columns, no evidence for them remains.

CONCLUSIONS

In addition to the remarkably preserved and accessible architecture thus far traced, with its attendant carved, moulded, painted and inscribed decorative features, a rich variety of similarly well preserved artifactual material has been recovered from the site of Kellis, both from surface clearance and from the initial limited tests discussed in this report. This includes ostraca, papyrus, bronze coins and statuettes, pottery, worked wood, textiles, baskets, sandals and rope. These finds, it may be stressed, are only a suggestion of the wealth of material, (subsequently and) still to be found, nearly intact and in last use contexts, below the depths of sand which have sealed the site since its abandonment. The substantial duration of the site, probably of several centuries, is attested to by the complexities of the architecture, which include a primarily agglutinative pattern of neighbourhood and town growth, as well as ample evidence of alteration, repairs and rebuilding. Dating evidence from the pottery remains imprecise, largely because the local sequence is still under study. More extensive excavation and analysis of sealed stratified deposits is in progress. At the time of writing (1985) no pottery of Ptolemaic date has been identified, the earliest dateable forms being from the Roman Period. The most recent types are from the early Byzantine Period, after which the town appears to have been abandoned. Analysis of reliefs, inscriptions, paintings and artifacts can also be expected to yield relative dating criteria, but a definitive chronology will most likely be constructed following the recovery and translation of documentary evidence such as coins, ostraca, papyri and codices, all of which offer the potential for very precise dating information.

It is clear from the architectural survey that the town grew to major local size and stature and enjoyed regional administrative and religious importance. Although the causes of the relatively quick and complete abandonment of the town are not yet understood, several explanations will bear testing during future work on the site. The answer most likely lies in a combination of environmental factors. The rapid accumulation of sand on the site has already been discussed in the introduction. The question remains whether this may have coincided with an over-exploitation of water resources. It is well attested that the introduction of the water-wheel or *saqiya* into Egypt, particularly into peripheral areas like the oases, allowed for significant expansion of agriculture in the Roman Period. The extent of irrigated field systems during this time in the Dakhleh Oasis was one of the most common observations of the survey (Mills 1979, 1980, 1981). The analysis of well preserved plant and animal remains from midden or stratified deposits at Kellis will certainly shed light on agricultural practices and land use, and might yield evidence of soil depletion and salination over the several centuries duration of the site. The delicate balance of water management and sustainable agricultural practices still influence land use and associated settlement patterns in the oasis today (Brookes 1989; Kleindienst *et al.*, Chapter 1, this volume). As one of the professed aims of the Dakhleh Oasis Project is to develop a better understanding of the complex interaction of man with his environment through time, the history of the agrarian and economic development of such a town site, and of its collapse, ought to provide a valuable contribution to this investigation.

Kellis, because of both its exceptional preservation and exceptional ease of archaeological recovery, affords a rich opportunity to investigate life in a Saharan town on the fringes of the Roman Empire, where ancient and Classical traditions mingled. With the appearance of Christianity by the 3rd Century AD, yet another provocative dimension was added to the social, religious and political complexion of the community. The town site, in preserving the evidence for this particular period of transition, presents the possibility of exploring the setting, the nature and the course of this complex interaction.

Acknowledgements
We wish to thank Joyce Haynes for supervising the test excavations in the churches, Colin Hope, who identified the pottery, Alan Hollett for taking some of the photographs and for having many of them printed, Alison Easson for examining the coins, Bryan Boyle, photographer at the Royal Ontario Museum, and John Glover, photograper in the Faculty of Arts ansd Science, University of Toronto, who prepared and printed the photographs and plans. Thanks are due to Nicholas Millet for arranging the (then) Egyptian Department to pay for ??? photo work and to Rufus Churcher for paying for the work of John Glover from his NSERC grant A1760. The analysis of the pottery

has been undertaken by Colin Hope, who has subsequently been conducting excavations at ancient Kellis (Ismant el-Kharab) to the present time. We are chiefly indebted to Tony Mills for his adroit orchestration of the Dakhleh Oasis Project, providing facilities, labour and transport with unfailing good humour. Other members of the Project provided collegial support and encouragement. Finally, many thanks are due to C.S. Churcher for sharing the onerous task of preparing our manuscript for publication.

Address for Authors

James E. Knudstad and Rosa A. Frey, Cassacawn Cottage, Blisland, Bodmin, Cornwall, England PL30 4JU

REFERENCES

Appendix II. This volume. List of Archaeological Sites Indexed, 251–266.

Brookes, I.A. 1989. Above the salt: sediment accretion and irrigation agriculture in an Egyptian oasis. *Journal of Arid Environments* **17**, 335–348.

Davies, J.G. 1952. *Origin and development of early Christian architecture*. New York: Studies in Christian Mission Press, 152p.

Fakhry, A. 1951. *The Necropolis of el-Bagawat in Kharga Oasis*. Cairo: Government Press (Service des antiquités de l'Égypte), 202p.

Hope, C.A. 1983. Dakhleh Oasis Project: Preliminary report on the study of the pottery – Fifth season, 1982. *Journal of the Society for the Study of Egyptian Antiquities* **13**: 142–157.

Hope, C.A. 1985. Dakhleh Oasis Project: Report on the 1986 excavations at Ismant el-Kharab. *Journal of the Society for the Study of Egyptian Antiquities* **15**: 114–125.

Hope, C.A. 1986. Dakhleh Oasis Project: Report on the 1987 excavations at Ismant el-Kharab. *Journal of the Society for the Study of Egyptian Antiquities* **16**: 74–91.

Hope, C. [A.] 1988. Three seasons of excavation at Ismant el-Gharab in Dakhleh Oasis, Egypt. *Mediterranean Archaeology (Australian and New Zealand Journal for the Archaeology of the Mediterranean World)* **1**: 160–178.

Kleindienst, M.R, C.S. Churcher, M.M.A. McDonald, and H.P. Schwarcz. This volume. Chapter 1. Geography, Geology, Geochronology and Geoarchaeology in the Dakhleh Oasis Region: An interim report, 1–54.

Krautheimer, R. 1965. *Early Christian and Byzantine Architecture*. Penguin Books: Harmondsworth, 390p.

Mills, A.J. 1979. The Dakhleh Oasis Project: Report on the first season of survey: October-December 1978. *Journal of the Society for the Study of Egyptian Antiquities* **9**: 163–185.

Mills, A.J. 1980. The Dakhleh Oasis Project: Report on the second season of survey, September-December, 1979. *Journal of the Society for the Study of Egyptian Antiquities* **10**: 251–282.

Mills, A.J. 1981. The Dakhleh Oasis Project: Report on the third season of survey, September-December, 1980. *Journal of the Society for the Study of Egyptian Antiquities* **11**: 176–192.

Mills, A.J. 1982. The Dakhleh Oasis Project: Report on the fourth season of survey, October 1981–January 1982. *Journal of the Society for the Study of Egyptian Antiquities* **12**: 93–101.

Osing, J., M. Moursi, Do. Arnold, O. Neugebauer, R.A. Parker, D. Pingree, M.A. Nur-el-Din, eds. 1982. *Denkmäler der Oase Dachla aus dem Nachlass von Ahmed Fakhry*. Deutsches Archäologisches Institut, Abteilung Kairo, Archäologisches Veröffentlichungen **28**, 1–117.

Wilkinson, J. G. 1843. *Modern Egypt and Thebes II*. London: John Murray, 364p.

Winlock, H. E. 1936. Ed Dakhleh Oasis. *Journal of a camel trip made in 1908*. New York: Metropolitan Museum of Art, 77p.

14

POTTERY MANUFACTURE IN THE DAKHLEH OASIS

Colin A. Hope

with a contribution by Daniel M. Tangri

INTRODUCTION

Throughout the course of the survey of the Dakhleh Oasis a detailed study of the large quantity of pottery collected has been undertaken. This material is predominantly from surface collections made at each of the sites discovered, but also includes a significant body derived from excavations or tests conducted at selected sites. The earliest pottery dates from the Epipalaeolithic Period and finds have been made which enable a sequence to be developed, albeit an interrupted one, extending into the Islamic Period. It is, therefore, possible to study the manufacture of pottery and its use in the oasis for a time span of at least eight thousand years.

Several preliminary reports have been published on the study of this material and the pottery kilns and workshops which have been found (Hope 1979, 1980, 1981a, 1983, 1993; Edwards and Hope 1989). The earlier ones are republished together in Edwards *et al.* (1987) with some corrections and additions. The pottery types characteristic of each of the periods identified have been illustrated and briefly described in these reports, which have focused primarily upon dating the material. This has been one of the major aspects of the study as, in the absence of other categories of datable material and the general abundance of ceramics on each site, the pottery serves as a guide to the identification of any period or periods of occupation. While vessel morphology plays an important role in this dating process, technical aspects such as method of manufacture, surface finish and decoration and the selection and treatment of raw materials also contribute significant information.

In assigning material from Dakhleh to many of the periods of the pharaonic history of Egypt, dated parallels from within the Nile Valley have been used extensively. This has been necessitated by the paucity of secure internal dating criteria and the poorly defined archaeological context of much of the material. In using data from the Nile Valley to date the pottery found in Dakhleh Oasis it is assumed that no significant time lapsed between the development of a particular feature or group of features by the Valley potters and their adoption in or transmission to the oasis.

Complementing this aspect of the study has been a much broader approach aimed at elucidating the general nature of pottery manufacture in the oasis. This has entailed the identification of features which appear to characterise discrete ceramic assemblages, in most cases representing different periods of manufacture, and the comparison of each of these to establish their relation one to the other and with the ceramics of surrounding regions. The information derived from the ceramic material may then be used to assist in the identification of the cultural affinities of the Dakhleh population and in the isolation of indigenous aspects of their material culture.

In this paper an overview will be presented of the current state of our knowledge of ceramic manufacture in the Dakhleh Oasis and the traditions which have been identified. This will be divided into three main sections: the Epipalaeolithic and Neolithic Periods, the Pharaonic Period, and the Ptolemaic-Byzantine Periods, each of which will be sub-divided. No discussion is included of the Islamic material (for which see Keall 1981). As representative selections of illustrations of the Dakhleh pottery have been published elsewhere (Hope 1979, 1980,

'Reports from the Survey of Dakhleh Oasis, Western Desert of Egypt, 1977–1987', edited by C.S. Churcher and A.J. Mills. Dakhleh Oasis Project: Monograph 2. Oxbow Monograph 99.

1981a, 1983; Edwards *et al.* 1987; Edwards and Hope 1989), reference will be made to those publications and no new corpora provided herein. However, the dating of some of the material has been changed in the light of further research. The discussion will focus on the ceramics recorded by the Dakhleh Oasis Project and discovered during the course of the survey of the oasis, but the invaluable material excavated by L'Institut Français d'Archéologie Orientale du Caire (IFAO) at the sites of Qila' el-Debba (Dabba) and 'Ain Aseel (Ain Asil) will of course be utilised to complete the picture.

EPIPALAEOLITHIC AND NEOLITHIC PERIODS

The Epipalaeolithic Period in the Dakhleh Oasis has been termed the Masara Cultural Unit; the Neolithic Period has been divided into two units: the Bashendi Cultural Unit and the Sheikh Muftah Cultural Unit, the former probably being the earlier of the two (McDonald, Chapter 7, this volume). Masara Unit sites have yielded very little pottery to date. Sherds are more common on Bashendi Unit sites while the Sheikh Muftah Unit sites invariably yield fairly abundant quantities. While the pottery from all of these units has been recorded, its detailed analysis is incomplete and the comments presented here should therefore be regarded as preliminary (see Postscript).

The Masara and Bashendi Cultural Units by Daniel Tangri

Masara Cultural Unit

Potsherds have been found on three Masara Unit sites. Most of these resemble in form, finish and fabric pottery of the Bashendi Unit and are probably to be attributed to that unit, given the partial complimentary distribution pattern of Masara and Bashendi Unit sites. However, there are three sherds which do not overly resemble any Neolithic pottery hitherto discovered in the Dakhleh Oasis. Two are from Loc. 076 on the escarpment at Maohoub, a wholly Masara Unit site, and are probably Epipalaeolithic. (Loc. 076 is within the Dakhleh Oasis Project's Index list of Prehistoric Archaeological Loci, Appendix III; the Locality Number cited here is from an additional system used by M.R. Kleindienst and M.M.A. McDonald for recording prehistoric loci outside the grid system based on the mapped area of the oasis, see Appendix II, this volume). The sherds are thick, sandy and coarse, with large shell and shale inclusions and are irregularly fired a brownish-grey to light brown colour. The other sherd, a fragment of a rounded base, was found at 30/420–C4–2. It has large chert inclusions and is granular in texture. Finger impressions on the exterior may indicate that it was constructed by pinching. It too is irregularly fired, but the exterior surface is also cracked and exfoliated post-firing. This probably reflects exposure to heat and

may indicate that the pot was used for cooking. The roughness of these three sherds contrasts with contemporary pottery from elsewhere in the eastern Sahara (Banks 1984; Gabriel 1979), as does the lack of decoration. The sample is too small, however, to draw any major conclusions from these differences.

Bashendi Cultural Unit

Pottery has been discovered on 23 Bashendi Cultural Unit sites. If some of the sherds from Masara Unit sites indeed represent the Bashendi Unit, this brings the total to 25 sites, or 571 sherds (counting joining fragments as one sherd). The range of fabrics is quite diverse, but generally the sherds contain differing proportions of sand and fine to coarse shale. The range of variation includes the two extremes of very fine shale with little sand and a very sandy fabric with little shale. Three of the very sandy sherds contain a little chaff. Otherwise, there are a few sherds (38) of a silty fine fabric, the majority from 30/435–N9–1. There are also four sherds of a fabric containing opaque flakes of white limestone, and two odd sherds. One is chaff-rich with coarse shale inclusions, not unlike the coarse shale wares produced during the Old Kingdom in Dakhleh (see below); similar sherds have been found on Sheikh Muftah sites. The final sherd, from 32/435–M10–1, is chaff-rich with very little sand. A burnished example of this fabric has been found on a Sheikh Muftah site.

It appears that Bashendi Unit pots, like those of the Sheikh Muftah Unit, were coil-built. Most of the shale wares are fired irregularly reddish-brown, though some of the finer variants are reduced. A few sherds with blackened rims may have been oxidised and then reduced (see below). Firing patterns are also similar to those of the Sheikh Muftah Unit.

Seven provisional shape groups have been identified among the material. These are:

a) Shallow open bowls with rim diameters from 120 to 260 mm.
b) Small restricted bowls with convex sides and rim diameters from 130 to 260 mm.
c) Open conical bowls with rim diameters from 130 to 170 mm.
d) Deep conical, open bowls with rim diameters from 180 to 240 mm.
e) Deep restricted bowls with convex sides which occasionally curve outwards slightly at the rim, with rim diameters from 90 to 240 mm.
f) Straight-sided versions of e).
g) Wide-bodied jars which narrow at the shoulder to a short neck and then curve out obliquely towards the rim; only one example is known, from 30/450–B10–1.

Many vessels bear holes drilled in their walls, whether for suspension or repair is unknown. One sherd bears an applied handle-stump, possibly from a lug.

There are nine sherds from four sites that are coated on

both surfaces with a dusky red slip. One sherd is slipped and burnished; 78 burnished sherds have been discovered at ten sites. Thirty-seven sherds from five sites are compacted; 33 of these derive from site 30/450–C6–1. Apparently only refined fine shale fabrics were compacted, although sherds of various sand and shale fabrics or silty wares might be burnished.

Most pots, however, were smoothed in some way. On occasion a tool may have been used for finishing, as scratches from such were observed on one sherd from 30/450–B10–1. The majority were smoothed by running the fingers over the coil junctions, which had already been pinched together, leaving 'finger-tracks' from the rim to the base (Fig. 14.1c). Other sherds betray nothing about the manner of their smoothing, other than that, from the fact that their surfaces are not rough, they were smoothed. Finger-tracks are ubiquitous among Sheikh Muftah material and, in the Bashendi Unit, large vessels were most commonly finished in this manner. Red slip has also been found on Sheikh Muftah pottery. Burnished sherds that are hard and reddish in colour have been found on sites of both Cultural Units.

Decoration is scarce, leaving aside sherds that cannot be clearly assigned to either unit (McDonald, Chapter 7, this volume). A rim sherd from a jar or deep bowl from 31/435–A6–3 bears parallel vertical notches on the rim (the 'milled' rim of Arkell's 1949, 84, terminology). Six fragments from the same vessel from 30/450–C6–1 are covered with basket impressions; this method of decoration is paralleled at the Sheikh Muftah site 30/450–B4–1 (Edwards and Hope 1987, 10, fig. 2g; Tangri 1991b; see below also). The finger-tracks on some pots may have been intended to have a decorative effect, as may the red slip. Otherwise, a few sherds with blackened rims appear to have been oxidised and then reduced in the manner of Nilotic black-topped wares (Davies 1962, 20–23; Edwards and Hope 1987, 4; Rizkana and Seeher 1987, 26). Such local 'black-topped' pots were also found on a site that is not definitely assignable to either unit, in conjunction with Nilotic black-topped imports (see below).

In summary, Masara and Bashendi Cultural Units pottery is simple in form and fabric, handmade and mostly coarse with some smoothing of the exterior. Burnished, slipped and compacted wares occur, though decoration is scarce.

Sheikh Muftah Cultural Unit (Fig 14.1–14.3, Pl. 14.1)

The pottery of the Sheikh Muftah Unit presents us with a clear tradition of handmade wares, either modelled from a single piece of clay in the case of the smaller vessels, or coil-built in the case of the larger forms. It would all appear to have been fired in what Edwards has termed a 'proto-kiln' situation, i.e., "on a smouldering bed of fuel, (e.g., dung) and then more fuel was heaped over them, thus resulting in a heavy reduction firing atmosphere. A

reasonable degree of heat conservation due to the fuel heaped up over the stack of pots would have occurred." (Edwards and Hope 1987, 4). On the whole the vessels were made from a limited range of fabrics, all with fairly abundant temper, and surfaces are characterised by unevenness, lack of compaction or surface coatings and infrequent elaborate decoration.

The local clay deposits which were exploited provided the potters with an iron-rich body containing a high percentage of tempering material, predominantly in the form of sand and shale. While some of these clays may have been treated to remove the larger inclusions, all of the fabrics distinguished among the Sheikh Muftah Unit material contain abundant non-plastic temper. The predominant bodies are a coarsely sand-tempered fabric with gritty surface, a finer sand-tempered fabric with smooth surface, and a range of sand-and-shale tempered fabrics with inclusions of fine and medium size (Edwards and Hope 1987, 2–5). All of these display firing colours varying from pale red and light brown to dark brown, grey cores and frequently have grey inner surfaces. Variation of fired colour on a single vessel or sherd is

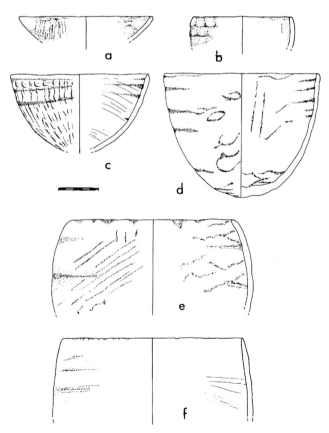

Fig. 14.1. Neolithic pottery of the Sheikh Muftah Cultural Unit. Note potter's finger marks in c, coil junctions in c, d and possibly e and f, and modelling below rim in b and c. a – from 31/405–K10–5; b – from 30/435–C3–2; c – from 30/435–B5–1 (object no. 4); d – from 30/450–F9–1 (object no. 1); e – from 31/405–E8–1; f – from 31/420–C10–1. Scale bar = 50 mm.

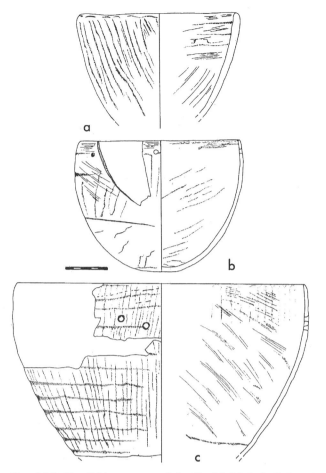

Fig. 14.2. *Neolithic pottery of the Sheikh Muftah Cultural Unit, from 30/435–J6–2. Note potter's finger marks in* a, *coil junctions in* c, *and perforations near rim in* b *and on body of* c. *Scale bar = 50 mm.*

uncommon. The principal surface feature of bowls and possibly also jars is a marked degree of unevenness. This may have partly resulted from the manufacturing processes but it frequently takes the form of vertical, oblique or random striations which appear to have been produced by running the fingertips over the moist surface of the already-formed vessel while exerting pressure (Figs 14.1–14.3) (Edwards and Hope 1987, figs 1c–i, 2c–e); these are the 'finger-tracks' referred to in the discussion of the Bashendi Unit pottery. In some cases this has been done with greater care to produce a slightly more regular finish and was undoubtedly intended to be decorative (Edwards and Hope 1987, fig. 1h, i). This treatment occurs on vessels often accompanied by a blackening of the upper body and/or rim. This darkening is also very irregular and obviously quite carelessly effected, displaying nothing of the control exhibited by the Nile Valley potters in the manufacture of black-topped wares. It was probably produced in the same manner as the latter.

A few sherds from Sheikh Muftah Unit sites display more elaborate decoration. Rim sherds from open bowls made in either coarsely sand-tempered fabrics or sand-and-shale tempered fabrics preserve rim top decoration of short oblique incisions, cross-hatching (Hope 1981a, 237, pl. XXIII), or nicks (Hope 1983, fig. 1), probably

common and is to be expected from the type of firing practised. The fabrics are not markedly different from those of the Bashendi Unit.

As far as may be determined, similar shapes were made in all of these fabrics. The range of forms is dominated by bowls (Figs 14.1–3; also Edwards and Hope 1987, figs 1–2), either open or restricted, which vary from shallow to very deep. Their sides may be convex or straight with conical and rounded shapes occurring; bases are either round or pointed and rims unaccentuated. Jars, when encountered, are of small to medium size with round- or ovoid-body shape and no neck formation. Again, bases appear to have been round or pointed and rims direct. The majority of the forms produced appear to have been used in the preparation and storage of food and, to judge by the general porosity of most of the fabrics, mainly dry foods. It may be suggested that fluids were stored in animal skins. Perforations of the vessel wall made after firing are not uncommon and, while many are to be regarded as repair holes, some may have been for suspension (Figs 14.2b–c, 14.3b).

As mentioned, surface coatings are rare and compaction

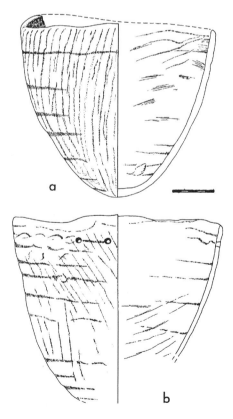

Fig. 14.3. *Neolithic Pottery of the Sheikh Muftah Cultural Unit from 30/435–J6–2. Note potter's finger marks, coil junctions and perforations. Scale bar = 50 mm.*

executed with the fingernail. Such decoration is not common but has been noted among material from several sites. At one such site, 31/420–C10–2, a short-necked jar, the only one of its kind discovered so far, carried an incised design of cross-hatching on the exterior of its rim (Pl. 14.1) (Hope 1983, pl. X.a). Originating from two sites only, 31/405–G6–1 and 33/390–I9–1/2, are a small number of body sherds in a sand-and-shale tempered fabric with incised lines either placed at random or parallel to one another.

Site 31/420–C10–2, which may prove to have Bashendi Unit affiliations (McDonald, Chapter 7, this volume), has also yielded evidence for yet more complex designs. Six rim sherds and one upper body sherd were recovered from what appear to have been straight-sided bowls with modelled rims, decorated in incised and impressed techniques. The motifs include incised pendant triangles filled with either vertical or horizontal rows of impressed punctates or incised cross-hatching between incised horizontal lines, and bands of horizontal rows of impressed punctates (Hope 1983, fig. 1). These sherds were made from a finely tempered sand-and-shale fabric, of the type commonly encountered, but fired black or grey. Only one other comparable decorated piece has been found in the oasis, at 31/405–G6–1. This sherd, from a restricted vessel, carries an incised design which may be identified as either a zigzag or triangle motif with adjoining areas alternately filled with either vertical or horizontal lines. Its exterior is covered with a red coating. While the fabric of the sherds from 31/420–C10–2 indicates that they were made within the oasis itself, it is possible that the sherd from 31/405–G6–1 is not a local product.

To conclude this survey of the decorated material found on Sheikh Muftah Unit sites, a large jar from 30/450–B4–1 must be mentioned. In addition to being the only large, necked jar recovered so far – it has a wide globular body, round base, concave flaring neck and internally thickened rim (Edwards and Hope 1987, fig. 2g) – it is unusual in having a basketry design impressed into its entire exterior surface. The jar is made from a dense sand-tempered fabric, fired dark brown at the exterior and dark grey on the interior. While the exterior impressions may have been decorative, it is possible that they resulted from the vessel having been constructed within a basket for support. The only parallels to this vessel discovered in Dakhleh are six body sherds, possibly from one vessel, found at 30/450–C6–1. They derive from a closed form (a jar?) and, while they have thicker walls than the vessel from 30/450–B4–1, they are similar in all other respects. In addition to this vessel, and the usual selection of typical Sheikh Muftah Unit wares, 30/450–B4–1 also yielded nine sherds in black-topped wares and a small, ceramic spoon-shaped object (Edwards and Hope 1987, fig. 2f).

In seeking parallels to the pottery types which are characteristic of the Sheikh Muftah Unit ceramic assemblage an interesting picture emerges. While similar shapes are encountered on various sites within the north-eastern Sahara and the Nile Valley, they are of such widespread distribution and of such basic profiles that, in general, vessel morphology offers few concrete indications of cultural affinity. The striated surface finish and the rim blackening, in the roughness of their execution, do not recall the rippled surfaces of black-topped wares of neighbouring regions. The paucity of elaborately executed decoration is a further distinguishing feature.

In relation to the small amount of decorated pottery which does occur, a connection with the widely attested ceramic traditions of the Saharo-Sudanese horizon may exist. Incised rim designs are common (e.g., Arkell 1953, pls 31, 32, 35, 37; Chlodnicki 1984, fig. 2) though frequently in conjunction with elaborate incised and impressed body decoration. The motifs on the seven sherds from 31/420–C10–2 and the isolated sherd from 31/405–G6–1 are all found on material of this ceramic horizon (Chlodnicki 1984; McHugh 1975, fig. 5; Nordstrom 1972, pls 25, 41). However, these similarities should be treated with caution as the Dakhleh material in general lacks the diversity of motifs for which this horizon is noted. Even the most cursory of glances at the material recently published from a number of sites stretching from the Nile to the Gilf el-Kebir is sufficient to show how dissimilar the oasis material is in general from the traditions apparent among that ceramic assemblage (Banks 1980, 1984; Krzyzaniak and Kobusiewicz 1989, *passim*; Kuper 1981, fig. 27; 1988).

In terms of their decoration, morphology and fired colour, the sherds from 31/420–C10–2 may prove to be related to the black-fired, burnished and incised ware known from the Naqada I period onwards in Egypt (Petrie's N ware; Petrie 1921, pl. XXVI; Petrie and Quibell 1896, pl. XXX). It would appear that this ware is of Nubian or Sudanese affiliation (Arkell 1953; Hassan 1988,158; Kaiser 1957; Payne forthcoming).

That the ceramic traditions of Predynastic Egypt may have influenced the Dakhleh Neolithic potters is indicated by a small number of sherds found on five sites. 31/405–G6–1 yielded three sherds from red-coated and polished black-topped vessels which appear to be of Nile Valley manufacture (Segnit *in* Edwards and Hope 1987), as does a single sherd from 30/450–B4–1 in an unburnished, smooth brown ware with a black top (Tangri 1991a). Each of these sites has also produced what are undoubtedly imitations of these black-topped wares in local sand-and-shale tempered fabrics with a variety of surface treatments (Segnit *in* Edwards and Hope 1987). They can be distinguished from other Sheikh Muftah manufactures by the degree of control exercised in producing the black top and their shapes, predominantly small ovoid jars (Hope 1981a, pl. XXIII.a) and restricted bowls. The number of such imitations identified to date is quite small, e.g., eight sherds from 30/450–B4–1, and four others from three separate sites. The occurrence of red-coated and/or burnished surfaces on pieces of local manufacture may possibly also attest Nile Valley influence. The ceramic

Pls 14.1–14.6

1, *Shiekh Muftah Unit: short-necked jar with incised design at neck from 31/420–C10–2 (object no. 1). 2, Early Dynastic Period jar from Grave 1 at 32/390–L2–1 (object no. 1). 3, Late Old Kingdom: pottery vessels from Grave 2 at 33/390–L9–2. 4, Late Old Kingdom: carinated bowl from the surface of 33/390–19–2 (object no. 4). 5, Late Old Kingdom: squat jar from Grave 3 at 33/390–19–2 (object no. 9). 6, Late Old Kingdom: spouted bowl from Grave 4 at 33/390–19–2 (object no. 19).*

'spoon' from 30/450–B4–1 should also be compared to Nile Valley examples (Tangri 1991a).

These sherds and a few others of late Predynastic Period date are also of importance in establishing chronological links between the Dakhleh Neolithic and Predynastic Egypt (McDonald, Chapter 7, this volume; Tangri 1991a). For example, there are a rim and upper body sherds from necked jars in a pink-fired marl (Petrie's L ware) from 30/435–C3–1, body sherds in the same ware from the former site, and from 30/435–C3–2, 31/420–D10–3 and 31/405–M10–3, and an intact jar in cream-fired, sand-tempered marl fabric which was an isolated surface find. These pieces may prove to be of the late Predynastic or Early Dynastic Period.

No exact parallels to the large jar with basketry impressions on its exterior have yet been found (Tangri 1991b). It is possible that the sherds with incised random or horizontal lines from 33/390–I9–1/2 and 31/405–G6–1 may be paralleled by sherds from a single vessel found in Kharga Oasis (Caton-Thompson 1952, 41, fig. 5). While the context of the pieces and the associated lithics did not enable Caton-Thompson to assign a precise dating to them, she did think them local with perhaps some Nubian affinities. Parallels may exist between these Dakhleh pieces and the 'rough-faced' ware known from the Fayum and Gebel Uweinat (Banks 1980, 310–313). It is indeed to be lamented that so little in the way of ceramics was found on the Neolithic sites in Kharga, and the few found were wind-blasted to the extent that only the briefest of descriptions could be provided (Caton-Thompson 1952, 38, 40). It is in this region, and perhaps in the oasis of Farafra, that one might expect to find pottery most similar to the rough products of the Dakhleh Neolithic. To date, however, nothing comparable has been reported from Farafra nor regions immediately to the north of Dakhleh, and the material from coastal Mediterranean regions shows no clear resemblance to that studied here.

To summarise, it is possible to say that the ceramic traditions of the Sheikh Muftah Unit were primarily indigenous to the oasis, resembling those of the Bashendi Unit, and that they show but little connection with either those of Predynastic Egypt or the Neolithic of neighbouring Saharan regions. They lasted unchanged in their essential characteristics until the end of the Old Kingdom at least, despite the arrival of the Egyptians in force with their own, quite different and more advanced, ceramic traditions and technology. Sheikh Muftah Unit pottery has been found in association with late Old Kingdom material on 13 separate sites (Hope 1980, 286; McDonald, Chapter 7, this volume). There is nothing to show that Egyptian ceramic traditions of the Old Kingdom influenced the local, while there is in fact a possibility that the reverse did happen in one respect at least (see below). The discovery of a local, handmade sherd in the fill of a tomb of Second Intermediate Period date (Hope 1980, 286) is to be regarded as fortuitous.

PHARAONIC PERIOD

Early Dynastic Period to Early Old Kingdom

With the arrival of the Pharaonic Egyptians in Dakhleh Oasis we encounter quite a different picture of ceramic manufacture. This change must have been equally as profound in all areas of human activity (Giddy 1987; Mills 1984, 1985, Chapter 10, this volume; Redford 1976).

Evidence for contact between the Nile Valley and this oasis before Dynasty VI is scarce. The ceramic evidence comes from one grave in the cemetery 32/390–L2–1, surface finds at several rock art sites at the eastern edge of the oasis and from a handful of sherds from sites of late Old Kingdom date. The group of vessels from 33/390–L9–2, Grave 2, which was originally dated to the early Old Kingdom (Hope 1980, 291–292, pl. XVIII) would seem better attributed to the late Old Kingdom, the two painted jars being residual (Pl. 14.2). Grave 1 at 32/390–L2–1 yielded three vessels: a necked storage jar with a pronounced roll-rim (Pl. 14.2) and two deep, restricted bowls (Hope 1980, 288–289, pl. XVII.b, c). These are made in a fine-grained silty material which is fired light brown in the case of the jar and pinkish in the case of the bowls. The exterior of the jar has a cream coating and the bowls a streaky red coating inside and out. Their shapes most closely recall Early Dynastic Period parallels and neither is found among the shapes of the later Old Kingdom in the Oasis. Despite Giddy's (1987, 166, 215, note 28) assertion to the contrary, I have not observed identical features among pottery shown to me from the IFAO excavations at 'Ain Aseel and Qila' el-Debba, nor are any referred to in the recent publications dealing with those sites (Ballet and Picon 1990; Valloggia with Henein 1986). During the 1988 field season a jar similar to that from grave 1 at 32/390–L2–1 and rim sherds from others were found at several sites in the eastern end of the oasis associated with rock art. While these pieces, and the other ceramic material from these sites, await detailed study, they are clearly of Early Dynastic Period date and closely parallel material from the Nile Valley.

Sherd material attests the occurrence of the early, classical form of the so-called 'Meydum' bowl, with its tall sides and pronounced, sharp carination. The sherds are made in a dense, pink-fired marl (Fine Marl A, variant 1, Nordström and Bourriau 1993, 176) with light red surfaces and fine polish. They are quite distinct from the more common examples with less pronounced carination made in a brown-fired body which is red-coated and burnished, and which belong to a later stage of development (Arnold 1982, 48) as has been verified by study of material from 'Ain Aseel in the oasis (Ballet 1987). They would appear to date from Dynasties IV and V, and as the earliest installations at 'Ain Aseel are tentatively dated to Dynasty V (Giddy 1987, 207) it is only to be expected that pottery of that period should be found in the oasis. All of the pieces alluded to were probably manufactured in the Nile Valley. Some locally-made examples have been found, associated with forms of a late Old Kingdom date (Hope 1979, pl. XX.2,5,9).

Late Old Kingdom to First Intermediate Period

The paucity of Early Dynastic Period and early Old Kingdom material is amply compensated for by the large quantities of pottery datable to the late Old Kingdom (Dynasty VI) and First Intermediate Period which have been found on various sites discovered during the course of the survey and in the excavations carried out at Qila' el-Debba and 'Ain Aseel near modern Balat, first by Ahmed Fakhry and then by IFAO. These latter sites have yielded inscriptional evidence which enables activity there to be dated mainly to Dynasty VI (Giddy 1987, 182–184, 201–203) and immediately thereafter.

The industry attested by these finds employed both wheelmade and handmade construction techniques, firing in up-draught kilns, the specialised use of certain clay bodies and surface treatments in the manufacture of a set range of categories of vessel shapes (e.g. bowls, jars, etc.) – the choice of clay body and surface treatment being dependent upon function – and a variety of specifically function-related vessel forms with a prescribed range of permissible variations.

This ceramic assemblage comprises three broad categories of material, distinguished by reference to ware types, vessel morphology and manufacturing techniques. These categories may be termed groups 1–3 for convenience here, and their characteristics summarised as follows:

Group 1. Fine wares made in a reddish-brown or brown-fired fabric tempered with quartz, some calcite and occasionally chaff, all of small sizes; grey cores are common. Surfaces may be uncoated but also smoothed, red coated or red coated and burnished. Shapes made in the uncoated ware include large and small necked jars, large deep bowls and stands (Pl. 14.3) (Hope 1979, pl. XX.13–14; Ballet and Picon 1990, pls 26–30). Those occurring in red-coated or red-coated and burnished wares are similar, including a wide range of bowls, basins and ewers, small and medium size jars and stands (Pls 14.3–9) (Hope 1979, pl. XX.1–12; Ballet and Picon 1990, pls 15–25). Manufacturing techniques employed the use of the wheel in the initial formation and secondary shape refinement by scraping, usually of the lower body and base. This applies to all of the shapes referred to except the large deep bowls. Discussions of this manufacturing technique and others employed until the New Kingdom and the types of wheel which were used have been provided by Arnold (1976; 1982, 47–48; 1985; 1993) and Holthoer (1977, 5–37).

Group 2. A rough ware made in a brown-fired fabric tempered with quartz and a large amount of both fine and coarse chaff; grey cores common. Surfaces are neither smoothed nor coated but left irregular, showing clearly elongated pores which have resulted from the burning out of the chaff. Shapes made in this ware include bread moulds (Pl. 14.10), shallow oval or round dishes (Pl. 14.11), elongated jars, conical vessels and small shallow or deep, round or oval bowls, some of which have finger-modelled, small birds or serpents(?) applied to the interior of the bases (Pl. 14.12) (Arnold 1982, pl. 11g–h, k–l; Hope 1979, pl. XIX.2–4, pl. XXI.1; Mills 1979, pl. XV.1, 4; Ballet and Picon 1990, pls 31–36). Examples of the latter type with finger-modelled, small birds found by Ahmed Fakhry at Qila' el-Debba have been dated to the Middle Kingdom by Arnold (1982, 52, pl. 11g–h). However, their close similarity to those found on various sites by the Dakhleh Oasis Project and at Qila' el-Debba by IFAO (Valloggia 1978, 68, pl. XXXVI.c; 1986, pls LXXVII, XCIV) would favour a late Old Kingdom and First Intermediate Period date, as with examples lacking the modelled element (Ballet and Picon 1990, 147). Of the Group 2 shapes most are completely handmade except the bread moulds, which were made either over a pre-shaped mould or on a wheel, as is indicated by experiments in replicating their manufacturing techniques carried out by Andrew Jamieson (Hope 1987a). The exterior of the handmade shapes is extremely uneven; that of the small, deep round or oval bowls frequently has impressed, vertical or oblique grooves, formed by the potters' fingers.

Group 3. Very coarse wares made in a heavily shale-tempered fabric fired a wide range of colours from pale red to brown and occasionally with multi-coloured shale inclusions. These inclusions vary in size from small to very large and both their size and quantity would have prevented the use of this fabric in the manufacture of vessels using a wheel. The shapes, predominantly medium and large size, deep bowls (Hope 1979, pl. XXI.2; Ballet and Picon 1990, pls 37–38) occur with uncoated or red-coated surfaces.

Material of Groups 1 and 2 occurs frequently while Group 3 is much rarer (cf. Ballet and Picon 1990, fig. 41). These categories accord with those identified by Ballet among material from the IFAO excavations at 'Ain Aseel and Qila' el-Debba (Ballet and Picon 1990; Giddy 1987, 243–247), and Maurice Picon (Laboratoire de Céramologie de Lyon) has provided a technical discussion of the clay materials used in their manufacture (Ballet and Picon 1990, 75–84). In addition to the fabrics outlined above, there also occurs infrequently a pale green-fired marl which was used for some open bowls and small and large, necked jars (cf. Ballet and Picon 1990, 119–121). Additional illustrations of material from Ain Aseel and Qila' el-Debba will be found in Arnold (1982), Minault-Gout (1980, 1981), Valbelle (1978), Valloggia (1978) and Vallogia with Henein (1986).

All pottery would appear to have been fired in simple up-draught kilns. Three kiln complexes, two associated with pottery workshops, have been found to date, in which

Pls 14.7–14.12

7, *Late Old Kingdom: potstand from the surface of 33/390–I9–2 (object no. 2).* **8**, *Late Old Kingdom: necked jar from the surface of 33/390–I9–2 (object no. 1).* **9**, *Late Old Kingdom: slender necked jar from Tomb 1 at 32/390–J3–1 (object no. 8).* **10**, *Late Old Kingdom: breadmould from Tomb 1 at 32/390–J3–1 (object no. 6).* **11**, *Late Old Kingdom: rough-ware, shallow bowl from the surface of 33/390–I9–2 (object no. 3).* **12**, *Late Old Kingdom: rough-ware, shallow bowl with modelling in sides and top and applied decoration on the interior, from Grave 2 at 33/390–L9–2 (object no. 3).*

material of the types described above was fired. Two of these served the communities at the western end of the oasis (Hope 1980, 303–307; 1993, 121–123) and one the large urban centre at 'Ain Aseel and its cemetery at Qila' el-Debba in the east (Soukassian *et al.* 1990). The design of several of these kilns closely resembles that of the kiln found at Buhen (Emery 1963, fig. 1). These complexes, in the absence of any from the Nile Valley within Egypt, will form the basis of our understanding of kiln technology during the Old Kingdom and later, enabling a far better appreciation of this aspect of pottery manufacture than is possible from the depiction of kilns in reliefs (Holthoer 1977, 34–37). The location of these kiln sites indicates a degree of regionalisation in the manufacture of pottery at the time, though to date no differences have been detected in the manufactures of the east and the west of the oasis.

In examining the characteristics of this material it is quite apparent that we are dealing with a predominantly Egyptian ceramic tradition, one which was developed by the potters of the early Old Kingdom in the Memphite region and which dominated pottery production within the country until the end of the Old Kingdom (Arnold 1982, 48–49). It was taken out to Dakhleh to provide for the domestic and funerary needs of the Egyptian settlers. Whether, as Arnold (1982, *passim*) has intimated, influence directly from Memphis can be detected is uncertain. Trade between Dakhleh and the Nile Valley at this time appears to have followed the Darb el-Tawil, leaving Middle Egypt in the region of Assiut (Leprohon 1986).

The Egyptian nature of the manufacture of this pottery can be seen clearly, not only in the range of vessel shapes produced and their morphological development (Ballet 1987), manufacturing techniques and the types of kiln used, but also in the selection and treatment of the raw materials employed. The fabric employed for the ceramics of Group 1 above resembles the fine and medium Nile silts employed within Egypt for exactly the same range of vessel shapes, with the same surface treatments, as are found in Dakhleh. The fabric of Group 2 recalls the chaff-tempered Nile silt used, as in Dakhleh, for coarse jars, bread moulds etc. Obviously the potters were determined to make their products look as Egyptian as they could. Fortunately, they were able to employ raw materials not too different, at least superficially, from those used in the Nile Valley. These were generally selected in preference to the shaly clays which were used by the local Sheikh Muftah people. These latter clays were employed in a small way in the manufacture of vessels of Group 3, possibly under the influence of indigenous potters.

This situation is perhaps best accounted for by the supposition that Egyptian potters were actually sent out to Dakhleh accompanying either one or more expeditions and took up residence there. This has also been suggested by Arnold (1982, 50). That such may have been Egyptian practice is indicated by a much later reference on a stela of Year 8 of Ramesses II (Holthoer 1977, 23), which implies that potters were sent on missions to provide for

the needs of stone masons. The discovery of an Egyptian pottery manufacturing installation in the vicinity of Haruba, 12 kilometres east of el-'Arish, and quantities of Egyptian pottery in North Sinai (Oren 1987) also lend support to the idea. It seems highly unlikely that local potters who had operated within the traditions of the Sheikh Muftah Unit pottery production would have been trained in the Egyptian traditions to such an extent that they were able to produce material which so closely resembled that made within the Nile Valley. Arnold (1982, 50–51) has suggested that contact with the Nile Valley trends was maintained by means of consignments of pottery (as containers for various commodities) sent out to Dakhleh, some pieces being retained for comparison (see also Ballet 1987, 16). This has received some verification as a result of trace element analysis carried out on 36 sherds of Old Kingdom to First Intermediate Period date, six of which proved to have close affinities with Nile Valley material. It is possible that the marl clay vessels of this date found in the oasis were imported from the Valley (Ballet and Picon 1990, 119–120, but note comment on 164).

While operating within the Egyptian ceramic traditions, it is possible that the Dakhleh potters did develop a few variations of their own. The use of shale fabrics has already been mentioned. Ahmed Fakhry (*fide* Arnold 1982, 51) believed that the handmade, small deep, oval and round bowls were 'the typical pottery of the 6th dynasty of the oases' manufactures. However, as Arnold has shown, they are encountered on Nile Valley sites, but there they are of a slightly earlier date and they became less common during the late Old Kingdom (Arnold 1982, 49). On the other hand, there are no parallels to those pieces carrying applied elements (birds and ?serpents) on their interior (Arnold 1982, 52). Such vessels seem to occur primarily in cemeteries where they may be accompanied by pottery offering tables. The latter are either square or rectangular, supplied with short legs at their corners, the top bearing rather crude, incised representations of offerings (Mills 1979, 172, pl. XV). Both the bowls and the offering tables may be Dakhleh features.

In addition, we may note a tendency to apply spouts to various shapes of bowl with greater frequency than in the Nile Valley and the use of in-turned, modelled rims on deep basins in preference to everted rims (Giddy 1987, 184, 199). It is possible that other variations will be identifiable when all material of this date is published. One type of vessel also deserves comment: a broad shouldered jar with a short, vertical neck and internal ledge. Either the ledge or the upper shoulder may be perforated; the shoulder and upper body are decorated with incised, pendant triangles filled with either short incisions or punctates (Hope 1980, 289–290, pl. XVII.d–f). Examples are all made in a sand-and-chaff tempered, orange-fired fabric. Both the shape and decoration find parallels among Predynastic material from Egypt, while the motifs resemble those found on Syrian pottery from the First Dynasty tombs at Abydos (Hope 1980, 289–290;

Brunton and Caton-Thompson 1928, pl. XL.14.k; Quibell 1898, pls XI.7, XX.6). They are also found on the indigenous Sheikh Muftah decorated pottery described above. Whether these jars are to be regarded as solely Dakhleh products is not yet certain. Their occurrence on sites alongside pottery of a late Old Kingdom date, by which time they were no longer to be encountered within the Nile Valley, indicates that they were at least being made in Dakhleh long after the time of their restricted appearance in Egypt.

So far the characteristics of the ceramic products of the Old Kingdom and the First Intermediate Period have been discussed collectively. It is now necessary to distinguish between them. This is largely possible as a result of the detailed study of material excavated at the pottery-manufacturing complex immediately to the south of the main mound of 'Ain Aseel, ascribed to the First Intermediate Period, and its comparison with that from 'Sondage b' by Ballet (Ballet and Picon 1990, 143–149, 150–157). The conclusions are confirmed by the pottery discovered at 33/390–K9–1 in the western end of the oasis (Hope 1980, 291, 305–307). Forms characteristic of Dynasty VI disappear, such as the late version of the 'Meydum' bowl, with its short upper side and modelled rim (Ballet 1987, fig. 10; Hope 1979, pl. XX.9), the deep basin with concave sides and internally modelled rim basin (Ballet 1987, fig. 2.3; Hope 1979, pl. XX.12) and its associated spouted ewer (Ballet 1987, fig. 2.4), the large restricted spouted bowl (Hope 1979, pl. XX.5) and the coarse-ware jar (Ballet and Picon 1990, pl. 34). Deep open bowls of varying sizes, with or without spouts, replace open forms (Ballet and Picon 1990, 152–154, pls 15–21) and small, globular-bodied jars with necks of varying heights increase in frequency (Hope 1980, pl. XIX.a; Ballet and Picon 1990, pl. 22). However, atypically, bread moulds of the standard Old Kingdom type (Jacquet-Gordon 1981, 12, fig. 3, type A2) continued in use (Ballet and Picon 1990, 165).

These features are well documented within the Nile Valley as having developed early in the First Intermediate Period, by what Seidlmayer has termed his Stufe IIC at Qâu-Matmar and IIB/C at Dendera (Seidlmayer 1990, Abb. 42, 83, 168). They are further attested in the oasis by finds within the subsidiary tombs at Qila' el-Debba (Seidlmayer 1990, 373–375), the dating of which is confirmed by inscribed material (Andreu 1981; Koenig and Koenig 1980; Leprohon 1983; Osing 1982, 33, no. 43; Pantalacci 1985; Valloggia 1985). Arnold (1982, 52–54) has also ascribed some of the pottery from Fakhry's excavations at Qila' el-Debba to this period. Of the diagnostic First Intermediate Period forms (Arnold 1972, 44–45; 1977, fig. 2.27–34; Kemp 1975; O'Connor 1974; Seidlmayer 1990, passim) only the 'drop-shaped' jar (Hope 1979, pl. XX.7) and the quatrefoil-mouthed jar (Ballet and Picon 1990, 121, pl. 39) occur, and then rarely. The same applies to one of the few decorative motifs of the period, namely incised undulating lines (Ballet and

Picon 1990, 148, pl. 39). However, this does not mean that the potters working in Dakhleh during this period were largely cut off from, or ignorant of, the developments within the Nile Valley. Seals and stone vessels found in the oasis are identical to those in use in the Valley, indicating that direct contact was maintained (Seidlmayer 1990, 374–375).

Middle Kingdom to Late Period

Despite the impression created by a fairly extensive body of inscriptional evidence from the Nile Valley (Giddy 1987, 53–98; Redford 1976; Valloggia 1981) and from Dakhleh itself (Gardiner 1933; Janssen 1968; Mills 1983, 128; Osing 1982, 33–41), the archaeological record from the oasis would at present suggest only a token Egyptian presence during these periods (Mills 1985, 128; Chapter 10, this volume). In addition, it should be noted that no trace of the local Sheikh Muftah ceramic traditions has been encountered nor any other which may be called indigenous to Dakhleh and dated to these periods. The pottery which has been found is all morphologically comparable to that from sites within the Nile Valley. It derives mostly from cemeteries and, except in the case of the Second Intermediate Period and possibly the Late Period, consists of only a few vessels or fragments from each period.

Middle Kingdom to Second Intermediate Period

Pottery which can be definitely ascribed to the Middle Kingdom has been found at three locations only: the area of the main cemetery at Qila' el-Debba (Arnold 1982, 54–56), Kôm I of the southern cemetery at Qila' el-Debba (Ballet 1990a) and 31/435–D5–2, the cemetery of 'Ein Tirghi (Frey 1986). Of the few pieces discovered at the former, one, a marl clay jar, would appear to have been made in Egypt probably some time after the reign of Amenemhat III. Arnold has suggested a connection with the Memphite pottery tradition for these vessels. The dating of the material from the other locations is based primarily upon a comparison of the morphology of the drinking bowls discovered with the sequence determined by Arnold for this form in the Nile Valley (e.g., Arnold 1988, 140–141). By this process Ballet (1990a, 27) has ascribed Tombs 16 and 1 at Kôm I of the southern cemetery at Qila' el-Debba to early and late Dynasty XII respectively and Tombs 42, 53 and 57 at the cemetery of 'Ein Tirghi belong to this same time span. As these latter tombs were excavated following the completion of the survey of the oasis a detailed discussion of their contents falls beyond the scope of this study. It was suggested in an earlier report (Hope 1981a, 233) that some Middle Kingdom pottery had been found at 31/405–G10–1, Mut el-Kharab. This material is now ascribed to the late Old Kingdom.

Pottery of the Second Intermediate Period has also been found at the cemeteries of 'Ein Tirghi (31/435–D5–

2; Hope 1983, 144–147) and Kôm I at Qila' el-Debba (Ballet 1990a), and at a single cemetery in the west of the oasis, 32/390–K1–2 (Pls 14.13–19)(Hope 1980, 293–298). A few pieces of similar date, including two Pangrave sherds, have been found on a settlement in the western part of the oasis (32/390–I5–1; Hope 1980, 287–288). Recent excavations at 'Ein Tirghi have produced a sizeable body of material, which displays a considerable variety of forms and, in some cases, variations upon types known from the Nile Valley. One of the main diagnostic features is again the drinking bowl which has become deeper than the Middle Kingdom types and in many examples has developed a slight s-shaped profile ('swing'; Arnold 1979, 34, 36–37; 1988, 140–141).

As with the pottery of the late Old Kingdom, that from these sites closely resembles the Nile Valley material in all respects and it is again possible to suggest that they were manufactured by potters from the Nile Valley working in the oasis, though no centres of production have been identified. Despite variations in surface finish and coatings, the predominant fabric employed is a light brown-fired, soft, iron-rich body tempered liberally with chaff. While analysis of a few examples of this fabric show it to have been made locally, just such a chaff-tempered fabric is characteristic of Nile Valley products (Bourriau, forthcoming). Only two marl clay vessels have been discovered at sites examined during the survey (Pl. 14.14) (Hope 1983, 144–147), the fabric of one of which (Hope 1983, fig. 2.n) so closely resembles one of the fine, Nile Valley marls that it may have originated there. Three have recently been excavated at Kôm I at Qila' el-Debba (Ballet 1990a, 24, no. 19) and a Nile Valley origin proposed. One import from the Nile Valley has definitely been identified on the basis of its fabric, i.e., the small, one-handled juglet (Pl. 14.15) from the lower burial in Grave 1 at 32/390–K1–2 (Hope 1980, 296–297, pl. XX.d). A jar from Tomb 1 at Kôm I, Qila' el-Debba (Ballet 1990a, 26, no. 23), and a neck fragment from another of similar shape from 32/390–K1–2 Grave 4 (Hope 1980, pl. XXII.c), may prove to be of Palestinian origin or inspiration (Ballet 1990a, 26).

The technology of these vessels is also in accord with that of Second Intermediate Period pottery from the Nile Valley. They have all been made on a pivoted wheel with secondary shape modification restricted to scraping of the bases. A few pieces show that their bases were produced entirely during the throwing process (e.g., Hope 1980, pl. XIX.d; 1983, figs 2b, n–p, 3a). This feature is attested on open forms (e.g., Hope 1983, fig. 2b) from the early Second Intermediate Period and on restricted forms (Pls 14.19–20) (Hope 1980, pl. XIX.d; 1983, figs 2n–p, 3a) mainly from the end of that period (Arnold 1976; Bourriau, forthcoming). The rarity of this feature and the morphological characteristics of the material indicate that the majority of these vessels should be ascribed to the early Second Intermediate Period, (XIII Dynasty and immediately thereafter) as defined by Bourriau (forthcoming).

Only a few are slightly later in date (Pls 14.19–20) (e.g., Hope 1980, pl. XIX.d; 1983, fig. 3a–e).

Among this material, as with that of the late Old Kingdom, the frequency of spouted forms may be noted. Two types occur: a deep, restricted bowl with a long curved spout (Pl. 14.16) (Hope 1980, pl. XXI.d; 1983, figs 2k–l, 3e) and a sharply carinated, restricted bowl with a medium to long spout, either curved or straight (Pl. 14.17) (Hope 1980, pls XIX.g, XXl, XXII.i; 1983, fig. 2b–c). While such spouted vessels are not encountered among the published corpora of Second Intermediate Period material from the Nile Valley, Bourriau (pers. comm., 1980) has pointed out that spouted forms are frequent in the material to be published from Lisht. Despite this, they do seem to have been popular in Dakhleh and the deep, restricted bowls with spouts recall similar products of the late Old Kingdom. Arnold (pers. comm., 1980) has pointed out another possible oasis feature among this material. In commenting upon the pottery from 32/390–K1–2 Grave 3, she has drawn attention to a small drinking bowl (Hope 1980, pl. XXI.i) which carries a red coating on its exterior, a feature not noted among examples from the Valley, where such bowls have thin red rim bands (Arnold 1988, 135, 140; Bourriau, forthcoming). This red coating is found frequently on such bowls in the oasis (Hope 1980, 294–296; 1983, fig. 2e–j).

New Kingdom

Pottery datable to the New Kingdom is at a premium in Dakhleh. Fragments from round-bottomed bread moulds have been found on the surface and built into the walls at Mut el-Kharab (Hope 1983, 147). Such moulds, known mainly from temple sites, have been clearly shown to be of New Kingdom date by Jacquet-Gordon (1981, 19, fig. 5) and are not of the Middle Kingdom as Giddy (1987, 217, note 64) has suggested. A few other pieces, including a decorated amphora (Pl. 14.21), have been found at the cemetery 31/435–D5–2 (Hope 1983, 147–148). They all appear to have been made within the oasis according to Egyptian traditions. Sherds ascribed to the New Kingdom are reported to have been found in the vicinity of Mastaba V at Qila' el-Debba (Vercoutter 1977, 278) and the author has observed others at 'Ain Aseel. The decorated amphora was initially ascribed to early Dynasty XIX (Hope 1983, 147–148), but in all probability it should be dated to the later Dynasy XIX or Dynasty XX, as suggested by Aston (1992, 74). This paucity of material is of particular interest, not only in the light of the textual evidence for New Kingdom activity in the oases (Giddy 1987, 65–98), but also as Dakhleh appears to be a possible source for the cobalt pigment used during that period on ceramics and in the manufacture of glass and faience (Kaczmarczyk 1986; Segnit in Edwards and Hope 1987).

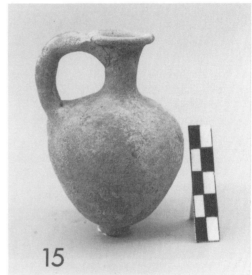

Pls 14.13–14.17

13, Second Intermediate Period: pottery vessels from Grave 4 at 32/390–K1–2 (object nos 1–5). 14, Second Intermediate Period: marl-clay, necked jar with linear decoration in brown from Grave 1 at 32/390–K1–2 (object no. 7). 15, Second Intermediate Period: one-handled juglet from Grave 1 at 32/390–K1–2 (object no. 20). 16, Second Intermediate Period: deep, spouted bowl from Grave 1 at 32/390–K1–2 (object no. 11). 17, Second Intermediate Period: spouted, carinated bowl from Grave 1 at 32/390–K1–2 (object no. 1).

Pls 14.18–14.21

18, *Second Intermediate Period: wide-bodied, narrow necked jar (rim damaged) from Grave 1 at 32/390–K1–2 (object no. 18)*. **19**, *Second Intermediate Period: large, necked jar from Grave 1 at 32/390–K1–2 (object no. 3)*. **20**, *Second Intermediate Period: feminoform jar from Grave 26 at 31/435–D5–2 (object no. 1)*. **21**, *XIX–XX Dynasty: decorated amphora from Grave 8 at 31/435–D5–2 (object no. 11, two views)*.

Third Intermediate Period to Late Period

For material of the Third Intermediate Period to Late Period we must again turn to the cemetery at 31/435–D5–2 for the major finds. Here cartonnage cases of the Third Intermediate Period and the Saite Period were found in Tombs 8 and 22 respectively, and coffins of the 5th–4th centuries BC in Tomb 14 (Mills 1983, 128–129). No pottery was found in Tomb 22. Tomb 8 yielded the New Kingdom amphora mentioned above along with a jar of the Second Intermediate Period and another of the Late Period (Hope 1983, pl. XI) similar to a jar from Tomb 14. The latter contained various grave goods and ceramics (Hope 1983, figs 3g–4i). These included tall-sided drinking vessels, spouted bowls with ring bases, globular-bodied jars with flaring rims, large wide-mouthed jars and a water keg with tall neck and pronounced, folded rim. This is the first datable occurrence of the latter form which was to become a standard component of later ceramic assemblages and a version of which is still manufactured in the oasis. There was also an unusual jar with a bulbous neck, slender upper body and wide lower body. All of these vessels were thrown on a fast kick-wheel, which appears to have been in use in the Nile Valley from the New Kingdom onwards (Hope 1981b; Lacovara and Vandiver 1985/86). In relation to the fabrics used, which appear to be local, it may be noted that they are denser than those of preceding periods, a feature also noted among material from the Nile Valley (Bourriau 1981, 80; Jacquet-Gordon, forthcoming). Vessel morphology indicates the beginnings of distinctly local traditions. Tomb 14 contained several other burials not in coffins, which cannot be dated with precision and it was not possible to determine which of the burials the pottery vessels had accompanied.

Confirmation of a Late Period date for the pottery from Tomb 14 may be found in parallels to one of the tall-sided drinking vessels from Mendes (Wilson 1982, pl. XIV.11) and to the elaborate jar from Nebesheh (Petrie 1888, pl. III) and Saqqara (French 1988, 80, 83, no. 7). These parallels are from Dynasty XXVI. However, examples of kegs resembling closely the one found in Tomb 14 have been excavated at Elephantine in Dynasty XXVII contexts (D. Aston, pers. comm., 1994). Forms similar to those from Tomb 14 were found in Tomb 17 (Hope 1983, figs 4j–5j). This contained the body of a small jar (Hope 1983, fig. 5j), the original complete shape of which would have resembled one from Tomb 23 (Hope 1983, fig. 5k). The latter and the other vessel from that tomb (Hope 1983, fig. 5l) both have parallels among material from the Nile Valley dating from the Third Intermediate Period and more frequently to Dynasty XXVI (Engelbach 1915, pl. XXXIX.112–113; Hansen 1967, fig. 11; Paice 1986/87, fig. 7.9; Petrie 1888, pls V.29, XXXIV.25). A small bowl with a pronounced foot from Tomb 17 (Hope 1983, fig. 4n) also has Late Period parallels in the Nile Valley (Jacquet-Gordon, forthcoming; Mostafa 1988b, 22, fig. 11; Petrie 1888, pl. XXXIV.14; Wilson 1982, pl. XV.3).

Similar bowls have been found at various sites in Dakhleh (Pl. 14.22), at one of which, 31/405–E8–2 (Hope 1981a, pl. XXV), they were associated in a grave with a fragmentary jar of typical Late Period date (Hope 1981a, pl. XXV.j), several examples of which have been found in the oasis (Pl. 14.23) (of Dynasty XXVI date – cf. Anthes 1959, fig. 3.33; Bourriau 1981, no. 153; Paice 1986/87, fig. 7.1; Petrie 1888, pl. XXXIV.21). This tomb also contained a deep spouted bowl, a jar with a pronounced undulating profile – 'double-gourd' jar – and a small asymmetrical keg with a narrow neck. Vessels resembling the 'double-gourd'-shaped jars have been found in Late Period (Dunham 1955 *passim*; Mostafa 1988a, 17, no.14; Petrie 1888, pl. XXXIV.23–24) and Ptolemaic Period contexts (e.g., Petrie and Mackay 1915, pl. XLV). Their undulating profile recalls that of larger jars known from the Third Intermediate Period onwards. The small keg is similar to one from Defenneh ascribed to the Late Period (Petrie 1888, pl. XXXIV.29). These three forms are found elsewhere associated with vessels which would appear to date to the Ptolemaic Period (Hope 1980, pls XXII–XXI; 1981a, pls XXIII–XXVI). This raises the possibility that certain forms were manufactured in the oasis after their abandonment in the Nile Valley and also indicates the timespan over which some forms continued in popularity. Jacquet-Gordon (forthcoming) has also raised this possibility in relation to Egyptian forms found on Sudanese sites which are dated to periods later than their *floruit* in Egypt. It may be noted that the three vessels published from Tomb 2 at cemetery 31/435–G2–2 (Hope 1983, fig. 6b–d) are probably to be dated to the Late Period also; for additional forms see Plates 14.24 and 14.25. Sherd material of the Third Intermediate Period and Late Period has been identified among surface finds at 31/405–G10–1, Mut el-Kharab, as might be expected from the discovery of the two Dakhleh stelae within its vicinity. Late Period ceramics have also been found during the excavations by the Egyptian Antiquities Organisation in the cemeteries near Mut el-Kharab.

PTOLEMAIC TO BYZANTINE PERIODS

For present purposes the Roman Period will be considered as extending up to the end of the 3rd Century AD and the Byzantine Period as commencing thereafter. There is growing evidence from the oasis that in terms of pottery manufacture major changes did occur during the late 3rd and early 4th centuries. While, however it is possible to distinguish the pottery of the Byzantine Period from that of the Roman Period, it is not as yet possible to present a clear picture of the Ptolemaic Period manufactures nor to isolate with certainty sub-phases within the Roman Period.

This situation has arisen due to the lack of precisely datable find contexts for most of the pottery. The majority of the material derives from the surfaces of sites and it is, therefore, not possible to use the evidence of numismatics or inscribed pieces, which might also be found on these sites, to assist in ascribing precise dates to the ceramics. While pottery undoubtedly of this period has been excavated in stratified deposits at both temple and settlement sites, and in some cases fairly large groups have been found within cemeteries, it is rarely the case that other categories of material are found in association with them to provide independent dating criteria. Vessel morphology and decoration provide the only clues.

Ptolemaic Period

The temple site of Ain el-Azizi, 31/405–M9–1, has yielded a range of ceramics, some dating to the Byzantine Period (Mills 1981, 181). The material is dominated by fragments from tall-necked water kegs and lentoid flasks which litter the site. They are not known from Romano-Byzantine contexts elsewhere in the oasis, and are tentatively ascribed to the Ptolemaic Period. The shape of some of the water kegs resembles that of the example dated to the Late Period from 31/435–D5–2 Grave 14, mentioned above, particularly in having tall, ribbed necks. Others possess shorter necks. Fragments preserving sections of the body indicate that while kegs of similar size to that from Tomb 14 at 31/435–D5–2 are present, so are much larger types. These vessels are made from a dense-bodied, ferruginous fabric tempered with quartz; they are hard and fired either grey or black, and carelessly finished. The lentoid flasks are of fairly large size with tall necks and have small, vestigial handles attached to the lower neck and upper body. Numerous examples of these kegs and flasks have been excavated at Karnak North and some have been found at the Luxor end of the Luxur-Farsut Road (Darnell and Darnell 1993, 1994), showing their use in the transport and storage of commodities over long distances. Associated with them at Ain el-Azizi are fragments, mainly from small- and medium-sized, open bowls in a light weight, porous marl fabric, fired pale green, occasionally with a pinkish core. A collection of pottery in this same fabric was excavated at the much ruined, mud-brick temple at 32/405–A2–1 (Hope 1981a, 234; Mills 1981, 181–182). The forms included open bowls, deep bowls with ring bases and thick modelled rims, some with spouts, restricted neckless jars, small 'double-gourd'-shaped jars and water kegs. This marl clay fabric is quite unlike any from the Nile Valley; however, certain of the deep bowls with ring bases do resemble Nile Valley forms known from the Late Period onwards (Jacquet-Gordon, forthcoming).

Vessels of similar shape have been found among the pottery from several cemeteries, though not always made in this particular marl fabric. The associated forms include deep bowls with ring bases, some having elaborate rim formation and decoration, a variety of small squat jars, frequently decorated, spouted jars (Pl. 14.26), handled jars and flasks (Hope 1980, pls XXII.k--XXIV.d; 1981a, pls XXIII.h–XXV.e, XXVI.a–o). Several of these find parallels among Ptolemaic Period pottery from the Nile

Valley (e.g., Hope 1981a, pls XXIII.i, t, XXIV.g, i, XXV.c–d, XXVI.b, e), while one vessel has parallels dating back to the Late Period (Hope 1981a, pl. XXIII.r). The oasis examples, however, frequently appear less well manufactured and represent degenerate versions (cf. Hope 1980, pl. XXIII.i: compare Hope 1981a, pl. XXIV.i with Bourriau 1981, no. 167). Decoration, where it occurs, is executed in monochrome black or dark brown and the motifs are predominantly linear, though some floral motifs do occur (Pls 14.27–28) (Hope 1980, pl. XXVIb–d; 1981a, pls XXVa–c, e, XXVII–o). Such decoration is attested from the Ptolemaic Period (Bourriau 1981, no. 167; Jacquet-Gordon, forthcoming; Mysliwiec 1987, nos 857–924) but is also known to have continued into the Roman Period, as finds from various sites in Dakhleh and at Dush in Kharga Oasis indicate (Rodziewicz 1985, 240).

In terms of imported material, attention may be drawn to a fragment from a deep, straight-sided bowl in a black-fired and polished fabric found on the surface at Mut el-Kharab, 31/405–G10–1, and a few sherds of what may be Eastern Sigillata. The former is a common Ptolemaic Period product in the Nile Valley, while the latter may have originated in Syria (Hayes 1972, 8).

Roman Period

There is abundant evidence from Dakhleh Oasis for extensive activity during what is here designated the Roman Period, and it would appear that the population level reached its maximum for any period during its history (Mills 1979, 1980, 1981, 1982, 1983 passim, 1985, Chapter 10, this volume). Concomitant with this we have a flourishing ceramic industry attested by large quantities of pottery and also by numerous kiln sites often associated with pottery workshops (Hope 1979, 197–200; 1980, 307–311; 1981a, 238–239; 1983, 142; 1993, 123–126). The kilns, while still of the simple up-draught type, are now of large dimensions and furnished with perforated stacking platforms. They are clearly designed to cope with large quantities of vessels of diverse sizes. The volume produced by the potters of the time is immense, as finds from all parts of the oasis show, in no small measure due to the use of fast kick-wheels. The discovery of unfired pottery in several kilns and of prepared clay associated with them, as well as the evidence of the fired material, indicates a preference for ferruginous clays. Marls were utilised but less frequently than may have been the case in the preceding period. Those attested tend to be dense-bodied rather than of the open-textured type described above, though a few occurrences of this have been noted.

In general the forms manufactured show a development of earlier types. The characteristics of the period may be summarised as follows. The preferred fabric seems to have been an iron-rich body of medium density, containing quartz, some carbonates and occasionally a little chaff temper. It was employed for a variety of wares in which were made a wide selection of domestic shapes. In the case

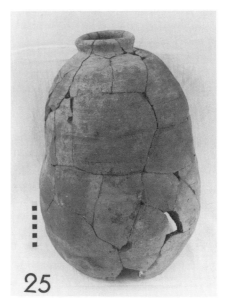

Pls 14.22–14.26

22, *Late Period (XXVI Dynasty): footed bowl from Room 1 in Tomb 1 at 32/390–K4–1 (object no. 4).* **23**, *Late Period (XXVI Dynasty): necked jar from Room 1 in Tomb 1 at 32/390–K4–1 (object no. 16).* **24**, *Late Period (XXVI Dynasty): spouted jar with two handles from Room 1 in Tomb 1 at 32/390–K4–1 (object no. 17).* **25**, *Late Period (XXVI Dynasty): narrow-necked, large jar from Room 1 in Tomb 1 at 32/390–K4–1 (object no. 1).* **26**, *Ptolemaic Period: two spouted vessels from Grave 2 at 32/390–K1–1 (objects nos 9 [left] and 4 [right]).*

of large jars there seems to have been a deliberate attempt to produce grey- or black-fired bodies, a feature noticed among the earlier Ptolemaic material from Ain el-Azizi. Undecorated wares predominate. Characteristic shapes include large jars with wide bodies, short necks and a ledge at the transition to the neck (Hope 1979, pl. XIX.6–7; 1981a, pl. XXVII.j), short-necked, globular-bodied jars (or cooking pots) sometimes supplied with small, vertical handles and which are similar to Nile Valley types (Hope 1979, pl. XIX.5; 1981a, pl. XXVII.d–h) and pigeon nesting pots (Hope 1979, pl. XIX 11); spouted forms continued to be made (Hope 1981a, pl. XXVII.i, k). The dating of some examples of the pigeon nesting pots is not certain and it appears possible that they continued to be manufactured into the Byzantine Period and later. Barrel-shaped water kegs were also made in this fabric, some with strap handles and strainers inside the neck (Hope 1979, pl. XIX.14). In place of the tall necks of the examples of Late Period and Ptolemaic Period dates, those of the Roman Period have short necks with modelled rims (Hope 1981a, 235–237). Rarely examples of this type of vessel were made in an open-textured, green-fired marl.

Of more specialised use were two types of shale-tempered fabrics, which now make a reappearance, having seemingly been out of fashion since the late Old Kingdom. One of these fabrics is exceptionally dense and hard-fired; it has a pinkish-grey colour in the section and a greyish-brown surface. The shale inclusions are often of fairly large size and are accompanied by fragments of limestone; it has the appearance of a marl clay fabric. Its use was restricted mainly to the manufacture of water kegs, which often have a rough surface; such vessels must have been very unwieldy. The second type resembles the quartz-tempered fabric described above, but with the addition of small- and medium-size inclusions of shale. It seems to have been fairly low fired and generally has a brown colour; red surface coatings are common. This fabric was employed mainly in the manufacture of cooking pots with globular bodies, round bases, either with or without a neck and having modelled rims. They are similar in shape to the jars made in the quartz-tempered fabric and, like them, often have either an internal thickening of the rim or a ledge within the neck, presumably to support a lid (Hope 1979, pl. XIX.5; 1981a, pl. XXVII.e–h). Bowls seem to have served this purpose. These cooking pots may have either vertical or horizontal handles, though many of these are of such small size, or so squashed against the wall of the vessel, that they can have been of little assistance in lifting.

As mentioned in the discussion of Ptolemaic Period material, decoration, though not common, comprises simple linear, abstract and stylised floral motifs. These are encountered either on uncoated surfaces or on a red or cream background colour, and may be executed in monochrome maroon, brown or black, or in bichrome red and brown or black. The pigments are iron ochres, available plentifully within the oasis, and appear to have

been fired onto the vessel. The same motifs occur on either the monochrome or bichrome decorated wares. These include bars and bands of colour, cross-hatching, festoons, crosses, palm fronds and other floral elements. They occur on certain short-necked jars, tall-necked jars and amphorae, as well as the small jars, amphorae and spouted vessels referred to above. Bowls received a decoration of rim ticks, normally on a pale background colour (Hope 1979, pl. XIX.9). Similar decorated material occurs at Dush in Kharga Oasis (Ballet 1990b).

A few sherds attest more elaborate decoration, also similar to pieces found at Dush and dated to the late 3rd to early 5th centuries AD (Rodziewicz 1985, 236, pl. II.1–2). Such a dating is also possible for the Dakhleh pieces, though their find spot, on the surface of the temple site of 'Ein Birbiyeh, 31/435–K5–1, provides no information on this. It may be noted that their decoration is quite unlike that found on Byzantine material elsewhere in Dakhleh. They are bichrome decorated on a pale background colour with motifs including lozenges between parallel lines, crosses, 'butterfly' shapes and an open, eight-petalled flower. Three of these pieces have, in addition, blue-coloured dots, which may have been applied after firing. These, and the Dush pieces, appear to be unconnected with Nile Valley decorated material. However, Alexandrine prototypes have been suggested for one decorated jar from Dush (Rodziewicz 1985, pl. I.4), the shape of which resembles a jar from Dakhleh (Hope 1981a, pl. XXVIII.g). The decoration of this piece is unlike either the Dush vessel or Alexandrine pieces (Rodziewicz 1985, pl. I; Hayes 1976, 40, no. 192) and resembles that of the Byzantine material from Dakhleh in the use of spirals. It differs from that material, however, in the use of a red background colour. The vessel undoubtedly belongs to the family of wares designated as 'Coptic Painted Wares' and the shape is that of a 'krater'; dated examples from Karanis range from the late 3rd to mid-5th centuries (Johnson 1981, pls 13–14, nos 105–110).

While the shapes of many of the vessels manufactured during this period are local to the oasis, others are clearly affiliated with Roman pottery from the Nile Valley and other parts of the Roman world. The general similarity of pottery of this period from many parts of the Mediterranean has been commented upon by Adams (1978, 131; 1986, 50, 51, 91, 207), undoubtedly a reflection of the widespread trade networks of the time, though Egyptian products have distinctive traits (Hayes 1976, 37). Imports into the oasis are few and take the form of a small number of sherds in dense, light-coloured fabrics, from what are probably amphorae, among which Nile delta and Antioch types have been identified. Of great interest is the occurrence at 33/390–F10–1 (Mills 1979) of several fragments, probably from two similarly shaped vessels: a deep, mould-made, bowl originally with two loop-handles, decorated with a vine motif (Pl. 14.29). They have been identified by Hayes as local or Nile Valley imitations of a Knidian prototype made in silver. Chemical analysis of

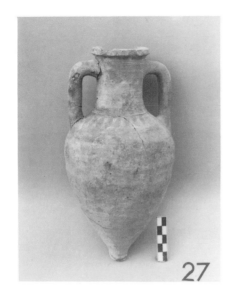

Pls 14.27–14.31

27, *Ptolemaic Period: small, decorated amphora from Grave 2 at 32/390–K1–1 (object no. 10).* **28**, *Ptolemaic Period: small, decorated, spouted amphora from Grave 2 at 32/390–K1–1 (object no. 11).* **29**, *Late Ptolemaic-Early Roman Period: mould-made bowls with vine motif, imitating a Knidian prototype in silver, from the surface of 33/390–F10–1 (both catalogued as object no. 1; Royal Ontario Museum 983.25.97).* **30**, *Byzantine Period: cooking jar from Grave 4 at 33/390–N6–1 (object no. 1).* **31**, *Byzantine Period: fragmentary, decorated two-handled flask from the surface of 33/390–I7–1 (unregistered).*

Pls 14.32–14.35

32, *Byzantine Period: one-handled jar from 31/435–H4–1 (Test 1, object no. 2).* **33**, *Byzantine Period: two-handled flask from 31/435–H4–1 (Test 1, object no. 4).* **34**, *Byzantine Period: fragmentary, decorated necked vessel from Grave 4 at 33/390–N6–1 (object no. 2).* **35**, *Byzantine Period: 'Oasis Red Ware' bowls from the gateway of 31/435–K5–1 ('Ein Birbiyeh).*

the pieces indicates that two different fabrics are represented. A dating within the 1st Century BC to 1st Century AD has been suggested for these vessels, now deposited in the Royal Ontario Museum (Egyptian Collection, 983.25.97).

Byzantine Period

The ceramic assemblage from Dakhleh ascribed to the Byzantine Period is undoubtedly the most well-defined of all the later material. Its identification and dating have resulted from the almost invariable combination of a series of easily recognisable wares, each used for specific shapes, which have been found associated with imported North African Red Slip wares, Egyptian Fine Wares and amphorae, and both ostraca and papyri inscribed in Coptic and Greek. Test excavations carried out at several sites have yielded stratified material of this date and, at the church site of Deir Abu Metta (Hope 1981a, 235; Mills 1981, 185) and the large settlement of Ismant el-Kharab (Hope 1983, 149–153; Mills 1982, 99–100), it has been found in conjunction with coins of the Byzantine Period. Excavations in progress at Ismant el-Kharab have further confirmed the definition of this assemblage (Hope 1985, 1986, 1987c, 1988; Hope *et al.* 1989) and important material is being excavated at the temple site of 'Ein Birbiyeh (Hope 1987b, 31).

Many of the traditions of the Roman Period continued into the Byzantine Period. This is particularly evident in the use of the quartz-tempered fabrics and in the shapes of the large, necked storage jars (Hope 1985, fig. 4), water kegs (Hope 1983, fig. 9), some of the cooking pots (Hope 1983, figs 7–8; 1985, figs 4–5) and, of course, the bowls. Both grey- or black-fired and brown-fired versions of these fabrics continued to be produced and they were still the dominant domestic fabrics. An innovation in the repertoire of shapes during the Byzantine Period seems to have been the manufacture of very large, deep bowls with ring bases and heavy, folded rims. We may note the disappearance of spouted forms. While no kilns or pottery workshops definitely datable to the period have been located, the manufacturing and firing techniques as witnessed by the material itself attest no changes from the preceding period. A brief discussion of some of the manufacturing techniques is given by Patten (1991).

Despite this, certain new fabrics made their appearance while others ceased to be used. The two Roman shale wares were no longer employed. Water kegs, formerly often made in the dense shale-fabric were now made from the common quartz-tempered fabric and the cooking pots in a fine, brittle fabric, which is one of the hallmarks of the period (Hope 1979, 196; 1985, 123). It is tempered with fine quartz and shale, fired either grey or pinkish-grey and was often given a red surface coating which turned dark grey during firing. It was used predominantly for thin-walled cooking pots (Pl. 14.30), some necked or with handles (Hope 1983, figs 7d–e, h, 8k–m; 1985, figs

4j–n, 5c, o–r), but also lids (Hope 1985, fig. 4f) and bowls, some decorated (Hope 1983, fig. 7a; 1985, fig. 5n). The cooking pots closely resemble contemporary Nile Valley shapes (e.g., Bailey 1982, 20–30) as do the lids.

A second shale-and quartz-tempered fabric also made its appearance. It is medium-textured and less compact than the one just described, fired pale orange to pink and is usually cream-coated and decorated; its use was restricted mainly to bowls (Hope 1985, 123, fig. 4d) and handled flasks (Pl. 14.31) (Hope 1980, pl. XXV.i–k; 1983, fig. 6e; 1985 figs 4q–r, 5a). A very similar ware is attested at sites in Kharga Oasis (Ballet 1990b). We may also note the use of a porous, light-weight, green-fired marl during this period for water bottles of the 'qulleh' type and large flasks (Pls 14.32–33) (Hope 1983, fig. 7f, pl. XII.c–d).

Amphorae do not appear to have been manufactured by the local potters who produced kegs and flasks in their place. All examples which have been found are of the typical Nile Valley types, predominantly those with a tall neck, ribbed body and stump base made in a dense brown silt ware (Hope 1985, fig. 6a–b); a black resinous coating on their interiors is frequent (e.g., Bailey 1982, 16–20; 1984, 17). A few fragments of the so-called 'Abu Mena' type amphora have been found.

Decoration occurs mainly on bowls and handled flasks. While the use of dark rim ticks on a light coloured ground applied to the rims of bowls continued, the floral motifs of the Roman Period largely disappeared. Motifs are predominantly linear and abstract (Pl. 14.31), while the swastika and *ankh* appear for the first time, and spiral motifs are especially common (Hope 1980, pl. XXV.d–k; 1983, figs 6e, 7a–c, g, 8a–d, g–i; 1985, figs 4d, 5n, 6c; 1986). One vessel attests the use of certain floral motifs (Hope 1980, pl. XXV), including what has been identified as a representation of the olive tree by Rodziewicz (1985, pl. II.2–3) (Pl. 14.34). All of these motifs and many of the vessel shapes they decorate are well known from Nile Valley material (e.g., Egloff 1977; Jacquet-Gordon 1972; Mysliwiec 1987).

In addition to the similarities with Nile Valley products of the period, noted above, and the use of amphorae made therein, like that region, the population of Dakhleh had access to the fine, imported North African Red Slip wares (Hope 1980, pls XXIV.l-XXV.b; 1986, 87, fig. 8). Whether these wares were traded into Dakhleh from the Nile Valley or from North Africa via Siwa Oasis remains, as yet, uncertain. Types dating from the late 3rd or early 4th to 5th centuries AD have been found, though it is possible that, as luxury items, they may have been in use after their apparent periods of manufacture. Their arrival in Dakhleh seems to have stimulated the local potters, and those in Kharga Oasis also, into producing imitations. These are found frequently throughout both oases. The ware is a red-fired shale fabric which is quite dense and covered with a red slip, roughly burnished; it is easily distinguishable from the prototype. The repertoire of shapes is dominated by bowls (Pl. 14.35) (Hope 1980, pl.

XXIV.e–k; 1986, figs 8i–9ff; Rodziewicz 1987), a feature of the North African industry itself (Hayes 1972), which like their source of inspiration, were mould-made. Lamps in this ware are not uncommon and some restricted forms are known (Rodziewicz 1987). Based upon evidence from Dush, Rodziewicz has suggested a period of manufacture throughout the 4th and 5th Centuries AD. The evidence from Dakhleh would tend to support this.

Partly contemporary with the import of the North African wares into Dakhleh, though apparently largely subsequent to it, is the import of Egyptian Fine Wares. This term is adopted from Bailey (1983, 27–36), replacing Hayes' (1972, 387–397) designation Egyptian Red Slip A; it includes the O and W wares of Rodziewicz (1976, 54–64). These wares appear to have been manufactured primarily in the Aswan region and were widely distributed throughout Egypt and Nubia (Adams 1986, 525ff; Ballet and Picon 1987, 43–48). Examples dating from the 5th to 7th Centuries AD have been found in Dakhleh. Accompanying these, as they do in Egypt, are coarser local products in the form of red coated and polished, wheel-made bowls with flanged rims, often with rows of short incisions below the rim. These are Hayes' (1972, 397–399) Egyptian Red Slip B and Rodziewicz's (1976, 50–53) 'K' ware. Some examples carry black painted decoration on the interior of the rims.

By means of its association with these two groups of imported material it may eventually prove possible to divide the Byzantine ceramic assemblage into two phases, the first of the 4th to early 5th centuries AD and the second of the mid-5th to 7th Centuries AD. Few differences, however, in the local material associated with these two groups of imports have, as yet, been noted. The manufacture of pottery in the traditions of the late Byzantine Period undoubtedly continued well into the Islamic Period.

CONCLUSIONS

During the course of the study of the pottery found in the Dakhleh Oasis throughout the survey and the preparation of this overview of the material, it has become apparent that three phases of pottery manufacture may be isolated. During the first of these, which corresponds with the Neolithic cultural units, we encounter a local ceramic tradition which has few affinities with material from neighbouring regions. This lasted until the arrival of the ancient Egyptians in force at the end of the Old Kingdom, when it would appear to have given way to the more specialised and advanced traditions of Nile Valley pottery manufacture. This is the second phase, when material found in the oasis dating from the late Old Kingdom to the Late Period appears to have been manufactured entirely under the influence of the trends identifiable as characteristic of this time span within the Valley. While some Dakhleh features are detectable, these are restricted to relative frequencies and minor morphological variations.

The third phase, from the Late Period to the Byzantine Period, witnessed the continuation of influence from the Nile Valley upon pottery manufacture in Dakhleh but also saw the emergence of local traditions. These are evident in the development of certain categories of vessel shapes and in the use of various fabrics which do not resemble those of the Nile Valley. Undoubtedly the clearest example of this is the manufacture of an Oasis fine 'table' ware (Oasis Red Slip) in imitation of imported North African Red Slip Wares (Hope 1985; Rodziewicz 1987).

The study of the ceramics discovered in the Dakhleh Oasis illustrates the extent to which the material culture of the Nile Valley became dominant in the region throughout its entire historical period. The pottery is perhaps the most reliable tool available in assessing this cultural assimilation. This is a consequence of its abundance, widespread distribution, occurrence on all types of site in diverse social contexts and the fact that nearly all of the major periods are attested by pottery finds, unlike other categories of material.

In concluding, it is worth noting that whatever innovations in pottery manufacture occurred during the centuries of the Islamic Period, many features of the Romano-Byzantine Period continued largely unaltered in the ceramic repertoire and are still evident to this day. This may be observed among the modern potters working at Qasr el-Dakhleh in terms of vessel morphology, particularly that of jars, water bottles and kegs, and wheel and kiln technology (Henein 1997; Patten 1991).

ADDENDUM

Since the final revision of the text of this study further evidence has been accumulated concerning parallels between the Neolithic pottery of Dakhleh and that of the Nile Valley which can be mentioned briefly here.

R.F. Friedman (1994, 891–893) in her Ph.D. thesis, *Predynastic Settlement Ceramics of Upper Egypt: A comparative Study of the Ceramics from Hemamieh, Nagada and Hierakonpolis,* drew attention to the existence of shale-tempered wares in the Hierakonpolis region dating to the Amratian Period which may resemble those typical of the Dakhleh Neolithic. They occur in both the Bashendi and Sheikh Muftah Cultural units. However, despite the similarities of some shapes made in shale-tempered wares identified by Friedman amongst material found in both areas, I think great caution must be exercised in interpreting this similarity. The sources of the clays used for each appear to be local to both regions and the shapes manufactured in these wares are extremely basic. Friedman (1994, 900) correctly points out that there may be no connection at all, though she also posits the possibility of a common ancestor

The small jar illustrated here (Pl. 14.1) from 31/420–C10–2, a site with both Bashendi Unit and Sheikh Muftah Unit affinities, is the only one found to date in the oasis.

It has been suggested that it may be a Lower Egyptian import (B. Adams, pers. comm., 1996). It certainly resembles the small jars known from Ma'adi on shape (Rizkana and Seeher 1987, 37; pls 34–35), but the use of incised cross-hatching on the upper neck and rim is not paralleled amongst that material which employs a red slipped and burnished ware (ware II) with impressed dsigns (Rizkana and Seeher 1987, 28, 39–40). The Dakhleh jar has an irregularly-fired, red-grey surface and is neither coated nor burnished. However, larger jars from Ma'adi do have incised designs (Rizkana and Seeher 1987; pls 39–41).

Acknowledgements
The original manuscript of this study was prepared in 1987 and revised in 1988, 1989, 1991 and 1994. For their comments upon various aspects of the study I am most grateful to Pascale Ballet, Janine Bourriau, Maxine Kleindienst, Mary McDonald and Anthony Mills. In addition, I wish to thank the following for their assistance with the initial dating of material discovered by the Dakhleh Oasis Project: Dorothea Arnold, Janine Bourriau, Maureen Kaplan and John Hayes. For allowing me early access to their manuscripts on the pottery of the Predynastic Period, Second Intermediate Period and the Third Intermediate Period-Ptolemaic Period to appear in *An Introduction to Ancient Egyptian Pottery* prior to their publication, I am most grateful to Joan Crowfoot Payne, Janine Bourriau and Helen Jacquet-Gordon. It is with great pleasure that I record my debt to Pascale Ballet for allowing me access to pottery from the IFAO excavations at 'Ain Aseel and Qila' el-Debba, for numerous discussions on the pottery from the oasis and sharing her knowledge of the pottery of the Late Roman Period. Finally, I wish to thank all my collegues in the Dakhleh Oasis Project, past and present, for their assistance in all stages of the collection and study of the ceramics from Dakhleh. I am particularly indebted to Bruce Parr and Shirley Patten whose contributions to the drawing and analysis of so much of the material have been invaluable.

POSTSCRIPT: ADDITIONAL OBSERVATIONS ON THE HOLOCENE CERAMICS

by Colin A Hope

The following comments supplement and, in some places, replace those given in the text of this chapter, and result from a re-examination in 1988 of the pottery from the Holocene cultural units, focusing on the material of the Masara and Bashendi Cultural Units.[1] Of necessity they will be kept to a minimum.

Most of the sherds discussed are isolated finds from a broad surface cultural scatter: thus the cultural unit noted here may not always be the identity under which the locus is listed in Appendix II.

EARLY HOLOCENE: MASARA CULTURAL UNIT

Dated between 9,200–8,500 BP on the basis of 12 uncalibrated radiocarbon dates (McDonald, In press).

A distinctive fabric profusely tempered with shale occurs on several Masara A and B sites. It is fired a wide range of colours including greyish-green, brown, yellow, pink and black, often with numerous colours on the same sherds, and may be grey-black on the interior. It has uncoated and compacted surfaces and is fairly resistant to abrasion (Mohr 4.5–6.5). It should be noted that these features may have resulted from exposure to sand and wind blasting, a phenomenon which makes difficult the identification of original secondary treatments on this and all early to mid-Holocene ceramic material, of which the vast majority comes from surface collections. The ware was used to manufacture medium-thick and thick-walled (generally 4–7 mm), coil-built vessels. No diagnostic pieces have been found but the vessels appear all to have been open forms. It has been found at the following sites:

Masara A sites. Loc 076 (N.N.): on top of the Escarpment at Maohoub: 1 sherd.
    Loc 259 (30/420–D7–1): 8 sherds.
Masara B site. Loc 200 (30/420–C5–1): 5 sherds.

In addition, considerable quantities were collected 200 m east of the Bashendi B Cultural Unit site Loc 271 (30/435–P9–1). Here three collections comprise the following: 12 sherds from one vessel with a wall thickness varying from 5.5 to 14 mm, with one sherd having a variation of 7.5 to 10.5 mm; 15 sherds from one vessel, with notable inclusions of red pebbles; and 87 sherds, possibly from one vessel or several vessels with very similar firing patterns.

Examples of this ware have been noted occasionally on sites of later cultural units, namely:

Bashendi B sites. Loc 252 (30/435–N9-1): 1 sherd.
    Loc 257 (30/450–E4–2): 2 sherds.
Sheikh Muftah sites. Loc 135 (30/450–B4–1): 1 sherd.
    Loc 136 (30/450–B3–2): 1 sherd.

---

[1] This reassessment was prompted by discussions with members of Rudolph Kuper's *Besiedlungsgeschichte der Ost-Sahara* Project and Mary M.A. McDonald in light of her establishment of a firmer radiocarbon chronology for the early and middle Holocene cultural units. I am most grateful to all of them for their comments. Daniel A. Tangri's study of this material was undertaken before the radiocarbon chronology was developed to its present extant. His belief that the ceramics of the Bashendi and Sheikh Muftah Cultural Units were variations of one tradition without significant temporal distinction, as reflected in his undergraduate thesis presented at Sydney University in 1989, and his published studies (1991b, 1992, though not 1991a), can now be shown to be incorrect. The radiocarbon chronology is discussed in McDonald (In press).

This scarcity, however, seems to indicate that it is not to be attributed to a later cultural unit. Its coarseness may in itself indicate production by a group experimenting with ceramic manufacture and which had not yet discovered the benefit of levigating the clay body. It could also be indicative of manufacture by people not permanently resident in the oasis and who were either unaware of, or who did not have the time to exploit, more suitable clay deposits. Interesting though such speculation may be, it must be remembered that amongst the ceramic bodies used by the occupants of the oasis during the Old Kingdom there was an equally coarse, shale-tempered fabric. The other fabrics so characteristic of the later Holocene cultural units and the Old Kingdom are rarely found amongst the ceramics on Masara Unit sites. At Loc 243 (29/450–D4–1) and in its containing basin, four typical thin-walled, fine shale-and-sand tempered Bashendi fabric sherds were found; a single sherd of the same fabric was found at Loc 259. In addition, it should be emphasised that the coarse shale-tempered fabric was the only fabric noted at three separate findspots on Loc 271 and also on Loc 259. These factors appear to confirm its identification as an early Holocene manufacture and serve as another indicator of the exceptional character of the Masara Unit. It seems to be the only Early Holocene cultural unit noted to date which is ceramic-producing north of the Salima Sandsheet, Keseiba and Nabta Playa, though pottery does occur on contemporary and earlier sites to its south in the Laqiya region (Kuper 1994, 129–130) and elsewhere in northwest Africa from possibly as early as 10,060 ± 150 yr BP (Close 1995). The sherd from Loc 218 (30/420–C4–2), noted in the main text as chert-tempered, is probably to be identified as Islamic on the basis of other occurrences in the oasis and its temper identified as ground, vitrified clay.

MID-HOLOCENE: BASHENDI CULTURAL UNITS

The following time frames have been established on the basis of some 50 separate radiocarbon dates:

Bashendi A – 7,600–6,800 BP with clusters of dates around 7,300 and 6,900 BP, respectively termed Early and Late Bashendi A Cultural Subunits.
Bashendi B – 6,500–5,200 BP: half of the relevant dates fall between 6,400 and 6,100 BP.

Early Bashendi A has no ceramics: they are first recorded in Late Bashendi A and become more common in Bashendi B, but note that Locs 261 (29/450–F4–1) and 270 (30/450–F10–2) have yielded some dates in the 7,300s BP.

Late Bashendi A site Locs with ceramics are:

088 (31/420–H7–2), 103 (32/435–M10–1), 174 (30/450–F8–3), 196 (30/420–D2–2), 261 (30/450–F4–1), 270 (30/450–F10–2), 275 (30/435–P10–1), 278 (30/450–F10–3), 304 (30/450–D9–1), 306 (30/450–F10–5), and 307 (30/450–F10–5).

Specific dates:

Loc 261 – 7,380 ± 70 yr BP.
Loc 270 yielded 12 dates spanning nearly 1,000 years from 7,340 BP, averaging 6,920 BP.
Locs 306 and 307 are contemporary with Loc 270.
Locs 174 and 275 are early 7th millenium BP.

Bashendi B site Locs with ceramics are:

074 (31/420–C10–2), 104 (31/420–M9–1), 116 (31/435–A6–3), 184 (30/450–F7–5), 212 (30/450–C6–1), 228 (30/450–A9–1), 252 (30/435–N9–1), 254 (30/450–B10–1), 258 (30/450–E5–1), and 302 (N.N.).

Specific date:

Loc 212 – 5,480 ± 120 yr BP.

Late Bashendi A Cultural Subunit

Loc 270 has yielded the only excavated sherd found to date: it derives from a sealed deposit. It is small, eroded, and affected by salt, and its original shape cannot be determined. It is made from an extremely fine clay with a close-grained matrix and few visible inclusions other than fine sand; it is fired brown (7.5YR 5–6/4). Other sherds from the surface of this site and those listed above are generally made from a fine sand-and-shale tempered fabric, which may have surface compaction but is otherwise uncoated, and which was used for thin and medium thick-walled, well-constructed vessels, predominantly open bowls. One sherd from Loc 304 has a plum red exterior coating. Other fabrics are rare; Loc 103 yielded four sherds in an uncoated sand-rich, chaff-tempered ware which resembles that used for the basket-impressed sherd from the Bashendi B site Loc 212 (see below). One sherd from Loc 307 has highly compacted surfaces and a brown exterior with a deliberately blackened rim.

Loc 275 has produced a small but extremely important collection of sherds. Fifteen pieces in all have been found in a distinctive sand-rich fabric, which also contains small black, red and white pebbles. It has a medium wall thickness, 6–8 mm, and a zoned firing pattern with brown (5YR 5/6–7.5YR 5–6/2–4) to reddish (2.5YR 5/6) surfaces. Five of these have overall punctate decoration in rows, two have rows of punctates and incised lines, one has crescentic rows of punctates and one has festoons and rows of punctates. An undecorated sherd in a similar fabric was found at Loc 103. The fabric indicates that these pieces were probably not manufactured in Dakhleh, while the decoration is reminiscent of the Saharo-Sudanese horizon similar to pieces found at Abu Ballas and north of the Gilf el-Kebir (Kuper 1994, 129 and fig. 3). The latter are made in a sand-and-shale tempered fabric which is similar to that of the typical Late Bashendi A material (R. Kuper, pers. comm. 1998).

Bashendi B Cultural Subunit

A greater variety is encountered amongst the ceramics of this phase, though the dominant material continues to be the fine sand-and-shale tempered fabric produced in the Late Bashendi A phase, regularly with highly compacted surfaces and sometimes streak burnishing on the exterior. It was used for thin-walled vessels, mainly bowls. Other fabrics contain less noticeable shale, but all have sand temper; some are very fine-grained. One distinctive group has a profuse white temper, which includes microfossils and gypsum; rare occurrences of this have been noted on Late Bashendi A sites. Loc 212 has produced four thick-walled, basket-impressed sherds in a sand-and-chaff tempered fabric. Decoration may comprise notched rims and lightly striated exteriors, random incised lines or rows of finger-nail incisions; deliberately blackened rims occur sporadically. More elaborately decorated sherds, with incised triangles filled with dashes or punctates between lines, occur on a few sherds made in the typical fine sand-and-shale tempered fabric with compacted, blackened surfaces. These come from Loc 074, as does a necked jar (Pl. 14.1), a site which is now thought probably to be Bashendi B rather than early Sheikh Muftah Unit. If this is the case, these decorated sherds are of particular interest as the motifs clearly have parallels with those found elsewhere in Northwest Africa, including the A-Group (references in the main text above). Pottery with various A-Group affinities has also been found in Wadi Shaw in the Laqiya area to the south, but dating after 5,000 BP (Kuper 1994, 133). The shape of many of the bowls and the use of notching upon the rims find parallels amongst material from Abu Munqar and in the region of the Gilf el-Kebir, while in the Gilf area, the Salima Sandsheet and the region of Laqiya hard, thin-walled, burnished or polished wares were produced (Kuper 1994, 129–130). Sand-and-shale tempered fabrics are also attested in the regions to the south of Dakhleh (R. Kuper, pers. comm. 1998).

LATE MID-HOLOCENE: SHEIKH MUFTAH CULTURAL UNIT

Only two reliable dates have been obtained to date: 5,070 and 4,310 BP.

The typical pottery fabric is still a sand-and-shale tempered fabric, but the exterior surfaces are regularly striated either vertically or obliquely and are irregularly fired with blackened tops. Compaction and burnishing are not common; vessel walls are generally thicker but still coil-built. There are numerous variants on the standard fabric, varying in quantities of sand and shale. The material in most cases seems to be less carefully constructed and finished. Parallels to the wares and forms, predominantly conical-shaped bowls, are to be found amongst the ceramics from areas to the south of Abu Ballas and in the Gilf el-Kebir (R. Kuper, pers. comm. 1998).

A few additional comments on pieces with Nile Valley affinties may be made here. Loc 035 (31/405–G6–1) has yielded a single sherd with a design of incised, hatched triangles resembling A-Group material; the piece is made in a sand-and-shale tempered fabric which is typical of most Holocene pottery from Dakhleh. Completely alien to the Sheikh Muftah tradition are two sherds with profuse straw tempering and some sand. One, from Loc 139 (N.N.) atop the Escarpment near Teneida, is from the base of a restricted vessel, probably a jar; it has a brown-fired exterior with a vertical streak burnish. Similarities may exist with material found in Buto Strata I-II (D. Faltings, pers. comm. 1998). The other piece is from Loc 136 and is the rim and wall from a straight-sided bowl, red coated and polished outside, and polished inside. It is undoubtedly from the Nile Valley. Finally, a small sherd from a so-called Tasian beaker was found near Loc 304 southeast of Teneida; that site has a general scatter of Bashendi B Cultural material. The sherd is brown-fired with a black surface which carries the typical incised design.

COMMENTS

In relation to what is known of the trends in the manufacture of ceramics during the Early and Middle Holocene in Northwest Africa, that from Dakhleh Oasis presents some interesting variations. Early Holocene ceramics in Dakhleh are undecorated unlike those from elsewhere (Close 1995); the Mid-Holocene ceramics are characterised by thin-walled vessels with compacted or burnished surfaces, and the majority is also undecorated. Ceramics decorated in the techniques and motifs of early Holocene traditions elsewhere only occur in the Mid-Holocene Bashendi Cultural Unit (Late A Subunit) and may be imports. Undecorated and compacted wares apparently occur much earlier than in other parts of the region, from at least 7,380 ± 120 yr BP at Loc 261, for example, rather than ca. 6,000 BP, as has been noted elsewhere (Close 1995, 26, Kuper 1994, 130). In general, the Mid-Holocene ceramics of Dakhleh Oasis appear to resemble more those from the Gilf el-Kebir than from elsewhere (Kuper 1994, 129).

Addresses for Authors

Colin A. Hope, Centre for Archaeology, Monash University, Clayton, Melbourne, Victoria, Australia 3168

Daniel M. Tangri, c/o Deartment of Archaeology, University of sydney, Sydney, New South Wales, Australia 2006

REFERENCES

Adams, W.Y. 1978. Ceramics, 126–133. *In* Hochfield, S. and E. Riefstahl, eds, *Africa in Antiquity. I The arts of ancient Nubia and the Sudan. The essays.* Brooklyn, The Brooklyn Museum, 143p.

Adams, W.Y. 1986. *Ceramic industries of medieval Nubia, 2 vols.* Lexington, University of Kentucky Press, 663p.

Andreu, G. 1981. La tombe à l'ouest du Mastaba II de Balat et sa stèle funéraire. *Bulletin de l'Institut Français d'Archéologie Orientale* **81**: 1–7.

Anthes, R. 1959. *Mit Rahineh, 1955.* University of Pennsylvania, University Museum Monograph 16, 93p.

Arkell, A.J. 1949. *Early Khartoum, an account of the excavation of an early occupation site carried out by the Sudan Antiquities Service in 1944/5.* London, Oxford University Press, 145p.

Arkell, A.J. 1953. *Shaheinab, an account of the excavation of a Neolithic occupation site carried out for the Sudan Antiquities Service in 1949/50.* London, Oxford University Press, 114p.

Arnold, Do. 1972. Weiteres zur Keramik von el-Târif. *Mitteilungen des Deutschen Archäologischen Instituts, Abteilung Kairo* **28**: 33–46.

Arnold, Do. 1976. Wandbild und Scherbenfund. *Mitteilungen des Deutschen Archäologischen Instituts, Abteilung Kairo* **32**: 1–34.

Arnold, Do. 1977. Gefässe, Gefässformen, Gefässdekor. *Lexicon der Ägyptologie* **2**: 483–501.

Arnold, Do. 1979. Die Keramik, 29–40. *In* Arnold, D. and Do. Arnold, *Der Tempel Qasr el-Sagha.* Deutsches Archäologisches Institut, Abteilung Kairo, Archäologische Veröffentlichungen 27: 1–41.

Arnold, Do. 1982. Keramikfunde aus Qila 'el-Dabba, 42–56. *In* Osing, J., M. Moursi, Do. Arnold, O. Neugebauer, R.A. Parker, D. Pingree and M.A. Nur-el-Din, *Denkmäler der Oase Dachla aus dem Nachlass von Ahmed Fakhry.* Deutsches Archäologisches Institut, Abteilung Kairo, Archäologische Veroffentlichungen 28, 117p.

Arnold, Do. 1985. Töpferei, Töpferwerkstatt, Töpferofen, Töpferscheibe. *Lexicon der Ägyptologie* **6**: 616–621.

Arnold, Do. 1988. Pottery, 106–146. *In* Arnold, D., *The south cemeteries of Lisht, vol. I. The pyramid of Senwosret I.* Publications of The Metropolitan Musem of Art, **22**: 156p.

Arnold, Do. 1993. Techniques and traditions of manufacture in the pottery of Ancient Egypt, Fasc. 1, 11–102. *In* Arnold, Do., and J. Bourriau, eds, *An introduction to ancient Egyptian pottery.* Deutsches Archäologisches Institut, Abteilung Kairo, Sonderschrift 17, 190p.

Aston, D.A. 1992. Two decorative styles of the Twentieth Dynasty. *Cahiers de la Céramique Égyptienne* **3**: 71–80.

Bailey, D.M. 1982. Four groups of late Roman pottery, 11–39. *In* Spencer, A.J. and D.M. Bailey, *Ashmunein (1981).* British Museum, London, Occasional Paper No. 41, 1–79.

Bailey, D.M. 1983. More groups of late Roman pottery, 26–52. *In* Spencer, A.J., D.M. Bailey and A. Burnett, *Ashmunein (1982).* British Museum, London, Occasional Paper No. 46, 1–141.

Bailey, D.M. 1984. The ceramic material and glass from Area B, 16–28. *In* Spencer, A.J., D.M. Bailey and W.V. Davies, *Ashmunein (1983).* British Museum, London, Occasional Paper No. 53, 131p.

Ballet, P. 1985. La céramique, 155–158. *In* Soukassian G., P. Ballet, L. Pantalacci and M. Wuttmann, *Balat: Raport préliminaire des fouilles à 'Ayn-Asil, 1983 et 1984. Annales du Service des Antiquités de l'Égypte* **70**: 151–161.

Ballet, P. 1987. Essai de classification des coupes type *Maidum-Bowl* du sondage nord de 'Ayn-Asil (Oasis de Dakhla). Typologie et évolution. *Cahiers de la Céramique Égyptienne* **1**: 1–16.

Ballet, P. 1990a. Annexe. La céramique du Kôm I, 18–28. *In* Aufrère, S., *La nécropole sud de Qila' al-Dabba (oasis de Dakhla, secteur de Balat). Un palimpseste archéologique. Bulletin de l'Institut Français d'Archéologie Orientale* **90**: 1–28.

Ballet, P. 1990b. Annexe II. La céramique du site urbain de Douch/Kysis, 298–301. *In* Reddé, M., *Quinze années de recherches françaises à Douch. Vers un premier bilan. Bulletin de l'Institut Français d'Archéologie Orientale* **90**: 281–301.

Ballet, P. and M. Picon. 1987. Recherches préliminaires sur les origines de la céramique des Kellia (Égypte). Importations et productions égyptiennes. *Cahiers de la Céramique Égyptienne* **1**: 17–48.

Ballet, P. and M. Picon. 1990. La production céramique, 75–165. *In* Soukassian, G., M. Wuttmann, L. Pantalacci, P. Ballet, and M. Picon. *Balat III. Les ateliers de potiers d''Ayn-Asil. Fin de l'Ancien Empire, première period intermediaire.* Fouilles de l'Institut, l'Institut Français d'Archéologie Orientale du Caire 34: 174p.

Banks, J.M. 1980. Ceramics of the Western Desert, 299–315. *In* Wendorf, F. and R. Schild, eds, *Prehistory of the eastern Sahara.* New York, Academic Press, 414p.

Banks, J.M. 1984. Early ceramic bearing occupations in the Egyptian Western Desert, 149–161. *In* Krzyzaniak, L. and M. Kobusiewicz, eds, *Origin and development of early food-producing cultures in north-eastern Africa.* Poznan, Polish Academy of Sciences, 503p.

Bourriau, J. 1981. *Umm el-Ga'ab: pottery from the Nile Valley before the Arab Conquest.* Cambridge, Fitzwilliam Museum, 142p.

Bourriau, J. Forthcoming. Second Intermediate Period to the reign of Tuthmosis I, *In* Arnold, Do., and J. Bourriau, eds, *An introduction to ancient Egyptian pottery.* Deutsches Archäologisches Institut, Abteilung Kairo, Sonderschrift (in prep.)

Brunton, G. and G. Caton-Thompson. 1928. *The Badarian civilization.* London, British School of Archaeology in Egypt, 128p.

Caton-Thompson, G. 1952. *Kharga Oasis in prehistory.* London, Athlone Press, 213p.

Chlodnicki, H. 1984. Pottery from the Neolithic settlement at Kadero (central Sudan), 337–342. *In* Krzyzaniak, L. and M. Kobusiewicz, eds, *Origin and development of early food-producing cultures in north-eastern Africa.* Poznan, Polish Academy of Sciences, 503p.

Close, A.E. 1995. Few and far between. Early ceramics in North Africa, 23–37. *In* Barnett, W.K. and J.W. Hoopes, eds, *The emergence of pottery: technology and innovation in ancient societies.* Washington, Smithsonian Institution Press, 285p.

Darnell, J.C. and D. Darnell. 1993. The Luxor-Farshût Desert Road Survey. *The Oriental Institute 1992–1993 Annual Report,* 48–55.

Darnell, J.C. and D. Darnell. 1994. The Luxor-Farshût Desert Road Survey. *The Oriental Institute 1993–1994 Annual Report,* 40–48.

Davies, P.O.A.L. 1962. Red and black Egyptian pottery. *Journal of Egyptian Archaeology* **48**: 19–24.

Dunham, D. 1955. *The royal cemeteries of Kush II: Nuri.* Boston, Museum of Fine Arts, 295p.

Edwards, W.I. and C.A. Hope. 1987. The Neolithic ceramics from the Dakhleh Oasis: a brief note, 1–10. *In* Edwards, W.I., C.A. Hope and E.R. Segnit, *Ceramics from the Dakhleh Oasis: preliminary studies.* Melbourne, Victoria College, Archaeology Research Unit Occasional Paper 1 (Dakhleh Oasis Project Monograph 1), 106p.

Edwards, W.I. and C.A. Hope. 1989. A note on the neolithic ceramics from the Dakhleh Oasis (Egypt), 233–242. *In* Krzyzaniak, L. and M. Kobusiewicz (eds.), *Late prehistory of the Nile Basin and the Sahara. Studies in African Archaeology* 2. Poznan, Poznan Archaeological Museum, 547p.

Edwards, W.I., C.A. Hope and E.R. Segnit. 1987. *Ceramics from the Dakhleh Oasis: preliminary studies.* Melbourne, Victoria College, Archaeology Research Unit, Occasional Paper 1 (Dakhleh Oasis Project Monograph 1), 106p.

Egloff, M. 1977. *Kellia: La poterie copte: Quatre siècles d'artisanat et d'échanges en Basse Egypte.* Recherches Suisses d'Archéologie Copte III. Geneva, Georg, Librarie de l'Université, 233p.

Emery, W.B. 1963. Egyptian Exploriation Society. Preliminary report on the excavations at Buhen, 1962. *Kush* 11: 116–120.

Engelbach, R. 1915. *Riqqeh and Memphis VI*. London, British School of Archaeology in Egypt, 38p.

French, P. 1988. Late Dynastic pottery from the Berlin/Hanover excavations at Saqqara, 1986. *Mitteilungen des Deutschen Archäologischen Instituts, Abteilung Kairo* 44: 79–89.

Frey, R.A. 1986. Dakhleh Oasis Project: Interim report on excavations at the 'Ein Tirghi cemetery. *Journal of the Society for the Study of Egyptian Antiquities* 16: 92–102.

Friedman, R.F. 1994. Predynastic Settlement Ceramics of Upper Egypt: A comparative study of the ceramics from Hemamieh, Nagada and Hierakonpolis. Ph.D. Thesis: University of California at Berkeley, 971p.

Gabriel, B. 1979. Gabrong-Achttausendjahrige Keramik im Tibesti-Gebirge, 189–196. *In Sahara: 10.000 Jahre zwischen Weide und Wüste*. Köln, Museen der Stadt, 470p.

Gardiner, A.H. 1933. The Dakhleh stela. *Journal of Egyptian Archaeology* 19: 19–30.

Giddy, L.L. 1987. *Egyptian Oases*. Warminster, Aris and Phillips, 305p.

Hansen, D. 1967. Mendes 1964. *Journal of the American Research Center in Egypt* 4:31–37.

Hayes, J.W. 1972. *Late Roman pottery*. London, The British School at Rome, 477p.

Hayes. J.W. 1976. *Roman pottery in the Royal Ontario Museum: a catalogue*. Toronto, Royal Ontario Museum, 125p.

Hassan, F. 1988. The Predynastic of Egypt. *Journal of World Prehistory* 2: 135–185.

Henein, N.H. 1997. *Poterie et Potiers d'AL-QASR*. Institut Français d'Archéologie.

Holthoer, R. 1977. *New Kingdom Pharaonic sites: the pottery*. Scandinavian Joint Expedition to Sudanese Nubia. Lund, Scandanavian University Books, 190p.

Hope, C.A. 1979. Dakhleh Oasis Project: Report on the study of the pottery and kilns. *Journal of the Society for the Study of Egyptian Antiquities* 9: 187–201.

Hope, C.A. 1980. Dakhleh Oasis Project - Report on the study of the pottery and kilns. *Journal of the Society for the Study of Egyptian Antiquities* 10: 283–313.

Hope, C.A. 1981a. Dakhleh Oasis Project: Report on the study of the pottery and kilns: Third season - 1980. *Journal of the Society for the Study of Egyptian Antiquities* 11: 233–241.

Hope, C.A. 1981b. Two ancient Egyptian potters' wheels. *Journal of the Society for the Study of Egyptian Antiquities* 11: 127–133.

Hope, C.A. 1983. Dakhleh Oasis Project: Preliminary report on the study of the pottery - Fifth season, 1982. *Journal of the Society for the Study of Egyptian Antiquities* 13: 142–157.

Hope, C.A. 1985. Dakhleh Oasis Project: Report on the 1986 excavations at Ismant el-Gharab. *Journal of the Society for the Study of Egyptian Antiquities* 15: 114–125.

Hope, C.A. 1986. Dakhleh Oasis Project: Report on the 1987 excavations at Ismant el-Gharab. *Journal of the Society for the Study of Egyptian Antiquities* 16: 74–91.

Hope, C.A. 1987a. Experiments in the manufacture of ancient Egyptian pottery, 103–105. *In* Edwards, W.I., C.A. Hope and E.R. Segnit, *Ceramics from the Dakhleh Oasis: preliminary studies*. Melbourne, Victoria College, Archaeology Research Unit Occasional Paper 1 (Dakhleh Oasis Project Monograph 1), 106p.

Hope, C.A. 1987b. The Dakhleh Oasis Project. *Bulletin de Liaison du Groupe International d'Étude de la Céramique Égyptienne* 12: 30–32.

Hope, C.A. 1987c. The Dakhleh Oasis Project: Ismant el-Kharab-1988–1990. *Journal of the Society for the Study of Egyptian Antiquities* 17: 157–176.

Hope, C. [A.] 1988. Three seasons of excavation at Ismant el-Gharab in Dakhleh Oasis, Egypt. *Mediterranean Archaeology* 1: 160–178.

Hope, C.A. 1993. Pottery kilns from the oasis of el-Dakhla, Fasc. 1, 121–127. *In* Arnold, Do., and J. Bourriau, eds, *An introduction to Ancient Egypt*. Deutsches Archäologisches Institut, Abteilung Kairo, Sonderschrift 17, 190p.

Hope, C.A., O.E. Kaper, G.E. Bowen and S.F. Patten. 1989. Dakhleh Oasis Project: Ismant el-Kharab 1991–92. *Journal of the Society for the Study of Egyptian Antiquities* 19: 1–22.

Janssen, J.J. 1968. The smaller Dâkhla stela. *Journal of Egyptian Archaeology* 54: 165–172.

Jacquet-Gordon, H. 1972. *Les ermitages chrétiens du désert d'Esna III: céramique et objects*. Publications de l'Institut Français d'Archéologie Orientale du Caire, 98p.

Jacquet-Gordon, H. 1981. A tentative typology of bread moulds, 11–24. *In* Arnold, Do., ed., *Studien zur altägyptischen Keramik*. Deutsches Archäologisches Institut, Abteilung Kairo, 228p.

Jacquet-Gordon, H. Forthcoming. From the Twenty-First Dynasty to the Ptolemaic Period, *In* Arnold, Do., and J., eds, *An introduction to ancient Egyptian pottery*. Deutsches Archäologisches Institut, Abteilung Kairo, Sonderschrift.

Johnson, B. 1981. *Pottery from Karanis. Excavations of the University of Michigan*. The University of Michigan, Kelsey Museum of Archeology Studies 7, 127p.

Kaczmarczyk, A. 1986. The Source of cobalt in ancient Egyptian pigments, 369–376. *In* Olin, J.S. and M.J. Blackman, eds, *Proceedings of the 24th International Archaeometry Symposium*. Washington, Smithsonian Institution Press, 517p.

Kaiser, W. 1957. Zur Inneren Chronologie der Naqadakultur. *Archaeologia Geographica* 6: 69–77.

Keall, E. 1981. Some observations on the Islamic remains of the Dakhleh Oasis. *Journal of the Society for the Study of Egyptian Antiquities* 11: 213–223.

Kemp, B.J. 1975. Dating Pharaonic cemeteries, Part I: non-mechanical approaches to seriation. *Mitteilungen des Deutschen Archäologischen Instituts, Abteilung Kairo* 31: 259–291.

Koenig, V. and Y. Koenig. 1980. Trois tombes de la Première Période Intermédiaire à Balat. *Bulletin de l'Institut Français d'Archéologie Orientale* 80: 35–43.

Krzyzaniak, L. and M. Kobusiewicz. 1989. *Late prehistory of the Nile Basin and the Sahara. Studies in African Archaeology 2*. Poznan, Poznan Archaeological Museum, 547p.

Kuper, R. 1981. Untersuchungen zur Besiedlungsgeschichte der östlichen Sahara - Vorbericht über die Expedition 1980. *Beitrage zur Allegemeinen und Vergleichenden Archäologie* 3: 215–275.

Kuper, R. 1988. Neuere Forschungen zur Beseidlungsgeschichte der Ost-Sahara. *Archäologisches Korespondenzblatt* 18: 127–142.

Kuper, R. 1994. Prehistoric research in the southern Libyan Desert. A brief account and some conclusions of the B.O.S. project. *Cahiers de recherches de l'Institut de Papyrologie et d'Egyptologie de Lille* 123–140.

Lacovara, P. and P. Vandiver. 1985/86. An outline of technical changes in Egyptian pottery manufacture. *Bulletin of the Egyptological Seminar* 7: 53–85.

Leprohon, R.J. 1983. Dakhleh Oasis Project: 1982 season: a new stela. *Journal of the Society for the Study of Egyptian Antiquities* 13: 188–192.

Leprohon, R.J. 1986. The dating of the Dakhleh Oasis epigraphic material. *Journal of the Society for the Study of Egyptian Antiquities* 16: 50–56.

McDonald, M.M.A. This volume. Chapter 7. Neolithic cultural units and adaptations in Dakhleh Oasis, 117–132.

McDonald, M.M.A. In Press. The Late Prehistoric Radiocarbon Chronology for the Dakhleh Oasis within the wider environmental and cultural setting of the Egyptian Western Desert. *In* Marlow, M., ed., *The Dakhleh Oasis Papers I: Proceedings of the First International Symposium of the Dakhleh Oasis Project.* Oxford, Oxbow Monograph 97.

McHugh, W.P. 1975. Some archaeological results of the Bagnold-Mond expedition to the Gilf Kebir and Gebel 'Uweinat, southern Libyan Desert. *Journal of Near Eastern Studies* 34: 31–62.

Mills, A.J. 1979. Dakhleh Oasis Project: Report on the first season of survey: October-December 1978. *Journal of the Society for the Study of Egyptian Antiquities* 9: 163–185.

Mills, A.J. 1980. Dakhleh Oasis Project: Report on the second season of survey, September-December, 1979. *Journal of the Society for the Study of Egyptian Antiquities* 10: 251–282.

Mills, A.J. 1981. Dakhleh Oasis Project: Report on the third season of survey: September-December, 1980. *Journal of the Society for the Study of Egyptian Antiquities* 11: 175–192.

Mills, A.J. 1982. Dakhleh Oasis Project: Report on the fourth season of survey. October 1981–January 1982. *Journal of the Society for the Study of Egyptian Antiquities* 12: 93–101.

Mills. A.J. 1983. Dakhleh Oasis Project: Report on the fifth season of survey: October, 1982–January, 1983. *Journal of the Society for the Study of Egyptian Antiquities* 13: 121–141.

Mills, A.J. 1984. Research in the Dakhleh Oasis, 205–210. *In* Krzyzaniak, L. and M. Kobusiewicz, eds, *Origin and early development of food-producing cultures in north-eastern Africa.* Poznan: Polish Academy of Sciences, 503p.

Mills, A.J. 1985. The Dakhleh Oasis Project, 125–134. *In Melanges Gamal Eddin Mokhtar, vol. 2.* L'Institut Français d'Archéologie Orientale du Caire, *Bibliothèque d'Étude* 17: 1–401.

Mills, A.J. This volume. Chapter 10. Pharaonic Egyptians in Dakhleh Oasis, 171–178.

Minault-Gout, A. 1980. Rapport préliminaire sur les première et seconde campagnes de fouilles du Mastaba II à Balat (Oasis de Dakhleh), 1979–1980. *Bulletin de l'Institut Français d'Archéologie Orientale* 80: 271–286.

Minault-Gout, A. 1981. Rapport préliminaire sur la troisième campagne de fouilles du Mastaba II à Balat (Oasis de Dakhleh). *Bulletin de l'Institut Français d'Archéologie Orientale* 81: 207–214.

Mostafa, I.A. 1988a. Tell Fara'on-Imet. *Bulletin de Liaison du Groupe International d'Étude de la Céramique Égyptienne* 13: 14–18.

Mostafa, I.A. 1988b. Tell Fara'on-Imet. *Bulletin de Liaison du Groupe International d'Étude de la Céramique Égyptienne* 13: 19–22.

Mysliwiec, K. 1987. Keramik und Kleinfunde aus der Grabung in Tempel Sethos' I. in Gurna. Deutsches Archäologisches Institut, Abteilung Kairo, Archäologische Veröffentlichungen 57, 199p.

Nordstrom, H-Å. 1972. *Neolithic and A-Group sites.* Scandinavian Joint Expedition to Sudanese Nubia. Lund, Scandanavian University Books, 259p.

Nordstrom, H-Å. 1986. Ton. *Lexicon der Ägyptologie* 6: 629–634.

Nordström, H-Å. and J. Bourriau. 1993. Ceramic technology: clays and fabrics, Fasc. 2, 147–190. *In* Arnold, Do. and J. Bourriau, eds, *An Introduction to ancient Egyptian pottery.* Deutsches Archäologisches Institut, Abteilung Kairo, Sonderschrift 17, 190p.

O'Connor, D.B. 1974. Political systems and archaeological data in Egypt: 2600–1780 B.C. *World Archaeology* 6: 15–38.

Oren, E. 1987. The 'Ways of Horus' in North Sinai, 69–119. *In* Rainey, A.F., ed., *Egypt, Israel and Sinai*: Archaeological relationships in the Biblical period. Jerusalem, Tel Aviv University, 171p.

Osing, J. 1982. Die beschrifteten Funde, 18–41. *In* Osing, J., M. Moursi, D. Arnold, O. Neugebauer, R.A. Parker, D. Pingree and M.A. Nur-el-Din. *Denkmäler der Oase Dachla aus dem Nachlass von Ahmed Fakhry.* Deutsches Archäologisches Institut, Abteilung Kairo, Archäologische Veröffentlichungen 28, 117p.

Paice, P. 1986/87. A preliminary analysis of some elements of the Saite and Persian pottery from Tell el-Maskhuta. *Bulletin of the Egyptological Seminar* 8: 95–107.

Pantalacci, L. 1985. Une nouvelle stèle de la nécropole de Balāt. *Bulletin de l'Institut Français d'Archéologie Orientale* 85: 255–257.

Patten, S. 1991. Dakhla Oasis, Ismant el-Kharab. Notes on pottery manufacture in Dakhla Oasis; ancient and modern. *Bulletin de Liaison du Groupe International d'Étude de la Céramique Égyptienne* 15: 37–40.

Payne, J.C. Forthcoming. Prehistory B: from Naqada I to the end of the Archaic Period, *In* Arnold, Do., and J. Bourriau, eds, An introduction to ancient Egyptian pottery. Deutsches Archäologisches Institut, Abteilung Kairo, Sonderschrift (in prep.).

Petrie, W.M.F. 1888. *Tanis. II, Nebesheh (Am) and Defenneh (Tahpanhes).* London, Egypt Exploration Fund, Memoir 4, 116p.

Petrie, W.M.F. 1921. *Corpus of prehistoric pottery* and palates. London, British School of Archaeology in Egypt, 7p.

Petrie, W.M.F. and E. Mackay. 1915. *Heliopolis, Kafr Ammar and Sharafa.* London, British School of Archaeology in Egypt, 55p.

Petrie, W.M.F. and J.E. Quibell. 1896. *Naqada and Ballas: 1895.* London, Egyptian Research Account, 79p.

Quibell, J.E. 1898. *El Kab.* Egyptian Research Account, 1897. (British School of Archaeology in Egypt, London), Memoir 3, 23p.

Redford, D.B. 1976. The oases in Egyptian history to Classical times. *Journal of the Society for the Study of Egyptian Antiquities* 7: 7–10.

Rizkana, I. and J. Seeher. 1987. *Maadi I: the pottery of the Predynastic settlement.* Deutsches Archäologisches Institut, Abteilung Kairo, Archäologisches Veröffentlichungen 62, 1–112p.

Rodziewicz, M. 1976. *La céramique romaine tardive d'Alexandrie.* Warsaw, editions Scientifiques de Pologne, 72p.

Rodziewicz, M. 1985. On the origin of the Coptic painted pottery in Kharga Oasis, 235–241. *Mélanges Gamal Eddin Mokhtar, vol. 2.* L'Institut Français d'Archéologie Orientale du Caire, Bibliothéque d'Étude 97, 401p.

Rodziewicz, M. 1987. Introduction à la céramique à engobe rouge de Kharga (Kharga Red Slip Ware). *Cahiers de la Céramique Égyptienne* 1: 123–136.

Segnit, E.R. 1987. Evaporite minerals from the Dakhleh Oasis, 97–102. *In* Edwards, W.I., C.A. Hope and E.R. Segnit, *Ceramics from the Dakhleh Oasis: preliminary studies.* Melbourne, Victoria College, Archaeology Research Unit Occasional Paper 1 (Dakhleh Oasis Project Monograph 1), 106p.

Seidlmayer, S.J. 1990. *Gräberfelder aus dem Übergang vom Alten zum Mittleren Reich. Studien zur Archäologie der Ersten Zwischenzeit.* Studien zur Archäologie und geschichte Altägyptens 1, 465p.

Soukassian, G., M. Wuttmann, L. Pantalacci, P. Ballet and M. Picon. 1990. *Balat III. Les ateliers de potiers d''Ayn-Asil. Fin de l'Ancien Empire, première Periode intermediaire.* Fouilles de l'Institut, l'Institut Français d'Archéologie Orientale du Caire 34, 174p.

Tangri, D.M. 1991a. Dakhla Oasis, the Neolithic pottery. *Bulletin de Liaison du Groupe International d'Étude de la Céramique Égyptienne* 15: 31–36.

Tangri, D.M. 1991b. Neolithic basket-impressed pottery from Dakhleh Oasis, Egypt: new evidence for regionalism in the Eastern Sahara. *Sahara* 4: 141–143.

Tangri, D.M. 1992. A reassessment of the origins of the predunastic in Upper Egypt. *Proceedings of the Prehistoric Society* 58: 111–125.

Valbelle, D. 1978. Une tombe de la fin de l'ancien empire à Balat.

Bulletin de l'Institut Français d'Archéologie Orientale **78**: 53–63.

Valloggia, M. 1978. Rapport préliminaire sur la première campagne de fouilles à Balat (Oasis de Dakhleh). *Bulletin de l'Institut Français d'Archéologie Orientale* **78**: 65–80.

Valloggia, M. 1981. This sur la route des Oasis. *Bulletin du Centenaire, Supplément au Bulletin de l'Institut Français d'Archéologie Orientale* **81**: 185–190.

Valloggia, M. 1985. La stèle d'un chef d'expédition de la Première Période Intermédiaire. *Bulletin de l'Institut Français d'Archéologie Orientale* **85**: 259–266.

Valloggia, M. with N.H. Henein. 1986. *Balat I: le mastaba de Medou-Nefer.* Fouilles de l'Institut, l'Institut Français d'Archéologie Orientale du Caire 31, 239p.

Vercoutter, J. 1977. Les travaux de l'Institut Français d'Archéologie Orientale en 1976–77. *Bulletin de l'Institut Français d'Archéologie Orientale* **77**: 271–286.

Wilson, K. L. 1982. *Cities of the Delta, Part II. Mendes, preliminary report on the 1979 and 1980 seasons.* American Research Center in Egypt, Reports 5, 43p.

LIST OF CATALOGUE NUMBERS OF OBJECTS ILLLUSTRATED IN PLATES 1 – 35

Plate No.	Field Number	Egyptian Antiquities Organisation Register Book No.	Royal Ontario Museum Egyptian Collection No.	Plate No.	Field Number	Egyptian Antiquities Organisation Register Book No.	Royal Ontario Museum Egyptian Collection No.
1	31/420–C10–2/1	734	983.25.236	13	32/390–K1–2/4/1	379	
2	32/390–L2–1/1/1	244		13	32/390–K1–2/4/2	443	
3	33/390–L9–2/2/1	283	983.25.45	13	32/390–K1–2/4/3	442	983.25.204
3	33/390–L9–2/2/2	263		13	32/390–K1–2/4/4	Not on object	983.25.93
3	33/390–L9–2/2/3	262	983.25.64	13	32/390–K1–2/4/5	441	983.25.212
3	33/390–L9–2/2/4	264	983.25.237	14	32/390–K1–2/1/7		
3	33/390–L9–2/2/5	265		15	32/390–K1–2/1/20	320	
3	33/390–L9–2/2/6	282	983.25.180	16	32/390–K1–2/1/11	329	
3	33/390–L9–2/2/7	266	983.25.226	17	32/390–K1–2/1/1	256	
3	33/390–L9–2/2/8	267	983.25.249	18	32/390–K1–2/1/18	321	
3	33/390–L9–2/2/9	268		19	32/390–K1–2/1/3	254	
3	33/390–L9–2/2/10	269	983.25.228	20	31/435–D5–2/26/1	1019	
3	33/390–L9–2/2/11	270	983.25.213	21	31/435–D5–2/8/11	807	
3	33/390–L9–2/2/12	271	983.25.108	22	32/390–K4–1/1/1/4	454	983.25.215
3	33/390–L9–2/2/13	272	983.25.147	23	32/390–K4–1/1/1/16	450	
3	33/390–L9–2/2/14	273		24	32/390–K4–1/1/1/17	451	983.25.118
3	33/390–L9–2/2/15	274	983.25.238	25	32/390–K4–1/1/1/1	427	983.25.246
3	33/390–L9–2/2/16	275	983.25.46	26 left	32/390–K1–1/2/9	302	
3	33/390–L9–2/2/17	276	983.25.211	26 right	32/390–K1–1/2/4	307	
4	33/390–I9–2/0/4	35	983.25.183	27	32/390–K1–1/2/10	281	983.25.98
5	33/390–I9–2/3/9	12		28	32/390–K1–1/2/11	301	
6	33/390–I9–2/4/19	34		29	33/390–F10–1/0/1	208	983.25.97
7	33/390–I9–2/0/2	46	983.25.162	30	33/390–N6–1/4/1	324	983.25.138
8	33/390–I9–2/0/1	43	983.25.120	31	33/390–I7–1	Unregistered	
9	33/390–J3–1/1/8	174		32	31/435–H4–1/1/2	820	983.25.166
10	33/390–J3–1/1/6	173	983.25.202	33	31/435–H4–1/1/4	821	983.25.139
11	33/390–I9–2/0/3	45		34	33/390–N6–1/4/2	323	983.25.126
12	33/390–L9–2/2/3	262	983.25.64	35	(31/435–K5–1)	Composite plate	

Note. Absence of a Royal Ontario Museum registration number (series 983.25.--) indicates that the object remains in Egypt. Object 983.25.93 has no Egyptian Antiquities Organisation Registration Book number recorded either on it or on the catalogue card.

Appendix I

DAKHLEH OASIS PROJECT
BIBLIOGRAPHY

Titles published by members of the project on the work of the project or by associates on materials collected by members of the project in both scholarly and popular journals. This list includes publications to the end of 1996.

Alcock, A., I. Gardner and P. Mirecki. 1997. Magical spell, Manichaean letter,1–32. *In* Mirecki, P. and J. BeDuhn, eds, *Emerging from Darkness to Light*. Leiden: E.J. Brill, 294p.

Alcock, A., I. Gardner and W.-P. Funk, eds. 1999. *Coptic Documentary Texts*. Dakhleh Oasis Project Monograph 9. Oxford: Oxbow Books.

Bagnall, R.S., ed. 1997. *The Kellis Agricultural Account Book*. Dakhleh Oasis Project Monograph 7. Oxford: Oxbow Monograph 92, 253p.

Bowen, G.E., C.A. Hope and O.E. Kaper. 1992. Excavations at Ismant el-Kharab – 1992. *Bulletin of the Australian Centre for Egyptology* 3: 41–49.

Bowen, G.E., C.A. Hope and O.E. Kaper. 1993. A brief report on the excavations at Ismant el-Kharab in 1992–1993. *Bulletin of the Australian Centre for Egyptology* 4: 17–28.

Brookes, I.A. 1983. Dakhleh Oasis – A geoarchaeological reconnaissance. *Journal of the Society for the Study of Egyptian Antiquities* 13: 167–177.

Brookes, I.A. 1986. Quaternary geology and geomorphology of Dakhleh Oasis and environs, south central Egypt: Reconnaissance findings. *York University, Toronto: Department of Geography Discussion Paper* No. 32, 90p.

Brookes, I.A. 1989a. Above the salt: Sediment accretion and irrigation agriculture in an Egyptian oasis. *Journal of Arid Environments* 17: 335–348.

Brookes, I.A. 1989b. Early Holocene basinal sediments of the Dakhleh Oasis region, south central Egypt. *Quaternary Research* 32: 139–152.

Brookes, I.A. 1990. Anthropogenic irrigation deposits, Dakhla Oasis, south-central Egypt, 113–126. *In* Bottema S., G. Entjes-Nieberg and W. van Zeist, eds, *Man's Role in the Shaping of the Eastern Mediterranean Landscape*. Proceedings of the International Union for Quaternary Research (INQUA) Symposium, Groningen, Netherlands, March, 1989. Rotterdam: A.A. Balkema, 349p.

Brookes, I.A. 1991. Desert climate: The past is the key to understanding dryland response to change. *Geotimes* 36: 22–25.

Brookes, I.A. 1993. Geomorphology and Quaternary geology of the Dakhla Oasis Region, Egypt. *Quaternary Science Reviews* 12: 529–552.

Churcher, C.S. 1980. Dakhleh Oasis Project: Preliminary observations on the geology and vertebrate palaeontology of northwestern Dakhleh Oasis. *Journal of the Society for the Study of Egyptian Antiquities* 10: 379–395.

Churcher, C.S. 1981. Dakhleh Oasis Project: Geology and Paleontology: Interim report on the 1980 field season. *Journal of the Society for the Study of Egyptian Antiquities* 11: 194–212.

Churcher, C.S. 1982. Dakhleh Oasis Project: Geology and Palaeontology: Interim report on the 1981 field season. *Journal of the Society for the Study of Egyptian Antiquities* 12: 103–114.

Churcher, C.S. 1983. Dakleh Oasis Project: Palaeontology: Interim report on the 1982 field season. *Journal of the Society for the Study of Egyptian Antiquities* 13: 178–187.

Churcher, C.S. 1986a. Equid remains from Neolithic horizons at Dakhleh Oasis, Western Desert of Egypt, 413–421. *In* Meadow, R.H. and H.-P. Uerpmann, eds, *Equids in the Ancient World*. Tübinger Atlas des Vorderen Orients, A (Naturwissenschaften) 19: 1-423.

Churcher, C.S. 1986b. Dakhleh Oasis Project: Palaeontology: Interim report on the 1985 field season. *Journal of the Society for the Study of Egyptian Antiquities* 16: 114–118.

Churcher, C.S. 1987a. The zooarchaeology of Dakhleh Oasis. *Canadian Mediterranean Institute, Bulletin* no. 7, 3.

Churcher, C.S. 1987b. Neolithic faunas from Dakhleh Oasis, Western Desert of Egypt (Abstract). *Society for American Archaeology, 52nd Annual Meeting, Program and Abstracts, May 6–10, Toronto*, 59.

Churcher, C.S. 1987c. Dakhleh Oasis Project: Palaeontology: Interim report on the 1988 Field Season. *Journal of the Society for the Study of Egyptian Antiquities* 17: 177–181.

Churcher, C.S. 1988a. Palaeontology: Interim report on the 1987 field season. *Journal of the Society for the Study of Egyptian Antiquities* 16: 114–118.

Churcher, C.S. 1988b. The Neolithic environment of Dakhleh Oasis. *Série de Conférences canadiennes sur l'Archéologie, Canadian Club, Cairo, Feb. 16, 1988*, 1–7.

Churcher, C.S. 1988c. Marine vertebrates from the Duwi Phosphor-

---

'Reports from the Survey of Dakhleh Oasis, Western Desert of Egypt, 1977–1987', edited by C.S. Churcher and A.J. Mills. Dakhleh Oasis Project: Monograph 2. Oxbow Monograph 99.

ites, Dakhleh Oasis, Western Desert of Egypt. *Abstracts of Papers, Forty-Eighth Annual Meeting, Society of Vertebrate Paleontology, Drumheller, Alberta, Journal of Vertebrate Paleontology,* **8** (supplement to no. 3): 11A.

Churcher, C.S. 1990. Dogs from a Roman Tomb in Dakhleh Oasis, Western Desert of Egypt (Poster). *Sixth International Conference of the International Council for Archaeozoology, Washington, DC, May 21–25.*

Churcher, C.S. 1991a. The Egyptian fruit bat *Rousettus aegyptiacus* in Dakhleh Oasis, Western Desert of Egypt. *Mammalia* **55**: 139–143.

Churcher, C.S. 1991b. The scales of *Stratodus apicalis* Cope 1872 (Abstract). Society of Vertebrate Paleontology, 51st Annual Meeting, San Diego, California, October 24–26. *Journal of Vertebate Paleontology* **11** (Supplement to no. 3): 39 (22A).

Churcher, C.S. 1992. Ostrich bones from the Neolithic of Dakhleh Oasis, Western Desert of Egypt. *Palaeoecology of Africa and Surrounding Islands* **23**: 67–71.

Churcher, C.S. 1993a. Romano-Byzantine and Neolithic diets in Dakhleh Oasis. *Canadian Mediterranean Institute, Bulletin* no. 13, 1–2.

Churcher, C.S. 1993b. Dogs from Ein Tirghi Cemetery, Balat, Dakhleh Oasis, Western Desert of Egypt, 39–60. *In* Clason, A., S. Payne and H.-P. Uerpmann, eds, *Skeletons in her Cupboard: Festschrift for Juliet Clutton-Brock.* Oxford: Oxbow Monograph 34, 259p.

Churcher, C.S. 1995. Giant Cretaceous lungfish *Neoceratodus tuberculatus* from a deltaic environment in the Quseir (= Baris) Formation of Kharga Oasis, Western Desert of Egypt. *Journal of Vertebrate Paleontology* **15**: 845–849.

Churcher, C.S. This volume. Chapter 2. A note on the Late Cretaceous vertebrate fauna of Dakhleh Oasis, 55–67.

Churcher, C.S. This volume. Chapter 8. Holocene faunas of the Dakhleh Oasis, 133–151.

Churcher, C.S., M.R. Kleindienst and M.F. Wiseman. 1997. A Mid-Pleistocene fauna from the Dakhleh Oasis, Western Desert of Egypt, 17–18. (Abstract). *British Columbia Paleontological Symposium, May 9–11, Vancouver, Program and Abstracts.* Vancouver: British Columbia Paleontological Alliance, 25p.

Cook, M. 1993. Detection of DNA in ancient skeletal remains using DNA flow cytometry. *Biotechnic and Histochemistry* **68**: 260–264.

Cook, M. 1994. The mummies of Dakhleh, 259–277. *In* Herring, A. and L. Chan, eds, *Strength in Diversity: A reader in physical anthropology.* Toronto: Canadian Scholars' Press, 458p.

Cook, M., E. Molto and C. Anderson. 1987. Possible case of hyperthyroidism in a Roman period skeleton from the Dakhleh Oasis, Egypt, diagnosed using bone histomorphometry. *American Journal of Physical Anthropology* **75**: 23–30.

Cook, M., E. Molto and C. Anderson. 1989. Fluorochrome labelling in Roman period skeletons from Dakhleh Oasis, Egypt. *American Journal of Physical Anthropology* **80**: 137–143.

de Jong, T. and K.A. Worp. 1995. A Greek horoscope from 373 A.D. *Zeitschrift für Papyrologie und Epigraphik* **106**: 235–240.

Edwards, W.I. and C.A. Hope. 1989. A note on the Neolithic pottery from the Dakhleh Oasis (Egypt), 233–242. *In* Krzyzaniak, L. and M. Kobusiewicz, eds, *Late prehistory of the Nile Basin and the Sahara. Studies in African Archaeology, vol. 23.* Poznan: Poznan Archaeological Museum, 547p.

Edwards, W.I., C.A. Hope and E.R. Segnit. 1987. Ceramics from Dakhleh Oasis: preliminary studies. *Victoria College, Melbourne: Archaeology Research Unit, Occasional Paper 1* (Dakhleh Oasis Project Monograph 1), 106p.

Fairgrleve, S.I. 1993. *Amino Acid Residue Analysis of Type I Collagen in Human Hard Tissue: An assessment of cribra orbitalia in an ancient skeletal sample from Tomb 31, Site 31/*

435–D5–2, Dakhleh Oasis, Egypt. Ph.D. Thesis, University of Toronto, 261p.

Frey, R.A. 1986. Dakhleh Oasis Project: Interim report on excavations at the 'Ein Tirghi cemetery. *Journal of the Society for the Study of Egyptian Antiquities* **16**: 92–102.

Gardner, I. 1993a. A Manichaean liturgical codex found at Kellis. *Orientalia* **62**: 30–59.

Gardner, I. 1993b. The Manichaean community at Kellis: Progress report. *Manichaean Studies Newsletter* **11**: 18–26.

Gardner, I. 1993c. The Manichaean community at Kellis: Progress report. *Acta Orientalia Belgica* **8**: 79–87.

Gardner, I. 1995a. An abbreviated version of Medinet Madi Psalm LXVIII found at Kellis, 129–138. *In* A. van Tongerloo, ed., *The Manichaean NOYΣ,* Louvain: International Association of Manichaean Studies, 323p.

Gardner, I. 1995b. Glory be to Mani! *Divitiae Aegyptae* **1995**: 105–112.

Gardner, I. 1996. *Kellis Literary Texts I.* Dakhleh Oasis Project Monograph no. 4. Oxford: Oxbow Monograph 69, 188p.

Gardner, I. 1997. The Manichaean community at Kellis, 161–175. *In* P. Mirecki and J. BeDuhn, eds, *Emerging from Darkness to Light.* Leiden: E.J. Brill, 294p.

Gardner, I. and S.N.C. Lieu. 1996. From Narmouthis (Medinet Madi) to Kellis (Ismant el-Kharab): Manichaean documents from Roman Egypt. *Journal of Roman Studies* **1996**: 146–169

Gardner, I. and K.A. Worp. 1997. Leaves from a Manichaean Codex. *Zeitschrift für Papyrologie und Epigraphik* **117**: 139–155.

Hodges, W.K. 1980. *Patterns of Environmental Change and Land-use Hydrology in a Hyperarid Desert: A preliminary survey of ed-Dakhleh Oasis, Western Desert, Egypt.* Unpublished Dakhleh Oasis Project Report, 99p.

Hollett, A.F. 1985. Tomb with a Phew. *Royal Ontario Museum Archaeological Newsletter, series II,* no. 8, 1–4.

Hollett, A.F. and C.S. Churcher. This volume. Chapter 9. Notes on the Recent fauna of the Dakhleh Oasis, 153–170.

Hope, C.A. 1979. Dakhleh Oasis Project: Report on the study of the pottery and kilns. *Journal of the Society for the Study of Egyptian Antiquities* **9**: 187–201.

Hope, C.A. 1980a. Dakhleh Oasis Project – Report on the study of the pottery and kilns. *Journal of the Society for the Study of Egyptian Antiquities* **10**: 283–313.

Hope, C.A. 1980b. Dakhleh Oasis, Survey (Dakhleh Oasis Project, University of Toronto). *Bulletin de Liaison du Groupe International d'Étude de la Céramique Égyptienne* **5**: 18–20.

Hope, C.A. 1981a. Dakhleh Oasis Project: Report on the study of the pottery and kilns: Third season – 1980. *Journal of the Society for the Study of Egyptian Antiquities* **11**: 233–241.

Hope, C.A. 1981b. Dakhleh Oasis, Survey (Dakhleh Oasis Project, University of Toronto). *Bulletin de Liaison du Groupe International d'Étude de la Céramique Égyptienne* **6**: 20–21.

Hope, C.A. 1983a. Ceramics and the Dakhleh Oasis Project, 59–66. *In* Hope, C.A. and J. Zimmer, eds., *Ancient Middle Eastern ceramics and Australian archaeology in the Middle East.* Melbourne: Royal Melbourne Institute of Technology, 186p.

Hope, C.A. 1983b. Dakhleh Oasis Project: Preliminary report on the study of the pottery – Fifth season, 1982. *Journal of the Society for the Study of Egyptian Antiquities* **13**: 142–157.

Hope, C.A. 1983c. The Dakhleh Oasis Project (University of Toronto). *Bulletin de Liaison du Groupe International d'Étude de la Céramique Égyptienne* **8**: 31–32.

Hope, C.A. 1985a. Dakhleh Oasis Project: Report on the 1986 excavations at Ismant el-Gharab. *Journal of the Society for the Study of Egyptian Antiquities* **15**: 114–125.

Hope, C.A. 1985b. Dakhleh Oasis Project: 1985 Season. *Bulletin de Liaison du Groupe International d'Étude de la Céramique Égyptienne* **10**: 32–33.

Hope, C.A. 1986a. Dakhleh Oasis Project: Report on the 1987

excavations at Ismant el-Gharab. *Journal of the Society for the Study of Egyptian Antiquities* **16**: 74–91.

Hope, C.A. 1986b. The Dakhleh Oasis Project (University of Toronto). *Bulletin de Liaison du Groupe International d'Étude de la Céramique Égyptienne* **11**: 45–47.

Hope, C.A. 1987a. Dakhleh Oasis Project: Ismant el-Kharab 1988–1990. *Journal of the Society for the Study of Egyptian Antiquities* **17**: 157–176.

Hope, C.A. 1987b. 7. Experiments in the manufacture of ancient Egyptian pottery, 103–105. *In* Edwards, W.I., C.A. Hope and E.R. Segnit, *Ceramics from the Dakhleh Oasis: preliminary studies*. Victoria College, Melbourne: Archaeology Research Unit Occasional Paper 1 (Dakhleh Oasis Project Monograph 1), 106p.

Hope, C.A. 1987c. 17. The Dakhleh Oasis Project. *Bulletin de Liaison du Groupe International d'Étude de la Céramique Égyptienne* **12**: 30–32.

Hope, C. [A.] 1988. Three seasons of excavation at Ismant el-Gharab in Dakhleh Oasis, Egypt. *Mediterranean Archaeology (Australian and New Zealand Journal for the Archaeology of the Mediterranean World)* **1**: 160–178.

Hope, C.A. 1990a. Excavations at Ismant el-Kharab in the Dakhleh Oasis. *Bulletin of the Australian Centre for Egyptology* **1**: 43–54.

Hope, C.A. 1990b. Dakhleh Oasis Project 1988–1989. *Bulletin de Liaison du Groupe International d'Étude de la Céramique Égyptienne* **14**: 30–32.

Hope, C.A. 1991. The 1991 excavations at Ismant el-Kharab in the Dakhleh Oasis. *Bulletin of the Australian Centre for Egyptology* **2**: 41–50.

Hope, C.A. 1993. Pottery kilns from the oasis of el-Dakhla, Fasc. 1, 121–127. *In* Arnold, Do., and J. Bourriau, eds, *An introduction to Ancient Egypt*. Deutsches Archäologisches Institut, Abteilung Kairo, Sonderschrift 17, 190p.

Hope, C.A. 1994a. Excavations at Ismant el-Kharab in the Dakhleh Oasis. *Egyptian Archaeology* no. 5, 17–18.

Hope, C.A. 1994b. Isis and Serapis at Kellis: A brief note. *Bulletin of the Australian Centre for Egyptology* **5**: 37–42.

Hope, C.A. 1995a. Ismant el-Kharab (Ancient Kellis) in the Dakhleh Oasis, Egypt. *Mediterranean Archaeology* **8**: 138–143.

Hope, C.A. 1995b. The excavations at Ismant el-Kharab in 1995: a brief report. *Bulletin of the Australian Centre for Egyptology* **6**: 51–58.

Hope, C.A. 1997. The archaeological context of the discovery of leaves from a Manichaean codex. *Zeitschrift für Papyrologie und Epigraphik 117*: 156–161.

Hope, C.A. 1999. Ismant el-Kharab. *In* Bard, K., ed., *The Archaeology of Ancient Egypt: An Encyclopedia*. London, 222–226.

Hope, C.A. This volume. Chapter 14. Pottery manufacture in the Dakhleh Oasis, 215–243.

Hope, C.A., O.E. Kaper and G.E. Bowen. 1992. Excavations at Ismant el-Kharab – 1992. *Bulletin of the Australian Centre or Egyptology* **3**: 41–49.

Hope, C.A., O.E. Kaper, G.E. Bowen and S.F. Patten. 1989. Dakhleh Oasis Project: Ismant el-Kharab 1991-92. *Journal of the Society for the Study of Egyptian Antiquities* **19**: 1-26.

Hope, C.A. and M. Riddle. 1983. Early Christianity in the Egyptian Sahara – new finds, 159–162. *In* Horseley, G.R.H., ed., *New Documents Illustrating Early Christianity*. North Ryde, New South Wales: Macquarie University, Ancient History Documentary Research Centre, 182p.

Jenkins, R.G. 1995a. The prayer of the emanations in Greek from Kellis. *Le Museon* **108**: 243–263.

Jenkins, R.G. 1995b. Papyrus 1 from Kellis: A Greek text with affinities to the Acts of John, 197–216. *In* Bremmer, J.N., ed., *The Apocryphal Acts of John*. Kampen, 197–216.

Kaper, O.E. 1987. How the god Amun-Nakht came to Dakhleh Oasis. *Journal of the Society for the Study of Egyptian Antiquities* **17**: 151-156.

Kaper, O.E. 1991. The god Tutu (Tithoes) and his temple in the Dakhleh Oasis. *Bulletin of the Australian Centre for Egyptology* **2**: 59–67.

Kaper, O.E. 1992. Egyptian toponyms of Dakhla Oasis. *Bulletin de l'Institut français d'Archéologie orientale* **92**: 117–132.

Kaper, O.E. 1993. 'Nieuwe' Tempels in de Oase Dachla. *Phoenix* **39**: 11–25.

Kaper, O.E. 1995a. The astronomical ceiling of Deir el-Haggar in the Dakhleh Oasis. *Journal of Egyptian Archaeology* **81**: 175–195.

Kaper, O.E. 1995b. Doorway decoration patterns in the Dakhleh Oasis. *In* Kurth, D., ed., 3. *Ägyptologische Tempeltagung Hamburg, June 1–5, 1994: Systeme und Programme der ägyptischen Tempeldecoration*, Wiesbaden: Harrassowitz, 99–114.

Kaper, O. E. 1997. *Temples and Gods in Roman Dakhleh. Studies in the indigenous cults of an Egyptian oasis*. Groningen: privately printed. 216p.

Kaper, O.E. In press. Local perceptions of the fertility of the Dakhleh Oasis in the Roman Period, *In* M. Marlow,ed., *The Oasis Papers I: The Proceedings of the First International Symposium of the Dakhleh Oasis Project, Durham, July 5–9, 1994*. Dakhleh Oasis Project Monograph no. 5. Oxford: Oxbow Monographs no. 97.

Kaper, O.E. accepted. A painting of the Gods of Dakhleh in the Temple of Tutu, *In* Quirke, S., ed., *The Temple in Ancient Egypt*. London: British Museum Press.

Kaper, O.E. and K.A. Worp. 1995. A bronze representing Tapsais of Kellis. *Revue d'Egyptologie* **46**: 107–118.

Keall, E. 1981. Some observations on the Islamic remains of the Dakhleh Oasis. *Journal of the Society for the Study of Egyptian Antiquities* **11**: 213–223.

Kleindienst, M.R. 1985. Dakhleh Oasis Project: Pleistocene archaeology: Report on the 1986 season. *Journal of the Society for the Study of Egyptian Antiquities* **15**: 136–137.

Kleindienst, M.R. 1987. Pleistocene archaeology of the Dakhleh Oasis, Egypt: Background to the Holocene adaptations (Abstract). *Society for American Archaeology, 52nd Annual Meeting, Program and Abstracts, May 6–10, Toronto, Ontario*, 88.

Kleindienst, M.R. 1991. Pursuing Pleistocene people: geo-archaeological and archaeological work at the Dakhleh Oasis, Egypt [*incorrectly published as* 'Preserving Pleistocene people at Dakleh Oasis, Egyptian Sahara']. Abstract. *Canadian Archaeological Association, 24th. Annual Meeeting, St. John's, Newfoundland, Programme and Abstracts, May 8–11*, 34.

Kleindienst, M.R. 1993. What is the Aterian? *26th Annual Meeting, Canadian Archaeological Association, Montreal, Quebec, Program and Abstracts, May 5–9*, 47.

Kleindienst, M.R. This volume. Chapter 5. Pleistocene archaeology and geoarchaeology of the Dakhleh Oasis: A status report, 83–108.

Kleindienst, M.R., C.S. Churcher, M.M.A. McDonald and H.P. Schwarcz. This volume. Chapter 1. Geography, Geology, Geochronology and Geoarchaeology of the Dakhleh Oasis Region: An interim report, 1–54.

Kleindienst, M.R., H.P. Schwarcz, K. Nicoll, C.S. Churcher, J. Frizano, R.W. Giegengack and M.F. Wiseman. 1996a. Pleistocene geochronology and palaeoclimates at Dakhleh and Kharga Oases, Western Desert, Egypt, based upon Uranium-Thorium determinations from spring-laid tufas, Abstract 57. *In* Krzyzaniak, L. and M. Kobusiewicz, eds, *13th Biennial Meeting, Society of Africanist Archaeologists, Poznan, Poland, Sept. 4th., 1996*.

Kleindienst, M.R., H.P. Schwarcz, K. Nicoll, C.S. Churcher, J.

Frizano, R.W. Giegengack and M.F. Wiseman. 1996b. Pleistocene geochronology and palaeoclimates at Dakhleh and Kharga
Oases, Western Desert, Egypt, based upon Uranium-Thorium
determinations from spring-laid tufas, Abstract. *Nyame Akuma*
no. 46, 96.

Kleindienst, M.R. and M.F. Wiseman. 1996a. Pleistocene archaeology and geoarchaeology at Dakhleh Oasis, Western Desert,
Egypt: 19 seasons of exploration, Abstract 58. *In* Krzyzaniak,
L. and M. Kobusiewicz, eds, *13th Biennial Conference, Society
of Africanist Archaeologists, Poznan, Poland, Sept. 4th., 1996.*

Kleindienst, M.R. and M.F. Wiseman. 1996b. Pleistocene archaeology and geoarchaeology at Dakhleh Oasis, Western Desert,
Egypt: 19 seasons of exploration, Abstract. *Nyame Akuma* no.
46, 96.

Knudstad, J.E. and R.A. Frey. This volume. Chapter 13. Kellis:
The Architectural Survey at the Romano-Byzantine Town at
Ismant el-Kharab, 189–214.

Krug, J.C. and R.S. Khan. This volume. Chapter 3. Soil Fungi from
eastern Dakhleh Oasis, 69–71.

Krug, J.C., R.S. Khan and R.S. Jeng. 1994. A new species of
Gelasinospora with multiple germ pores. *Mycologia* **86**: 250–
253.

Krug, J.C., R.S. Khan and S. Udagawa. 1994. A reappraisal of
Areolospora bosensis. *Mycologia* **86**: 581–585.

Krzyzaniak, L. 1987. Dakhleh Oasis Project: Interim report on the
first season of the recording of petroglyphs, January/ February
1988. *Journal of the Society for the Study of Egyptian Antiquities*
17: 182–191.

Krzyzaniak, L. 1990. Petroglyphs and the research on the development of the cultural attitude towards animals in the Dakhleh
Oasis (Egypt). *Sahara* **3**: 95–97.

Krzyzaniak, L. 1994. Dakhleh Oasis: Research on Rock Art 1993.
Polish Archaeology in the Mediterranean **5**: 97–100.

Krzyzaniak, L. and K. Kroeper. 1985. Dakhleh Oasis Project: Report
on the reconnaissance season of the recording of petroglyphs,
December 1985. *Journal of the Society for the Study of Egyptian
Antiquities* **15**: 138–139.

Krzyzaniak, L. and K. Kroeper. 1990. The Dakhleh Oasis Project:
Interim report on the second (1990) and third (1992) seasons of
the recording of petroglyphs. *Journal of the Society for the
Study of Egyptian Antiquities* **20**: 77–88.

Krzyzaniak, L. and K. Kroeper. 1991. A face-mask in the prehistoric
rock art of the Dakhleh Oasis? *Archaeo-Nil* **1**: 59–61.

Leahy, L.M.M. 1980. Dakhleh Oasis Project: the Roman wall-
paintings from Amheida. *Journal of the Society for the Study of
Egyptian Antiquities* **10**: 331–378.

Leprohon, R.J. 1983. Dakhleh Oasis Project 1982 season: a new
stela. *Journal of the Society for the Study of Egyptian Antiquities*
13: 188–192.

Leprohon, R.J. 1986. The dating of the Dakhleh Oasis epigraphic
material. *Journal of the Society for the Study of Egyptian
Antiquities* **16**: 50–56.

McDonald, M.M.A. 1980. Dakhleh Oasis Project: Preliminary
report on lithic industries in the Dakhleh Oasis. *Journal of the
Society for the Study of Egyptian Antiquities* **10**: 315–329.

McDonald, M.M.A. 1981. Dakhleh Oasis Project: second preliminary report on lithic industries in the Dakhleh Oasis. *Journal of
the Society for the Study of Egyptian Antiquities* **11**: 225–
231.

McDonald, M.M.A. 1982a. Dakhleh Oasis Project: Third preliminary report on the lithic industries in the Dakhleh Oasis. *Journal
of the Society for the Study of Egyptian Antiquities* **12**: 115–
138.

Mcdonald, M.M.A. 1982b. Sequences without stratigraphy:
investigating the prehistory of the Dakhleh Oasis. *Royal Ontario
Museum Archaeological Newsletter* no. 204, 4p.

McDonald, M.M.A. 1983. Dakhleh Oasis Project – Fourth prelimin-

ary report on the lithic industries in the Dakhleh Oasis. *Journal
of the Society for the Study of Egyptian Antiquities* **13**: 158–
166.

McDonald, M.M.A. 1985. Dakhleh Oasis Project: Holocene
prehistory: Interim report on the 1984 and 1986 seasons. *Journal
of the Society for the Study of Egyptian Antiquities* **15**: 126–
135.

McDonald, M.M.A. 1986. Dakhleh Oasis Project: Holocene
prehistory: Interim report on the 1987 season. *Journal of the
Society for the Study of Egyptian Antiquities* **16**: 103–113.

McDonald, M.M.A. 1987. Adaptations in Dakhleh Oasis in the
early to mid-Holocene (Abstract). *Society for American
Archaeology, 52nd Annual Meeting, Program and Abstracts,
May 6–10, Toronto*, 98.

McDonald, M.M.A. 1990a. The Dakhleh Oasis Project: Holocene
Prehistory: Interim report on the 1988 and 1989 seasons. *Journal
of the Society for the Study of Egyptian Antiquities* **20**: 24–53.

McDonald, M.M.A. 1990b. The Dakhleh Oasis Project: Holocene
Prehistory: Interim report on the 1990 season. *Journal of the
Society for the Study of Egyptian Antiquities* **20**: 54–64.

McDonald, M.M.A. 1990c. The Dakhleh Oasis Project: Holocene
Prehistory: Interim report on the 1991 season. *Journal of the
Society for the Study of Egyptian Antiquities* **20**: 65–76.

McDonald, M.M.A. 1990d. New evidence from the Early to Mid-
Holocene in Dakhleh Oasis, South-Central Egypt, bearing on
the evolution of cattle pastoralism. *Nyame Akuma* no. 33, 3–9.

McDonald, M.M.A. 1991a. Origins of the Neolithic in the Nile
Valley as seen from Dakhleh Oasis in the Egyptian Western
Desert. *Sahara* **4**: 41–52.

McDonald, M.M.A. 1991b. Systematic reworking of lithics from
earlier cultures in the Early Holocene of Dakhleh Oasis, Egypt.
Journal of Field Archaeology **18**: 269–273.

McDonald, M.M.A. 1991c. Technological organization and
sedentism in the Epipalaeolithic of Dakhleh Oasis, Egypt.
African Archaeological Review **9**: 81–109.

McDonald, M.M.A. 1992a. Neolithic of Sudanese tradition or
Saharo-Sudanese Neolithic? The view from Dakhleh Oasis,
South Central Egypt, 51-70. *In* Sterner, J. and N. David, eds, *An
African Commitment: papers in Honour of Peter Lewis Shinnie.*
Calgary, University of Calgary Press, 248p.

McDonald, M.M.A. 1992b. The roots of Egyptian Civilization as
seen from the Dakhleh Oasis in the Western Desert, 257–261.
In Harrak, A., ed., *Contacts between Cultures: West Asia and
North Africa*, vol. 1. Lewiston/Queenston Lampeter, The Edwin
Mellen Press, 508p.

McDonald, M.M.A. 1993. Cultural adaptations in Dakhleh Oasis,
Egypt, in the early to mid-Holocene, 199–209. *In* Krzyzaniak,
L., M. Kobusiewicz and J. Alexander, eds, *Environmental
change and human culture in the Nile Basin and northern Africa
until the 2nd millenium BC*. Poznan, Polish Academy of
Sciences, 494p.

McDonald, M.M.A. 1996. Relations between Dakhleh Oasis and
the Nile Valley in the mid-Holocene: A discussion, 93–99. *In*
Krzyzaniak, L., K. Kroeper and M. Kobusiewicz, eds, *Inter-
regional Contacts in the Later Prehistory of Northeastern
Africa*. Poznan, Polish Academy of Sciences, 490p.

McDonald, M.M.A. 1999. Dakhleh Oasis: Prehistory. *In* Bard, K.,
ed., *The Archaeology of Ancient Egypt: An Encyclopedia.*
London and New York, 226–229.

McDonald, M.M.A. This volume. Chapter 7. Neolithic cultural
units and adaptations in Dakhleh Oasis, 117–132.

Melbye, F.J. 1983. Human remains from a Roman Period tomb in
the Dakhleh Oasis, Egypt: A preliminary analysis. *Journal of
the Society for the Study of Egyptian Antiquities* **13**: 193–201.

Mills, A.J. 1979a. Dakhleh Oasis Project: Report on the first season
of survey: October-December 1978. *Journal of the Society for
the Study of Egyptian Antiquities* **9**: 163–185.

Mills, A.J. 1979b. The basis of an oasis. *Royal Ontario Museum Archaeological Newsletter*, n.s., no. 168, 4p.

Mills, A.J. 1979c. Dakhleh Oasis Project 1978 Season. *Nyame Akuma*, no. 14: 16.

Mills, A.J. 1980a. Dakhleh Oasis: 1979 season. *Nyame Akuma*, no. 16: 5–6.

Mills, A.J. 1980b. Lively paintings: Roman frescoes in the Dakhleh Oasis. *Rotunda (Bulletin of the Royal Ontario Museum)* **13**: 18–25.

Mills, A.J. 1980c. Dakhleh Oasis Project: Report on the second season of survey, September-December, 1979. *Journal of the Society for the Study of Egyptian Antiquities* **10**: 251–282.

Mills, A.J. 1981a. Dakhleh Oasis Project: Report on the third season of survey: September-December, 1980. *Journal of the Society for the Study of Egyptian Antiquities* **11**: 175–192.

Mills, A.J. 1981b. Little fleas have bigger fleas .... *Royal Ontario Museum Archaeological Newsletter*, n.s., no. 197, 1–4.

Mills, A.J. 1982a. A spectacular find reburied. *Canadian Collector (Toronto)* **17**: 55–57.

Mills, A.J. 1982b. Dakhleh Oasis Project: Report on the fourth season of survey. October 1981 – January 1982. *Journal of the Society for the Study of Egyptian Antiquities* **12**: 93–101.

Mills, A.J. 1982c. The Dakhleh Oasis Project: a report on the first two seasons. *Annales du Service des Antiquités de l'Egypte (Le Caire)* **67**: 71–78.

Mills, A.J. 1983a. Dakhleh Oasis Project: Report on the fifth season of survey: October, 1982 – January, 1983. *Journal of the Society for the Study of Egyptian Antiquities* **13**: 121–141.

Mills, A.J. 1983b. O tempora, O templa. *Royal Ontario Museum Archaeological Newsletter*, n.s., no. 216, 1–4.

Mills, A.J. 1984a. The Dakhleh Oasis Project: Report on the sixth season of survey: 1983 – 1984. *Journal of the Society for the Study of Egyptian Antiquities* **14**: 81-85.

Mills, A.J. 1984b. Research in the Dakhleh Oasis, 205–210. *In* Krzyzaniak, L. and M. Kobusiewicz, eds, *Origin and early development of food-producing cultures in north-eastern Africa*. Poznan: Polish Academy of Sciences, 503p.

Mills, A.J. 1985a. The Dakhleh Oasis Project, 125–134. *In Melanges Gamal Eddin Mokhtar*, vol. 2. Cairo: L'Institut Français d'Archéologie Orientale du Caire, 401p.

Mills, A.J. 1985b. The Dakhleh Oasis Project: An interim report on the 1984 – 1985 field season. *Journal of the Society for the Study of Egyptian Antiquities* **15**: 44–45.

Mills, A.J. 1985c. Dakhleh Oasis Project: A preliminary report on the field work of the 1985/1986 season. *Journal of the Society for the Study of Egyptian Antiquities* **15**: 105–113.

Mills, A.J. 1986. The Dakhleh Oasis Project: report on the 1986/1987 field season. *Journal of the Society for the Study of Egyptian Antiquities* **16**: 65–73.

Mills, A.J. 1987. The Dakhleh Oasis Project: Report on 1987/1988 field season. *Journal of the Society for the Study of Egyptian Antiquities* **17**: 142–150.

Mills, A.J. 1990a. The Dakhleh Oasis Project: Report on the 1988–1989 field season. *Journal of the Society for the Study of Egyptian Antiquities* **20**: 1-6.

Mills, A.J. 1990b. The Dakhleh Oasis Project: Report on the 1989–1990 field season. *Journal of the Society for the Study of Egyptian Antiquities* **20**: 7–10.

Mills, A.J. 1990c. The Dakhleh Oasis Project: Report on the 1990–1991 field season. *Journal of the Society for the Study of Egyptian Antiquities* **20**: 11–16.

Mills, A.J. 1990d. The Dakhleh Oasis Project: Report on the 1991-1992 field season. *Journal of the Society for the Study of Egyptian Antiquities* **20**: 17–23.

Mills, A.J. 1993. The Dakhleh Oasis columbarium farmhouse. *Bulletin de la societé archéologique d'Alexandrie* **45**: 192–198.

Mills, A.J. 1999. 'Dakhleh Oasis, Dynastic and Roman Sites'. *In* Bard, K., ed., *The Archaeology of Ancient Egypt: An Encyclopedia*, London and New York, pp. 220–222.

Mills, A.J. This volume. Introduction, vii–x.

Mills, A.J. This volume. Chapter 10. Pharaonic Egyptians in the Dakhleh Oasis, 171–178.

Molto, J.E. 1986. Dakhleh Oasis Project: Human skeletal remains from the Dakhleh Oasis, Egypt. *Journal of the Society for the Study of Egyptian Antiquities* **16**: 119–127.

Molto, J.E. 1990. The people of ancient Dakhleh: Their story from bones. *Canadian Mediterranean Institute, Bulletin no.* **10**, 1–3.

Nicoll, K., M.R. Kleindienst, H.P. Schwarcz, R. Giegengack and M.F. Wiseman. 1996. New uranium-series ages for Quaternary travertines at Refuf Pass, Kharga Oasis. Abstract. *Egyptian Geological Survey Centennial Meeting, Cairo, Egypt, November 19–22*, 141–142.

Patten, S. 1991. Dakhla Oasis, Ismant el-Kharab. Notes on pottery manufacture in Dakhla Oasis; ancient and modern. *Bulletin de Liaison du Groupe International d'Étude de la Céramique Égyptienne* **15**: 37–40.

Patten, S.F. 1993. Dakhleh Oasis Project, 1992. *Bulletin de Liaison du Groupe International d'Étude de la Céramique Égyptienne* **17**: 37–40.

Patten, S.F. 1994. Dakhleh Oasis Project. *Bulletin de Liaison du Groupe International d'Étude de la Céramique Égyptienne* **18**: 61–67.

Patten, S.F. 1996. Dakhleh Oasis Project, 1994 Season. *Bulletin de Liaison du Groupe International d'Étude de la Céramique Égyptienne* **19**: 51–55.

Ritchie, J.C. 1980. Preliminary observation on the botany of the Dakhleh Oasis. *Journal of the Society for the Study of Egyptian Antiquities* **10**: 379–422.

Ritchie, J.C. 1986. Modern pollen spectra from Dakhleh Oasis, Western Egyptian Desert. *Grana* **25**: 177–182.

Ritchie, J.C. 1993. Imagined and real applications of pollen analysis in reconstructing a Holocene Sahara. *Sahara* **5**: 111–114.

Ritchie, J.C. This volume. Chapter 4. Flora, vegetation and palaeobotany of the Dakhleh Oasis, 73–81.

Ritchie, J.C., C.H. Eyles and C.V. Haynes. 1985. Sediment and pollen evidence for an early to mid-Holocene humid period in the eastern Sahara. *Nature* **314**: 352–355.

Sha'aban, M.M. 1984. Trephination in Ancient Egypt and the report of a new case from Dakhleh Oasis. *Ossa* **9–11**: 135–142.

Sha'aban, M.M. 1988. *Palaeodemography of a pre-Roman population from el-Dakhleh, Egypt: evidence from the skeletal remains at site 31/435–D5–2*. Department of Anthropology, University of Toronto, Ph.D. thesis, 369p.

Sharpe, J.L. 1987. Dakhleh Oasis Project: The Kellis codices. *Journal of the Society for the Study of Egyptian Antiquities* **17**: 192–197.

Sharpe, J.L. 1991. Exciting discoveries in the Egyptian Desert. *Duke University Libraries* **5**: 8–12.

Sharpe, J.L. 1992. The Dakhleh tablets and some chronological considerations. *In* Lalou, E., ed., *Les tablettes* à écrire de l'antiquité à l'époque moderne. *Bibliologia* **12**: 127–148.

Sheldrick, P.G. 1980a. Human remains from the Dakhleh Oasis. *Journal of the Society for the Study of Egyptian Antiquities* **10**: 423–427.

Sheldrick, P.G. 1980b. "Skinny bones" from the Dakhleh Oasis. *Paleopathology Newsletter*, no. 30, 7–10.

Sheldrick, P.G. This volume. Chapter 11. Pathologically slender human long bones from the Dakhleh Oasis, 179–182.

Tangri, D. 1991a. Dakhla Oasis, the Neolithic pottery. *Bulletin de Liaison du Groupe International d'Étude de la Céramique Égyptienne* **15**: 31–36.

Tangri, D. 1991b. Neolithic basket-impressed pottery from Dakhleh

Oasis, Egypt: new evidence for regionalism in the Eastern Sahara. *Sahara* **4**: 141–143.

Tangri, D. 1992. A reassessement of the origins of the Predynastic in Upper Egypt. *Proceedings of the Prehistoric Society* **58**: 111–125.

Wiseman, M.F. 1993. The Dakhleh Oasis during the Terminal Pleistocene: Is anyone home?, 283–285. *In* Jamieson, R.W., S. Abonyi and N.A. Mirau, eds, *Culture and Environment: A fragile coexistence*. Calgary: University of Calgary Archaeological Association, 443p.

Wiseman, M.F. This volume. Chapter 6. Late Pleistoccene prehistory in the Dakhleh Oasis, 109–115.

Worp, K.A. 1997. A new wooden board from the temple at Kellis. Akten des 21. International Papyrologenkongresses in Berlin 1995. *Archiv für Papyrusforschung [Berlin]* **43**: 1014–20.

Worp, K.A., J.E.G. Whitehorne and R.W. Daniel, eds. 1995. *Greek Papyri from Kellis: I*. Dakhleh Oasis Project Monograph 3. Oxford: Oxbow Monograph 54, 281p.

Worp, K.A. and A. Rijksbaron, eds. 1997 *The Isocrates Codex from Kellis*. Dakhleh Oasis Project Monograph 5. Oxford: Oxbow Monograph 88, 292p.

Zielinski, A.K. 1984. Preservation treatment of the decorated tomb of Kitinos in Ezbet Bashendi, Dakhleh Oasis. *Journal of the Society for the Study of Egyptian Antiquities* **14**: 86–87.

Zielinski, A.K. 1986a. Excavation at Dakhleh Oasis, Egypt. *International Council on Monuments and Signs (ICOMOS) Canada, Newsletter* **7**: 10–12.

Zielinski, A.K. 1986b. Conservation at Dakhleh, 203–212. *In Preventative measures during excavation and site protection*. Proceedings of the Conference of the International Centre for the Study of the Preservation and Restoration of Cultural Property (ICCROM), Rijksuniversiteit, Gent: 318p.

Zielinski, A.K. 1989. In-situ conservation of the temple of Amun Nakht, Ayn Birbiyeh, Dakhleh Oasis in Egypt. *Association for Preservation Technology Bulletin* **21**: 49–60.

Zielinski, A.K. This volume. Chapter 12. Conservation, preservation and presentation of monuments and objects in the Dakhleh Oasis, 183–188.

Appendix II

INDEX LIST OF ARCHAEOLOGICAL SITES SURVEYED BY THE DAKHLEH OASIS PROJECT

Collated by C. S. Churcher and A. J. Mills

INTRODUCTION

The reference system for indexing the various archaeological sites within Dakhleh Oasis is explained in by A.J. Mills in 'Dakhleh Oasis Project: Report of the first season of survey, October-December 1978 *(Journal of the Society for the Study of Egyptian Antiquities*, 1979, **9**(4): 167–168) and see Mills (Introduction, this volume). In brief, it is based on the "Egypt 1:25,000" series of maps, which were the best large-scale coverage of the oasis available in 1978. Each of the thirteen map sheets is numbered on a national system, e.g., "33/390", and the project has established an alpha-numeric 1–km grid of 150 squares on each map, e.g., "E10". Finally, each individual archaeological occurrence is serially numbered within its square. A complete location number thus reads, e.g., "33/39–E10–4".

An additional three digit numerical system was developed for computer sorting the Palaeolithic and Neolithic prehistoric localities, both within the mapped regions of Dakhleh Oasis and the areas of the extended palaeoasis. These have are given (in parentheses) after the descriptive note for loci assigned such numbers. For a list of these localities, see Appendix III.

The dating evidence for post-New kingdom sites is currently under revision. It would be premature to include these reassessed site ascriptions here, while omitting others, for lack of complete study. Dr. Colin Hope has drawn attention to the problems of dating this material during the survey years in the *Journal of the Society for the Study of Egyptian Antiquities* **11**: 234.

Sites with multiple cultural occupations may have different descriptions for different recorded phases, represented by the abbreviations noting additional phases under each period or age.

ABBREVIATIONS

The following abbreviations are used within this index:

1IP	First Intermediate Period.
2IP	Second Intermediate Period.
3IP	Third Intermediate Period.
Arc	Archaic (Early Dynastic Period).
Bal	Balat Unit(within ESA).
Bash	Bashendi Cultural Unit.
Byz	Byzantine (Christian).
CSS	Calcareous Silty Sediment.
ESA	Earlier Stone Age (includes Balat Unit).
EAO	Egyptian Antiquities Organization.
FSS	Ferruginous Sandy Sediment.
IFAO	Institut français d'Archéologie orientale.
Indet	Indeterminate.
Isl	Islamic
Late	Late Period.
Loc	Locality.
Mas	Masara Cultural Unit.
MK	Middle Kingdom.
Mod	Modern.
MSA	Middle Stone Age.
Muf	Sheikh Muftah Cultural Unit.
N.N.	Off mapped area, no map location number assigned.
Neo	Neolithic
NK	New Kingdom.
OK	Old Kingdom.
P1	Alluvial fan gravels resting on oldest pediment surface.
P2	Alluvial fan gravels resting on second-oldest pediment surface.

'Reports from the Survey of Dakhleh Oasis, Western Desert of Egypt, 1977–1987', edited by *C.S. Churcher and A.J. Mills. Dakhleh Oasis Project: Monograph 2. Oxbow Monograph 99.*

P3		Alluvial fan gravels resting on youngest pediment surface.
Pet		Petroglyph site.
PSA		Pleistocene Stone Age.
Ptol		Ptolemaic.
Rom		Roman.
Subloc		Sublocality.
Unc		Uncertain historical date.
+		indicates additional cultural units within the site location.

PLEISTOCENE (c.400,000 – -12,000 BP)

General

30/435–M2–1	Artifacts	CSS sediments with Pleistocene fauna, some artifacts. (348) +Rom +Byz.
30/435–M2–6	Handaxe	Acheulean, together with sherds and fresh lithics. (355) +Rom +Byz.
30/435–M5–1	Artifacts	A few artifacts on CSS remnants. (349)
30/435–P3–1	Flakes	Surface of CSS outcrop; Pleistocene faunal bone. (350)
30/435–P3–2	Artifacts	Surface & *in situ* finds of artifacts and fossil bone in basal CSS. (351)
30/450–A4–2	Artifacts	Various pieces from eroded CSS. (352)
30/450–B & C2–4	Bone & Lithics	Surface of CSS; mixed with Holocene bone. Spread over 6 squares. (356) +Neo +OK +Rom
30/450–B4–3	Fauna	Mixed Pleistocene fauna on & in CSS, Camelthorn Basin. (357)
30/450–C5–1	Artifacts	Flint scatter on CSS bench; ?MSA indet. (211)
30/450–D2–1	Artifacts	3 Flints on P2 gravels; ?MSA indet. (213)
30/450–D3–1	Artifacts	Sparse scatter on P2 & P3 gravels, el-Akoulah Basin; PSA indet. (360)
31/405–B6–1	Industry	Workshop on ferruginous quartzite (ironstone) outcrop; ?ESA. (223)
31/420–F7–2 (F9–4, 1997)	Artifacts & Fauna	Scarce artifacts *in situ* with bones in CSS; PSA. (362)
31/420–F9–4	Artifact	Core *in situ* in CSS; PSA indet.
31/420–H6–3	Artifacts	Flint scatters on 2 spring terraces (FSS); PSA indet. (155) +ESA +Bal/+ESA +MSA.
31/420–I5–1	Artifacts	Scatter atop CSS. Some flakes *in situ*. (353) +ESA.
31/420–L10–1	Artifacts	2 Indet Flakes, *in situ*, CSS terrace deposit. (151) +MSA on surface.
31/435–M2–1	Industry	Workshop, flaked geodes or 'chert balls'; ?ESA/MSA. (128)
31/450–var.	Artifacts	General collection, PSA var – Recent; Wadi el-Battikh. (290) +Rom.
32/390–I3–1	Artifacts	Flake & small biface scatter on rejuvenated spring mound conduits & eroded surface; ?MSA indet. (162)
32/450–var.	Artifacts	General collection, PSA var – Recent; Wadi el-Battikh. (290) +Rom.
33/390–I9–6	Artifacts	Flake scatter, various raw materials, on eroded spring mounds; ESA/MSA indet. (209)
N.N.	Industry	Workshop, 8 large quartzite flakes. (249) +?MSA +Neo.

N.N.	Raw Material	Surface scatter on inverted wadi, desert SE of Teneida. (285)
N.N.	Occupation	Surface scatter on P1 terrace, 700 × 100 m; ?late MSA/PSA indet. (287)
N.N.	Artifacts	Surface scatter on P2/P3 terrace, 60 × 100 m, Wadi el-Battikh; late PSA/PSA indet (or early Masara Unit). (288)

Earlier Stone Age (includes Balat Unit) (c.400,000 – 250,000 BP)

29/420–C1–1	Artifacts	Cores, flakes, scattered over several km² along SST rim. (337) +MSA.
29/420–C1–2	Artifacts	Bifaces, cores, flakes; several km² scatter. (338) +MSA.
30/420–C4–3	Artifacts	Tools, flakes, cores in basin & on sandstone. (340) +MSA.
30/420–D5–1	Artifacts	20 m² Scatter of cores, flakes & hammerstones in chert and chert-ball matrix. (289) +MSA.
30/450–D4–3	Artifacts	Scatter on P2 gravels, 500 m W of 361, el-Akoulah Basin. (366) +MSA.
31/405–B6–1	Industry	Workshop on ferruginous quartzite. (223)
31/405–D7–3	Artifacts	Flint scatter on breached spring mound, above 31/405–D7–1 & 2; ESA, ?Upper Acheulian. (007) +?Bal/ESA +MSA +Neo +Rom.
31/405–E8–2	Artifacts	Biface scatter on spring mound. (367) +Rom.
31/405–L10–3	Artifact	Biface on cemetery hill. (055) +Rom +Byz.
31/420–Var.	Artifacts	Isolated finds in general area. (327) +MSA.
31/420–E5–1	Artifacts	Biface & flake *in situ* on P2 gravels. (084)
31/420–F10–3	Artifacts	Balat-type biface *in situ* in FSS; hammerstone, flake. (323)
31/420–G7–4	Artifacts	Flint scatter. (236) +MSA +Neo.
31/420–H6–2	Artifacts	9 Bifaces & flakes between spring mounds, 20 m²; Balat Unit. (091) +Bal/ESA.
31/420–H6–3	Artifacts	2 Flint scatters on spring mound; Balat Unit. (155) +PSA indet +MSA.
31/420–I1–1	Artifact	Biface on P2 gravels. (216) +MSA.
31/420–I3–1	Artifacts	Flint scatter, mint, on spring mounds & P2 gravels. (193) +MSA.
31/420–I4–1	Artifacts	Surface finds, including 1 Levallois point, on CSS. (322) +MSA.
31/420–I5–1	Artifacts	Flakes *in situ* & scatter, on CSS. (353) +PSA.
31/420–I5–2	Artifacts	Biface scatter on sandstone; Balat Unit. (359)
31/420–K1–1	Artifacts	Biface scatter on P2 & P3 gravels. (217) +MSA.
31/420–L3–1	Artifacts	Biface scatter on sandstone ridge; Balat Unit. (081) +Bal/ESA.
31/420–L9–2	Artifacts	Flakes & biface on spring mound. (150)
31/420–L9–3	Artifacts	Cores & flake scatter on 2 spring mounds. (191) +MSA.
31/420–N4–1 & N4–2	Artifacts	Flints from spring mound conduits; Balat Unit. (147) +MSA. [Excavated by Schild & Wendorf.]
31/420–N4–3	Artifacts	Flint scatter on P2 gravels & talus; Balat Unit. (147) +Bal/ESA +MSA.
31/450–var.	Artifacts	General collection, PSA var – Recent; Wadi el-Battikh. (290) +Rom.

32/390–L1–1	Artifacts	Biface scatter around spring mound. (001) +MSA +Neo +Unc.
32/420–E8–1	Artifacts	Flint scatter on P2 gravels. (156) +MSA.
32/420–E8–2	Artifacts	Biface scatter on P1 gravels. (157) +MSA.
32/420–L6–1 Sublocs A-E	Artifacts	Biface scatter on P2 gravels; Upper 'Acheulian' & Balat Unit. (187) +Bal/ESA +MSA +Mas.
32/420–L7–1	Artifacts	Levallois chert flaking material. (188) +MSA.
32/435–K10–1 & L10–1 & 2	Artifacts	Biface scatter on P3 or younger gravels. (161; cf. 124) +MSA. (Same locus as Pet 32/435–L10–1 & Neo 32/435–L10–2; 124.)
32/435–M5–1	Artifacts	Biface scatter, flint & limestone, on P2 gravels; Upper Acheulian type. (159)
32/435–N9–1	Artifacts	Scattered cores, flakes, tools on basin floor. (296) +MSA.
32/450–var.	Artifacts	General collection, PSA var – Recent; Wadi el-Battikh. (290) +Rom.
33/390–I9–1	Artifacts	Biface scatter, quartzite, on spring mound surface; Upper 'Acheulian' type. (002) +MSA +Neo +Bash.
33/390–I9–5	Artifact	Biface, small, cordiform, on spring mound. (208)
33/390–N2–1	Artifacts	Biface scatter on P2 gravels. (199) +MSA.
33/405–A2–1	Artifacts	Biface scatter on P3 gravel lag. (198) +MSA.
33/450–Var.	Artifacts	Isolated finds in wadi drainage. (312) +MSA.
33/450–H7–1	Artifact	Isolated Acheulian biface. (340)
33/450–H8–1	Artifact	Biface on limestone, East Rim, North Wadi. (240)

Middle Stone Age (c.250,000 – 38,000 BP)

29/420–A1–1	Artifacts	Cores, flakes, tools; Aterian & Khargan; scattered over several km². (335)
29/450–var.	Artifacts	Isolated Dakhleh Unit finds in various squares in the **29–30/450** map sheets. (341)
29/420–A1–2	Artifacts	Cores, flakes, tools scattered over several km². (336)
29/450–G3–2	Occupation	15 Hut Circles, Masara C, Kharga Road. (265)
29/450–G3–4	Occupation	Hearths & bone, Masara C, Kharga Road. (308)
29/450–G3–6	Occupation	Workshop, Masara C, Kharga Road. (300)
29/450–H4–2	Occupation	8 Hut circles, chipped stone in varied raw materials, grinding slab, ostrich egg shell & bone, Masara Unit C, Kharga Road. (309)
30/405–I2–2	Artifacts	Flint scatter, small. (043)
30/405–I2–3	Artifacts	Flint scatter, extensive. (051) +Isl.
30/405–L1–1	Artifacts	Flint scatter on hilltop. (057) +OK +Pet.
30/405–L1–3	Artifacts	Flint scatter on spring mound. (054) +Unc.
30/405–M1–2	Artifacts	Flint scatter, sparse, on sand. (060)
30/420–var.	Artifacts	Isolated finds in Sheikh Muftah Valley area. (327) +ESA.
30/420–A8–1	Artifacts	Chert flakes and ?cores & flakes in quartzite and chalcedony. (319) +Neo.
30/420–B9–1	Artifacts	Flakes & cores scattered in lag on sandstone. (291)

30/420–B9–2	Artifacts	Chert & chalcedony flakes and core on sandstone bench. (292)
30/420–C4–3	Artifacts	Tools, flakes, cores scattered on basin & sandstone rim. (340) +ESA.
30/420–D1–2	Artifacts	Extensive scatter (into **E2**) of ?Aterian materials. (331)
30/420–D2–3	Artifacts	Flakes & cores in chert and quartzite. (293)
30/420–D2–4	Artifacts	?Khargan tools, flakes & cores; Sheikh Mabruk Unit. (332)
30/420–D3–3	Artifacts	Late MSA (Khargan) cores, flakes & tools. (339)
30/420–D5–1	Artifacts	20m² Scatter of cores, flakes & hammerstones in chert. (289) +ESA.
30/420–E1–1	Artifacts	2 Flint scatters on FSS. (203A & B)
30/420–E1–2	Occupation	Scatter, 200 × 200 m (into **F1**), of tanged pieces, cores, flakes & tools; Aterian. (325)
30/420–E1–3	Occupation	Discrete cluster of Aterian and Khargan on FSS terrace surface, spreading into **F1**. (328)
30/420–E1–4	Artifacts	Scatter on sandstone & FSS rim of cores, flakes & tools(?Khargan), spreading into **F2**. (329)
30/420–E2–1	Artifacts	Flint scatter below spring terrace remnants. (214)
30/420–E2–2	Artifacts	Flint scatter between spring terrace remnants. (215)
30/420–E2–4	Artifacts	Concentration of ?Aterian materials. (330)
30/420–L1–1 (31/420–L10–1, 1998)	Artifacts	Flint scatter on & below CSS bench. (151) +PSA indet.
30/420–L1–2 (31/420–M10–1, 1998)	Artifacts	Cores & flakes on eroded spring mound. (153)
30/435–F6–1	Artifacts	Flint scatter at foot of hill. (096) +Muf.
30/435–J5–1	Artifacts	Flint scatter, including tanged 'Aterian' point. (094) +Muf.
30/435–J5–2	Artifacts	Flint scatter around base of hill. (095) +Muf +OK +Pet.
30/435–L2–2	Artifacts	Surface scatter of small MSA tools, cores, scrapers. (346)
30/435–L3–1	Artifacts	Flint scatter, abraded artifacts. (120) +Neo.
30/435–M2–2	Artifacts	Flint scatter on wadi floor, 3,000 m². (121)
30/435–M2–4	Artifacts	Flint scatter on sandstone ridge; '?Aterian'. (130)
30/435–M2–6	Artifacts	Fresh lithics on CSS knoll; Acheulean handaxe. (355) +Rom +Byz.
30/435–M3–1	Artifacts	Small cores, flakes, & retouched tools in surface scatter. (345)
30/435–P6–1	Raw Materials	'Chert balls' *in situ* in upper Mut Fm shales; Holocene usage. (347)
30/450-var.	Artifacts	Isolated Dakhleh Unit finds in various squares in the **29–30/450** map sheets (341)
30/450–A9–1	Artifacts	Scatter ca. 1 km diam. of hearths and Bashendi 'A' artifacts eroding from silts. (228) +Bash.
30/450–C5–1	Artifacts	Scattered flakes & cores; in ferruginous sandstone, chert & limestone. (211)
30/450–D4–1	Artifacts	Large artifacts. (361)
30/450–D4–3	Artifacts	Scatter on P2 gravels, 500 m W of 361, el-Akoulah Basin. (366)
30/450–D2–1	Artifacts	3 Isolated pieces on pediment gravels; 1 scraper on Levallois point. (213)
30/450–L3–1	Artifacts	Individual pieces on P2 remnant. Levallois cores, flakes & tools. (286)

31/405–D7–3	Artifacts	Flint scatter on breached spring mound. (007) Above 31/405–D7–1 & D7–2. +ESA +?Bal/ESA +Neo +Rom.
31/405–F9–6	Artifacts	Flint scatter on spring mound, 50 x 100 m. (040)
31/405–K1–1	Artifacts	10 Flint pieces clustered on gravel terrace. (029)
31/405–K10–6	Artifacts	Flint scatter near spring mound, 30 m². (050) +1 Neo sherd.
31/405–L1–1	Artifacts	Flint scatter on gravel terrace 2 km long, 9 pieces in general collection. (030)
31/405–L10–5	Occupation	Artifact scatter. (053) +Muf.
31/405–L10–6	Occupation	Flint scatter, mixed. (056) +Neo.
31/405–M1–1	Artifacts	Sparse flint scatter on Qusseir (= Mut) Fm Shale. (234)
31/405–M2–1	Artifacts	Flint scatter, mint, & Levallois core *in situ*, in P3 gravels. (233)
31/405–M3–2	Artifacts	Flint scatter on gravel & hill, 500–600 m². (034) (Associated with cemetery 31/405–M3–1) +Rom +Byz.
31/405–M4–2	Artifacts	Flint scatter on wadi or P3gravels, 1 km². (031) +Neo.
31/405–N1–1	Artifacts	Flint scatter on wadi fan or dissected P3 gravels, 3 km². (033)
31/420–var	Artifacts	Isolated finds in Sheikh Muftah Valley area. (327) +ESA.
31/420–A5–1	Artifacts	Flint scatter, sparse, disturbed. (058)
31/420–E2–3	Artifacts	Scatter of small sized artifacts on or below FSS. (326)
31/420–E10–3	Artifacts	Flakes, mint, *in situ*, in spring mound conduit sediments; also surface finds. (146)
31/420–F8–1	Artifacts	MSA specialized flake in FSS, with Neo surface scatter. (354) +Neo.
31/420–F10–1	Artifacts	Sparse flint scatter below spring terrace. (067)
31/420–F10–4	Artifacts	Scatter of small sized artifacts, 100 × 50 m. (324)
31/420–G7–4	Artifacts	Flint scatter below spring terrace. (236) +ESA +Neo.
31/420–H6–1	Artifacts	Flint scatters, in 0.5 km long depression between spring mounds. (090)
31/420–H6–3	Artifacts	2 Flint scatters, on spring mound & spring terrace (FSS), core *in situ*. (155) +PSA indet +ESA +Bal/ESA.
31/420–I1–1	Industry	Flint scatter & workshops, & 'Aterian' tanged artifacts, on P2 gravels. Systematic collection area. (216) +ESA.
31/420–I1–2	Artifacts	Workshop: Levallois & blade cores, flakes, on terrace remnant. (342)
31/420–I2–1	Artifacts	Flint scatter on P3 gravels. (230)
31/420–I3–1	Artifacts	Cores & flakes, some fresh, on spring mound & P2 gravels. (193) +ESA.
31/420–I4–1 (H6–4, 1998)	Artifacts	Surface finds on northernmost CSS; 1 Levallois point. (322) +ESA.
31/420–I6–2	Artifacts	Cores & flakes on spring mound. (160)
31/420–J2–1 & J3–1	Artifacts	Cores & flakes on P3 gravels; 1 tanged piece. (231)
31/420–K1–1	Artifacts	Cores & flakes on P2 & P3 gravels. (217) +ESA.
31/420–L1–1	Artifacts	Flint scatter, ?'Aterian', on sandstone ridge. (082)
31/420–L3–2	Artifacts	Surface collection on sandstone ridge. (280)
31/420–L6–1	Artifacts	Flint scatter on spring mound. (154) +Isl.
31/420–L9–1	Artifacts	Core *in situ* in spring mound deposit & surface finds. (149)
31/420–L9–3 (L9–4, 1998)	Artifacts	Flint scatter on spring mound. (192)
31/420–M5–1	Artifacts	Mixed finds on SST scattered across squares **M5, 6 & 7**; Bifaces, cores, flakes, tangs. (344)
31/420–M7–2	Artifacts	Blowout scatter on CSS buttes, Sheikh Mabruk Unit. (367)
31/420–M9–3 (L9–3, 1998)	Artifacts	Cores & flakes on spring mound. (191) +ESA.
31/420–M10–1 (M9–1, 1998)	Artifacts	Cores & flakes on 2 spring mounds; 1 core *in situ*. (152)
31/420–N2–1	Artifacts	Flint scatter on trenched spring mound. (080) +Unc.
31/420–N4–1 & N4–2	Artifacts	Flint scatter on P3 gravels. (147) +ESA +Bal/ESA. [Schild & Wendorf]
31/420–N4–3	Artifacts	Flint scatter on P2 gravels & talus. (147) +ESA +Bal/ESA.
31/420–P5–2	Artifacts	Flint scatter on P3 gravel lag. (148)
31/435–A1–1	Artifacts	Flint scatter on P3 gravels around spring mound. (079)
31/435–J & K1–2 (J1–2, 1998)	Artifacts	Sparse scatter over wide sandstone (281)
31/435–K1–2	Artifacts	Surface scatter on gravel-capped knolls. (282)
31/450–B6–1	Artifacts	Flint scatter on P1 gravels. (158)
32/390–I3–1	Artifact	Core from eroded spring deposit. (162) +PSA indet.
32/390–L1–1	Artifacts	Flint scatter on deflated spring mound. (001) +ESA +Neo +Unc.
32/405–A7–3	Artifacts	3 Artifact clusters, dense piles, (assembled for construction uses, indicating reuse in historic times). (032) +?Mod.
32/405–C3–1	Artifacts	Flint scatter at base of Libyan Escarpment, 4 × 1 km. (023)
32/405–D6–1	Artifacts	Flint scatter on & around sandstone hill, 800 m². (026)
32/405–P9–1	Artifacts	Flint scatter on wadi fan gravels. (232)
32/420–D8–1	Artifacts	Flint scatter on P2 gravels. (202)
32/420–E8–1	Artifacts	Flint scatter on P2 gravels. (156) +ESA.
32/420–E8–2	Artifacts	Core & flake scatter on P1 gravels. (157) +ESA.
32/420–K4–1	Artifacts	Scattered cores & flakes on colluvium. (343)
32/420–L5–1	Artifacts	Cores, flakes & tools scattered on base of colluvium. (334)
32/420–L6–1 Sublocs A-E	Artifacts/ Industry	Artifact scatter, diffuse, & workshops, on P2 gravels. Systematic collection area. (187) +ESA +Bal/ESA +Mas.
32/420–L6–2 & L7–2: Sublocs A & B	Artifacts	Flint scatter on P3 gravels. (189)
32/420–L7–1 Sublocs A & B	Artifacts	Flint scatter & clusters on P1 gravels. Systematic collection area. (188) +ESA
32/420–L7–3 Sublocs A & B	Artifacts	Flint scatter on Duwi Fm bench & P3 gravel lag. (190)
32/420–P6–1	Artifacts	Aterian cores, flakes & tanged points, on P3 gravels. (333)
32/435–I3–1	Workshop	Cores & flakes scattered on steep colluvium slope. (317)
32/435–I4–1	Artifacts	Scatter of workshop materials on 6 P2 remnants; spreading into square **I5–1**. (316 & 316E)

32/435–I5–1	Artifacts	Scattered workshop debitage – chert cores & flakes. (315)
32/435–J6–1	Industry	Workshops on P2 gravels. (201)
32/435–J6–2	Workshop	Cores, flakes & tools atop high hill. (318)
32/435–J6–3	Artifacts	Scatter in derived gravels, some Aterian. (321)
32/435–K5–1	Artifacts	Sparse scatter of fresh material on alluvial gravel. (319)
32/435–K10–1 & L10–1	Artifacts	Flint scatter, incl. 'Aterian' tanged points, on P3 or younger gravels. (161) +ESA. Area includes Pet 32/435–L10–1 and Neo 32/435–L10–2. (124)
32/435–L9–1	Artifacts	2 Clusters of cores, flakes, tanged tools. (294)
32/435–L9–2	Artifacts	Scattered cores, flakes, tools in lag on SST. (295) +Mas.
32/435–L9–3	Artifacts	Bifoliate scatter in small sandstone depression, W of 295. (364)
32/435–L10–2	Artifacts	Flint scatter at base of sandstone hills, 32/435–L10–1. (363) +Bash +OK +Pet.
32/435–M9–1	Artifacts	Surface veneer on sandstone, Aterian. (283)
32/435–P8–1	Artifacts	Large cores and points on P3 gravel ridge, 400 × 4 m. (310)
32/435–P9–1	Artifacts	Sparse scatter on P3 terrace, Dakhleh Unit. (299) +Isl.
32/450–var.	Artifacts	Flint scatters, Wadi el-Tawil. (204)
32/450–A6–1	Artifacts	Scattered workshop materials on P3 terrace. (311)
33/360–K10–1	Artifacts	Sparse concentration of flakes & debitage. (320)
33/390–B7–1	Artifacts	Discontinuous, in pockets on limestone bedrock. (003)
33/390–F5–1	Artifacts	4 Artifact concentrations on spur near foot of Libyan Escarpment. (004)
33/390–I9–1/2	Occupation	Artfact scatter & debris, 1 km². (002) +ESA +Bash +Neo.
33/390–I9–6	Artifacts	Raw materials & flakes. (209)
33/390–N2–1	Artifacts	Core & flake scatter on P2 gravels. (199) +ESA.
33/405–A2–1	Artifacts	Cores & flakes on Duwi Fm bench, & on P3 gravels &/or P3 gravel lag. (198) +ESA.
33/405–B5–1	Artifacts	Flint scatter, diffuse, on ?wadi &/or P3 gravel terrace below Libyan Escarpment. (005)
33/450–Var.	Artifacts	Isolated finds in wadi drainage. (312) +ESA.
33/450–C10–1	Artifacts	Flint scatter on P3 lag gravels, Lower Dakhla Fm shale. (237)
33/450–D9–1	Artifacts	Flint scatter on P3 gravel fan. (238)
33/450–D9–2	Industry	Work stations, & cores & flakes, on P2 bench. (239)
33/450–E10–1	Workshop	Cores, flakes on P2 terrace. (313)

The following sites, designated 'N.N.', are located in the desert South or Southeast of Grid Locality 30/450–A9–1 (228)

N.N.	Occupation	Core, flake & tool scatter; ironstone, quartzite & chert, & 1 'Aterian' tanged point, at SE base of small hill. (225)
N.N.	Artifacts	Core, flake & tool scatters, 2 concentrations, chert, quartzite & ironstone. (245)
N.N.	Industry	Workshop, quartzite. (246)
N.N.	Artifacts	Ironstone flakes on abraded hilltop. (247)
N.N.	Artifacts	Ironstone flake-blades on hilltop. (248)
N.N.	Occupation	Flint & ground stone scatter. (249) +PSA +Neo.
N.N.	Artifact	'Aterian' tanged point, isolated. (255)
N.N.	Occupation	Small surface scatter. (284)
N.N.	Occupation	Surface scatter on P1 terrace, 700 × 100 m. (287) +PSA indet.

HOLOCENE

Epipalaeolithic (Masara A & B) (c.9,200 – 8,500 BP)

29/450–D3–1	Occupation	Sparse flint scatter by dry pan. (242)
29/450–D4–1	Occupation	Sparse flint scatter & 2 hearths. (243)
29/450–F3–1	Occupation	700 m² Scatter of blade tools & grinders; hut circles. (263)
29/450–F4–1	Occupation	Scattered material around hut circles & hearths. (261) +Bash.
29/450–G3–1	Occupation	Cluster of ± 20 hut circles; & lithics. (264)
29/450–G3–3	Occupation	Artifact scatter amongst hut circles; knapping areas. (268)
29/450–G4–1	Occupation	Stone oval 36 × 48 m with scatter of material. (267)
29/450–H3–1	Occupation	Lithic scatter at base of Winkler's rock art Site 62. (262)
29/450–H4–1	Occupation	13 Hut circles with scattered lithics. (260)
30/405–N3–1	Occupation	Artifact scatter. (224)
30/420–B3–1	Occupation	Flint clusters in basin, 320,000 m². (226)
30/420–B3–2	Occupation	Flint scatter in basin, 15,000 m². (227)
30/420–C1–1	Occupation	Artifact clusters in basin. (075)
30/420–C4–1	Industry	Quartzite knapping floors. (207)
30/420–C4–2	Occupation	Flint scatters in basin, 40,000 m². (218)
30/420–C5–1	Occupation	Artifact scatter on playa margin. (200)
30/420–C7–1	Occupation	Artifact scatter in basin, 600 m². (206)
30/420–D1–1	Occupation	Artifact scatter in basin, 8,400 m². (194)
30/420–D2–2	Occupation	Artifact scatter on Libyan scarp. (196) +Bash.
30/420–D3–2	Occupation	Artifact clusters in basin, 60,000 m². (195) +Bash.
30/420–D4–1	Occupation	2 Artifact scatters in basin. (205)
30/420–D7–1	Occupation	Artifact scatter in basin. Blades; no burins, Masara 'A'. (259)
30/435–P8–2	Occupation	650 m² Scatter with chert knapping, quartz & geometrics. (274)
30/450–H8–1	Occupation	Mixed scatter of hammerstones, grinders, chipped stone & sherds. (266) +Bash.
31/420–G4–1	Industry	Knapping floor in hill area, 12,000 m². (083)
31/420–F8–1	Occupation	Surface scatter of artifacts on FSS cap. (354) +MSA.
31/420–H10–1	Occupation	Artifact scatter, 1,400 m². (085)
31/420–H10–2	Occupation	Artifact scatters on Libyan scarp. (186) +Bash.
31/435–B4–3	Occupation	Artifact scatter on oval mound, 27,500 m². (098) +Neo +OK +Rom.
32/420–L6–1	Industry	Flint scatter, fresh blade cores & removals, rare isolated work stations, on P2 gravels. (187B) +ESA +Bal/ESA +MSA.
32/435–L9–2	Artifacts	Scattered lithic materials in sandstone lag. (295) +MSA.

33/435–C6–1	Hunting Stations	Arrowheads, blades, etc., on plateau. (163)
33/435–C6–3 & C7–3	Occupation	Chipped and ground stone in playa muds; knapping; Libyan Plateau. (166)
N.N.	Occupation	Clusters of chipped stone, grinding slabs & handstones; area 500 m diameter, Libyan Plateau, above Maohoub; probably Masara 'A'. (076)
N.N.	Occupation	Flint scatter, dense, on playa edge, Libyan Plateau. (140) +Bash.
N.N.	Artifacts	Surface scatter on P2/P3 terrace, 60 × 100 m, ?early Masara Unit. (288) +Late PSA/PSA indet.

General Neolithic (c.7,800 – 4,000 BP)

29/420–C2–1	Artifacts	Rough bifaces, desert far SW of Sheikh Muftah. (305)
30/420–A8–1	Occupation	Hut circles atop small sandstone hill. (314) +MSA.
30/435–L3–1	Occupation	Artifact cluster within wider scatter, including MSA, all worn. (120) +MSA.
30/435–M2–3	Occupation	Sherd scatter, heavy mauls, & 2 hearths, 700 m². (123). +Rom.
30/435–M2–5	Occupation	Flint, sherd & heavy maul scatter, mixed. (131) +Rom.
30/435–P2–1	Occupation	Flint & sherd clusters, heavy mauls, & hearth, mixed. (132) +OK +Rom.
30/435–P8–1	Structure	5.4 × 3.35 m structure of stone slabs, standing to 0.70 m. No associated artifacts, but Masara site nearby (P8–2; 274). (273)
30/435–P10–2	Occupation	Dense scatter over 40,000 m² of hearths, chipped stone, ground stone & pottery. (276)
30/450–B2–1	Bone	Animal bone from Holocene brown silts, mixed with CSS-derived bone & lithics. Spread over squares **B** and **C2,3, & 4**. (356) +PSA.
30/450–B3–1	Occupation	Concentration of ceramics, grinders & chipped stone. (134)
30/450–B3–2	Occupation	60 m² Scatter of bone, grinders, chipped stone & ceramics. (136)
30/450–B4–1	Occupation	Scatter over 1 km² of pottery, chipped stone & bone. (135)
30/450–B4–4	Fauna	Bones in pan sediments. (358)
31/405–D7–3	Occupation	Flint scatter & Roman sherds. (007) +ESA +?Bal/ESA +MSA +Rom.
31/405–H6–1	Occupation	Artifact scatter on spring mounds. (065) +OK +Rom.
31/405–K10–5	Occupation	Artifact scatter & knapping areas. (048) +OK.
31/405–K10–9	Occupation	Artifact scatter. (049)
31/405–L10–6	Occupation	Flint scatter, mixed. (056) +MSA.
31/405–M4–2	Occupation	Artifact scatter, 1 km². (031) +MSA.
31/405–P8–1	Occupation	Flint scatter on Islamic brick ruin. (061) +Isl.
31/420–G7–4	Occupation	Flint scatter. (236) +ESA +MSA.
31/435–B4–2	Occupation	Artifact scatter on 2 spring mounds. (097) +OK +Rom.
31/435–B4–3	Occupation	Artifact scatter on oval mound, 27,500 m². (098) +Mas +OK +Rom.
31/435–D1–1	Occupation	Flint and ground stone scattered over disturbed area. (078)
31/435–J1–2	Workshop	Small flakes & hammerstones on quartzite surface; quarry. (279)
32/390–H5–2	Occupation	Artifact scatter around 32/390–H5–1. (013)

32/390–J3–1	Cemetery	300 Graves, mixed & plundered, on large hill; flexed burials in oval pits. +OK +Rom.
32/390–L1–1	Occupation	Flint scatter, 1 km², concentration in NW corner. (001) +ESA +MSA +Unc.
32/390–P5–1	Occupation	Flint & pottery scatter, 35,000 m². (020) +OK +Rom.
32/405–A1–1	Occupation	Flints, in brick building. (024) +Byz.
32/405–A2–1	Occupation	Flints, from temple site. (027) +Late +Ptol +Rom +Byz.
32/405–A2–2	Artifact	Flint flake, in brick building. (025) +Rom +Byz.
32/405–A7–1	Ground Axe	Found within church. (041) +ROM
32/435–M10–2	Artifacts	Scattered materials on basin floor. (297) +MSA.
32/435–N10–1	Artifacts	Scattered materials on P3 terrace. (298) +MSA.
33/360–K10–2	Settlement	12 Stone hut circles; chipped & ground stone. (301)
33/390–H5–1	Industry	Sherds, lithics, ash on low mound. (016) +Neo.
33/390–H8–1	Occupation	Extensive Islamic village with some lithics. (019) +Rom +Isl.
33/390–H9–1	Occupation	Artifact clusters on playa & spring mound. (008)
33/390–I4–1	Occupation	Artifact scatter on 2 mounds. (009) +OK.
33/390–I5–1	Occupation	Sherd & flint scatter, 50 × 30 m; stone walls. (010) +OK.
33/390–I6–2	Occupation	Sherd & flint scatter on 4 mounds. (011) +Muf +OK.
33/390–I8–2	Cemetery	Flexed burials in stone-lined graves; area deflating, 175 × 50 m.
33/390–I9–1/2	Occupation	Artifact scatter & debris, 1 km². (002) +ESA +MSA +Bash.
33/435–C7–2	Occupation	Flint scatter on playa terrace, Libyan Plateau. (164)
N.N.	Cave	Sparse lithics from within cave. Libyan Plateau, above Aweina. (044)
N.N.	Occupation	Chipped stone scatter, Libyan Plateau, above Aweina. (045)
N.N.	Occupation	Chipped stone scatter, N of and denser than 045, Libyan Plateau, above Aweina. (046)
N.N.	Occupation	Flint & ground stone scatter. (249) +PSA +MSA.
N.N.	Occupation	Artifact scatter. (251)

Bashendi Neolithic (c.7,500 – 5,500 BP)

29/420–C2–1	Artifacts	Desert far SW Sheikh Muftah. (305)
29/450–F1–1	Occupation	40 × 80 m Oval and 2 hut circles. (269)
29/450–F4–1	Occupation	Scattered materials around hut circles and hearths. (261) +Mas.
30/420–D2–2	Occupation	Flint scatter on Libyan scarp. (196) +Mas.
30/420–D3–2	Occupation	Flint clusters in basin, 60,000 m². (195) +Mas.
30/420–E3–1	Occupation	Flint scatters, 15,000 m². (197)
30/435–M9–1	Occupation	Flint & pottery scatter, sparse, & hearths. (253)
30/435–N9–1	Occupation	Artifact & pottery scatter, sparse, & hearths. (252)
30/435–P9–1	Occupation	250 m² Mound at N edge of 30/450–G8–2 basin. *In situ* ash, bone, flints. (271)
30/435–P10–1	Occupation	Dense scatter of hearths and chipped stone, beads & ceramics over 30,000 m². (275)

30/450–A4–1	Occupation	Flint scatter at base of hill, 440 m². (137)
30/450–A7–1	Hut Circle	On ridge north of 228. (277) +later Neo.
30/450–A9–1	Occupation	1 km diam scatter of hearths & artifacts, eroding from basin silts. (228) +MSA.
30/450–B8–1	Occupation	Thin, small scatter of chert. (272)
30/450–B10–1	Occupation	Flint, pottery, etc., scatter & hearth mounds. (254)
30/450–C6–1	Occupation	Flint & pottery scatter, & hearths, 180,000 m². (212)
30/240–D8–1	Occupation	Scatter, N of Trig Point Hill 180; Bashendi B. (303)
30/450–D9–1	Occupation	Scatter, N of trig Point Hill 180; Bashendi B. (304)
30/450–E4–2	Occupation	Scatter of chipped stone. (257)
30/450–E5–1	Occupation	Surface scatter of lithic & ceramic materials. (258)
30/450–E7–1	Occupation	Ironstone scatter, sparse, 550 m². (183)
30/450–F7–1	Occupation	Arrowhead scatter, 315 m². (176)
30/450–F7–2	Industry	Bead manufactory, 1,700 m². (179)
30/450–F7–3	Occupation	Artifact scatter & hearths, 90 m². (181)
30/450–F7–4	Occupation	Hearths with artifacts, 3 m². (182)
30/450–F7–5	Occupation	Artifact scatter & hearths, 2,700 m². (184)
30/450–F8–1	Occupation	Artifact scatter & hearths, 11,250 m². (172)
30/450–F8–2	Occupation	Artifact scatter in basin, 700 m². (173)
30/450–F8–3	Occupation	Flint, stone & other artifact clusters around hearths, 4,320 m². (174)
30/450–F8–4	Occupation	Material scatter, sparse, 700 m². (177)
30/450–F8–5	Occupation	Artifact scatter & hearths, 325 m². (178)
30/450–F8–6	Occupation	Artifact scatter on hillslope. (210) +OK +Pet.
30/450–F9–1	Occupations	Artifact scatters & hut circles on hilltop. (180) +OK.
30/450–F10–2	Occupation	150+ Hut circles; flakes, sherds & grindstones; on outcrop. (270)
30/450–F10–3	Occupation	Surface scatter on interfluve around 270. (278)
30/450–F10–4	Occupation	Structures & grindstones, E of 270; Late Bashendi A. (306)
30/450–F10–5	Occupation	Structures & pottery, SW of 270; Late Bashendi A. (307)
30/450–G8–1	Occupation	Flint & sherd scatter, 1,500 m². (175)
31/420–C10–2	Occupation	Flint & pottery scatter, 1,500 m². (074)
31/420–F9–1	Occupation	3 Artifact clusters, mixed. (070) +Muf.
31/420–G8–1	Occupation	Artifact scatter, 15,000 m². (086)
31/420–H7–2	Occupations	Flint clusters, 300 m long. (088) +Muf.
31/420–H10–2	Occupation	Artifact scatter over Libyan scarp. (186) +Mas.
31/420–M9–2	Occupation	Artifact concentration & hearths, 1,200 m². (104)
31/420–P5–1	Occupation	Artifact scatter & hearths. (101)
31/435–A6–3	Occupation	Flint & sherd, etc. scatter on gravel plain, 7,200 m². (116)
31/435–L1–1	Occupation	Flint, sherd & bone scatter, 300 m². (125)
32/390–D2–2	Occupation	Artifact scatter, dense; butchering. (006) +Muf +OK +Rom.
32/405–A2–3	Occupation	Flint clusters on spring mound. (022)
32/420–L7–4	Occupation	Knapping debris, cores, blades, flakes & tools, scattered on P3. (219)

32/435–L10–2	Occupation	Flint clusters around hills of 32/435–L10–1. (124) +MSA +OK (+Pet 32/435–L10–1).
32/430–L10–3	Hut Circles	2 Stone hut bases on hilltops; flints & pots. (235) +OK.
32/435–M10–1	Occupation	Flint scatter in basin, 11,500 m². (103)
33/360–K10–2	Settlement	12 Stone hut circles; chipped & ground stone. (301)
33/390–I9–1/2	Occupation	Artifact scatter & debris, 1 km². (002) +ESA +MSA +Neo.
33/435–C6–1	Camps	Hunting stations; Libyan Plateau (Miramar Basin). (163)
33/435–C7–1	Occupation	Artifacts & ostrich egg shell; Libyan Plateau (Miramar Basin). (165)
N.N.	Occupation	Mixed scatter of flint, grindstones, hearths & ostrich eggshell, 700 × 300 m; Libyan Plateau above Maohoub; Bashendi 'B'. (077)
N.N.	Occupation	Flint scatter, dense, on edge of Libyan Plateau. (140) +Mas.
N.N.	Industry	Knapping floor; Libyan Plateau. (141)
N.N.	Occupation	Artifact scatters in basins. (185)
N.N.	Occupation	Artifact scatter, Bashendi Unit, Kharga Road S of TV tower (302)

Sheikh Muftah Neolithic (c.5,300 – 4,000 BP)

30/420–P1–1	Occupation	Artifact scatter, 520 m². (105)
30/420–P2–1	Occupation	Artifact scatter, 108 m². (144)
30/435–A2–1	Occupation	Artifact cluster, 77 m². (106)
30/435–B3–1	Occupation	2 Artifact clusters, each 8 m in diameter. (107)
30/435–B3–2	Occupation	Artifact cluster, small, on wadi floor. (108)
30/435–B3–3	Occupation	Artifact clusters in wadi bed. (109)
30/435–B5–1	Occupation	Artifact cluster, small, around hearths. (171)
30/435–B6–1	Occupation	Artifact scatter, small; whole pots. (143)
30/435–C3–1	Occupation	Artifact cluster, 20 m². (111) +Arc.
30/435–C3–2	Occupation	Artifact clusters, 10,200 m². (112)
30/435–C6–1	Occupation	Artifact cluster, 100 m². (110)
30/435–D4–1	Occupation	Artifact scatter in wadi, 1,500 m². (113)
30/435–F6–1	Occupation	Flint & sherd scatter, sparse, at base of hill. (096) +MSA
30/435–I3–1	Occupation	Artifact clusters. (117)
30/435–J2–1	Occupation	Artifact scatter & clusters. (093)
30/435–J5–1	Occupation	Artifact scatter, 3,500 m². (094) +MSA.
30/435–J5–2	Occupation	Artifact scatter at base of hill. (095) +MSA +OK +Pet.
30/435–J6–1	Occupation	Artifact clusters & hearths, 75,000 m². (221)
30/435–J6–2	Occupation	Artifacts, hearths & whole pots, scattered, 13,500 m². (222)
30/435–J9–1	Occupation	Sparse artifact scatter. (220)
30/435–K3–1	Occupation	Artifact scatter, 500 m². (119)
30/435–L2–1	Occupation	Sparse artifact scatter, with clusters, 6,400 m². (129)
30/435–P2–2	Occupation	Artifact scatter on plain, 600 m². (133)
30/450–B & C2–4.	Bone & Lithics	Surface of CSS; mixed with Holocene bone. Spread over 6 squares. (356) +PSA +OK +Rom.
30/450–B3–1	Occupation	Artifact scatter, 100 m². (134)
30/450–B3–2	Occupation	Artifact scatter, 2,800 m². (136)
30/450–B4–1	Occupation	Artifact scatter & clusters, along 1 km of basin edge. (135)

31/405–E8–1	Occupation	Artifact scatter on spring mound. (039) +Rom.
31/405–F7–1	Occupation	Artifact scatter on spring mounds. (038) +OK +Rom +Isl.
31/405–G6–1	Occupation	Artifact scatter on spring mound. (035) +OK +Rom.
31/405–G6–2	Occupation	Artifact clusters on spring mound. (064)
31/405–G7–2	Occupation	Artifact scatter on spring mound, 600 m². (036) +OK.
31/405–G7–3	Occupation	Artifact scatter on spring mound. (037) +Isl.
31/405–G7–4	Occupation	Artifact scatter on spring mounds. (062)
31/405–G7–5	Occupation	Artifact scatter on spring mound. (063)
31/405–H4–2	Occupation	Artifact scatters on spring mounds. (066) +OK +Rom.
31/405–K10–3	Occupation	Scraper, near building. (047) +Byz.
31/405–L10–4	Occupation	Artifact clusters. (052) +Rom.
31/405–L10–5	Occupation	Artifact scatter. (053) +MSA.
31/405–M10–3	Occupation	Mixed scatter of flint, sherds, grindstones & bone. (059) +OK?
31/420–C10–1	Occupation	Artifact scatter at base of spring mound. (073)
31/420–C10–3	Occupation	Artifact scatter & clusters, 2,000 m². (118)
31/420–C10–4	Occupation	Artifact cluster, small, & hearths. (142)
31/420–D9–1	Occupation	Artifact clusters around spring mounds. (072) +OK.
31/420–D10–3	Occupation	Artifact clusters. (069)
31/420–E10–1	Occupation	Artifact cluster. (071)
31/420–E10–2	Occupation	Artifact clusters in yardang field. (122)
31/420–E10–4	Burial	Skeleton eroding from clays. (365)
31/420–F9–1	Occupation	3 Artifact clusters, mixed. (070) +Bash.
31/420–F9–3	Occupation	Debris cluster, 700 m². (092)
31/420–F10–2	Occupation	Artifact clusters & knapping floor. (068)
31/420–G7–3	Occupation	Artifact clusters. (089) +OK.
31/420–H5–1	Occupation	Artifact scatters around 3 spring mounds. (087)
31/420–H7–2	Occupations	Artifact clusters, 300 m diameter. (088) +Bash.
31/420–M6–1	Occupation	Artifact scatter & 4 hearths, on playa, 350 m². (168)
31/420–N6–1	Occupation	Artifact clusters along 200 m of playa edge. (145)
31/420–N6–2	Occupation	Artifact scatter & 2 hearths, 150 m². (167)
31/420–N7–1	Occupation	Artifact scatter on playa, 950 m². (169)
31/420–N7–2	Occupation	Artifact scatter. (170)
31/420–P6–1	Occupation & Cemetery	Artifact scatter & human burials, 8,000 m². (100)
31/435–A6–2	Occupation	Artifact cluster, large, & 2 hearths, 100 m². (115)
31/435–A7–1	Occupation	Artifact cluster, small. (114)
31/435–M1–1	Occupation	Artifact clusters & quartzite mauls. (126)
32/390–D2–2	Occupation	Artifact scatter, dense; butchering. (006) +Bash +OK +Rom.
33/390–I6–2	Occupation	Flint & sherd scatter on 4 mounds. (011) +Neo +OK.
N.N.	Occupation	Artifact scatters on playa edge, Libyan Plateau. (139)
N.N.	Occupation	Small rock shelter. (244)
N.N.	Occupation	Artifact concentration. (250)

HISTORICAL

Pharaonic

Archaic (Early Dynastic Period) (c 3,100 – 2,700 BC)

30/435–C3–1	Occupation	Sherd scatter, mixed. (111) +Muf.
30/450–F10–1	Artifact	Archaic jar. (241)
32/390–L2–1	Cemetery	60 Graves, mixed, plundered; Grave 1 with flexed burial & Archaic pots. +OK +Rom.

Old Kingdom (c 2,700 – 2,180 BC)

30/405–L1–1	Settlement	2 Hut circles, on hilltop. (057) +MSA +Pet.
30/420–F3–1	Occupation	Hilltop lookout with 3 hut circles, pottery & petroglyphs.
30/435–J5–2	Occupation	Sherd scatter on earlier site. (095) +MSA +Muf +Pet.
30/435–P2–1	Occupation	Sherd & flint scatter, mixed with Roman industry. (132) +Neo +Rom.
30/450–B & C2–4.	Bone & Lithics	Surface of CSS; mixed with Holocene bone. Spread over 6 squares. (356) +PSA +Neo +Rom.
30/450–C4–1	Occupation	3 slab structures on gebel; sherds, lithics & petroglyphs. +Rom.
30/450–D4–2	Outpost	Slab structure with petroglyphs.
30/450–E4–1	Occupation	Debris in small scatter; pottery & chipped stone. (256)
30/450–F8–6	Occupation	Sherd & flint scatter on hillslope. (210) +Bash +Pet.
30/450–F9–1	Occupations	Artifact scatters & hut circles on hilltop. (180) +Bash.
30/450–G8–2	?Tannery	3 Hut circles, on hilltop. (229)
31/405–F7–1	Occupation	Sherd & flint scatter on spring mounds. (038) +Muf +Rom +Isl.
31/405–G6–1	Occupation	Sherd scatter on spring mound. (035) +Muf +Rom.
31/405–G7–2	Occupation	Sherd scatter on spring mound, 600 m². (036) +Muf.
31/405–G10–1	Settlement	'Mut el-Kharab' (Mothis), brick enclosure, 240 × 180 m, on spring mound; surface sherds; temple & brick buildings. (042) +NK +3IP +Late +Ptol +Rom +Byz.
31/405–H4–2	Occupation	Sherd scatter on spring mounds. (066) +Muf +Rom.
31/405–H6–1	Occupation	Sherd scatter on spring mounds. (065) +Neo +Rom.
31/405–K4–1	Caves	4 Shafts, & sherd scatter on surface. +Rom +Byz.
31/405–K10–5	Occupation	Sherd scatter, mixed in earlier site. (048) +Neo.
31/405–M10–3	Occupation	Mixed scatter of sherds, flints & bone. (059) +Muf.
31/420–D9–1	Occupation	Artifact clusters around spring mounds. (072) +Muf.
31/420–G7–3	Occupation	Artifact clusters. (089) +Muf.
31/435–B4–2	Occupation	Sherd scatter on surface. (097) +Neo +Rom.
31/435–B4–3	Occupation	Sherd scatter on oval mound, 27,500 m². (098) +Mas +Neo +Rom.
31/435–B4–4	Occupation	Sherd & flint scatter on spring mound. (099) +Rom.
31/435–G2–1/2	Cemetery	'Kila ed-Debba' (incl. `Kom Sud'), IFAO excavation site. +1IP +MK +2IP +Late +Rom +Byz.
31/435–I1–1	Town	'Ain Aseel', IFAO excavation site. +1IP +MK +2IP +NK +3IP +Late +Ptol +Rom.

31/435–I4–1	Occupation	Sherd scatter, 70,000 m². (127) +Byz.
31/435–J1–1	Building	Brick remains, 30 × 35 m.
31/435–L2–4	Occupation	Stone hut circles, sherds & flints. (102)
31/435–L9–2	Occupation	Sherd scatter, 500,000 m². +Rom +Byz.
32/390–L9–2	Cemetery	100 Graves, mostly disturbed by erosion.
32/390–D2–2	Occupation	Artifact scatter, dense; butchering. (006) +Bash +Muf +OK +Rom.
32/390–I4–3	Settlement	Sherd & flint scatter on surface. (014) +Rom.
32/390–I5–1	Settlement	Sherd & flint scatter; VI Dynasty. (018)
32/390–K2–1	Cemetery	75 Graves, some intact, 10,000 m².
32/390–K2–2	Settlement	Sherd, flint & debris scatter, brick structures & kiln, 500 × 150 m; VI Dynasty. (017)
32/390–L2–1	Cemetery	60 Graves, mixed, plundered; Grave 3 OK. Archaic pots. +Arch. +Rom.
32/390–L3–1	Settlement	Sherd scatter among Roman brick buildings. +Rom.
32/390–N4–1	Habitation	Sherd & flint scatter, 500 m². (015) +Rom.
32/390–P5–1	Occupation	Sherd & flint scatters, 35,000 m². (020) +Neo +Rom.
32/435–L10–2	Occupation	Artifacts, from hills around 32/435–L10–1. (124) +MSA +Bash (+Pet 32/435–L10–1).
32/435–L10–3	Hut Circles	2 Stone hut bases on hilltops, flints & pots. (235) +Bash.
33/390–H5–1	Occupation	Sherd, flint & ash scatter, no structures, on 80 × 40 m mound. (016) +Neo.
33/390–I4–1	Occupation	Artifact scatters on 2 mounds. (009) +Neo.
33/390–I5–1	Occupation	Sherd & flint scatter, & stone walls, 50 × 30 m. (010) +Neo.
33/390–I6–2	Occupation	Sherd & flint scatter on 4 mounds. (011) +Neo +Muf.
33/390–I9–2	Cemetery	200 Tombs, rock-cut, in 3 small hills, plundered. (028)
33/390–I9–3	Settlement	Brick structures & kilns, 300 × 600 m. (012)
33/390–I9–4	Cemetery	150 Graves & rock-cut tombs, plundered.
33/390–K6–1	Industry	Sherd scatter, ash & slag, 30,000 m². +Rom +Isl.
33/390–K7–1	Habitation	Sherd & flint scatter on spring mound. +Rom.
33/390–L9–2	Cemetery	100 Graves, mostly disturbed by erosion.
N.N.	Campsite	Sherd & flint scatter, 'fishtail' knife, & hearths; Libyan Plateau. (138)

First Intermediate Period (c.2,180 – 2,050 BC)

31/435–G2–1/2	Cemetery	'Kila ed-Debba' (incl. 'Kom Sud'), IFAO excavation site. +OK +MK +2IP +Late +Rom +Byz.
31/435–I1–1	Town	'Ain Aseel', IFAO excavation site. +OK +MK +2IP +NK +3IP +Late +Ptol +Rom.
32/390–L2–1	Cemetery	60 Graves, mixed & plundered. +Arc +Rom.
33/390–K9–1	Industry	Sherd scatter, brick structures & kilns, 37,500 m².

Middle Kingdom (c.2,050 – 1,785 BC)

31/435–G2–1/2	Cemetery	'Kila ed-Debba'(incl. 'Kom Sud'), IFAO excavation site. +OK +1IP +2IP +Late +Rom +Byz.
31/435–I1–1	Town	'Ain Aseel', IFAO excavation site. +OK +1IP +2IP +NK +3IP + Late +Ptol +Rom.
31/435–D5–2	Cemetery	''Ein Tirghi', 100+ tombs & graves disturbed, often reused. +2IP +NK +3IP +Late +Ptol.
31/435–D9–1	Settlement	'El-Qasaba', IFAO excavation site.

Second Intermediate Period (c.1,785 – 1,567 BC)

31/435–D5–2	Cemetery	''Ein Tirghi', 100+ tombs & graves disturbed, often reused. +MK +NK +3IP +Late +Ptol.
31/435–G2–1/2	Cemetery	'Kila ed-Debba' (incl. 'Kom Sud'), IFAO excavation site. +OK +1IP +MK +Late +Rom +Byz.
31/435–I1–1	Town	'Ain Aseel', IFAO excavation site. +OK +1IP +MK +NK +3IP +Late +Ptol +Rom.
32/390–I5–1	Settlement	Sherd & flint scatter, ash & debris, & brick walls.
32/390–K1–2	Cemetery	50 Graves, end-pit, disturbed.

New Kingdom (1,567 – 1,085 BC)

31/405–G10–1	Settlement	'Mut el-Kharab' (Mothis), 240 × 180 m brick enclosure on spring mound; surface sherds; temple & brick buildings. (042) +OK +3IP +Late +Ptol +Rom +Byz.
31/435–D5–2	Cemetery	''Ein Tirghi', 100+ tombs & graves, disturbed, often reused. +MK +2IP +3IP +Late +Ptol.
31/435–I1–1	Town	'Ain Aseel', IFAO excavation site. +OK +1IP +MK +2IP +3IP +Late +Ptol +Rom.

Third Intermediate Period

31/405–G10–1	Settlement	'Mut el-Kharab' (Mothis), 240 × 180 m brick enclosure on spring mound, surface sherds, temple & brick buildings. (042) +OK +NK +Late +Ptol +Rom +Byz.
31/435–D5–2	Cemetery	''Ein Tirghi', 100+ tombs & graves, disturbed, often reused. +MK +2IP +NK +Late +Ptol.
31/435–I1–1	Town	'Ain Aseel', IFAO excavation site. +OK +1IP +MK +2IP +NK +Late +Ptol +Rom.

Late Period (1,085 – 332 BC)

31/405–D7–1	Settlement	Brick domestic buildings & kilns. +Rom.
31/405–E8–2	Cemetery	300 Graves, in spring mound, plundered. (367) +Rom.
31/405–F6–1	Cemetery	100+ Tombs, plundered. +Ptol +Rom +Byz.
31/405–F9–3	Cemetery	16 Brick tombs, vaulted, plundered. +Ptol +Rom.
31/405–G10–1	Settlement	'Mut el-Kharab' (Mothis), 240 × 180 m brick enclosure, on spring mound, surface sherds, temple & brick buildings. (042) +OK +NK +3IP +Ptol +Rom +Byz.
31/405–K6–1	Settlement	Sherd scatter on spring mound, 60,000 m² & wall traces. +Ptol +Rom +Byz +Isl

31/420–D10–1	Cemetery	Several tombs, multi-chambered, plundered. +Rom.
31/435–D5–2	Cemetery	''Ein Tirghi', 100+ tombs & graves, disturbed, often reused. +MK +2IP +NK +3IP +Ptol.
31/435–G2–1/2	Cemetery	'Kila ed-Debba' (incl. `Kom Sud'), IFAO excavation site. +OK +1IP +MK +2IP +Rom +Byz.
31/435–I1–1	Town	'Ain Aseel', IFAO excavation site. +OK +1IP +MK +2IP +NK +3IP +Ptol +Rom.
31/435–N3–1	Settlement	Brick buildings, rectangular. +Rom.
32/390–K4–1	Cemetery	Brick tombs, many rooms, underlying settlement, disturbed. +Rom +Isl.
32/390–M4–1	Settlement	Brick walls, 15+ ovens; ash, 80 m diam. +Rom.
32/405–A2–1	Temple	Brick temple, 9 rooms, 17 × 30 m; 3+ building phases; painted plaster. (027) +Neo +Ptol +Rom +Byz.
33/390–E9–2	Cemetery	1500 Tombs, rock-cut or vaulted, plundered. +Rom.

Ptolemaic Period (332 – 30 BC)

30/405–M1–1	Cemetery	120 Tombs, plundered. +Rom +Byz.
31/405–F6–1	Cemetery	100+ Tombs, plundered. +Late +Rom +Byz.
31/405–F9–3	Cemetery	16 Brick tombs, vaulted, plundered. +Late +Rom.
31/405–G10–1	Settlement	'Mut el-Kharab' (Mothis), 240 × 180 m brick enclosure, on spring mound, surface sherds, temple & brick buildings. (042) +OK +NK +3IP +Late +Rom +Byz.
31/405–H9–2	Cemetery	40 Brick tombs, in spring mound, plundered. +Rom.
31/405–H10–3	Cemetery	200 Tombs, plundered, in spring mound. +Rom +Byz.
31/405–K6–1	Settlement	Sherd scatter on spring mound, 60,000 m² & wall traces. +Late +Rom +Byz +Isl.
31/405–L4–2	Temple	Brick structure, 14 rooms, 26 × 19 m, standing 1.3 m. +Rom +Byz +Isl.
31/405–M9–1	Settlement	'Ain el-Azizi', brick buildings, temple enclosure & kilns, 1.5 km². +Rom +Byz.
31/420–C5–1	Cemetery	Multiple burials in ~300 cave tombs in low hill NW of & adjacent to Ismant el-Kharab. +Rom.
31/420–D6–1	Settlement	'Ismant el-Kharab' (Kellis), brick village; 2 temples, 3 churches, administrative buildings, bath house, residences & mausolea, standing to 7 m. +Rom.
31/435–D5–2	Cemetery	''Ein Tirghi', 100+ tombs & graves, disturbed, often reused. +MK +2IP +NK +3IP +Late.
31/435–I1–1	Town	'Ain Aseel', IFAO excavation site. +OK +1IP +MK +2IP +NK +3IP +Late +Rom.
31/435–K5–1	Temple	''Ein Birbiyeh', buried axial sandstone temple, usual Egyptian plan, 35 × 21 m, standing 4 m. Gateway dedicated by Augustus Caesar. +Rom +Byz.
32/390–K1–1	Cemetery	150 Brick tombs, vaulted & plundered. +Rom.
32/405–A2–1	Temple	Brick temple, 9 rooms, painted plaster, 17 × 30 m; 3+ building phases. (027) +Neo +Late +Rom +Byz.

33/390–M5–2	Temple	Stone temple dedicated to 'Thoth, Twice Great of Hermopolis', in later domestic buildings at Qasr, intact door jambs. +Rom +Isl.

Roman Period (30 BC – 300 AD)

30/405–H1–1	Structure	Brick house, 4 rooms; domestic. +Byz.
30/405–I1–1	Settlement	Sherd scatter, 25,000 m². +Byz.
30/405–I2–1	Structure	Brick, 7 rooms, enclosed. +Byz.
30/405–L1–2	Cemetery	75 Tombs & pits, rock-cut & plundered.
30/405–M1–1	Cemetery	120 Tombs, plundered. +Ptol +Byz.
30/420–A1–1	Cemetery	300+ Tombs, plundered. +Byz +Isl.
30/420–D2–1	Settlement	Sherd scatter & brick structures, 125,000 m². +Byz.
30/420–D3–1	Cemetery	50 Graves, plundered. +Byz.
30/435–J1–1	Occupation	Sherd scatter, 20,000 m².
30/435–K1–1	Occupation	Brick house & sherd scatter, 375,000 m². +Byz.
30/435–K1–4	Cemetery	8 Tombs, rock-cut & plundered.
30/435–K1–5	Temple	Brick temple, standing 4 m, 6–8 occupation floors, 10 × 15 m & debris.
30/435–M2–1	Graves	Looted grave shafts atop hill. (348) +PSA +Byz.
30/435–M2–3	Occupation	Sherd scatter & heavy stone mauls., (123) +Neo.
30/435–M2–5	Occupation	Sherd scatter & heavy stone picks & mauls (?quarrying tools). (131) +Neo.
30/435–M2–6	Cemetery	Looted grave shafts ringing a CSS knoll. (355) +PSA +Byz.
30/435–P2–1	Industry	Heavy quartzite implements, on sandstone hill with rectangular cut holes; Roman pottery. (132) +Neo +OK.
30/450–B & C2–4.	Bone & Lithics	Surface of CSS; mixed with Holocene bone. Spread over 6 squares. (356) + PSA +Neo +OK.
30/450–C4–1	Occupation	3 Slab structures on gebel; sherds, lithics, petroglyphs. +OK.
31/390–K1–1	Settlement	Sherd scatter, 1.5 km².
31/405–C4–1	Settlement	Spring mound area with multi-roomed buildings & sherds, 4,000 m².
31/405–D5–1	Building	Brick house, 25 rooms, on small hill.
31/405–D5–2	Settlement	Several farmhouses, 37,500 m² area.
31/405–D7–1	Settlement	Brick domestic buildings & kilns. +Late.
31/405–D7–2	Cemetery	25 Brick tombs, multi-chambered, plundered.
31/405–D7–3	Sherds	Roman sherds, & flint scatter. (O07) +ESA +?Bal/ESA +MSA +Neo.
31/405–E8–1	Sherds	Sherd & flint scatter. (039) +Muf.
31/405–E8–2	Cemetery	300 Graves, in spring mound, plundered. (367) +Late.
31/405–E8–3	Structure	Brick house, 3 rooms, 8 × 7 m. +Byz.
31/405–F2–1	Cemetery	25 Graves, in shale, disturbed. +Byz.
31/405–F6–1	Cemetery	100+ Tombs, plundered. +Late +Ptol +Byz.
31/405–F7–1	Sherds	Sherd scatter over spring mounds. (038) +Muf +OK +Isl.
31/405–F9–1	Cemetery & Kiln	400+ Tombs & mausolea, some decorated plaster, plundered; & kiln.
31/405–F9–3	Cemetery	16 Brick tombs, vaulted, plundered. +Late +Ptol.
31/405–F9–4	Occupation	Sherd scatter on spring mound, 700 m². +Byz.
31/405–F9–5	Cemetery	60 Graves, plundered. +Byz.
31/405–G6–1	Occupation	Sherd scatter on spring mound. (064) +Muf +OK.
31/405–G7–1	Cemetery	3 Graves, plundered.

31/405–G9–2	Cemetery	EAO excavation.
31/405–G10–1	Settlement	'Mut el-Kharab' (Mothis), 240 × 180 m brick enclosure, on spring mound, surface sherds, temple & brick buildings. (042) +OK +NK +3IP +Late +Ptol +Byz.
31/405–H4–2	Occupation	Sherd scatter on spring mounds. (066) +Muf +OK.
31/405–H6–1	Occupation	Sherd scatter on spring mounds. (065) +Neo +OK.
31/405–H8–1	Buildings	Brick walls, 1,600 m² area. +Byz.
31/405–H9–2	Cemetery	40 Brick tombs, in spring mound, plundered. +Ptol.
31/405–H9–3	Occupation	Sherd scatter on spring mound. +Byz.
31/405–H10–1	Buildings	Brick walls & sherd scatter, 10,000 m² area.
31/405–H10–2	Settlement	Sherd scatter with brick remains, 75,000 m². +Byz.
31/405–H10–3	Cemetery	200 Tombs, in spring mound, plundered. +Ptol +Byz.
31/405–K4–1	Caves	4 Shafts & sherd scatter on surface. +OK +Byz.
31/405–K6–1	Settlement	Sherd scatter on spring mound, 60,000 m² & wall traces. +Ptol +Late +Byz +Isl.
31/405–K9–1	Cemetery	3 Brick tombs, vaulted, plundered.
31/405–K10–1	Tomb	Brick tomb, vaulted, plundered.
31/405–K10–2	Occupation	Midden debris with hand-made pottery.
31/405–K10–4	Settlement	Sherd scatter & brick walls, 20,000 m². +Byz.
31/405–K10–7	Cemetery	3 Brick tombs & graves, plundered. +Byz.
31/405–K10–8	Occupation	Sherd scatter on spring mound.
31/405–L4–2	Temple	Brick structure, 14 rooms, standing 1.3 m, 26 × 19 m. +Ptol +Byz +Isl.
31/405–L9–1	Cemetery	3 Brick tombs, vaulted & other graves, plundered. +Byz.
31/405–L9–2	House	Brick house, several rooms. +Byz.
31/405–L10–1	Cemetery	20 Tombs, vaulted, plundered. +Byz.
31/405–L10–2	House	Brick house, 7 rooms, 11.5 m square. +Byz.
31/405–L10–3	Cemetery	100 Graves, plundered. (055) +ESA +Byz.
31/405–L10–4	Occupation	Artifact clusters. (052) +Muf.
31/405–M3–1	Cemetery	200 Graves, in shale hill, plundered. +Byz.
31/405–M4–1	Cemetery	200 Graves, plundered, 500,000 m². +Byz.
31/405–M9–1	Settlement	'Ain el-Azizi', brick buildings, temple enclosure & kilns, 1.5 km². +Ptol +Byz.
31/405–M10–1	Cemetery	300+ Graves, plundered. +Byz +Isl.
31/405–N3–2	Structure	Brick building, multi-roomed. +Byz.
31/420–B9–1	Settlement	Brick walls on low mound, 12,500 m². +Byz.
31/420–B9–2	Settlement	Brick walls on mound, 30 rooms, 2,000 m². +Byz.
31/420–B10–1	Cemetery	'Beyout el-Ghoreish', 300+ graves & 10 brick mausolea standing to cornices, plundered.
31/420–C5–1	Cemetery	Multiple burials in 300 cave tombs tombs in low hill NW of & adjacent to Ismant el-Kharab. +Ptol.
31/420–C5–2	Cemetery	300 Simple pits with single burials in flat area N of Ismant el-Kharab. +Byz.
31/420–C7–1	Settlement	Brick buildings, buried to wall tops, 300+ rooms, 87,500 m². +Byz.
31/420–C9–1	Occupation	Sherd scatter, 100 × 100 m. +Byz.
31/420–D6–1	Settlement	'Ismant el-Kharab' (Kellis), brick village; 2 temples, 3 churches, administratve buildings, bath house, residences & mausolea, standing to 7 m. +Ptol.
31/420–D10–1	Cemetery	Several tombs, multi-chambered, plundered. +Late.
31/420–D10–2	Settlement	Sherd scatter & brick structures, 250,000 m².
31/420–F9–2	Colombarium	Brick, 5.9 × 6.9 m.
31/420–G6–2	Temple	'Qasr el-Halakeh', brick 3–storey structure, 40 rooms, standing 8 m on bedrock rise, 25 × 50 m.
31/420–G6–3	Settlement	Sherd scatter & brick traces, 1,600 m².
31/420–G7–2	Settlement	Brick walls & colombarium above, 22,500 m².
31/420–G9–1	Cemetery	200 Graves, in low scarp, plundered.
31/420–G9–2	Building	Brick wall & sandstone cornice block.
31/420–H7–1	Cemetery	300 Graves & rock-cut pits, plundered.
31/420–I6–1	Cemetery	24 Tombs, rock-cut, plundered.
31/420–J4–2	Occupation	Sherd scatter & ?structural remains, 2,000 m².
31/420–M7–1	Graves	5 Pits, disturbed.
31/420–M8–1	Graves	6 Pits, disturbed.
31/420–M9–1	Occupation	Sherd scatter, 1,300 m². +Byz.
31/420–N10–1	Cemetery	75 Graves, plundered.
31/435–A6–1	Occupation	Brick remains, sherds, kilns & ?temple, 200,000 m².
31/435–B3–1	Settlement	Brick temple, 25 × 6 m, & other buildings, low mounds, 150,000 m².
31/435–B4–1	Cemetery	Brick mausolea & 13+ other graves, plundered.
31/435–B4–2	Occupation	Sherd scatter on surface. (097) +Neo +OK.
31/435–B4–3	Occupation	Sherd scatter on oval mound, 27,500 m². (098) +Mas +Neo +OK.
31/435–B4–4	Occupation	Sherd & artifact scatter. +OK.
31/435–B7–1	Settlement	Sherd scatter. +Byz +Isl.
31/435–C6–1	Settlement	Brick ruins, vaulting, white plaster, ?kilns, & sherds, 375,000 m².
31/435–D3–2	House	Brick walls, 500 m². +Byz.
31/435–D5–1	Graves	6 Graves, on small knoll.
31/435–E3–1	Settlement	Colombarium, 7 m², & nearby building, 10 rooms.
31/435–F3–1	Settlement	2 Brick houses. +Byz.
31/435–F6–1	Cemetery	100 Brick tombs & graves, plundered.
31/435–G2–1/2	Cemetery	'Kila el-Debba'(incl. `Kom Sud'), IFAO excavation site. +OK +1IP +MK +2IP +Late +Byz.
31/435–I1–1	Town	'Ain Aseel', IFAO excavation site. +OK +1IP +MK +2IP +NK +3IP +Late +Ptol.
31/435–I2–1	Cemetery	8 Stone tombs, plundered; includes decorated tomb of 'Kitinos' and domed tomb of 'Sheikh Bashendi'.
31/435–I2–2	Settlement	Sherd scatter; brick & stone temple structure & kilns, 70,000 m².
31/435–I3–1	Settlement	2 Sherd scatters & brick traces.
31/435–J4–2	Structure	Brick building, 18 rooms, & kiln, atop small hill. +Byz.
31/435–K1–1	Occupation	Sherds in later building. +Isl.
31/435–K2–1	Colombarium	Brick structure, nesting boxes in walls.
31/435–K3–1	Temple	Brick axial structure, 4 rooms, 30 m long, standing to 5 m. Within 31/435–K3–2.

31/435–K3–2	Settlement	Sherd scatter with brick domestic structures, 1.5 km². Includes 31/435–K3–1.
31/435–K3–3	?Saqia	Brick enclosure, 8.7 m diameter & run-off channel. +Byz.
31/435–K5–1	Temple	"Ein Birbiyeh', buried axial sandstone temple, usual Egyptian plan, 35 × 21 m, standing 4 m. Gateway dedicated by Augustus Caesar. +Ptol +Byz.
31/435–K5–3	Settlement	3 Circular interconnected brick structures, each 3 m diameter.
31/435–L2–1	Cemetery	500 Graves & tombs, plundered. +Byz.
31/435–L2–2	Cemetery	20 Brick tombs, vaulted, plundered.
31/435–L2–3	Cemetery	15 Brick tombs, plundered. +Byz.
31/435–L3–1	Settlement	Brick walls, deflated bases.
31/435–L9–2	Occupation	Sherd scatter, 500,000 m². +OK +Byz.
31/435–M3–1	Temple	Brick temple structures (2 stratified), decorated plaster, on 40 m diameter mound. +Byz.
31/435–M4–2	Settlement	Sherd scatter & few brick remains, 15,000 m².
31/435–M7–1	Cemetery	20 Brick tombs, plundered.
31/435–M8–1	Cemetery	300+ Tombs & graves, plundered.
31/435–N2–1	Cemetery	40 Tombs, rock-cut, plundered. +Byz.
31/435–N3–1	Settlement	Brick buildings, rectangular. +Late.
31/435–N6–2	Settlement	Brick & rough stone buildings, including 3 brick axial temples, atop sandstone plateau. +Byz.
31/435–N6–3	Cemetery	24 Tombs, rock-cut, plundered.
31/435–P3–1	Cemetery	2500 Tombs & graves, rock-cut, plundered.
32/390–D1–1	Habitation	3 Brick rooms. Within 33/390–E9–2.
32/390–D2–1	Structure	Sherd scatter & brick remains, 50,000 m².
32/390–D2–2	Occupation	Artifact scatter, dense; butchering. (006) +Bash +Muf +OK.
32/390–E1–1	Industry	Brick walls, ash, grinding stones, on mound, 135 × 90 m.
32/390–E10–1	Cemetery	60 Graves & brick tombs, plundered.
32/390–F7–1	Cemetery	100 Graves, plundered.
32/390–F9–1	Settlement	9 Brick buildings, 2–storey, 2 km².
32/390–G6–1	Cemetery	12 Graves & vaulted tombs, plundered.
32/390–G6–2	Mine	15 Pits, 2.5–3 m deep, in sandstone outcrop, no galleries.
32/390–G7–1	Cemetery	Tombs, brick and rock-cut, plundered.
32/390–H5–1	Structure	Building, 8 rooms, atop 2.9 m high yardang.
32/390–H5–3	Cemetery	60+ Graves, rock-cut, plundered.
32/390–H9–1	Settlement	4 Brick houses, many rooms, 10,000 m².
32/390–I4–1	Cemetery	Sherds, bricks & coffin fragments; scatter, 180 m².
32/390–I4–2	Structure	Brick building, 12 rooms, 19 × 16.5 m.
32/390–I4–3	Settlement	Sherd & flint scatter on surface. (014) +OK.
32/390–I6–1	Cemetery	20 Graves & brick tombs, disturbed.
32/390–I6–2	Settlement	2 Brick buildings; 1 with 20 rooms.
32/390–I6–3	Cemetery	15 Pits, plundered.
32/390–J3–1	Cemetery	300 Graves, mixed & plundered, in hill. +Neo +OK.
32/390–J3–2	Settlement	3 Brick buildings, many rooms, 50 × 75 m.
32/390–J6–1	Settlement	2 Brick rooms, denuded.
32/390–J10–1	Cemetery	100+ Tombs, rock-cut, plundered, along 1 km of hillside.
32/390–K1–1	Cemetery	150 Brick tombs, vaulted & plundered. +Ptol.
32/390–K1–3	Settlement	Brick walls, 200 m square.
32/390–K1–4	Settlement	2 Brick columbaria, & another building on spring mound.
32/390–K2–3	Cemetery	200 Graves, plundered, in large hill.
32/390–K4–1	Cemetery	Brick tombs, many rooms, underlying settlement, disturbed. + Late +Isl.
32/390–L2–1	Cemetery	60 Graves & brick vaulted tombs, mixed & plundered. +Arc +OK.
32/390–L3–1	Settlement	2 Brick structures, colombarium & villa. +OK.
32/390–L3–2	Structure	Brick building, 12 rooms, 2 storeys.
31/435–L9–1	Village	10 Brick & adobe houses, small & poor. +Ptol +Isl.
32/390–M4–1	Settlement	Brick walls, 15+ ovens; ash, 80 m diam. +Late.
32/390–N4–1	Habitation	Sherd & flint scatter, 500 m². (015) +OK.
32/390–N8–1	Cemetery	75 Graves, plundered, & brick tombs. +Isl.
32/390–P5–1	Occupation	Sherd & lithic scatter, 35,000 m². (020) +Neo +OK.
32/390–P7–1	Settlement	Sherds & 44 brick buildings, 40,000 m².
32/405–A2–1	Temple	Brick temple, 9 rooms, 17 × 30 m; 3+ building phases. (027) +Neo +Late +Ptol +Byz.
32/405–A2–2	Structure	Brick room, 3.75 × 3.1 m. (025) +Neo +Byz.
32/405–A8–1	Cemetery	25 Brick tombs, vaulted, plundered, under settlement. +Byz.
32/405–B2–1	Cemetery	6 Brick tombs, plundered.
32/405–C7–4	Settlement	Brick houses, several, many rooms, white plaster, stone steps, 60,000 m². +Byz.
32/405–D10–1	Cemetery	6 Tombs & 10 graves, plundered. +Byz.
32/405–I10–1	Cave	Cave, 6 × 10 m, neat entrance, with animal bones. +Isl.
32/435–J10–1	Cemetery	5 Tombs, rock-cut, plundered.
33/390–D8–1	Settlement	Brick building with atrium, pigeon loft & kiln.
33/390–D8–2	House	Brick walls.
33/390–D9–1	Colombarium	Brick, isolated.
33/390–E8–1	Settlement	Brick colombarium & traces of other buildings.
33/390–E9–1	Settlement	3 Colombaria & other brick structures, 37,500 m².
33/390–E9–2	Cemetery	1500 Tombs, rock-cut or vaulted, plundered. Includes 32/390–D1–1. +Late.
33/390–F7–1	Settlement	5 Colombaria, in village.
33/390–F7–2	Structure	Brick building, 3 storeys, with pigeon lofts, 35 × 44 m.
33/390–F8–1	Occupation	Brick structures & industrial mounds, 2 main areas.
33/390–F9–1	Temple & Settlement	'Deir el-Haggar', sandstone temple of 1st Century AD; extensive adjacent domestic brick structures.
33/390–F9–2	Lime kilns	Brick kilns: 1 round & 1 rectangular, 24 × 21 m.
33/390–F10–3	Settlement & Cemetery	Industrial area; some brick graves; cow, buried with demotic ostraca, 4,000 m².
33/390–G9–1	Occupation	Industrial area, 3,000 m².
33/390–H5–3	Cemetery	Tombs, rock-cut, largely destroyed.
33/390–H6–2	Settlement	11 Colombaria, in village.

33/390–H7–1	Cemetery	'El-Muzzawaka', 300 tombs, rock-cut, plundered; incl. decorated tombs of `Petosiris' & `Pedubastis'. EAO excavations.
33/390–H7–3	Occupation	Industrial area, 17,500 m².
33/390–H8–1	Settlement	Sherds mixed into later site. (019) +Neo +Isl.
33/390–I6–3	Occupation	Sherd scatter on small hill.
33/390–I6–4	Occupation	Sherd scatter on small hill.
33/390–K5–1	Habitation	4 Brick structures, simple. +Isl.
33/390–K6–1	Industry	Sherd scatter, ash & slag, 30,000 m². +OK +Isl.
33/390–K6–2	Habitation	3 Brick rooms, courtyard & kiln.
33/390–K7–1	Settlement	Brick rooms on spring mound. +OK.
33/390–K7–2	Settlement	Several brick rooms on spring mound.
33/390–K9–2	Village	Brick structures, traces, 8 low mounds.
33/390–K9–3	Habitation	Sherd scatter & traces of brick walls, 25,000 m².
33/390–K9–4	Cemetery	3000 Graves & tombs, decorated plaster, plundered. Adjacent to 33/390–L9–1.
33/390–L5–1	Cemetery	17 Tombs, rock-cut, plundered.
33/390–L7–1	Cemetery	50 Tombs, plundered.
33/390–L7–3	Cemetery	12 Pits, rectangular.
33/390–L9–1	Settlement	'Amheida' (Trimethis),1500 × 750 m town mound, kilns, industrial area, painted rooms, temple block, good brick architectural preservation. +Byz.
33/390–M5–1	Cemetery	25 Tombs, small, rock-cut, plundered.
33/390–M5–2	Habitation	Sherds in exposed well face at Qasr. +Ptol +Isl.
33/390–N6–1	Settlement	6 Brick houses, many rooms, scattered. +Byz.
33/390–N7–1 = 33/390–N6–1		Cancelled.
33/405–A6–1	Habitation	Brick walls.
33/405–B8–1	Cemetery	Graves, many, plundered.
33/405–B8–2	Cemetery	6 Graves, disturbed. +Byz.

Byzantine Period (c.300 – 700 AD)

30/405–H1–1	Structure	Brick house, 4 rooms. +Rom.
30/405–I1–1	Settlement	Sherd scatter, 25,000 m². +Rom.
30/405–I2–1	Structure	Brick building, 7 rooms & courtyard. +Rom.
30/405–M1–1	Cemetery	120+ Tombs, plundered. +Ptol +Rom.
30/420–A1–1	Cemetery	300+ Tombs, plundered. +Rom +Isl.
30/420–D2–1	Settlement	Sherd scatter & brick structures, 125,000 m². +Rom.
30/420–D3–1	Cemetery	50 Graves, plundered. +Rom.
30/435–K1–1	Occupation	Sherd scatter & brick house, 375,000 m². +Rom.
30/435–M2–1	Graves	Looted grave shafts atop hill. (348) +PSA +Rom.
30/435–M2–6	Cemetery	Looted grave shafts ringing a CSS knoll. +PSA +Rom.
30/450–B & C2–4.	Bone & Lithics	Surface of CSS; mixed with Holocene bone. Spread over 6 squares. (356) +Neo.
31/405–D5–3	Cemetery	100 Graves, E-W, undisturbed.
31/405–E8–3	Structure	Brick house, 3 rooms, 8 × 7 m. +Rom.
31/405–F2–1	Cemetery	25 Graves, dug in shale, disturbed. +Rom.
31/405–F6–1	Cemetery	100+ Tombs, plundered. +Late +Ptol +Rom.
31/405–F9–4	Occupation	Sherd scatter on spring mound, 700 m². +Rom.
31/405–F9–5	Cemetery	60 Graves, plundered. +Rom.
31/405–G1–1	Tomb	Rock-cut chamber, isolated, plundered. +Isl.
31/405–G9–3	Cemetery	EAO excavation.

31/405–G10–1	Settlement	'Mut el-Kharab' (Mothis), 240 × 180 m brick enclosure, on spring mound, surface sherds, temple & brick buildings. (042) +OK +NK +3IP +Late +Ptol +Rom.
31/405–H4–1	Cemetery	100 Graves, plundered, 7,500 m². +Isl.
31/405–H8–1	Structures	Brick walls, 1,600 m². +Rom.
31/405–H8–2	Structure	Brick room on spring mound.
31/405–H9–3	Occupation	Sherd scatter on spring mound. +Rom.
31/405–H10–2	Settlement	Sherd scatter & brick walls, 75,000 m². +Rom.
31/405–H10–3	Cemetery	200 Tombs, plundered, in spring mound. +Ptol. +Rom.
31/405–H10–4	Structure	Brick walls, ?non-domestic, 60 × 30 m, on hilltop.
31/405–I2–1	Cemetery	30 Graves, some brick, disturbed. +Isl.
31/405–J1–1	Structure	Brick building, 5+ rooms, 700 m².
31/405–K4–1	Caves	4 Shafts, & sherd scatter outside. +OK +Rom.
31/405–K6–1	Settlement	Sherd scatter on spring mound; brick wall traces, 60,000 m². +Late +Ptol +Rom +Isl.
31/405–K6–2	Cemetery	150 Graves, 11,250 m². +Isl.
31/405–K8–1	Habitation	Brick & sherd scatter, 5,000 m².
31/405–K10–3	Structure	3 Brick rooms. (047) +Muf.
31/405–K10–4	Settlement	Brick walls & dense sherd scatter, 20,000 m². +Rom.
31/405–K10–7	Cemetery	3 Brick tombs & other graves, plundered. +Rom.
31/405–L4–1	Structures	3+ Brick houses, many rooms.
31/405–L4–2	Occupation	Sherds in brick temple. +Ptol +Rom +Isl.
31/405–L9–1	Cemetery	3 Brick tombs, vaulted, & other graves, plundered. +Rom.
31/405–L9–2	Structure	Brick house, several rooms. +Rom.
31/405–L10–1	Cemetery	20 Tombs, vaulted & plundered. +ESA +Rom.
31/405–L10–2	Structure	Brick house, 7 rooms, 11.5 m². +Rom.
31/405–L10–3	Cemetery	100 Graves, plundered. (055) +ESA +Rom.
31/405–M3–1	Cemetery	200 Graves, in shale hill, plundered. +Rom.
31/405–M4–1	Cemetery	200 Graves, plundered, 500,000 m². +Rom.
31/405–M6–1	Church	'Deir el-Molouk', domed brick building, bi-apsidal nave, 9 rooms, 17.5 × 15.5 m.
31/405–M9–1	Settlement	'Ain el-Azizi', brick buildings, temple enclosure & kilns, 1.5 km². +Ptol +Rom.
31/405–M10–1	Cemetery	300+ Graves, plundered. +Rom +Isl.
31/405–N3–1	Settlement	Brick walls, standing 2.8 m, 145 rooms on largest mound, white plaster, area of mounds 30,000 m².
31/405–N3–2	Structure	Brick building, many rooms. +Rom.
31/420–B9–1	Settlement	Brick walls on low mound, 12,500 m². +Rom.
31/420–B9–2	Settlement	Brick walls, 30 rooms, on 2,000 m² mound. +Rom.
31/420–C5–2	Cemetery	?2,000 Simple pits with single burials in flat area N of Ismant el-Kharab. +Rom.
31/420–C7–1	Settlement	Brick buildings buried to wall tops, 300+ rooms, standing 3–4 m, 87,500 m². +Rom.
31/420–C9–1	Occupation	Sherd concentration, 100 × 100 m. +Rom.
31/420–F7–1	Cemetery	10 Graves, disturbed, & brick structure, 4 rooms.

31/420–G6–4	Habitation	Sherd scatter & brick buildings, 7,500 m².
31/420–M9–1	Occupation	Sherd concentration, 1,300 m². +Rom.
31/435–B7–1	Settlement	Sherd scatter around buildings. +Rom +Isl.
31/435–D3–1	Cemetery	150 Graves, simple, in low mound.
31/435–D3–2	Structure	Brick walls, 500 m². +Rom.
31/435–D5–2	Cemetery	''Ein Tirghi', 100+ tombs & graves disturbed, often reused. +2IP +NK +Late +Rom.
31/435–E7–1	Settlement	Brick walls on sides of active spring mound & kilns.
31/435–F3–1	Structures	2 Brick domestic buildings, adjacent. +Rom.
31/435–G2–1/2	Cemetery	'Kila ed-Debba' (incl. 'Kom Sud'), IFAO excavation site. +OK +1IP +MK +2IP +Late +Rom.
31/435–G2–3	Occupation	Sherd scatter & brick wall traces, 125,000 m².
31/435–H4–1	Settlement	150 Rooms, in close association, standing 3.5+ m.
31/435–I4–1	Occupation	Sherd scatter & brick building, 20 rooms. +OK.
31/435–J4–1	Cemetery	50 Brick tombs, plundered.
31/435–J4–2	Structure	18 Brick rooms on small hill, & kiln. +Rom.
31/435–K3–3	?Saqia	Brick enclosure, 8.7 m diameter, & run-off channel. +Rom.
31/435–K5–1	Occupation	''Ein Birbiyeh'. Reuse of areas of temple for ?light industry. +Ptol +Rom.
31/435–K5–2	Settlement	Brick walls & kiln; few sherds.
31/435–K5–4	Settlement	Brick wall traces.
31/435–L2–1	Cemetery	500 Graves & tombs, plundered. +Rom.
31/435–L2–3	Cemetery	15 Brick tombs, plundered. +Rom.
31/435–L2–5	Settlement	Brick buildings & kilns, 30,000 m².
31/435–L4–1	Structure	Brick building, 2 storeys, in 175 m² mound.
31/435–L5–1	Occupation	Sherd scatter, 700 m².
31/435–L6–1	Settlement	Brick buildings, several, 75,000 m².
31/435–L9–1	Village	10 Brick & adobe houses, small & poor. +Ptol +Isl.
31/435–L9–2	Occupation	Sherd scatter, 500,000 m². +OK +Rom.
31/435–M3–1	Temple	Brick temple structure (2 rooms stratified), decorated plaster, on 40 m diameter mound. +Rom.
31/435–N2–1	Cemetery	40 Tombs, rock-cut, plundered. +Rom.
31/435–N2–2	Settlement	Brick traces & sherds, 20 × 20 m.
31/435–N6–1	Structure	Brick building, substantial, 14.8 m long.
31/435–N6–2	Settlement	Stone & brick buildings on sandstone plateau, including 3 axial brick temples; Coptic graffito. +Rom.
31/435–N10–1	Settlement	6 Brick structures, scattered on plain.
31/435–P2–1	Industry	Brick kiln, large, 2–chambered.
32/405–A1–1	Building	Brick room, heavy, 2.5 × 3.85 m. +Neo.
32/405–A2–1	Habitation	Sherd scatter denotes reuse of earlier temple. (027) +Neo +Late +Ptol +Rom.
32/405–A2–2	Building	Brick room, 3.75 × 3.1 m. (025) +Neo +Rom.
32/405–A7–1	Church & Settlement	'Deir Abu Metta' or 'Deir el-Uthman'; ?3+ brick architectural phases predate brick church, standing 2+ m high. (041) +Neo.

32/405–A8–1	Settlement	Brick domestic building, over earlier cemetery. +Rom.
32/405–B4–1	Cemetery	10 Brick tombs, plundered.
32/405–B4–2	Structures	Brick domestic buildings, many rooms, 10,000 m².
32/405–C7–1	Structure	Brick building, 4 rooms, 12.3 × 6 m.
32/405–C7–2	Cemetery	Extensive cemetery, multi-roomed mausolea, largely undisturbed. +Isl.
32/405–C7–3	Settlement	Brick buildings on sandstone hill.
32/405–C7–4	Buildings	Brick houses, many rooms, white plaster, stone steps, 60,000 m². +Rom.
32/405–D6–2	Mine or Quarry	2 Caves & shallow excavations in shale, & shale talus piles.
32/405–D9–2	Settlement	Brick walls, 1,500 m².
32/405–D10–1	Cemetery	6 Tombs & 10 graves, plundered. +Rom.
32/405–E9–1	Settlement	Brick & stone walls, rude. ?Stables.
32/405–E10–1	Cemetery	100 Graves, some disturbed.
32/405–G10–1	Mine	6 Adits, in Qusseir (= Mut) Fm shale.
32/405–J10–1	Mine	5 Adits to gallery in Qusseir (= Mut) Fm shale.
32/435–H10–2	Habitation	Sherd scatter, 5,000 m².
33/390–F10–1	Settlement	Brick rooms in 2 contiguous ranges.
33/390–F10–2	Cemetery	27 Graves, some intact.
33/390–H3–1	Camp	7 Stone hut circles, 4 m average diameter.
33/390–I6–1	Settlement	2 Dwellings, part cave/part brick walled.
33/390–I7–1	Settlement	Brick buildings, 2 storeys, 150 × 75 m.
33/390–I7–2	Cemetery	41 Pit graves, intact.
33/390–L9–1	Settlement	'Amheida' (Trimethis),1,500 × 750 m town mound, kilns, industrial area, painted rooms, temple block, good brick architectural preservation. +Rom.
33/390–N6–1	Settlement	6 Brick houses, many rooms, scattered. +Rom.
33/390–N7–1 = 33/390–N6–1		Cancelled.
33/390–P7–2	Cemetery	2 Brick tombs, plundered.
33/405–B8–2	Cemetery	6 Graves, disturbed. +Rom.
33/405–C10–1	Habitation	Brick house & stone wall remnants on hill, 3,000 m². (021) +Neo +Isl.

Islamic Period (c.700 AD to recent)

30/405–I2–3	Occupation	Sherd scatter, extensive. (051) +MSA.
30/420–A1–1	Cemetery	300+ Tombs, plundered. +Rom +Byz.
30/450–B & C2–4.	Bone & Lithics	Surface of CSS; mixed with Holocene bone. Spread over 6 squares. (356) +Neo.
31/390–L1–1	Settlement	Adobe domestic complex, on spring mound.
31/390–L2–1	Settlement	Adobe enclosure & interior structures.
31/405–B2–1	Building	Adobe room & bins.
31/405–B4–1	Settlement	Brick houses & sherd scatter, 500 m².
31/405–C6–1	Settlement	Adobe & brick rooms, several.
31/405–D1–1	Cemetery	Tomb complex, 3 rooms, ca. 100 bodies.
31/405–F3–1	Settlement	5 Brick houses & field system.
31/405–F7–1	Occupation	Sherd scatter over spring mounds. (038) +Muf +OK +Rom.
31/405–G1–1	Tomb	Chamber, rock-cut, isolated, plundered. +Byz.
31/405–G7–3	Occupation	Sherd scatter on spring mound. (037) +Muf.
31/405–H4–1	Cemetery	100 Graves, plundered, 7,500 m². +Byz.

31/405–I2–1	Cemetery	30 Graves, some brick, disturbed. +Byz.
31/405–J3–2	Occupation	Sherd scatter, 10,000 m².
31/405–K4–2	Occupation	Sherd concentration & ?field system, 1,000 m².
31/405–K6–1	Settlement	Sherd scatter & brick wall traces, on spring mound, 60,000 m². +Late +Ptol +Rom +Byz.
31/405–K6–2	Cemetery	150 Graves, 11,250 m². +Byz.
31/405–L4–2	Occupation	Sherds in brick temple. +Ptol +Rom +Byz.
31/405–M10–1	Cemetery	300+ Graves, plundered. +Rom +Byz.
31/405–P8–1	Settlement	'Kharabet el-Naguda', brick ruin on spring mound, 3 building phases. (061) +Neo.
31/420–L6–1	Sherd	(154) +MSA.
31/435–B7–1	Settlement	Sherd scatter around adobe buildings. +Rom +Byz.
31/435–D6–1	Occupation	Sherd scatter & field system, 13 km².
31/435–D8–1	Settlement	Brick walls, 300 m².
31/435–D9–1	Settlement	'El-Qasaba', IFAO excavation site.
31/435–D10–1	Village	6 Brick houses.
31/435–E2–1	Settlement	40 Brick & adobe rooms.
31/435–G9–1	Occupation	Sherd scatter on deflated fields.
31/435–I3–2	Settlement	Adobe rooms, in 3 groups.
31/435–J9–1	Kiln	Brick kiln, isolated, 1.1 m interior diameter.
32/390–J10–2	Wall	Adobe enclosure 20 m long (?byre), adjacent to ?saqia & field system.
31/435–K1–1	Settlement	2 Adobe huts, 2 rooms each, in spring mound eye. +Rom.
31/435–L9–1	Village	10 Brick & adobe houses, small & poor. +Ptol +Byz.
32/390–K4–1	Farmstead	Adobe house & palms/fields over Roman cemetery. +Late +Rom.
32/390–N8–1	Fields	Sherd scatter over field systems adjacent to cemetery. +Rom.
32/390–P6–1	Village	Brick houses, several, many rooms, buried in dune.
32/390–P6–2	Settlement	Sherd concentration & brick structures, includes ovens & storage bins, 15,000 m².
32/405–A7–2	Kilns	10–15 Pottery kilns & nearby brick ?workshops. Kiln intact to above stacking platforms.
32/405–B7–1	Settlement	Brick buildings with small rooms, 4,800 m².
32/405–B7–2	Settlement	Brick architecture & pottery kilns on mound, 250 × 175 m.
32/405–C7–2	Cemetery	Extensive cemetery, multi-roomed mausolea, undisturbed. +Byz.
32/405–D9–1	Cemetery	12+ Graves, disturbed.
32/405–I10–1	Cave	Cave, neat entrance & animal bones, 6 × 10 m. +Rom.
32/435–H10–1	Habitation	Sherd scatter, 3,000 m².
32/435–P9–1	Cairn Grave	On terrace. (299) +MSA.
33/390–H8–1	Settlement	Adobe houses, kiln & field systems. (019) +Neo +Rom.
33/390–K5–1	Habitation	4 Brick structures, simple. +Rom.
33/390–K6–1	Industry	Sherd scatter, ash & slag, 30,000 m². +OK +Rom.

33/390–L6–1	Settlement	Brick & adobe houses.
33/390–M5–2	Town	'Qasr', medieval town with brick architecture, dated & named door lintels, mosques, etc. Presently inhabited. +Ptol +Rom.
33/390–N7–2	Cemetery	7 Graves, no local tradition of use.
33/405–A5–1	Habitation	Brick houses of village, adobe enclosures & small field system.
33/405–C10–1	Habitation	Brick house & stone walls, on hill, 3,000 m². (021) + Neo +Byz.

Uncertain Historical Date

30/405–L1–3	Cemetery	20 Tombs, rock-cut, ?Late, plundered. +MSA.
31/405–J3–1	Cemetery	100 Graves, disturbed, on plain.
31/420–B6–1	House	Brick building, rooms around courtyard.
31/420–G7–1	Cemetery	12 Graves, small, no artifacts.
32/405–H9–1	Cave	Empty, 3 deep × 3 wide & 0.9 m high.
32/405–H10–1	Cave	Empty, 3 deep × 5 wide & 1 m high.
33/390–F10–4	Occupation	Brick walls & 3 small ovens, under aqueduct dredgeate.
33/390–H7–2	House	5 Brick rooms on hills of 33/390–H7–1. Fill contained several funerary objects.
33/390–L7–2	Mine	Several pits, in ancient spring mound.
33/390–M5–3	Mine	8 Pit entrances to galleries in shale.
33/390–N4–1	Mine	12 Pits, in shale.
33/405–A4–1	Mine	60–100 Entrance pits to galleries in shale.
33/405–A4–2	Mine	12 Entrance pits, with shoring.
33/405–A6–2	Graves	Graves, few, no cultural remains.

PETROGLYPHS

30/405–L1–1	Rock Pictures	On building stones of Old Kingdom huts. (057) +MSA +OK.
30/420–F3–1	Art Mobilier	Engravings on rock fragments and hilltop, ?Libyan, of gazelle, dogs, geometric designs & 'OII≡IIO'. OK.
30/435–J1–2	Rock Pictures	200+ animals, signs & games.
30/435–K1–2	Rock Pictures	Animals, feet & humans.
30/435–K1–3	Rock Pictures	Animals, signs; some paint.
30/450–B & C2–4	Bone & Lithics	Surface of CSS; mixed with Holocene bone. Spread over 6 squares. (356) +Neo.
30/450–B4–2	Rock Pictures	Camels, horses, other animals & human feet.
30/450–C4–2	Rock. Pictures	Various styles from Neolithic animals to boats & Islamic camels.
31/420–J4–1	Rock Pictures	Group of 7 horned quadrupeds.
32/435–L10–1	Rock Pictures	2 Adjacent hills, with animals, humans, game holes & human feet. +MSA +Bash +OK (32/435–L10–2; 124).

Appendix III

INDEX LIST OF PREHISTORIC ARCHAEOLOGICAL LOCALITIES

Surveyed by M. M. A. McDonald, M. R. Kleindienst, M. F. Wiseman and A. L. Hawkins

Compiled by M. R. Kleindienst & M. M. A. McDonald and collated by C. S. Churcher

INTRODUCTION

In order to accomodate the realities of the way in which prehistoric evidence is found preserved, especially for Pleistocene archaeological units (cf. Kleindienst, this volume, Chapter 5), and in order to simplify computer sorting, McDonald and Kleindienst have adopted the procedure initiated by Caton-Thompson and Gardner at Kharga Oasis (1932, 1952; see Chapter 5, this volume) for sequentially numbering prehistoric 'loci' (localities = Loc. Numbers).

Some prehistoric localities encompass later evidence, or occur together with evidence from historic time periods at the same map point. Some 'area collection numbers' cover several grid squares within the DOP Grid system of 'site' designation. McDonald has also assigned Loci Numbers to some Holocene historic sites with lithic remains.

A three digit numerical system was developed for computer sorting the Palaeolithic and Neolithic prehistoric localities, within the mapped regions of Dakhleh Oasis and peripheral areas of the extended palaeoasis. This system overlaps the Grid-based reference system so that prehistoric localities within the oasis basin bear two identifiers. This List allows such localities to be cross-referenced without searching Appendix 2.

Loci are given in numerical order with years of recognition, followed by Grid Reference identifiers for sites where appropriate. Epochs and cultural remains on each site are noted in the third column. Subdivided loci are indicated by numbers or letters following the Locality Number; numbers followed by a comma indicate that there is a sublocus without a suffix and a sublocus with a suffix, e.g., NW, S, etc.

The DOP Grid-based reference system is explained by A.J. Mills in 'Dakhleh Oasis Project: Report of the first season of survey, October-December 1978 (*Journal of the Society for the Study of Egyptian Antiquities*, 1979, 9(4):167–168): also see Mills (Introduction, this volume). Sites within this system are listed in 'Index List of Archaeological Sites Surveyed by the Dakhleh Oasis Project' (Appendix 2).

Additional information regarding the numbered Archaeological Localities (Loci) in this appendix may be found by keying to the master 'Index List' in Appendix 2. Sites with multiple cultural occupations may have different descriptions for different recorded phases. These phases are noted here in column three.

ABBREVIATIONS

The following abbreviations are used within this index:

Arc	Archaic (Early Dynastic Period).
Bal	Balat Unit(within ESA).
Bash	Bashendi Cultural Unit (Neolithic), A and B variants.
Byz	Byzantine (Christian).
ESA	Earlier Stone Age (Upper Acheulian *sensu stricto*, or Balat Unit).
ESA-Ach	Upper Acheulian *sensu stricto*.
ESA-Bal	Balat Cultural Unit (latest Earlier Stone Age).
Hol	Holocene Epoch
Isl	Islamic Period.
Mas	Masara Cultural Unit (Epipalaeolithic); A, B, and C variants.

'Reports from the Survey of Dakhleh Oasis, Western Desert of Egypt, 1977–1987', edited by C.S. Churcher and A.J. Mills. Dakhleh Oasis Project: Monograph 2. Oxbow Monograph 99.

Mod	Modern.
MSA	Middle Stone Age, undifferentiated.
MSA-Dak	Middle Stone Age-Dakhleh Cultural Unit (Aterian Technocomplex).
MSA-Mab	Middle Stone Age-Sheikh Mabruk Unit (Khargan Technocomplex).
Muf	Sheikh Muftah Cultural Unit (Neolithic).
N.N.	Outside Grid map area; no map location identitifyer assigned.
Neo	Neolithic.
OK	Old Kingdom.
palaeo	Pleistocene faunal or vegetal remains.
pet	Petroglyphs present.
Pleist	Pleistocene epoch.
PSA	Pleistocene Stone Age evidence.
Ptol	Ptolemaic.
Rom	Roman.
Unc	Uncertain historical date.

Periods in parenthses are the less important periods on a site and the cultures are prefaced by '+'.

Corrections to Grid Site identifiers are shown as the old identifier with the year of correction in parentheses.

LIST OF ARCHAEOLOGICAL LOCALITIES

Locality = Loc. No.	DOP Grid Identifier	Geological Periods & Cultural Units (See above for key)
1978–79		
001	32/390–L1–1	Pleist (& Hol): ESA, MSA, MSA-Dak, +Mas?, Neo, Unc.
002	33/390–I9–1	Pleist (& Hol): ESA-Ach, MSA, +Neo, Bash.
003	33/390–B7–1	Pleist: MSA.
004	33/390–F5–1	Pleist: MSA.
005	33/405–B5–1	Pleist: MSA.
006	32/390–D2–2	Hol: Muf, Bash, OK, Rom, Mas
007	31/405–D7–3	(Pleist &) Hol: ESA-Ach, MSA, Neo, Rom.
008	33/390–H9–1	Hol: Neo.
009	33/390–I4–1	Hol: Neo, OK.
010	33/390–I5–1	Hol: Neo, OK.
011	33/390–I6–2	Hol: Neo, Muf, OK.
012	33/390–I9–3	Hol: OK.
013	32/390–H5–2	Hol: Neo.
014	32/390–I4–3	Hol: Rom.
015	32/390–N4–1	Hol: OK, Rom.
016	33/390–H5–1	Hol: Neo.
017	32/390–K2–2	Pleist (& Hol): ESA-Bal, +OK.
018	32/390–I5–1	Hol: OK.
019	33/390–H8–1	Hol: Neo, Rom, Isl.
1980		
020	32/390–P5–1	Hol: Neo, OK, Rom.
021	33/405–C10–1	Hol: Neo, Byz, Isl.
022	32/405–A2–3	Hol: Bash.
023	32/405–C3–1	Pleist: MSA.
024	32/405–A1–1	Hol: Neo?, Byz.
025	32/405–A2–2	Hol: Neo, Rom, Byz.
026	32/405–D6–1	Pleist: MSA.
027	32/405–A2–1	Hol: Neo, Ptol, Rom, Byz, Unc.

028	33/390–I9–2	Hol: OK.
029	31/405–K1–1	Pleist: MSA.
030	31/405–L1–1	Pleist: MSA
031	31/405–M4–2	Pleist (& Hol): MSA, +Neo
032	32/405–A7–3	Hol (Pleist): MSA.
033	31/405–N1–1	Pleist: MSA.
034	31/405–M3–2	Pleist (& Hol): MSA, +Byz.
035	31/405–G6–1	Hol: Muf, OK, Rom.
036	31/405–G7–2	Hol: Muf, OK.
037	31/405–G7–3	Hol: Muf, Isl.
038	31/405–F7–1	Hol: Muf, OK, Rom, Isl.
039	31/405–E8–1	Hol: Muf, Rom.
040	31/405–F9–6	Pleist (& Hol): MSA, +Neo, Rom.
041	32/405–A7–1	Hol: Neo, Rom.
042	31/405–G10–1	Hol: OK, Ptol, Rom, Byz, Unc.
043	30/405–I2–1	Pleist (& Hol): MSA, +Byz.
044	N.N.	Pleist: PSA, MSA?
045	N.N.	Pleist: PSA, MSA?
046	N.N.	Pleist: PSA, MSA?
047	31/405–K10–3	Hol: Muf, Byz.
048	31/405–K10–5	Hol: Neo, OK.
049	31/405–K10–9	Hol: Neo.
050	31/405–K10–6	Pleist (& Hol): MSA, +Neo.
051	30/405–I2–3	Pleist (& Hol): MSA, +Neo, Rom, Isl.
052	31/405–L10–4	Hol: Muf, Rom.
053	31/405–L10–5	Pleist (& Hol): MSA, +Muf.
054	30/405–L1–3	Pleist (& Hol): MSA, +Byz.
055	31/405–L10–3	Pleist (& Hol): ESA?, +Rom, Byz.
056	31/405–L10–6	Pleist (& Hol): MSA, +Neo.
057	30/405–L1–1	Pleist (& Hol): MSA, +OK?; pet.
058	31/420–A5–1	Pleist: MSA.
059	31/405–M10–3	Hol: Muf, OK?
060	30/405–M1–2	Pleist: MSA.
061	31/405–P8–1	Hol: Neo, Isl.
1981–82		
062	31/405–G7–4	Hol: Muf, OK?
063	31/405–G7–5	Hol: Muf.
064	31/405–G6–2	Hol: Muf.
065	31/405–H6–1	Hol: Neo, OK, Rom.
066	31/405–H4–2	Hol: Muf, OK, Rom.
067	31/420–F10–1	Pleist: MSA.
068	31/420–F10–2	Hol: Muf.
069	31/420–D10–3	Hol: Muf.
070	31/420–F9–1	Hol: Bash, Muf.
071	31/420–E10–1	Hol: Muf.
072	31/420–D9–1	Pleist (& Hol): ESA-Bal, MSA-Dak, +Muf, OK.
073	31/420–C10–1	Hol: Muf.
074	31/420–C10–2	Hol: Bash.
075	30/420–C1–1	Hol: Mas A.
076	N.N.	Hol: Mas A.
077	N.N.	Hol: Bash B.
078	31/435–D1–1	Hol: Neo.
079	31/435–A1–1	Pleist: MSA.
080	31/420–N2–1	Pleist: MSA, MSA-Dak.
081	31/420–L3–1	Pleist: ESA-Bal, MSA.
082	31/420–L1–1	Pleist: MSA, MSA-Dak.
083	31/420–G4–1	Hol: (Pleist): Mas, +MSA.
084	31/420–E5–1	Pleist (& Hol): ESA-Bal, MSA, +Mas.
085	31/420–H10–1	Hol: Mas A.
086	31/420–G8–1	Hol.Bash.
087	31/420–H5–1	Hol: Muf.
088	31/420–H7–2	Hol: Bash, Muf.
089	31/420–G7–3	Hol: Muf, OK.
090	31/420–H6–1	Pleist: MSA, MSA-Dak.

091	31/420–H6–2	Pleist: ESA-Bal.
092	31/420–F9–3	Hol: Muf.
1982–83		
093	30/435–J2–1	Hol: Muf.
094	30/435–J5–1	Pleist (& Hol): MSA, MSA-Dak, +Muf.
095	30/435–J5–2	Pleist (& Hol): MSA, Muf, +OK; pet.
096	30/435–F6–1	Pleist (& Hol): MSA, +Muf.
097	31/435–B4–2	Hol: Neo, OK, Rom.
098	31/435–B4–3	Hol: Mas, Neo, OK, Rom.
099	31/435–B4–4	Hol: OK, Rom.
100	31/420–P6–1	Hol: Muf.
101	31/420–P5–1	Hol: Bash B.
102	31/435–L2–4	Hol: OK.
103	32/435–M10–1	Hol: Bash.
104	31/420–M9–2	Hol: Bash B.
105	30/420–P1–1	Hol: Muf.
106	30/435–A2–1	Hol: Muf.
107	30/435–B3–1	Hol: Muf.
108	30/435–B3–2	Hol: Muf.
109	30/435–B3–3	Hol: Muf.
110	30/435–C6–1	Hol: Muf.
111	30/435–C3–1	Hol: Muf, Arc.
112	30/435–C3–2	Hol: Muf.
113	30/435–D4–1	Hol: Muf.
114	31/435–A7–1	Hol: Muf.
115	31/435–A6–2	Hol: Muf.
116	31/435–A6–3	Hol: Bash B.
117	30/435–I3–1	Hol: Muf.
118	31/420–C10–3	Hol: Muf.
119	30/435–K3–1	Hol: Muf.
120	30/435–L3–1	Pleist (& Hol): MSA, MSA-Mab, +Neo.
121	30/435–M2–2	Pleist: MSA, MSA-Mab.
122	31/420–E10–2	Hol: Muf.
123	30/435–M2–3	Hol: Neo, Rom, raw material.
124	32/435–L10–2	Hol: Bash, OK; pet.
125	31/435–L1–1	Hol: Bash.
126	31/435–M1–1	Hol: Muf.
127	31/435–I4–1	Hol: OK.
128	31/435–M2–1	Pleist: PSA.
1984		
129	30/435–L2–1	Hol: Muf.
130, N	30/435–M2–4	Pleist: MSA-Dak, MSA-Mab.
131	30/435–M2–5	Hol: Rom?
132	30/435–P2–1	Hol: Rom?
133	30/435–P2–2	Hol: Muf.
134	30/450–B3–1	Hol: Muf.
135	30/450–B4–1	Hol: Muf.
136	30/450–B3–2	Hol: Muf.
137	30/450–A4–1	Hol: Bash B.
138	N.N.	Hol: OK.
139	N.N.	Hol: Muf.
140	N.N.	Hol: Mas A, Bash B.
141	N.N.	Hol: Bash.
1986		
142	31/420–C10–4	Hol: Muf.
143	30/435–B6–1	Hol: Muf.
144	30/420–P2–1	Hol: Muf.
145	31/420–N6–1	Hol: Muf.
146 1,2	31/420–E10–3	Pleist: MSA
147 1–4	31/420–N4–1 & 2	Pleist: ESA-Bal, MSA.
148	31/420–P5–2	Pleist: MSA, raw material.
149 1,2	31/420–L9–1	Pleist: MSA.

150	31/420–L9–2	Pleist: ESA-Bal.
151	30/420–L1–1	Pleist: PSA, MSA. (= 31/420–L10–1, corrected 1998)
152 1,2	31/420–M10–1	Pleist: MSA. (= 31/420–M9–1, corrected 1998)
153	31/420–L1–2	Pleist: MSA. (= 30/420–M10–1, corrected 1998)
154	31/420–L6–1	Pleist (& Hol): MSA, +Isl.
155 1–6	31/420–H6–3	Pleist: PSA, ESA-Bal, MSA.
156	32/420–E8–1	Pleist: ESA, MSA.
157	32/420–E8–2	Pleist: ESA, MSA.
158	31/450–B6–1	Pleist: MSA.
159	32/435–M5–1	Pleist: ESA-Ach.
160	31/420–I6–2	Pleist: MSA.
161	32/435–K & L10–1	Pleist (& Hol): ESA, MSA, MSA-Dak, +Neo; pet.
162 1,2	32/390–I3–1	Pleist: PSA, MSA.
163	33/435–C6–1	Hol: Mas, Bash.
164	33/435–C7–2	Hol: Mas?
165	33/435–C7–1	Hol: Bash B.
166	33/435–C6 & 7–3	Hol: Mas A.
167	31/420–N6–2	Hol: Muf.
168	31/420–M6–1	Hol: Muf.
169	31/420–N7–1	Hol: Muf.
170	31/420–N7–2	Hol: Muf.
171	30/435–B5–1	Hol: Muf.
172	30/450–F8–1	Hol: Bash.
173	30/450–F8–2	Hol: Bash A.
174	30/450–F8–3	Hol: Bash A.
175	30/450–G8–1	Hol: Bash.
176	30/450–F7–1	Hol: Bash.
177	30/450–F8–4	Hol: Bash.
178	30/450–F8–5	Hol: Bash.
179	30/450–F7–2	Hol: Bash.
180	30/450–F9–1	Hol: Bash, OK.
181	30/450–F7–3	Hol: Bash.
182	30/450–F7–4	Hol: Bash B.
183	30/450–E7–1	Hol: Bash B.
184	30/450–F7–5	Hol: Bash B.
1987		
185	N.N.	Hol: Bash.
186	31/420–H10–2	Hol: Mas, Bash.
187 A-E	32/420–L6–1	Pleist (& Hol): ESA-Ach, ESA-Bal, MSA, MSA-Dak, +Mas.
188 A,B	32/420–L7–1	Pleist: MSA.
189 A,B	32/420–L6 & 7–2,	Pleist: ESA-Bal, MSA, MSA-Dak.
190 A,B	32/420–L7–3	Pleist: MSA.
191 1,2	31/420–M9–3	Pleist: MSA (= 31/420–L9–3, corrected 1998)
192	31/420–L9–3	Pleist: MSA. (= 31/420–L9–4, corrected 1998)
193	31/420–I3–1	Pleist: ESA-Bal, MSA.
194	30/420–D1–1	Hol: Mas B.
195	30/420–D3–2	Hol: Mas, Bash.
196	30/420–D2–2	Hol: Mas, Bash.
197	30/420–E3–1	Hol: Bash.
198 1–3	33/405–A2–1	Pleist: ESA, MSA.
199	33/390–N2–1	Pleist: ESA, MSA.
200	30/420–C5–1	Hol: Mas B.
201	32/435–J6–1	Pleist: MSA.
202	32/420–D8–1	Pleist: MSA.
203 A,B.	30/420–E1–1	Pleist: MSA, MSA-Mab.
204	32/450–var. several squares	Pleist (& Hol): ESA, MSA, +Unc, Mod.
205	30/420–D4–1	Hol: Mas A.
206	30/420–C7–1	Hol: Mas A.
207	30/420–C4–1	Hol: Mas.

208	33/390–I9–5	Pleist: ESA.
209	33/390–I9–6	Pleist: ESA, MSA.
210	30/450–F8–6	Hol: Bash, OK, pet.
211, NW,NE	30/450–C5–1	Pleist (& Hol): MSA, +OK; pet.
212	30/450–C6–1	Hol: Bash B.
213	30/450–D2–1	Pleist: MSA.
214	30/420–E2–1	Pleist: MSA.
215	30/420–E2–2	Pleist: MSA.
216, N	31/420–I1 & 2–1	Pleist: ESA, MSA, MSA-Dak.
217 A,B	31/420–K1–1	Pleist: ESA, MSA.
218	30/420–C4–2	Hol: Mas.
219	32/420–L7–4	Hol: Bash.
220	30/435–J9–1	Hol: Muf.
221	30/435–J6–1	Hol: Muf.
222	30/435–J6–2	Hol: Muf.
223	31/405–B6–1	Pleist: ESA? raw material.
224	30/405–N3–1	Hol: Mas A.
225	N.N.	Pleist (& Hol): MSA-Dak, +Muf.
226	30/420–B3–1	Hol: Mas A.
227	30/420–B3–2	Hol: Mas.
228	30/450–A9–1	Hol: Mas, Bash.
229	30/450–G8–2	Hol: OK; pet.
230	31/420–I2–1	Pleist: ESA-Bal, MSA.
231	31/420–J2 & 3–1	Pleist: MSA, MSA-Dak.
232	32/405–P9–1	Pleist: MSA.
233	31/405–M2–1	Pleist: MSA.
234	31/405–M1–1	Pleist: MSA.
235	32/435–L10–3	Hol: Bash, OK; pet.
236	31/420–G6 & 7–4	Pleist: ESA-Bal, MSA, MSA-Dak.
237	33/450–C10–1	Pleist: MSA.
238	33/450–D9–1	Pleist: MSA.
239	33/450–D9–2	Pleist: MSA.
240	33/450–H8–1	Pleist: ESA.
241	30/450–F10–1	Hol: Arc.

1989

242	29/450–D3–1	Hol: Mas A.
243	29/450–D4–1	Hol: Mas A.
244	N.N.	Hol: Muf.
245	N.N.	Pleist: MSA.
246	N.N.	Pleist: MSA.
247	N.N.	Pleist: MSA
248	N.N.	Pleist: MSA.
249	N.N.	Pleist(& Hol): MSA?, +Neo.
250	N.N.	Hol: Muf.
251	N.N.	Hol: Neo.
252	30/435–N9–1	Hol: Bash B
253	30/435–M9–1	Hol: Bash B.
254	30/450–B10–1	Hol: Bash B.
255	N.N.	Pleist: MSA-Dak.

1990

256	30/450–E4–1	Hol: OK.
257	30/450–E4–2	Hol: Bash B.
258	30/450–E5–1	Hol: Bash.
259	30/420–D7–1	Hol: Mas A.
260	29/450–H4–1	Hol: Mas C.
261	29/450–F4–1	Hol: Mas, Bash.
262	29/450–H3–1	Hol: Mas.
263	29/450–F3–1	Hol: Mas A.
264	29/450–G3–1	Hol: Mas. C.
265	29/450–G3–2	Hol: Mas. C.
266	30/450–H8–1	Hol: Mas, Bash.
267	29/450–G4–1	Hol: Mas. C.
268	29/450–G3–3	Hol: Mas. C.
269	29/450–F1–1	Hol: Bash.
270	30/450–F10–2	Hol: Bash A.

1991

271	30/435–P9–1	Hol: Bash B.
272	30/450–B8–1	Hol: Bash.
273	30/435–P8–1	Hol: Neo.
274	30/435–P8–2	Hol: Mas C.
275	30/435–P10–1	Hol: Bash A.
276	30/435–P10–2	Hol: Bash B.
277	30/450–A7–1	Hol: Bash.
278	30/450–F10–3	Hol: Bash.
279	31/435–J1–3	Hol: Neo, raw material.
280	31/420–L3–2	Pleist: MSA.
281	31/435–J & K1–2 (= 31/435–J1–2, corrected 1998)	Pleist (& Hol): ESA?, MSA, MSA-Dak, +Neo.
282	31/435–K1–2	Pleist: MSA.
283 1,2	32/435–M9–1	Pleist (& Hol): ESA, MSA-Dak, +Neo, pet.
284	N.N.	Pleist: MSA.
285	N.N.	Pleist: MSA, raw material.
286	30/450–L3–1	Pleist: PSA.
287 1,2	N.N.	Pleist (& Hol): PSA, +Mod.
288	N.N.	Pleist: PSA.
289	30/420–D5–1	Pleist: ESA, MSA.
290	31/ & 32/450–var. several squares	Pleist (& Hol): PSA, +Rom.
291 1,2	30/420–B9–1	Pleist: MSA.
292	30/420–B9–2	Pleist: MSA.
293	30/420–D2–3	Pleist: MSA, MSA-Dak.

1992

294 1–3	32/435–L9–1	Pleist: MSA-Dak.
295	32/435–L9–2	Pleist (& Hol): ESA, MSA, MSA-Dak, +Neo.
296	32/435–N9–1	Pleist: ESA, MSA.
297	32/435–M10–2	Pleist (& Hol): MSA, MSA-Dak, +Neo, OK; pet.
298	32/435–N10–1	Pleist (& Hol): MSA, +Neo.
299	32/435–P9–1	Pleist (& Hol): MSA-Dak, +Isl.
300	29/450–G3–6	Hol: Mas C.
301	33/360–K10–2	Hol: Neo.
302	N.N.	Hol: Bash B.
303	32/450–D8–1	Hol: Bash B, pet.
304	30/450–D9–1	Hol: Bash B, pet.
305	29/420–C2–1	Hol: Mas, Bash.
306	30/450–F10–4	Hol. Bash A.
307	30/450–F10–5	Hol: Bash A.
308	29/450–G3–4	Hol: Mas C.
309	29/450–H4–2	Hol: Mas C.
310	32/435–P8–1	Pleist: MSA.
311	32/450–A6–1	Pleist: MSA, MSA-Dak.
312	33/450–var. several squares	Pleist: ESA?, MSA.
313	33/450–E10–1	Pleist: MSA.
314	30/420–A8–1	Pleist: MSA.
315	32/435–I5–1	Pleist: ESA, MSA.
316 A-F	32/435–I4 & 5–1	Pleist: MSA.
317	32/435–I3–1	Pleist: MSA, MSA-Dak.
318, N	32/435–J6–2	Pleist: MSA.
319 N,S	32/435–K5–1	Pleist: MSA, MSA-Dak.
320	33/360–K10–1	Pleist: MSA, MSA-Dak.
321	32/435–J6–3	Pleist: MSA.
322	31/420–I4–1 (= 31/420–H6–4, corrected 1997)	Pleist: MSA-Mab.
323	31/420–F10–3	Pleist: ESA-Bal.
324	31/420–F10–4	Pleist: MSA-Mab.
325	30/420–E & F1–2	Pleist: MSA-Dak.
326	31/420–E2–3	Pleist: MSA, MSA-Mab.

327	30/ & 31/420–var. several squares	Pleist (& Hol): ESA-Bal, MSA, MSA-Dak, MSA-Mab, +Bash, Muf.

1993

328	30/420–E & F1–3	Pleist: MSA, MSA-Dak, MSA-Mab.
329, K	30/420–E & F1–4	Pleist: MSA, MSA-Dak, MSA-Mab.
330	30/420–E2–4	Pleist: MSA-Dak, MSA-Mab.
331	30/420–D & E1 & 2–2	Pleist: ESA-Bal, MSA, MSA-Mab.

1994–1995

332	30/420–D2–4	Pleist:MSA-Mab.
333	32/420–P6–1	Pleist: MSA-Dak.
334	32/420–L5–1	Pleist: MSA-Dak.
335	29/420–A, B & C1 & 2–1	Pleist: ESA, MSA, MSA-Dak, MSA-Mab.
336	29/420–A, B & C1 & 2–2	Pleist: MSA.
337	29/420–C, D1 & 2–1	Pleist: MSA.
338	29/420–C, D1 & 2–2	Pleist (& Hol): ESA, MSA, +Neo.
339	30/420–D3–3	Pleist (& Hol); MSA, MSA-Mab, +Mas, Bash.
340	30/420–C4–3	Pleist (& Hol): ESA, MSA, +Mas.
341	29 & 30/450–var. several squares	Pleist (& Hol): MSA-Dak, +Mas, Bash.
342	31/420–I1–2	Pleist: MSA-Dak.
343	32/420–K4–1	Pleist: ESA,MSA.
344, S	31/420–M5, 6–1	Pleist (& Hol): ESA-Bal, MSA, MSA- Dak, +Neo, Byz.

1996

345	30/435–M2&3–1	Pleist (& Hol): MSA, MSA-Dak, MSA-Mab, +Mod; pet.
346	30/435–L2–2	Pleist: MSA-Mab.
347	30/435–P6–1	Pleist (& Hol): MSA, +Neo, raw material.
348	30/435–M2–1	Pleist (& Hol): PSA, +Byz; palaeo.
349	30/435–M5–1	Pleist: PSA; palaeo.
350, W,S	30/435–P3–1	Pleist: PSA, MSA; palaeo.
351	30/435–P3–2	Pleist: PSA, MSA; palaeo.
352, N	30/450–A4–2	Pleist: PSA, palaeo.
353	31/420–I5–1	Pleist: ESA-Bal; palaeo.

1997

354	31/420–F8–1	Pleist (& Hol): MSA, +Neo.
355	30/435–M2–6	Pleist (& Hol): PSA, +Byz; palaeo.
356	30/450–B & C2–1	Pleist (& Hol): PSA, +Muf, OK, pet & palaeo.
357	30/450–B4–3	Pleist (& Hol): PSA, MSA, +Neo; Rom, Isl; palaeo.
358	30/450–B4–4	Pleist?/Hol?: palaeo.
359	31/420–I5–2	Pleist: ESA-Bal.
360	30/450–D3–1	Pleist: PSA, MSA-Mab.
361	30/450–D4–1	Pleist: MSA, MSA-Mab.
362	31/420–F7–2 (= 31/420–F9–4, corrected 1997).	Pleist: PSA.
363	32/435–L10–2	Pleist: MSA-Dak.
364	32/435–L9–3.	Pleist: MSA-Dak.
365	31/420–E10–4	Hol: burials, Muf?
366	30/450–D4–3	Pleist: ESA,MSA.

1998

367	31/420–M7–2	Pleist:MSA, MSA-Mab.
368	31/420–L7–1	Pleist: ESA-Bal, MSA, MSA-Mab.
369	31/420–L8–1	Pleist: MSA-Mab.
370	31/420–L & N8, 9 & 10–2	Pleist: ESA-Bal, MSA.
371	31/420–N8–1	Pleist: PSA, ESA-Bal?
372	31/420–N8–2	Pleist: ESA-Bal; palaeo.
373	31/420–L9–4	Pleist: ESA-Bal.
374	31/450–D4–4	Pleist: MSA.
375	31/420–E10–5	Hol: burials, Neo.
376	30 & 31/420–var. several squares	Pleist (& Hol): MSA, MSA-Mab, +Mas, Neo.
377 E,W	30/420–M1–1	Pleist: MSA.
378	30/450–var. several squares.	Pleist (& Hol): ESA, MSA, +Neo.
379	31/420–N10–2	Pleist: palaeo.
380	31/420–E9–1	Hol: Muf.
381	31/420–E10–6	Hol: Muf.
382	31/420–E10–7	Hol: Muf.
383 to 389	(not yet assigned)	
390 1,2	30/420–M4–1	Pleist: ESA.
391	30/450–D4–7	Pleist: MSA.
392	30/450–D4–8	Pleist: MSA.
393	31/420–D10–4	Pleist: MSA.